The PHOTOSHOP 7 WOW! BOOK

Jack Davis

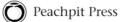

Peachpit Press

The Photoshop 7 Wow! Book, Windows/Mac Edition

Jack Davis

Peachpit Press
1249 Eighth Street
Berkeley, CA 94710
(510) 524-2178
(510) 524-2221 (fax)

Find us on the World Wide Web at:
http://www.peachpit.com/wow

Peachpit Press is a division of Pearson Education

Copyright © 2003 by Jack Davis and Linnea Dayton
Cover design: Jack Davis
Book design: Jill Davis
Production and prepress: Jill Davis and Jonathan Parker
Direct-to-plate printing: CDS Publications / Medford, Oregon

ISBN 0-321-12397-2

0 9 8 7 6 5 4 3 2 1

Printed and bound in the United States of America.

To Him, from whom all
blessings flow...

— Jack

ACKNOWLEDGMENTS

Although the edition you're holding may have only one author's name on the cover, it is still largely the end-result of a collaboration with my former co-author of 10 years, Linnea Dayton. With a new grandchild and a renowned marine biologist husband who finally has a traveling partner again, Linnea has chosen to take a break from the world of *Photoshop Wow!* and focus on other projects.

But you will find that much of this current edition of *Wow!* builds upon the complete revision of the book that we did together for Photoshop 6—the largest upgrade ever for our beloved Photoshop, and our most comprehensive how-to book ever. So enjoy this edition and you will still be benefitting from the gifted communication of Linnea — a great friend and a phenomenal writer/author.

This book would not have been possible without a great deal of support. First, I would like to thank the Photoshop artists who have allowed us to include their work in the "Gallery" sections of the book; their names are listed in the Appendix. As always, I appreciate the support of the folks like Russell Brown, Julieanne Kost, and Gwyn Weisberg at Adobe Systems, Inc., who kept me up to date on the development of Photoshop, answered my technical questions, and always inspired me. And my thanks goes to Stephen French and others at Corbis Images who made it possible for us to include photos from their Royalty Free collections as part of our tutorials, and to Richard Lopinto of Nikon, Rich Harris from Wacom, and Dan Steinhardt of Epson for providing us with their most excellent and indispensable products.

I am grateful to my wife and business partner Jill Davis, whose book design and layout of this edition allowed me to focus more on the "fun stuff," and to Lisa and Stephen King and Lynn Fleschutz for helping update the (literally) thousands of graphics in this edition, and to Cristen Gillespie for helping with the frantic final proofreading, editing, and indexing.

And many thanks to Jonathan Parker, an eternal and absolutely essential part of the team, who once again made room in his design studio's schedule to do final production and prepress for this edition.

I'd like to thank the friends, family, and colleagues, including many at Peachpit Press, who have supported us through nine editions of this endeavor. In particular, I thank our editor Cary Norsworthy and publisher Nancy Ruenzel for their continuing support, Victor Gavenda and Heidi Jonk-Sommer for their technical expertise and for checking and engineering the CD-ROM, and production coordinator Connie Jeung-Mills.

Finally, I'd like to thank those readers of previous editions who have let me know that *The Photoshop Wow! Book* has been inspirational as well as educational to them, and to those who have just quietly used and appreciated it. Thanks also for pointing out where we could improve the book so all of us can continue to get the most "Wow!" from our favorite tool — Photoshop. This edition, as always, was a labor of love — our love of the creative process and our love of communicating. I hope you enjoy it!

CONTENTS

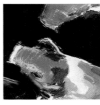

On the Wow CD-ROM

Tutorial "Before" and "After" Image Files • Wow Presets • Wow Miscellaneous Goodies • Other Wow Books • Third-Party Demos and Try-outs

Welcome to The Photoshop 7 Wow! Book

One of the greatest new features of Photoshop 7 is the File Browser — much more than an interactive "contact sheet" of the contents of a folder, it's a whole new way of managing your digital creations. Here the viewing method is set to Large Thumbnail with Rank–Rank being the easiest way to prioritize a set of images by simply assigning selected images a letter from A through E.

In the Detail view (accessible through the pop out menu in the upper right corner of the File Browser or via the pop up menu at the bottom of the window) you can scan the specifics of multiple images - from file size to dimensions to embedded copyright information and color profile. Below the Preview (which is to the right of the currently highlighted image) is the "Metadata pane" where a digital photograph's seemingly endless EXIF (Exchangeable Image File) information can be seen.

ADOBE PHOTOSHOP, ESPECIALLY IN COMBINATION with Adobe Image-Ready, is one of the most powerful visual communication tools ever to appear on the desktop. Together the two programs allow the new generation of information architects to forge ahead in creating on-screen imagery for the Web and other interactive digital delivery systems. Photoshop has also expanded the visual vocabulary of traditionally print-oriented designers, illustrators, and fine artists. And Photoshop 7 makes it even easier for photographers to do the retouching, resizing, cropping, and basic color correction of production work, both for printed output and for the Web. Beyond that, it provides a laboratory for synthesizing textures, patterns, and all kinds of visual imagery that can be applied to photos, graphics, video, or film. It can even automate many of these tasks — everything from routine production operations to extensive graphics special effects.

WHAT'S NEW IN PHOTOSHOP 7 & IMAGEREADY 7

In terms of making your work quicker and easier, the step up to version 7 of Photoshop has great potential — especially for those doing retouching and natural media illustrations and art. Photoshop 7 brings numerous improvements that long-time Photoshop users will appreciate, both for creating images and for making production workflow more efficient. If you're new to Photoshop, you can consider yourself lucky to be starting out with a version that's more versatile and potentially easier to use than ever.

Many of the most important changes to Photoshop 7 are introduced on the next nine pages, with pointers to sections of the book where they are put to use step-by-step.

The File Browser

Lauded by many as the most timesaving new feature to be added in Photoshop 7, the File Browser is far more than just a "contact sheet" of a folder's content. Rather, it's an entire asset management environment contained right within the program where you can sort, rank, move, delete, rotate, rename, and view scalable thumbnails of the files, as well as any information that might be "along for the ride," such as the EXIF (Exchangeable Image File) shooting information supplied by most digital cameras.

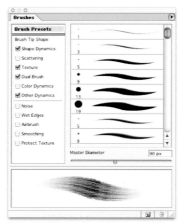

Photoshop 7's new Brush Engine contains hundreds of new options for creating dynamic natural media tools. Here the Expanded View of the brushes palette shows not only the currently available brush tips, but also the categories of variables on the left-hand side and a preview of the current settings in action at the bottom.

By saving all the customizable brush options (like Texture, Dual Brush and Shape Dynamics) as Tool Presets, we have created the Wow Art Media Brushes, which have sets that can be used with the Brush Tool (some samples are to the right), the Art History Brush and the Pattern Stamp Tool.

An original stylized photograph was converted to a painting using the Wow-PS (Pattern Stamp) Dry Brush group of tool presets. See page 281 for more on cloning with the Pattern Stamp tool.

By default, the File Browser is broken up into four panes:

- The **Tree Pane,** showing the disk and folder hierarchy where your images are located
- The **Thumbnail Pane,** which displays the contents of a selected disk or folder in one of five size options: Small, Medium, Large, Large with Rank, and Detail
- The **Preview Pane,** where a larger version of a selected images' thumbnail appears
- The **Metadata Pane,** which displays information about the currently selected image — this can include everything from associated keywords and captions, to resolution and bit depth, to camera exposure and white balance settings

In addition to sorting images by name, size, type, date, etc., you can right-mouse button click (or Ctrl/click on a single button Mac) on an image and assign it a letter ranking (and perform several other operations) via a context-sensitive menu.

Right-clicking (Ctrl-click on a single-button Mac mouse) on any thumbnail in the File Browser brings up a context-sensitive menu of available options.

Energetic Brushes

Photoshop 7's painting engine provides hundreds of new features to all of the brush-based tools within the program. In regard to imitating natural media effects, these new capabilities allow Photoshop to go where it has never gone before — into the realm of *dynamic*

The new Jitter feature in Photoshop 7's brush engine allows for subtle "random" changes to a brush's behavior, like permitting a 10% hue shift in the Wow preset shown above. See Chapter 6 for multiple methods of taking advantage of these new features.

brushes. With multiple brush sizes, shapes, and tips available, the dynamic brushes can interactively change orientation based on the direction that you are moving your mouse or stylus, and simultaneously interact with the variable paper and canvas textures potentially built into them. Combine these capabilities with the ability to choose percentage values of random "jitter" variables (like allowing the color, size or shape of a brush to "organically" vary, say by 10% for example, during a single brush stroke).

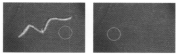

The Healing Brush is an excellent new addition to Photoshop's arsenal of image fixing tools. Kind of like the Clone Stamp on steroids, the Healing Brush samples a source area (above left) to paint over a problematic one, but does so while maintaining the shading, lighting and texture of the original (above right).

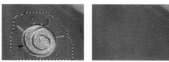

The related Patch Tool works with selections to fix larger areas, and uses the same magical mathematics to attempt to seamlessly blend the Source over the Destination. (See pages 137–138 for more on the Healing Brush.)

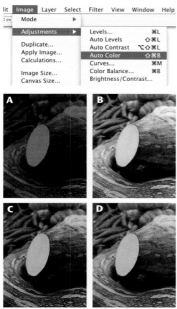

The Auto Color feature joins with Auto Levels, and Auto Contrast to round out some very powerful "quick fix" options in Photoshop 7's Image, Adjustments menu. Notice how it pulled out shadow detail (D) from the original (A) like Auto Levels (B), while maintaining the correct color cast like Auto Contrast (C).

Healing and Patching

The Healing Brush (and its close relative the Patch Tool) lets you easily remove unwanted artifacts like dust, scratches, and blemishes, and it allows you to reduce elements such as wrinkles and bags under the eyes in a very controlled and natural fashion. (See page 137 for a fast and flexible technique using this tool.) Photoshop performs this digital alchemy by replacing the offending element with a sample taken from a surrounding area, while maintaining the shading, lighting and texture of the original location.

Auto Corrections

Adding to the "auto" button that has been a part of Photoshop's levels and Curves dialog boxes for ages, and the Auto Contrast option that became available in version 6, Adobe has created another Auto feature: **Auto Color.** By looking at shadow and highlight color, as well as midtones, many times Auto Color can get rid of stubborn color casts with a single click.

These Auto Color Correction features are available in the Image, Adjust menu, but are also accessible via the Options subdialog in both the Levels and Curves Adjustment layers.

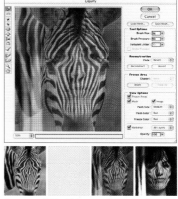

Because of Liquify's new ability to view the background image that you are trying to conform the currently active layer to, this enhanced Photoshop "filter" offers dynamically greater precision and control. (See page 226 for more on Liquify.)

Liquify Enhancements

The image warping capabilities of Liquify (found at the top of the Filter menu) have expanded to include the abilities to zoom and pan within its preview window, perform multiple undo's, and save a "distortion mesh." By creating a distortion mesh on a low-resolution version of a file, you can later reapply that mesh to a high-resolution counterpart. Perhaps the most useful new feature of Liquify is that it lets you see all the layers below the currently active one that you are manipulating, thus giving you more creative control while allowing for greater precision in warping one image in relation to another.

A Preset for Everything!

Being able to save custom settings for everything from gradients to patterns, styles to custom shapes, has been possible in Photoshop for awhile, but the flood gates have opened in 7.0 with the ability to save both tool and workspace settings as presets as well. Set up anything in Photoshop just once (a custom brush to get rid of red-eye, for example, with settings for color, blend mode, and opacity), just the way you like it, then save those settings and call them up instantly the next time you have a similar need. Perhaps you'd like to set the Marquee's style to a fixed aspect ratio of 8x10 in the Option bar, and save this as a preset for future use. It's even applicable for how you set up your workspace. For retouching photos, for instance, you may arrange your palettes and brushes one way; you can save this arrangement via the Window, Workspace menu. Then if you create graphics for the web you can set up your palettes, View options, and colors another way, and save this organization as a preset as well.

Other additions and Improvements

Depending on how you use Photoshop, you may consider some of the other additions to 7.0 as either simply helpful to you, or, they may be a dream-come-true. (For some Photoshop users, being able to double-click on a layer's name and change it right within the palette is worth the price of upgrading alone!) Whatever your needs, here are a few other improvements that are sure to come in handy in your adventures in Photoshop:

- A **Spell Checker** has been built into Photoshop 7, accessible through the Edit menu. It can search and replace, check multiple languages, and correct spelling on just one text layer or all text layers in the same document.

- **Picture Package** (File, Automate) now lets you print multiple page sizes, add labels or text to each image, print more than one image per page, and output files as "flat," or with layers intact.

- Acrobat 5.0's **Security Settings** are now completely supported, allowing you to add passwords and other protection devices to Photoshop PDF files before you share them with others or upload them to the web.

- The new **Pattern Maker** plug-in (found along with Extract and Liquify at the top of the Filters menu) is useful for creating larger

Tool Presets (along with the other new and existing presets like Workspaces and Layer Styles) are perhaps the biggest time savers to be extended in Photoshop 7 – with their ability to save almost every possible option (like foreground color and blend mode for the Red Eye-Neutralize preset above) for every possible tool, they give everyone the ability to create their own instantly accessible custom "time savers" – like the whole set of Wow-Image Fix brushes shown above (see page 9 for more on using these presets).

Picture Package has been improved in Photoshop 7 to allow for more page sizes, the addition of titles and labels, the combining of different images on a single page and the option of outputting the results as a flattened document or one with all the elements on separate layers.

By adding Security features to its PDF saving options, Photoshop 7 allows for tighter control over your documents in workgroup or online publishing situations.

Photoshop 7 has finally integrated the long-awaited Spell Checker (and an associated Find and Replace feature).

The new Pattern Maker filter can take a small portion of an image (for example from the large rock above) and generate a non-repeating texture of unlimited size.

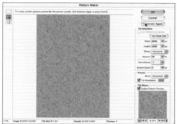

The results could be used for full-sized backgrounds (like the 10Mb result above) or smaller tiling versions could be used for web pages or fabric patterns.

Features aimed at designing for the Web haven't been overlooked. A new Remap to Transparency option in both Photoshop 7 and ImageReady 7 can help graphics with solid edges be easily repurposed by simply selecting the color in a question and clicking a button.

And the Rollovers palette in ImageReady has been completely redesigned to show all of a file's slices, rollovers, image maps and animations in one organized location. (See the introduction to Chapter 9 for more.)

background fill patterns from smaller selections of an existing texture — like rock, sand, or grass — by using some elaborate randomizing algorithms to reduce the appearance of those unsightly repeating seams.

- There are now more sophisticated templates available for you to choose within the **Automate/Web Photo Gallery** dialog, including ones with auto-advance slide show capabilities. A new security option allows you to place type (file name, copyright, URL, etc.) directly onto each photo, either as solid text or as a watermark.

New Style templates are available in Photoshop 7's Web Photo Gallery, as well as a new function which allows you to add custom watermarks to every one of your images on the site. (See page 423 for samples.)

Improvements to ImageReady

Photoshop's symbiotic web application, ImageReady, wasn't overlooked when all the improvements were being made. Here's a brief list of some of the new additions to ImageReady (see the opening section of Chapter 9 on page 412 for more.)

- Now you can easily **remap multiple colors to make them transparent** with a click of a button in the color table's palette, as well as choose to have any transparencies in a GIF file (like those used in a soft edged drop shadow) maintained using the **Transparency Dither** option.

- For JPEG files, you can **Modify Quality Settings** to help text and shape layers maintain better edge fidelity by giving compression priority to their outlines.

ImageReady (along with Photoshop's built-in Save For Web) now has a Transparency Dither feature to better integrate images with soft edges into different backgrounds.

- Photoshop and ImageReady now let you Preview and Save For Web in **WBMP format,** commonly used for displaying images on PDAs and wireless devices.

- The new **Rollovers Palette** allows you to see *all* the slices, rollovers, image maps, and animations of a document in one easily managed location, as well as add a layer-based rollover with a single click. And the new Selected State in ImageReady 7 helps with creating elements like navigation bars with simultaneous rollover effects.

Photoshop fundamentals are covered primarily in Chapter 1, and in the introductory pages of the other chapters.

HOW TO USE THIS BOOK

The aim of *The Photoshop 7 Wow! Book* is to provide the kind of inspirational examples and practical "nuts-and-bolts" info that will help you maximize the program's performance and your own creativity and productivity with it.

You'll find **six kinds of information** in this book: (1) basic information about how Photoshop's tools and functions work, (2) short tips for making your work quicker and easier, (3) step-by-step techniques for particular kinds of projects, (4) "Galleries" of work done by experienced Photoshop artists, (5) illustrated lists, or "catalogs," of related techniques, and (6) the Wow! companion CD-ROM.

1 You'll find the **Basics** sections at the beginning of each of the nine chapters of this book. Whether or not you start by reading Chapter 1, at some point you're going to come up against the need for some "Photoshop fundamentals." When you do, here's where to look for frequently asked questions:

- To **maximize your efficiency** — from stocking your system with RAM and disk storage space, to constructing your files to give yourself as many options as possible for later changes later, to recovering from mistakes — read the "**Working Smart**" section of Chapter 1.

- To learn how to **scan a photo or artwork so you get enough information** to make a good print, read "**Setting Up a Scan**" in Chapter 1.

- To **get the color you expect** when you print, read "**Getting Consistent Color**" in Chapter 2.

- For a quick exploration of how **Layer Styles** work to produce special effects, read about Styles starting on page 352 at the beginning of Chapter 8, "Special Effects for Type & Graphics." Then see "**Anatomy of a Layer Style**" on page 366, and try out the other techniques in Chapter 8.

- To find out how to **make a clean selection** of part of an image without spending all day at it, read "**Making Selections**" and "**Modifying Selections**" in Chapter 1.

- For pointers on choosing component images and making them work together in a seamless **montage**, read "**Extracting an Image**" and "**Assembling a Still Life**" in Chapter 4 and "**Combining with Light**" in Chapter 5.

- For a quick tutorial on using **layer masks** to combine several elements into an effective **montage**, see "**Quick Masking & Blending**" in Chapter 4.

- To **set up assembly-line production and reliable repeatability**, read "**Automating with Actions**" in Chapter 1.

- To decide which **Web-preparation** tasks to do in Photoshop and which in ImageReady, see Chapter 9.

INSTALLING WOW PRESETS

In Photoshop 7, installing presets couldn't be easier. Drag the PS7 **Wow Presets** icon (depending on your operating system, this icon will be different — this is actually a folder containing all of our presets), shown below, into the **Presets** folder within the Adobe Photoshop 7 **Application** folder and restart Photoshop. That's it! Photoshop will find the 38 different Wow sets of presets and automatically load them into the appropriate menus where they can be selected via the associated menu's pop-out Options menu. Once a set is loaded (such as Wow 7–12 Plastic Styles), you can access the specific presets (Wow-Plastic 06, for example) contained within that style set. See page 9 for further information on loading the Wow Presets

2 To collect the kind of hands-on information that can make you instantly more efficient, flip through the book and scan the **Tips**. You can easily identify them by the gray title bar on top. The tips are nuggets of information that are positioned alongside the basics and techniques where they'll be the most helpful. But each one also stands on its own, and you can quickly pick up a lot of useful information simply by flipping through the book and reading them. You can identify **tips about keyboard shortcuts** by the yellow background behind them.

3 Each **Technique**, presented in 1 to 6 pages, is designed to give you enough step-by-step information so you can carry it out in Photoshop. Our goal was to provide enough written and pictorial instructions so you wouldn't have to hunt through the *Adobe Photoshop 7.0 User Guide* or continuously consult Photoshop's online Help to follow the steps. But to spare you a lot of repetition, we've assumed you know the basic Windows or Mac interface — how to open and save files, for instance. Some of the techniques are simple and introductory; others are more advanced and challenging. If something isn't clear to you, you may find it helpful to go back to review Chapter 1, as well as the introductory pages for the chapter you're working in.

   "**Before**" and "**after**" versions of the files used in the techniques have been provided on the **Wow CD-ROM** in the pocket at the back of the book. You can use these files to follow the steps and check your results, before trying the techniques on other images. (Many of the original photographs for the "before" and "after" files have been generously provided by Corbis Images Royalty Free, whose license agreement is also provided on the CD.)

   The techniques sections are like recipes — you follow the directions to combine the ingredients. When you want an approach that's more like a microwavable meal than a recipe, turn to the automated **Wow 7-Styles** or **Wow 7-Photoshop Actions** on the CD-ROM. After you've enjoyed a no-fuss-no-muss Style or Action, you can dissect the resulting file along with the Style or Action itself, to learn about that particular technique and to pick up pointers for making your own Styles or Actions.

   As you work with Photoshop 7, you'll notice that there seem to be at least a dozen ways to do everything — you can choose from a menu, use a keyboard shortcut, or click a button; you can cut and paste, or drag and drop; you can combine images using layer masks or blend modes or both; you can apply color adjustments or special effects directly, or add Adjustment layers or a Layer Style to do it. Because of the variety of possibilities, you'll find varied approaches used in the techniques sections, so you'll get a broad exposure to the different ways Photoshop can work. But, in general, the methods that are presented are the most efficient and effective — approaches

3c

"Before" and "after" files are organized by chapter on the Wow CD-ROM.

that will save you time, produce top-quality results, and leave you with the most flexibility to make the inevitable last-minute changes.

4 The images in the **Galleries** are for inspiration, but their captions also include a lot of useful information about how the artwork was produced. Many of the methods mentioned in the Galleries are described more fully elsewhere in the book.

5 Throughout the book are illustrated "**catalogs**" of options for treatments of images or graphics, such as "Quick Tone & Color Adjustments" in Chapter 3, Filtered Frames" in Chapter 5, "Art History Examples" in Chapter 6, and "Chrome Style Variations" in Chapter 8.

6 Don't miss the **Wow CD-ROM** with its "before" and "after" files; the Wow Layer Styles and Wow Rollover Styles, Gradients, and Patterns; and the Wow Actions. It also includes demo programs and product information from third-party companies.

Experiment! The aim of this book is to get you started using the tools if you're new at it, and to give you some new insight and ideas if you're an old hand. As you read the book and try out the tips, techniques, Styles and Actions, we hope you'll use them as a jumping off place for your own fearless experimentation.

4

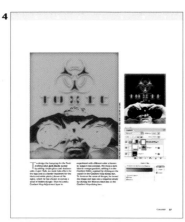

Without taking you through projects step-by-step, "Gallery" sections provide insight into artists' techniques, with enough detail so you can see how to apply their methods to your own work.

5

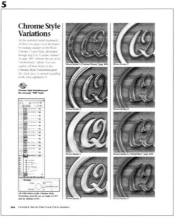

An illustrated "catalog" page shows several quick examples of related techniques.

6

The Wow Button Sampler on page 455 shows the Wow Button Styles and Wow Rollover Styles found on the CD-ROM that comes with this book and provides tips for applying them to your own graphics.

If you already own the Adobe Photoshop 7 One-Click Wow! book from Adobe Press, and have loaded the presets from its CD-ROM, there is no need to load the presets from the Wow CD that comes with the book you're holding in your hands. All the presets associated with The Photoshop 7 Wow! Book are merely a subset of the 800 or more presets that come with the 100-page reference One-Click book. All the names of the presets are the same as in this book, and they are organized in the same fashion. If you have loaded presets from The Photoshop 6 Wow! Book, you can also move them out of Photoshop 7's multiple folders since they also are only a small subset of the ones in the Adobe Photoshop 7 One-Click Wow! book (nor are they organized so nicely by use and appearance).

Installing the Wow Presets

In Photoshop 7, installing presets couldn't be easier. Drag the **PS7 Wow Presets** icon **A** (this is actually a folder containing all our presets) into the **Presets** folder within the Adobe Photoshop 7 **Application** folder **B** and restart Photoshop. That's it! Photoshop will find the 38 different Wow sets of presets and automatically load them into the appropriate menus where they can be selected via the associated menu's pop-out Options menu. Once a set is loaded (such as Wow 7-12 Plastic Styles), you can access the specific presets (Wow-Plastic 06, for example) contained within that style set. Below are the categories of the Wow Presets and the sets they contain.

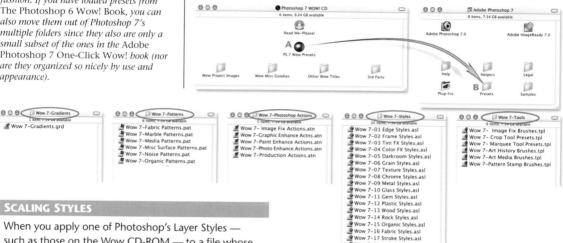

SCALING STYLES

When you apply one of Photoshop's Layer Styles — such as those on the Wow CD-ROM — to a file whose resolution (dpi) is different from the resolution of the file the Style was originally created in, Photoshop automatically scales the Style — whether you want it to or not. To avoid the unwanted scaling, you can temporarily and nondestructively change the resolution of the target file as described on page 348. Or you can right-click (Windows) or Control-click (Mac) directly on the *"f"* icon *for the layer where you've applied the Style* and choose Scale Effects from the context-sensitive menu that pops up. Here are some scale factors for common file resolutions:

• If the Style was created at **72 dpi** (as were the Wow 7-20 Button Styles) and your target file is 225 dpi, use 32% for the Scale. If your target file is 300 dpi, use 24% for the Scale.

• If the Style was created at **225 dpi** (as were the rest of the Wow 7 Styles) and your target file is 300 dpi, use 75% for the Scale. If your target file is 72 dpi, use 312% for the Scale.

• If the Style was created at **300 dpi** and your target file is 225 dpi, use 133% for the Scale. If your target file is 72 dpi, use 417% for the Scale.

IMAGEREADY

ImageReady doesn't automatically find presets unless they are in the appropriate labeled folders in the main Presets folder, which is located within the Adobe Photoshop 7 Application folder. If you think you will be designing or creating rollovers in ImageReady, you have one more step to take. Since Layer Styles are the only category of presets that work within ImageReady, the easiest way to have the **Wow 7 Styles** available in both Photoshop and ImageReady is to move the **Wow 7-Styles** folder **A** out of the **PS7 Wow Presets** folder and put it in the **Styles** folder **B** located within the main presets folder and restart both programs.

USING THE WOW! IMAGE FIX BRUSHES

When you have a lot of files to tweak in a hurry, try these quick "fix-it" tools to tackle the problems.

*Try the **Wow 7-05 Darkroom Styles 11–15** on a non-background layer to brighten and tint an image. See page 12 for tips on applying styles.*

To correct red-eye, use the Wow-Red Eye brushes to first neutralize the red and restore color to the iris if necessary (center), and then darken the pupil if needed (right). You can use the bracket keys to change brush size — [to go smaller,] to enlarge.

*Rather than aiming for a "Hollywood" smile, use the **Wow-White Teeth** brushes to subtly neutralize specific stained areas (center), then whiten them (right).*

*If the built-in color of the **Wow-Red Skin-Neutralize** brush isn't right for your image, hold down the Alt/Option key and click in the image to sample a desired skin color.*

*Before (left) and after lightening with the **Wow-Dodge & Burn-Subtle** Preset, using white paint, a large soft brush tip, and low Opacity.*

WITH THE ADVENT OF PHOTOSHOP 7'S NEW **Tool Presets** feature, you can create quick "fix-it" tools — available at a moment's notice — which can be especially helpful if you need to tweak dozens of images at once. (Can you say "Wedding Photographer?")

We have created a number of these requested "time-savers" as part of the **Wow 7-Styles, Wow 7-Tool Presets,** and **Wow 7-Actions.** Please read page 9 for loading instructions on how to install the **Wow Presets.**

The process of improving a photo should start with overall tone and color adjustments and then proceed to retouching tasks. Here are some pointers for success:

1 Duplicate your background image. Type Ctrl/⌘-J to duplicate your background layer (or any layer); that way you'll always have your original to refer to.

2 Make any necessary corrections to overall tone and color. You can try one of the **Wow 7-Image Fix Actions** as a start to correcting overall tonality problems. If the result isn't quite what you want, in the Layers palette drag the Adjustment layer made by the Action to the trash icon at the bottom of the palette, then try a different Wow-Image Fix Action. Other subtle "quick fixes" you can try are **Wow 7-05 Darkroom Styles 11–15**; these styles focus attention on the center of an image by darkening the edges and lightening and tinting the center of a layer. (See page 12 for more on applying styles.)

3 To work with the **Wow 7-Image Fix Brushes,** choose the Brush tool from Photoshop's Tools palette, then open the Tool Presets palette (Window, Tool Presets). Choose Wow-Image Fix Brushes from the palette's pop-out list, and experiment:

- To even the lighting in an image, in the Tool Presets palette, choose a **Wow-Dodge & Burn** tool from the Tool Presets palette, and paint with it, switching between black (to darken) and white (to lighten). Aim for subtle changes. For a more controlled method of Dodging & Burning (though not as fast), see page 120.

- To get rid of "red-eye," first use the **Wow-Red Eye-Neutralize** brush at an appropriate size to carefully paint away the red in the pupil (and the iris if necessary). If you do have to remove red from the iris, restore color with one of the three **Wow-Red Eye-Replace** brushes and select any existing color remaining in the eye by Alt/Opt-clicking with the brush. And if the pupil needs darkening, use the **Wow-Red Eye-Darken** brush.

- To whiten teeth or eyes, dab with an appropriate-size **Wow-White Teeth-Neutralize** brush to get rid of stains. (Stay away from lips and gums.) Use the **Wow-White Teeth-Brighten** brush to lighten.

- To take the "heat" out of red patches on the face but still leave some of the natural blush, use the **Wow-Red Skin-Neutralize** brush.

USING THE WOW! ACTIONS

These "try 'em, you'll like 'em" Wow! Actions meet everyday Photoshop challenges and can create some spectacular effects.

*Some of the **Wow Actions** start by making a duplicate file from whatever is visible in your image file. The Action then runs on that copy.*

Adobe Photoshop

For this Action, select an object/s within your image. Preferably the selection should extend off the bottom of the image. If you don't have one already, press the Stop button below and make the selection. Then click the lit Action button (if in Button Mode), or the Play arrow on the bottom of the Actions palette (if in List mode).

Stop   Continue

Actions	Actions
Wow-Photo Enhance (button reset)	Wow-Photo Enhance (button reset)
Wow-Soft Focus-Lighten	Wow-Soft Focus-Lighten
Wow-Soft Focus-Darken	Wow-Soft Focus-Darken
Wow-Soft Focus-Overlay	Wow-Soft Focus-Overlay
Wow-Soft Focus-Soft Light	Wow-Soft Focus-Soft Light
Wow-Color Background	Wow-Color Background
Wow-Background Blur-Digital Camera	Wow-Background Blur-Digital Camera
Wow-Background Blur-Film Grain	Wow-Background Blur-Film Grain
Wow-Filtered Watercolor 1	Wow-Filtered Watercolor 1
Wow-Filtered Watercolor 2	Wow-Filtered Watercolor 2

If your Actions palette is set to Button Mode via the pop-out menu in the palette's upper right hand corner, click the button to start the Action (above). It's important to read and carry out the directions in any "Stop" message. Then click the button again (it will be red, so you can find it) to continue.

THERE ARE FIVE SETS OF WOW-ACTIONS — "mini-programs" you can run in Photoshop for image fixing, dimensional effects for graphics, photo enhancements, enhancements for paintings, and production shortcuts.

1 Set up the Actions palette. Once you've loaded the **Wow Presets** as described on page 9, open the Actions palette (choose Window, Actions). By default the palette appears in List Mode, but you can toggle it to a compact and colorful set of buttons by choosing Button Mode from the menu that pops out from the palette's upper right corner. Each **Wow 7-Photoshop Actions** set that you choose from the bottom of that menu will be added to the palette.

2 Prepare the file. Open the file you want to run a Wow Action on. Make sure the image you want to start with is what's showing on-screen. That is, all the layers, masks, and Styles that make up the image must be visible. Also, target the layer you want the Action to work on (click on the layer's name in the Layers palette).

3 "Play" the Action. In the Actions palette, click the button for the Action you want to run. Basically, that's it — the Action runs!

Briefly, here are the **Wow Actions**, and some of their capabilities:

- **Wow 7-Image Fix Actions.** Among these is **Wow-Dust & Scratches Layer**, which helps you remove those tiny, annoying specks; it's faster than using Photoshop's Healing Brush, and you do the work on a separate layer (see page 134 for an understanding for this technique). **Wow-Auto Levels-All 7 Variations Sampler** adds several Levels Adjustment layers for correcting common tone and color problems; after running the Action you can view the effect of each Adjustment layer and choose which works best and remove what doesn't.

- **Wow 7-Graphics Enhance Actions.** These routines turn your active graphics or type layer into dimensional materials with characteristics like light refraction or flaming glows, which are too complex to achieve with a single Style.

- **Wow 7-Paint Enhance Actions.** Try these after using the Wow painting and cloning Presets, to emphasize brush strokes or pooled paint effects.

- **Wow 7-Photo Enhance Actions.** Try any of these 28 enhancements, such as watercolor, line work, mezzotint, and framing, and see what happens. (These may even help that poorly-taken photograph of your boss pass as art!)

- **Wow 7-Production Actions.** These are shortcuts (especially in Button Mode) for everyday operations, like rotating a digital photo 90°, duplicating a flattened copy of your file or deleting hidden layers.

Layer Styles: "One-Click" Flexibility

Layer Styles can provide an ideal way to get the quality, speed, and flexibility that make for successful Photoshop solutions. With Layer Styles you can design, save, and reapply an almost limitless number of combinations of colors, tones, gradients, strokes, and images (in the form of patterns and textures), plus the dimensionality of bevels, shadows, glows, and "reflections." Once you've designed and saved it as a preset, a Style also provides you with the extremely practical opportunity to apply it to any other type, graphic, or photo and have it automatically conform to the shape of the new recipient.

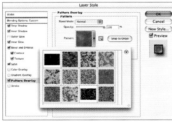

The Wow Styles that come on this book's companion CD are a sampling taken from the book/CD Adobe Photoshop 7 One-Click Wow, and are organized into 20 categories — all of which are titled: **Wow 7-**, then the number of the set (**01-20**), followed by the name of the set (**Glow Styles**, for example). See page 9 for more.

 Mentawai files

LAYER STYLE EFFICIENCY

Layer Styles, like other presets, use RAM and scratch disk space. See "Managing Presets" on page 23 for pointers on keeping your presets handy without sacrificing efficiency.

Preparing the File

A layout was assembled, with each element on a separate layer. Type was set in two separate layers in Arial Black, so we would be able to apply different Styles to the two settings. We wanted to be able to use a Style to assign a texture or image to the background of our composition. But since the Background is the only kind of layer than can't accept a Style, we double-clicked on the Background's thumbnail to turn it into a "Style-friendly" layer with potential for transparency.

A *The converted background layer*

B *The headline type*

C *The photos*

D *The small type*

"One-Click" Application

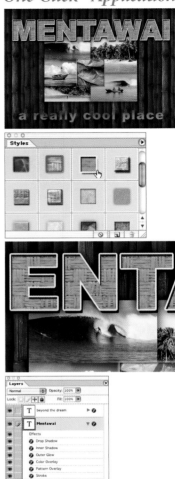

With the **PS 7 Wow Presets** installed, and the specific style set loaded from the pop-out menu in the upper-right of the Styles palette, each layer was targeted by clicking its name in the Layers palette, and with one click in the Styles palette a Style was applied:

A *Wow-Organics 16 (found in the Wow 7-15 Organic Styles set), a Style made with a photographic Pattern Overlay*

B *A variation on Wow-Organics 05, which is a dimensional Style made with shadows and glows, with a photographic pattern and a tint*

C *Variations on Wow-Halo 03 (found in the Wow 7-18 Halo Styles set) with the Color Overlay option turned off*

D *Wow-Stroke 01 (found in the Wow 7-17 Stroke Styles set)*

Instant Style Changes

Scale Layer Effects

Scale:	20	▸	%	OK
				Cancel
				☑ Preview

A Layer Style can be changed instantly. You can either assign a different Style with one click in the Styles palette, as we did here for the background layer, headline type, and photos. Or you can leave the same Style in place and change its parameters, either individually in the Layer Style dialog box or by scaling the entire effect, as shown here for the small type.

A *Wow-Rocks 20 (found in the Wow 7-14 Rock Styles set), made with a fine-grained pattern used as the Pattern Overlay and Texture components of the Style*

B *Wow-Rocks 16*

C *A variation of Wow-Tint FX 01 (found in the Wow 7-03 Tint FX Styles set), made with a sepia-toned Color Overlay at 60% Opacity in Color blend mode to allow some of the original color to show through*

D *Wow-Stroke 01, scaled to look more like the Style was originally designed to look*

✳ = TEXTURE

In the Styles palette, an "✳" at the end of the name of a Wow Style indicates that a pixel-based texture was used to create this style, so care should be taken when scaling it. See page 369 for more.

Instant Content Changes

If you change the content of a layer to which a Style has been applied, the Style instantly conforms to the new content, as shown with these type changes. (For the small type a different Style was also applied.)

A *Wow-Rocks 20 (unchanged)*

B *Wow-Rocks 16 (unchanged)*

C *Wow-Tint FX 01 (unchanged)*

D *Wow-Metals 07 (found in the Wow 7-09 Metal Styles set)*

Scaling the File

Image Size		
Pixel Dimensions: 774K (was 3.03M)		OK
Width: 606	pixels	Cancel
Height: 436	pixels	Auto...
Document Size:		
Width: 5.39	inches	
Height: 3.875	inches	
Resolution: 112.5	pixels/inch	
☑ Constrain Proportions		
☑ Resample Image: Bicubic		

To repurpose the composition for the Web, a duplicate can be resized. Resizing by changing the "Resolution" (not the "Width" or "Height") keeps all the Styles in proportion. (This process is described on page 337.)

Rollover Styles

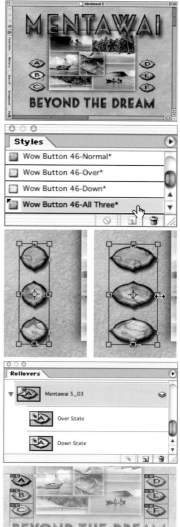

In ImageReady, with one click in the Styles palette (like Wow-Button 46, shown here, found in the Wow 7-20 Button Styles set), you can apply combined Rollover Styles. Like other Styles, Rollover Styles conform to the shape of the layer content, so it's simple to transform the button shape (as here from circular to oval). Combined Rollover Styles include interactivity for states such as Normal, Over, and Down. Automatic layer-based slicing ensures that the active area of the button conforms to the current button shape. (Creating and applying Rollover Styles is described step-by-step starting on page 449.)

FUNDAMENTALS OF PHOTOSHOP

THIS CHAPTER IS DESIGNED to give you an overview of how Photoshop 7 works — how it organizes information when you create or edit an image, and how you interact with the program. It will also give you some general pointers on using the program easily and efficiently. But it won't replace the *Adobe Photoshop 7.0 User Guide* or on-screen Help as a comprehensive source of basic information.

WHAT IS A PHOTOSHOP FILE?

Back when Photoshop was born, more than ten years ago, the answer to the question "What is a Photoshop file?" was a lot simpler. It was a digital picture made up of a monolayer of *picture elements*, or *pixels* for short — tiny square dots of color. Today a Photoshop file is a lot more complex, but also a lot more powerful.

You can think of a typical Photoshop image file as a stack of **layers**, kind of like a big open-face sandwich. The image that you see on-screen or that gets printed is what you would see if you looked down at the layer stack from the top. There are several different kinds of layers that can be in the stack:

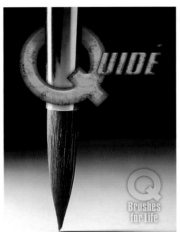

- There can be a ***Background*** at the bottom of the stack, completely filled with pixels.

- **Transparent layers** can also hold pixels, but these layers can have areas that are completely or partly transparent, so that any pixels from the layers underneath show through the clear areas.

- **Adjustment layers** don't contribute any pixels to the image at all. Instead, they store instructions that change the color or tone of the pixels in layers below.

- **Type layers** hold — you guessed it — type, in a "live," or *dynamic*, form that can be edited if you need to change the spelling of the words or the spacing of the characters or the font or color or any other characteristics of the type.

- **Shape layers** and **Fill layers** are also dynamic. Instead of including *pixels* of color, they include *instructions* for what color they should be and what parts of them should be allowed to show.

Photoshop 7's Layers palette shows how the elements of an image stack up. Layer stacks are important in almost every aspect of Photoshop work, as you'll see in the techniques throughout the book. Layers can be linked, grouped, made into sets, and color-coded. These relationships are covered thoroughly in Chapter 4, "Combining Images," since they are very important in making composite images.

Each of these kinds of layers, except the *Background*, can include one or two *masks* — a pixel-based *layer mask* or an instruction-based *vector mask*. And each mask can hide part of the layer's con-

continued on page 16

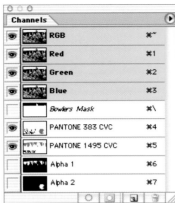

Alpha channels are listed at the bottom of the Channels palette. They aren't really related to the color channels (which hold primary colors and spot colors) that appear above them. Instead alpha channels mainly store information that can be used to select different areas of the image. But color channels and alpha channels are conveniently stored together in one place. The layer mask of the currently active layer is a "transient" resident in the Channels palette, appearing only as long as that particular layer is active. Its name appears in italic.

The Paths palette stores vector-based outlines that you can make with the Pen and Shape tools. The vector mask of the currently active layer also appears in the Paths palette. The Work Path is the path that's currently being drawn and hasn't been saved yet. Because the vector mask and the Work Path are transient, their names appear in italic.

tribution to the overall image. All of these layers, again with the exception of the *Background*, can also include a *Layer Style*, which is a "kit" of instructions for creating special effects like shadows, glows, bevels, and color or pattern fills, that follow the shape of the content of that layer.

In the "sandwich" of the Photoshop file, the difference between the pixel-based elements and the instruction-based elements is an important one. We might think of the pixel-based layers of the file as, for example, the paté, cream cheese, bologna, lettuce, marinated eggplant, and bread put together in the sandwich. Then we could think of the instruction-based elements as little notes that say "put two tablespoons of guacamole between the paté and the cream cheese" or "spread a mixture of mayonnaise and mustard on the bread, but on the left side only" or "trim this piece of bologna into a heart shape and curl the edges" or even "put a slice of roast beef here." Magically, in a Photoshop "sandwich" the computer translates the instructions into an on-screen picture that shows us in advance what the complete result will be like.

The advantage of using these instructions is obvious — it's a lot easier to change your mind. You can decrease the guacamole to one tablespoon or swap peanut butter for the mustard-mayonnaise mixture or trim the bologna to the edges of the bread or decide to leave out the beef. If these elements had already been added to the "sandwich" or "trimmed and curled" in *pixel* form, it would be a lot harder to "revise" the sandwich. Changing the *instructions* is a clean operation that doesn't leave behind a residue or make us wish we hadn't cut something off. The instructions can be changed right up until the "sandwich is served," or until the layered file is rendered as a monolayer of pixels to be printed or put on a Web page.

If we think of the layers — including their masks and Styles — as sandwich components, we might think of the color channels as the protein, carbohydrate, fat, and vitamin components of the food. Instead of keeping track of the image as layers in a stack, the color channels store information about the amounts of each primary color in the image. It's a different way of separating or analyzing the information in the file, and one that's important for the way Photoshop works.

The sandwich analogy can only be pushed so far. It's hard to translate layer masks into sandwich lingo, for instance. But at least it's a start at understanding the importance of layering and of the difference between *pixels* and *vector-based* or *procedural instructions*.

In addition to the layers (with masks and Styles) and color channels, Photoshop files can also have *Paths* and *alpha channels*. These provide two different ways to store information that you can use to select and reselect areas of the image to work on.

If you can't dedicate an entire hard disk or a multi-gigabyte partition to be the scratch disk for Photoshop and you have to use a disk that also stores files, be sure to *optimize* the disk regularly. The process of optimizing a hard disk collects all of the small pieces of fragmented storage space that result when a disk is used and reused over time. The goal is to join all the free disk space into a single large contiguous block. This makes it more efficient for Photoshop to store and work on a file when the scratch disk function is used, swapping parts of the file from RAM to the hard disk and back.

• On a Windows-based system run the Scan Disk program and then run Disk Defragmenter. Both can be found by choosing Start, Programs, Accessories, System Tools.

• On the Mac use a defragmenting program such as Norton Utilities' Speed Disk.

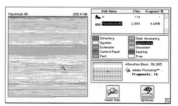

Before defragmenting, the empty space (indicated by white, above) is in many small noncontiguous blocks.

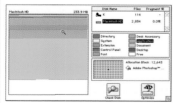

After Disk Defragmenter or Norton Utilities' Speed Disk (shown here) is applied, the empty space is consolidated in a single large block or blocks.

WHAT IT TAKES TO RUN PHOTOSHOP

Photoshop files tend to be large — the number of layers in a Photoshop file is limited only by your computer's capacity to keep track of them, which brings us to what kind of equipment is needed to work with Photoshop.

CPU Speed and RAM

A great deal of information has to be stored to record the color of each of the thousands or millions of pixels that make up an image. Vector-based elements (such as Shape and type layers) and procedural instructions (such as those in Layer Styles) take less storage space than pixel-based layers, but they all add up. So it can take quite a bit of computer processing just to open a file (which brings that information into the computer's working memory, or RAM) or to apply a Style or filter effect (which can involve complicated calculations for evaluating and changing the color of every pixel in the image). Photoshop needs a lot of RAM to hold an image while it works on it, especially with the addition of improvements to efficiency such as the History palette, which "remembers" earlier stages of the file, and with the ability to keep many presets available — palettes of Layer Styles, Brushes, Patterns (which are pixel-based), and other kinds of presets as well. Although you can do good Photoshop work on a smaller, slower, less powerful computer system, the program works best if you have a very fast computer, a great deal of RAM, a monitor displaying full 24-bit photorealistic color, and a very large, fast hard disk drive with plenty (multiple gigabytes) of optimized free space.

Requirements for running the program on Windows and Macintosh platforms are identical, except for the operating system, of course. Here's what you need:

• **The operating system** — a **Windows** Pentium-class III or faster processor with the Windows 98 (Special Edition), Windows NT 4.0, Millennium edition, Windows 2000, or Windows XP; or a **Macintosh** system with a PowerPC or faster processor running MacOS 9.1 through OSX, 10.1.3 or later

• **A monitor** — capable of displaying at least 800 x 600 pixels and at least 16-bit color (thousands of colors)

• **RAM** — 128 MB, although 192 MB is suggested; this doesn't include any memory required for the operating system or for running other programs at the same time.

• **Free hard disk space** — at least 320 MB

• **A CD-ROM drive** — to install the program

To get the full benefit of Photoshop's vector-based and live-type capabilities, you will also need a **PostScript printer**, and to have any fun you'll need a **desktop color printer**. For input, especially if you plan to use Photoshop for painting, a **graphics**

tablet with pressure-sensitive stylus will make a big difference. And if you're running on a Mac, for convenience you may want to replace the standard one-button mouse with a **two-button mouse** so you can right-click instead of having to reach for the Control key for many of the important Photoshop functions, available via context-sensitive menus. And then, of course, you'll want a scanner, a CD-ROM-burner, a digital camera, and then . . .

Scratch Disk

If Photoshop doesn't have enough room to handle a file entirely in RAM, it can use hard disk space for memory — that's *virtual memory*, or in Photoshop parlance *scratch disk*. In that case, two factors become important. The first is the amount of empty hard disk space (beyond the 320 MB required, you'll want at least as much space as you have RAM *plus* at least five times the size of any file you work on). The second factor is the transfer rate of the disk drive, or the speed at which data can be read off a disk. Consider dedicating an entire fast multi-gigabyte hard disk drive as a scratch disk. Disk space is relatively cheap these days, and this will give Photoshop plenty of "elbow room." Second best would be to dedicate a multi-gigabyte partition of a hard disk as the scratch disk. Either way, because you won't be storing anything on it permanently, the drive or partition won't become fragmented, which is important for speed, and so you won't have to run a defragmenting program periodically (as described on page 17) to keep your system in top-notch form.

HOW PHOTOSHOP WORKS

As with virtually all graphics programs for the computer, you work with Photoshop by operating tools and by making choices from menus, palettes, or dialog boxes. But for most of the tools and commands, before you can make changes to an image, you have to tell Photoshop which *part* of the image you want to change, by targeting a layer or one of its masks, and sometimes by making a *selection* within the layer. If you don't make a selection, Photoshop assumes that you don't want to limit your changes, and it applies them everywhere on the layer or mask you're working on. ("Selecting," later in this chapter, tells how to operate many of Photoshop 7's selection tools and commands. And just as important, it tells how to choose a selection method based on the image you're using and what kind of image material you want to select. It also tells how to store selections, refine and edit them, and reactivate them later.)

Photoshop's User Interface

Photoshop 7's user interface, where it presents its tools and commands for your use, is more compact and in some ways more predictable than in previous versions. Below is one way to set up an efficient Photoshop "working environment." (ImageReady 7's toolbox is shown on page 412, and its unique palettes are explored in the techniques in Chapter 9.)

*Photoshop 7's **Options bar** is a kind of context-sensitive palette that offers the appropriate choices for the tool or command that's active.*

*A shortcut for File, **Open** is to Ctrl/⌘-click on the title of the file to open a menu with the location and folder hierarchy of the current document so you can locate and open another file.*

Palettes can be "nested" (stacked behind one another) by dragging the title tab of one palette onto the body of another. To bring a palette to the front of the nest, just click on its title tab.

*If your monitor is big enough so the **palette well** appears at the right end of the Options bar, you can drag palettes into the well and open them by clicking their title tabs. Palettes stored in the well close as soon as you click in the working window.*

*Working at **100%** gives you the most accurate view. If you have to work at a smaller magnification in order to see enough of your image, choose 50%, 25% or some other division of 100 by a multiple of 2. Likewise, when you zoom up for a close view, use exact multiples of 100%, such as 200%, 300%, and so on. The "zoom" box in the lower left corner is "live" — you can type in a specific percentage.*

*This **little box** can be set up to view file sizes, color profile, efficiency (an indicator of how often Photoshop runs out of RAM and has to use scratch disk space), and other factors (as described on page 22).*

*Right-click (or Control-click on a Mac with a one-button mouse) on almost anything to bring up a **context-sensitive menu** of choices.*

Palettes can by "docked" (attached "head to toe") by dragging the title tab of one onto the bottom edge of another, until the bottom edge shows a double line. Docked palettes have a single open/close and a single expand/collapse button.

*Here's one way to set up a 1024 x 768-pixel screen for **working efficiently in Photoshop** with most of the palettes handy. Palettes that you want "at the ready" but that you don't use all the time (here the Swatches, Styles, Actions, and History palettes) can be stored in the "well" at the right end of the Options bar. Palettes that you want to keep open can be "nested" together, like the Layers, Channels, and Paths palettes shown here. Palettes can also be "docked" so they can be opened, closed, and moved together. Some Photoshop artists extend their working space by using a second monitor for the palettes.*

Photoshop's Toolbox

*The **pop-out palettes** in Photoshop 7's toolbox name the tools and present the keyboard shortcuts for toggling between tools that share a space in the toolbox. By default you use the Shift key with the shortcut letter to change tools. Photoshop 7's new Healing Brush and Patch Tools are invaluable additions to its retouching arsenal.*

*The Path Component Selection and Direct Selection tools are used for **moving and editing paths.***

*The **Magnetic Pen** is now available in the Options bar as an option for the Freeform Pen.*

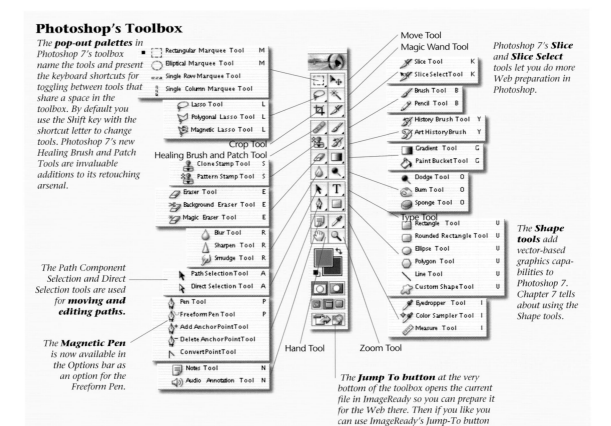

Rectangular Marquee Tool	M
Elliptical Marquee Tool	M
Single Row Marquee Tool	
Single Column Marquee Tool	
Lasso Tool	L
Polygonal Lasso Tool	L
Magnetic Lasso Tool	L

Crop Tool
Healing Brush and Patch Tool

Clone Stamp Tool	S
Pattern Stamp Tool	S
Eraser Tool	E
Background Eraser Tool	E
Magic Eraser Tool	E
Blur Tool	R
Sharpen Tool	R
Smudge Tool	R
Path Selection Tool	A
Direct Selection Tool	A
Pen Tool	P
Freeform Pen Tool	P
Add Anchor Point Tool	
Delete Anchor Point Tool	
Convert Point Tool	
Notes Tool	N
Audio Annotation Tool	N

Move Tool
Magic Wand Tool

Slice Tool	K
Slice Select Tool	K
Brush Tool	B
Pencil Tool	B
History Brush Tool	Y
Art History Brush	Y
Gradient Tool	G
Paint Bucket Tool	G
Dodge Tool	O
Burn Tool	O
Sponge Tool	O

Type Tool

Rectangle Tool	U
Rounded Rectangle Tool	U
Ellipse Tool	U
Polygon Tool	U
Line Tool	U
Custom Shape Tool	U
Eyedropper Tool	I
Color Sampler Tool	I
Measure Tool	I

Hand Tool
Zoom Tool

*Photoshop 7's **Slice** and **Slice Select** tools let you do more Web preparation in Photoshop.*

*The **Shape tools** add vector-based graphics capabilities to Photoshop 7. Chapter 7 tells about using the Shape tools.*

*The **Jump To button** at the very bottom of the toolbox opens the current file in ImageReady so you can prepare it for the Web there. Then if you like you can use ImageReady's Jump-To button to jump back to Photoshop.*

Menus

*Many of Photoshop's commands have **keyboard shortcuts** for quick application.*

✓ Selection Edges	
✓ Target Path	⇧⌘H
Grid	
✓ Guides	⌘;
Slices	
Annotations	
All	
None	
Show Extras Options...	

*A **check mark** next to a menu item means that feature is turned on; clicking the item toggles it off or on.*

Dialog Boxes

*Pressing the **Escape key** is like clicking Cancel.*

*Pressing the **Enter key** is like clicking OK.*

Dust & Scratches

OK
Cancel
☑ Preview

100%

Radius: 4 pixels
Threshold: 15 levels

*Holding down the **Alt/ Option key** changes the Cancel button to Reset.*

Palettes

__Close__ and put away

__Title__ tab

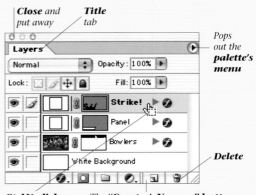

Layers

Normal   Opacity: 100%
Lock: ☐ / ✛ ⬛   Fill: 100%

👁 ✏ Strike!
👁 Panel
👁 Bowlers
👁 White Background

*Pops out the **palette's menu***

__Delete__

__Ctrl/⌘-click__ on almost any palette entry to load it as a selection.

*The **"Create A New . . ." button** at the bottom of a palette makes a new layer, channel, color swatch, or whatever the palette houses.*

WORKING SMART IN PHOTOSHOP 7

Once your system is set up with lots of RAM and a fast hard disk drive, there are some other things you can do to make your "Photo-shopping" time more productive. Assuming that you want to produce the highest-quality artwork, as quickly as possible, and with as much flexibility as you can manage, here are some pointers that can help.

Getting Prepared

Here are a few things you can do to make your work more efficient, either to speed up the rate at which your computer works or to make your own fingers more efficient.

Opening several files at once. You can open several files at once from the Desktop by Shift-clicking their icons or names to select them all and then dragging them onto the Photoshop icon or a Photoshop alias or shortcut icon. The files need not be Photoshop files, as long as they are in a format Photoshop can open. All open files appear in Photoshop's Window, Document menu, so it's easy to get to a document, even if it's behind others in the working window.

Learning the shortcuts. Photoshop has a keyboard shortcut for each of its tools and most of the commands in its menus. To memorize them all would probably take more time and effort than it's worth. But there are certain shortcuts that are definitely worth knowing and practicing until they become automatic. Some good ones are presented in "Essential Shortcuts" on page 56.

"Essential Shortcuts" on page 56.

MAKE ME ANOTHER ONE

When you choose File, New, you can base the new file size on any document that's open in Photoshop: Just pull down the Window menu and choose from the files listed at the bottom to open a new file with the same dimensions, resolution, and color mode. This trick also works with the Image Size and Canvas Size dialog boxes.

AUTOMATIC ACTIVATION

Photoshop's Move tool has an Auto Select Layer feature, which you can turn on and off in the Options bar when the Move tool is active. In Auto Select mode, clicking the tool on an image will automatically activate the uppermost layer with information (pixels) under the pointer. This is designed to make it easier to activate the layer that holds the part of the image you want to work on. However, there are a few conditions that affect which layer is activated:

- If the Opacity control for the layer is set at less than 50%, Auto Select won't "see" the pixels, even though *you* can see them fine.

- An element with more than 50% Opacity may nevertheless be invisible to you, or nearly so, in the composite image because of the blend mode used for its layer. But the Auto Select option will still "see" and select it.

Even with Auto Select Layer on, you can choose which of the layers under the pointer is activated: Right-click to display a menu of layers with pixels under the cursor.

The small box in the lower left corner of the Photoshop window holds a lot of information:

• **How big is the file?** In *Document Sizes* mode the box shows the current open size of the file with all its layers and channels (right) and the size it would be if it was flattened to one layer with all alpha channels removed (left) — that is, the amount of data that will be sent to the printer or other output device.

• **What is the color profile of the file?** In *Document Profile* mode the box shows the color profile assigned to the file, or lists it as "untagged" if no profile has been assigned.

• **Is the scratch disk being used?** In *Scratch Sizes* mode the box shows roughly how much RAM is available for Photoshop to use (right) and how much memory is currently tied up by all open Photoshop files, the clipboard, Snapshot, and so on (left). If the left-hand figure exceeds the right-hand figure, it means Photoshop is using virtual memory to carry out its functions.

• **Would more RAM help?** You can watch the *Efficiency* indicator to see how much Photoshop is using RAM alone, rather than swapping data with the scratch disk. A value near 100% means the scratch disk isn't being used much, so adding more RAM probably wouldn't improve performance. A value less than about 75% means that assigning more RAM would probably help.

• **How long did that take?** In *Timing* mode the box tells how long the last operation took. So you can walk away from your computer leaving it to filter a large file, and find out when you return how long it took, so you'll know for future filtering.

• **What tool am I using?** With the ability to choose Brush Size or Precise cursors instead of picture icons (File, Preferences, Display and Cursors), and with the ability to hide all palettes, including the toolbox (press the Tab key), it can be hard to tell what tool is active. Before you click or drag and make a mistake you'll have to undo, you can check the *Current Tool* listing for the name of the active tool.

• **How will it print?** Pressing on the numbers themselves opens a box that shows the size of the image relative to the page size currently selected in File, Page Setup.

• **What are its specs?** Holding down the Alt/Option key while pressing the numbers shows the dimensions (in pixels and in the Rulers units, set with File, Preferences, Units & Rulers), the resolution (in pixels per inch or pixels per cm, as set with Image, Image Size, Resolution), the color mode, and the number of channels in the image file.

Holding down the Ctrl/⌘ key while pressing the numbers shows the number and size of the rectangular "tiles" that make up the image. The tiles are the blocks of information Photoshop uses to store the image. (If Photoshop is working back and forth from the scratch disk, you can see them appear one by one as the screen is redrawn when you work on a file.) The amount of additional memory required by each layer depends on how many of these tiles its pixels occupy. For instance, in a nine-tile file, a layer with a small circle of pixels at the center of each tile would require more memory than a layer with all the small circles aggregated in one tile.

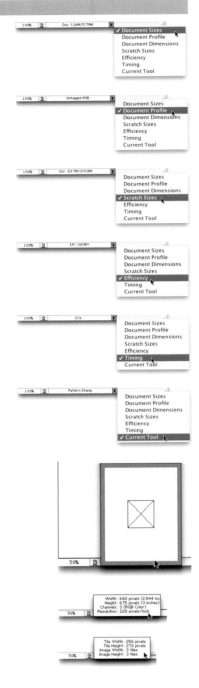

Changing the view (displayed in the file's title bar and editable in the lower left corner of the working window) doesn't change the pixels in the image file — it just changes your on-screen view of them.

- When you view an image at **100%**, it doesn't mean you're seeing it at the dimensions it will print. It means that every pixel in the image file is represented by 1 pixel on-screen.

- **Higher percentages** mean that more than 1 screen pixel is being used to represent 1 pixel of the image file. For instance, at 200% each pixel in the image file is represented by a 2 x 2-pixel block on-screen.

- **Lower percentages** mean just the opposite: 1 on-screen pixel represents more than 1 image pixel. For instance, at 50% each pixel on-screen represents a 2 x 2 block of pixels in the image file.

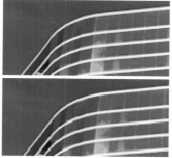

The views at 100% (top), 50%, and 25%, look much smoother and are more accurate for on-screen editing than odd settings like 33.3%, 66.7%, or the 104% view shown here (bottom), which can give you the impression that your image has been somehow corrupted.

Mastering the art of selection. Knowing the ins and outs of making, cleaning up, storing, and recalling selections is at the heart of successful montage and image editing. Take the time to make sure you understand how to choose and use Photoshop's many selection methods, especially the Extract command. These topics are covered in "Selecting" later in this chapter, and the use of Extract is covered step-by-step in "Extracting an Image" on page 162.

Taking advantage of History. Understanding how Photoshop's History palette works can make your sessions more efficient. To get familiar with it, read "The History Palette" later in this section.

Managing Presets

Photoshop 7 has a system for managing Tools, Brushes, Styles, Patterns, Custom Shapes, Gradients, Swatches, and Contours, so they can all be handy for you to grab and apply in your work. Each individual Brush or Style is called a ***preset.*** A set of one or more presets is saved in a ***preset file.*** When a preset file is loaded into Photoshop, its presets appear as thumbnails or lists in the **Preset Manager** (opened by choosing Edit, Preset Manager). They also appear in the appropriate palettes and dialog boxes throughout the Photoshop interface. For instance, Layer Styles appear in the Styles palette (opened by choosing Window, Show Styles) and in the Styles pop-out in the Options bar for the Pen tool and other places; Patterns appear in the Options bar for the Paint Bucket and in pop-out palettes in the Fill dialog box and in the Pattern Overlay and Texture Overlay sections of the Layer Style dialog box.

Loading a preset file that includes many individual presets can use a significant amount of RAM and scratch disk memory, especially if the presets are pixel-based elements, such as Patterns or the pattern-based effects in Layer Styles. Here are some tips for managing presets so you have access to all you want, but at the same time keep your RAM and scratch disk memory freed up so Photoshop has plenty of "elbow room" for working.

Creating individual presets. The Layer Style dialog box (described starting on page 352), the brush-editing interface (page 264), and the Gradient Editor (page 266) are just some of the parts

Choosing Edit, Preferences, General and turning on *Show Tool Tips* can be very helpful in navigating Photoshop 7's streamlined but complex interface. If you pause the cursor over almost anything in the interface, a cheery little note will pop up to tell you what you're looking at.

To save a set of presets using the Preset Manager, select all the ones you want to save, and then click the Save Set button.

Saving presets files (either loose or in a folder) inside the Presets folder in the Adobe Photoshop 7 folder makes these files "visible" to Photoshop's Preset Manager and thus available in the list at the bottom of the pop-out menu in the Preset Manager and in other palettes throughout Photoshop. Choosing from this list is the quickest way to load preset files.

In the Preset Manager you can delete several presets at the same time by Shift-selecting them and clicking the Delete button. To save memory, load a preset file and then delete any individual presets that you know you won't use. Then save a new, smaller set under a new name. (All the presets you removed will still be available in the original larger presets file, which you can load again if you need them.)

of the Photoshop interface where you can design elements that can be named and added to the appropriate palettes as presets. Each of these parts of the interface provides some way to add an individual preset that you've designed. In some cases — such as the Brush-editing panel — it's a Create A New Preset button (the tiny dog-eared page icon); in other cases there's a "New . . ." button — for instance, in the Gradient Editor the button says simply "New"; in the Layer Style dialog it says "New Style." **Caution:** Naming a preset and adding it to the palette does not permanently save it in a way that preserves it against crashes or accidental deletion. The way to do that is to **save it as part of a preset file,** as described next.

Saving presets files. Be sure to save a set that includes any new presets you make. Start by opening the Preset Manager. **Select the presets** you want to save, and **then choose Save Set**. If you save your presets in small "batches," then loading the set you need for a particular job (like adding dimensional effects or styling buttons) won't take up any more memory than necessary.

If you don't save the presets you make, you risk losing your carefully crafted presets in case of a crash or an accidental deletion. For instance, any preset that you delete when you use the "Removing presets" method described on page 25 **will be lost for good** unless they have been saved in a set.

Saving into Photoshop's Presets folder. When you save a preset file, it's a good idea to **store the file in the Presets folder inside the Adobe Photoshop 7.0 folder** on your hard disk. Photoshop can "see" all the preset files in this folder (and in folders nested within this folder), so they will be listed at the bottom of the pop-out menu in the appropriate palettes and in the Preset Manager (as shown at the left). That way you can load a set whenever you want it by clicking its name in the list rather than choosing Load and searching through a hierarchy of folders.

Loading presets. There are several different ways to load a file of presets. You can **choose from the list of preset files at the bottom of the pop-out menu** in the Preset Manager or in a palette (as described in "Saving into Photoshop's Presets folder" above).

In a pop-out palette such as the one for editing brushes or any of the ones for choosing patterns, the "Create A New . . ." button lets you name the current element and add it as a new preset. This gives you a way to save a brush that you've changed, for example, or make a Pattern preset from a Pattern Overlay included in a Style.

You can change the ruler units by right-clicking on one of the rulers (Control-click on a Mac with a one-button mouse).

Column Size

| Width: | 1.8 | inches |
| Gutter: | 1 | picas |

Double-click on a ruler to open the Units & Rulers section of the Preferences dialog box, so you can see or change the Column Width or Gutter. Photoshop can use Column Width as a unit of measure for creating a new file or resizing an image.

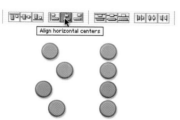

The same options provided in Photoshop's Align Linked and Distribute Linked commands from the Layer menu are also provided as buttons in the Options bar when the Move tool is chosen. They let you line up or evenly space the contents of several linked layers. To line up buttons for a Web page, for instance, this is much quicker than hand-placing Guides from the rulers and then aligning elements to the guides. If you have elements contained on several layers (left), you can align them by clicking to activate one of the layers, then clicking in the column next to the Eye icon in each of the other layers to link them, and finally choosing Layer, Align Linked and selecting the type of alignment you want, or clicking the appropriate alignment button, as shown above. The elements will be aligned according to your choice (right).

Another way to load is to use the Load button in the Preset Manager, or choose Load . . . from the pop-out menu in an appropriate palette. Or you can double-click the icon for your presets file on the Desktop. Once the presets are loaded, you may want to "thin them out" as described in "Removing presets," next.

Removing presets. If you have limited memory and you feel that presets files with many presets are too large to keep "open" all the time (like the Wow Styles files on the CD-ROM that comes with this book), another option is to "thin out" the individual presets you don't need:

- **To remove a preset from within a palette,** simply Alt/Option-click on it to delete it with the scissors cursor.
- **To remove one or more presets using the Preset Manager,** Shift-select the ones you want to remove and click the Delete button. Or if you want to remove all but a few of the presets in the Preset Manager, select all the presets (Ctrl/⌘-A), then Shift-click any that you *don't* want to remove (so they are no longer selected) and then click the Delete button.
- **To unload all the presets in a palette at once** (except the default set supplied by Adobe), choose Reset . . . from the pop-out menu of the Preset Manager or a palette.

Caution: Any time you create a new Style or Pattern or Gradient and save it as a preset by clicking the Create A New Preset button (the dog-eared page icon) or the New button as you are working, before you remove them to thin out the palette, be sure to save them as part of a **named presets file** that you'll be able to load later. Otherwise any presets that you delete will be gone for good.

Taking Advantage of the "Precision" Tools

Photoshop 7 is equipped for precision. You can toggle the **rulers** on and off (Ctrl/⌘-R), and change the ruler units by right-clicking (or Control-clicking on a Mac with a one-button mouse) on a ruler to open a context-sensitive menu of units. Double-clicking on a ruler opens the Units & Rulers section of the Preferences dialog box, where you can see and reset the column size.

You can also create **Guides** simply by dragging from either the top or the side ruler, and set up a custom **Grid** by choosing Preferences, Guides & Grid. You can toggle visibility on and off for these Guides (Ctrl/⌘-') and Grid (Ctrl-Alt-' or ⌘-Option-'), and make them magnetic by choosing the Snap options in the View menu. (For more information about Guides and Grid, see the "Drawing on the Grid" tip on page 301 and "Styled Steel" on page 405.)

The **Move** tool and the **Distribute Linked** and **Align Linked** commands from the Layer menu automatically accomplish even spacing and alignment of elements respectively. The **Options bar for the Transform and Free Transform commands** allows you to enter precise specifications for angles and distances. (See "Transforming" on page 26.)

Here scaling (left) and skewing of the shadow layer were done with only one Transform session. Pressing Ctrl/⌘-T brought up the Transform frame; dragging the top center handle downward scaled the shadow; then with the cursor inside the box, right-clicking (Windows) or Control-clicking (Mac) brought up the context-sensitive menu so Skew could be chosen, and the top center handle was dragged to the left.

△ 0.0 °	⟋ H: 25 °	V: 0.0 °

The Options bar for the Transform commands reflects any changes you make by hand by manipulating the center point and handles of the Transform frame. Or you can enter numbers for the parameters you want to change, such as the rotation angle and horizontal or vertical skew in the part of the Options bar shown here.

Actions
1-unsharp mask	F1
2-gaus blur	F2
3-levels adj	F3
4-hue/sat adj	F4
5-paste©notice	F5
6-paste style	F6

Things that you're likely to do again and again like adding a Levels Adjustment layer or copying and pasting Layer Styles, are great candidates for Actions. The Actions palette can be stored in Button mode as shown here, for one-click operation.

Transforming

Photoshop provides powerful **Transform** and **Free Transform** commands from the Edit menu for scaling, rotating, skewing, distorting, creating perspective, or flipping. These can be carried out "freehand" or with numeric precision by making entries in the Options bar. You can use either command, or use the keyboard shortcut, Ctrl/⌘-T to open a Transform frame with a centerpoint and handles for transforming. You can move the center of rotation if you like by dragging it to a new position, as described in "Animating by Transforming" on page 434. Often you'll want to carry out more than one transformation at a time — a scale and then a skew for a cast shadow, for instance. You can **right-click (Windows) or Control-click (Mac) in the Transform frame to open a context-sensitive menu to switch the kind of transformation,** working back and forth between the different transformations until you get exactly what you want. Finally, press the Enter key to complete the transforming session. Each transforming session can cause softening of the image. So rather than making a series of individual transformations, each time pressing the Enter key and then starting another one, **do all the transforming operations you can in a single "session"** before pressing Enter.

Once you've completed a Transform session, you can repeat the transformation on the same element by using the Edit, **Transform Again** command or pressing Ctrl/⌘-Shift-T. Or make a duplicate and transform the duplicate "again" in one operation by adding the Alt/Option key (Ctrl-Alt-Shift-T for Windows; ⌘-Option-Shift-T for Mac).

Maintaining Flexibility

Keeping your options open is an important part of developing a Photoshop file. By planning ahead, using "procedural," or instruction-based, methods such as Layer Styles and Adjustment layers rather than pixel-based adjustments to your original, and knowing how to undo, you can increase the flexibility of your files and the ease of your work flow. Procedural methods allow you to go back and "change the instructions" later without degrading the image, and it may keep the file size smaller.

Using Layer Styles. Applying special-effects treatments by means of a Layer Style gives you tremendous flexibility. First, you can make repeated changes to the effects themselves without degrading the image. Second, you can apply the Style to one or more other layers in the same file or even in other files. And third, you can even change the contents of the layers you've applied them to and the effects will automatically and instantly "rewrap" themselves to fit the new contents. For a demonstration of the flexibility of Layer Styles, see page 12. To learn how to put Layer Styles to work, see

"Working with Layer Styles" on page 348 and the sections that follow in Chapter 8, especially "Anatomy of a Layer Style" on page 366.

Working with Adjustment layers. If you store color and tone corrections in Adjustment layers, you can readjust without having to start over and without degrading the original image by adding one alteration to another. Adjustment layers also let you save settings from dialog boxes that don't include a Save button, such as Color Balance. (See "Color Adjustment Options" starting on page 74 and "Working with Adjustment Layers" starting on page 114.)

Recording your actions. Any time you make changes that you think you might someday want to make to other images, record the process using the **Actions palette**. Recording doesn't take extra time or RAM, and it may very well produce a useful "macro." Actions work better for recording some processes than for others. Not everything you can do in Photoshop 7 can be recorded in an Action. For instance, brush strokes with painting and toning tools are left out. To get a start on recording and applying Actions, see "Automating with Actions" later in this chapter.

Saving selections as you work. If you're using one of the selection tools or commands to make a complex selection, save the selection periodically by making it into an alpha channel. With a backup version of the selection saved with the file, if you accidentally drop the selection and it's too late to use the Reselect command (found in the Select menu), you won't have to start over completely. Be sure to save the selection again when it's finished, so you can reselect exactly the same area if you need to later.

Making a "repairs" or "painting" layer. If you're using the Sharpen/Blur, Smudge, or Clone Stamp tool to make repairs to an image, you can add the repairs to a separate, transparent top layer, making sure that Use All Layers is selected in the tool's Options palette ("Seamlessly Tiling Patterns" on page 378 shows examples.) That way the sharpening, blurring, smudging, or stamping strokes will use a composite of all layers of the image to make the repairs. With a repairs layer the new work doesn't actually get mixed into the image. So if you want to undo part of your repair work, you can erase, or select and delete, that part from the layer, leaving intact the rest of the repairs, as well as the layers beneath. A related approach can be used for applying the Dust & Scratches filter to remove such blemishes from a photo, as shown in "Fixing a Problem Photo" on page 134.

Besides repairs, you can use a separate layer for adding brush strokes to a painting without risking the work you've already done. When you're sure you like the new work, you can merge it with the layer below (Ctrl/⌘-E), then add another new layer and experiment with more brush strokes.

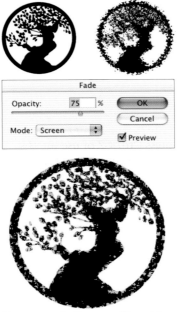

Here we started with a scan of line art (top left), then applied the Spatter filter (top right) and used the Fade command to change its Opacity to 75% and its blend mode to Screen. In Screen mode, the black "spatters" had no effect; only the light spots were combined with the original black artwork.

In a dialog box like Color Balance, where there are a number of settings that can be adjusted, use Ctrl/⌘-Z to undo the last slider setting or typed entry. You can also hold down the Alt/Option key to change the Cancel button to a Reset button, restoring the starting values for all sliders in the box.

You can purge any or all of Photoshop's various caches to free up RAM. Keep in mind, though, that choosing Histories or All purges not only the current document but also any other open files.

Duplicating a layer. Sometimes you may want to make changes to a particular layer but you want an "escape hatch" to get back to the previous version, or you want the flexibility of combining the changed version with the original. In that case, copy the layer and work on the copy. You can do this by dragging the layer name in the Layers palette to the New Layer icon at the bottom of the palette, or typing Ctrl/⌘-J.

Saving files for reference. When you've finished and saved a multilayered image, and you've flattened a copy and printed it, it's a good idea to store the original in its layered form in case you'd like to be able to go back someday and see how you accomplished the look you got in the final printed piece — how the elements were layered and what blend modes, Opacity settings, type specifications, Styles, Blending Options, layer masks, alpha channels, Adjustment layers, and clipping groups you used — in case you want to get a similar effect in another image.

If you can't afford the space to store the entire full-size file, try saving a "thumbnail" version. Choose Image, Image Size to reduce a copy of the layered file to a small low-res version. You could never use it for print — unless the entire image was made with vector-based and procedural elements such as Shape layers, type, and Layer Styles — but it will store the layer information, including Styles, live type, shapes, and Adjustment layer settings, in much less space.

Recovering

Even if you use Layer Styles, Adjustment layers, Shape layers, and other procedural methods to give yourself as much flexibility as possible for making changes later, you may sometimes go too far in a pixel-based process or overdo an application of a filter and need to recover. Here are a few ways to do that:

Undoing. Photoshop's **Ctrl/⌘-Z** (for Edit, **Undo**) will undo your last operation, and the History palette can be set up to let you go much further back than the most recent single step in your work, either by clicking the states in the palette (for more, see "The History Palette" later in this section) or by using **Ctrl/⌘-Shift-Z** to step backward through your most recent changes. The History States setting (Edit, Preferences, General) determines how many steps backward you can undo. You can also **use "Undo" inside a dialog box** that has more than one entry box or slider, pressing **Ctrl/⌘-Z** to undo the last setting you changed.

Resetting a dialog box. In any dialog box that lets you enter at least one value and that has a Cancel button, holding down the **Alt/Option** key changes the Cancel button to the **Reset** button;

If RAM is limited, there are several ways you can "copy and paste" a selection, a layer, a channel, or an entire image without using the clipboard, which requires RAM.

• **To duplicate a selection in the same file,** press Ctrl/⌘-J (for Layer Via Copy).

• **To duplicate the content of a layer,** drag its thumbnail to the Create New Layer button. Press Ctrl/⌘-J.

• **To duplicate a selected area or a layer from one file to another,** drag and drop with the Move tool from one document to the other; to center the selection in the new file, press and hold the Shift key before you stop dragging. Or use the Layer, Duplicate Layer command.

• **To duplicate a channel from one image into another,** drag the channel from the Channels palette into the other image.

• **To copy an entire image as a new file,** either with all layers intact or flattened, choose Image, Duplicate.

• **To duplicate a Snapshot from one file to another,** drag its thumbnail from the History palette into the other file.

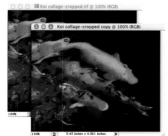

When you copy a file by using the Image, Duplicate command or the History palette's Create New Document, the new file is named but not saved. As soon as you duplicate a file, it's a good idea to choose File, Save As (Ctrl/⌘-Shift-S) so you'll be able to rename and permanently save the document.

clicking this button leaves the box open but returns all the settings to the state they were when you first opened the box.

Fading. Immediately after you apply a filter, or a color adjustment command, or painting strokes — before you do anything else — you can use the Edit, Fade command to reduce the effect or change the blend mode.

Reverting. The File, Revert command takes the file back to its condition the last time it was saved. (The Revert command can be undone if you change your mind — press Ctrl/⌘-Z or use the History palette.) You can also revert to any stage you've saved as a Snapshot in the History palette.

Optimizing Performance

If your find that Photoshop's performance is slowing down or if you notice that the Efficiency rating in the lower left corner of the working window is consistently well below 100% (see page 22), there are some things you can do to free up some RAM or to operate in ways that don't require as much memory.

Purging the clipboard and other caches. If you cut or copy something to the clipboard so you can paste it elsewhere, the material is retained in RAM even after you've pasted a copy in place. In addition, Photoshop always remembers what the image was like before your most recent changes, in case you decide to use Edit, Undo (Ctrl/⌘-Z) or use the History palette. Since some of Photoshop's commands can be carried out only in RAM (not by using the scratch disk), it's good strategy to release the RAM by clearing out a large clipboard selection, purging all History states, or deleting a step you know you won't need to Undo. Just choose **Edit, Purge**; any choices that aren't grayed out indicate that something is stored and can be purged. When you Purge Histories, the *states,* or step-by-step changes, are deleted, but the History Snapshots remain. *Caution*: Choosing Edit, Purge, Histories or Edit, Purge, All affects not only the currently active file but *all open files.* Use the Clear History command from the History palette's pop-out menu to purge only the History for the active file.

Closing other applications. If your main goal is to work in Photoshop, open Photoshop first, before opening any additional applications. This gives Photoshop first claim on RAM. As you work, if you find that you need more RAM, close any other programs you've opened. Even if you aren't doing anything with them, open applications reserve their assigned amount of RAM, which may cut down on the amount available to Photoshop.

Reducing the number of presets. See "Managing Presets" on page 23.

Working at low resolution saves time and disk space. Several designs for the Healthy Traveler book cover were worked out at 72 dpi before one was chosen for development at high resolution.

History Options

☑ Automatically Create First Snapshot
☑ Automatically Create New Snapshot When Saving
☑ Allow Non-Linear History
☑ Show New Snapshot Dialog by Default

OK
Cancel

The settings in the History Options dialog box determine how the History palette operates.

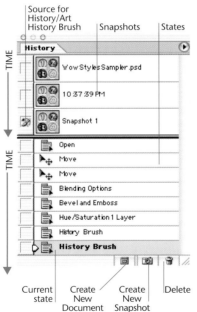

Source for History/Art History Brush

Snapshots

States

TIME

History

TIME

Wow Styles Sampler.psd

10:37:39 PM

Snapshot 1

Open
Move
Move
Blending Options
Bevel and Emboss
Hue/Saturation 1 Layer
History Brush
History Brush

Current state

Create New Document

Create New Snapshot

Delete

The History palette stores step-by-step states at the bottom, recording everything you do to the file. Snapshots, made when you choose to preserve the file at a particular stage of development, are stored at the top of the palette. The History brush icon in the source column means that the state or Snapshot next to the brush icon will be the source if you paint with the History Brush, the Art History Brush, or the Eraser in Erase To History mode, or if you use the Fill command with the History option turned on.

Using "low-overhead" alternatives for copying. The Copy and Paste commands use the clipboard and thus occupy RAM. The "Low-Overhead Copies" tip on page 29 tells about other ways of copying.

Building a file in stages. If you're planning to modify and combine images in a very complex collage illustration, try doing the modifications on the separate, smaller parts first, and then combine them into a larger file. Instead of having a separate layer for every piece of the image, build "modules": Build one component of several layers, then copy those layers into a single layer (Ctrl/⌘-Shift-C copies all visible layers within a selection boundary); create other components the same way; then manipulate the combined copies to make the final image. Chapter 4 tells more about compositing images using layers.

Starting out in low resolution. Especially with the new Layer Styles and vector-based Shape layers and layer clipping paths, you can sometimes do your planning and "sketching" in a lower-resolution file than you will ultimately need for output. For instance, working at low resolution can reduce the processing time needed for creating and changing a number of comps. Although you'll have to make some of the changes again when you choose a direction and create the higher-res file, vector-based elements made at lower resolution can be dragged and dropped, then scaled up in the larger file. If you make tone and color changes as Adjustment layers, you can drag and drop them from the Layers palette of the low-resolution image into the bigger file. If an Adjustment layer includes a layer mask, however, the layer can't be successfully dragged and dropped to the higher-resolution file because the mask will be too small. To learn more about Adjustment layers, start with "Adjustment Layers" on page 73 and "Color Adjustment Options" on page 74. (Settings for some of the Image, Adjust commands that can't be applied as Adjustment layers, such as Variations, can be saved and loaded again later, using the Save and Load buttons in their dialog boxes.)

Like Adjustment layers, active Layer Styles from a low-resolution file can often be successfully transferred into a high-res version, in this case by copying and pasting. To successfully move Layer Styles from a low-res to a high-res file, you'll need to scale them. Some useful scaling factors for Styles are shown on page 9.

The History Palette

The History palette (Window, Show History) lets you go back to a previous state of the image in the current work session and work from there. You can return to a previous state of the entire image, or use History as a source for painting with the previous version, one brush stroke at a time. The Eraser tool and the Fill command can also use History as a source.

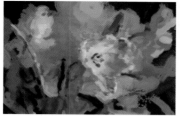

The Art History Brush generates brush strokes that automatically follow the color and contrast contours in an image, using a Snapshot or state from the History palette as a source. With carefully chosen settings and details added afterwards, you can produce a pleasing Art History Brush "painting."

HISTORY TROUBLE

If you make a Snapshot from the Full Document, you can run into trouble later if you've added any layers in the meantime. If you try to paint on one of your new layers with the History Brush or Art History Brush from the Full-Document Snapshot, you'll see a warning:

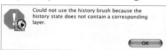

And if you try to use the Eraser tool or the Fill command, the History option will be dimmed and unavailable.

You can **avoid** this problem by choosing Merged Layers when you make a Snapshot:

But if you've already made a Full-Document Snapshot and you get the "Could not use . . ." message or find the History option dimmed for the Eraser or Fill, there's a way to **remedy** the situation: Click on the Snapshot's thumbnail to activate it, then take another Snapshot — merged this time — and then drag the old one to the trash at the bottom of the palette if you no longer need it for anything.

States and Snapshots. The History palette "remembers" the most recent *states,* or steps, of your current work session — the work you've done since you opened the file. This gives you the potential for multiple Undo's, since you can work backwards state by state. However, once you finish your current work session and close the file, the History palette is emptied — it no long retains step-by-step information about what you did.

In practice, the History palette's "memory" can be quite limited. In order to keep from tying up too much RAM, by default the palette retains only the last 20 steps. You can increase the number of steps, but this increases the amount of RAM used and potentially slows down all Photoshop operations.

The History palette automatically adds a state for every change you make to the image. When the list of states in the bottom section of the History palette reaches the number set in the General Preferences (Edit, Preferences, General), the older states at the top of the list are deleted to make room for more at the bottom.

A **Snapshot** is a stored version of the file you're working on. You can make a Snapshot by choosing New Snapshot from the palette's pop-out menu or by clicking or Alt/Option-clicking the Create New Snapshot button at the bottom of the palette.

There are several settings in the History Options dialog box (opened by choosing from the History palette's pop-out menu) that control the making of Snapshots, as shown at the left. These are the benefits of turning on all the options:

- **Automatically Create First Snapshot** gives you access to the file in its original state when you opened the document, even when the early states have cycled off the palette. This option lets you go back even beyond when you last saved the file!

- **Automatically Create New Snapshot When Saving** provides access to the important "milestones" in the

HOLDING ONTO HISTORY

History "evaporates" when you close a file, which means that you can no longer use it for multiple Undo's or for working from any Snapshots you've previously made. But with a little planning and effort you can hold onto the Snapshots, though not the individual states:

Before you close the file, drag a Snapshot to the Create New Document From Current State button, at the left at the bottom of the History palette.

Repeat this process for any of the other Snapshots you want to preserve. Close and save all the files before you quit. When you're ready to work on the image again, open it and all the duplicates you made. Drag the initial Snapshot from each one's History palette into the original file. The dragged Snapshots will be added to the current History palette.

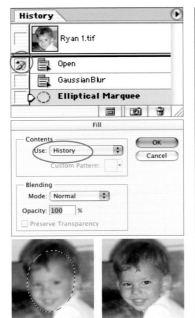

The History palette and Fill command can be used to restore part of a previous version of the image. This method was used here to focus attention on the face: First the image was blurred and the face area was selected with a feathered lasso. Then the original sharp version of the image (the Open state) was chosen as the source, and Edit, Fill, History was used to fill the selected area.

BUTTON, BUTTON . . .

If you put the Actions palette in Button mode (by choosing Button Mode from the palette's pop-out menu or by using the method in the "Quick Changes" tip on page 33), you can use a multicolumn layout that takes up less space per button: Simply drag the lower right corner to widen the palette slightly to two or more columns; the individual buttons will get narrower.

Actions	
Vignette (selec...	Frame Channel ...
Wood Frame - ...	Cast Shadow (t...
Water Reflectio...	Custom RGB to ...
Molten Lead	Make Clip Path ...
Sepia Toning (I...	Quadrant Colors
Save As Photos...	Gradient Map
Wow-Paint Enh...	Wow-Paint Edg...
Wow-Paint Edg...	Wow-Impasto E...
Wow-Impasto E...	Wow-Impasto E...
Wow-Graphics ...	Wow-Silver
Wow-Gold	Wow-Chrome
Wow-Crystal	Wow-Distressed ...

development of the image by making Snapshots of the versions you saved, naming them according to when they were saved.

- **Allow Non-Linear History** lets you go back to an earlier state or Snapshot (by clicking on its thumbnail in the palette) and make changes to the file without throwing away all the states that came after.

- **Show New Snapshot Dialog By Default** automatically opens the New Snapshot box when you click the Create New Snapshot button (you don't have to Alt/Option-click to get the dialog box), and this allows you to choose **From: Merged Layers**, which can be important for using History as a source for painting or filling (see the "History Trouble" tip on page 31.)

An efficient approach to working with History is to **limit the number of states to 20 or fewer** and **duplicate any current state** that you think you might want to refer back to by clicking on that state in the History palette and saving a copy (File, Save As, Save: As A Copy).

Automating with Actions

Even with the arrival of Layer Styles, which can package a set of dimensional or tone-and-color effects for one-click application via the Styles palette, Photoshop's Actions palette still has a lot to offer — for automating the Photoshop functions that can't be included in Styles and also for repetitive production tasks and batch processing. The Actions palette offers a way to record a series of Photoshop operations and play them back in order, on a single file or a whole batch. In a nutshell the process is as follows: You turn on Photoshop's recording apparatus, carry out the operations you want to record, stop recording, and play the Action back on another file whenever you want to. In Photoshop 7 you can also turn an Action into a ***droplet***, a "stand-alone" macro with its own icon that can sit on the Desktop and run the Action on any files whose icons are dragged onto it, as described on page 35.

The Actions palette. Actions are displayed by name in the Actions palette (opened by choosing Window, Show Actions). Within the palette they are grouped in sets, indicated by folder icons. Here are some important things about this organization:

- The **small triangle** to the left of the name of a set or an Action in the Actions palette is a toggle. Clicking it expands the set or Action to show all of its components, or collapses it to hide them.

- An Action's position in a set can be changed simply by **dragging the Action's name to a new position** in the Actions palette.

- You can **play an entire set of Actions** by clicking on the set (the folder) in the Actions palette and clicking the Play (triangle) button at the bottom of the palette. This makes it possible to

A **check mark** next to a command indicates that it is active; if no check mark appears, the command is currently turned off and will not be carried out when the Action is played.

A **check mark** next to the Action name shows that the Action is active and will play as part of a set. A **red check mark** alerts you to the fact that some commands in the Action are currently not active and won't play when the Action is played.

A red dialog box icon in the **modal control column** indicates that some steps in a set or Action will stop and wait for input via a dialog box or the Enter/Return key. If the icon is black, there will be a stop at *every* step where input is possible.

Click to **expand or close** the listing.
Set
Action
Command

Click to **stop recording** or playing.

Click to **record**; red indicates that recording is in progress.

Click to create a **new set**.

Click to create and name a **new Action**.

Click to **Delete** the Action or command.

Click to **play** a selected Action or to play from a selected command onward; **Ctrl/⌘-click** to play only the selected command and then stop.

assemble sets of Actions as "toolkits" that are appropriate for particular jobs, and you can include the same Action in several different toolkits.

• **A set can (and should!) be permanently saved** with the Save Actions command in the Actions palette's pop-out menu.

• An Action can be **moved from one set to another** simply by dragging.

• An Action can be **copied,** either within the same set or to a different one, by Alt/Option-dragging to the position in the palette where you want the duplicate.

Recording an Action. The process of recording an Action differs, depending on whether you want to make a clickable button to choose a single menu item or whether you want to record a multi-step process.

• **To turn any Photoshop command into a clickable button or an F-key shortcut** that chooses a command, open the Actions palette and click the Create New Action button at the bottom of the palette. Name the Action and assign a color or function key shortcut if you like; then click Record. Choose Insert Menu Item from the pop-out menu and select the command you want from a menu or submenu (for instance, Unsharp Mask). Then click the square Stop button at the bottom of the palette to complete the recording.

Now whenever you play that Action in the Actions palette, Photoshop should respond as if you had chosen the command from its menu. And if the command includes a dialog box, the box should open so you can enter the settings you want, just as it would if you were choosing it from the menu.

• **To record a multistep operation** so you'll be able to apply the whole series of commands again, open a file like the ones you want to work on, and click the Create New Action button at the bottom of the Actions palette. Name the

In an Action the effect of a toggle command like Snap To Guides or Show/Hide Guides will depend on the state of the file when the command is played as part of an Action. In other words, even though the command you recorded when you made the Action was Show Guides, if guidelines are already showing when the Action plays the Show Guides command, it will *Hide Guides* instead.

There are some things that are worth recording at the beginning of almost any Action:

- **Start the Action by making a copy of the file's "pre-Action" state** with the Image, Duplicate command. That way you'll have a way to recover your original if you don't like the "actioned" file.

- For some Photoshop operations the file has to be in a certain mode. For instance, the Lighting Effects filter runs only in RGB Color mode. Also, you can't convert an RGB or CMYK file directly to Bitmap or Duotone without going through Grayscale mode first. If your Action requires that the file be in a specific mode, you can avoid problems by inserting the **File, Automate, Conditional Mode Change** command, which will change the mode if necessary.

Action, click Record, and start performing operations, tailoring your choices within the limitations of "actionable" operations mentioned in "What's 'Actionable,'" which follows this section. The round Record button at the bottom of the Actions palette will stay red (indicating that recording is in progress) until you press the square black Stop button to end the recording session.

What's "Actionable." Many of Photoshop 7's commands and tool operations, including the new Shape tools, are "actionable" — able to be recorded as part of an Action and played back on other files. Also, choices made in the **Layers, Channels, Paths, History,** and **Actions palettes can be recorded.** Since the Actions palette is one of the palettes for which choices can be recorded, you can **nest an existing Action within the one you're currently recording** by playing it as you record. Click in the Actions list to select the Action you want to include, then press the Play button. This Action will be added as a step in the one you're recording.

For many of the commands and operations that can't be recorded directly, there are workarounds.

- **Paths drawn "by hand" with the Pen tools won't be recorded as you draw them,** but you can include a path as part of an Action by drawing the path, saving it in the Paths palette with a unique name, then selecting the path in the Paths palette and choosing the **Insert Path** command from the Actions palette's pop-out menu. When the Action is played on another file, the original path will be added to the new file's Paths palette, and further commands in the Action can use that path. (Completing and saving paths can be tricky; see "Two-Phase Options Bars" on page 290 and "Pen Tools" starting on page 299 for information.)

- **Brush strokes made with the paint tools** (Paintbrush, Healing Brush, Clone Stamp, Eraser, and Smudge), **the focus tools** (Sharpen and Blur), and **the toning tools** (Dodge, Burn, and Sponge), as well as the Background Eraser, **aren't recorded.** Instead you can insert a pause, complete with directions for what to do during the pause, so the user can stop and paint. To put a pause in the Action, choose the **Insert Stop** command from the Actions palette's pop-out menu, as described on page 35.

- Some of the choices made in the **Options bar, palettes, and dialog boxes** are recorded and some are not. Again, you can include the Insert Stop command for a choice that isn't recorded, with directions so the person playing the Action can make the appropriate settings. To tell which choices are recorded, you can watch the Actions palette as you record to see what choices add a step to the Action.

Many of the dialog box and palette settings that *can* be recorded

When you choose Insert Stop from the Actions palette's pop-out menu so that your Action will stop running and display a message or give the user a chance for input, you have the opportunity to "Allow Continue." If you check this box, the message that's displayed when the Action stops to include a Continue button will make it easier for the user to continue the Action.

WHEN YOU "INSERT"...

Using the **Insert Menu Item** command as you record an Action will indeed add the command to the Action. But *it won't carry out the command during the recording session.* So if you need a nonrecordable command to be carried out in order for the rest of the Action to be recorded correctly, you'll have to both **carry out the operation in its nonrecordable form** (to do the job in the file you're recording from) *and* **use the Insert Menu Item command** (to get the operation recorded so that it will be carried out when the Action is played).

The Playback Options from the Actions palette's pop-out menu can be used to make Actions run speedily (Accelerated, the default) or one step at a time so you can see the result of each step before the Action continues (good for diagnosing a problematic Action) or with a pause. By default, an Action will pause to finish playing any annotation recorded as part of an Action before the Action continues, but you can turn off this option.

are recorded only if they are changed from an existing setting. So if you want to record a current setting, you have to change to another setting before recording so you can record the process of changing it back to the desired setting.

- Commands that affect the working "environment" rather than an individual file — such as changing Preferences or Color Settings, showing a CMYK Preview or Gamut Warning, zooming your view, or turning Snap To Guides on or off — won't be recorded directly as part of a multistep Action. Instead this kind of command has to be recorded by choosing **Insert Menu Item** from the Actions palette's pop-out menu. Then choose the command, or type the command's name into the Insert Menu Item dialog box.

- Of course, your Action will only work if the **conditions of the file** you're working on will allow it to work. For instance, if your Action includes a step to add a layer mask, you won't be able to do that if the layer that's active when that step is played is the *Background* layer, which can't have a mask. So you have to be sure that you include in the Action all the steps necessary to prepare the file for each step of the Action to work — or a Stop step that explains the requirements so the user can pause and get the file ready: Choose **Insert Stop** from the palette's pop-out menu, and type the message. Select the Allow Continue option if you want the user to be able to proceed with the Action after reading the message. Leave the Allow Continue box unchecked anytime that some input is *required* before the Action can proceed. When you've finished making entries in the Record Stop dialog box, click OK.

Playing an Action. Once you've recorded an Action or loaded an Action that was recorded by someone else (see "Loading Actions" on page 37), you can play it back on a single file or on all the files in a folder.

- **To run an Action or set of Actions,** click its name in the Actions list and click the triangular Play button at the bottom of the palette.

- **To play an Action from a specific step** forward, select that step in the Actions list and then click the Play button.

- **To play a single step** of an Action, click on that step to select it, and then Ctrl/⌘-click the Play button.

Automating Actions. To run an Action on a whole batch of files, put the files into a folder and use the File, Automate, **Batch** command. Or create a standalone **droplet** application from the Action by choosing File, Automate, Create Droplet. Choose the Action you want to play and choose a Destination for the altered files. If you choose Save And Close, the old files will be overwritten by the altered ones. If you choose to save the files to a designated folder, you have tremendous flexibility in naming the files.

Automate	▶	Batch...
File Info...		Create Droplet...
		Conditional Mode Change...
Page Setup...	⇧⌘P	Contact Sheet II...
Print with Preview...	⌘P	Fit Image...
Print...	⌥⌘P	Multi-Page PDF to PSD...
Print One Copy	⌥⇧⌘P	Picture Package...
Jump To	▶	Web Photo Gallery...

If you click on the name of an Action in the Actions palette's list mode and then choose the File, Automate, Create Droplet command, the Create Droplet dialog box opens, where you can choose to bypass any Open and Save As commands that exist as part of your Action. In Photoshop 7 you can choose how your processed document will be named. Here the word "-Sharp" and the file extension are added to the document name for files processed by an Unsharp Mask droplet so it's easy to tell that the file has been sharpened.

When you click OK in the Create Droplet box, the Action is exported as a standalone macro on the Desktop. You can run the Action saved in the droplet by dragging a file or folder icon onto the droplet icon.

You can choose from the pop-out File Naming lists, or type in your own choices. This makes it possible, for instance, to create a numbered or lettered series of files with the same basic name. Once you've made a droplet, you can drag a file or a folder of files onto the droplet's icon on the Desktop to launch Photoshop if necessary, run the Action on the file(s), and save the result into the folder you chose. You can also run more than one Action at a time on a batch of files or via a droplet: Create a New Action, and then record the File, Automate, Batch command to play each of the Actions you want to run.

Editing Actions. If you want to modify an Action you've recorded or loaded, here are some easy methods:

- **To remove a step** (or even an entire Action or set) from the Actions list, drag it to the trash button at the bottom of the palette.

- **To duplicate a step** in an Action, hold down the Alt/Option key and drag the step's name to the point where you want the copy in the Actions list.

- **To change dialog box settings** for a step that opens a dialog box, double-click the command's name in the Actions palette, enter new settings, and click OK.

- **To insert a new command** (or commands) in the Actions list, click the command you want the new command to come after. Then click the round Record button, record the new command(s), and click the square Stop button.

- **To change the order of steps,** drag their names up or down to new positions in the Actions list.

- To make the Action **pause within a step** so the user can change the settings in a dialog box, click in the **modal control column** just to the left of the command's name. A dialog box icon will appear in the column to show that the command will pause with its dialog box open. Clicking again in this column toggles the pause function off.

  The modal control works not only for dialog boxes but also for operations that require pressing the **Enter/Return key** or double-clicking to accept the current settings, such as using the Free Transform command or the Crop tool.

- To **temporarily disable a step** so it isn't carried out when you play an Action, without permanently removing the step from the Action (or to disable an Action without permanently removing it from the set), click the check mark in the farthest left column of the Actions palette. Click in this column again to bring back the check mark and re-enable the step.

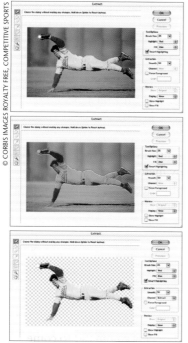

When using the Extract command, make sure to take advantage of Smart Highlighting, which helps you follow the edge of the element you want to select, and the Cleanup and Edge Touchup tools, for improving the edge of an extracted image before leaving the Extract dialog box. (For step-by-step instruction on using Extract, see "Extracting an Image" on page 162.

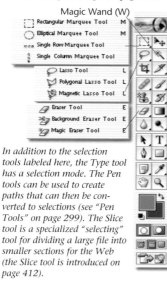

In addition to the selection tools labeled here, the Type tool has a selection mode. The Pen tools can be used to create paths that can then be converted to selections (see "Pen Tools" on page 299). The Slice tool is a specialized "selecting" tool for dividing a large file into smaller sections for the Web (the Slice tool is introduced on page 412).

Loading Actions

You can load a saved Actions palette either as an addition to the current palette (choose **Load Actions** from the palette's pop-out menu), or you can load it *instead of* the current palette (choose **Replace Actions**. *Note*: Before you replace Actions, make sure you've saved the current set so you'll be able to retrieve it again.

SELECTING

To work effectively with Photoshop, you need to know about selections: how to make them, how to store them, how to activate them again from storage, how to combine them, and how to modify them.

Selections can be made with choices from the **Select menu**, with the **Extract command** from the Filter menu, with **selection tools,** or by modifying a copy of one of the file's **color channels** — for instance, the Red, Green, or Blue channel of an RGB image.

Two selection tools, the Magic Eraser and Background Eraser, along with the Extract command, automatically make their selections permanent by isolating the selected subject on an otherwise transparent layer. But with the other selection tools, when you make a selection, a flashing boundary (sometimes referred to as "marching ants"), lets you see what part of the image is selected. The selection boundary disappears if you click outside it with a selection tool or press Ctrl/⌘-D or choose Select, None. Photoshop provides a safety net in case you need a selection back after you've deselected. You can restore the most recent selection, even after you've made changes to the image — as long as you haven't made another selection — by choosing Select, **Reselect.**

A more permanent way to preserve a selection is to store it permanently as an **alpha channel** (as described later in this section) or as a **Path** or **vector mask** (economical vector-based ways to store a hard-edged selection). A selected area can be turned into a **layer** of its own or the selection can become a **layer mask**, which limits how much of a particular layer is hidden or revealed. Layer masks are covered on page 154. A selection can also serve as the mask for an **Adjustment layer** (which can use its built-in mask to target a color or tone change to a particular part of an image; Adjustment layers are discussed on page 114).

Making Selections

In general, selections that are made *procedurally* — that is, by using information like color or brightness that's intrinsic to the image — rather than by drawing a selection boundary by hand, are often faster and more accurate. But the tool or command that works best for making a selection depends on what you want to select. Each of the selection tools and commands has its own advantages and disadvantages. To decide which to use, you need to analyze the area

If you deselect and then find that
you need your selection back,
choose Select, Reselect (Shift-Ctrl/
⌘-D). Even if you've made other
changes to the file since you deselected — painting, adding layers,
and so on — as long as you haven't
made another selection in the
meantime, the selection you want
will be restored.

Select	
All	⌘A
Deselect	⌘D
Reselect	⇧⌘D
Inverse	⇧⌘I

You can use the Magic Wand to
check a silhouetted image to make
sure the background is spot-free, or
check a vignette, drop shadow, or
glow to see exactly how far it extends:
In the Magic Wand's Options bar,
set the Tolerance to 0 and make
sure Anti-aliased is deselected. Then
click on the background. The "marching ants" boundary will show where
the edge of the color change is, and
any stray "sparkles" will indicate
spots in the background.

*The Magic Wand can help you see the
extent of soft-edged effects and unwanted
spots in a solid-color background.*

*The Options bar for the Magic Eraser looks
very much like the Magic Wand's. In fact,
this tool works like a Magic Wand that
"clears" instead of selecting. An example is
shown on page 264.*

you want to select. Is it organic or geometric? Is it fairly uniform in
color, or is it multicolored? Does it contrast with its background or
blend into it, or do some parts of it contrast and others blend in?
Then you can choose the tool, command, or combination of techniques that will do the job. The three sections that follow —
"Selecting by Color," "Selecting by Shape," and "Selecting by
Shape *and* Color" — tell how to choose and use the appropriate
selection methods.

Sometimes the best way to select is to use one selection method
and then add to the selection, subtract from it, or transform it by moving or reshaping the selection boundary. "Modifying Selections" later
in this section tells how to accomplish these changes.

Selecting by Color

Cleanly silhouetting a subject by color can help you grab elements
such as a purple flower among pink ones, or a brown dog on a
green lawn. Selecting by color is a *procedural* method. It uses the
image's hue, saturation, or brightness information (or some combination of these) to define the selection. To make a selection of all
the pixels of a similar color, you can use the Magic Wand tool or
the Select, Color Range command, or develop a selection from one
of the color channels.

Using the Magic Wand. One advantage of the **Magic Wand**
tool is that it's quick and easy. It's good for selecting one uniformly
colored area or a small number of similarly colored areas in an
image where there are other spots of the same color but you don't
want to select them all. By default, Magic Wand selections are **anti-
aliased**, or smooth-edged.

- **To make a selection with the Magic Wand**, just click it on
  a pixel of the color you want to select. By default the wand is in
  Contiguous mode, so it selects the pixel you clicked and all
  similarly colored pixels for as far as that color continues without interruption. You can add to the color-based selection by
  Shift-clicking similarly colored areas with the Magic Wand, or
  by first choosing the Add To Selection option in the Options
  bar and then clicking with the Wand again.

- You can use the Wand to **select *all* pixels of the same color**,
  whether they're contiguous or not, by turning off the default
  Contiguous feature in the Options bar.

- **To specify how broad a range of color the Magic Wand
  should include in a selection**, set the Tolerance value in the
  Options bar to a number between 0 and 255. The lower the
  number, the smaller the range of colors. (The Magic Wand's Tolerance setting also controls the color range used by the Grow
  and Similar commands from the Select menu, as explained in
  "Modifying Selections" later in this section.)

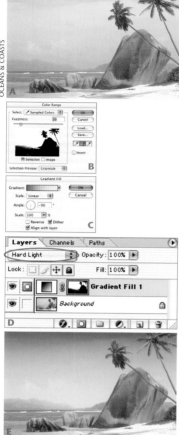

*Use the Select, Color Range command in Sampled Colors mode to select a broad expanse of closely related colors. Here the challenge was to add drama to the sky without having to make a manual selection in a photo **A** with a subtle gradation at the hazy horizon and complex shapes (the palms) that had to be excluded. The Color Range eyedropper was dragged across the sky to select a range of blues. Then the Alt/Option key was held down and the eyedropper was clicked on the colors we wanted to exclude. Fuzziness was adjusted between 15 and 30 — a good range for Fuzziness in general — to antialias the selection around the palms and "feather" the horizon area **B**. With the selection active, we clicked the Create New Fill/Adjustment Layer button at the bottom of the Layers palette and chose Gradient for the type of Fill. We chose a gradient **C** and a layer mask was automatically made from the active selection. We chose Hard Light for the new layer's blend mode **D**, which added the color ramp while retaining some of the subtle cloud structure from the original sky **E**.*

- **To control whether the selection is based on the color of only a single layer or of all visible layers** combined, turn Use All Layers off or on in the Options bar.

Using the Magic Eraser. Often, the goal of making a selection is to isolate the selected subject on a layer of its own, so you can use it in a layered composition. When the subject you want to select appears on a contrasting background, the Magic Eraser is ideal for silhouetting it by removing that background. When you use the magic eraser, the result is not the ephemeral marching ants that you get with the Magic Wand, but instead **a subject isolated on an otherwise transparent layer**.

- **To make a selection with the Magic Eraser**, click it on a pixel of the color you want to make transparent. By default, the Magic Eraser, like the Magic Wand, is in Contiguous mode, and the edge of the transparent area is antialiased.

- **To allow the transparency to replace every occurrence of the color you clicked on**, turn off the Contiguous setting before you click on the color you want to eliminate.

- **To specify how broad a range of color** the Magic Eraser should include in a selection, set the Tolerance value as described for the Magic Wand on page 38.

- **To control the degree of transparency**, use the Opacity slider — the higher the Opacity setting, the greater the erasing effect and therefore the more transparent the area will become.

Selecting by Color Range. The **Select, Color Range** command is complex, but it's well worth learning to use. In some cases it offers more control of what's selected than the Magic Wand does, and it **shows the extent of the selection more clearly**.

The little preview window in the Color Range dialog box shows a grayscale image of the selection. White areas are selected; gray areas are partially selected, with the degree of selection decreasing as you go toward black, which indicates areas that are completely deselected. With its many levels of gray, this picture is much more informative than the marching ants you see when you use the Magic Wand.

The **Fuzziness** is like the Magic Wand's Tolerance setting, but it's easier to work with, since the entire range is spread out on a slider scale and the preview window instantly shows the effect of changing it. Keeping the setting above 16 to 32 will usually prevent jagged edges in the completed selection.

The **"Select" field** at the top of the box lets you choose the color selection criteria:

- **To select based on colors sampled from all visible layers of the image as if they were merged,** choose Sampled Colors, then choose the dialog box's leftmost Eyedropper tool and click on the image, just as you would with the Magic Wand. The

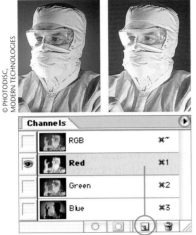

©PHOTODISC, MODERN TECHNOLOGIES

To start a mask to select the surgeon, we found that the Red channel showed good contrast between the subject and the background (above). So we duplicated it to make an alpha channel (below).

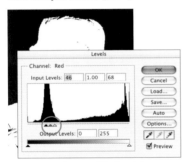

Contrast was increased in the alpha channel by adjusting the Input Levels (Image, Adjust, Levels). The Airbrush and Paintbrush tools were used to touch up the alpha channel with black and white paint, getting rid of unwanted gray pixels.

The completed alpha channel was loaded as a selection, and Image, Adjust, Variations was used to change the overall color and lighting.

selection extends throughout the image (or the existing selection, if there is one), as if you had made a Magic Wand selection with Contiguous turned off.

- **To select based on color sampled from a single layer**, first make all other layers invisible by clicking off their Eye icons in the Layers palette. Then choose Select, Color Range and click with its Eyedropper.

- **To extend or reduce the range of colors in the current selection,** click or drag with the + or – Eyedropper to add new colors or to subtract colors. Or click or drag with the plain Eyedropper, with Shift (to add) or Alt/Option (to subtract). You can also expand or contract the selection by adjusting the Fuzziness, but pixels whose colors are at the extremes of the selected color range are only partially selected.

- **To select a family of colors,** choose from the color blocks in the "Select" list. The color families are predefined — you can't change the Fuzziness or use the Eyedroppers to expand or shrink the range.

- **To select only the light, medium, or dark colors,** choose Highlights, Midtones, or Shadows. Again, there's no opportunity to make adjustments to these ranges.

- The **Invert box** provides a way **to select a multicolored subject on a plain background:** Use the Color Range Eyedropper to select the background, and then click the Invert box to reverse the selection.

Using a color channel as a starting point. The color information that Photoshop stores in individual color channels, such as the Red, Green, and Blue values of an RGB image, can be useful for selecting. Often the contrast between a subject and its surroundings is a lot more pronounced in one of the color channels than in the others.

   To use a color channel as a starting point for making a selection, look for a channel where the subject is very light and the surrounding area very dark, or vice versa. Then copy that channel to make an alpha channel by dragging the color channel's name to the Create New Channel button at the bottom of the Channels palette. Use the Levels command on the alpha channel to increase the contrast between the areas you want to select and those you want to leave unselected. Finally, load the alpha channel as a selection; you can do this by Ctrl/⌘-clicking on the channel's name in the Channels palette. (This technique is illustrated at the left.)

Selecting by Shape

If the subject you want to select is not distinctly different in color from its surroundings, then using the Magic Wand, the Magic Eraser, the Color Range command, or a color channel, won't be effective. So you may want to select it by outlining its shape. In

For a vignette effect with a hard or soft (feathered) border, use the Rectangular or Elliptical Marquee.

FEATHERING A SELECTION

A feathered edge can be useful for making a "seamless" change when part of an image is selected, modified, and then released back into its original unmodified surroundings. Feathering extends the selection outward but at less than full opacity so that some of the surrounding image is included. At the same time the opacity of the image is also reduced for a distance inside the selection border. It's the Feather Radius that determines how far this transition extends.

• **To feather a Lasso or Marquee selection as you make it**, enter a Feather setting in the Options bar and then make the selection.

• If you forget to set the Feather ahead of time, or if the selection method you used didn't have a Feather option, **you can feather the selection after you've made it** (but before you move or change it): With the selection active choose Select, Feather and set the Feather Radius.

A type-based clipping group or vector mask provides greater flexibility than using the Create Mask Or Selection option for the Type tool, shown here.

that case the Marquee tools, the Lassos, and the Pens are the tools you'll need to choose from. Since the Magnetic Lasso, Background Eraser, and Extract command employ both color and shape, they are covered in "Selecting by Shape *and* Color" later in this section, rather than here with the completely "hand-operated" tools. (Operation of the vector-based Pen tools is covered in Chapter 7, "Type, Shapes, Paths & PostScript," starting on page 300.)

Selecting geometric or custom shapes. To "frame" a selection, you can use the Rectangular or Elliptical Marquee tool, as explained next, or use one of the Shape tools to draw a more complex shape (as explained in "Shape Tools and Shape Layers" on page 298) and then convert the Shape to a selection (as described in the "Convertibility" tip on page 304). The Marquee tools offer a variety of options for selecting:

• The default mode for the Marquee tools is to start the selection from the edge. But many times you have better control of exactly what you select if you draw the selection from the center out. **To draw a selection from the center,** press and hold the Alt/ Option key at any time while you're drawing the Marquee.

• **To select a square or circular area,** constrain the Rectangular or Elliptical Marquee by holding down the Shift key as you drag.

• **To make a selection of a particular width-to-height ratio,** choose Constrained Aspect Ratio for the Style in the Options bar and set a particular width-to-height ratio. Now the Marquee will make selections of those proportions.

• **To make a selection of a specific size**, choose Fixed Size for the Style and enter the Width and Height measurements in pixels (adding "px" to the number), inches (add "in"), or centimeters (add "cm").

• **To make a soft-edged selection,** you can set the Feather in the Options bar before you make the selection, or make the selection and then apply the Select, Feather command (see the "Feathering a Selection" tip at the left for more information).

• You can **adjust the position of a selection Marquee** either as you draw it or afterwards. If, for instance, you start to draw a Marquee from the middle but find that it's developing a little off-center of the element you want to select, you can **hold down the spacebar** while you drag to move it, and then release the spacebar and continue to drag to finish the selection.

To reposition a completed selection boundary without moving any of the pixels inside it, put the selection tool's cursor inside the selection and drag.

The Type selection and mask options. Photoshop 7's Type tool (its operation is covered in "Type," starting on page 292) offers

To select an area that has a complex outline and shares colors with its surroundings so it's hard to select by color, use the Lasso tool.

Holding down the Alt/Option key lets you switch between dragging the Lasso in its freeform mode and clicking it as a Polygonal Lasso.

○ ○ ○ ≡ AVI0039D.jpg @ 100% (RGB)

100%

With the Alt/Option key held down, you can click or drag the lasso outside the boundaries of the image, to make sure your selection doesn't miss any pixels at the edges.

HYBRID SELECTIONS

To make a selection that's partly sharp-edged and partly feathered, set the Feather in the Options bar and make the feathered selection first; then set the Feather to 0 and add the unfeathered selection by holding down the Shift key as you select. (If, instead, you make the sharp-edged selection first and then the feathered, the feather softens the junction of the two selections.)

The feathered selection was made first; then the sharp-edged selection was added.

the option to make a type-shaped *selection* instead of setting live (editable) type, by clicking the button with the "T" made of dashed lines. The selection option was more useful in previous versions of the program, for masking images inside of type, for instance. But in Photoshop 7 it's almost always better to set editable type in a layer below the image you want to mask and then make the type layer the base of a clipping group (by Alt/Option-clicking the border between the image layer and the type layer in the Layers palette). Or create a *Work Path* from the type (Layer, Type, Create Work Path). Then use the *Work Path* to make a vector mask (a smooth, resolution-independent mask) on the image layer by clicking the name of the image layer in the Layers palette and then Ctrl/⌘-clicking the Add A Mask button at the bottom of the palette. The clipping group approach allows more flexibility, since the type remains live and editable. (The process of masking an image inside type by using a clipping group is described in "Typography, Groups, and Layer Styles," starting on page 308, especially in step 9, and in "Blending Images & Type," starting on page 168.)

Selecting irregular shapes. To select a multicolored area, especially if the thing you want to select shares colors with its surroundings so that you can't select procedurally as described on pages 38–40, you may need to "hand-draw" the selection border with one of the Lasso or Pen tools. If the boundary of the element you want to select is defined by smooth curves, use a Pen (see page 300). If the boundary is complex with detailed "ins and outs," try a Lasso:

- For **very detailed edges**, drag the standard **Lasso**.
- Clicking a **series of short line segments with the Polygonal Lasso** is often an easier and more accurate way **to define a fairly smooth region of a boundary** than trying to trace the edge by dragging the Lasso.
- Holding down the **Shift key** as you use the **Polygonal Lasso** restricts its movement to **vertical, horizontal, or 45° diagonal**.
- Holding down the **Alt/Option key** lets you **operate the tool as either** the Lasso or the Polygonal Lasso, switching back and forth between them. (You can even switch between these two tools and the Magnetic Lasso, described on page 43.)

There's another advantage of holding down the Alt/Option key: Holding down the key **keeps the selection from closing up** if you accidentally let go of the mouse button before you've finished selecting. If you make a mistake, you can **"unravel" the selection boundary** you're drawing, pressing the Delete key as well as holding down the Alt/Option key until you get back to the "good part." And if you want **to make sure your Lasso selection extends all the way to the edges** of the image without missing any pixels, you can hold down the Alt/Option key and click or drag the tool outside the image.

The Magnetic Lasso's Options bar, most of
which is shown above, includes the four
buttons characteristic of the Options bar for
all selection tools. There you can specify
whether the selection you are about to
make will be (left to right) a new selection,
an addition to the current selection, a
subtraction from it, or the intersection.

EASIER SELECTING

No matter what selection tool or
procedural method you use, selecting can be made easier if you exaggerate the color or tone contrast
between the area you want to
select and its surroundings before
you try to make the selection. For
instance, in a shadowed area a Levels Adjustment layer can be added
above the image layer to lighten
the image, which will make color
differences more obvious than they
were in the dark shadows. Then you
may be able to select by color, or at
least have a better view of an area
you're selecting by hand. When the
selection is complete, the Adjustment layer can be deleted.

A temporary
Levels Adjustment
layer can make it
easier to use the
Magnetic Lasso to
select the subject.

TWO-HANDED SELECTION

When you use the Magnetic Lasso
(or Magnetic Pen), you can decrease
or increase the Width by pressing
the bracket keys: [and]. This means
you can **shrink or enlarge the
tool's footprint** with one hand
while you operate the tool with
the other hand, tailoring its size to
the nature of the edge as you work.

Selecting by Shape *and* Color

Some of Photoshop's selecting tools are designed to let you take
advantage of color contrast anywhere it exists, but to also substitute
manual selection in areas where the contrast breaks down. These
tools include the Magnetic Lasso and Magnetic Pen, the Extract
command, and the Background Eraser.

The Magnetic Lasso. The operation of the Magnetic Lasso is very
similar to the operation of the Magnetic Pen, described starting on
page 300. Basically, it works like this: You click the center of the circular cursor somewhere on the edge you want to trace and then
"float" the cursor along, moving the mouse or stylus without pressing its button. The tool automatically follows the "edge" created by
color or tone contrast. The settings in the Options bar control the
way the Magnetic Lasso performs. Parameters that can be set include **Width, Frequency**, and **Edge Contrast**, just as for the
Magnetic Pen. In addition, with the Magnetic Lasso you can set the
Feather, and if you have a graphics tablet, you can turn on the
Stylus Pressure option.

For an explanation of how Width, Frequency, and Edge Contrast
affect the operation of the Magnetic Pen, see page 301. Here are
some pointers for using the tool:

- As for most other tools whose cursor size can vary, you can use
the left and right **bracket keys** to change the Width as you
operate the Lasso, as described in the "Two-Handed Selection"
tip at the left, or use a graphics tablet and turn on **Stylus Pressure**. With increasing pressure the Width becomes smaller.

- If you're tracing a **well-defined edge**, use a large Width and
move the tool quickly. **To increase the contrast at the
edge,** and thus make the tool easier to operate, you can use a
temporary Adjustment layer as described in the "Easier Selecting" tip at the left. **If there are other edges or distinct
objects** near the edge you want to trace, use a small Width and
keep the cursor carefully centered on the edge you're tracing. **If
the edge is soft** with little contrast, use a smaller Width and
trace carefully. **Where there is no contrast** for the Magnetic
Lasso to follow, you can operate the tool like the Polygonal
Lasso, clicking from point to point. **Or hold down the Alt/
Option key to have access to all three Lassos**, switching
between the Magnetic Lasso (by floating), the Polygonal Lasso
(by clicking), and the Lasso (by dragging).

- Increase the **Frequency** to put down more fastening points,
which determine how far back the selection border will be
"unraveled" each time you press the Delete key.

- Increase the **Edge Contrast**, which determines how much contrast
the tool should be looking for in finding the edge, if the subject contrasts strongly with it surroundings. Use a low setting for a soft edge.

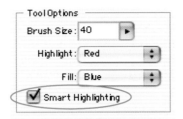

Smart Highlighting turned on for "magnetic" operation of the Edge Highlighter

PROCREATE KNOCKOUT

procreate KnockOut is an image extraction and masking plug-in that goes beyond the selecting capabilities of Photoshop's Extract command. For silhouetting subjects with difficult edges, like a photo of fine wisps of hair or a glass or anything else that you can't successfully Extract, the KnockOut program is invaluable.

In the procreate KnockOut sample (top), you define what's definitely inside and what's definitely outside the part of the image you want to isolate, and the program very successfully deals with the "border area" in between. It provides tools for identifying and selecting complex color transitions and soft edges such as shadows. On the left above is the procreate KnockOut selection, with the Photoshop Extract selection on the right for comparison.

The Extract "Filter." The Extract command (now located under the Filter menu) isolates a part of an image by erasing all other pixels on that layer, leaving transparency in their place. Choosing Filter, Extract opens a dialog box that lets you set the stage for Photoshop to do its "intelligent masking." In Photoshop 6, three improvements were made to make the process much easier: The **Smart Highlighting** function makes it easier to select distinct, high-contrast edges. After the initial masking, the **Cleanup tool** can subtract from the edge or restore parts of the edge that were removed. And the **Edge Touchup tool** can sharpen or smooth rough edges. The Extract interface can be confusing, but one fairly direct way to proceed is outlined below. (For a step-by-step tutorial and tips on using Extract, work through the example in "Extracting an Image" on page 162.)

1 With the **Edge Highlighter** tool selected, set the Brush Size in the Tool Options section. Choose a size that's big enough so you can easily drag it around the edge of the area you want to isolate (the subject). But keep in mind that anything within this edge is fair game for Extract to make fully or partially transparent. Try to keep this transition area tight. When you come to an area of high edge contrast, to trace the edge "magnetically," switch to **Smart Highlighting** (by clicking the check box in the Tool Options section of the Extract dialog box, or by holding down the Ctrl/⌘ key). When contrast gets low again, turn off Smart Highlighting.

2 Drag the Highlighter around the edge to enclose the subject. If the area you want to select extends to the edge of the image, you can draw just to the edge — you don't have to drag around the border. You can use the bracket keys as described in "Two-Handed Selection" on page 43 to change the tool's footprint as you drag.

3 Choose the dialog box's **Fill tool** and click inside the highlight-bordered subject area in order to be able to preview.

4 Click the **Preview** button to see the extracted subject. You can zoom in for a closer look at the edge with the dialog box's **magnifier** tool. To check the quality of the edge, you can change the preview's background color by choosing from the pop-out **Show** list in the Preview section of the dialog box; this is a good way **to check the integrity of the edge**. You can also toggle the view to compare the extracted subject with the original by choosing from the **View** settings.

If the Preview shows that the extracted subject isn't to your liking, you have several choices for making corrections:

• If the Extract process has left **problems at the edge** — extra pixels outside the edge, or semitransparency where the subject's edge should be solid — use the **Cleanup tool to erase excess** material from the edge, or use the **Cleanup tool with Alt/ Option held down to restore** material at the edge. Use the

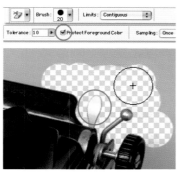

The Background Eraser's Protect Foreground Color option makes this a very powerful selection tool. It lets you sample a color that you want to protect from being erased. An example is shown in "Assembling a Still Life" on page 174.

Edge Touchup tool to consolidate and remove "pixel debris" at the edge. As you touch up the extraction, keep in mind that **it's better to leave too much material at the edge (you can remove it later) than not enough** (it won't be easy to restore the missing material once you leave the Extract dialog box).

- If the edge looks so sloppy that you want **to start over** completely, hold down the Alt/Option key to change the Cancel button to **Reset**, click the button, enter a **new Brush Size**, and start again.

- If the edge itself looks good but there are areas that are completely inside the edge but that need to be eliminated — such as **small patches** of sky showing through the leaves of a tree you've selected — you don't need to highlight the edge of each patch. Instead, click OK to close the Extract dialog box and then use the **Background Eraser** as described next.

The Background Eraser. The Background Eraser tool, which shares a spot with the other Erasers in the toolbox, is sort of like the Extract command in a wand. It erases the pixels you drag it over, leaving transparency instead. The "+" in the center of the tool's cursor indicates the "hot spot," and the footprint around it defines the tool's "reconnaissance area." When you click the Background Eraser tool, it samples the color under the hot spot. And as you drag the tool, it evaluates the color of pixels within the reconnaissance area, to see which ones should be erased. Which pixels get erased depends on how you customize the settings in the Options bar.

    Tolerance affects the range of colors that are erased. A **high Tolerance** setting erases a **broader range of color** than a low setting. With a setting of **0**, pixels of only a **single color** are erased — the specific color under the hot spot when you click.

    For the type of **Sampling**, you can choose Continuous, Once, or Background Swatch.

- **To erase every color you drag the Background Eraser's hot spot over**, choose **Continuous** sampling, which repeatedly updates the color to be erased.

- **To erase only the color that's under the hot spot when you first push the button down** on your mouse or stylus, choose **Once**. When you push the button down, the Background Eraser will choose the color to erase. It will erase this color as you drag, until you release the mouse button. When you push the button down again, it will resample and choose the new color that's now under the hot spot.

- **To set a single specific color or color family to be erased**, regardless of when you press and release the mouse button, choose **Background Swatch**. Set the Background color

Sometimes you don't notice a "fringe" of background pixels surrounding a silhouetted subject until you've layered it on top of a new background (left). But it isn't too late to remove it. Choose Layer, Matting, Defringe before you merge the layer with the composite. The Defringe command pushes color from the inside of the selection outward to replace the edge pixels, thus eliminating the fringe.

by clicking the Background square in the toolbox and either specifying a color in the Color Picker or clicking in your image to sample a color. This type of sampling, combined with adjustments to the Tolerance settings, provides a great deal of control.

For the **Limits**, you can choose Discontiguous, Contiguous, or Find Edges.

• **To erase any occurrence of the color anywhere within the brush's footprint** as it moves along, choose **Discontiguous**.

• To erase **only pixels whose color continues uninterrupted** from the pixel under the hot spot, choose **Contiguous**.

• **Find Edges** is like Contiguous, but it pays special attention to **preserving sharp edges**.

The **Protect Foreground Color** option in the Options bar lets you sample and protect one color at a time as you erase. This is useful for preserving an element that's close to the color you want to erase.

Modifying Selections

Photoshop provides several ways to make a selection larger or smaller, or to change its position or shape while the selection is still active. In addition to the techniques presented below, be sure to see the "Fingers and Thumbnails" tip at the left for quick, easy-to-remember shortcuts.

• To make a "hand-drawn" **addition to, subtraction from, or intersection with** the current selection, click one of the buttons at the left end of the selection tool's Options bar and then make the new selection.

• To **expand** a selection outward, picking up more pixels at the edge, use **Select, Modify, Expand**. To **contract** a selection inward, dropping the edge pixels, choose **Select, Modify, Contract**.

• To **add pixels that are similar in color and adjacent to the current selection**, you can choose **Select, Grow**. Each time you use the command, the range of colors selected gets larger. The amount that the color range grows is controlled by the Tolerance setting in the Options bar for the Magic Wand.

• To **add all pixels in the image that are similar in color** to the pixels in the current selection, choose **Select, Similar**. The Tolerance setting in the Options bar for the Magic Wand determines how similar the additional pixels have to be. A setting of "0" adds only pixels that are exactly the same colors as pixels in the existing selection.

• **To move the selection boundary** without moving any pixels, drag inside the selection with a selection tool.

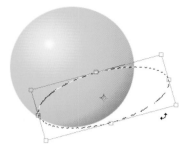

The Transform Selection command is great for angling and skewing selections. Here it's used in the process of shaping a shadow. We Ctrl/⌘-clicked the layer's thumbnail to load the shape of the ball as a selection. Then we chose Select, Transform Selection. Dragging inside the transform box moved the selection, dragging handles inward and outward scaled it, and dragging outside a corner handle rotated it. It's also possible to skew or otherwise distort the selection: Right-click (Windows) or Control-click (Mac) to open a context-specific menu, where you can choose the transformation you want. When you've finished, press the Enter key to accept the changes.

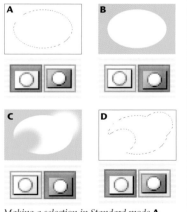

Making a selection in Standard mode **A**, converting to Quick Mask mode **B**, changing the selection mask by adding to the mask with black paint and removing from the mask with white paint **C**, and turning the altered mask back into a selection **D**

- **To skew, scale, distort, or flip the selection boundary,** choose Select, Transform Selection. Then right-click (or Control-click on a Mac with a one-button mouse) to bring up a context-sensitive menu where you can choose the kind of transformation you want to make. Drag the center point or handles of the Transform frame, and press Enter to complete the transformation.

Using Quick Mask. By making a selection and then clicking the Quick Mask button (on the right side near the bottom of the toolbox), you can turn an active selection into a clear area in a semitransparent mask. In Quick Mask mode you can see both image and mask, so you can do some fairly subtle mask modification. As you edit it with painting tools or filters, the Quick Mask remains stable, preserving the selection while you work on it. When you've finished modifying the mask, you can turn it back into a selection boundary by clicking the Standard mode button (to the left of the Quick Mask icon).

Cleaning up a selection. Sometimes, despite the most careful selecting, the selected part of the image retains a tinge of background color, visible around the edge. To get rid of this unwanted "fringe," you can use the commands of the Layer, Matting submenu. Note that these commands work only after the selected material has been separated from its surrounding pixels, by being made into a layer of its own, for instance.

- **To eliminate an "edging" picked up by an image selected from a black (or white) background,** choose Layer, Matting, Remove Black Matte (or Remove White Matte).

- **To remove edging in a color other than black or white,** try the Layer, Matting, Defringe command. This will "push" color from the inside outward into the edge pixels. Be careful, though — using a Defringe setting of more than 1 or 2 pixels can create "spokes" or "rays" of color at the edge.

- Besides the Layer, Matting commands, **another way to remove color edging** is to **"choke"** the layer, to shrink the edges inward just slightly, so what's causing the edging is excluded. Load the layer's content outline (also called its *transparency mask*) as a selection by Ctrl/⌘-clicking the layer's

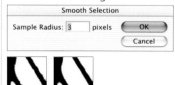

In this "hand-tinting" project we saved the skin selection **A** *in an alpha channel* **B**. *Then we could make a rough selection of the dress, without tracing the neck or arm* **C**. *We Ctrl-Alt-clicked (Windows) or ⌘-Option-clicked (Mac) the alpha channel in the Channels palette to subtract it from the rough selection so we could color the dress* **D**.

thumbnail in the Layers palette. Next choose the Select, Modify, Contract command to shrink the selection, then invert the selection (Ctrl/⌘-Shift-I) and press the Delete key to remove the troublesome outer edge.

- A nondestructive way to modify the edge (called "nondestructive" because no pixels are permanently removed) is to use a layer mask, as described in step 4 of "Extracting an Image" on page 166. "Extracting an Image" also has other important pointers for fitting a selected and silhouetted subject into a new background.

Storing Selections in Alpha Channels

Photoshop's alpha channels provide a kind of "subfile" for storing selection boundaries so you can load them back into the image and use them later. A selection stored in an alpha channel becomes a mask, with white areas that can be loaded as an active selection, black areas that protect parts of the image where changes shouldn't apply, and gray areas that expose the image to changes proportionally to the lightness of the gray.

To make an alpha channel from an active (marching ants) selection:

- Choose Select, Save Selection, choose New Channel, and click OK.

- Or click the Save Selection As Channel button, second from the left at the bottom of the Channels palette. To name the channel as you make it, Alt/Option-click the Save Selection As Channel button to open the New Channel dialog box.

To load an alpha channel as a selection:

- Ctrl/⌘-click on its name in the Channels palette. You can also add the selection to or subtract it from a currently active selection using the techniques described in the "Fingers and Thumbnails" tip on page 46.

- Or choose Select, Load Selection. In the Load Selection dialog box, choose the document and channel you want to load. This command gives you the added ability to load an alpha channel from any open document of the same pixel dimensions as the one you're working on.

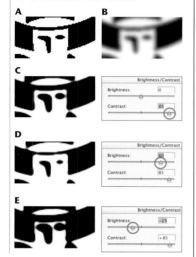
UNDERSTANDING RESOLUTION AND RESAMPLING

Besides understanding the basic "anatomy" of a Photoshop file and knowing how to select the part of the image that you want Photoshop's tools and commands to work on, another fundamental concept that's important for working in Photoshop is ***resolution***. *Resolution* is the term used to describe the **amount of information** in an image file. Typically, the more data, the larger you can print the image before it starts to look pixelated and lose detail. Resolution is sometimes expressed as the number of dots, pixels, or ink spots per unit of measure (pixels per cm, or lines per inch, for example). Alternatively, resolution may be stated as pixel dimensions — 640 x 480 pixels, for instance. This way of expressing resolution is often used for images designed to be displayed on-screen, such as images for the Web.

Getting enough information

When you're trying to decide on a resolution for scanning or creating an image, the goal is to gather (or create) enough image information to print the image successfully — keeping the color transitions smooth and the details sharp. Although you want to be sure to use a high enough scan resolution, you don't want to overdo it — because the higher the scan resolution, the bigger the file size. The bigger the file size, the more disk space you need to store it, the more RAM and scratch disk space you need to work on it in Photoshop, and the longer it takes to open, work on, save, and print.

Resampling

Regardless of how well you plan, there are likely to be times when you need to *resample* — either resample down or resample up. *Resampling down* means decreasing the file size. You might do this because you have more information than you need for printing and you want to reduce the bulk of the file. *Resampling up* increases the file size. In a case where you can't rescan the original again at the correct settings, you might need to do this in order to have enough information to reproduce the image at the size and screen frequency or display resolution you want. (Consider using LizardTech Software's Genuine Fractals PrintPro if you have to resample up; you can find information and a try-out version at **www.genuinefractals.com**.)

To resample, you can use the Image Size dialog box, or use the Resize Image Wizard/Assistant — it's easier, as demonstrated on page 52, but it doesn't give you as much "hands-on" control. If you use the Image Size dialog box, make sure that Constrain Proportions is checked (so the image stays in proportion as it's resized). The Resample Image box should also be checked, and Bicubic (the highest quality interpolation and the default) should be chosen from the Resample Image pop-out list.

In the **Pixel Dimensions** section at the top of the Image Size dialog box, you can see the size that the image file will be in its flattened form for printing or displaying on-screen. You can also see the Width and Height in pixels.

Image Size			
Pixel Dimensions: 6.08M			OK
Width:	1350	pixels	Cancel
Height:	1575	pixels	Auto...
Document Size:			
Width:	6	inches	
Height:	7	inches	
Resolution:	225	pixels/inch	
☑ Constrain Proportions			
☑ Resample Image: Bicubic			

In the **Document Size** section of the box, you can see the Width and Height and the Resolution in pixels per inch or centimeter. When you change any of the numbers in the Document Size section, the result you get depends on whether the Resample Image option is turned on. **If Resample Image is unchecked**, changing any of the settings in the box will not change the number of pixels in the file and thus will not change the file size. For instance, if you decrease the dimensions, the Resolution will increase so that the file size stays the same. **If the Resample Image box is checked**, changing the dimensions or Resolution will not cause a change in the other to compensate. Instead, the image will be resampled, and the file size will change.

- **To change the image dimensions,** in the Document Size section, enter a new value in the Height or Width field. The other dimension will change automatically, the Resolution will stay the same, and so the file size will change.

- **To change the image resolution,** in the Document Size section, set Height and Width units to anything but pixels. Then enter a new value in the Resolution field. The dimensions will stay the same but file size will change with the change in resolution.

SIZING FOR COLUMNS

If you're sizing images for a publication whose column width you know, choose File, Preferences, Units & Rulers and enter the column and gutter widths. Then when you size an image in the Image Size dialog box, you can choose Columns as the unit of Width and set the number of columns wide that you want the image to be. If you specify more than one column, the calculation automatically takes the gutter measure into account.

Column Size		
Width:	1.8	inches
Gutter:	1	picas

When an image is resampled, Photoshop recalculates the color of each pixel in the resized file; this can cause some softening of the image. The same kind of recalculation can occur when you use the Transform commands to rotate, scale, or skew part of an image. After you've resampled or transformed, run the Unsharp Mask filter to "bring back" some of the detail lost in recalculation.

SCANNING AND OTHER FORMS OF INPUT

Scanners — desktop, mid-range and high-end — turn photos into image files that can be manipulated in Photoshop. Today there are inexpensive desktop flatbed scanners that can capture photographic prints, other hard copy, and even some three-dimensional objects in millions of colors or even billions of colors. The more color depth your scanner offers, the more shadow and highlight detail it will be able to record. Photoshop 7 can use the extra information to help make finer color and tone adjustments as described in "Correcting 16-Bit Images" on page 121, or you can do the correction even before the scan is imported into Photoshop, using the scanner's own software, as described in "Raw File Tweaking," a tip on page 122.

Desktop slide scanners and some transparency adapters for flatbed scanners make it possible to capture images from transparencies in sizes from 35 mm to 8 x 10 inches, though the quality of transparency adapters varies greatly. Another input option is to **have your images scanned by a service bureau** using scanners with optical-mechanical systems that are more precise than those of desktop scanners. The quality of the scan will depend on the skill of the person operating the scanner.

When your scanner shows you a preview of your image, use the scanning software's cropping tool to identify the area you want to scan.

For a color scan, set the type of scan to "Millions of Colors" or "24-bit color" (top) and adjust your scanner's Resolution and Scaling settings. (If you're using the "double-checking" method described at the right, the Image Size value in K or MB should now match or slightly exceed the New Image Size number that you get in step 5. At this point, if you have a challenging photo with lots of shadow or highlight detail, and if your scanner is capable of "billions of colors," you can choose that option (bottom). The file size will go up automatically. Then complete the scan.

Setting Up a Scan

Scanners allow you to prescan your image so you can identify the area of the image that you want to scan. Then you can specify the color mode and scan resolution (dpi) that you want, and enter a scale factor (a percentage) if the final printed size will be larger or smaller than the original.

To figure out the scan resolution to specify for print, you can multiply the print resolution (number of lines per inch, or lpi, in the halftone screen) by 1.5 or by 2. The 1.5 multiplier (for example, 1.5 x 150 lpi = 225 dpi for the file) can work well for photos of natural scenery without stark geometric patterns, sharp color boundaries, or ultra-fine details (most of the images in this book, including the cover, fit in this category). A multiplier of 2 (typically 2 x 150 lpi = 300 dpi for the file) works well for photos of man-made structures, which tend to have straight lines and sharp color breaks, or for close-up "beauty" photography with details like fine eyelashes. Above 2, you increase file size without making the picture look significantly better.

Note: The difference in file size between a file that's 1.5 and 2 times the line screen is almost double, which is a lot of extra weight to carry around if you don't really need it.

If you plan to use the scanned image to develop art for the Web, it's a good idea to scan at twice or four times the 72 dpi resolution you'll need for the finished art. With the larger file, selecting will be easier, fine line work will ultimately be smoother, and you'll have the flexibility of being able to use the art for other (higher-resolution) purposes later.

Double-checking. If you want to double-check and make sure you're using the right scanner settings to get the amount of information you need in a scan for print, you can use a "dummy" file in Photoshop to calculate the required file size. Then cross-check this calculated file size with the file size the scanner software comes up with. Here's a way to do it:

1 Setting the color mode of the scan. One of the things that will affect the amount of information collected is the color mode used for the scan. For example, a full-color scan records three times as much information as a grayscale scan (for more about color modes, see "Color Modes" on page 64). Create a new file (File,

SCANNING IN 3D

By placing a small object on a flatbed scanner, you may be able to capture its dimensionality. One or more sides of the object may show, depending on where on the bed you place it. The farther you move the object toward an edge or corner of the scan bed, the more of its sides will show.

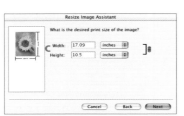

Steps 1 and 2 *To figure out how big (how many MB) a scan file should be, start by opening a "dummy" file in Photoshop and setting the color mode. You don't have to worry about setting the Height, Width, or Resolution at this point.*

Step 3 *Choose Help, Resize Image and choose Print in the first screen of the Resize Image dialog box. Click Next and enter the dimensions at which you want to print the scanned image.*

Step 4 *In the next screen, choose a halftone screen.*

Step 5 *Choose the quality level you want (1.5 or 2 or somewhere in between) and read the New Image Size in the Results section. Compare this value to the size of the file indicated by your scanning software (you can ignore the Original Size and the Pixels Per Inch values). Then click the Cancel button.*

New). This dummy file will not be used to make an image, only to calculate scan resolution. The first step is to set the mode (see **A** at the left):

- For both color and grayscale images, the mode used for scanning should be RGB Color; grayscale images typically turn out better if you scan in color and then convert to Grayscale in Photoshop. (See "From Color to Gray" on page 98 for conversion tips.)

- Use Grayscale mode for scanning black-and-white line art. Line art usually turns out better (with smoother, more consistent lines) if it's scanned in Grayscale mode and then perfected with Image, Adjust, Levels. Then it can be left as Grayscale or converted to Bitmap mode, depending on how you want to use it.

2 Setting the size of the image you want to scan. In the New dialog box, enter the Width and Height of the area of the image you're starting with (see **B** at the left). You can use the dimensions that your scanner reported when you cropped the prescan. With the mode and dimensions set, click OK to close the New dialog box. (For the purposes of this dummy file, the Resolution setting is irrelevant; you can set it at 72 dpi if you like.)

3 Using the Resize Image Wizard/Assistant. The amount of scan data you need for print depends on the printed size and the halftone screen frequency. Choose Help, Resize Image to open the Resize Image Wizard/Assistant, which will ask you to enter this information and will calculate the file size that's needed. First you'll specify that you want the image for **Print**. Then you'll enter one of the dimensions of the finished size — either Height or Width (see **C** at the left). The Height and Width are linked, so if your final crop will be different than the aspect ratio you set up in the prescan, use the dimension that makes the image larger than you need the final image to be, rather than smaller, so that both Height and Width are at least as big as the dimensions of the image you need. In other words, you can let one dimension be larger than you need, but don't let either dimension be smaller.

4 Factoring in the screen frequency. In the next Resize Image screen you'll account for the halftone screen. Choose the appropriate number of lines per inch (see **D** at the left). If you don't know the screen frequency for printing, it's better to guess high than low. Typical screen frequencies are 110 lpi for newspapers, 150 lpi for books like this one and for magazines, and 175 lpi for some fine-art publications.

5 Reading the new file size. In the Quality slider, choose 1.5 or 2, the same value you used to multiply the halftone screen when you entered the Resolution in your scanner software. (If a warning about enlarging appears at the bottom of the box, you can ignore it, since this file you're working on is just a dummy.) In the Results section, note the New Image Size (see **E** at the left). This is the file

When you scan an image that has already been printed, the halftone screen pattern used to print it can interact with the scanner's sampling pattern to produce an unwanted moiré pattern. Many desktop and other scanners have built-in descreening algorithms for eliminating the moiré.

Shown here are scans made with (bottom) and without (top) turning on the scanner's descreening function.

A high-quality digital camera such as the Nikon D100 that captured this photo, can produce an image that's clearer than you can get with many film-based cameras.

size (in K or MB) of the scan you will need. In other words it's the amount of data the scanner will need to gather to support the size and halftone screen you've chosen. Compare the New Image Size number to the file size your scanner arrives at, to see if they are approximately the same. Then you can click the Cancel button to close the Resize Image box. If the two file sizes — the one from the scanner and the one from the Resize Image approach — are very different, you may need to look at the problem again to see where the mistake is.

Other Input Options

Besides inputting images by scanning, you can also buy collections of photos and other artwork already scanned and provided on CD-ROM, such as all the Corbis Royalty Free images used throughout this book and on the Wow CD-ROM. The wealth of stock images, patterns, textures, and illustrations available on CD-ROM continues to grow, with a variety of arrangements for use and payment.

Kodak Photo CD, Picture CD, and Pro Photo CD technology provides an easy and inexpensive way to have images from film (35 mm negatives or slides or even larger-format film) stored on a compact disc. The easiest and least expensive way to get your images in one of these formats is to take your exposed film to a photofinisher who offers the Kodak service, though you can also take previously developed slides or negatives. The images on the disc are relatively high-quality scans, efficiently compressed and stored so they can be opened in several different resolutions, or file sizes. There are many other picture-on-CD formats, and the quality varies.

Digital cameras, which bypass film altogether and record images as digital files, are another extremely popular source of images for manipulation in Photoshop. Many come with USB or Firewire connections for loading images directly to the Desktop or into Photoshop, as if the camera were a hard disk drive. The quality/price ratio of digital cameras continues to dramatically improve. A camera such as the Nikon D100 can produce very high-quality 6-megapixel images that are large enough (over 10 MB) to be printed with film quality at 11 x 14 inches on desktop photo printers. With enlarging technologies such as Alta Mira's Genuine Fractals (**www.genuinefractals.com**) digital photos can be successfully printed even larger.

The image quality that can be achieved with very low-cost digital cameras is not as good as film. If an image is to be extensively manipulated for a photo-illustration, or reproduced at a small size, or used only at a fairly low resolution — for instance, for placement in a Web page — the convenience of having the "photo" instantly available may outweigh the quality difference.

Video — directly from a video camera or cassette — can be brought into Photoshop through the File, Import command, using

Cher Threinen-Pendarvis used Photoshop with a Wacom Intuos tablet and a laptop computer with 192 MB of RAM to draw sketches (top two) for her Alps Study *on location, then completed the painting on her desktop computer, also with the Intuos. To optimize Photoshop's performance while working on location and the "natural media" feel of the painting tools, she painted on the Background layer only and purged History often.*

a plug-in module provided with a *video frame grabber,* a hardware-software combination designed to acquire video signals or images.

For imitating traditional art media such as the paintbrush, pencil, airbrush, or charcoal, a **pressure-sensitive graphics tablet** with stylus — for example, any of those in Wacom's Intuos line — has a more familiar feel than a mouse and also provides much better control. Photoshop's painting tools (see Chapter 6) are "wired" to take advantage of pressure sensitivity for controlling opacity, brush size, and fade.

OUTPUT: PROOFING AND PRINTING

Like other desktop color files, Photoshop images can be printed on inkjet, thermal transfer, or dye sublimation printers, color laser printers that can accept digital input, or film recorders (as negatives or positive transparencies). Typically, inkjet, thermal transfer, or dye sublimation printing is used to show generally how the image and the color will look when printed on an offset press (see "Color Views" on page 72 and "Getting Consistent Color" on page 79), or to achieve a particular kind of art print quality. *Giclée,* a fine-art digital printing method achieved by "spraying" ink, is growing as a way of producing an edition of fine-art prints. Originally done on an Iris printer, Giclée is now more and more done on six- and seven-color archival desktop and large-format printers from companies such as Epson. A key factor in this method of printing is the development of archival-quality printing inks and papers that can reproduce a wide range of color whose fidelity will last up to 100 years, as is the case with Epson's UltraChrome Inks).

Photoshop documents, alone or placed in page layouts, can also be produced as color-separated film for making plates for offset printing, by using imagesetters or high-end color-separation systems. Or, as the pages of this book were, the files can be output direct-to-plate, which bypasses film, or even direct-to-press, which bypasses both film and plates.

When color separations for offset printing are made by the traditional halftone screening method, the *match print,* which a printer and client agree is the color standard to be matched on the printing press, is usually a laminated print made from the film that will be used to make the printing plates. However, as stochastic screening (shown on page 55), direct-to-plate, and direct-to-press printing technologies replace halftone film for most printing jobs, the "soft" proof (often printed directly from the digital file on an inkjet or dye sublimation printer rather than from color-separated film) becomes more important.

FILE FORMATS

Photoshop can open and save images in many different file formats. Here are some tips for saving files, depending on what you want to do with them:

In scans and screen displays, images are made up of pixels. The pixels are all the same size but vary in color.

Many printed images are composed of overlaid screen patterns of halftone dots. These dots vary in size, but the number of lines of halftone dots per inch remains constant. The spectrum of printed colors results because the eye "mixes" the dots of color.

Stochastic screening, used in most desktop printers and some high-end printing presses, uses very tiny but uniformly sized dots that vary in number. Because the tiny dots are not clumped together to make larger dots, no halftone pattern is generated, and more image detail can usually be seen.

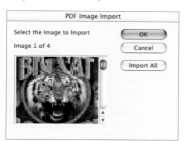

In Photoshop 7 you can open individual images embedded in a PDF document. Choosing File, Import, PDF Image and choosing a PDF file opens the PDF Image Import dialog box. There you choose which image(s) to import, as shown here. Another PDF-import function (the Multipage PDF To PSD command in the File, Automate menu) converts each page of a PDF to a separate Photoshop file, with file names that include sequential numbering.

For flexibility in what you can do with the file in the future, save in **Photoshop** format. It preserves all the layers, channels, paths, live (editable) type, Styles, and annotations.

To place Photoshop images in a page layout program, TIFF and EPS are typically the formats of choice. **TIFF** files can have lossless compression, making the file smaller for storage and transport without degrading the image at all, and they can include clipping paths. **EPS** files can include vector information, including clipping paths, but are much larger than TIFFs. It's a good idea to check with your imagesetting or printing service to see how they suggest saving and placing the files. For instance, not all services will accept TIFFs with clipping paths. (The extended TIFF options that show up in the Save As dialog box if you choose Edit, Preferences, Saving Files and turn on Enable Advanced TIFF Save Options now allow clipping paths, layers, alpha and spot channels, and annotations, with several options for file compression. But not all page layout programs and imagesetting or printing services are happy to accept TIFFs with these "extras.")

Another very flexible format is **Photoshop PDF**, the format to use if you want the file to be readable in a PDF viewer such as Adobe Acrobat. Like the Photoshop format, it can preserve the layers, channels (including alpha and spot color), and annotations. In the PDF Options dialog box that opens when you choose to save a file in Photoshop PDF format, choosing **Include Vector Data** retains paths and type as vector-based (non-pixel) information. Then you can choose to Embed Fonts or Use Outlines For Text:

- Choosing **Embed Fonts** ensures that type will be displayed as you designed it, whether or not the font exists on the system where the PDF will be displayed.

- If embedding fonts makes the file too large, you can preserve crisp type edges by choosing **Use Outlines For Text**. You preserve the look of the type but lose its editability, and it can't be searched as text by the PDF viewer.

- If **neither option** is chosen, the type will be live text in a PDF viewer, but it may not look exactly like you designed it, as the viewer will substitute a font if the one you used isn't present on the system.

For information about opening, importing, and saving files **for use with PostScript programs**, see "Using Photoshop with Other PostScript Programs" on page 304. For file formats used **for the Web**, see "Optimizing Web Art," starting on page 419.

Essential Shortcuts

Here are some keyboard shortcuts that are worth remembering, for tools and commands you're likely to use almost every day.

CONTEXT-SENSITIVE MENUS

Right-clicking on almost anything in Photoshop's working window or palettes brings up a **context-sensitive menu** with choices appropriate for the element you clicked on. (On a Mac with a one-button mouse, Control-click.)

HIDE/SHOW PALETTES

To get an uncluttered view of your image, press the **Tab** key to **hide all palettes**; press Tab again to show the palettes. Press **Shift-Tab** to toggle on and off **all palettes except the toolbox**.

ESSENTIAL TOOLS

All the tools have keyboard shortcuts you can use to select them. Two tools you'll need again and again are the **Move tool** (press **V**) and the selection **Marquee** (press **M**). Also, to turn any tool into the **Move tool** temporarily, hold down the **Ctrl/⌘** key. Release the key to change back.

TRANSFORMING

Press **Ctrl/⌘-T** for Edit, **Free Transform**. To make the same transformation again, for an additive effect, Transform Again by pressing **Ctrl/⌘-Shift-T**. To **duplicate and transform** the copy, press **Ctrl-Alt-Shift-T** (Windows) or **⌘-Option-Shift-T** (Mac).

Free Transform	⌘T
Transform ▶	Again ⇧⌘T
Define Brush	Scale

REPEATING A FILTER

Once you apply a filter, you can **filter again** with the same setting by pressing **Ctrl/⌘-F**. To apply the filter again but open the dialog box so you can change the settings, press **Ctrl-Alt-F** (Windows) or **⌘-Option-F** (Mac).

COPY MERGED

If you use the standard Edit, Copy command (Ctrl/⌘-C), it copies the selected area of the currently active layer. But if you add the Shift key (**Ctrl/⌘-Shift-C**), a merged copy is made that includes everything that's visible within the selection, from all layers.

Copy	⌘C
Copy Merged	⇧⌘C
Paste	⌘V

UNDO

Ctrl/⌘-Z is the long-standing shortcut for Edit, **Undo**; press this combination again to **Redo**. In Photoshop 7 by default **Ctrl-Alt-Z** (Windows) or **⌘-Option-Z** (Mac) is "**multiple Undo**" — it steps backward through your recent changes. But you can change the shortcut so Ctrl/⌘-Z is multiple Undo instead of the Undo/Redo toggle: Choose Edit, Preferences, General (Ctrl/⌘-K is the shortcut) and choose Ctrl/⌘-Shift-Z for the Redo key.

HAND-TOOL TOGGLE

You can temporarily switch from the currently active tool to the **Hand tool** for moving the image around in the working window by pressing the **spacebar**. (The exception is that if the Type tool is active and in editing mode, the spacebar types a space.)

SAVE AS / SAVE A COPY

To open the Save As dialog box so you can save the current file under a new name or in a different format or save a copy, press **Ctrl/⌘-Shift-S**.

FILLING WITH COLOR

To fill a selected area or a layer with the **Foreground color**, press **Alt/Option-Delete**. To fill with the **Background color**, press **Ctrl/⌘-Delete**.

To limit the fill so that **only non-transparent pixels** are affected and transparency is maintained, add the **Shift** key to the combination. Partially transparent pixels will stay partially transparent, but their color will be replaced with the Foreground or Background color.

BRUSH SIZE

Use the bracket keys — **[** and **]** — to **reduce** or **increase the brush size** as you paint.

MASK TOGGLES

To view a layer mask instead of viewing the image, **Alt/Option-click** on the layer mask's thumbnail in the Layers palette. Alt/Option-click again to restore the image view.

To temporarily turn off the masking effect of a layer mask or layer clipping path, so you can see the unmasked image, **Shift-click** on the mask's thumbnail. Shift-click again to turn it back on.

SELECTING

To add to the current selection, hold down the **Shift** key as you select. **To subtract,** hold down the **Alt/Option** key as you select. To **select the intersection** of the current selection and the one you're making, hold down **Alt/Option and Shift**.

BLACK AND WHITE

Press the **D** key to make the Foreground and Background colors the **D**efault black and white. Press **X** to e**X**change the Foreground and Background colors.

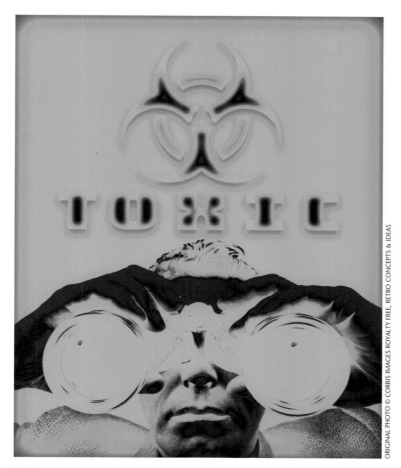

ORIGINAL PHOTO © CORBIS IMAGES ROYALTY FREE, RETRO CONCEPTS & IDEAS

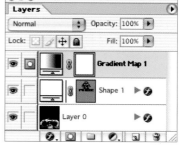

To design the *hang-tag for the Toxic clothing label,* **Jack Davis** started by adding simple glows and shadows with a Layer Style, to create halo effects for the logo and as a border treatment for the black-and-white photo (shown at the right), which he had chosen to convey a sense of hidden danger. Then he used a Gradient Map Adjustment layer to experiment with different color schemes to support that concept. He chose a dark blue to orange gradient, editing it in the Gradient Editor, opened by clicking on the swatch in the Gradient Map dialog box. To increase the sense of danger, he turned the image and logo into a negative simply by clicking the Reverse check box in the Gradient Map dialog box.

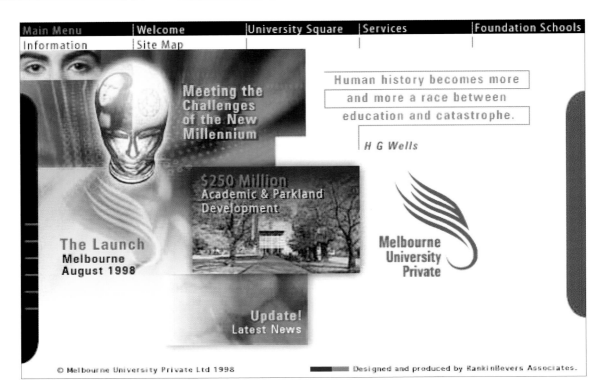

© Melbourne University Private Ltd 1998   ▬▬▬ Designed and produced by RankinBevers Associates.

In designing a *Web site for Melbourne University Private,* **Wayne Rankin** drew on the designs already created for the CD-ROM (shown on page 457). In this case however, the client wanted a white background. Despite the change, Rankin maintained a similar look and feel so that the Web site is clearly related to the visual style established for the CD-ROM, using black border areas as one of the ways of tying the disc and Web site together.

Like the CD-ROM graphics, the Web art makes use of repeating elements that vary in color. Graphics for the Web artwork tend to be simpler than those used on the CD-ROM. The files are smaller, for quick downloading, and the sound and video elements created for the CD-ROM were eliminated with the same goal in mind.

The navigational system for the site is understated, with "buttons" that are small blocks of plain type. The initial splash screen lists the browser requirements for getting the most out of the site, and a site map uses a simple, easy-to-remember layout to show how information is organized.

The image shows a stamp sheet titled "PLANET OCEAN" featuring six 45c Australian stamps depicting: WEEDY SEADRAGON, SOUTHERN RIGHT WHALE, MANTA RAY, WHITE POINTER SHARK, BOTTLE NOSED DOLPHIN, and GIANT SQUID.

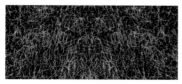

esigner **Wayne Rankin** created *Planet Ocean* as a special souvenir stamp sheet for Australia Post's Stamp Collecting Month and also to commemorate the United Nations International Year of the Ocean. The sheet features six stamps, each highlighting a sea creature native to the waters surrounding Australia. The animals were generated from 3D models provided by Viewpoint Datalabs (**www.viewpoint.com**). These models (at left, top) were then customized in 3D Studio Max using photographic reference and advice from marine experts to match the characteristics of the Australian species (left, center). The texture and bump maps applied to make the 3D models look realistic were created both from photographic sources and by painting directly in Photoshop.

To cast watery highlights and shadows on the creatures when they were rendered in the 3D program, Rankin used an imported black-and-white image as a lighting gel (left, bottom). This mottled image was created in Photoshop by drawing white lines and swirls over a solid black background with the Airbrush tool, then applying a slight Gaussian blur to further soften the lines, and finally extending the texture by duplicating parts of the drawing and flipping and rotating the copies.

The background for *Planet Ocean* was created directly in Photoshop using the Airbrush tool and the Motion Blur filter to blend together scanned photos and painted areas. The type for each stamp and the layout of stamp outlines were created in Adobe Illustrator. The Illustrator artwork was rasterized into the Photoshop file as a separate layer (File, Place), to help with positioning each creature over the background. For final output, visibility for the line work layer was turned off before the flattened file was made, and the final layout was assembled in Illustrator.

EUROAIR
FRANCE

TRANS INTERNATIONAL

Mike Kungl produces his art deco posters, such as *Euroair France* shown here, often starting with photo reference, and then working in Adobe Illustrator, Photoshop, and procreate Painter. For Euroair he built a hobby-shop model of the DC-3, then photographed it at the angle he needed to match the reference photo he had for the Eiffel Tower.

Kungl does his initial design and drawing in Illustrator, using as a template a scanned sketch made from his photos. When he finishes the Illustrator part of the process, he has a working layout of shapes filled with flat color. With the goal of using these shapes as "friskets" in Painter, Kungl translates the paths into Photoshop alpha channels. Then he saves the file — an RGB Photoshop PSD document that consists of a single empty layer and numerous channels — and opens it in Painter, where the Photoshop alpha channels appear as masks in the Masks section of Painter's Objects palette.

Kungl uses the masks with Painter's custom textures and brushes to paint his artwork, keeping individual elements on separate layers. He saves the file in Photoshop format and reopens it in Photoshop, where the layer hierarchy created in Painter is preserved. In this multilayer Photoshop file he can touchup the edges of the artwork and make color adjustments with Levels, Hue/Saturation, and Selective Color and by changing layer Opacity. Finally he converts the file to CMYK.

The 24 x 36-inch posters, as well as a 10 x 15-inch version, are output as editions of 250 Giclée prints by Classic Editions in Costa Mesa, California, using archival inks and a UV-protective coating on 330-pound Somerset Velvet paper.

William Low's painting *Wedding* was created by working back and forth between Photoshop and procreate Painter. Using a scanned photo for reference he painted each element of the image on a separate layer, using the Paintbrush with round, hard-edged brushes. He could then use the Move tool to arrange the composition of the many figures. The rice effect was created on a layer in Painter. The texture on the car and on the upper right corner of the background was created by applying a paper texture in Painter, then returning to Photoshop to run the Paint Daubs filter.

A Original

B After Auto Levels

C High Pass alone

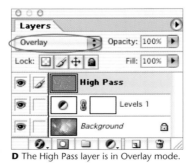

D The High Pass layer is in Overlay mode.

I n the cloud scapes on these pages, both taken with a Nikon D100, Davis used a 2-step process to enhance the inherent "glory" of the moments.

For the original late afternoon cloud shot *Tampa God Rays* (above) **A,** a Levels Adjustment Layer was created and the Auto button clicked to instantly expand the tonal range of the photo to extend from full black to complete white **B.** Next, a duplicate of the *Background* layer was created (Ctrl/⌘-J) and placed above the Adjustment Layer and the High-Pass filter (found under Filter, Other) was applied **C.** This left the layer a mostly neutral gray (50%), with areas of contrast turned to darker or lighter grays (or even pure white).

By changing the Blend Mode of this filtered layer to Overlay **D,** the middletone grays would have no effect on the layers below (50% gray being a "neutral color" in Overlay mode). However, the lighter and darker shades would automatically act as an instant Dodge & Burn treatment, just where it was needed most—around existing shapes and areas of contrast—to further exaggerate the feeling of dimension and space, or in this case, the impression of light and shadows.

For *Cloud Column* and *NYC Clouds* on the facing page, Davis employed the same techniques to add additional drama to the images.

Original image

Original image

COLOR IN PHOTOSHOP

PHOTOSHOP 7 HAS A POWERFUL SET OF FEATURES DEDICATED TO choosing, mixing, applying, and modifying color. It has highly technical tools that are numerically precise, such as the Info palette, the Levels dialog box, and color management functions, developed to ensure that color remains consistent from image creation to final output. But it also has very intuitive tools, such as the painting tools, the Swatches palette, and the Variations dialog box. Working efficiently with color in Photoshop starts with understanding a certain amount about how on-screen and printed color differ.

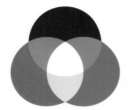

In a subtractive *color model (represented by the top illustration), cyan, magenta, and yellow inks combine to make a dark, nearly black color. In* additive *color (bottom), red, green, and blue light combine on-screen to make white light.*

The Channels palette shows the primary colors of the current color mode for the file. Shown here is the Channels palette for a file in RGB mode (left) and a file in CMYK mode (right).

COLOR MODES

Photoshop uses several different systems of color representation. These systems — Bitmap, Grayscale, Duotone, Indexed Color, RGB Color, CMYK Color, Lab Color, and Spot Color — can be selected through the Image, Mode submenu. The *gamut,* or range of colors that can be produced in that color system, varies from mode to mode, as described below.

In any color system the *primary colors* are the basics from which all other colors can be mixed. Photoshop stores the color data for each of the primary colors in a *color channel*. These channels are shown in the Channels palette, with the first listing in the palette representing the combination of the primary channels.

RGB Color

Computer monitors generate colors by mixing the primary colors of light (called *additive primaries*) — red, green, and blue, or RGB. When all three colors are turned on at full intensity, the result is white light; when all are turned off, black results. The various brightnesses of the three colors

continued on page 66

There are 256 different brightness settings for each of the three primary colors (red, green, and blue) of most computers' RGB color systems. This means that there are potentially 256 x 256 x 256 (or more than 16 million) colors that can be mixed. This gamut provides enough colors to realistically represent the world we see.

It takes 8 bits of computer data (a bit is a 1 or a 0, an ON or OFF signal) to represent 256 different values (2^8 = 256), as needed for each primary color channel. To represent three sets of brightness settings — one set for each channel — takes 24 bits (2^8 x 2^8 x 2^8 = 2^{24} = 16.7 million). So full color as displayed on the computer screen is called "24-bit color," or millions of colors.

Photoshop's 3D Transform, Lens Flare, and Lighting Effects filters work *only* in RGB mode. Others — the Artistic, Brush Strokes, Sketch, Texture, and Video filters, as well as Smart Blur, Diffuse Glow, Glass, Ocean Ripple, and Glowing Edges — work in RGB, Grayscale, Duotone, and Multichannel, but not in CMYK. However, you may be able to get the effect you want on a CMYK file by filtering the color channels one by one. Click on a single channel's name in the Channels palette, run the filter, then click another channel, rerun the filter (Ctrl/⌘-F), and so on.

Converting to Indexed Color in order to reduce the color palette is better done through the Optimize section of the Save For Web dialog box or ImageReady's Optimize palette (shown here) than by choosing Image, Mode, Indexed Color.

mix visually to form all the colors of the RGB spectrum. Unless your work in Photoshop requires a particular color mode for some specialized purpose, RGB is usually the best color mode to work in, since it offers the most function and flexibility. All of Photoshop's tools and commands work in this mode, whereas other modes have a more limited set of functions. You may have to switch to some other mode to get your Photoshop file where it's going — to print (CMYK mode) or to the Web (a reduced, or indexed, palette of colors). But you'll probably be doing most of your creative work in RGB color, since it offers a broader *gamut,* or range of colors, than most other modes.

Within the RGB mode there can be many different *color spaces,* or subsets of the RGB gamut, that different scanners, digital cameras, and monitors can reproduce. These are defined by the color capabilities of a particular monitor or input device, such as a digital camera or scanner. Photoshop can use ICC profiles, which are descriptions of these color spaces, in its color management system. ("Color Management," starting on page 80, tells more about profiles.)

CMYK Color

CMYK, or *four-color process,* printing is the type of commercial printing most often used for reproducing the photos, illustrations, and other works created in Photoshop. The CMYK primaries (called *subtractive primaries*) are cyan, magenta, and yellow, with the addition of black to intensify the dark colors and details. Adding black makes dark colors look crisper than darkening with a heavier mix of cyan, magenta, and yellow. Darkening with black also requires less ink; this can be important because a press has an upper limit to the amount of ink it can apply to the printed page before the ink will no longer adhere to the paper cleanly. The Color Settings dialog box (opened by pressing Ctrl/⌘-Shift-K) offers several standards for CMYK printing that can be used when Photoshop converts from RGB (for image development) to CMYK (for printing), or you can choose Custom and Custom CMYK and enter the specific Separation Options recommended by your printer. (For more about converting from RGB to CMYK, see "Making RGB-to-CMYK Conversions" on page 84.)

Indexed Color

The process of assigning 256 or fewer colors to represent the millions of colors potentially in a full-color image is called *indexing.* The Indexed Color command (Image, Mode, Indexed Color) used to be important for preparing art for the

When you choose the Image, Mode command, you may find that certain of the modes in the submenu are "grayed out" and not available. That's because some modes are accessible only if the file is currently in RGB or Grayscale mode. For instance, to get to Bitmap or Duotone mode, you have to go through Grayscale. To get to Indexed Color mode, you have to go through Grayscale or RGB.

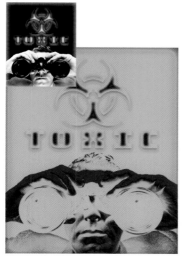

The Gradient Map Adjustment layer provides a better way to "remap" the colors in an image than using the Custom choice in Indexed color. Here the Gradient Map was used to convert a black-and-white image to a "toxic" palette.

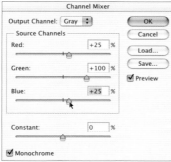

When converting from color to grayscale, a Channel Mixer Adjustment layer provides control of the contribution of each color channel. In most cases this can produce a much better conversion (shown on the right) than using Image, Mode, Grayscale (shown in the center), as described in step 4 of "From Color to Gray" on page 98.

Web or for special color effects. Now you can do the Web conversion in Photoshop's Save For Web dialog box or in ImageReady's Optimize palette, choosing from the same **Perceptual, Selective,** and **Adaptive** palettes that are available when you choose Image, Mode, Indexed Color. All three of these palettes are "adaptive" or "local" in the sense that they are chosen with regard to reproducing the colors of the current image. They are sets of 2 to 256 colors chosen to best represent the colors in the currently active image (Local) or in a group of images for which a shared (Master) palette has been prepared in ImageReady.

- A **Perceptual** palette takes into consideration the parts of the spectrum where the human eye is most sensitive, assigning more of its palette spots to colors in those particular ranges.

- A **Selective** palette is optimized to favor Web colors and colors that occur in large areas of flat color.

- An **Adaptive** palette is one that's adapted, or optimized, to reproduce the colors that occur most often in the image.

For more about these three kinds of adaptive palettes and how to use them, see "Optimizing Web Art" on page 419.

A **Custom** palette is a set of colors selected for some particular purpose. Choosing Mode, Indexed Color, Custom opens the Color Table dialog box, where you can choose one of several Custom palettes that are supplied with the program, or make your own palette by clicking the individual squares of the Color Table and choosing new colors to fill them. In Photoshop 7, the special color effects that used to be done with a Custom palette can be accomplished better by using a **Gradient Map,** which maps the range of tones in an image into the range of colors in a gradient. An example is shown at the left (top). A Gradient Map Adjustment layer can be added by clicking the Create New Fill/Adjustment Layer button at the bottom of the Layers palette and choosing Gradient Map from the pop-out list.

"SHAPING" ADAPTIVE PALETTES

"SHAPING" ADAPTIVE PALETTES

You can "weight" the colors of the Adaptive, Perceptual, or Selective palette in favor of the colors in a selected area. For instance, you may want to preserve the skin tones in a portrait, giving less weight to the clothing colors or background colors. Simply select an area of the image that contains the important colors and save it as an alpha channel before you begin working with the Optimize function of Photoshop or ImageReady. Then click the mask button next to the palette type in the Optimize palette and choose the alpha channel you saved.

The image on the left was optimized with the palette "weighted" toward the skin tones by using an alpha channel made from the selection shown. The same number of colors was used to optimize the image on the right, but without weighting.

PHOTO: JILL DAVIS

Photoshop's Duotone mode provides curves that store information for printing a grayscale image in one to four ink colors. The program comes with several sets of preset duotone, tritone, and quadtone curves. Or you can shape the curves yourself.

By drastically reshaping curves as in this quadtone, you can make different colors predominate in highlights, midtones, and shadows. You may also choose a more standard duotone from the ones in the Presets/Duotones folder supplied with Photoshop 7.

The **Previous** palette is the set of colors that was used the last time, within the current Photoshop session, that a file was indexed with a Custom or adaptive palette. This option can be useful for converting a number of images so they share a single custom palette.

Lab Color

Instead of being separated into three colors (plus black in the case of CMYK color), color can be expressed in terms of a brightness component and two hue/saturation components. Photoshop's **Lab Color** mode uses such a system, as does Kodak Photo CD (its Photo YCC color system), and analog color television. Because its gamut is large enough to include the CMYK, RGB, and Photo YCC gamuts, Photoshop's Lab Color mode serves as an intermediate step when Photoshop converts from RGB to CMYK or from Photo YCC to RGB.

Grayscale

An image in Grayscale mode, like a black-and-white photo, includes only *brightness* values, no data for the *hue* or *saturation* characteristic of color images. Only 8 bits of data are required for storing the 256 shades (black, white, and grays) in most Grayscale gamuts. For the best reproduction of a color photo in black-and-white, the Channel Mixer offers more control and flexibility than a conversion through the Image, Mode submenu. See page 94 for more on channel mixing.

Duotone

Even though a Grayscale image can include 256 levels of gray, most printing processes can't actually produce that many different tones with a single ink color. But with two inks (or even one color of ink applied in two passes through the press) it's possible to extend the tonal range. By adding a second color in the highlights, for example, you increase the number of tones available for representing the lightest tones in an image. Besides extending tonal range, the second color can "warm" or "cool" a black-and-white image, tinting it slightly toward red or blue, for example. Or the second color may be used for dramatic effect or to visually tie a photo to other design elements.

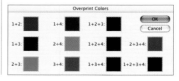

Black

Yellow

In Duotone mode you can't see the individual color plates that will be used for printing. To look at them, you can convert the file to Multichannel mode temporarily, open a second window, and view a different channel in each window. (If you want to see the plates in color, choose Preferences, Display & Cursors, Color Channels In Color). Follow these steps exactly: Open the Channels palette (Window, Show Channels) and open a second view of the image (Windows, Documents, New Window). Then choose Image, Mode, Multichannel. Activate a different Channel (by clicking on its name in the Channels palette) for each window. View both plates, but don't try to edit. You won't be able to get back to Duotone mode with the edits intact. After you've looked at the plates, Undo (Ctrl/⌘-Z) or step back in the History palette to go back to Duotone mode.

In Photoshop's Duotone mode, a set of *curves* determines how the grayscale information will be represented in each of the ink colors. Will the second color be emphasized in the shadows but omitted from the highlights? Will it be used to color the midtones? The Duotone image is stored as a grayscale file and a set of curves that will act on that grayscale information to produce two or more separate plates for printing. Duotone mode also includes tritone and quadtone options, for producing three or four color plates.

Bitmap

Bitmap mode uses only 1 bit of "color" data to represent each pixel. A pixel is either OFF or ON, producing a gamut of two "colors" — black and white.

Other Choices from the Mode Submenu

In addition to the color modes themselves, the Image, Mode submenu includes more choices: Multichannel, 8 Bits/Channel, 16 Bits/Channel, Color Table, Assign Profile, and Convert To Profile.

Multichannel mode can be useful for viewing the plates of a Duotone image, as shown at the left. Color images automatically become Multichannel files when one of the color channels is deleted.

The **8 Bits/Channel** and **16 Bits/Channel** choices let you choose the *color depth,* or how many bits per pixel are used to store color data in each color channel of the file. Using the 16 Bits/ Channel setting, Photoshop can perform some of its operations in files with 10, 12, or even 16 bits per channel. So if you have a scanned image with more than 8 bits per pixel of color information (sometimes referred to as the "billions of colors" option in scanning software), you can open it in Photoshop, and make tonal and color adjustments using this extra information — for instance, fine-tuning the shadow detail. "Correcting 16-Bit Images" on page 121 tells how to correct tone and color in 16-bit images.

Photoshop's standard operating mode is 8 Bits/Channel. So if you start out in 16 Bits/ Channel mode and you've made all the corrections you can, you may need to choose 8 Bits/Channel so that you can use all of Photoshop's other functions, such as Layers, a feature which is unavailable in the 16-bit mode.

Color Table lets you view and edit the colors in an Indexed Color image. You can also name and save the colors in

ADJUSTING IN 16 BITS/CHANNEL

According to Photoshop's online Help, even if you start with an image in 8 Bits/Channel mode, you may be able to get better results with color adjustments (from the Image, Adjust submenu) if you convert to 16 Bits/ Channel temporarily to make the adjustments, and then switch back. For many purposes, however, the increase in color detail will be imperceptible when printed. Also, you'll have to flatten the file to work in 16 Bits/Channel mode, and the file can be as much as twice as large.

When you add a spot color channel, it appears below color channels but above alpha channels in the Channels palette.

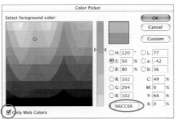

A spot color channel can be useful for adding a custom color to a CMYK printing job, as described in the "Trapping Spot Color" tip on page 105.

Photoshop's default Color Picker lets you simply click to choose a color by eye or enter numeric values to mix colors in the RGB, CMYK, Lab, and HSB (hue, saturation, brightness) modes. Or you can click one of the round buttons to switch between color models. Clicking on Custom lets you choose from several custom color-matching systems. The Color Picker also has a check box that lets you restrict the Color Picker's choices to those in the Web palette, as shown here, and a box that provides the hexadecimal code for the current color.

the Color Table, and load previously saved Color Tables and Swatches files.

The **Assign Profile** and **Convert To Profile** commands give you a way to efficiently handle a file that doesn't have a profile embedded but that's from a known RGB color space, especially if it's very different from the monitor color space you're currently using (See the tip "When 'Assign Profile' May Be Worth a Try" on page 83).

SPOT COLOR

Spot colors, or custom colors, are special premixed ink colors other than the standard cyan, magenta, yellow, and black. Among the most popular spot colors are inks formulated to the Pantone Matching System. They are used to print specific colors, instead of trying to produce these colors by overlapping the tiny halftone dots of the standard CMYK process ink colors. In Photoshop you can use spot colors in Duotones or in spot color channels, added by choosing New Spot Channel from the Channels palette's pop-out menu.

Spot color channels can be used along with the CMYK inks or instead of CMYK. A spot color channel can be used when an absolute color standard has to be met for a corporate color or logo — the ink is premixed to the standard, so that the printed color always looks the same. Or it can be used for colors that are outside the CMYK printing gamut, such as certain oranges or blues, fluorescents, or metallics. Spot color channels can also be used to maintain control over the individual printing plates — for posters, T shirts, and so on, or to apply a clear, shiny, or dull varnish. Using spot colors is covered in "Spot Color Overlays" on page 100.

CHOOSING OR SPECIFYING COLORS

The **Foreground and Background color squares** in the toolbox in Photoshop and ImageReady show what color you'll get when you paint on any layer (the Foreground color) or erase on the *Background* layer (the Background color). You can choose Foreground and Background colors simply by clicking on one of the squares to open the **Color Picker** and then choosing or specifying a color. Or you can click with the **Eyedropper** tool to set a new Foreground color by sampling color from any open document; Alt/Option-click to sample a Background color.

Other tools for choosing color include the two **color palettes** (Color and Swatches), which can be opened from the Window menu and are ideally suited for certain ways of choosing colors. The **Color palette**, with its different modes and sliders, lets you mix colors scientifically (by reading the numbers as you move the sliders) or "by feel" (by sampling from the Color Bar at the bottom of the palette). By default, the **Swatches palette** shows a set of

The Color palette has a color bar from which colors can be sampled. The color space of the bar can be changed by choosing from the palette's pop-out menu. Or Shift-click on the bar to toggle through the four color bar choices: RGB Spectrum **A**, *CMYK Spectrum* **B**, *Grayscale Ramp* **C**, *and Current Colors (Foreground To Background)* **D**. *You can also choose to make the sliders or color bar Web-safe.*

Using a Solid Color Fill layer with a mask that targets the color allows you to experiment with color changes without degrading the original image. This method is used for applying a particular custom color for a printed catalog in "Controlled Recoloring" on page 90.

125 color samples. You can click a swatch to select a Foreground color or Alt/Option-click to select a Background color. You can add to this scrollable palette by sampling a new Foreground color and clicking the Create New Swatch button at the bottom of the palette. Or you can add an entire set of colors by choosing Load Swatches from the palette's pop-out menu and choosing a palette, such as the System or Web-safe colors in the Color Palettes folder.

APPLYING COLOR

In Photoshop, color has always been applied with the **painting and filling tools** and the **Edit, Fill** command. These are covered in Chapter 6, "Painting." Photoshop 6 introduced the ability to apply color with a Fill layer or a Shape layer. Choose a **Fill layer** by clicking the Create New Fill/Adjustment Layer button (the black-and-white circle at the bottom of the Layers palette) and choosing a type of fill. It adds a layer filled with the current Foreground color, with a pattern, or with a gradient. A Fill layer has a built-in layer mask that you can alter with painting tools or fill operations to hide or reveal parts of the color layer. A **Shape layer** provides the same kind of color-filled layer, but the built-in mask is a vector-based *layer clipping path*, formed by drawing with a Shape tool or with the Pen tool. Both Fill layers and Shape layers provide flexibility, because you can change the color simply by clicking the layer's thumbnail in the Layers palette and choosing a new fill, without degrading the layer content or worrying about traces of the old color being left behind at an antialiased or feathered edge. (To learn about using Shape layers, see "Shape Tools and Shape Layers" on page 298.)

Still another way to apply color is with an **Overlay** effect, as part of a Layer **Style**. The Color, Pattern, and Gradient Overlays allow you to assign color as part of the Layer Style — a portable combination of effects that can be saved and applied to other elements and in other files. The application of Layer Styles is described step-by-step in techniques throughout the book, but especially in Chapter 8 (see "Overlays" on page 354 and "Anatomy of a Layer Style" on page 366 to learn more about how they work).

ASSESSING COLOR

When you want to know what mix of primary colors makes up a color in your image, you can use the Info palette and the Color Sampler tool. The **Info palette**, shown on the next page, provides an interactive display of color composition — as you move the mouse, the color composition is shown for the pixel currently under the cursor. When you apply a color or tonal adjustment such as Levels or Hue/Saturation, the Info palette displays two sets of numbers — the color composition both *before* and *after* the change — in the dialog box. You can choose two color modes for

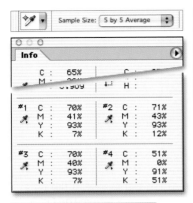

In Photoshop you can establish as many as four stationary samplers with the Color Sampler tool. These samplers feed color information to the Info palette. Color samplers let you pinpoint important areas of an image and watch how their color composition changes as you make adjustments to tone and color. In the Options bar you can set up the Sample Size of the Color Sampler to sample the color of a single pixel or the average color from a 3 x 3-pixel or 5 x 5-pixel area. The same Sample Size setting is shared by the Eyedropper tool; changing the setting for either tool will also change it for the other. The sample size of the Eyedroppers in the Levels and Curves dialog boxes are also controlled by this setting. (See "Adjusting Overall Tone and Color" on page 114 for more about Levels and Curves.)

By default, the Gamut Warning uses gray to indicate colors that may change when the file is converted to CMYK mode.

the composition readout, set by choosing the Palette Options in the Info palette's pop-out menu.

In Photoshop you can also set up to four "permanent" color sampling sites in your image, each of which will provide a separate readout in the Info palette. To set up the samplers, choose the **Color Sampler** tool (it shares a position with the Eyedropper in the toolbox) and click as many as four locations where you want the Info palette to provide readouts. Once the points are established, you can use the tool to drag them around, or Alt/Option-click on a point to remove it.

Color Views

In the View menu you'll find three commands that relate to color. The **Proof Colors** command is designed to let you see how the color in your RGB image will look under the conditions you choose with the **Proof Setup** command. You can choose to see the Working CMYK, which uses the CMYK specifications in the Color Settings dialog box, or you can choose individual or combined printing plates, again according to the Color Settings CMYK specifications. You can also choose to preview how the color will look when viewed in the standard RGB Macintosh or Windows color space. Or choose Custom to load a profile for your desktop printer, for example. Unlike choosing Mode, CMYK Color to convert the file

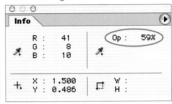

The out-of-gamut warning and the "not Web safe" warning from Photoshop 7's Color Picker

Photoshop offers on-screen "proofing" of files through the View, Proof Colors command. If you have accurate profiles of your monitor and of the output device on which the file will be printed or displayed, you can see what will happen when the file is converted from the RGB color mode as displayed by your monitor to another RGB color space or to CMYK printing colors. (Before choosing Proof Colors, you can choose View, Proof Setup, Custom to open the Proof Setup dialog box and load the profile for a specific output device.) If the Gamut Warning is turned on (like it was for the smaller image above), the second view will show flat gray for colors that may change when the file is converted.

from RGB to CMYK, the Proof Colors option doesn't actually make the conversion, so you don't lose the RGB color information as you would if you converted it. Opening a second view of your RGB file (Window, Documents, New Window) and then choosing View, Proof Color lets you see the file in both your working RGB color space and the CMYK or alternate RGB space (the new view) at the same time.

The **Gamut Warning,** also chosen from the View menu, identifies the colors in your RGB image that will be adjusted to bring them inside the printable or viewable color range that you've chosen with the Proof Setup command. By default, a flat medium gray is displayed to show that colors are out-of-gamut. If flat gray doesn't contrast well with your image, you can change the Gamut Warning color by choosing Edit, Preferences, Transparency & Gamut, clicking the color box under Gamut Warning, and choosing a color with the Color Picker.

ADJUSTING COLOR

Photoshop provides a powerful array of tools for adjusting color and contrast. Many of them are found in the Image, Adjustments submenu and in the list of Adjustment layers that pops up if you click the Create New Fill/Adjustment Layer button (the black-and-white circle) at the bottom of the Layers palette. Depending on which kind of Adjustment layer you choose, you can target your color changes to specific colors or to specific parts of the brightness range of an image — highlights, midtones, or shadows. You can also target the change to a particular place in the image by adding a mask to the Adjustment layer or by selecting an area before you choose the Image, Adjust command.

Adjustment Layers

Using an Adjustment layer is almost always preferable to using a direct command. It provides greater flexibility in adjusting color, because the changes are made without permanently changing the original color of the image, and you can reset them later if you need to. "Adjusting Overall Tone and Color" and "Working with Adjustment Layers," starting on page 114, as well as many of the technique sections in Chapter 3, tell step-by-step how to use Photoshop's color adjustment options.

One of the hardest things about making color adjustments in Photoshop is deciding which is the right tool for the job. "Color Adjustment Options," starting on page 74, tells how the various Adjustment layers differ and provides tips for choosing the right one for the job you need to do. And "Quick Color & Tone Adjustments" on page 124 provides some practical suggestions for using Adjustment layers for "quick fixes" to improve the quality of photos.

COLOR ADJUSTMENT OPTIONS

 When the Layers palette doesn't have room for the detailed thumbnail for an Adjustment layer, a generic thumbnail appears.

These three pages point out the special talents of each of the commands in the Image, Adjustments submenu, with references to where in the book you can find more information. If a command can be applied as an Adjustment layer, its Layers palette thumbnail is shown. Adjustment layers provide flexibility, because you can change their settings later without degrading the image.

Levels

Through its **histogram** the Levels dialog box provides more information and more interactive feedback about how the tones and colors in your image are distributed than any other color or contrast adjustment interface. It's excellent for overall tone and sometimes color adjustment (see "Adjusting Overall Tone and Color," starting on page 114).

Auto Levels

Auto Levels is a **"one-button fix"** that's often effective as a complete adjustment to color and tone, or as a starting point. Examples are shown in "Quick Tone & Color Adjustments" on page 124. Unless you're working in 16 Bits/Channel mode where you can't have more than one layer, apply Auto Levels by means of a **Levels Adjustment layer** rather than through the Image, Adjust submenu. This gives you the flexibility to vary its Opacity (and therefore its intensity) and change its blend mode, and you can undo it at any point later.

Auto Contrast

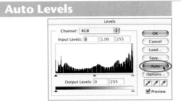

Auto Contrast adjusts tonality without affecting color. You can achieve the same result as the Auto Contrast command while using an Adjustment Layer by clicking the **Options** button in either the Levels or Curves dialog box and selecting **Enhance Monochromatic Contrast**. This preserves the overall color relationship while making highlights appear lighter and shadows appear darker.

Auto Color

The Auto Color command adjusts the contrast and color of an image by searching the actual image rather than the channels' histograms for shadows, midtones, and highlights. It neutralizes the midtones and clips the white and black pixels based on the values set in the **Auto Correction Options** dialog box. You can achieve the same result as the Auto Color command while using an Adjustment Layer by selecting the **Find Dark & Light Colors** and the **Snap Neutral Midtones** options within the Levels or Curves **Options** dialog box.

Curves

The Curves dialog box lets you identify and **adjust specific tonal ranges** in your image without adjusting overall "exposure." For instance, you can lighten shadow tones to bring out detail, as described in "Correcting Particular Exposure Problems" on page 118. The Curves dialog box can also be used for **special color effects** such as solarization (some tones are left positive and others are switched to negative), or to create the look of iridescence. Also, the **Contour** and **Gloss Contour** settings for the Shadow, Glow, and Bevel And Emboss components of a Layer Style are based on Curves settings (see page 368).

Color Balance

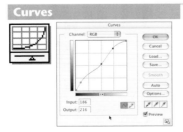

A Color Balance Adjustment layer lets you **target color changes to the highlights, midtones, and shadows *separately*.** Also, its **three color sliders can make it easier to correct a color problem:** Simply find the slider that controls the color you have too much of (such as Red) and drag toward the opposite end of the line (Cyan).

Brightness/Contrast

Brightness/Contrast is **useful for adjusting the edges of masks**, as described in the "Cleaning Up Masks" tip in Chapter 1. But for adjusting the color of an image, its restricted set of controls **can compromise the color or tonal range of an image**, lightening or darkening the image overall when the Brightness is changed and reducing detail when you adjust Contrast.

Hue/Saturation

The Hue/Saturation dialog box is very versatile because it gives you **separate control of hue** (shifting color around the color wheel), **saturation** (making a color more neutral and gray or more vivid and intense), and **lightness**. Or you can make a "monotone" adjustment, tinting the image by checking the **Colorize** box. Besides changing color overall, you can **target different changes to any of the six color "families" independently** (Reds, Yellows, Greens, Blues, Cyans, or Magentas), and the slider bars let you **expand or shrink the targeted color ranges** and **control the transition** between the changed and unchanged colors — you can make it gradual or sharp. You'll find examples of general and targeted changes to Hue/Saturation on pages 120, 127, and 147 for images and on page 371 for Layer Styles.

Desaturate

The Desaturate command is a way of "removing" color to produce a grayscale look but leaving the capacity for color in the file so color can be added back. The Desaturate command is a "one-click fix," but since it can't be applied as an Adjustment layer, it permanently changes the image. And for most images, it doesn't provide the best conversion to black-and-white, so it's **better to use the Saturation slider in a Hue/Saturation Adjustment layer (set to Color mode) or a monotone Channel Mixer Adjustment layer.**

Replace Color

The Replace Color dialog box includes some powerful controls. It lets you make a selection based on sampled color and then change the hue, saturation, or lightness of the selected color, all in one operation. Its preview lets you see how the selection changes as you experiment with the color adjustment and with the Fuzziness, which controls the transition between the changed and unchanged areas. The problem is that it **doesn't provide flexibility for making changes later**. There's no way to save the selection boundary, and Replace Color **can't be applied as an Adjustment layer.**

Selective Color

Selective Color is designed for adding or subtracting specific percentages of cyan, magenta, yellow, and black inks. You can target the changes to any of the six color families as well as Black, White, or Neutrals. It can be **ideal for making adjustments based on a color proof** that shows that you aren't getting the target color you want. **When the printer tells you that you need to add a certain percentage of one of the primary colors, you can do it** with Selective Color. If you're used to thinking in terms of inks, Selective Color can also be useful for adjusting color as you develop an image.

Channel Mixer

The Channel Mixer is excellent **for adjusting the individual color channels** of an image or for **converting a color image to black-and-white** (you'll find examples on page 99).

The Gradient Map adjustment **replaces the tones of an image with the colors of a gradient** you choose. It offers great **flexibility for trying out a variety of creative color solutions** simply by clicking to choose a different gradient. You can **invert the order** in which the original tones are remapped to the gradient's colors by clicking the Reverse box.

The Invert command **changes colors and tones to their opposites.** Besides creating a "negative" look, it can be very **useful for making an "opposite" layer mask.** You can use the Invert command to make a background mask from a foreground mask, or vice versa. (If you're working on a layer mask, you'll have to use the Invert command or keyboard shortcut [Ctrl/⌘-I] rather than an Invert Adjustment layer, since Adjustment layers work on the layer content, not on the mask.)

The Equalize command can be good for **seeing extraneous pixels of color** in an area that appears to be pure black or white, or for seeing when a soft edge has been flattened by cropping too close. Choosing Image, Adjust, Equalize exaggerates the contrast between pixels that are close in color so you can see where the specks or edges are. Then undo (Ctrl/⌘-Z) and fix the problem. Equalize used to be useful for finding the extent of a soft edge, so you didn't accidentally trim it off in cropping the image. But now the Image, **Trim** command can do that kind of cropping job automatically (see page 112 for more about Trim).

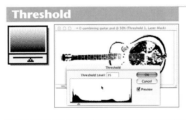

The Threshold command converts each pixel in an image to either black or white. A slider in the Threshold dialog box lets you control where in the tonal range of the image the black/white divide occurs. It can be useful for creating **single-color treatments of photos or for simulating line drawings.**

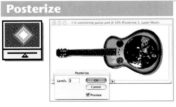

The Posterize command or Adjustment layer simplifies an image by reducing the number of colors (or tones in a grayscale image). It can provide a **good start for reducing the palette of an image for the Web,** to reduce file size and thus download time. Sometimes you get better results if you blur the image slightly (Filter, Blur, Gaussian Blur or Filter, Noise, Despeckle) and then Posterize. Another option for a posterized effect is the Cutout filter (Filter, Artistic, Cutout).

The Variations command has the dual appeal of being able to handle a wide array of color adjustments — hue, saturation, and lightness controlled independently for highlights, midtones, and shadows — and letting you preview several different options for change so you can choose between them. It **may suggest color adjustment options that hadn't occurred to you.** For instance, you may be thinking that an image (or a selected area) needs more red, but the Variations window may show you that increasing magenta would do a better job of achieving the color you want. A major drawback to Variations is that it can't be applied as an Adjustment layer.

AVOIDING RAINBOWS

To reduce the rainbow sheen that can appear when you scan a 3D object, select the area and use a Hue/Saturation Adjustment layer to desaturate. In the pop-out list of colors at the top of the box, sequentially adjust only the Reds, Greens, and Blues (not Cyans, Magentas, or Yellows) by moving the Saturation slider. The color will remain but the rainbow glare will be lessened. Another option is to scan in Grayscale mode and colorize the image afterward.

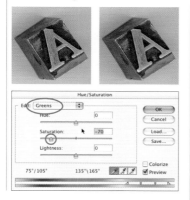

BEHIND = LOCK

Using Behind mode in the Brush Options bar is like the reverse of using the Lock Transparency button at the top of the Layers palette. Instead of protecting transparent areas from applied color, Behind protects *non-transparent* areas.

Toning Tools

The toning tools — Dodge and Burn — can be thought of as "Levels in a wand." They can be used to change brightness, contrast, and thus detail, with independent control of the highlights, shadows, and midtones, chosen in the Options bar. The other tool that shares the same spot on the palette — Sponge — controls saturation. With all their powerful variables, the toning tools can be difficult to control (see page 120 for more about the tools and for a more flexible method for pinpoint control of contrast, brightness, and detail).

Blend Modes

Blend modes control how the colors of a layer or brush stroke interact with the image you apply them to. In Normal mode, color is applied like paint — at full Opacity it covers whatever is "below" it in the image. But the other blend modes change how the color interacts with existing color.

In Photoshop 7, the blend modes (available in the Layers palette, the Options bar for the painting tools, and the dialog boxes for Layer Style, Fade, Fill, Calculations, and Apply Image) are organized by their "neutral colors" (differentiated from each other by those light-colored dividing lines you may have noticed in the palette) — certain colors (actually the neutral "colors" are black, white, and gray) in an overlying layer will have no effect (or be neutral) on the layers below if they are in the particular blend mode.

If a layer is in **Normal** mode, the color stays normal-looking and doesn't interact with color in the layers underneath.

At full opacity, **Dissolve** mode is just like Normal. But reducing the Opacity setting, instead of pushing all the pixels toward transparency, makes a dither (randomized dot) pattern, with some pixels completely transparent and others at full opacity. The lower the Opacity setting, the more pixels disappear.

Darken mode makes the same comparison as Lighten does, but chooses the darker channel component in each case.

The effect of **Multiply** mode is like putting two slides together in the same slide projector slot and projecting them. Where both of the slides have color, the projected color is darker than either. White is neutral in Multiply mode; that is, the white parts of a layer are like the clear parts of a slide — the white has no effect on the

SHADING WITH TONING TOOLS

Although they can be difficult to use for correcting exposure problems in photos, the Dodge and Burn tools can be useful for highlighting and shading flat color artwork.

Here the Burn tool is used for shading, as described on page 327.

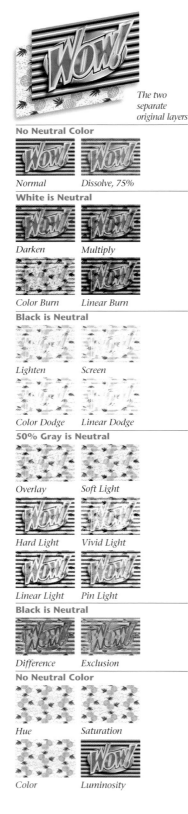

The two separate original layers

No Neutral Color

Normal   Dissolve, 75%

White is Neutral

Darken   Multiply

Color Burn   Linear Burn

Black is Neutral

Lighten   Screen

Color Dodge   Linear Dodge

50% Gray is Neutral

Overlay   Soft Light

Hard Light   Vivid Light

Linear Light   Pin Light

Black is Neutral

Difference   Exclusion

No Neutral Color

Hue   Saturation

Color   Luminosity

layers below. Multiply mode is good for applying shadows without completely eliminating the color of the shaded areas in the layers underneath and for layering line work over color or vice versa, as in step 5 of "Coloring Clip Art" on page 324.

Color Burn increases the contrast of the image underneath, intensifying the color by changing the hue and saturation. **Color Dodge** lightens as it brightens (because it decreases the contrast of the image underneath), and Color Burn darkens. With Color Dodge, light colors affect the composite more. With Color Burn, dark colors have more effect.

Linear Burn darkens what is underneath by decreasing the brightness component.

Lighten mode compares pixels in the overlying layer and the image underneath, channel by channel — that is, it compares the Red channels of both, the Blue channels, and the Green channels — and chooses the lighter channel component in each case.

Screen mode is like projecting two slides from separate slide projectors onto the same spot on the wall, or like overlapping colored spotlights. The result is to lighten the composite. Black is a neutral color in Screen mode, causing no effect. Screen mode is good for applying highlights to an image.

Linear Dodge brightens the base color to reflect the blend color by increasing the brightness.

Overlay, Soft Light, and **Hard Light** provide three different complex combinations of Multiply and Screen, acting differently on dark colors than on light colors. For all three, 50% gray is neutral. Overlay mode, used with a 50%-gray-filled layer, is useful as a substitute for the Dodge and Burn tools, as described on page 120. These modes are useful in general for applying special effects.

Vivid Light burns or dodges the colors by increasing or decreasing the *contrast*, depending on the blend color. If the blend color (light source) is lighter than 50% gray, the image is lightened by decreasing the contrast. If the blend color is darker than 50% gray, the image is darkened by increasing the contrast.

Linear Light burns or dodges the colors by decreasing or increasing the *brightness*, depending on the blend color. If the blend color (light source) is lighter than 50% gray, the image is lightened by increasing the brightness. If the blend color is darker than 50% gray, the image is darkened by decreasing the brightness.

Pin Light replaces the colors, depending on the blend color. If the blend color is lighter than 50% gray, pixels darker than the blend color are replaced, and pixels lighter than the blend color do not change. If the blend color is darker than 50% gray, pixels lighter than the blend color are replaced, and pixels darker than the blend color do not change.

Difference mode does a complex calculation to compare the overlying layer and the image underneath. Black results if there is

The blend mode for painting, filtering, or color adjustment can be changed using the Fade command. For instance, if you sharpen an image (Filter, Sharpen, Unsharp Mask) and find that the sharpening has created an unwanted increase in color contrast, you can change the blend mode to Luminosity to leave the overall sharpening effect intact but eliminate the color problem.

Edit	Image	Layer	Select	Fi
Undo Unsharp Mask				⌘Z
Step Forward				⇧⌘Z
Step Backward				⌥⌘Z
Fade Unsharp Mask...				⇧⌘F
Cut				⌘X

Fade

Opacity: 100 %   OK
Cancel
Mode: Normal   ☑ Preview

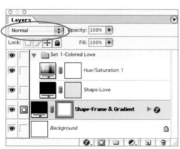

The default mode for a layer set (collected layers, represented by a folder in the Layers palette) is Pass Through, which allows the blend modes of the individual layers within the set to be passed through to affect layers below. An example of using a layer set in Pass Through mode can be found on page 336. If you change the blend mode of a layer set to Normal (as shown above), it's as if all the component layers were merged (combined into a single layer) and then this layer's mode was set to Normal. This allows any Adjustment layers in the set to affect only what's inside the set. The "Limiting a Color Change" tip on page 373 tells more about it.

no difference in the pixel colors, and black is also the neutral color for Difference mode, causing no change in the image underneath. Since Difference mode usually results in more intense colors, it's good for creating psychedelic color effects. It's also good for comparing two images to see if there is any difference between the two. **Exclusion** is like a subdued, grayed-back version of Difference.

Hue, Saturation, and **Luminosity** modes each apply only one of the three attributes of the pixels in the overlying layer. Hue is good for shifting color without changing brightness or value. Luminosity is the mode to use if you want to transfer only the light-and-dark information from a texture onto an image underneath.

Color mode is like a combination of Hue and Saturation modes. The layer contributes all the information except Luminosity (the brightness information).

Behind mode allows color to be applied only to transparent areas of a layer. Any already colored pixels are protected. It's as if color was being applied only *behind* the existing color. Available only for painting and filling tools and for the Edit, Fill command, the Behind mode can't be applied to layers.

Pass Through mode applies only to layer sets, which are groups of layers organized together so that some of their attributes, such as Opacity and blend mode can be controlled as a unit. (For more about layer sets, see "Layer Sets and Layer Colors" on page 157.) The Pass Through mode is the default for layer sets. It allows each individual layer in the set to keep its own blend mode. If you choose any other blend mode for the set, it's as if the layers of the set (with their individual blend modes) had been merged to form a single layer and then the set's blend mode had been applied to that layer.

GETTING CONSISTENT COLOR

In producing color artwork on the computer, you may have noticed some differences in the way color is represented on different monitors and on printed pages. There are several fundamental factors that make on-screen and printed color look different from each other.

- First of all, the transmitted (additive) RGB **color from a monitor looks brighter** than the color produced by light reflected from CMYK or custom inks on paper (subtractive color).

- Second, because the *gamut,* or range of colors that can be displayed or printed, is bigger for RGB than for CMYK, **not all the colors that can be displayed on-screen can be printed.** That means it's possible to develop colors in RGB files that can't be reproduced on the printed page. (Although the CMYK gamut is smaller overall than the RGB gamut, there are also some CMYK colors that are outside the RGB gamut and can't be displayed on-screen.)

- Third, when you convert RGB colors to CMYK for printing, you're moving from a three-color to a four-color system in which

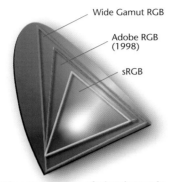

Wide Gamut RGB

Adobe RGB (1998)

sRGB

The gamut, or range of colors that can be displayed or printed, varies for different RGB working spaces. The sRGB space recommended by Adobe as part of the Web Graphics Defaults Settings in the Color Settings dialog box is smaller than the Adobe RGB (1998) color space recommended as part of the U.S. Prepress Defaults Settings that Adobe recommends for Photoshop files destined for print. The Wide Gamut RGB color space, available at the bottom of the pop-out list of RGB options in the Color Settings dialog box, is bigger still.

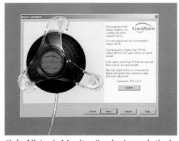

ColorVision's Monitor Spyder is a relatively low-cost hardware-software device that attaches to your screen and characterizes your monitor, producing an ICC-compatible profile that can be used in Photoshop's Color Settings dialog.

black can partially substitute for mixes of the other three colors. Because of this fourth "primary color," **there are many ways to represent a particular RGB color in the CMYK system,** and because of the way ink pigments interact, the results of all these ways can look slightly different from each other.

• Finally, **variations** in halftone screen density (lines per inch), film separation processes, paper, ink, proof printers, presses, and press operators also affect the color in the final printed product.

Color Management

As if the differences between on-screen and printed color weren't enough, there are also differences in the way various scanners record colors and the way various monitors display them. Different kinds of input and display devices operate in different *color spaces,* or subsets of the full range of RGB color. There are also differences in the way particular presses or desktop printers interact with inks and paper to produce printed color. To compensate for this variability, Photoshop offers a color management system to translate color accurately between devices. The **Color Settings** dialog box (Shift-Ctrl/⌘-K) is where you can choose how to configure Photoshop to produce consistent color from scan to print or to the Web.

In a perfect world — one in which every component of every computer graphics system was calibrated (adjusted so that its color stayed consistent over time and was standardized to a universal benchmark), and in which we knew each component's ICC profile (that component's color characteristics according to an international standard designed to help reproduce colors accurately) — the color management system built into Photoshop could work perfectly. It would allow color to stay consistent no matter what device or graphics program was used to display or print Photoshop documents. Unfortunately, the world isn't perfect yet in this regard.

Many Photoshop users, especially if they are designers working alone and **if they don't share their files during the Photoshop image-creation process,** prefer to choose the "Off" options in the Color Management Policies section of the Color Settings dialog box. This way they can avoid any complications that might arise because the file was passed from or to another graphics program that doesn't include the same color management functions, such as many Web page applications and HTML editors. But by also turning *on* the Embed Color Profile option in the Save As dialog box (File, Save As) when a file is saved, they can still include information about the color space they were using when the file was developed, in case it's of use to the next person in the workflow.

On the other hand, if the workflow involves passing files back and forth from one person to another for different stages of the creative process, it may be worth implementing the color management system within the work group and sharing the profiles. Setting up and using the color management system will involve

In the Adobe Gamma Assistant (Mac OS9) or Wizard (Windows) dialog box, clicking the Step By Step button and then clicking Next starts the Adobe Gamma Wizard or Assistant, to lead you through the process of calibrating your monitor and creating an ICC-compliant profile.

In the first Adobe Gamma Wizard (or Assistant) screen, enter a name for the monitor profile you'll be producing with Adobe Gamma.

After the Wizard/Assistant has led you through the calibration process, click the Finish button and give the profile the same name as you did in the first screen, as described above.

You can use Mac OSX's built-in Display Calibrator Assistant to walk you through the profile creation process.

searching out or creating the ICC profile for each scanner, digital camera, monitor, and output device (with various settings for different resolution and paper settings); keeping each component in the workflow calibrated so that the ICC profile is meaningful for that component; and studying the recommendations in Chapter 4 ("Producing Consistent Color") of the *Adobe Photoshop 7.0 User Guide* and the sections of the on-screen Help recommended there. (Color management is a complex subject, and there is a great deal of discussion — and disagreement — online and in print about choosing an RGB Working Space, developing ICC profiles, and related topics.)

Your "Color Environment"

To get consistent color, not only the monitor but also the viewing environment has to be constantly maintained because changes in lighting conditions can change your perception of colors on the screen. Here are some ways to keep environmental color conditions from interfering with your on-screen color work:

- Position the room's light source above and in back of the monitor, and keep it dimmed and constant.
- If your room lighting is controlled by a rheostat, mark the knob and the base plate so you can always restore the lighting to the same level.
- The wall behind you should be neutral in color, with no bright posters or other images.
- Wear neutral colors when doing color-critical work, to minimize color reflection from your clothes to the screen.
- Use a neutral Desktop color (medium gray works well), with no bright colors or distracting pictures.

Calibrating and Characterizing Your Monitor

In order for your computer monitor to show you consistent color — so the same file displayed on the screen today looks the same as it did last week and as it will next week — the monitor has to be calibrated periodically to bring it into compliance with the standards it was designed to meet. Some monitors come with special calibration software. If yours didn't, you may want to try a hardware-software combination package that either actually adjusts your monitor or tells you which settings need correcting so you can manually adjust it before the software then creates a profile that describes how your monitor is currently reproducing color. That way, the color management system can accurately translate color between your monitor and various input and output devices.

Another possibility for calibration in Windows or Mac OS9 is to use the Adobe Gamma control panel that comes with Photoshop to do a simplified calibration, and build an ICC profile. Opening the control panel and choosing the Step By Step option will lead you through the monitor calibration and profiling process. In the very first screen of the Adobe Gamma Wizard (Windows) or Assistant (Mac), enter a new name for the profile you are building. Remember the name because you'll need it again when you finish the process. By naming the profile here and giving it the same name when you click the Finish button at the end of the process and save the profile, you designate this profile as the default for the Monitor RGB working space in the Color Settings dialog box. Mac OSX has a

*The process described in "**A 'Back-to-Front' Calibration System**" on page 86 was used to calibrate the monitor that was used in creating and preparing the images for this book, using printed pages from a previous edition of the book. In the Color Settings dialog box, we started with "Photoshop 5 Default Spaces" chosen for the Settings, then clicked the Advanced check box so we could load our customized Monitor RGB profile for the RGB Working Space. (The CMYK Working Space setting was irrelevant, since we were using "back-to-front" calibration rather than using the Proof Color command.) The finished files were saved and then opened on another computer system for conversion to CMYK, with the "Leave as is" option chosen in the Missing Profile or Profile Mismatch dialog box and with a custom ICC profile loaded into the Color Settings dialog box as the CMYK Working Space. (The printing company had sent their own profile for us to load.) The files were converted in batches using an Action that opened each file and executed the Image, Mode, CMYK Color command, then saved a copy of the file.*

*Clicking the **Advanced Mode** check box allows you to load profiles other than those listed in the pop-out Working Spaces menus by choosing Load or Custom.*

*Adobe recommends starting with the Settings that best describe the output process that will be used to produce your images — typically, **Web Graphics Defaults** or **U.S. Prepress Defaults**. Then you can change individual Working Space settings to match your actual workflow. For instance, you can change RGB to the monitor characterization produced with the Adobe Gamma utility or with a hardware-software-based profiling device. You might also want to change the CMYK Working Space according to custom CMYK Setup settings provided by the printer who will be producing a specific job. The printer may also provide Custom Dot Gain settings for a black-only or spot color printing job. As soon as you change any settings in the Color Settings dialog box, the Settings entry changes to **Custom**.*

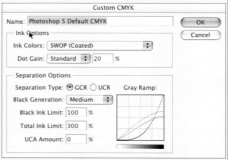

Choosing Custom CMYK opens the CMYK Setup dialog box, where you can choose Separation Options. Alternatively, you can Load a CMYK profile supplied by the printer who will be producing a specific job.

*If the **Ask When Opening** boxes are checked, as Adobe recommends, you are offered the opportunity to override the Color Management Policies whenever you open a file or paste an element whose profile doesn't match the current working space.*

*Your choice of **Color Management Policies** determines what will happen if you open a file that doesn't have an embedded profile or whose profile isn't the same as the current working space, and the Ask When Opening box is unchecked.*

The MonacoEZColor system is designed to measure color and build ICC-compatible profiles for your scanner and printer. EZColor uses a target file, a printed target, and characterization software to characterize both the scanner and the printer at the same time. The scanner profile can then be used by Photoshop to accurately display scanned images. The printer profile can be used in previewing printed files through Photoshop's Proof Setup and Proof Color commands. You can find more information on the Wow CD-ROM or at **www.monacosys.com***.*

ProfileCity.com is an online service that will make ICC-compliant profiles for your equipment, based on test prints that you make from downloaded files and mail back to ProfileCity for analysis.

built-in Display Calibrator Assistant to walk you through the profile creation process.

Color Settings

In the Settings section of the Color Settings dialog box, you can choose one of the predefined color management options offered by Photoshop to produce consistent color results for the most widely used on-screen and print workflows. Each setting can be used "as is" or you can modify it — for instance, by loading the characterization for your particular monitor that was generated with Adobe Gamma or with a hardware-software device. Adobe recommends that you leave the "Ask When Opening" options turned on, so that you will be alerted whenever you open a file that has no embedded profile or that has a profile that doesn't match the one in your Color Settings dialog box for the color mode of the file. For more about working with Color Settings, see Chapter 4 of *The Adobe Photoshop 7.0 User Guide.*

"Color-Managing" Your Local Workflow

Once your monitor is calibrated and its profile has been built, consistent color management requires that other devices in your

WHEN "ASSIGN PROFILE" MAY BE WORTH A TRY

Suppose you open an image that came from somewhere other than your own system and not only does it look bad on your monitor but it hasn't been tagged with an embedded profile to tell your system about the color characteristics of the device it came from — so your system can't correct the way the file is displayed. For instance, it may be that the person who created the image chose not to embed a profile, or the image may have come from a scanner or digital camera that can't embed profile information. You could just go ahead and use Photoshop's color-adjustment tools and commands to get the image looking the way you want, but there may be another option that will save you some time and work. If you can find out what device it came from (or make a good guess), and if you can get a profile for that system, you can try using Assign Profile to make the image look better — more like it looked to the person/system that produced it. The **Image, Mode, Assign Profile** command may change how the image looks on your screen, depending on how different the color space of origin was from your working color space. But it **doesn't change the color information in the file.** It may show you an on-screen version of the image that's more like what the originator of the file "intended" the image to look like. If the profile you assigned actually makes the image worse instead of better, you can undo (Ctrl/⌘-Z) and try another profile if you like.

The **Convert To Profile** command converts an image from its embedded RGB, CMYK, or Grayscale color space — whether it was embedded originally or assigned with the Assign Profile command — to the current working space that's set in your Color Settings dialog box. This **changes the actual color data in the file** to the color data that your system with its current Color Settings would use to create an image that looks like what you're seeing on-screen. With the profile converted, you can make changes to the file to get it looking the way you want it, embed your own system's profile when you save the file (File, Save As, Embed Color Profile), and pass it on.

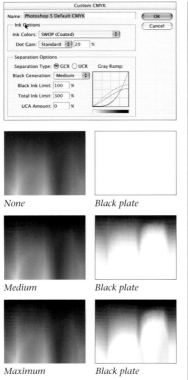

None   *Black plate*

Medium   *Black plate*

Maximum   *Black plate*

The parameters for converting RGB to CMYK color can be customized in the Custom CMYK dialog box (top). There are several options for Black Generation, which controls how much of the dark colors is contributed by black ink and how much is contributed by a mix of cyan, magenta, and yellow. Shown here are results of converting from RGB to CMYK color using each of three different Black Generation settings in the CMYK Setup dialog box.

workflow — such as your scanner and desktop color printer used for proofing — also be calibrated, or at least have ICC-compliant profiles, so that color can be accurately translated from one device to the next. Although you can obtain profiles created by the manufacturers of your equipment, the actual scanner or printer (and the paper you are using) may vary from the manufacturer's profile standard, and there may not be an easy way to calibrate the equipment to bring it into compliance with the profile. A better solution is to generate profiles for the specific scanner and printer you own. One relatively inexpensive and successful system that has been developed to do that is MonacoEZColor, shown at the left. Another option for building custom profiles is a profiling service such as that provided by ProfileCity (**www.profilecity.com**), which gives advice on preparing your printer to deliver its best output and also supplies a file for you to print and mail in; ProfileCity analyzes the print to develop an ICC-compatible profile for your particular printer.

Making RGB-to-CMYK Conversions

If you're preparing an image for print, unless you use a desktop printer or a photo emulsion printer that actually prints using an RGB color space, the image will eventually need to be turned into CMYK color primaries. This can be done at several different stages in the development of the image. For instance:

- You can choose CMYK Color mode when you first create a new Photoshop file (File, New, Mode: CMYK Color).

- Some scanning services (and even some desktop scanning software) can make the CMYK conversion for you. The quality of the result depends on the sophistication of the software and the suitability of its settings for the kind of printing you want to do, or on the skill of the professional scan operator. (For more about scanning, see "Setting Up a Scan" in Chapter 1.)

- If you start in RGB, you can choose Photoshop's Image, Mode, CMYK Color at any point in the development of an image to convert from the RGB working space to the CMYK working space chosen in the Color Settings dialog box. But once you make the conversion you can't regain the original RGB color by choosing Image, Mode, RGB Color. Instead, if you don't like the result, you will have to step back through the History palette's states, if enough are preserved, to get back to the point when the conversion was made, or choose a Snapshot made before the conversion, or choose File, Revert to go back to the last saved version of the file. (Using History is explained in "The History Palette" in Chapter 1.)

- Or you can keep the file in RGB Color mode, place it in a page layout, and allow the page layout program or color separation utility to make the separation.

*If you are developing Photoshop artwork that will be output with more than one printing method, the ColorBlade plug-in for Photoshop may be helpful. With the goal of automatically controlling and predicting color output across different media and devices, it lets you preview your color image on-screen in side-by-side ICC profile comparisons. Information about ColorBlade can be found at **www.creativepro.com**.*

PREVIEW TOGGLE

To toggle back and forth between the RGB view and the CMYK preview, the shortcut for View, Proof Colors is **Ctrl/⌘-Y**.

Both color fidelity and longevity took a big leap forward with the arrival of Epson's Stylus Photo 2200 Printer (and its bigger brother, the 7600). The 2200 is the first large-format desktop photo printer (up to 13" wide) to use 7 pigment-based inks (it adds a "light black" — typically known as "gray" — for added shadow and highlight detail, as well as for beautiful black-and-white prints), and has the highest color gamut of any pigment ink jet printer and archival-rated light-fastness of up to 100 years. With the included Fire Wire connection, roll paper holder and automatic cutter, it's truly a dream come true!

- Or, if your final destination is a desktop printer, you can leave the file in RGB and let the printer's software do the conversion "on the fly." Many desktop printers will even convert a CMYK file back to RGB, just so they can do their own conversion.

How do you decide which one of these options is best for converting from RGB to CMYK? Here are some tips to help you choose when (or if) to convert:

- The single advantage of working in CMYK from the beginning is that it prevents last-minute color shifts, since it keeps the image within the printing gamut during the entire development process.
- But if you're working in CMYK mode and your printing specifications change (a different paper may be chosen for the job, for instance), the CMYK working space you chose may no longer apply. In that case, for the highest-quality separations it's better to start over from an RGB version of the final image.
- Working in RGB and putting off the CMYK conversion to the last possible moment allows more freedom, so you can get just the color you want on-screen and then work with Photoshop's Hue/Saturation, Levels or Curves adjustments to tweak out-of-gamut colors to get CMYK alternatives that are as close as possible to your original colors.
- Another very significant advantage of working in RGB is that some of Photoshop's finest functions (for example, the Lighting Effects and Glass filters, described in Chapter 5 and applied in several of the techniques in Chapter 8) don't work in CMYK mode.
- With Photoshop's Preview Color and Gamut Warning available, it makes sense to work in RGB, preview CMYK in a second window, and do the actual RGB-to-CMYK conversion at the end of the process. Or work in just one window and toggle back and forth between the RGB and the CMYK previews as needed.

KEEP AN RGB VERSION

Before you convert an RGB file to CMYK mode, save a copy in RGB mode. That way, if you need to, you can make changes to the file or the Color Settings criteria to make a new CMYK version, starting with the full RGB gamut.

BOOST SATURATION IN CMYK

Photoshop's Gamut Warning is designed to let you identify the colors in your image that may not translate successfully from the RGB working space to CMYK. For some CMYK printing processes the Gamut Warning is conservative, "predicting" more color problems than will actually be encountered. Instead of reducing saturation or shifting colors in RGB to eliminate all the problem areas indicated by the Gamut Warning, you can try making the conversion to CMYK and then using the Saturation slider in a Hue/Saturation Adjustment layer to restore color intensity, targeting the adjustment to the particular color range that has become dull in the conversion process.

As a CMYK file to use for back-to-front calibration, the **Ole No Moire.tif** file (from the Photoshop 7 CD-ROM's Goodies folder) provides fine-tuned color and good shadow detail so you can be confident about whether a printed proof is accurate. It also includes standard color swatches that your printer can check with a densitometer. The eight gray levels in the black ink scale will show you what's happening to the highlight and shadow tones in your image.

MAKING A STEP WEDGE

To make a kind of photographer's step wedge that will allow finer discrimination about tonal distinctions than you get with the eight-step black scale in **Ole No Moire.tif**, you can add your own gray scale with 5% tone steps: Add canvas to the **Ole No Moire.tif** file (Image, Canvas Size) and fill a long rectangular selection with a black-to-white gradient. Then posterize it (Image, Adjust, Posterize, 21 Levels).

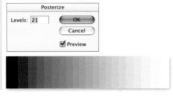

Back-to front monitor calibration involves comparing a printed piece or a proof as you adjust your monitor's settings using Adobe Gamma, as described at the right.

- You may be able to bow out of the conversion process altogether for many jobs. The printer you work with may have a separation utility that can do an excellent job of converting most of your RGB images to CMYK, "tweaked" specifically for their particular printing environment. If that's the case, you can save yourself some time and angst by using this method, although there may be an additional charge.

At whatever point you make the conversion, the specifications in Photoshop's Color Settings dialog box and the profiles that support those settings will affect the final result.

A "Back-to-Front" Calibration System

Whether or not you decide to use a color management system with Photoshop, you can do a sort of "backwards calibration" to make sure your monitor's screen display is an accurate predictor of the color you'll get in a print or proof. Here's a way to do it:

1 **Use a piece that was previously printed with the same production and printing methods** — for instance, an earlier version of a brochure or annual report cover. Or print or proof a color file; this could be an image of your own, but you may also want to include the **Ole No Moire.tif** image from the Photoshop 7 program CD-ROM. Either:
   - print the file on the same system you'll be using for final printing,
   - or print the file on a proofing printer that your press operator assures you will be a good predictor of final color,
   - or produce film and a laminate proof that your printing press operators can check and assure you they can match on press.

   Going all the way to press, rather than stopping at a proof, is better, but often it isn't practical.

2 **In your controlled-light environment** (see "Your 'Color Environment'" on page 81) open the file on-screen. Hold the print or proof up to the screen to compare color.

   The back-to-front system calibration process depends on changing the *display characteristics of the monitor* at this point, *not the file itself*. So don't do any work in Photoshop during the process — that is, *don't change the file*. Instead, readjust your monitor with the Adobe Gamma control panel until the on-screen image looks like the printed piece. Use the Finish button in the Adobe Gamma Wizard/Assistant to save the settings for future use in projects that will use the same printing process. Once your monitor has been readjusted so the on-screen image matches the print or proof, you can assume that for files you produce in the future, when the image looks the way you want it on the screen, the print or proof will look like the screen. (In the Color Settings dialog box, you can load the Gamma setting you saved by clicking the Advanced check box and choosing Load RGB for the RGB Working Space.)

Duotones & Other Tint Effects

Overview *Apply one of six coloring techniques: (1) preparing a Duotone, (2) colorizing a gray version of the image, (3) partially desaturating the image, (4) shifting the hue of the desaturated image, and (5) applying a Gradient Map, (6) Tinting with Layer Styles*

"Duotone Tint" "before" and "after" files

1a   **1b**

Original image   Converted to grayscale

1c

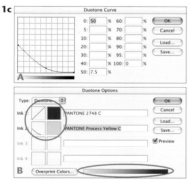

The curve for the yellow ink was adjusted to color the highlights **A**. The Overprint Colors bar in the Duotone Options dialog box **B** predicts how the ink mix will look throughout the full range of tones, with yellow dominating in the highlights and deep purple in the shadows **C**.

IF YOUR PRINTING BUDGET LIMITS YOU to two-color design, Photoshop's Duotone mode can deliver a sophisticated look that's quick, easy, and flexible. Even for a four-color print job, the coloring of a duotone, a tint, or a gradient-based color scheme may be just what you're looking for. Here are six ways to achieve subtle (or not so subtle) color effects; you can start with a color image, as we did, or start with a Grayscale file and convert it to the mode you need — Duotone for the technique in step 1, or RGB for the methods in steps 2 through 5 and the tip on page 88.

1 Making a duotone. Photoshop's Duotone mode gives you precise control of how each of your two spot colors is applied to the range of tones in your image, through the curves for Ink 1 and Ink 2 in the Duotone Options dialog box. To set up your Duotone, if your image is RGB **1a,** convert it to Grayscale, since a Photoshop Duotone is actually a grayscale image with Curves information stored with it. We used Image, Mode, Grayscale to convert this image **1b;** other conversion methods are described in "From Color to Gray" on page 98.

"FULL-COLOR" DUOTONES

You can get interesting results using Photoshop's Duotone mode and two complementary colors (opposites on the traditional artist's color wheel), but **Powertone 1.5** is a plug-in (available from creo.com) that goes well beyond simple mapping of spot colors to lights and darks. It uses two colors (from the plug-in's color sets or your own choices) to generate the best Duotone match it can make, based on the original colors of the image. See below for an example of blues kept blue and oranges kept orange.

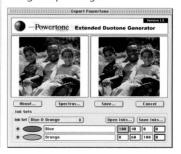

Now you can convert to Duotone mode (Image, Mode, Duotone) and choose Duotone from the Type pop-out menu. You can then set up your two color curves, as described in the next paragraph, or click the Load button and select one of the Duotone color sets supplied in the Duotones folder inside Photoshop 7's Presets folder.

To make your own set of curves as we did, click the color squares for Ink 1 and Ink 2 in turn and choose a color from the color sets offered when you click the Custom button in the Color Picker dialog box. Once the colors are chosen, if you click the Curves box next to each color square in the Duotone Options dialog box, dragging to change the curve will modify the color treatment **1c.** You can watch the image change as you adjust the curves. For this example, we left the dark purple (Ink 1) at its default setting and changed the curve for the yellow (Ink 2) so that a 50% tint of yellow was applied to the highlights. The yellow faded to 0% at the dark end of the tonal scale, so that the deepest shadows would remain pure purple.

Using the Colorize option in a Hue/Saturation Adjustment layer to tint an image

2 Colorizing. To create a sepia or other subtle tinting effect, start with a grayscale image converted to RGB (Image, Mode, RGB) or with a color file desaturated (Image, Mode, Desaturate). Then add an Adjustment layer by clicking the Create New Fill/Adjustment Layer button at the bottom of the Layers palette and choosing Hue/Saturation from the pop-out list. In the Hue/Saturation dialog box, click the Colorize box (to produce a monotone) and experiment by moving the Hue and Saturation sliders until you get the color you like **2.**

3 Desaturating a color image. Start with an RGB image and add an Adjustment layer by Alt/Option-clicking the Create New Fill/Adjustment Layer button at the bottom of the Layers palette and choosing Hue/Saturation from the pop-out list. In the New Layer dialog box, which opens because you used the Alt/Option key when you added the Adjustment layer, be sure to choose Color as the Mode and click OK. Move the Saturation slider in the Hue/Saturation dialog box to the left to reduce the color **3;** we set it at –75.

Toning down a color image by adding a Hue/ Saturation Adjustment layer in Color mode

TINTING WITH STYLE

An easy way to tint an image is with Layer Styles. Simply select Color Overlay from the Layer Styles pop-out from the bottom of the Layers Palette and set the Blend Mode to Color and then click on the swatch

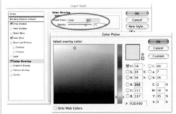

to the right and select a color. If you would like some of the color of the original to show through you can lower the Opacity. And while you are in the Styles dialog you may want to experiment with a subtle Inner Glow or Drop Shadow effect as well (as we did for the opening image on page 87).

4

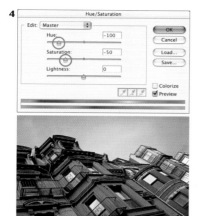

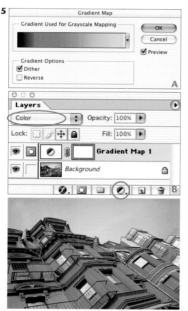

Changing the Hue to go from a warm to a cool color scheme

5

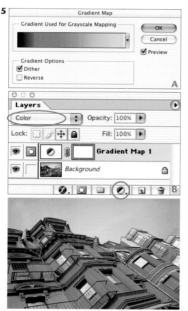

*Because of its dark-to-light progression of the gradient we selected, when it's applied as a Gradient Map, the tonality of the "remapped" image is similar to that of the original image **A**. (You can open the Gradient Editor by clicking the large Gradient swatch anywhere it occurs.) We set the Gradient Map Adjustment layer to the Color Blend mode **B**.*

4 Changing the tint. You can experiment with other color schemes by simply moving the Hue and the Saturation sliders in the Adjustment layer that was added at step 3. To make the change, double-click the Adjustment layer's thumbnail in the Layers palette to open the Hue/Saturation dialog box, and then move the Hue slider. Moving the slider to the left shifted the color of our image from its original warm tones to cool, but maintained the range of subtle color differences **4**.

5 Remapping the color.

Photoshop 7's Gradient Map lets you recolor an image — either full-color or desaturated — by replacing the luminosity values with the colors of a gradient of your choice. Gradient Map can be applied directly to a layer (Image, Adjust, Gradient Map) or as an Adjustment layer. If you use a gradient that goes from a dark color on the left through a medium-bright color to a light color on the right, such as the one we used here **5**, you can roughly maintain the original lights and darks of your image as you add the color. If you haven't already loaded the Wow Presets from the companion CD-ROM that comes with this book, go to page 7 for installation instructions.

To add a Gradient Map Adjustment layer, click the Create New Fill/Adjustment Layer button at the bottom of the Layers palette and choose Gradient Map from the pop-out list. In the Gradient Map dialog box, click the tiny triangle to the right of the gradient swatch and choose from the pop-out palette, then click OK. With the Gradient Map layer in place, experiment by changing the blend mode for the layer. The blend mode was set to Color to produce the image shown at the left.

SCROLLING BLEND MODES

Holding down the Shift key and pressing the "+" or "–" key changes the blend mode. Use **Shift-+ to work forward** (down) in the pop-out blend mode list or **Shift-hyphen to work backwards**. This results in a mode change for the currently active layer, or for the Blend Mode choice in the Options bar if the currently chosen tool has this option. (If one of the two path selection tools is chosen, the keyboard shortcut doesn't work at all.)

Controlled Recoloring

Overview *Add a custom color swatch as a Fill layer to a CMYK image file; select the part of the image that you want to recolor; create another Fill layer in Hue mode using the selection and the custom color; if necessary, experiment with changes to the color of the Fill layer and the luminance of the original image.*

"**Controlled Recolor**" "before" and "after" files

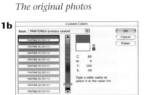

1a The original photos

1b Choosing the color for the Fill layer

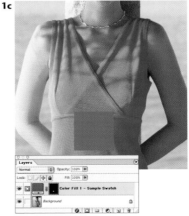

1c The "swatch" layer in place

JHD / ORIGINAL PHOTOS: © CORBIS IMAGES ROYALTY FREE, TROPICAL ESCAPE (LEFT) AND MODERN TEENS (RIGHT)

FOR MOST PHOTOSHOP PRINT APPLICATIONS it makes sense to work in RGB color, then make a duplicate file in CMYK mode at the end when you need to save the image for printing. For instance, if you need to make a color change to get "pleasing color" rather than a specific color match, you can make the change in RGB using the method described in "'Quick & Dirty' Color Change" on page 93. But if your goal is to match a particular custom color — for a clothing catalog, for instance — it works better to tackle the project in CMYK from the beginning. That way the swatch you're trying to match is a stable target — one that you can check with a process color chart like those from Pantone, and that won't change during an RGB-to-CMYK conversion.

1 Making an on-screen swatch. Open the photo you want to recolor; we wanted to change the color of the dress and shirt in the two photos **1a** to a custom green. If the file isn't yet in CMYK mode, choose Edit, Color Settings and *pick the color settings given to you by the printer.* Then choose Image, Mode, CMYK Color. We received the preseparated CMYK file from the client.

Make a color swatch using a Fill layer, as follows: Make a selection in the size and location you want the swatch; starting with the dress photo, we used the Rectangular Marquee to make a selection in an area that was neither heavily shaded nor blown out by the

2

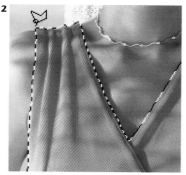

Selecting the dress

3a

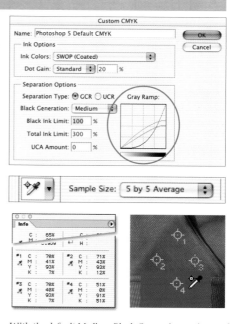

Adding a Solid Color Fill layer in Hue mode

relatively strong lighting in our photo. Then click the Create New Fill/Adjustment Layer button (the black-and-white circle) at the bottom of the Layers palette and choose Solid Color, at the top of the pop-out list. When the Color Picker opens, choose the color you want to match; we needed to match Pantone Process 293-1, so we chose Custom, Pantone Process and scrolled to this color and clicked it **1b**, then clicked OK to finish adding the Fill layer **1c**.

2 Selecting the element to recolor. Next, select the item you want to recolor (you can find tips on choosing a selection method in Chapter 1). Because the area we wanted to select had distinct (rather than soft) edges but included detailed shadows that could confuse an automated selection process such as Color Range, it was easier to make the selection by hand, using Lasso tools **2**.

WHY NOT DO IT BY THE NUMBERS?

When your goal is to match a particular CMYK (for Cyan, Magenta, Yellow, blacK) process color, you may be tempted to try to do it "by the numbers": "Why couldn't we use the Color Sampler tool to set up some samplers on the selected part of the image whose color we want to change and one more sampler on a swatch of the custom color we're trying to match? Then we could use Photoshop's color-and-tone-adjusting functions — such as Hue/Saturation, Color Balance, Levels, and Curves — to change the color in our image until its CMYK composition matched the target swatch, couldn't we?"

Maybe if you were both extremely patient and very lucky, you could do the job this way. But in a production environment, where time matters, this wouldn't be a practical option, for the following reason: There are many different ways to mix cyan, magenta, yellow, and black inks to produce a particular color.

Depending on how the CMYK image you're trying to recolor was converted from RGB to CMYK, the colors in the image could have been darkened with black ink only. At the other extreme, it could be that *no* black ink was used for darkening; instead the colors might have been darkened by increasing the amounts of all three color inks (C, M, and Y) to make up the black component. (When Photoshop converts RGB to CMYK, it uses different CMYK mixes, depending on which presses and paper stocks will be used for printing.) If C, M, and Y inks were in fact used for darkening the colors in the image, but they weren't used in this same way to arrive at the color makeup of your target swatch, the Color Samplers in your image will show C, M, and Y values that are higher overall than for your swatch (which also includes some black). This discrepancy will be true even when the match looks great to your eye. So by concentrating on matching the *numbers* rather than producing a *visual* match, you may be setting yourself a task that's virtually impossible — or at least very time-consuming, and also unnecessary.

With the default Medium Black Generation setting used to separate the image (top), the cyan, magenta, and yellow inks are used along with black ink for darkening colors. But in the target color swatch, much of the darkening comes from black ink alone. Therefore, even if you set the Color Samplers to average the color over a 5 x 5-pixel area to allow for shading due to the weave of the fabric, the color composition shown by the samplers in the image (#1, #2, and #3) won't match the sampler on the swatch (#4), even though the colors themselves look very similar.

3b

The mask in the Solid Color Fill layer targeted the color change to the dress. Putting this layer in Hue mode allowed the detail from the image to show through.

4a

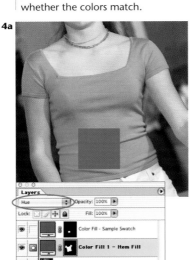

For the shirt, just putting the Fill layer in Hue mode wasn't enough. The new color of the shirt was too light.

3 Recoloring. With the selection active and the image layer targeted, add another Solid Color Fill layer in your custom color as in step 1, but this time hold down the Alt/Option key as you click the button. The New Layer dialog box will open **3a**, where you can name the layer and choose the blend mode — Hue, and then click OK. Choose the same custom color as in step 1.

Now compare the swatch to the new color of the element you selected. We found that applying the color to the dress in Hue mode had worked well **3b**. If your "before" and "after" colors were close in intensity — that is, the two colors are about equally bright and saturated — the recoloring process will probably be complete now, as it was for our dress photo. But if your two colors are very different in intensity, as they are for the shirt in our second photo, you may need to add another step or two. As described in step 4, you'll need to make some changes to the luminance of the element you're recoloring to match it to the luminance of the target swatch. Or you may even need to adjust the saturation of the color you're adding.

4 Tweaking the recoloring. On our second model we repeated steps 1 through 3, adding a color swatch, selecting the shirt, and adding a Solid Color Fill layer in Hue mode. But the color of the

4b

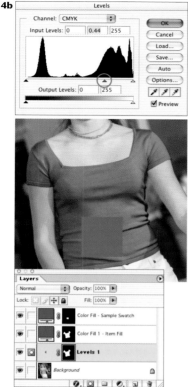

Shifting the gamma in a Levels Adjustment layer above the Background *improved the color.*

4c

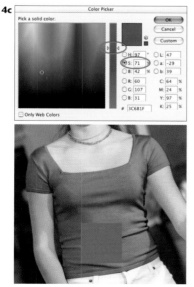

Slightly decreasing the saturation of the Fill layer finally produced the result we wanted.

shirt was too light **4a**. To fix that problem, we used Levels to adjust the luminance of the underlying shirt: We loaded the shirt selection by Ctrl/⌘-clicking the thumbnail for its mask in the Fill layer. Then we clicked on the *Background* layer in the Layers palette to target it so the Levels Adjustment layer we were about to add would appear just above the original photo. We clicked the Create New Fill/Adjustment Layer button and chose Levels. In the Input Levels section, dragging the center (gray, gamma) slider to the right darkened the shirt. This improved the color, but the shirt still looked slightly "hotter" (more intense, or saturated) than the swatch **4b**, so we wanted to try toning down our new shirt color slightly.

In the Layers palette we double-clicked the color thumbnail (not the mask) for the shirt's Fill layer to open the Color Picker. The dialog box was still in Custom Colors mode from when we chose our Pantone color, so we clicked the Picker button to switch to Color Picker mode, then clicked the "S" button in the HSB section of the dialog box. This gave us a slider bar for controlling Saturation alone. We could drag the slider down slightly to decrease saturation, then release the mouse button to see the color change, experimenting until the shirt color more closely matched the swatch **4c**. 🖐

"QUICK & DIRTY" COLOR CHANGE

When it isn't necessary to match a specific custom color, a quick way to change the color of a selected area of an image is to use the Hue slider in a

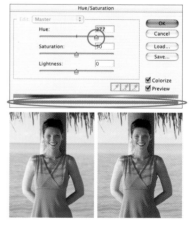

Hue/Saturation adjustment. With Colorize turned on in the Hue/Saturation dialog box, you can ensure that all the colors in the original will change toward a particular color, which shows up in the bottom color bar. Without the Colorize option, all colors would simply shift a certain amount around the color wheel. This would mean that if highlights or shadows in the original image had their own color cast, the color-shifted shadows might end up looking the wrong color, both in relation to the new color and in relation to the highlights and shadows elsewhere in the original image.

Channel Mixing

Overview Experiment with color and grayscale effects with a Channel Mixer Adjustment layer.

"**Channel Mix**" "before" and "after" files

1a

Original photo

1b

*Loading Adobe's **RGB Pastels.cha** preset provides a good start toward a hand-tinted look by adding to all color channels to lighten the colors in the image.*

2

*Adobe's **RGB Swap Red&Blue.cha** preset*

EVERYTHING FROM SUBTLE COLOR ADJUSTMENTS to radical colorizing to sepia tones to optimized grayscale conversions can be produced with the Channel Mixer, either as a command (Image, Adjust, Channel Mixer) or as an Adjustment layer. But using an Adjustment layer makes it a more practical image-manipulation tool.

It would take a great deal of space to show the settings for all the variables in the Channel Mixer dialog box. So for this example we've used the presets that Adobe supplies with Photoshop. One way to learn how to work this complex dialog box, with as many as 20 variables to set, is to apply a preset and study the settings that produce the result you see. Then experiment with the settings and watch the changes in the image. (Printed examples of Adobe presets are provided in "Channel Mixer Presets" on pages 96 and 97.)

1 Starting with pastels. Open an RGB image **1a**, open the Layers palette (Window, Show Layers), and Ctrl/⌘-click the Create New Fill/Adjustment Layer button (the half-black/half-white circle) at the bottom of the palette; from the pop-out menu, choose Channel Mixer. In the Channel Mixer dialog box, click the Load button and find and load the RGB Pastels preset (**RGB Pastels.cha**; it's on the Adobe Photoshop 7.0 CD-ROM in Goodies, Channel Mixer Presets). Inspect the settings in the Channel Mixer box for each Output Channel: Red, Green, and Blue. Notice that the dialog box tells you that the new Red channel now includes all the brightness information it originally contained (Red, 100%) plus 50% of the brightness information from the Green channel and 31% of the brightness information from the Blue channel. The brightness in the other Output Channels is similarly boosted. The effect of adding brightness to all three Output Channels (R, G, and B) is to lighten the colors, produc-

3

Wow-RGB Hula Color.cha (from the Wow CD-ROM)

4a

Blocking the effects of the Channel Mixer Adjustment layer with a painted layer mask

4b

*Starting with the **Wow-RGB Hula Color.cha** preset in step 3, we adjusted Blending Options to allow part of the original blue sky to show.*

ing pastels. Reducing the Constant setting to –11% balances the lightness somewhat by slightly darkening the image tone overall **1b**.

2 Swapping channels. While you're working in the Channel Mixer, try another option. Load Adobe's **RGB Swap Red&Blue.cha** preset to produce a color reversal. Because the Green channel stays intact, the image stays positive rather than becoming a negative **2**.

3 Heading toward fluorescent. Still in the Channel Mixer, load the **Wow-RGB Hula Color.cha** preset (from the Wow CD-ROM that comes with this book). Click OK to close the Channel Mixer dialog box **3**.

4 Restricting Channel Mixer effects. Now you can paint the Adjustment layer's built-in mask so it blocks the Wow-RGB Hula Color Channel Mixer effect from parts of the image: With the Channel Mixer layer active and with black as the Foreground color, choose the Paintbrush or Airbrush tool. In the Options bar, set the tool's Opacity or Pressure low, and paint. We blocked the Channel Mixer from affecting the flowers and skin tones **4a**.

To "drop out" the effect of the Channel Mixer from certain colors or tones in the image, double-click the Channel Mixer layer's name in the Layers palette to open the Blending Options section of the Layer Style dialog box. Adjust the "This Layer" and "Underlying Layer" sliders in the lower part of the box. To split a slider so color transitions are gradual rather than abrupt, hold down the Alt/Option key as you move one half of the slider. (For a more thorough explanation of how these sliders work, see pages 156 and 160–161). We tried splitting the right-hand slider in "This Layer," separating its halves but moving both to the left so the light colors of the channel mix didn't contribute to the image; we also split both "Underlying Layer" sliders and moved them inward so the channel mix applied to the midtones only, so part of the original sky showed through **4b**. We finally settled on Advanced Blending settings that removed the channel mix effect from the lightest colors **4c**.

Experimenting with gray. Try some conversions from RGB to Grayscale with Monochrome chosen in the Channel Mixer box, as at the right. 🐄

4c

The image at the top of page 94 was produced with the layer mask shown in figure 4a and with the Blending Options settings above, which protected the lightest colors, such as the white in the bathing suit, from change.

*A grayscale conversion made with the **Wow-RGB Hula Grayfx.cha** preset. See page 98 for other grayscale conversion methods.*

Channel Mixer Presets

Here are some of the Channel Mixer presets found in the Good-ies folder on the Adobe Photoshop 7.0 CD-ROM. A preset can serve as a starting point for color change. If you use an Adjustment layer to apply it, you can change the Opacity or add a mask to target the effect (see "Channel Mixing" on page 94 for the technique). And you can also go back and make changes to the channel mix later by double-clicking the Adjustment layer's thumbnail.

© CORBIS IMAGESROYALTY FREE, FAMILY TIME

Original photo

*The Red Output channel of the **RGB Pastels.cha** preset*

Channel Swaps: RGB Swap Green&Blue.cha

Channel Swaps: RGB Swap Red&Blue.cha

Channel Swaps: RGB Swap Red&Green.cha

Grayscale: CMYK to Gray.cha

Grayscale: Grayscale Standard.cha

Grayscale: Grayscale Yellows2.cha

Channel Mixer applied as an Adjustment layer

Special Effects: RGB Blacklight.cha

Special Effects: RGB Blueprint.cha

Special Effects: RGB Burnt Foliage.cha

Special Effects: RGB Easter colors.cha

Special Effects: RGB Holiday Wrap.cha

Special Effects: Inverted Warm Brass.cha

Special Effects: RGB Over Saturate.cha

Special Effects: RGB Pastels.cha

Special Effects: RGB Sepiatone subtle color.cha

Special Effects: RGB Sepiatone subtle color2.cha

Special Effects: RGB Sepiatone subtle color3.cha

Special Effects: RGB Warmer.cha

Special Effects: Yellows&Blues(RGBorCMYK).cha

YCC Color: RGB -> YCrCb.cha

From Color to Gray

Overview *Convert an RGB image using any of four methods.*

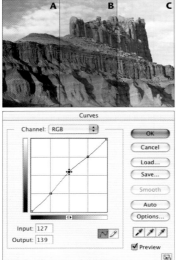

*The RGB photo **A** was converted to Grayscale **B**, and the midtones were lightened with a Curves Adjustment layer **C**.*

*The RGB image **A** was converted to Lab color. Then the two color channels were dragged to the trash icon and the file was converted to Grayscale **C**. The direct RGB-to-Grayscale conversion **B** is shown for comparison.*

IN PHOTOSHOP THERE ARE MANY WAYS to convert a color image to grayscale. The method you choose will depend on the characteristics of your original RGB image and whether you simply want to optimize the image for the best reproduction in one ink, or whether you want to achieve a particular photographic effect. In each case, making the conversion to gray may be only part of the process. You may also want to do some fine-tuning afterwards.

1 Making a "straight conversion." When your original RGB image shows good detail and tonal distinction, you can start with a direct conversion to grayscale and then fine-tune by adjusting Levels or Curves. For an image of canyon country we started by choosing Image, Mode, Grayscale. Then we lightened the midtones by adding a Curves Adjustment layer. By saving the file with the Adjustment layer as well as a flattened copy for printing, we would be able to make changes to the Curves if a proof showed they were needed. To add a Curves Adjustment layer, click the Create New Fill/Adjustment Layer button, the black-and-white circle at the bottom of the Layers palette.

In the Curves dialog box you can "peg" (lock) the areas of the curve that you want to remain the same, and then make your adjustments. We wanted to preserve the highlights and shadows, so we clicked on the diagonal line at 25% and 75% of its length. Then we lightened the midtones by dragging the 50% point slightly up and to the left **1**. (Fine-tuning with Curves or Levels can also be done if needed after using a technique from step 2, 3, or 4.)

ADJUSTING CURVES

In the Curves dialog box, you can use the arrow keys to reshape the curve in tiny steps, instead of dragging. Click on the curve to make a point or select an existing point; then press any of the arrow keys.

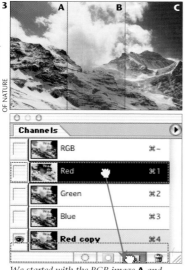

*We started with the RGB image **A** and duplicated the Red channel as an alpha channel. Then the three color channels were deleted and the file was converted to Grayscale **C**. The direct RGB-to-Grayscale conversion **B** is shown for comparison.*

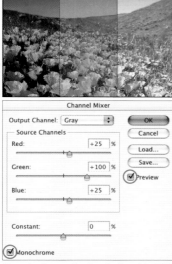

*To make the poppies "pop" when this RGB image **A** was converted to black-and-white, we used a channel mix that included a 100% contribution from the Green channel and just 25% from the Red and Blue **C**. The direct RGB-to-Grayscale conversion, shown for comparison **B**, lacked contrast, since the oranges in the poppies varied in hue but not much in tone.*

2 Reducing noise. If the image you start with is "noisy" with film grain or you simply want a softer look or want to see if this method will produce subtly better tonal range than the straight conversion described in step 1, you can do the conversion to grayscale by going through the Lab Color mode. To reduce the film grain in this RGB image as we converted it to grayscale, we first chose Image, Mode, Lab Color. Then we removed the two color channels ("a" and "b") by dragging "a" and then "Alpha 2" to the trash icon in the Channels palette **2**, leaving only the Lightness channel. The image was now in Multichannel mode, which happens when you remove one or more of the color channels of an RGB, CMYK, or Lab file. Next we chose Image, Mode, Grayscale to finish the conversion.

3 Creating special photographic effects. To imitate the look of a photo taken with infrared film or with a color filter and black-and-white film, you can try picking your favorite grayscale version from the color channels of the RGB file. For this mountainscape, we opened the Channels palette of the RGB image and clicked in the eye column to toggle the visibility of the channels off and on so we could view each channel alone as a grayscale image. (If your single-channel images are in color, you can switch to a grayscale display by choosing Preferences (Ctrl/⌘-K), Display & Cursors, and clicking the check box to turn off the Color Channels In Color option.) We duplicated the Red channel as an alpha channel by dragging its thumbnail to the Create New Channel button at the bottom of the palette **3.** Then we deleted the three color channels by dragging each one to the trash button. This left only the alpha channel, with the file in Multichannel mode. So we chose Image, Mode, Grayscale to complete the conversion.

4 Mixing channels. In an image whose colors have distinctly different hues but similar values (lights and darks), the Channel Mixer can be invaluable. With your image in RGB Color mode, add an Adjustment layer by clicking the Create New Adjustment Layer button as described in step 1, but this time choose Channel Mixer from the list. In the Channel Mixer dialog box, turn on the Monochrome option by clicking the check box and making sure the Preview box is checked. Then move the Red, Green, and Blue color sliders to experiment with different contributions from each channel **4,** keeping in mind that film grain and scanning noise are usually found mostly in the Blue channel. When you have a mix that you like, make a flattened duplicate of the image (Image, Duplicate, Duplicate Merged Layers Only) so the Channel Mixer adjustment will be retained in your original when you convert your copy to grayscale (Image, Mode, Grayscale).

The image at the top of page 98 was converted two different ways using Channel Mixer Adjustment layers. The sample on the left is made up mostly of the color file's Red channel, and the sample on the right is made mainly from the Green channel.

Spot Color Overlays

Overview *Prepare the background image; set type and create graphics as white-filled Shape layers to make knockouts for the spot colors; use the transparency masks of the knockouts to make the spot color channels; add tinted areas to the spot channels.*

"**Spot Colors**" "before" and "after" files

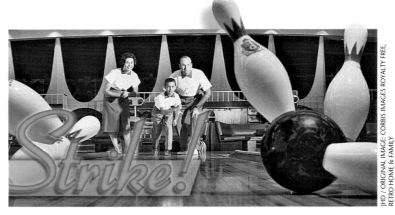

JHD / ORIGINAL IMAGE: CORBIS IMAGES ROYALTY FREE, RETRO HOME & FAMILY

CUSTOM COLOR — OR *SPOT COLOR* — is a great option when you need to exactly match a standard corporate color, or get that brilliant orange, green, or metallic look that you know you just can't achieve with process CMYK inks, or prepare a file for screen printing a T-shirt or a poster. For this hang-tag for a clothing company, we started with a grayscale image and added the brand's standard colors. The coloring process for the tag depended on using Photoshop's layers to construct knockouts in the grayscale image where we wanted the color to print, then using spot color channels to deploy the custom inks. (You can use a similar approach for adding spot color to a full-color image.) To enhance the "retro" look of the tag we added airbrushed shadows and glows around the type and panel, and varied the opacity of the spot colors in order to tint selected parts of the image.

1a

The original photo

1b

Painting the Quick Mask with white to silhouette the bowling pin

1 Preparing the image. Adjust contrast (and color if you're using a color background image); if you need pointers on adjusting contrast or color, see pages 114 and 124–127. Make any other adjustments necessary to produce the background you want **1a.** To dramatize the action in our image, we wanted to silhouette and shadow the largest bowling pins at the top of the image. First we turned the image from a *Background* to a transparent layer so we'd be able to add a layer mask (to make the conversion, double-click on the original *Background* in the Layers palette to open the New Layer dialog, name the layer if you'd like, and click OK).

Next we used the Rectangular Marquee to select up to the top of the wall in our photo, leaving out the ceiling and the tops of the two bowling pins. We clicked the Quick Mask icon in the toolbox to temporarily turn the selection into a mask so we could modify it by painting. When Quick Mask is activated, it automatically sets its Foreground color to black and its Background color to white, so we pressed the "X" key (for eXchange), making white the Foreground color. We chose the Paintbrush and a round, hard-edged brush and altered the mask by painting to reveal the tops of the two pins **1b.** To turn the mask back into a selection, we clicked the Standard Mode icon (to the left of Quick Mask in the toolbox). To hide the un-

1c

A layer mask made from the edited selection hides the top of the image.

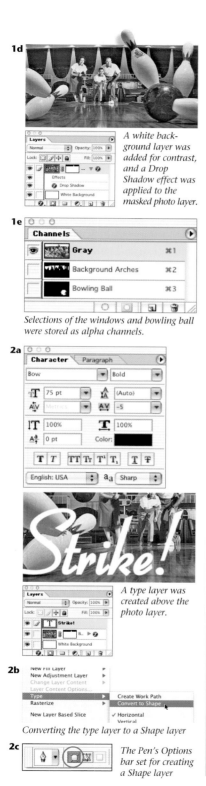

1d

A white background layer was added for contrast, and a Drop Shadow effect was applied to the masked photo layer.

1e

Channels

Gray ⌘1

Background Arches ⌘2

Bowling Ball ⌘3

Selections of the windows and bowling ball were stored as alpha channels.

2a

Character | Paragraph

Bow | Bold

A type layer was created above the photo layer.

2b

New Fill Layer
New Adjustment Layer
Change Layer Content
Layer Content Options...
Type ▶ Create Work Path
Rasterize ▶ Convert to Shape
New Layer Based Slice ✓ Horizontal
Vertical

Converting the type layer to a Shape layer

2c

The Pen's Options bar set for creating a Shape layer

wanted area at the top of the image, we made a layer mask by clicking the Add A Mask button at the bottom of the Layers palette **1c**.

To see how our flattened file would look, we added a white-filled layer below the silhouetted image: We clicked the Create A New Layer button at the bottom of the palette; we pressed "D" for Default Foreground and Background colors, and pressed Ctrl/⌘-Delete to fill the new layer with the Background color (white); finally, we dragged the new layer's name downward in the palette, below the image layer. We added a drop shadow effect on the image layer to make the bowling pin pop off the page. To add a drop shadow, click on the image layer's name to target it; then click the "*f*" button at the bottom of the palette and choose Drop Shadow from the menu. We set the Angle so the Drop Shadow, which follows the masked edge of the image, fell to the left and down, so the only place where the shadow showed was beside the highest pin **1d**.

We also used the Polygonal Lasso to trace the windows framed by the arches in the background, and stored the selection as an alpha channel (Select, Save Selection) for use later in directing a tint of spot color. For the bowling ball we used the Elliptical Marquee, holding down the Shift and Alt/Option keys to draw a perfectly circular selection from the center of the ball outward; then we chose the Polygonal Lasso, clicked the Subtract From Selection button in the Options bar, and drew around the end of the bowling pin to subtract it from the selection **1e**.

2 Preparing the type and graphics. In this hang-tag, the type and the panel behind it would appear in custom Pantone inks. The custom colors would also be used to tint parts of the photo. In some areas a knockout would be made in the grayscale image where the spot inks would be printed. In other areas the inks would print as tints or would be overprinted by the photo or by the fills, glows, or shadows created as Layer Styles for the type and graphic.

ADVANTAGES OF CONVERTING TYPE TO SHAPES

Converting a type layer to a Shape layer retains the vector information built into the type, for smooth output at the highest resolution the PostScript output device can produce. And it avoids some potential problems that can arise if you keep the type as type:

• Unless the type is converted, the font has to be present on the output system.

• If the type is *not* converted, you run the risk that a font with the same name but not exactly the same font is present, or that there are differences in font metrics (kerning and tracking specifications) between the computer of origin and the output device. Either can cause minor differences in the position of characters. This might not be a problem in a standard CMYK file. But in a spot-color file even a very slight difference can cause trouble, because the spacing of the live (vector-based) type that controls the knockout may be slightly different on the output system than it was when the type was rasterized to create the spot color channel. In that case the spot color and knockout won't match perfectly.

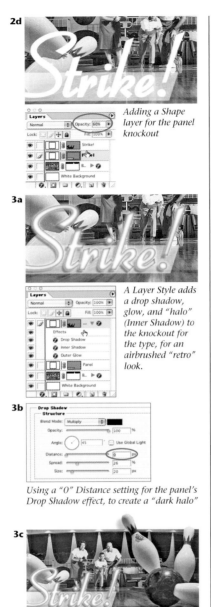

2d

Adding a Shape layer for the panel knockout

3a

A Layer Style adds a drop shadow, glow, and "halo" (Inner Shadow) to the knockout for the type, for an airbrushed "retro" look.

3b

Using a "0" Distance setting for the panel's Drop Shadow effect, to create a "dark halo"

3c

The file with Layer Styles in place for the photo, type knockout, and panel knockout; ready for the addition of custom colors

We set our type (in the Bow font) in white **2a**. When we had the style, size, tracking, and kerning as we liked, we pressed the Enter key, then converted the type to a Shape layer (Layer, Type, Convert To Shape) **2b** in order to avoid the problems described in the "Advantages of Converting Type to Shapes" tip on page 101.

Next we used the Pen tool to create a Shape layer to make the knockout for a color panel to underlie the type. Choose the Pen in the toolbox and click the Create New Shape Layer button in the left corner of the Options bar, and a Shape layer will be produced when you draw **2c**. With white as the Foreground color (as set in step 1) we clicked with the Pen to draw the straight lines to make a closed shape, holding down the Shift key where we wanted perfectly horizontal or vertical line segments. On-screen the shape filled with white as we drew it. We wanted a ghosted version of the underlying photo to show through the custom ink that would be applied, so we set the Opacity of this Shape layer to 60%. That way the knockout wouldn't be complete **2d**.

3 Adding stylized detail. To add airbrushed outlines and shading to the custom-color graphics, we applied Layer Styles to the converted type layer and to the Shape layer for the panel. To build the Style for each layer, we clicked the *"f"* button at the bottom of the Layers palette and from the pop-out menu chose the first effect we wanted to add. We gave the type a **Drop Shadow**, then chose **Inner Shadow** from the list on the left side of the Layer Style dialog box. We defined the Inner Shadow's Distance (which determines the offset) as 0, for an inner halo effect that followed the edge evenly. Finally we chose **Outer Glow** from the list (the Inner and Outer Glow effects have no Distance setting and therefore no offset) **3a**.

For the panel we added only a **Drop Shadow**, with the Distance set to 0 to create a "dark halo" effect rather than an offset shadow created by directional light **3b**. Because we had already set the Opacity of the layer, we could see how dark the shadow would be as we created it **3c**.

4 Creating the first spot color channels. With the knockouts and edge effects established, you can now use the shape information in the type and graphics layers to start to build the spot color channels that will tell Photoshop where you want to put the custom inks. First load one of these layers as a selection by Ctrl/⌘-clicking its name in the Layers palette; we started by loading the selection from the type layer **4a**. (Because the glow and dark halo around the type created a "soft" edge between the green and the black, it was not necessary to build in any trap; but if trap had been needed, this would have been the time to expand the selection if necessary, as described in the "Trapping Spot Color" tip on page 105.)

With the selection active, we chose New Spot Channel from the pop-out menu at the upper right corner of the Channels palette **4b**.

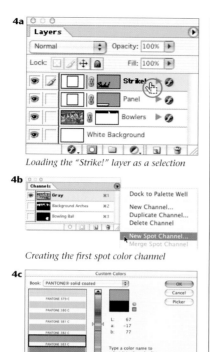

4a

Loading the "Strike!" layer as a selection

4b

Creating the first spot color channel

4c

Choosing the custom green color

4d

Solidity set at 0 for the transparent ink

4e

Loading the bowling ball selection

4f

In the Pantone 383 CVC channel (here viewed alone), the bowling ball selection was filled with 50% gray so that a tint of the green color would print in that spot.

PREVIEWING SPOT COLORS

Your printer can provide information about your spot color job that will help you set up your file for a more accurate on-screen preview. For instance, you should be able to get a Solidity value to plug into Photoshop's Spot Channel dialog box. The Solidity entry is designed to simulate on-screen how an overlapping spot color will look when printed. At 100% Solidity the spot color is opaque — it covers other inks virtually completely; at 0%, it's transparent. The Solidity setting doesn't actually affect the density of the printed ink; it's just for preview purposes. Generally, pastel colors (which contain opaque white), dark shades (which contain black), and metallics are more opaque, and purer colors and, obviously, varnish are more transparent.

Also, your printer can tell you, based on the spot colors you've chosen, in what order the plates will be printed. The on-screen preview of spot colors assumes that the inks will be printed in order starting with the one at the top of the Channels palette. To comply with this assumption, you can either add the spot colors with the first-to-print color added first, followed by the others in order, or you can add the spot colors in any order and then reorder them by dragging their channels up or down in the Channels palette.

We chose a color by clicking the swatch to open the Color Picker and then clicking the Custom button and choosing the set of inks (Pantone Coated) and the color we wanted (Pantone 383) **4c**. In the New Spot Channel dialog box we left the Solidity setting at 0 (see the "Previewing Spot Colors" tip above) and clicked OK **4d**. Since there was an active selection when we chose New Spot Channel, its shape was automatically used in making the channel — the selection filled with black. Black in a Spot channel represents where the custom ink will print at 100% density.

We wanted to add a tint of the Pantone green to the bowling ball in the background image. So we loaded the channel with the stored bowling ball selection by Ctrl/⌘-clicking its name in the Channels palette **4e**. Then with the green Spot channel active, we filled the selection with a medium gray (Edit, Fill, Use: 50% Gray). In this area the custom ink would print at half-density — that is, with a *50% screen* of the color **4f**, **4g**. (To use a lighter or darker gray for the mask, see the "Specifying Grays" tip on page 104. If you want a slight tint, use a light gray; for a heavier tint, use a darker gray.)

5 Creating the second spot color channel. For the panel spot color we carried out the same process as in step 4, except this time we had to cut out the area where the type overlapped the panel so the green ink for the type wouldn't overprint the orange ink for the panel. To do this we Ctrl/⌘-clicked the panel layer to load it as a selection, and then subtracted the type from the selection by Ctrl-Alt-clicking (Windows) or ⌘-Option-clicking (Mac) on the type layer's name **5a**. Now when we chose New Spot Channel, the new orange channel (Pantone 1495 CVC) automatically included a knockout for the type **5b**. To tint the arches in the background image, we Ctrl/⌘-clicked the alpha channel where we had stored

4g

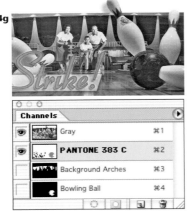

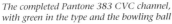

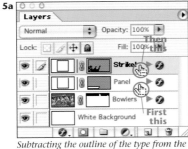

The completed Pantone 383 CVC channel, with green in the type and the bowling ball

5a

Subtracting the outline of the type from the panel selection

5b

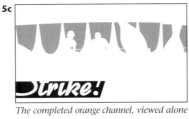

The completed panel selection, ready for creating the orange spot color channel

5c

The completed orange channel, viewed alone

5d

Channels

	Gray	⌘1
	PANTONE 383 C	⌘2
	PANTONE 1495 C	⌘3
	Background Arches	⌘4

The image file with both spot color channels complete

the windows selection to load it and filled this selection with 50% Gray as we had for the bowling ball **5c**. This completed the setup for the file **5d, 5e**.

Proofing and final output.
Some desktop color printers will convert a Photoshop spot color file to produce a color print that can be used as a comp for approval. If your printer *won't* do so, another way to produce a comp is to use a screen-capture utility to capture the image as displayed on your computer screen. Or use the screen-capture function built into the System software:

- On a **Windows**-based system press Alt-Print Screen to copy the active window to the clipboard. In Photoshop create a new file (File, New) and paste (Ctrl-V). Then crop out the window frame by dragging the Crop tool diagonally across the part you want to keep and double-clicking inside the Crop frame.

- On a **Mac** press ⌘-Shift-4 and drag to select the area you want to capture; the file will be stored on your hard drive and will be named "Picture *number*" using the lowest number not already in use in another Picture file name.

When a comp has been approved, you can output the file directly from Photoshop. Or to place it in a page layout program, save a copy of your file in encapsulated Postscript format (File, Save As, Photoshop DCS 2.0, As A Copy, Spot Colors), throwing away the alpha channels you used to build the file. In the DCS 2.0 format, the Include Vector Data box should be checked, and Include Halftone Screen and Include Transfer Function should be unchecked.

5e

*Because the panel is filled with black in the spot color channel **5d**, the transparent orange ink will print at full intensity. The image is partially visible through the panel because the knockout layer is at 60% opacity.*

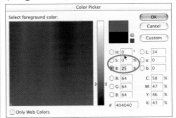

In artwork in which the color graphics or type have sharp edges with distinct color breaks, *trap* may be required. Trap is the precautionary overlap of colors. It prevents gaps in ink coverage that can occur if, for example, the paper shifts as it's going through the printing press, offsetting one of the colors.

For this clothing tag, we needed to build in trap for the Pantone 144 CVC type in order to prevent a potential white gap between the orange and the "knocked-out" background photo if the paper shifted during printing.

Since all spot color work in Photoshop is done with pixel-based channels rather than vector-based sharp edges, there is a certain amount of built-in trap that results from antialiasing or halftoning. But if your printer says you need to trap, there are two methods you can choose from. You need to pick the one that will better maintain the integrity of your graphics or type. You can either *choke* (shrink) the knockout or *spread* (expand) the spot color element. The method to choose will depend on the opacity of your custom ink. For instance, if the custom color is quite opaque, you should choke the knockout, because any expansion of the spot color element will make it look "fatter." But if the ink is quite transparent (as is usually the case), you should spread the spot color element **A**, because choking the knockout will make the spot color element look too "thin." Your printer or the ink manufacturer can provide information about ink opacity. Also, your printer can tell you how large to make the trap, based on his or her experience with press alignment.

Once you've created the knockout in a layer **B**, you can build the trap at the same time that you make the spot color plate. First load the knockout as a selection by Ctrl/⌘-clicking the name of its layer in the Layers palette. Then:

• If you need **to spread the spot color element** rather than shrink the knockout, expand the active selection by choosing Select, Modify, Expand **C**; the Expand By box calls for an entry in pixels. Often 1 or 2 pixels is plenty. But if your printer gives you the size of the trap in mm or as a fraction of an inch, you can convert that number to pixels as follows:

Trap (in pixels) = **Trap** (in mm or inches) **x Width of image** (in pixels) ÷ **Width of image** (in mm or inches)

Enter the appropriate pixel value for the trap in the Expand By box and click OK. Then in the Channels palette choose New Spot Channel from the palette's pop-out menu, choose the custom color you want **D**, set Solidity, and click OK to complete the channel **E**.

• On the other hand, **if you need to choke the knockout**, with the selection active, choose New Spot Channel from the Channels palette's pop-out menu, set Solidity, and click OK. Then go back to the Layers palette and click the knockout layer's name to make it the active layer. (If the layer is vector-based — that is, if it's a Shape layer or live type — you'll need to rasterize it before choking it: Choose Layer, Rasterize, Layer. Then activate the selection again by Ctrl/⌘-clicking the layer name. Choose Select, Modify, Contract and enter a Contract By value to shrink the selection by the trap amount, calculated as shown above. Then trim the knockout by inverting the selection (Ctrl/⌘-Shift-I) and pressing Delete.

The knockout was created by filling the logo with white in a transparent layer.

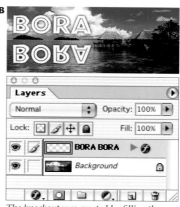

The logo was loaded as a selection by Ctrl/⌘-clicking its layer. Then the selection was expanded (Select, Modify, Expand) since the printer reported that the ink was very transparent.

Choosing New Spot Channel from the Channels palette's pop-out menu allowed us to choose our custom color. We left the Solidity setting at 0 for this transparent ink.

Clicking OK in the New Spot Channel dialog box created the spot color channel with its slightly expanded contours.

For this *three-color poster* design, **Jack Davis** started by taking a photo of a statue by Brian Curtis and Thomas Marsh, scanning the photo, and converting it to Grayscale ("From Color To Gray" on page 98 gives suggestions for converting). Davis planned to use black ink for the detail, and yellow and magenta inks for the color, applying the yellow over the entire image and adding tints of magenta in other areas to make reds and oranges.

So he could replace the overcast sky in the background, Davis traced the statue in the grayscale image with the Pen tool, saved the path and converted it to a selection, then reversed the selection and deleted the sky. He then added a new gray-filled layer below the statue layer and used the Airbrush tool to create the amount of detail he wanted for the black component of the abstract "sky." He also created a soft, dark outline for the statue by adding a Layer Style consisting of a Drop Shadow effect to the statue layer.

To control the coloring of the man, surfboard, and base of the statue separately, he started with the path he had saved and created separate selections for the base and the surfer, saving each one in an alpha channel. Then he loaded the overall selection from the path and subtracted the base and surfer to create the channel for the surfboard.

To increase the impact of the large flat areas in the base and the board, Davis reduced the amount of black by loading both alpha channels as a selection and then using Levels, moving the black Output Levels slider to the right.

Type was set in 75% gray and darkened with an Inner Shadow in a Layer Style. To make the type outline, the type was loaded as a selection, and the selection was expanded and then filled with white on a new layer created below the type. The Layer Style for the soft, dark outline was dragged from the statue layer and dropped on the expanded type layer.

With the black image complete, spot color channels for the yellow and magenta were added by Ctrl/⌘-clicking the Create New Channel button at the bottom of the Channels palette. Both spot channels were filled with black. The yellow channel was left that way, since Davis wanted the yellow to print at full strength over the entire poster. The selections for the base and board were loaded in the magenta channel and filled with 75% and 50% black respectively; the selection for the man was loaded and filled with white so no magenta would print there.

To make the type outline red, Davis loaded the expanded type's transparency mask as a selection, expanded it by 1 pixel more for trap, and filled the selection with 100% black. (For more about designing with spot colors, see "Spot Color Overlays" on page 100.)

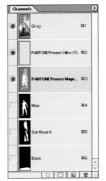

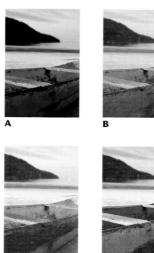

A   **B**

C   **D**

For this black and white edition of an original color photo of a Brazilian coast and canoe, **Jack Davis** used his Nikon D100 and began by making sure that he captured the shot in Nikon's raw 36-bit NEF format **A.** This "high-bit depth" format meant that each of the red, green, and blue channels that made up the full color image had thousands of tones to record the channels' information, rather than the limited 256 shades per channel of a typical 24-bit JPEG image. This extra information is extremely handy when working with images that need their highlight or shadow detail "rescued," or for photography that is destined for black-and-white applications, as was the case here.

Once the image was brought into Photoshop, Davis had to decide which method he should use for the conversion from color to grayscale. A straight Mode change produced a flat image with little distinction between the saturated reds and blues of the canoe **B.** Instead, he chose to use a Channel Mixer adjustment in order to customize the change from color to monochromatic. By mixing different percentages of the red, green, and blue channels, Davis could minimize the amount of blue that would contribute to the mix and subsequently lighten the interior of the canoe **C.** Or, as he did for the final image, he could maximize the blue channel's contribution and lighten the red component, making the boat's side stripe and seat nicely contrast with the canoe's interior as they did in the original color image **D.**

Curved Leaves is an example of an original color digital photograph transformed into a sepia-toned final print by the noted photographer **Christine Zalewski.** The original Background layer was first copied onto a separate layer and sharpened. The "eye" icon was then turned off on the Background layer, thus preserving a "safe-copy" original within the file itself. Next, a repair layer was added to correct a spot on one of the leaves, and the first Curves layer was added to darken a distracting leaf in the upper right-hand corner. The Channel Mixer layer desaturated the image in a much more controlled manner than either Desaturate or a Mode change would. Next, a Hue/Saturation layer was added in colorize mode, which used a setting that had been previously saved into Zalewski's "utility folder." Once the desired colorization was obtained for the sepia tone, a second Curves layer was added and masked to further enhance the print.

Although not shown in the screen shots here, there are several other layers in the master file which fine tune the print for the different printers in Zalewski's digital darkroom, a method of matching across different media that she finds preferable to the sometimes mystic science of color calibration and profiling.

Often it's the most subtle adjustments that can allow the inherent beauty of an image to shine through. **Christine Zalewski** has found that beautiful tones often exist in the files of her original digital photographs that may not be apparent when they are first opened. For instance, Pink Flush Tulips benefited greatly from minor adjustments, including Hue/Saturation, which was adjusted +28 for saturation and –8 for hue (Zalewski never adjusts brightness in the Hue/Saturation layer, but rather uses additional Levels or Curves layers to adjust brightness). To keep images realistic while using Hue/Saturation, adjustments should be kept relatively minor when increasing the saturation or moving the hue in either direction. Both of these adjustments can cause marked digital artifacts that vary in intensity depending on the colors of the original.

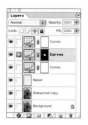

The first four steps of *Purple Anemone II* are identical to those described in the *Curved Leaves* description on page 108. A second Curves layer was added to this digital photograph to bring out the detail in the center of the flower. Finally, the third Curves layer improved the overall contrast without sacrificing the detail uncovered in the second adjustment layer. **Christine Zalewski** often works directly on the layer masks, using filters as well as paint tools, to perfect what is allowed of the adjustment to show through. This image exemplifies how Photoshop can be used to "recapture" a tonal range that is recorded by a digital camera, but is not entirely visible in a straight print of the file.

Using a technique she learned from Davis in a Photoshop WOW! seminar, **Christine Zalewski** created the framing effect found in *Peach* and *Yellow Tulip II*. First, the color- and tone-adjusted original was flattened and saved into a separate file. The background layer was duplicated (Ctrl/⌘-J), made active again, then filled with white. A layer mask was then created on the duplicated working layer by selecting the area to be framed, clicking the "add a mask" icon at the bottom of the layers palette, then softening the mask with Gaussian Blur, then with the Sprayed Strokes filter. Finally, to accentuate the effect, a black backing layer was added underneath the flower layer by creating an empty layer, reselecting the original framed area, filling it with black, and blurring it in a 10% proportion to the blur applied to the image layer mask. (See page 128 for more on this technique.)

RETOUCHING & ENHANCING PHOTOS

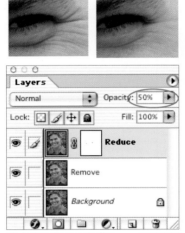

Photoshop 7's new Healing Brush is much more effective than the Clone Stamp tool for removing image problems or reducing some cosmetic artifacts — especially if you perform the "removal" step separately from the "cosmetic reduction" step, as shown on page 137.

The new Patch Tool, serving as a good counterpart to the Healing Brush, uses the same edge-blending and tone-matching technology as the Healing Brush (such as the Scratch Repair shown here), but which works on larger selections. Besides being able to cover up problems using these selected patches, it can duplicate specific areas to new locations.

THIS CHAPTER DESCRIBES SEVERAL TECHNIQUES for enhancing photos — from emulating traditional camera and darkroom techniques such as soft focus and vignettes, to retouching and hand-tinting. But much of the day-to-day production work done with Photoshop involves simply trying to get the best possible reproduction of a photo — a crisp and clear print or on-screen image, with the fullest possible range of accurate tone and color. If you ask an expert where to start in correcting a photo, you're almost sure to hear "It depends on the photo." That's certainly true. But most photos will typically need cropping, overall adjustments to tonality and color, "local" touch-up (using Photoshop 7's Healing and Patch tools), and sharpening to repair any "softness" introduced in the scan or the fixing process.

If the photo you start with is in 16 Bits/Channel mode and you want to keep it in 16-bit mode for output, you can still crop, adjust tone and color, fix specific color problems or blemishes, and sharpen it using all the functions described in the next few pages. But you'll need to adapt them a bit in order to deal with the fact that 16-bit mode allows only flattened images — no transparent layers or Adjustment layers. A method for working in 16 Bits/Channel mode is described in "Correcting 16-Bit Images" on page 121.

CROPPING

When you need to crop an image, Photoshop provides three ways to do the job:

- By making a selection of the area you want to keep and then choosing **Image, Crop**;
- By choosing **Image, Trim** and making choices in the Trim dialog box.
- Or by choosing the **Crop tool** and making choices in the Options bar.

Image, Crop

The advantage of the first method — **Image, Crop** — is that it's very simple. If you make your selection with the Rectangular Marquee, the image is cropped to the "marching ants" selection border. If you make the selection with any other method, the image will be cropped to the smallest rectangle that can completely contain the

continued on page 112

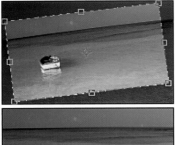

A one-step crop and rotation can be used to reorient the horizon.

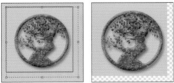

Dragging the Crop tool outward beyond the edges of the image adds more "canvas."

CROP SHORTCUTS

When you're using the Crop tool, you can cancel the cropping operation by pressing the Escape key or Ctrl/⌘-period.

To complete a crop, instead of clicking the ✓ you can press Enter/ Return or double-click inside the crop frame.

CROPPING NEAR THE EDGE

With the Snap option turned on (in the View menu) the Crop tool snaps its cropping frame to the edges of the image when you drag the tool close to them. To be able to crop near — but not at — the edge, open the View menu and turn off Snap, or choose Snap To and turn off Document Bounds.

selection, including any antialiasing or feathering inside the selection boundary, *but not including any exterior effects applied by a Layer Style,* such as a Drop Shadow, Outer Bevel, or Outer Glow (Styles are covered in detail in Chapter 8).

Trim

The **Trim** method is ideal for cropping images with soft edges, to get them to their smallest possible size — it's especially useful for Web graphics. It avoids the problem of accidentally clipping off part of a soft edge because you couldn't tell where the "softness" ended at the edge of the photo and the background color or full transparency began. To crop with the Trim command, choose Image, Trim and then choose the options you want in the Trim dialog box. You can choose to trim away any or all of the four edges of the image. The trim will be based on "cutting off" pixels from the edge inward, and it can be set to trim transparent pixels (you have to turn off visibility for any background layers before using), or pixels that are the same color as the top left or bottom right pixel.

The Crop Tool

The advantage of the using the **Crop tool** is that you can have much more control of what happens during the crop. For instance, once you drag the tool across your image to define the area you want to keep, you can:

- **Adjust the size or proportions of the cropping frame** by dragging on a side or corner handle. (To keep the ratio of height to width constant as you change size, Shift-drag.)

- **Change the orientation of an image** by dragging around just outside a corner handle to rotate the frame. This function lets you **straighten a crooked scan, level the horizon** in an image that was taken at a tilt, **or simply reframe an image in a different orientation.**

- **Crop and resize** the image in a single step, by making choices in the Options bar, as described in the "Controlling the Crop" tip on page 113.

- **Enlarge the "canvas"** around your image by dragging across the entire image, then making the working window bigger than the image, and dragging a corner handle of the cropping frame *outward* to "crop" beyond the image. (To get the extra working space you need, you can drag the lower right corner of the working window to enlarge the window, or shrink the image without shrinking the window [press Ctrl-Alt-hyphen for Windows or ⌘-Option-hyphen for Mac]. If this keyboard shortcut shrinks the window along with the image, it's because the Keyboard Zoom Resizes Windows option has been turned off [Edit, Preferences, General]. In that case pressing Ctrl/⌘-hyphen, without the Alt/ Option key, should do the trick.) This "hypercropping" can be

Continued on page 114

In the Options bar that appears when you choose the Crop tool, you can set the Height, Width, and Resolution of the image you want to end up with when the cropping operation is complete. The choices you make will determine whether the image will be resampled (that is, the number of pixels in the cropped area will change from what it was before the crop). If an image is resampled, it may need sharpening afterwards. Below are some tips for setting the Height, Width, and Resolution.

- **To freely drag the Crop tool to any dimensions** that look good to you, click the Clear button at the right end of the bar to "erase" all three entries, and then drag with the tool. When you finalize the crop, no resampling will take place. This can be useful if you simply want **to "reframe" the image,** cutting out unwanted elements at the edges.

- **With the Width and Height values set in pixels,** the cropping frame will hold its Width/Height proportions as you drag it. When you commit the crop (by clicking the ✓, for instance) the image will be resampled. You can use this method **to prepare images for the Web,** where pixel dimensions are important.

- **With the Width and Height set in units other than pixels** (for instance, if you type "in" or "cm" in the Height and Width fields) the image will be resampled if you change the Resolution but not if you leave it at the current value for the file, or if you leave it blank. This can be useful if you're preparing images for print and you want **to keep the current resolution but crop the image to fit in a particular amount of space.**

- **With the Resolution value set and the Height and Width left blank,** you can control the proportions of the crop freely, but the file will be resampled (unless the Resolution you specified is the same as the resolution of the file before you started the cropping operation).

- **To base the Height, Width, and Resolution entries on the active image**, click the Front Image button; these settings will persist until you change them. This can be useful if you need **to crop a number of images to the same dimensions.** The image will be resampled if the Resolution is not the same as the current resolution of the file you're cropping.

- **To get rid of perspective distortion as you crop,** use the Crop tool in any of the ways described above. Then, in the second phase of the Options bar, turn on Perspective using the check box. When you do this, the center point of the cropping frame will move to the center of the image; for best results, Adobe recommends leaving it there. Move the corners of the cropping frame so they are parallel to the slanted edges that you want to straighten, and complete the crop. The Perspective function can be used **to straighten a painting photographed on a wall, or a tall building photographed from street level.** *Note:* The Perspective option of the Crop tool is tricky to use. Another option is to not use the Crop tool at all, but use the Free Transform command instead: Press Ctrl/⌘-T to create the Transform frame; then hold down the Ctrl/⌘ key and drag on individual corner handles to Distort the image, or hold down Ctrl-Shift-Alt (Windows) or ⌘-Shift-Option (Mac) and drag a corner handle for a Perspective distortion.

© CORBIS IMAGES ROYALTY FREE, ARCHITECTURE & REAL ESTATE

*Using the Crop tool in Hide mode on a non-Background layer defined the "stage" for developing an animation **A** but left the cropped-out areas still available. The image could then be moved to different positions on the stage. Here **B** is the extreme left position, and **C** is extreme right. For a smooth animation, the transition could then be tweened in ImageReady.*

IMAGE Tug of War.psd and Tug of War.gif

CAUTION: "HIDDEN" CROP

When you use the Crop tool, if you choose to Hide rather than Delete the cropped-out areas, the areas outside the crop are retained in the file. In certain situations this can create problems. For instance, Photoshop continues to use **the entire image** (including the "off-stage" parts) for such operations as adjusting Levels or Curves, or filling with a pattern (which starts at the upper left corner of the image) or applying a displacement map when you run the Displace filter (the map aligns with the upper left corner and tiles or stretches to fit). If you forget the "hidden" image edges, any of these operations can produce results that are very different from what you intended.

STACKING ORDER

When you use more than one Adjustment layer to correct the contrast, exposure, or color in an image, it's as if you had applied the corrections in order: The lower the Adjustment layer is in the stack, the earlier its correction was made.

useful for adding more canvas on some edges than others, so your image is centered better on its canvas. Or to add canvas on all sides at once, Alt/Option-drag.

• **Straighten out perspective problems** in images that show distortion because they weren't photographed "straight-on," such as tall buildings that appear to narrow at the top, or pictures hanging on a wall. This process is described in the "Controlling the Crop" tip on page 113.

The Options bar for the Crop tool has two "phases": The first phase appears when you choose the tool, and the second appears after you make your choices in the first phase and drag the Crop tool to frame the area you want to keep. The second phase lets you choose how you want the area outside the crop to appear; you can **Shield** it with the color and Opacity you choose. If your image isn't flattened — that is, if it doesn't consist of a *Background* alone, with no other layers — you can also choose whether to **Hide** the area outside the cropping frame (keeping the cropped-out edge areas outside the image frame but still available) or **Delete** it (kissing it good-bye forever). Hiding allows flexibility — you can later decide to change the "framing" of the image. And it can be useful in animation — the cropped image defines the size of the "stage" area. The frames of the animation can be created by dragging the image, including the hidden parts, across the stage with the Move tool. But hiding can also cause trouble in certain situations, as described in the "Caution: 'Hidden' Crop" tip at the left.

Like the other Options bars that have two phases, the Crop tool's second-phase Options bar lets you complete or cancel the operation by clicking the ⊘ to escape the current cropping or by clicking the ✓ to "commit" the crop.

ADJUSTING OVERALL TONE AND COLOR

Once your image is cropped, you'll often want to make tone and color changes to the entire image or a selected area. You can apply these changes either by choosing commands from the **Image, Adjust** submenu or by means of an **Adjustment layer.** As you work with tone and color adjustments, remember that for your final image to match the preview that your screen shows you, your monitor and output system need to be calibrated and matched, as described in "Getting Consistent Color" in Chapter 2.

Working with Adjustment Layers

You can add an Adjustment layer by clicking the Create New Fill/Adjustment Layer button at the bottom of the Layers palette and choosing the type of adjustment you want from the pop-out menu. Because they provide so much flexibility, **it's almost always worthwhile to use an Adjustment layer** rather than choosing from the Image menu. (An exception is if you're working in 16

To add an Adjustment layer, click the Create New Fill/Adjustment Layer button at the bottom of the Layers palette and choose from the pop-out menu **A**. *In the dialog box that appears after you click, make your changes like clicking the Auto button in Levels or Curves* **B**. *A new addition to Photoshop 7 is the extended Options dialog, in which you can fine-tune your Auto Color Corrections, like we've done here by changing the default Enhance Per Channel Contrast to find dark and light colors (see page 116)* **C**. *To edit the changes later, you can double-click the layer's thumbnail* **D**.

Bits/Channel mode, where Adjustment layers aren't available, as described on page 121.) Here are some of the advantages of using Adjustment layers:

- Since the adjustments are stored as instructions rather than as permanent alterations to the pixels, it's easy to reopen the dialog boxes and **change the settings later** to fine-tune the image without degrading it as could happen if you further changed pixels that you already altered.

- You can **target the corrections** with each Adjustment layer's **built-in layer mask,** which you can customize when you apply the adjustment, or at any time later.

- An Adjustment layer's effect can **either apply to *all* layers below** it in the Layers stack, **or be restricted to *particular* layers.** To restrict the adjustment, either move the Adjustment layer *below* any layers you don't want it to affect, or if that isn't possible, make it part of a clipping group: To restrict the adjustment to the currently active layer only, you can hold down the Alt/Option key when you click the Create New Fill/Adjustment Layer button to make the Adjustment layer, and check the Group With Previous Layer box. Or you can form the clipping group *after* adding the Adjustment layer by Alt/Option-clicking between the Adjustment layer and the layer below, or by pressing Ctrl/⌘-G. ("Clipping Groups" on page 156 tells how clipping groups work.)

You'll find many examples of using Adjustment layers in this chapter and throughout the book. Look on pages 124–127 for a "catalog" of examples of tone and color corrections, many of which were done with Adjustment layers.

Increasing Contrast and Exposure

In an image with highlights and shadows, you'll usually want to get the broadest range of tones (and thus the largest amount of detail possible) by lightening the lightest area in the image to the lightest printable "white," and darkening the darkest area to the darkest printable "black," and thus spreading the in-between tones over a greater range of brightness. (The default settings for the lightest and darkest tones work for many images and printing situations. But if your printer recommends that you restrict the tonal range so it doesn't exceed what the printing process can success-

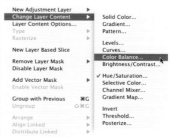

CHANGING LAYER CONTENT

If you try one kind of Adjustment layer and then decide you want to change it to another kind, choose Layer, Change Layer Content, and choose the kind you want to try. The appropriate dialog box will open so you can set the parameters.

By clicking the Options button in either the Levels or Curves dialogs, the Auto Color Correction Options will open and automatically try to balance the image's color and contrast.

As a default, *Enhance Per Channel Contrast* (the contrast for each color channel, independent of the others) alters the color cast. (As with all the Auto options, sometimes this is for the better, sometimes for the worst.) This option is the same as the Auto Levels feature found in the Image, Adjustments menu.

By adding the *Snap Neutral Colors* feature to any of the options above, the midtones in the newly-adjusted image that are **close** to neutral (made up of an equal mix of all the primary colors) will be mapped to a true neutral.

Enhance Monochromatic Contrast clips the contrast of each color channel identically so as not to change the current color balance — the same as using the Auto Contrast feature — and works well with images whose color is already correct.

Find Dark & Light Colors (in conjunction with *Snap Neutral Midtones*) analyzes the image to determine the shadow and highlight values and uses these areas to help balance color and contrast. These two options create the same result as Auto Color.

fully produce, you can find information about how to reset the target values for highlights and shadows by choosing Help, Help Contents, and clicking the Search tab. In the "Find Pages Containing:" entry box, type in "using target values to set highlights" and click the Search button.)

To see whether an image uses the full tonal range that's available, you can add a Levels Adjustment layer and in the Levels dialog box inspect the *histogram*, which is the graph that shows what proportion of the image's pixels (shown by the height of the bars) are in each of 256 tones or *luminance values* (which are spread along the horizontal axis, from black on the left to white on the right). The darkest pixels in the image are represented by the leftmost vertical bar of the histogram; the lightest pixels are represented by the bar at the right end. If the histogram doesn't extend all the way across the horizontal axis to the edges of the frame, it means the full range of tones isn't present in the image — the blacks are not really pure black and the whites are not pure white.

Using Auto Levels. Working in the Levels dialog box, you can expand the tonal range (and thus increase the contrast) by simply clicking the **Auto** button. This tells Photoshop to increase the contrast in the image, making the darkest existing pixels in the image black, making the lightest ones white, and spreading the intermediate ones over the full range of tones in between.

The Auto Levels adjustment works well for images that need a boost in contrast. In its default mode, Auto Levels can also affect color balance. That's because the Auto correction adjusts the "black" and "white" points *for each individual color channel* (red, green, and blue for an RGB image, or cyan, magenta, yellow, and black for a CMYK file). Always worth a try because it's so quick, the Auto correction can easily be undone if it doesn't do what you want: Just press Ctrl/⌘-Z, or hold down the Alt/Option key to change the Cancel button to Reset, and click the button. In Photoshop 7, the Options button in Levels brings up the Auto Color Correction Options dialog box, which enables you to select options that match all the Auto Settings in the Image, Adjustments menu: Auto Levels, Auto Contrast, and the new Auto Color (see samples on left).

AUTO LEVELS FLEXIBILITY

Sometimes Auto Levels, applied in a Levels Adjustment layer, *almost* works, but not quite.

If Auto Levels does too good a job and the image now looks like it has an unnatural amount of contrast, simply reduce the Opacity of the Adjustment layer, thereby reducing the intensity of the contrast adjustment.

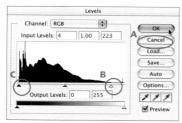

If an Auto Levels adjustment doesn't work, you can undo it (by holding down Alt/ Option to turn the Cancel button into Reset, and clicking it) **A**. *Then try adjusting "by hand." When you move the white Input Levels slider inward* **B**, *you're telling Photoshop that you want all pixels lighter than this value to become white. Likewise, moving the black point slider* **C** *says that you want all pixels darker than this value to be black. Unlike using the Auto button, this method lets you control overall tonal values without the possibility of causing a color shift.*

USING THE SET POINT DROPPERS

In the Levels dialog box, instead of using the black and white Input Levels sliders to adjust contrast, you can use the Set Black Point eye-dropper by clicking on the darkest pixel in the image that should be black, and Set White Point eyedropper by clicking on the lightest spot in the image that should be white. But there are some drawbacks:

• It can be hard to pick out the darkest or lightest pixel so you can know where to click.

• When you use the Set Point drop-pers, the change in the histogram is sudden and can't be fine-tuned, because unlike with the slider method, information is clipped when the "after" histogram is generated, and you can no longer see the histogram bars outside the black point and white point.

• Once you finish making changes in the Levels dialog box and close it, you can't get back to any of the "prechange" settings, even if you're using an Adjustment layer, without undoing *all* the Levels changes you made.

Setting Levels by hand. If the one-click Auto Levels method doesn't work for correcting overall problems of contrast and expo-sure, set the black point, white point, midtones, and neutral color by hand. You can do this as follows:

1 Look at the histogram and drag the black point slider just a little inside where the histogram's bars start. With the Preview option turned on you can see what happens as you drag, and experi-ment until you get the result you want. Sometimes you can identify a narrow "hump" at the extreme left end of the histo-gram that might come from any extraneous very dark pixels, such as those in a black border around the image. In that case you may get better results by dragging the black point slider inward to a position that just barely excludes the hump.

2 Look at the histogram again as you drag the white slider inward, as described in **1** for the black slider.

3 At this point you'll have a full range of tones from black to white. But the photo may still be suffering from incorrect expo-sure — the image is too dark overall (underexposed) or too light overall (overexposed). To remedy this, move the gray (gamma, middle) Input Levels slider to lighten or darken the image over-all. (If parts of the tonal range are still too dark or too light, see "Correcting Particular Exposure Problems" on page 118.)

4 Even with contrast and overall exposure adjusted, there may be an unwanted color cast in the image. To attempt to correct a color cast, choose the gray eyedropper (called Set Gray Point)

USING LEVELS IN THRESHOLD MODE

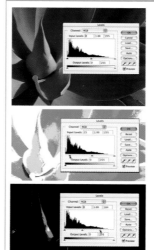

When you're making Levels adjustments, it can be useful to know exactly where the darkest and lightest points in your image are, and what tones you're forcing to be black or white as you move the black point and white point Input Levels sliders. For an RGB or Grayscale image, you can get this information by operat-ing the Input Levels sliders in Threshold mode: Hold down the Alt/Option key, put the cursor on the black slider and press the mouse button to see the black pixels. If you don't see any black, it means that none of the pixels are pure black. Slowly drag the slider inward; the first black pixels to show up are the darkest pixels in your image. Use Alt/Option with the white point slider in the same way to find the lightest pixels, which will be the first white pixels to show up.

By holding down the Alt/Option key and dragging each Input Levels slider, you can use Levels in Threshold mode to find the darkest and lightest pixels.

The Set Gray Point eyedropper, which is found in the Levels and Curves dialog boxes, can be useful in correcting a color cast. By clicking it on the image, you're telling Photoshop that the pixel you've clicked on is supposed to be a neutral gray, and Photoshop makes an overall adjustment to the color balance of the image to make that happen. Here clicking on the gray mountains fixed the color in this faded photo. If your image doesn't include anything that should be neutral gray, this method won't work, because you'll actually be adding a color cast as you try to force some colors to neutral.

PAUL K. DAYTON, JR.

and click it on a color in the image that should be a neutral middle-tone gray, with no color. If this overcorrects the original color cast and thus creates a different color problem, click around on other should-be-neutral spots until you find one that fixes the color. In general, choosing a spot that should be medium gray (rather than extremely light or dark) works best. (If you can't find a spot that works, see "Removing a Persistent Color Cast" below.)

Correcting Particular Exposure Problems

Once the overall exposure is adjusted, you can **adjust particular parts of the tonal range** using the **Curves** dialog box. With Curves you can bring out shadow detail without affecting other parts of the range. (You can also use Curves instead of Levels for overall exposure corrections, but the histogram in Levels gives you more information about what you're doing.)

Curves, like Levels, can be applied as an Adjustment layer or by choosing it from the Image, Adjust submenu. The "curve" in the Curves dialog box represents the relationship of tones before and after you make adjustments. It starts out as a straight line, until you add points and move them to reshape it into a curve.

If you move the cursor out of the Curves dialog box, it turns into an eyedropper. Clicking on a particular value in the image identifies the position of that tone on the curve, or **Ctrl/⌘-clicking automatically adds the point to the curve.** Then you can lighten or darken that part of the tonal range by moving the point, either by hand or with the arrow keys, as you preview the result.

A useful adjustment to an image with good overall exposure but hidden shadow detail can be made with an **"M" adjustment** to the curve. This is a correction that can't be made with Levels:

1 With the Curves dialog set up so the dark ends of the tone bars are at the bottom and left, anchor the middle of the curve by clicking on it to make a midpoint to anchor the curve.

2 Click a point in the lower quarter of the curve and raise it (drag it up and to the left) to lighten the shadow tones.

3 Click to make a point about a quarter of the way down from the top of the curve and raise it to slightly lighten the highlights if needed.

Caution: If you add more than one point to the curve and move them more than the slight corrections involved in an "M" curve, you can run into trouble. Anything more than a subtle move can cause solarizing or posterizing of the image.

Removing a Persistent Color Cast

If the image still seems to have color problems after you've expanded the tonal range, corrected for exposure, and used the Set Gray Point eyedropper in the Levels dialog box, you can try a Hue/Saturation

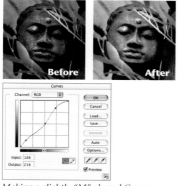

Making a slightly "M"-shaped Curves adjustment to bring out shadow detail and boost highlight tones

The family of colors you want to target may not be listed in the Edit menu of the Hue/Saturation dialog box. For instance, you may want to change the oranges in your image. In that case just choose one of the color families next to it on the color wheel — Yellows or Reds. Then use the "+" eyedropper to click and drag in the image to expand or move the range of targeted colors. The name of your targeted range may change — as it did here to "Reds 2" — to correctly name the range but distinguish it from the default Reds range.

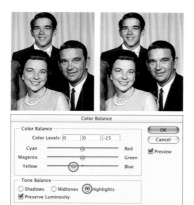

One way to remove a color cast is by adding the opposite of what you have too much of. Here a blue cast in the highlights was removed by adding yellow.

or Color Balance adjustment by choosing one of these options from the Image, Adjust menu — or, better yet, the pop-out menu of Adjustment layer types at the bottom of the Layers palette. Again, the Adjustment layer offers more flexibility.

- **To make overall color shifts** in highlights, midtones, and shadows all at once, you can use **Hue/Saturation:** With the Preview box checked, drag the Hue slider. At the bottom of the dialog box, the top spectrum bar shows the "before" state, and the bottom bar shows how colors have shifted in the "after" state.

- **To target color shifts to the highlights, midtones, or shadows individually,** use **Color Balance.** In the Color Balance dialog box, click to choose which of the three tonal ranges you want to change, then drag the sliders to add the opposite of what your image has too much of. For instance, if it shows a blue cast in the highlights, click the Highlights button and move the Blue/Yellow slider toward the Yellow end.

- **To correct the color of a particular area,** make a feathered selection and then create a Hue/Saturation or Color Balance Adjustment layer to fix it. (Chapter 1 has tips on selecting and feathering.)

- **To change one particular color or family of colors,** pick the appropriate color family from the Edit menu at the top of the **Hue/Saturation** dialog box, then use the dialog box's eyedropper to click in your image to target a particular color within that range. You can expand the range (shown by the dark gray bar that appears between the spectrum bars) by Shift-clicking or Shift-dragging over related colors. **To make a more gradual transition between the colors that change and those that don't,** you can drag the small white triangles outward to enlarge the light gray "fuzziness" bars, or drag them inward to make the transition sharper.

- **To constrain the color change to one area,** make a selection that includes the region you want to alter before you apply the Hue/Saturation change.

RETOUCHING "BY HAND"

Using Photoshop's retouching tools — Healing Brush/Patch Tool, Clone Stamp, Smudge, Sharpen/Blur, and Dodge/Burn/Sponge — involves "hand-painting," which can be tricky. Even with the option of using the History brush, it can be difficult to go back later and correct a several-stroke mistake. Here are some ways to do retouching so you don't permanently damage the image if you make a mistake, and so individual corrections can be easily seen and removed or repaired.

- **When using the new Healing Brush and Patch Tools,** since they can only work on the current layer that has the problem (as opposed to tools like the Clone Stamp that can "use all layers," see below), remember to first duplicate the layer that

Here are a few of the many ways to create a sepiatone effect in Photoshop. For any of these treatments, reducing the Opacity of the "browning" layer will allow some of the original color to show through.

Each of the treatments below started with this color photo, Sterling at Swami's.

Adding a Solid Color Fill layer in Hue mode will tint the existing colors brown, but it won't change the neutral colors — black, white, and grays.

Here the same Fill layer as above was used in Color mode, which tints the entire photo, including the neutrals.

A monotone effect is created by using a Hue/Saturation Adjustment layer with the Colorize option chosen, to apply a brown color by choosing an orange Hue and reducing the Saturation.

needs the fixing (⌘/Ctrl-J will do this automatically), and work on this copy, leaving the original layer intact. See page 137 for more on using these tools.

- **To remove dust and small scratches,** duplicate the image in a layer above and run the Dust & Scratches filter on this layer. Then add a black-filled layer mask to hide the entire filtered image, and finally paint the mask with white where you need the filtered image to hide the blemishes. This method is described step-by-step in "Fixing a Problem Photo" on page 134. Or if you're working on a 16-bit image, where you can't use multiple layers, use the History method described in "Retouching with History" on page 122.

- **To remove larger blemishes,** use the Clone Stamp on a transparent "repairs" layer above the image, first setting the tool to Use All Layers in the Options bar. The Clone Stamp works especially well in Non-aligned mode with a medium-soft brush tip. Alt/Option-click to pick up neighboring image detail, and click to deposit it. Since the repairs are on a separate layer, you can change your fixes at any time.

- **To blur or sharpen particular areas of the image,** add a duplicate layer as described above for removing dust and small scratches. Blur or sharpen this layer with the appropriate filter (Filter, Blur, Gaussian Blur, or Motion Blur; or Filter, Blur, Unsharp Mask). Add a black-filled layer mask and use the Paintbrush and white paint as you would for dust and scratches. For 16-Bit images, use the History method described in "Retouching with History" on page 122.

- **To increase the contrast, brightness, or detail of particular areas of an image,** add a layer above your image, putting this new layer in Overlay mode and filling it with 50% gray, which is neutral (invisible) in Overlay mode. (Alt/Option-clicking the Create A New Layer button at the bottom of the Layers palette opens the New Layer dialog box, where you can set the mode and the fill as you add the layer.) Then work on this layer by using black paint (to dodge), white paint (to burn), or shades of gray, with a soft Airbrush or Paintbrush, with Pressure or Opacity set very low. As you paint, be careful not to oversaturate the image. *(If oversaturation occurs, try changing the Blending mode of this gray-filled "Dodge & Burn" layer to Soft Light.)* This method is shown on page 121 and is also demonstrated in "Blending a Panorama" on page 180. **Note**: The Dodge and Burn tools can also target adjustments to contrast, brightness, and detail. But using these tools can be slow and a bit confusing. First, you have to contend with three different Range options for each tool (Highlights, Midtones, or Shadows) set in the Options bar. And second, when you hand-paint with the tools, you don't really know that you've reached the optimal result until you've overshot it and

Using a separate 50%-gray-filled layer in Overlay or Soft Light mode for "dodging" and "burning"

gone too far; then you have to undo and redo until you get it right. Worst of all, you can't make these adjustments on a separate "repairs" layer — that means you have to change the color in your original. So it often works better to use the "dodge and burn" layer method, described above.

- **To increase or decrease color saturation of certain areas in an image,** add a Hue/Saturation Adjustment layer and make a Saturation adjustment that cures the particular problem — for the moment, ignore what happens to the rest of the image. Fill the Adjustment layer with black, which will completely mask the Saturation change. Finally, use a soft Airbrush or Paintbrush to paint with white in the problem areas, altering the mask to let the saturation changes come through. ***Note***: The Sponge tool can also be used for saturation or desaturation, but it can be difficult to make the saturation changes you want without also changing contrast or affecting more of the image than you intended. Also, the Sponge can't be used on a separate "repairs" layer. So using a masked Hue/Saturation layer often works better than using the Sponge.

SHARPENING

Running the Unsharp Mask filter almost always improves a scanned photo. Usually it's the last thing that should be done to an image before it's prepared for the press, because the synthetic effects of sharpening can be magnified in other image-editing processes, such as increasing the color saturation. Sharpening is discussed more extensively in Chapter 5, starting on page 204.

CORRECTING 16-BIT IMAGES

With 10, 12, or 16 bits per color channel you have the possibility of thousands of tones per channel rather than just the 256 values that 8-bits-per-channel provides. Having the extra color depth of Photoshop's 16 Bits/Channel mode can make a significant difference in the results when you're struggling with Curves to bring out detail in the shadows or highlights. In Photoshop 7 you can do more with 16-bit images than you could in earlier versions. But there are still some workarounds needed to accomplish your goals:

- You can crop images with the Image, Crop command or the Crop tool as described on pages 110 through 114, although the Hide and Perspective options won't be available for the Crop tool. Unfortunately, the Trim command won't work in 16-bit images.

- Although you don't have the flexibility of Adjustment layers in 16 Bits/Channel mode, most of the same functions are available as commands in the Image, Adjust menu. So you can make overall changes to contrast, exposure, and color using the Levels, Curves, Hue/Saturation, and Color Balance manipulations described on pages 115 through 119.

When shooting photos with a digital camera, consider setting your camera's file format to "RAW" in order to take advantage of the enhanced manipulation possibilities with a "billions of colors" image. The various digital camera manufacturers have different names for their version of the Raw file format. For instance, Nikon's is called NEF (for Nikon Electronic Format). These "high-bit depth" files can be opened with the camera manufacturer's own software (an excellent example is Nikon's *Capture* **see below**), or with a Photoshop Plug-in like Adobe's new CamerRaw. Software such as these (as well as most scanner controlling software) let you adjust many of the critical elements of an image's color and contrast attributes, as well as sharpening and noise reduction, before the photograph is actually opened in Photoshop. Doing these adjustments while the image is in its most "robust" form creates the best possible original, with the greatest chance for shadow and highlight detail that doesn't "posterize" or degrade once manipulated. After the adjustments have been made, you can choose to open the image in 16-bit-per-channel mode, or in the standard 8-bit per channel (millions of colors) mode. If you do choose the later, the adjustments you set while the file was "Raw" will still carry over (for the most part) even with the reduced color space.

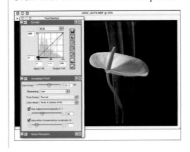

- You can use the Clone Stamp for fixing large blemishes, as described on page 120, though not on a separate layer.
- You can't add an extra layer as described in "Retouching 'By Hand'" on page 119 for removing dust and scratches, blurring and sharpening, dodging, burning, or adjusting saturation. And the Blur, Sharpen, Dodge, Burn, and Sponge tools don't work in 16-bit color. But there's still a way to get these corrections done efficiently and with the flexibility to make changes. The secret is in the History palette.

RETOUCHING WITH HISTORY

In many cases where you would use a second layer as described in "Retouching 'By Hand'" on page 119, you can use a History-based process instead, described step-by-step below specifically for eliminating dust & scratches. You can use essentially the same History process for blurring (use Filter, Blur, Gaussian Blur instead of the Dust & Scratches filter), for sharpening (use Filter, Sharpen, Unsharp Mask), or for changing saturation (use Image, Adjust, Hue/Saturation). Even for dodging and burning specific areas, you can make an overall Levels adjustment that fixes the spots you want to brighten or darken, then take a Snapshot, undo the change, and paint from the Snapshot with the History Brush. The History repairs process works for both 8-bit and 16-bit images, but it's especially useful for working in 16-bit color, where you don't have the luxury of extra layers for adjustments or repairs.

1 Run the Dust & Scratches filter on the entire image (Filter, Noise, Dust & Scratches), with settings high enough to hide all the problems (see "Fixing a Problem Photo" on page 134 for help).

2 To store a copy of the blurred image in the History palette, take a Merged Snapshot of the filtered image by Alt/Option-clicking the Create New Snapshot button at the bottom of the palette and choosing "From: Merged Layers" in the New Snapshot dialog box. (For 16-bit images, choosing Merged Layers instead of the default Full Document isn't essential, since there can be only one layer in the document. But for multilayer files, choosing Merged Layers can be important for avoiding problems with the Snapshot later.)

3 Press Ctrl/⌘-Z for Edit, Undo, to restore the image to its "prefiltered" state.

4 Click in the column to the left of the new Snapshot near the top of the History palette, to designate the Snapshot as the source for painting with the History Brush tool.

5 Choose the History Brush in the toolbox. In the Options bar choose Normal mode, pick a soft brush tip, and set Opacity to 100%. Then dab to paint the stored, filtered image over the dust and scratches. If you overdo it, you can drag the latest History

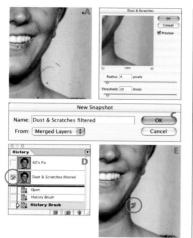

To fix a blemished image **A**, first run the Dust & Scratches filter on the entire image, with settings high enough to hide all the problems **B**. Then take a Merged Snapshot of the filtered image **C**. Undo the filter and set the new Snapshot as the source for the History Brush **D**. Paint with the smallest soft brush tip that will paint out the defects **E**. (History states and Snapshots are lost when you close the file. For a method that gives you more flexibility for making changes later, see "Fixing a Problem Photo" on page 134.)

© CORBIS IMAGES ROYALTY FREE, FOOD & INGREDIENTS

Silhouetting a subject with a clipping path allows it to be exported without its background, so you can layer it with other elements in your page layout program (see "Silhouetting Images & Type" in Chapter 7).

© CORBIS IMAGES ROYALTY FREE, ALTERNATIVE MEDICINE

Blurring the background (right) can eliminate detail that competes with the subject (see "Blurring the Background, but Keeping the Grain" on page 140).

state (at the bottom of the History palette) down to the trash button to undo the last brush stroke, working backwards until you've eliminated the problem.

SPECIAL EFFECTS FOR PHOTOS

There are times when you want to use a particular artistic treatment or when a photo *must* be used in a project but the photo just can't be redeemed by the normal correction processes. Here are some ideas for those kinds of photos:

- **To simplify and stylize an image,** use a filter such as Cutout (Filter, Artistic, Cutout) to create a posterized effect. You can choose the number of colors or shades of gray you want to use, and you can also control the smoothness and fidelity of the color breaks. The Cutout filter produces smoother, cleaner edges and more color control than you can get with the Posterize command or with a Posterize Adjustment layer. Or try Filter, Blur, Smart Blur as described in Chapter 5 on page 208.

- **To silhouette a subject against a bright background,** select the subject and fill it with black (press "D" for Default colors and Alt/Option-Delete to fill it with the Foreground color).

- **To get rid of unwanted detail in the background,** select the background and blur it as described in "Blurring the Background but Keeping the Grain" on page 140. Or use the Clone Stamp to paint over distracting background objects with other background texture.

- **To get rid of a background altogether,** select it and fill it with white or with a color. Or **replace the background with a different image,** as described in "Extracting an Image" on page 162. To be able to export a subject without its background, you can use a clipping path, as described in "Silhouetting Images & Type" in Chapter 7.

- Blending the part of the scene that continues from one photo to another — often this is the sky — is usually the hardest part of making a panorama sequence into a single image. **To piece together a problematic panorama,** one solution is to remove the sky and then replace it with a sky from a different photo, or a stretched version of the sky from one of the montaged images, or a synthetic sky created with a Gradient. See "Blending a Panorama" on page 180 for other tips on assembling panoramas.

- For **special artistic effects,** try one of the filters found in the Filter, Sketch submenu; many of these filters use the Foreground and Background colors to create their effects. So you can choose the colors before you run them, or change the color afterwards using an option like those in the "Sepiatones" tip on page 120.

Quick Tone & Color Adjustments

In Photoshop 7 there are many ways to approach the problem of making a bad photo look good or a good photo look great. But in most cases you'll be looking for the one that takes full advantage of Photoshop's power to save time, produce top-quality results, and leave you with a file that's flexible, in case you need to make further changes. The approaches on these four pages are presented with that in mind. In some cases using one of these "quick fixes" may not get you all the way to your goal, but it can provide a big head start.

Once you identify the main "need" for a particular photo, here are some general rules of thumb for approaching the problem:

- *For overall tone (and possibly color) corrections, try a Levels Adjustment layer, taking advantage of the Auto and Options buttons and the Set Gray Point dropper if you can (see pages 116–118 for tips).*

- *To correct specific parts of the tonal range, try Curves (page 118).*

- *To make overall color shifts, or to target color changes to particular colors, try Hue/Saturation (page 119).*

- *To control color changes separately for highlights, midtones, and shadows, try Color Balance (page 119).*

- *If needed, target your tone and color adjustments with soft selections and masks.*

Auto Levels

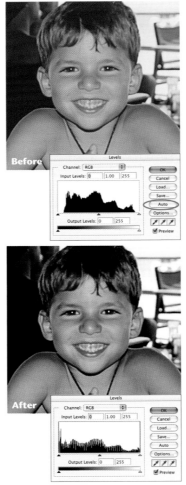

Simply applying Auto Levels often markedly improves the overall tonal range of a photo. You can apply it through a Levels Adjustment layer by clicking the circular black-and-white Create New Fill/Adjustment Layer button at the bottom of the Layers palette and choosing Levels from the pop-out list. With an Adjustment layer you can make additional changes later if needed, without ever affecting the original image below.

Selecting & Levels

An Auto Levels correction often works better if you first select the area that's most important for Photoshop to "consider" when it adjusts the contrast. For instance, in this photo **A**, when Auto Levels was applied without a selection **B**, the result was too dark because Photoshop found pure white in the border areas and therefore didn't "think" that it needed to lighten the image. When a selection was made before the Levels Adjustment layer was added, a mask was automatically generated for the Levels Adjustment layer, and the result was much better **C**. After making the Levels adjustment you can either delete the mask (by dragging its icon to the trash can button) or fill the entire mask with white.

Auto Levels & Opacity

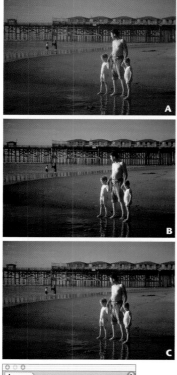

IMAGE Auto Levels-Opacity.psd

Sometimes treating an image **A** with Auto Levels can overshoot the tonal correction you're aiming for and increase the contrast too much **B**. Before you give up on Auto Levels and try to make the Levels adjustment "by hand," try reducing the effect of the Auto Levels correction. If you've applied Auto Levels through a Levels Adjustment layer — always a good idea — just experiment with reducing the Opacity **C**. If you used Image, Adjust, Auto Levels instead of an Adjustment layer, try reducing the Opacity with the Edit, Fade Auto Levels command, which is only available immediately after you apply Auto Levels directly (via the Image menu or Ctrl/⌘-Shift-L).

Levels & Luminosity

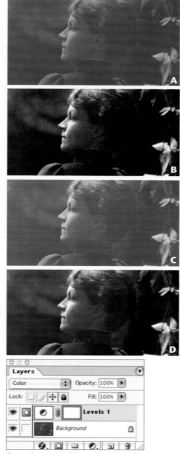

Sometimes treating an image with the default Auto Levels expands the tonal range but has an undesirable effect on color. Try putting the Levels Adjustment layer in Luminosity mode, so only the tonality, and not the color, is affected by the adjustment. For this sepiatone **A** the Auto Levels correction removed the color **B**. First we tried the Enhance Monochromatic Contrast feature in the Options sub dialog of Levels which brought back the color, but without the contrast we wanted **C**. Next we used the default Auto settings of Enhance Per Channel Contrast, then changed the Blend mode of the Levels Adjustment layer to Luminosity and we got the best of both worlds **D**. (Alternatively, if you want to keep the color correction produced by Auto Levels but don't want the change in tone, change the blend mode of the Levels layer to Color.)

IMAGE Levels-Luminosity.psd

Levels & Set Gray Point

If your original image **A** shows an unwanted color cast that isn't fixed by adjusting Levels **B**, try using the Set Gray Point eyedropper in the Levels dialog box. After you click the Auto button or adjust the black point and white point Input Levels sliders, if there are pixels in your image that should be a neutral gray, you can click on them with this dropper to adjust the color. If you undercorrect or overcorrect (introducing a different color cast) with the first click, you can continue to click around to try to locate a neutral medium gray, such as the suspenders in this image **C**.

IMAGE Levels-Set Gray Point.psd

Auto Contrast

If your original image **A** shows an unwanted color shift when the default Auto Levels is applied **B**, and changing the blend mode of the Levels Adjustment layer (as in "Levels & Luminosity" on page 125) eliminates the color shift but just doesn't seem to make the color "pop" **C**, go into the Levels Options dialog and change settings to Enhance Monochromatic Contrast and Snap Neutral Midtones (the same as choosing Auto Contrast from the Image, Adjustments menu).

Levels & Multiply

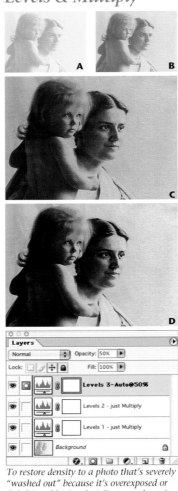

To restore density to a photo that's severely "washed out" because it's overexposed or faded **A**, add a Levels Adjustment layer in Multiply mode (by Alt/Option-dragging on the Create New Fill/Adjustment Layer button at the bottom of the Layers palette and choosing Levels from the pop-out list). In the New Layer dialog box, choose Multiply for the mode and click OK. When the Levels dialog box opens, click OK without making any adjustment. If this "blank" Levels layer hasn't improved the range of tones enough **B**, you can duplicate it (by dragging its thumbnail to the Create A New Layer button at the bottom of the Layers palette) **C**. If the image still looks washed out, try adding another Adjustment layer (this time in Normal mode) to apply Levels either manually or by using the Auto button as we did here. Adjust Opacity if needed **D**.

 Levels-Multiply.psd

Masking Curves

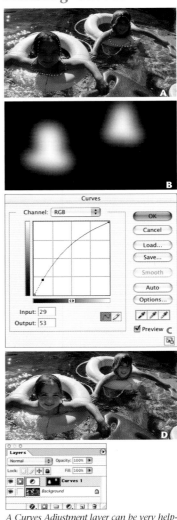

A Curves Adjustment layer can be very helpful when an image shows good color and contrast overall, but you want to lighten a particular tonal range or a particular area. In this image a feathered selection of the girls' faces was made **A** and then a Curves Adjustment layer was added by clicking the Create New Fill/Adjustment Layer button at the bottom of the Layers palette and choosing Curves from the pop-out menu. This automatically created a soft-edged layer mask **B** for the Curves layer. Ctrl/⌘-clicking on one of the faces, which were shadowed, made a point on the curve in the Curves dialog box. The point was then moved up **C** to lighten the area revealed by the mask **D**.

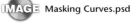 Masking Curves.psd

Color Balance

A Color Balance Adjustment layer can target a color change to the highlights, midtones, or shadows separately. You simply add the opposite of the color you have too much of. This image showed a yellow cast in the highlights **A**. *To remove the yellow, the Highlights option was chosen in the Color Balance dialog box and the Yellow-Blue slider was moved toward Blue. And to bring back a little warmth, the Cyan-Red slider was moved slightly toward Red* **B**, **C**.

 Color Balance.psd

Hue/Saturation

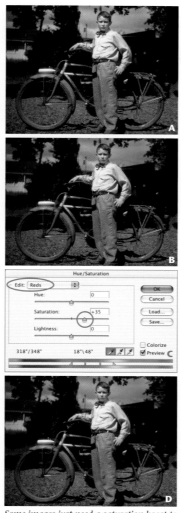

Some images just need a saturation boost to restore color — either generally or in a specific range of colors. For this image **A** *a Hue/Saturation Adjustment layer was added and the Saturation slider for the default Master channel was moved to the right to brighten up the color overall* **B**. *Then, to emphasize the bike and the bow tie, the Reds color family was chosen from the dialog box's Edit menu and its saturation was boosted separately as well* **C**, **D**. *Both changes were made in the same Adjustment layer.*

 Hue-Saturation.psd

Boosting CMYK

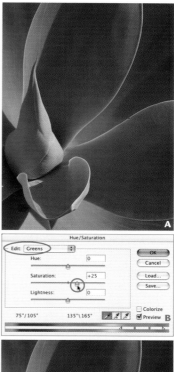

An RGB image whose colors look intense and lively can sometimes lose its "oomph" when converted to CMYK mode for printing **A**. *In that case a subtle Hue/Saturation change in an Adjustment layer can sometimes help restore some of the vibrancy of the color overall or of a particular color range. Here Green was chosen from the Hue/Saturation dialog's Edit menu and the Saturation was increased* **B**, **C**.

 Boosting CMYK.psd

Framing
with Masks

Overview *Inside your image make a rectangular selection of the area that you want to frame; make a layer mask from the selection; blur the mask; experiment with black and white backgrounds behind the image; for variations apply filters to the blurred layer mask.*

"**Framing**" "before" and "after" files

JHD / ORIGINAL PHOTO: © CORBIS IMAGES ROYALTY FREE, TRAVEL & ROMANCE

IT'S EASY TO CREATE CUSTOM EDGE TREATMENTS for photos by making a layer mask to define the area you want to frame, then blurring the black-and-white mask to create soft edges that blend into the page. As shown above, you can also create a well-defined, "dark-haloed" edge for the image within the soft vignetting.

1 Creating the layer mask. Open an image **1a** and open the Layers palette (Window, Show Layers). If your image consists of a single *Background* layer, you'll need to turn it into a layer with the capacity for transparency so that it can have a layer mask: Double-click the *Background* label in the Layers palette; in the New Layer dialog box, rename the layer if you'd like and click OK.

To add a layer mask, first choose the Rectangular Marquee tool (the keyboard shortcut is "M") and drag to select the part of the image you want to frame; make sure your selection is far enough inside your image so that any soft vignetting will not hit the edge of the canvas. Then turn the selection into a layer mask by clicking the Add A Mask button at the bottom of the Layers palette **1b.** (Before you modify the mask in the next step, store the frame shape for safekeeping: Open the Channels palette [Window, Show Channels] and drag the *Layer Mask* name to the Create New Channel button at the bottom of the palette.)

1a

Original image

1b

A layer mask was made from a rectangular selection used to frame the image.

> **AVOIDING HARD EDGES**
>
> Any time you create soft vignetting at the edge of an image, you risk having the soft edges cut off abruptly by running into the actual edge of the image. To avoid this, make sure the area of the image that you select to frame doesn't extend too close to the edges — a good rule of thumb is to allow a buffer of at least 1.5 times the Gaussian Blur setting you plan to use to soften the edge.

2 Softening the edges. Adding a white-filled layer below the image layer will give you a better look at the frame edges as you develop them: Alt/Option-click the Create A New Layer button at the

2

A white background layer was added and the mask was blurred to soften its edges. We used a Radius setting of 20 pixels for our approximately 1000-pixel-wide image.

3

A layer was added with a black-filled rectangle the same size as the original frame selection. This clearly defines the frame without eliminating the soft edges.

bottom of the Layers palette to create and name the layer. Then fill it with white (choosing Edit, Fill, Use: White is one way to do it). In the Layers palette, drag the layer down below the image-and-mask layer.

Now soften the edges of the mask: With the image layer targeted in the Layers palette and the layer mask active (click on the mask thumbnail to make the mask icon appear next to the eye), choose Filter, Blur, Gaussian Blur. Experiment with the Radius setting until you see the soft-edged fade-to-white effect you want.

At this point you may want to rename your image layer to include information about the Gaussian Blur setting. If so, right-click on the layer's name in the Layers palette (Control-click on a Mac with a one-button mouse), choose Layer Properties from the pop-out context-sensitive menu, and type a new name **2**.

3 Adding black to define the frame. For a well-defined frame in combination with the soft edge treatment **3**, add a black backing layer that will show through the softened edge of the masked image, creating "a dark halo": With the white background layer targeted, click the Create A New Layer button. Then activate the same selection you used to make the mask (if you haven't made a selection since creating the mask, choose Select, Reselect, or use the shortcut Ctrl/⌘-Shift-D; if reselecting doesn't work, in the Channels palette Ctrl/⌘-click the alpha channel you made in step 1). Fill the selection (Edit, Fill, Use: Black).

To soften the transition between sharp frame and soft edge, you can blur the black layer slightly. We used a Gaussian Blur with a Radius of 2 pixels for the result at the top of page 128.

Fancy framing. Experiment on the layer mask with filters to stylize either the edge area or the entire mask, as shown below. See pages 218–219 for examples of filtered edge treatments. 𝒲𝒶𝓊!

IMAGE SWAPPING

Once you have a framing file set up, it's easy to experiment with the same frame and another image of similar size: Start by targeting the image-and-mask layer and then drag-and-drop your new image into the file. Then press Ctrl/⌘-G to make a clipping group of the new image layer and the masked layer below.

The layer mask was targeted and the Texturizer filter was applied. The filter settings you need to create this and other "filtered edges" are on pages 218–219.

Softening the Focus

Overview *Duplicate the original image to a new layer; blur the copy with the Gaussian Blur filter; vary the blurred layer's Opacity, Blend Mode, and Blend If options (in the Layer Style dialog box) to produce a softening effect. Create a Dodge & Burn layer to exaggerate tonality.*

ORIGINAL PHOTO: © JJHDAVIS DESIGN

IMAGE
"Soft Focus" "before" and "after" files

1

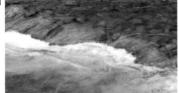

The original image duplicated to a new layer.

2

Blur the duplicate image. We used a radius of 10 pixels for our1500-pixel-wide image.

3

Reduce the Opacity of the blurred layer and change its Blend Mode mode to Overlay.

SINCE THE END OF THE 19TH CENTURY, photographers have used soft-focus and haze effects to impart a romantic quality to their images. Often the goal is to soften the appearance of skin or hair, or create a diffuse glow around highlights in the photo. In Photoshop you can accomplish these effects and more with the Gaussian Blur filter and a skillful blending of blurred and sharp layers.

1 Duplicating the image onto a new layer. To make another copy of the image, drag the image layer's name (ours is the original *Background* layer) to the Create New Layer button at the bottom of the palette, or type Ctrl/⌘-J **1**.

2 Blurring the duplicate layer. Choose Filter, Blur, Gaussian Blur to make the new layer look out-of-focus. The Radius setting in the Gaussian Blur dialog box will determine the amount of halo or softening you can achieve. We used a Radius of 10 pixels for our 1500-pixel-wide image **2**.

3 Adjusting Opacity and Blend Mode. Now experiment with the blurred layer's Opacity slider, its Blend Mode, and the Advanced Blend If's options:

- To reduce the haze effect but still apply it to all the tonal values in the image — highlights, midtones, and shadows — simply lower the blurred layer's Opacity.

- For our photo we left the Opacity at 100% but chose to change the Blend Mode to Overlay to exaggerate the contrast and increase saturation (Soft Light would create a similar effect without the increased saturation, and for the standard "Diffused Glow" treatment, Screen mode, with a reduced opacity would do the trick).

- Change both the Blend Mode and the Opacity. Here the Opacity was reduced to 60% **3**.

4

Limit the contribution of the light tones of the blurred layer using Blend If settings

5a

Set up the new "Dodge & Burn" layer

5b

Use a big soft brush tip and low Opacity to have the most control for dodging and burning.

5c

Turning off and on the visibility for the Dodge & Burn Layer

The finished "Dodge & Burn" layer for the stream photo, viewed by itself

4 Advanced Blending. A "hidden feature" that has been in Photoshop forever is Blend If (now part of the Layer Styles dialog). Without any hand selecting or masking you can easily change the "contribution" made by one layer's lights and darks in relation to the layer beneath. With the Layer Style box open to the Blending Options section, adjust the Advanced Blending, Blend If options by holding down the Alt key (Windows) or Option key (Mac) and dragging the left half-triangle of the white-point slider of "This Layer" to the left. Holding down the Alt/Option key allows the slider to split, and splitting the slider makes a soft transition between the light tones of the blurred version (This Layer) and those of the sharp version (Underlying) of the image. The tones to the left of the left half-triangle in the blurred image will contribute fully to the composite image. The tones between the two half-triangles will partially contribute, with the ones at the light end of this range contributing least. The effect was to prevent the brightest highlights of the blurred copy from contributing to the mix and "blowing out" the light areas **4.** The same method was used for reducing the amount that the darks in the blurred copy contributed.

5 Adding a Dodge & Burn layer. Photoshop's Dodge and Burn tools can be used to decrease or increase contrast and brightness in particular areas of an image. But using these tools can be slow and a bit confusing. By working with three different Range options for each tool (Highlights, Midtones, and Shadows), you don't know for certain if you've reached the optimal result until you've overshot it and gone too far. Most problematic of all, you can't make these adjustments on a separate "repairs" layer, which means that you have to change your original image. An easier way to make quick targeted adjustments to contrast and brightness is to create a separate "Dodge & Burn" layer.

Start by adding a layer above your image: At the bottom of the Layers palette, Alt/Opt-click the "Create a new layer" icon. When the New Layer dialog box opens, set the Mode to Overlay, and click the check box for "Fill with Overlay-neutral color (50% gray)" **5a.** The appearance of your image won't change, since you've added a layer filled with 50% gray, and 50% gray isn't visible (or "neutral") in Overlay mode.

Now you can work on this new layer by using black paint (to burn) or white paint (to dodge), applied with the Brush tool with a soft brush tip and a very low Opacity (try 5–10%) set in the Options bar **5b.** If you've overdone it with dark or light gray, you can fix the mistake by applying 50% gray to "neutralize" the dodging or burning.

We used a "Dodge & Burn" layer on this stream photograph to exaggerate the central focal point of the image by highlighting (dodging) the edge of the water as it rolled over the rocks and darkening (burning) the transition point where the white water churned beneath the "falls" **5c.**

Focusing Attention with Color

Overview *Apply a Hue/Saturation Adjustment layer with a layer mask to protect the subject from color change; use a Layer Style to add a drop shadow to make the subject stand out more; add type with a matching shadow.*

"**Attention**" "before" and "after" files

1a

The color photo

1b

Selecting the subject with the Pen tool

1c

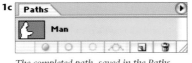

The completed path, saved in the Paths palette

2a

Choosing from the pop-out list of Adjustment layers

A POPULAR EFFECT BOTH IN PRINT AND VIDEO is to emphasize the subject of an image by *de*-emphasizing the background. This effect can be used to make the subject stand out, to simplify the background for overprinting type, or to tie an image to others in a series. In this case we've focused attention on the subject by removing most of the color from the background, at the same time tinting it with a color that contrasts with the subject. A slight shadow, or "dark halo," makes the subject "pop" even more. Type was colored to emphasize the color in the subject, and a matching drop shadow brings the type forward.

1 Isolating the subject. Choose a color photo **1a** and use an appropriate selection tool or command to select the subject (see Chapter 1 for tips on selection). We used the Pen tool to outline the man because his shape consisted largely of smooth curves **1b** (for help using the Pen tool, see page 300). When the outline was complete, we closed the path (a small circle next to the cursor tells you when you're close enough to the beginning anchor point so that a click will close the path). In order to name and save the path, we double-clicked the *Work Path* name in the Paths palette to open the Save Path dialog box, where we typed in a name ("Man") and clicked OK **1c**. Then we loaded the path as a selection by Ctrl/⌘-clicking on the name of the path.

2 Ghosting the background. When the subject is selected, switch the selection to the background instead (choose Select, Inverse, or press Ctrl/⌘-Shift-I). Create a Hue/Saturation Adjustment layer by clicking the Create A New Fill/Adjustment Layer button at the bottom of the Layers palette and choosing from the list **2a.**

The active selection will create a mask in the Adjustment layer that will protect the subject. So when you make changes in the Hue/Saturation dialog box **2b,** they will apply to the background

2b

Setting up the Hue/Saturation Adjustment layer to neutralize, tint, and darken the background

2c

The result of adding the Hue/Saturation layer

3a

Adding a "dark halo" to the Hue/Saturation Adjustment layer by using the Inner Shadow; shown here is the Inner Shadow section of the Layer Style dialog box.

3b

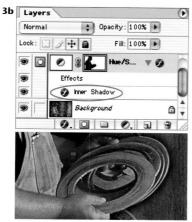

The dark halo makes the subject stand out from the background even more.

only **2c.** Decrease Saturation by moving the slider to the left. You can also click the Colorize checkbox, as we did, and adjust the Hue. Move the Lightness slider in a direction that boosts the contrast between background and subject; we darkened our image by moving the Lightness slider to the left. Adjust the Hue/Saturation box's three sliders interactively until you have the effect you want.

3 Adding a Layer Style based on a mask. When you apply a Layer Style to an Adjustment layer with a mask, the effects in the Layer Style will be applied to the edge of the mask. The mask made in step 2 is for the *background* rather than the *subject*. Therefore, if you were to apply a Drop Shadow to the Hue/Saturation layer, the shadow would appear *on* the subject instead of *behind* it, and the background would seem to be in front of the subject. To put the shadow in the right place to make a dark halo around the subject, you can use the Inner Shadow layer effect: With the Adjustment layer active, click the Add A Layer Style button (the *"f"*) at the bottom of the Layers palette and choose Inner Shadow from the pop-out menu. In the Layer Style dialog box, set the Distance to 0 so the dark halo won't be displaced off-center (since the Distance is 0, the Angle setting won't matter). Increase the Size to spread the shadow from the edge; increase the Choke to make the shadow denser **3a, 3b.**

4 Adding type with a matching shadow. To add type, choose the Type tool and then choose your type characteristics from the Options bar: the font (we used Aachen), orientation (horizontal or vertical), type style, size, kind of antialiasing, alignment, and color.

4

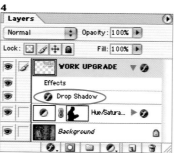

The Layers palette for the final image (see the top of page 132) shows the addition of a type layer with a Drop Shadow effect.

When you click the color swatch on the Options bar, the Color Picker opens and you can choose from its offerings; or move the cursor onto your image (the cursor becomes the Eyedropper tool) and click to sample a color you like. If you need more control — over kerning, tracking, leading, vertical or horizontal scaling, position relative to the baseline, or paragraph characteristics — click the Options bar's Palettes button to open the Character and Paragraph palettes. (For more about setting and styling type, see Chapter 7.)

To give the type a dark halo, add a Layer Style as in step 3, but this time choose Drop Shadow from the pop-out menu **4.** Again set the Distance to 0; match the Size you used for the Inner Shadow in step 3, and match the Spread to the Choke value you used.

Fixing a Problem Photo

Overview *Apply the Dust & Scratches filter through a hand-painted mask; make "cosmetic" changes with a "repairs" layer; use a Levels Adjustment layer to fix tonality and color cast.*

IMAGE

"Problem Fix" "before" and "after" files

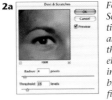

The original scan from the slide

2a 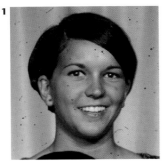 For the Dust & Scratches filter, setting the Radius at 4 and then adjusting the Threshold to 15 eliminated the spots in the image copy but retained the film grain.

2b

A black-filled layer mask was added to the filtered layer.

2c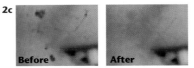

Defects were removed by dabbing white on the layer mask.

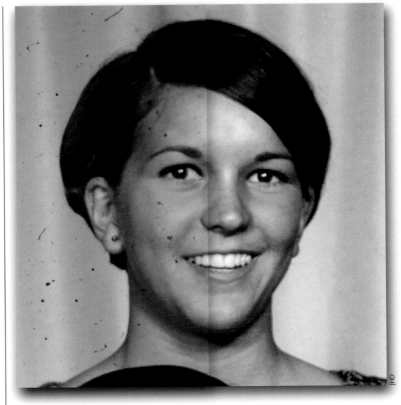

WHEN YOU NEED TO FIX A "PROBLEM PHOTO," you want a method that's as fast and automated as possible yet gives you precise control of the placement and quality of the "fixes," and that's flexible enough so you can make changes later if you need to. It pays to use the built-in power and speed of Photoshop filters and Adjustment layers to make global changes such as eliminating dust and scratches and adjusting color and tonality. But you also want the "human touch" to direct these "automatic" changes so they do precisely what you want. The image above shows the "before" (left) and "after" versions of a scanned color slide from the 1960's. Using the Healing Brush would have sufficiently completed the repairs needed on this photo, but the following technique removed the million bits of "junk" from our file in only about 3 minutes! And when the entire problem-fixing process was complete, including color correction, the original image remained untouched on the *Background* layer and the various changes were on their own layers, where they could easily be edited if necessary.

1 Analyzing your photo. Specific challenges vary from image to image, but many old photos show the problems seen in this scan **1**. The most obvious flaw was the "junk" caused by dust on the slide or deterioration of the emulsion. Another problem was the fading of

2d

After removing all the specks from the face by painting white onto the black-filled mask

the color. Start by identifying your photo's worst problem, so you can tackle it first. In this image the worst problem was the "junk."

2 Eliminating dust and scratches. To quickly get rid of dust or scratches, start by copying your original image to another layer: Drag its thumbnail in the Layers palette to the Create A New Layer button at the bottom of the palette (Ctrl/⌘-J). Next filter this copy to hide all the "junk," as follows: Choose Filter, Noise, Dust & Scratches. The Dust & Scratches filter looks for spots that differ from their surroundings in color or brightness; then it blurs the surrounding color into the spots to eliminate them.

To control the blurring, first move the Radius and Threshold sliders all the way to the left, to 0. Then slowly move the Radius slider to the right to make the problem spots disappear. When you reach the Radius setting where the spots are all hidden, you'll find that you've also eliminated any inherent noise or film grain. To restore the grain, leave the Radius slider where it is and move the Threshold slider to the right until the spots just begin to reappear; then "back off" by moving the slider just slightly to the left until the spots are gone again **2a.** What you've just done by increasing the Threshold is to make the filter "smarter" so that it blurs away only those spots that are very different from their surroundings. Small color differences such as those due to film grain are left unchanged.

Although the spots are gone and the grain is restored, you'll find that most of the important image detail has also been eliminated. That's because the Dust & Scratches filter can't tell the difference between a scratch and an eyelash, or a dust speck and the twinkle in an eye. To solve that problem, you can use a layer mask to hide the filtered image and then "paint it back" where you need it to hide the blemishes: Make a mask to hide the new filtered layer completely by Alt/Option-clicking the Add A Mask button at the bottom of the Layers palette **2b.** The palette should now show that the black-filled mask is active; in the toolbox white should be the Foreground color — it's the default when a mask is active.

Choose the Paintbrush, and in the Options bar choose a soft-edged brush tip that's about the size of the specks you need to hide. Dab with the brush where you see specks in detailed areas, such as the face in this image **2c.** The dabs will make white "holes" in the mask, allowing the filtered image to cover the spots in those areas **2d.**

Eliminating specks in large areas that have little detail can be done all at once by selecting these areas and filling them with white on the mask: Choose the lasso and in the Options bar set its Feather (we used a 3-pixel feather); surround the area you want to fill; then Alt/Option-Delete to fill the selected area of the mask with white, the current Foreground color **2e.**

3 Making cosmetic changes. If you want to make cosmetic changes to the image, it's best to add a "repairs" layer above the

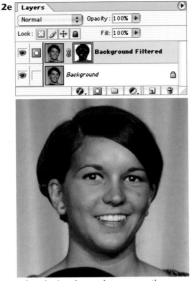

2e

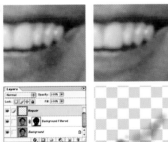

After altering the mask to remove the specks from the background of the image

3

A separate "repairs" layer was added and the Clone Stamp was used to smooth the color in the lip and other areas.

4a *A Levels Adjustment layer was added so that overall tonality and color cast could be corrected.*

4b

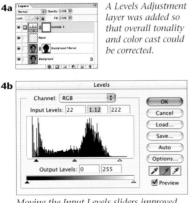

Levels

Channel: RGB

Input Levels: 22 1.12 222

OK
Cancel
Load...
Save...
Auto
Options...

Output Levels: 0 255

☑ Preview

Moving the Input Levels sliders improved the overall contrast and the Set Gray Point eyedropper helped remove the color cast.

filtered layer, where you can make your "hand-painted" alterations. This protects the image from painting mistakes and also makes it easy to make changes to your repairs later if you need to.

There are several ways to create a repair layer to make cosmetic changes. The Healing Brush (covered in "Healing in Stages" on page 137) works well for repairs, but it is unable to perform its magic on a separate layer. So for the simple fixes needed in this image, we used the Clone Stamp tool. The Clone Stamp lets you make quick repairs on a separate layer by using the inherent color variations that are found in your image, rather than "painting" the fix with a single choosen color.

Start by adding another layer (click the Create A New Layer button). To use the Clone Stamp for repairs, in the Options bar set the Opacity low and make sure the Use All Layers option is turned on. This option lets you sample color from the composite image formed by the layers below while you keep the repairs layer active for painting the changes. To start the repairs, hold down the Alt/Option key and click in an area near the flaw to sample an appropriate "source" area with the desired color and texture. Then paint over the flaw **3**.

4 Adjusting contrast and removing a color cast. A quick way to try an overall color/contrast correction is with a Levels Adjustment layer: Click the Create New Adjustment Layer button at the bottom of the Layers palette and choose Levels **4a**. In the Levels dialog box, we moved the black-point and white-point Input Levels sliders inward and the gamma (gray) slider left, experimenting until the tonality looked right **4b**. To get rid of the color cast we chose the center eyedropper (the Set Gray Point control) and clicked in the

4c

Removing a color cast by using the Set Gray Point eyedropper to sample an area that should be a neutral gray

4d

The final image, with all its problems fixed

image to sample an area that we thought *should* have been a *neutral gray* before the color of the image faded **4c**. If you don't get the color cast fixed on the first try, "hunt and peck" your way around until you hit upon the right gray tone to remove the cast **4d**. This "quick fix" often works well for color casts due to scanner malfunction, erroneous white balance settings in the camera (like what may happen when shooting under fluorescent lighting) or fading in old photos. If it doesn't solve the problem for your particular image (because neutral grays don't exist), see "Removing a Persistent Color Cast" on page 118.

Healing in Stages

Overview *Make a "Remove" layer to hide certain elements and a "Reduce" layer for minimizing others; make global and targeted adjustments to these corrections*

![IMAGE]

"**Healing Stages**" "Before" and "After" files

ORIGINAL PHOTO: ©JHDDAVIS DESIGN

The original photo

1a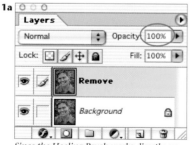

Since the Healing Brush works directly on the image (rather than allowing you to make a separate "repair" layer above it), start by duplicating the photo to a new layer (Ctrl/⌘-J – if you add the Alt/Opt key to the shortcut it will bring up the New Layer dialog where you can name the new layer at the same time). The opacity of this layer stays at 100%, leaving the original photo intact below for safe keeping.

AMONG OTHER THINGS, PHOTOSHOP 7'S HEALING BRUSH is very useful for hiding blemishes and softening wrinkles. We used an approach that does both with a degree of subtlety that doesn't make adult skin look unrealistically smooth. The goal was to make the person look like they were "having a really good day," or maybe make it appear that they were shot with flattering lighting, or even that their makeup was "just right" this day. But our goal was *not* to make our model look like she was someone else by completely removing their "character lines."

By simply dividing up the retouching process into the two stages of first: *Removal* of items you want to completely erase from the image (blemishes, scars, distracting elements in the background, etc.), and second: *Reduction* of elements that need "toning down" (wrinkles, circles under the eyes, etc.) you get a much more natural result, and in a way that is much quicker (and has greater flexibility for change later) than if you had tried to do everything at once on the original image.

1 Making a "Remove" Layer. After fixing any color or tone problems in your photograph, duplicate your original background layer (it's always good to retain the original photo intact) by typing Ctrl/⌘-J for New Layer Via Copy **1a.** Then choose the Healing Brush from the Tools palette.

On the new layer use the Healing Brush on anything that you want to remove completely, such as we did here for blemishes on the forehead and sun spots around the lips **1b.** Painting in short strokes, use a brush tip just big enough to cover up the offending area. On this layer you may also want to use the Healing Brush's

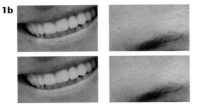

1b

Select a brush tip just big enough to cover up the offending area, painting in short strokes.

2a

When all the blemishes are hidden, duplicate this "healed" layer (Ctrl/1-J)

2b

On a duplicate of the Remove layer, completely hide all elements that you will later want to reduce.

3

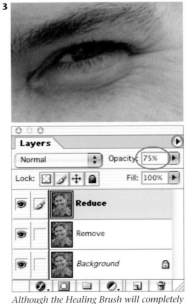

Although the Healing Brush will completely eliminate the wrinkles you use it on, you may now adjust the Opacity of this "Reduce" layer to let some of the original "character lines" show through.

"big sister," the Patch Tool, on larger problematic areas. We used it here to fill a "hole" in the upper right corner of the hedge behind the model. To use the Patch Tool, we selected the hole while making sure the tool's option bar was set to Source, then dragged the selection to a "clean" part of the hedge.

2 Making a "Reduce" Layer. When all the problems are hidden, duplicate this "healed" layer (Ctrl/⌘-J) **2a.** Then use the Healing Brush again on the new layer, this time on anything that you may not want to hide completely, such as wrinkles or freckles. Don't worry if the results look like a rubber mask from a bad sci-fi movie **2b,** because once you've completely covered the elements you want to reduce, the subsequent steps will enable you to "turn back the clock" as much or as little as you like.

3 Global Adjusting. Although the Healing Brush will completely eliminate the wrinkles you use it on, you can now "dial in" the Opacity of this "reduce" layer to let some of the original "character lines" show through **3.** You may want to set this opacity a little on the high side because the next step will let you adjust specific areas even further with absolute precision.

4 Targeted Adjusting. To finalize the reduction process, you can add a Layer Mask to the Reduce layer to allow a little more character to show through, like in the corners of the eyes. To do this, simply click the Add A Mask icon at the bottom of the Layers palette and paint on the resulting mask with a soft-edged brush. Give it a lower opacity and assign black as the foreground color in order to hide portions of the Reduce layer and allow more of the underlaying layer to show through **4.**

4

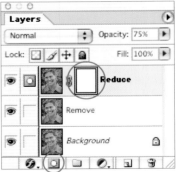

To further fine tune the reduction process, you can add a Layer Mask to the Reduce Layer to allow a little more character to show through by painting with black on the mask.

Skin Softening and Patching

Overview *Apply the Dust & Scratch filter; target the application of the filter with a Layer Mask; make a skin cover-up patch and move and transform it into place.*

"Skin Softening" "before" and "after" files

TO QUICKLY SOFTEN PROBLEMATIC SKIN, as well as get rid of small acne or sun spots, sometime the Dust & Scratches filter can be a big time saver. And when the Patch Tool "hits a wall" because it can't rotate or scale a patch to fit its surroundings, the good ol' feathered Lasso can do quite nicely.

1 Applying the Dust & Scratch Filter. Duplicate the original image to another layer (Ctrl/⌘-J) and run Noise, Dust & Scratches. Set the Radius just high enough to cover up or soften the problems, then set the Threshold high enough to bring back the subtle pores of the skin and the inherent noise of original photo **1.** Don't worry if detail is lost by the filtering, we'll bring it back in the next step.

Next adjust the opacity of this layer to tone down the overall effect. Then create a mask that will temporarily hide this filtered layer, but allow you to paint back in the softening where it's needed. Alt/Opt-clicking the Add a Mask icon at the bottom of the Layers Palette creates a mask that starts off filled with black, thus hiding everything on the current layer. To reveal the filtered copy, simply paint on the mask with a large, soft-edged paint brush (with white as your foreground color) in the areas you want to soften.

2 Making a Patch. To reduce or eliminate large skin "characteristics" you can still "patch" good over bad by using the Lasso. With its Feather setting fairly large (for this image it was set to 15), select the area you want to cover and with the Lasso tool still active, move the selection itself to a "clean" area that you want to use for the patching **2a.** Now copy this area to its own layer (Ctrl/⌘-J for New Layer Via Copy) and then type Ctrl/⌘-T to start to Transform it. Drag the area over the problem and scale or rotate the patch as needed to line up with the original below (moving the cursor out of the box allows you to rotate the selection) **2b.** Reduce the opacity of this layer if desired, or try changing its Blend Mode to Lighten.

Repeat these steps as needed. In this case we duplicated the Skin Coverup layer one more time (Ctrl/⌘-J) and again typed Ctrl/⌘-T (to move and Transform/Rotate the patch) to cover up the other problematic area of the neck.

1

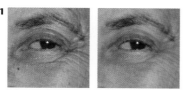

In the Dust & Scratches dialog, set the Radius just high enough to cover up or soften the defects, then set the Threshold high enough to bring back the subtle pores of the skin. Adjust the opacity of this layer and mask until you achieve the look you want.

2a

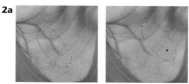

Set the Feather fairly large in the Lasso tool, select the area you want to cover, move the selection to an area that you want to use for the patching, then type Ctrl/⌘-J to put the patch on its own layer.

2b

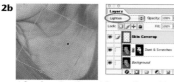

After dragging the patch over the problem, scale or rotate it as needed to line up with the background, then reduce its opacity or change its Blend Mode to Lighten.

Blurring the Background, but Keeping the Grain

Overview Select the part of the image you want to keep sharp — the subject — and cut it out of the background; blur either the background alone or both background and extreme foreground; use a Layer Style to restore film grain or digital noise in the blurred areas.

"Background Blur" "before" and "after" files

1a

© CORBIS IMAGES ROYALTY FREE, ARMED FORCES

Original image

1b

With the selection of the two men active, clicking the Save Selection As Channel button stored the selection as an alpha channel for safekeeping.

JHD

YOU CAN REMOVE DISTRACTING DETAIL from an image or focus attention on the subject by isolating the subject and keeping it in focus as you blur other parts of the picture. The Photoshop technique presented here imitates the effect you get with a *shortened depth of field,* traditionally achieved by opening up the camera's iris (setting the f-stop low). The blurring can be limited to the background (follow the step-by-step process below, stopping after step 3). Or, as shown here, the sharp subject can be sandwiched between blurred background and blurred foreground (continue through step 5). In either case, you'll need to make the blurred areas match the sharp ones by restoring the film grain or digital noise (the equivalent of film grain in an image taken with a digital camera) that was lost in the process of blurring.

DEFINING THE FOREGROUND

If you want to keep a foreground subject in focus while blurring only the background, it's a good idea to make sure the foreground subject bleeds off the bottom of the picture, even if it means cropping the image. Otherwise, if the subject is standing on the ground, it can be very tricky to make the transition from the in-focus ground at the feet of the subject to the out-of-focus background.

1 Making and saving selections. Select the subject using the appropriate Photoshop tools or commands. (For help in choosing a selection method, see "Choosing a Selection Method" in Chapter 1.) For this image **1a** we used the lasso to make the selection, then stored the selection as an alpha channel **1b** by clicking on the Save Selection As Channel button at the bottom of the Channels palette (to open the palette, choose Window, Channels). The stored selection would be useful later (at step 4) in making the selection of the sailor alone.

2 Making a separate subject layer. At this point, to avoid confusion later in the process, rename the *Background*. We double-clicked the *Background* thumbnail in the Layers palette which opened the New Layer dialog box. There we could rename it "Original Image," since the next steps in the process would involve add-

2a

The photo was duplicated as another layer and the two layers were renamed.

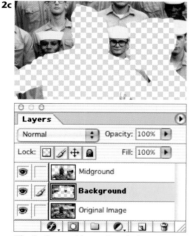

2b

Make a new layer by selecting the subject and cutting it out of the Background layer. By holding down the Alt/Option key as you choose from the menu or use the keyboard shortcut, you get the chance to name the layer as you create it.

2c

The Background layer viewed alone, complete with "hole" and ready for blurring

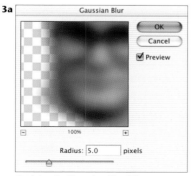

3a

Applying the Gaussian Blur filter

ing a layer to isolate the background of the photo, and we wanted to identify this first layer as the original.

To make separate layers for the subject and the background, first duplicate the image by Alt/Option-dragging the layer's name to the Create A New Layer button at the bottom of the Layers palette; this creates the duplicate layer and also lets you name it. We named the new layer "Background," since this is what it would soon contain **2a.**

Next cut the subject out of the new Background layer as follows: If the selection of the subject is no longer active, load the alpha channel for the subject by Ctrl/⌘-clicking its thumbnail in the Channels palette. To cut the subject to a layer of its own and at the same time open the New Layer dialog box so you can name it, hold down the Alt/Option key and choose Layer, New, Layer Via Cut **2b** (or press Alt-Ctrl-Shift-J on Windows, or Option-⌘-Shift-J on the Mac). We named our new layer "Midground," in anticipation of adding a blurred foreground later at steps 4 and 5.

You now have three layers: a top layer with the subject and no background, a Background layer beneath it with a "hole" where the subject used to be, and the full Original Image underneath **2c.** The hole will prevent colors from the subject from "smearing" into the background area, which would happen if you blurred the Background layer (as described in the next step) *without* cutting the hole. As it is, the hole itself will blur outward, so the edge of the hole will become semi-transparent. This would leave a partly clear "halo" around the subject, except that the Original Image underneath will show through and fill in the semi-transparent area.

3 Blurring the background. To blur the Background, first click its thumbnail in the Layers Palette to make it the active layer; then choose Filter, Blur, Gaussian Blur **3a.** We used a Radius of 5 pixels for this 1000-pixel-wide image to get the degree of blurring we wanted **3b.**

In some cases the image-editing will be complete at this point, with a sharp subject — in this photo the interaction between the officer and the sailor — emphasized against an out-of-focus background. Steps 4 and 5 change the focus of attention to the officer alone by blurring the sailor also. And step 6 adds back the film grain that was lost when parts of this grainy image were blurred.

4 Selecting the foreground for blurring. Next you'll select the area of the foreground that you want to be out-of-focus. To select the sailor we loaded the alpha channel made in step 1 and subtracted the officer from the selection — to subtract from an active selection, choose a selection tool, hold down the Alt/Option key, and select (or choose the tool and then click the Subtract From Selection button in the selection tool's Options bar and select) **4a.** We preserved the new selection as an alpha channel for safekeeping and also kept the selection active **4b** (the method is described in step 2).

To make a new foreground layer, your selection will probably have to be modified further in order to make the blurred foreground look

3b

After blurring the background. Top: Viewing only the Midground and Background layers shows the "halo" caused by the blurring of the hole in the Background. Bottom: With all layers in view, the Original Image layer fills in the semi-transparent edge of the hole.

4a

Click the Subtract From Selection button in the Options bar (or hold down the Alt/Option key). You can then lasso parts of the selection that you want to remove, in this case leaving the sailor alone.

4b

A new alpha channel created from the selection of the sailor in the foreground

4c

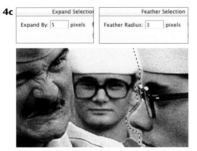

The selection of the sailor was expanded by 5 pixels so that blurring would not make his profile partly transparent. Feathering the expanded selection ensured that there would not be a visible edge between the blurred foreground and the midground and background behind it.

right in the composite. We knew that blurring the foreground area (which we were about to put on its own layer) would make its edge semi-transparent (as described for the hole in the background in step 3). We wanted to make sure the edge of the sailor's face wouldn't be removed when the blurred Background layer showed through, so we expanded the selection outward (as described in the next paragraph) so the sailor's profile would remain intact though blurred.

To expand our selection of the sailor by a few pixels more than the blur we would use, we chose Select, Modify, Expand, 5 pixels. We then softened the edge of the selection by choosing Select, Feather, with a Radius of 3 pixels **4c.** Once your selection is modified, target the Original Image layer in the Layers palette. Then duplicate the selected area as a layer of its own: Choose, Layer, New, Layer Via Copy; or press Alt-Ctrl-J (Windows) or Option-⌘-J (Mac). Name the new layer "Foreground" and drag it to the top of the palette **4d.**

5 Blurring the foreground. Now blur the new foreground layer, but less than you did the background, as if the camera had been focused on the officer with a very short depth of field; we applied a 3-pixel blur to the new layer (Filter, Blur, Gaussian Blur) **5a.** Inspect the image **5b.** If the edge of your subject doesn't look right, you can delete this layer by Alt/Option-clicking the trash can button at the bottom of the Layers palette; then load the alpha channel you saved at the beginning of step 4 (Ctrl/⌘-click its name in the Channels palette) and repeat the process of expanding and feathering the selection (using new numbers) and duplicating the selected area of the Original Image to a new layer.

6 Restoring film grain. At this point the blurred background and foreground had succeeded in focusing attention on the officer, but our trickery was obvious because the blurring had not only smoothed out the details but had also obliterated the pronounced film grain in this photo. We decided to treat the blurred Foreground and Background layers by creating a Layer Style consisting only of a Pattern Overlay of noise, to imitate film grain.

4d

Selecting the sailor from the Original Image layer and copying it to a new layer produced a separate layer for blurring.

5a

Blurring the foreground layer

5b

The image after the Foreground layer is blurred

6a

To put film grain back into the blurred layers, a Layer Style was added. We used a Pattern Overlay, choosing the Wow–Noise Small Strong Color Pattern (from the Wow 7–Noise Patterns Presets.

6b

The Pattern Overlay with Adjusted Blend Mode, Opacity, and Scale

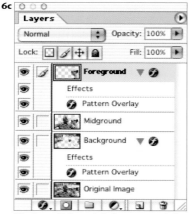

6c

The Layer Style created above was copied and pasted from the Foreground layer to the Background layer as well.

Before adding a Style to a layer, first make sure all the Wow Presets are loaded. Then target the foreground layer where you want to apply the film grain. Next select Pattern Overlay from the Layer Styles pop-up menu at the bottom of the Layers palette and click the little arrow on the right edge of the current picker. From there, click on the arrow in the upper right corner of the picker to load the Wow 7–Noise Patterns. Choose Wow–Noise Small Strong Color Pattern **6a**; now the Blending Mode, Opacity and Scale can be adjusted so the noise pattern will more closely match our film grain target. For this specific photo, the Overlay Blend Mode was used (Soft Light could work as well) Opacity was set to 75% and the scale to 150%. These adjustments tweaked the noise pattern just enough to pass for film grain **6b.**

One of the nice aspects of using a Layer Style for this technique was that once we created a film grain style that we liked, we could copy and paste it to the other layer that needed it. To do this, just right-click (or Ctrl/click on a Mac with a single button mouse) on the Style icon on the layer that you like, and choose Copy Layer Style from the context sensitive menu that appears. Now select the layer where you would like to apply this effect (in this case our Background layer) and repeat the menu shortcut, this time selecting Paste Layer Style from the menu **6c.**

To open a context-sensitive menu of the changes you can make to a Layer Style that has been applied to any layer, right-click (or Control-click if you have a Mac with a one-button mouse) directly on the "*f*" icon that appears to the right of the layer's name in the Layers palette. This menu contains all but one of the choices you would get if you chose Layer, Layer Style (Scale, Copy, Paste, and so on). The exception is Blending Options; to get to this choice directly, double-click the "*f*."

A quick and easy way to focus attention on a subject is to simply select it with the Rectangular Marquee tool, copy the selected area to make a new layer (Ctrl/⌘-J), and then blur the *Background* layer. For added emphasis, add a barely noticeable dark "halo" around the sharp area using a Layer Style (click the Create A Layer Style button — the "*f*" — at the bottom of the Layers palette; choose Drop Shadow from the pop-up list of effects and change the Distance setting to 0 pixels, which will put the shadow directly under the subject instead of offsetting it).

Coloring a Black-&-White Photo

Overview *Convert a grayscale image file to RGB; choose a few colors to use for hand-tinting and make a new layer for each color; paint the areas of the photo that you want to color; adjust the balance of the colors by controlling the opacity and blend mode of each color layer; create a layer set so you can also control the intensity of all the colors as a group.*

"Coloring B&W" "before" and "after" files

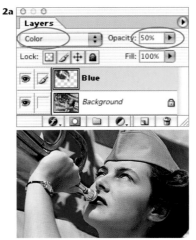

1

The original black-and-white photo

2a

A layer was added in Color mode at 50% Opacity, and was painted with the Airbrush in Normal mode at a low Pressure setting.

FROM VERY EARLY IN THE HISTORY OF PHOTOGRAPHY, photo-tinting specialists used paints and dyes to color black-and-white photos. The popularity of hand-colored photos decreased when color photography became widespread, but today the look is popular again — not a technicolor imitation of a color photo, but a subtle coloring reminiscent of the early hand-tinting processes. In Photoshop 7, using a separate layer for applying each color will give you a great deal of flexibility in controlling how each color interacts with the black-and-white image.

1 Preparing the photo. If your photo has been scanned and stored as a grayscale image, start by converting it to RGB (Image, Mode, RGB Color). The image's appearance won't change, but it will now have the potential for color **1**. (If your image is in color to begin with, the most controlled way to remove the color is by using the Channel Mixer, as described on page 99; alternative quick conversion methods are also described there.) If necessary, use Photoshop's Levels or Curves command to spread the tones to improve the tonality of the image or to bring out highlight or shadow detail.

2 Layering the color. Choose a few colors to use in the tinting process. We chose six main colors and isolated them in the Swatches palette (see "Collecting Your Colors" on page 145.)

As you work, you'll create a new layer for each of the colors you want to use. When tinting, you'll want to keep the original luminosity (darks and lights) of the image as you add color. A good way to do this is to put each of the layers in Color mode. This will ensure that you won't get any hard-edged, opaque-looking patches of color. Also, since you want to leave yourself the flexibility to

2b

The blue layer viewed alone, showing the loose application of color

2c

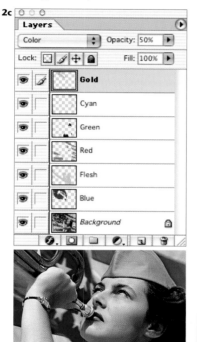

The painting with all colors in place and all layers in Color mode

2d

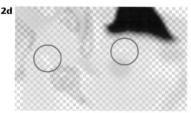

The color layers, viewed without the photo, showing the "holes" (circled above) erased for the watch face and the eyes . Notice also that because the layer is in Color mode and the cap was a light gray in the original photo, a thick application of dark green added only a little color to the cap. In contrast, a thin application of red makes the stripe in the flag quite intense, since this area was dark gray in the original.

COLLECTING YOUR COLORS

To make a limited set of colors easy to pick out as you work, store them together at the end of the Swatches palette: Choose Window, Show Swatches to open the palette. For each color, click on the palette to choose it, and then move the cursor to the empty space at the end of the palette's color samples. The cursor will become a paint bucket and you can click to "pour" the color into a new swatch.

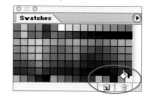

either increase *or* reduce color later, you can start with each layer at less than full opacity. To add the layer and set its blend mode and opacity at the same time, Alt/Option-click the Create New Layer icon at the bottom of the Layers palette to open the New Layer dialog box. Set the Mode to Color and the Opacity to 50%, and click OK.

To add color on the layer you've just created, choose the Paint Brush tool and check the Airbrush option. In the Options bar leave the Mode setting at the default Normal, and choose a soft brush from the pop-out Brush palette. Set the Pressure low for the most control, since the Airbrush works by building up color the longer you leave it in one place. You can set the Airbrush Pressure even lower if you find you need more control once you start to apply the color: Use the number keys to reset the Pressure percentage as you paint. You can type a single digit ("1"–"9" for 10%–90%, or "0" for 100%), or, if you're quick, type two digits (for example, "15" for 15%).

Paint with one of the colors you chose **2a**. In general, the darker the gray in the area where you apply color, the more intense the color will be.

As you paint, don't worry about perfect edges or perfectly uniform coverage. In traditional hand-tinting, the dyes weren't applied perfectly either **2b**.

With each color on a separate layer **2c**, it's easy to use the Eraser tool in Airbrush mode (set in the Options bar) to fix color overlaps or remove color in certain areas — in this case removing the skin tint from the watch and the eyes, for instance **2d**.

SETTING THE BLEND MODE

When you want to apply paint in Color mode (or Overlay, Difference, or some other blend mode), you'll get the same initial result whether you set the blend mode for the layer to Color and the blend mode for the painting tool to Normal, or vice versa. But for flexibility, it's better to use Color mode for the *layer* rather than the tool because you can change it later via the Layers palette if you need to.

If you put the layer in Normal mode instead and use Color for the tool's mode (through the Options bar), it will be harder to know how to make changes later. That's because, unlike the blend mode for the layer, which is clearly labeled and easy to change in the Layers palette, your many separate brush strokes will bear no record of the mode you used when you applied them.

3a

We gave the trumpet a metallic look by changing the blend mode of the Gold layer to Overlay and increasing the Opacity to 75%.

3b

Adjusting the Opacity of the individual layers balanced the colors.

4a

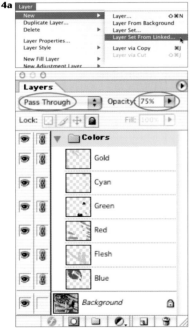

Linking the color layers and collecting them in a set in Pass Through mode allowed us to maintain the balance we had achieved, as we easily reduced the color intensity overall by lowering the set's Opacity to 75%. (Notice that the thumbnails of the layers are indented in the Layers palette to show that they are part of the set named "Colors.")

3 Balancing the colors.
When the color layers are complete, go back to the individual layers and make adjustments: To increase the brilliance of metallic objects, try changing the color layer's blend mode to Overlay, which boosts contrast and saturation **3a**. Also, adjust the Opacity of each layer to taste. To balance color intensity in our image, we reduced the Opacity of the Blue and Red layers and increased the Opacity of the Gold and Green **3b**.

4 Making a layer set. Once your colors are balanced, you may want the option to intensify or reduce the color overall, after the client looks at a proof, or for different output options. In that case you can group the color layers together in a set, and then control the color intensity with the set's Opacity slider: With one of the color layers targeted in the Layers palette, link the other layers to it by clicking in the Links column (just to the right of the Eye column) for each of the other color layers. (To target a whole stack of layers, you can just drag the cursor up or down the links column instead of clicking each one separately.) Next group the linked layers into a set by choosing Layer, New, Layer Set From Linked (or choose New Set From Linked in the Layers palette's pop-out menu).

In the New Set From Linked dialog box, choose Pass Through for the Mode, so the blend modes of the individual layers will not change when the layers are gathered in the set. Name the set if you like (we called ours "Colors") and click OK **4a**. When all the color layers are in the set, you can still control the intensity of each individual color (by means of its layer's Opacity slider). You can also change the intensity of all the colors together (with the Opacity slider for the set) **4b**.

4b

This detail from the final image (shown at the top of page 144) shows the overall reduction in color produced by lowering the Opacity of the Colors set.

CUTTING UP LAYERS
If you've set up your hand-tinting file with one color per layer, you may find that you want separate control over the blend mode and opacity of individual color "patches" on a single layer. For instance, you might have used a yellow color layer to tint both metallic and nonmetallic objects. In that case you could select the metallic items (with the Lasso or Rectangular Marquee, for instance) and move them to a separate layer by pressing Ctrl /⌘-Shift-J (which is the shortcut for Layer, New, Layer Via Cut). Then for a metallic look you could put this layer in Overlay mode and increase its opacity, leaving the original layer in Color mode.

JHD / MODEL: LATISHA TOLBERT / AGENCY: ANDERSON PHOTOGRAPHICS.COM

To edit this original portrait **A,** **Jack Davis** decided to combine three different effects to draw the viewer into the focal point of the photograph — the model's eyes. First, Davis wanted to do a quick Dodge & Burn treatment on the image to increase the contrast between the background and the hair, and to lighten the area around the eyes. To do this he Alt/Option-clicked on the New Layer icon at the bottom of the Layers palette, and in the dialog that opened he selected Overlay as the Blend Mode, and clicked the "Fill with Overlay–neutral color (50% Gray)" check box **B.** The resulting gray-filled layer had no effect on the Background below because of this Overlay Blend Mode, until Davis started painting on this layer with a large, soft-edged paint

brush set to a low opacity (5%) with black or white. By changing areas of this layer to something other than exactly 50% gray, he was able to rapidly darken or lighten the image where he wanted **C** without worrying about changing his original below (see "Softening the Focus" on page 130 for more on this technique).

Next, Davis experimented with reducing the color photo to monochrome by adding a Channel Mixer Adjustment Layer. By selecting Monochrome within the dialog **D** and balancing the mix of the contribution of the original's red, green, and blue channels, he could completely customize the look of the resulting "black-and-white" photo (see "From Color to Gray" on page 98 for more on Channel mixing).

Finally, he chose to take advantage of the Channel Mixer's built-in Layer Mask to selectively "reveal" some of the color of the adjusted image below. Davis clicked on the Mask thumbnail portion of the Channel Mixer Adjustment in the Layers palette **E,** and painted with light gray over the area of the model's hair and eyes. By Alt/Option-clicking on the mask thumbnail, he could toggle on and off a view of the mask as he worked **F.** The resulting "recoloring" framed the face of the woman with the hair, and locked the viewer onto the eyes, where the shared experience of the photograph occurs.

Susan Thompson creates her impressionistic images by shooting the photos with a vintage 1972 SX-70, the first Polaroid camera to use film with the dye encapsulated under a protective sheet of clear mylar. For about two hours after the image is shot, the dyes are fluid and can be rearranged by applying pressure. Thompson can see her images developing as she uses chopsticks, toothpicks, and other tools to swirl the dyes and "etch" lines in the photos. When the physical manipulation process is done, Thompson scans the image at about 170 MB and then uses many of Photoshop's Image, Adjust commands — Levels, Curves, Color Balance, Selective Color, and Variations — to digitally remaster the manipulated images to the colors she prefers. Her color adjustments can also make up for less-than-optimal lighting conditions when the photograph was

made, and can restore color intensity lost in the manipulation process. Whenever possible, she applies these changes by means of Adjustment layers so she can work interactively, balancing the changes made by the various commands.

The rich colors of *Grapes* (above) were achieved as follows: Starting with her scan (left), Thompson applied a Levels adjustment globally, moving the Input Levels black and white sliders inward a little to increase contrast and deepen the intensity of the colors. This adjustment pushed the background too far toward white, so she used the History Brush to restore the original subtle colors. (For tips on using the History Brush, see page 122.) Thompson used Selective Color Adjustment layers to saturate the greens in the leaves and some of the grapes, and the blues and magentas in other grapes.

To get the result she wanted for *Pancho's Surf Shop,* **Susan Thompson** wanted to remove the yellow cast from the car in the original image (left) but at the same time enrich the yellow in the surfboards on the roof. She used a Levels Adjustment layer to remove the yellow cast in the shadows and increase the contrast in the gray tones. ▶ *As a default, clicking the Auto button in the Levels dialog box adjusts the Input Levels for each of the color channels, so it can remove a color cast as well as increase contrast.*

To target other color changes, Thompson used Selective Color Adjustment layers, using masks made as follows: Each mask was started by selecting loosely with the Lasso tool. Thompson then converted to Quick Mask mode (this can be done by clicking the Quick Mask icon in the Tools palette or by pressing the "Q" key). She modified the Quick Mask with the

Paintbrush and a hard-edged brush tip using black to add to the mask material and white to add to the clear area. The edges were then softened by blurring the mask (Filter, Blur, Gaussian Blur). ▶ *You can turn a Quick Mask into an Adjustment layer mask by pressing "Q" to leave Quick Mask mode and convert the Quick Mask to a selection, then clicking the Create New Fill/Adjustment Layer button at the bottom of the Layers palette and choosing the type of adjustment you want.*

Thompson also used the Variations command (Image, Adjust, Variations) to add magenta to the highlights and blue and cyan to the midtones of selected areas; the Fine setting in the Variations dialog box allowed subtle adjustments.

Both *Pancho's Surf Shop* and *Grapes* (opposite) were output as numbered-edition Giclée prints on Somerset Velvet paper in three sizes by Harvest Productions in Placentia, California.

COMBINING IMAGES

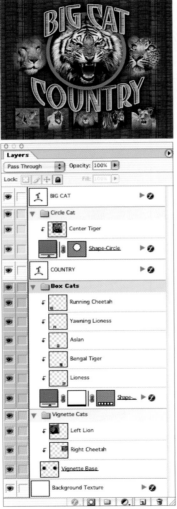

With live type, multiple masking techniques, and Layer Styles, "collaging" in Photoshop 7 is easily achieved. The image above is a variation of the technique presented step-by-step in "Collaging with Masks & Groups" on page 185.

IN TRADITIONAL PHOTOGRAPHY and photo-illustration, *montage* is a method of making a single photographic print by superimposing several negatives. *Collage* is the assembly of separate photos mounted together, sometimes with other nonphotographic elements. With Photoshop, the distinction between montage and collage breaks down. Layers containing photos, illustrations, original painting, and even type and graphics can easily be combined into a single image or an entire page layout, without the use of a darkroom or glue.

Some of Photoshop 7's most useful compositing techniques involve the following tools, commands, and settings:

- With the **Move tool** you can slide layers around until you're happy with the composition. Photoshop even preserves the parts of layers that you move outside the margins of the canvas. So if you change your mind, the entire element will still exist and you can move it back into the image frame.

- The **Clone Stamp** and **Pattern Stamp** can copy image material from one part of the composite and repeat it in another area, as shown in the "Making an 'Object Stamp'" tip on page 259.

- The soft edges of **feathered selections** allow images to blend into one another.

- The **Extract command** excels at making clean selections of elements with difficult organic edges, such as hair. You'll find an example of its use in "Extracting an Image" on page 162.

- In the Layers palette the **Opacity** setting can be adjusted to give layers a "ghosted" look.

continued on page 152

FEATHERING

You can make a feathered (soft-edged) selection in any of the following ways:

- Choose a selection tool and set the Feather radius in the Options bar before you select.

- Make the selection and then choose Select, Feather (or press Ctrl-Alt-D in Windows or ⌘-Option-D on the Mac) and set the Feather Radius.

- Make the selection and convert it to a Quick Mask (press the "Q" key). Then blur the mask (Filter, Blur, Gaussian Blur) and convert back to a selection (press "Q"). This is **the only way to interactively preview the feather** so you can see how soft the edge will be.

- If you're making a selection from a path, you can activate the path in the Paths palette and then Alt/Option-click the Load Path As Selection button at the bottom of the palette and set the Feather Radius.

The Overlay blend mode and a layer mask are two of the essential ingredients in applying the flag to the rock face in "Wrapping a 'Decal'" on page 194.

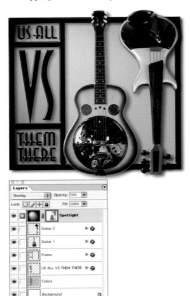

The Lighting Effects filter (applied to a gray-filled, masked top layer) was used to reinforce the lighting in the two original photos and in the layer Styles that had been applied to the various elements in this composite. The compositing process is presented step-by-step in "Combining with Light" on page 220 in Chapter 5.

- The **blend mode** of a layer controls the way colors from that layer affect the layers below. Blend modes are demonstrated in Chapter 2.

- **Masks** on layers — which can be either pixel-based *layer masks* or vector-based *vector masks* — can be used to control which parts of a layer are hidden or revealed as part of the composite image. You'll find examples of the use of masks in most of the techniques covered in the book, and "Quick Masking & Blending" starting on page 160 shows effective techniques for blending images with layer masks.

- In **clipping groups,** one layer acts as a mask for the layers above it. One powerful use of a clipping group is to mask an image (or some other pixel-based fill such as a gradient or pattern) inside live type. This technique is covered in "Blending Images & Type" on page 168.

- **"Blend If"** options are available through the Blending Options section of the Layer Style dialog box. They provide sophisticated "masking" controls based on color and tone. You'll find more about how they work in "Blending Options" on page 156.

Many image-compositing functions can be controlled via the Layers palette. Some of the important ones are identified on page 153.

CHOOSING AND PREPARING COMPONENTS

One requirement for creating a successful "seamless" photo montage, when that's your goal, is making sure that you choose component images that match in several important respects. For example, the light should be coming from the same direction, the color and amount of detail in the shadows and highlights should be about the same, and the "graininess" of the images should match. Some of these factors are more important than others:

- **Highlight and shadow detail can be manipulated** by using Curves and Levels, either as commands or as the more flexible Adjustment layers.

- A **color cast** — in a shadow, for instance— can be identified with the RGB or CMYK readings in the Info window (you can choose Window, Show Info to open it, or use the F8 default keyboard shortcut). Then the color cast **can be adjusted** — with Curves, Levels, or Color Balance.

- **Changing the direction of the light can be much more difficult** than managing shadow detail or color cast. If the elements you want to blend are fairly flat (like pictures on a wall), you may get good results with either the Lighting Effects filter or the Bevel And Emboss effect in a Layer Style. For instance, if the final effect you're looking for will tolerate it, you may be able to "overpower" the varied "native" lighting of the elements of a composite image by applying the same lighting effect to all the parts.

continued on page 154

Each layer has a **blend mode** that determines how the pixels on that layer affect the color of pixels below.

Reducing the **Opacity** of a layer below 100% allows the image below to show through.

The **Fill** percentage only affects the opacity of the Color, Gradient and Pattern Overlay portions of an applied Layer Style.

Any layer except the Background can have a layer mask, a vector mask, and a Layer Style. A **vector mask** is a vector-based, hard-edged mask whose shape reveals part of a layer and hides the rest.

A **Layer Style** is a set of editable effects that are applied to the layer. Some layer effects, such as the Drop Shadow, can be very useful in combining images.

A **layer mask** is a pixel-based, grayscale mask that reveals some parts of a layer and hides others.

You can use **color coding** to show that certain layers are related.

Linked layers can be moved or transformed together.

A **Shape layer** consists of a solid fill with a built-in vector mask.

Visibility can be toggled on and off for viewing all or just some of the layers in a composite.

The **Background** is a nontransparent bottom layer that establishes the canvas size (or boundaries) for an image. It can't have masks or a Layer Style.

Four toggle buttons in the **Lock** line allow you to protect a layer from change. From left to right, they lock transparent pixels, image pixels, position, and "all of the above."

A **Type layer** (plain or warped) is "live" and editable. It can be masked, and it can be included in a clipping group.

Collapsible **layer sets** can be useful for keeping the palette manageable as the number of layers grows. Masks on a layer set affect all the layers in the set.

A **clipping group** consists of a bottom layer that "clips" the other layers in the group so they are revealed only within the shape established by the image or masks or the clipping layer.

An **Adjustment layer** contains instructions for changing the color or tone of layers below it. Its effect can be targeted with masks, and it can be part of a clipping group. Adjustment layers can be useful in unifying color and lighting in a composite image.

A **Fill** layer applies a Solid Color, Pattern, or Gradient. It has a built-in layer mask.

Layers

Normal   Opacity: 100%

Lock: Fill: 100%

BIG CAT

Center Tiger

Effects
Inner Shadow
Outer Glow
Stroke

COUNTRY

Side Cats

Left Lion

Right Cheetah

Bottom Cats

Running Cheetah

Yawning Lioness

Aslan

Bengal Tiger

Lioness

Shape-Boxes

Background Elements

Shape - ©

Hue/Saturation 1

Pattern Fill 1

Background

Add A Layer Style

Create A New Set

Delete

Add A Mask

Create New Fill/ Adjustment Layer

Create A New (transparent) Layer

To make changes to a layer mask, click the mask thumbnail. An outline around the thumbnail and a little mask icon will show that the mask is active. You'll still be viewing the image rather than the mask, but any painting, filtering or other changes you make will affect the mask, not the layer.

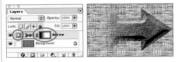

To make a *layer mask* visible instead of the image, Alt/Option-click the mask thumbnail. Alt/Option-click again to make the image visible again.

To see and edit the outline of a *vector mask* at the same time you're viewing the layer *or* the layer mask, click the thumbnail for the vector mask. An outline appears around the thumbnail and the path appears on-screen. You can then change the path with the Shape or Pen tools or with one of the Transform commands. Click the thumbnail again to turn off the outline.

To turn a layer mask or vector mask off temporarily so it has no effect, Shift-click the mask thumbnail. An "X" on the thumbnail shows that the mask is turned off. Shift-click again to turn it back on.

You can see examples of this in "Combining with Light" on page 220. You can also dodge and burn to create highlights and shadows (a nondestructive "dodging and burning" method is described in step 5 of "Blending a Panorama" on page 180). But if quick Lighting Effects or dodging and burning fixes won't work, you'll generally get better results if you continue your search for photos whose lighting matches, rather than trying to make further adjustments to correct the lighting.

- **Film grain can be simulated,** starting with the Add Noise filter, as described in step 4 of "Blending Images & Type'" on page 168 and step 6 of "Blurring the Background but Keeping the Grain" on page 140.

LAYER MASKS AND VECTOR MASKS

Each layer in a Photoshop file, except a *Background* at the bottom of the stack, can have two kinds of "masks" for hiding or revealing parts of the layer without permanently changing the actual pixels or type on the layer. Instead of erasing or cutting away part of an image, you can leave it intact but block it with a *layer mask* or a *vector mask*. There are some important differences between layer masks and vector masks.

A **layer mask** is a pixel-based, grayscale mask that can have up to 256 shades of gray, from white to black. Where the mask is white, it's transparent, and it allows the image on its layer to show through and contribute to the composite. Where the mask is black, it's opaque, and the corresponding portion of the image is blocked (masked out). Gray areas are partly transparent — the lighter the gray, the more transparent — and the corresponding pixels in the layer's image make a semitransparent contribution to the composite. A layer mask affects only its own layer — it doesn't mask the layers above or below, unless it's on the bottom layer of a clipping group

With a selection active, adding a layer mask by clicking the Add A Mask button makes a mask that *reveals* the selected area and hides the rest. In contrast, Alt/Option-clicking makes a mask that *hides* the selected area and reveals the rest. You can also make either kind of mask by choosing Layer, Add Layer Mask, Reveal, or Hide Selection.

You can create a vector mask to reveal the area inside the path by choosing a Pen or Shape tool and clicking the Add to Path Area button in the Options bar, then Ctrl/⌘-clicking the Add A Mask button, or by using the New Layer, Add Vector Mask menu option.

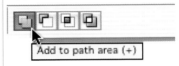

To *hide* the area inside the path, click the Subtract From Path Area button before Ctrl/⌘-clicking Add A Mask.

If the thumbnails for both the layer mask and the vector mask have borders around them as shown here, then both are active and ready to edit. If you choose a pixel-based tool such as the Paintbrush, Gradient, or Smudge tool, you'll automatically be working on the layer mask. If you choose one of the Shape tools or the Pen tool, your changes will show up on the vector mask. (Chapter 6 tells how to use the painting tools and Chapter 7 the drawing tools.)

A layer can be added to a clipping group at the time the layer is created by holding down the Alt/Option key while clicking the New Layer icon.

(as described below) or unless it's applied to a layer set, as described on page 336. You can **create a layer mask by clicking the Add A Mask button** at the bottom of the Layers palette. To make a mask that hides instead of reveals the selected area, Alt/Option-click.

As the name implies, a **vector mask** (previously referred to as a layer clipping path in Photoshop 6) is vector-based. Like other paths in Photoshop, it's resolution-independent so it can be resized, rotated, skewed, and otherwise transformed repeatedly without the deterioration you would see if you subjected a layer mask to the same contortions. And it creates a smooth outline when the file is output to a PostScript printer, regardless of the resolution (dpi) of the file. However, since it's vector-based, it has crisp edges and doesn't have the capacity for softness or partial transparency in the parts of the layer it reveals. Like a layer mask, a vector mask doesn't mask the layers above unless it's on the bottom layer of a clipping group or on a layer set. You can **create a vector mask by Ctrl/ ⌘-clicking the Add A Mask button** at the bottom of the Layers palette, or by using the New Layer, Add a Vector Mask menu option. The "Revealing or Hiding" tip on page 154 tells how to control what your new mask reveals and what it hides.

When a layer mask or vector mask is created, Photoshop assumes that the next thing you'll want to do is edit it. So the mask — rather than the image part of the layer — becomes active. Meanwhile, three things happen in the Layers palette to tell you how the mask relates to the image in the layer:

• A **thumbnail** appears to the right of the image thumbnail. The *layer mask* thumbnail shows the grayscale content of the layer mask. The *vector mask* thumbnail shows the area hidden by the layer clipping path (in gray) and the "revealed" area (in white), with the path (a black outline) separating them.

One way to mask an element inside part of an existing image is to use the Edit, **Paste Into** command: Select and copy (Ctrl/⌘-C) the element you want to paste, then activate the layer you want to paste into (by clicking its name in the Layers palette). Make a selection of the area where you want to paste, and choose Edit, Paste Into. The pasted element will come in as a new layer, complete with a layer mask that lets it show only within the area you selected.

If you hold down the Alt/Option key as you choose Paste Into, the effect will be to **Paste Behind** instead. Keyboard shortcuts are Ctrl/⌘-Shift-V for Paste Into and Ctrl-Alt-Shift-V (Windows) or ⌘-Option-Shift-V (Mac) for Paste Behind.

Typically, when you add a layer mask, the image and mask are linked, so moving or transforming the image moves or transforms the mask, too. But when you use Paste Into (as shown here) or Paste Behind, the mask and image are unlinked by default. That way you can move the image around, resize it, or make other transformations and still keep it "inside" or "behind" the selected area.

By creating a clipping group with a type layer as the bottom layer, you can mask a photo or hand-painted image inside the type and still keep the type "live," editable, and resolution-independent.

Using the Blending Options can be an important early step in developing a composite. Here the pixels of the hand layer are hidden where they overlap the light pixels in the clouds image. The slider is split (by Alt/Option-dragging) to make a smooth transition between the clouds and the hand. The Blending Options process is described in step 2b of "Blending Images & Type" on page 168.

- A **link icon** appears to the left of the mask thumbnail, to show that if you move or scale or otherwise transform the layer or the mask, the other one will move or be transformed along with it. (To move or transform the layer or mask separately, you can unlink by clicking to turn off the link icon.)

- In the case of a **vector mask,** a **mask icon** also appears in the narrow column next to the Eye (visibility) column to let you know that whatever you do will be done to the mask instead of the image. (The mask icon replaces the paintbrush icon that otherwise tells you that the image, not the mask, is targeted.)

- In the case of **a vector mask,** a **vertical line** also appears to the left of the link icon. It tells you that anything represented by the thumbnails to the left of the line will be masked by the layer clipping path. This may include the image and layer mask, or the image alone if the layer has no layer mask.

CLIPPING GROUPS

Another nondestructive compositing element, a ***clipping group,*** is a group of layers, the bottom layer of which acts as a mask. The outline of the bottom layer — including pixels and masks — "clips" all the other layers in the group so only the parts that fall within the outline can contribute to the image.

You can make a clipping group by **Alt/Option-clicking on the borderline** between the names of two layers in the Layers palette. The lower layer becomes the clipping mask, and its name is now underlined in the palette. The other layer is clipped; its thumbnails are indented and a down-pointing "tab"-like arrow points to the clipping layer below. To add more clipped layers to the group, you can just work your way up the Layers palette, Alt/Option-clicking more borderlines. (To be members of a clipping group, layers have to be together in the stack. You can't add one, skip one, add the next, and so on.)

A clipping group can also be set up (or added to) when a layer is first added to the stack. To do this, check the Group With Previous Layer box in the New Layer dialog box.

BLENDING OPTIONS

With the sliders in the Blending Options section of the Layer Styles dialog box, you can control how the pixels of the active layer (called "This Layer" in the dialog box) and the image underneath (called "Underlying Layer") will combine in the composite. (The term "Underlaying Layer" is a bit deceptive. It actually refers to the entire underlying image, whether only a single layer is visible or whether the image is made up of a composite of layers.)

The sliders of the **Underlying Layer** bar define what range of colors in the underlying image are available to be hidden by the active layer. So if you wanted to make it so that only the light pixels could be hidden, you would move the dark Underlying Layer slider inward so the darkest tones are outside the range and thus can't be hidden.

To create a clipping group comprised of the active layer and the layer below it, press Ctrl/⌘-G. If there is already a clipping group below, the active layer is added to it.

Ctrl/⌘-Shift-G releases the active layer from the clipping group, along with any other layers above it in the group.

A quick way to make a layer set from existing layers is to link them and then choose New Set From Linked.

Layer sets provide an easy way to "tidy up." With sets closed, the Layers palette takes up less room on-screen. And it can be much easier to locate and work on layers in a multilayer file if other layers are stowed out of sight.

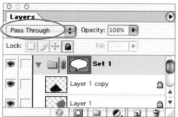

Click the folder in the Layers palette to see the Opacity and blend mode that it contributes to the layers in the set. The Pass Through mode, available only for folders, gives priority to the blend modes of the individual layers in the set. A layer mask or vector mask on a folder affects all layers in the set.

The sliders of the **This Layer** bar determine what range of colors in the active layer will be allowed to show in the composite image. These pixels will *hide* the corresponding underlying pixels if the active layer is in Normal mode, or will *blend* with them if the active layer is in some other blend mode. So if you want only the dark pixels of the active layer to show, move the white slider for This Layer inward so the light pixels are outside the range.

Together, the two sliders set up a sort of "If . . . then" proposition for each pixel in the underlying image. If the pixel in the underlying image falls within the range established in the Underlying Layer slider bar *and* the corresponding active-layer pixel falls within the range established in the This Layer slider bar, then the active layer's pixel is shown. Otherwise, the underlying pixel is left as it is, and the active one is ignored.

Holding down the Alt/Option key as you drag a slider will allow you to split the slider. This lets you smooth the transition by defining a range of colors that are only partially visible.

LAYER SETS AND LAYER COLORS

Photoshop 7 offers two features for organizing layers — sets and color coding. The **layer set** lets you collect layers into a "folder."

- You can collect existing layers in a set by targeting one of the layers in the Layers palette, then clicking (or dragging) in the column next to the Eye for all the other layers you want in the set (this will link these layers), and then choosing New Set From Linked from the palette's pop-out menu.

- You can add more layers to an existing set by dragging the layer thumbnails to the folder's thumbnail, or directly to the position where you want the layer in the stack.

- You can add a brand-new layer to a set by targeting the folder in the Layers palette and then clicking the Create A New Layer button at the bottom of the palette.

By clicking the little triangle to the left of the folder in the Layers palette, you can hide or show the list of layers inside the set. In a file with many layers, closing a set can make your Layers palette more compact, which makes it easier to locate and work with other layers.

A layer set also lets you control certain layer attributes for the entire set at once. The Opacity and blend mode for the folder don't replace the settings for the individual layers, they interact with them:

- **The folder's Opacity is a multiplier** for the Opacity of each layer in the set. At 100%, the folder's Opacity setting makes no change to the look of the composite. Below 100% the folder's Opacity reduces the opacity of the layers proportionally. So, for instance if you have a set with some layers at 50% Opacity and some at 80%, if you reduce the folder's Opacity to 50%, the cumulative effect is that some layers are now only 25% opaque (50% of 50% is 25%) and some are 40% opaque (50% of 80% is 40%).

To delete an entire layer set, drag the folder to the trash can button at the bottom of the Layers palette. Or target the folder in the Layers palette, click the trash can button, and when the caution box appears, click the **Set And Contents** button.

To keep the layers but toss the folder (so the layers are no longer in a set), target the folder, click on the trash can button, and click the **Set Only** button.

To move a layer set so that all its component layers move together, target the folder in the Layers palette, choose the Move tool, and then do one of the following:

• If all the layers in the layer set are linked, simply drag in the image window to move the set.

• If some of the layers in the set are *not* linked, *turn off the Auto Select Layer option* in the Move tool's Options bar and drag in the image window to move the set.

To transform a layer set with the Free Transform command (Ctrl/⌘-T) or any of the individual Transform commands, the folder has to be linked to at least one layer — either inside or outside the set.

• **The folder's default blend mode is Pass Through,** which simply means that each layer in the set keeps its own blend mode, the same as if it weren't in the set. If you choose any other blend mode for the folder, the result is as if you had merged all the set's layers (with their existing blend modes) into a single layer and then applied the folder's blend mode to the merged image.

A folder can't have image content of its own. In this respect it's simply a container for its layers. But a folder can have its own layer

In Photoshop 7 the terms *link*, *group*, and *clip* have more than one meaning, or they mean something different than what they mean in other familiar programs such as QuarkXPress, PageMaker, Illustrator, or InDesign. This can be confusing.

LINKING in Photoshop is a lot like what you can do with grouping in those other programs.

Linked layers. You can link layers to each other by targeting one of them in the Layers palette and clicking in the column next to the Eye for the other. You can also drag in the column to link as many consecutive layers as you like. When layers are linked to one another:

• Moving or otherwise transforming one linked layer also transforms the others.

• Dragging one linked layer from the *working window* and dropping it into another file drags the other linked layers along. However, a drag-and-drop of a layer from the *Layers palette* doesn't bring linked layers with it.

• You can quickly make a layer set that includes all of the linked layers by clicking on one of them in the Layers palette and choosing Layer, New, Layer Set From Linked. (Or choose it from the palette's pop-out menu.)

• Likewise, you can lock or unlock all the linked layers at once by choosing Lock All Linked Layers from the pop-out menu.

• You can also paste the same Layer Style to linked layers by copying the Style from a "donor" layer, then pasting to one of the linked layers.

Linked masks. By default, layer masks and layer clipping paths are linked to their layer. If you move or otherwise transform the layer, you transform the linked mask.

CLIPPING in Photoshop refers to specialized kinds of masking, done by clipping groups and image clipping paths. *GROUPING* can refer to making a clipping group or making a layer set.

Clipping Groups. A clipping group is a stack of associated layers that are all masked by the bottom ("parent") layer in the stack. The outline of the mask is determined by the nontransparent pixels on the parent layer and by the layer mask and vector mask, if any.

Clipping paths (also now called *image clipping paths*). A clipping path is a vector-based path, stored in the Paths palette, which you designate to show only part of your image, making everything outside the clipping path transparent when the image is exported and printed. You can save a clipping path with your file in PDF, DCS, Photoshop EPS, or TIFF format to be placed into another application file and output to a PostScript device.

To open the Layer Properties dialog so you can choose a color code for the active layer, Alt/Option-double-click the Layer's name (not its thumbnail) in the Layers palette.

MERGING OPTIONS

Several options for merging visible layers are available in the Layers palette's pop-out menu and in the main Layer menu. Others are available elsewhere, as noted below:

• **Merge Visible** (**Ctrl/⌘-Shift-E**) combines all visible layers and also keeps all the hidden layers.

• **Merge Down** (**Ctrl/⌘-E**) combines the active layer with the very next layer below it in the stack.

• **Merge Linked** (**Ctrl/⌘-E**) combines the active layer and any visible layers linked to it, discarding any hidden linked layers.

• When the bottom layer of a clipping group is the active layer, **Merge Group** (**Ctrl/⌘-E**) combines all the visible layers of the group, discarding the group's hidden layers.

• When the folder of a layer set is active, **Merge Layer Set** (**Ctrl/⌘-E**) combines all the visible layers of the group, discarding the set's hidden layers.

• Edit, **Copy Merged** (**Ctrl/⌘-Shift-C**) copies the selected area of all visible layers. Then Edit, Paste (Ctrl/⌘-V) can be used to turn the copy into a new layer.

• Image, **Duplicate** offers the **Merged Layers Only** option, which makes a merged copy of the file, discarding invisible layers.

• Unchecking the Layers box in the **Save As** dialog box saves a merged copy of the file.

mask and vector mask. This gives you an easy and efficient way to apply the same mask to several layers at once.

You can't apply a Layer Style to a folder, even if the folder has a layer mask or vector mask of its own. And a folder can't serve as the base for a clipping group. Also, a folder's masks aren't subject to the Layer Styles of the layers in the set.

Unlike a folder, **color coding** has no effect on the layers you apply it to. Its only purpose is to help you visually organize the layers in your Layers palette. You can assign the same color to layers that are somehow related. For example, you might color all the members of a layer set with the same color, so you can quickly see where sets begin and end when they are expanded in the palette. Or use a color to identify all the layers that were duplicated from a single original layer. (When a layer is duplicated, the new copy keeps the same color code.) Or use the same color to identify related elements in several different files. For instance, you might routinely make all "live" type layers yellow so you can quickly identify them when you want to simplify your file by converting them to Shape layers or rasterizing them. You can color-code a layer at the time you create it or afterward:

• When you create a layer, hold down the Alt/Option key as you click the Create A New Layer button at the bottom of the Layers palette; this will open the New Layer dialog, where you can choose a Color.

• To color-code an existing layer, activate it and choose Layer Properties from the Layers palette's pop-out menu.

• When you color a set (in the New Layer Set dialog or the Layer Set Properties dialog), it automatically colors all the layers within the set.

• Right-click on a Layer Eye icon and choose a color from the pop-out menu.

MERGING AND FLATTENING

When you've finished working on a series of layers and you no longer need to keep them separate and "live," you can reduce the number of layers — and the amount of RAM needed for the file — by merging or flattening them. When you merge or flatten a file, Layer Styles and masks are applied and then discarded, and type is rasterized. Alpha channels are retained.

Merging combines visible layers into one layer. The new combined layer takes its blend mode and opacity from the bottom layer of the merging series.

Flattening combines visible layers into a *Background*. A Caution box warns that hidden layers will be discarded, so you can reconsider. Any transparency in the combined image is filled with the current background color. 🖌

Quick Masking & Blending

Layer masks, Blending Options, and clipping groups provide a variety of options for blending images, as shown by the examples on these two pages. Five of the examples were made from a silhouetted hand layered above a cloudscape, with layer masking and Blending Options used to merge the two layers. "Blending Images & Type" on page 168 provides a step-by-step approach to combining several of these masking and blending techniques.

Hand-Cloud "before" file

Gradient Mask

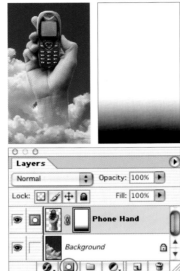

Adding a layer mask (by clicking the Add A Mask button) and filling it with a black-to-white gradient fades the hand into the clouds while keeping both originals intact.

"Blend If" Tonality

Double-clicking to the right of the name of the hand layer in the Layers palette opens the Layer Style dialog box to the Blending Options section. In the "Blend If" area you can adjust the sliders for "This Layer" and "Underlying Layer" to composite the two layers according to the color and tonality of each. Alt/Option-drag to split the sliders for a gradual blending. See "Blending Options" on page 156 for more.

Blurred Mask

To make a layer mask that fades the silhouetted subject at the edges, Ctrl/⌘-click on the subject's thumbnail in the Layers palette, click the Add A Mask button, and run the Gaussian Blur filter on the mask.

Painted Mask

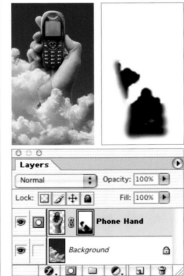

Hand-painting a layer mask allows precise control of how the composite is formed from the two images.

"Blend If" & Mask

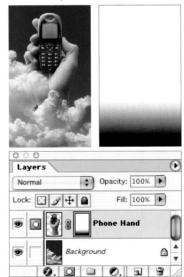

Masking and blending methods can be combined. Here a gradient-filled layer mask was added after the "Blend If" interaction above had been set up. The Layers palette shows the mask but not the "Blend If" changes.

"Blend If" & Mode

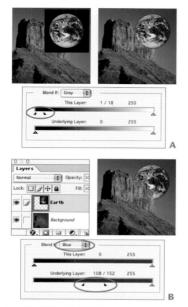

If there are clear differences of color or tone, the "Blend If" section of Blending Options may be useful for quickly "dropping out" a background. Here the default Gray setting for "This Layer" (the earth) could be used to hide the black background **A**. The sky and rock here are similar in brightness, so the default Gray setting for the "Underlying Layer" sliders couldn't distinguish between them. But the "Underlying Layer" sliders in the Blue channel worked well to give priority to the earth layer where the sky is blue and to hide the earth layer where the reddish rock occurs **B**. Putting the earth layer in Screen mode and reducing its Opacity completed this montage **C**.

 Earth-Rock.psd

Masking the Focus

To protect a central part of an image from a change, apply the change (here the Radial Blur filter) to the upper of two identical layers. Then add a layer mask to the upper layer, filled with a Radial black-to-white gradient. The gradient mask fades the changed image into the original.

Filtered Mask

For a custom-edged vignette treatment, "frame" the image with a layer mask, then blur the mask to create some gray at its edges and run a filter on the mask. See page 128 for the technique and pages 218 and 219 for filter ideas.

Masking a Transition

To show a transition from an original photo to a filtered version, start with two identical layers. Apply a filter to the top layer, then add a layer mask and fill it with a black-to-white gradient to create the transition.

Clipping Group

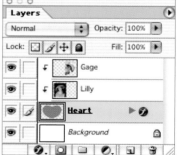

You can use the content of one layer to mask other layers above it by forming a clipping group by Alt/Option-clicking on the border between the layers. A Layer Style applied to the base layer (here a dark Inner Glow) affects the other grouped layers. Learn about using clipping groups on page 156 and in "Blending Images & Type" (page 168) and "Collaging with Masks & Groups" (page 185).

Extracting an Image

Overview *Use the Extract command to select the subject from the background; to improve the edge of the extracted subject, make a layer mask from the extracted subject's transparency mask and then modify the mask; import the new background; use Adjustment layers, with masks if needed, to modify the color of the ambient and directional lighting to make the two layers match.*

"**Extracting**" "before" and "after" files

JHD

1

The original subject and background photos

ORIGINAL PHOTOS: CORBIS IMAGES, ROYALTY FREE, CARIBBEAN GETAWAY

WHEN YOU WANT TO COMBINE a subject from one photo with a background from another, one of the main tasks is making a clean selection of the subject from its original background. If you're working with a portrait, that usually means solving "the hair problem": How do you make a selection that separates the hair from the background with a result that looks natural instead of too smooth or too spiky? There's no simple one-size-fits-all solution to this problem. The approach that works best depends on whether the hair color contrasts strongly with the background, and whether the wisps of hair are in sharp focus or soft, among other things. Photoshop 6's Extract made three improvements over past versions that makes it easier to select a subject: (1) the **Smart Highlighting** function makes the Edge Highlighter tool automatically follow the edge; (2) the **Cleanup tool** can subtract from or add to an extracted image; and (3) the **Edge Touchup tool** sharpens and smooths soft or rough edges of an extraction. (For more about using the Extract command, see "Extraction Pointers" (opposite). In Photoshop 7, the Extract command is unchanged, except for its relocation to the Filter menu.

Even when the hair problem is solved and the selection is made, there are other important factors that will help to make the subject at home in its new environment so the composite will be convincing:

- The ambient lighting, most evident in the color and density of

2a

Before the Extract command was used, we made a copy of the image for safekeeping.

EXTRACTION POINTERS

Here are some general rules of procedure for highlighting the edge when you use the Extract command (Filter, Extract) to isolate a subject from a background:

1 Some edges may be "fuzzy" because they are partly out of focus or partially transparent, or because they include highlights or shadows that have picked up color from the background. Typical edges of this kind include wisps of hair against a background, or tree leaves or blades of grass against the sky. To highlight fuzzy edges, use the Edge Highlighter tool with a broad brush (a large Brush Size setting).

2 Where the edge you want to select is distinct and high-contrast, turn on the Smart Highlighting option for the Edge Highlighter.

3 After you've surrounded the subject with highlight, filled the highlight with the Fill tool, and turned on Preview, use the *Cleanup tool* in spots where you want to take away from the extracted image and make it *more transparent*. Use the *Cleanup tool with the Alt/ Option key* held down where you want to restore the image so it's *more opaque.*

the shadows, has to look the same for both the subject and the background.

- The directional lighting also has to be consistent.

- The depth of focus has to look realistic. If the subject is entirely sharp and in focus, the background can be either in focus or blurred. But if the subject shows a short depth of field, with some parts in sharp focus and others soft, the background will need to be soft.

- The film grain or "noise" in the component images has to match (Simulating or adjusting film grain is covered in "Blurring the Background" on page 140.)

1 Analyzing the photos. Select the two photos you want to combine, and crop if necessary. In choosing the subject and background, look for images whose lighting doesn't "fight" uncontrollably. The sunset sky we chose for our ad image had ambient lighting that was opposite in color from the lighting in our portrait — a warm golden brown instead of a cool green **1**. But we knew we would be able to fix this difference by adjusting the color of the green-tinted highlights in the portrait (in step 5). The direction of the lighting in the background photo was straight into the camera, so there was nothing to conflict with the basic directional lighting in the portrait, which came from behind the woman and from her left (notice the highlights on the shoulders). So we were confident that the two images could be made into a convincing composite.

2 Starting the extraction. The Extract command (Image, Extract) is often Photoshop's best tool for solving the hair problem and other selection bugaboos. But using this command is a "destructive" process — it permanently removes pixels. So before you Extract, duplicate your image layer for safekeeping by dragging its name in the Layers palette to the Create A New Layer button at the bottom of the palette (the shortcut is Ctrl/⌘-J) **2a.** (Alternatively, you could make a Snapshot in the History palette, but History doesn't persist beyond the current working session, so making an extra layer is safer.) Click the Eye icon of the bottom image layer to turn off its visibility so you'll be able to see the result of your extraction.

Next open the Extract dialog box from the Filter menu. Choose a color from the popout Highlight menu. We changed the default Green to Red, since the background of the photo was green.

NAVIGATING THE PREVIEW

To temporarily turn on navigation tools in the Extract dialog box without dropping the Edge Highlighter, use these keyboard shortcuts:

- Hold down the **spacebar** for the **Hand tool**, to scroll around the image.

- Hold down **Ctrl/⌘-spacebar** for the **Zoom tool** and click to magnify the image.

- Hold down **Ctrl-Alt-spacebar** (Windows) or ⌘-**Option-spacebar** (Mac) and click to zoom out.

2b

Using the Edge Highlighter with a large brush size and Red as the Highlight color for areas that have transparency or have the background color showing through

2c

Turning on Smart Highlighting to trace the edge "magnetically"

2d **2e**

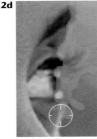 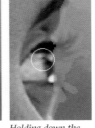

When the Edge Highlighter is in Smart Highlighting mode, the cursor changes.

Holding down the Alt/Option key turns the Edge Highlighter into a highlight eraser.

3a

Filling the completed highlight with the Fill tool makes the Preview button available.

With the Edge Highlighter tool chosen, set the Brush Size: A large brush works well for soft or fuzzy edges. We chose a relatively large Brush Size (40) to select the hair. Although on first inspection the contrast between the green background and the black hair looks strong, the depth of field for this photo is very short, so some of the hair is out-of-focus and soft; also, the green background has created green highlights in the hair. A large brush would allow us to drag along the edge quickly, catching all the fine curls of hair in one sweep. Drag the Edge Highlighter to draw a highlight that overlaps both the subject and the background where they meet **2b.** This highlight defines the band where the Extract function will look for the edge when it selects the subject. In the extraction process that follows, anything within the highlight band can be made transparent. In our image the broad strokes would help with selecting the fine detail, and would allow the hair to be selected as partially transparent, without the color cast from the background. When the extracted image was put against the new background, this semi-transparency of the hair would allow the new background to add its own color cast.

A smaller brush is better for a hard edge, or if there are two edges close together. In our image, we could use a small brush to make a sharp selection of the left side of the neck. But instead of resetting the Brush Size, we clicked the Smart Highlighting checkbox **2c.** With Smart Highlighting turned on, the cursor changes and the Edge Highlighter becomes "magnetic," automatically clinging to the edge as you drag the tool and *automatically narrowing the brush whenever possible.*

In our portrait there were really two high-contrast edges on the woman's profile — the green-against-white edge between the background and the highlight, and the white-against-brown

REPAIRS ON-THE-FLY

If you make a mistake with the Edge Highlighter and have to make a repair:

• You can quickly add by dragging the tool back over an area you missed.

• Or to remove some of the edge material you've applied, hold down the Alt/Option key to temporarily turn the Edge Highlighter into the Eraser.

CHANGING BRUSH SIZE

The control keys for resizing the brush tip for the Edge Highlighter, Cleanup, and Edge Touchup tools in the Extract dialog box are the same as for Photoshop's painting tools: You can use the **bracket keys to increase or decrease brush size** as you work by pressing "[" to shrink the brush, or "]" to enlarge it.

THE DUMB/SMART TOGGLE

Unfortunately, "Smart Highlighting" is really only smart about sharp, high-contrast edges. So as you drag from an area with a high-contrast edge to an area of low contrast, you'll need to turn off Smart Highlighting and operate the Edge Highlighter "by hand." Holding down the Ctrl/⌘ key automatically switches out of Smart Highlighting if you have it turned on, or switches into it if you have it turned off. Release the key to toggle back again.

3b

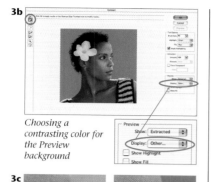

Choosing a contrasting color for the Preview background

3c

Switching the "Show" setting from Original (left) to Extracted to check the edge

3d

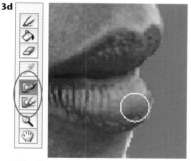

The Cleanup tool (shown here) and the Edge Touchup tool (below it in the Extract tool palette) become available after you click the Preview button, so you can refine the edge before finalizing the extraction.

3e

The subject layer after extraction

edge between highlight and normal skin tone. We zoomed in as described in the "Navigating the Preview" tip on page 163 for a close-up, in order to follow the edge **2d.** We had to switch back to "manual" operation of the Edge Highlighter (by holding down the Ctrl/⌘ key) to follow the highlight on the shoulders in order to "tell" the Edge Highlighter that we wanted to keep, not cut away, the hot white edges. Left to its own devices, Smart Highlighting would have followed the higher-contrast edge between the white highlight and the darker skin. To clean up the edge, we held down the Alt/Option key to erase existing highlighting **2e.**

The highlighting is complete when the subject is entirely enclosed within the highlight, except that you don't have to drag along the outside edges of the image. For instance, in this photo the highlight extended from the bottom edge of the photo on the left, up and around the profile to the right edge of the photo.

3 Completing the extraction. Before you can preview the selection you've made with the Edge Highlighter, you need to add a fill. Select the Extract box's Fill tool and click inside your highlight to fill the enclosed area and make the Preview button available **3a.** In the Extraction section of the dialog box, you can set the Smooth value to 100 to make an extraction with as little "debris" at the edge as possible; you'll be able to smooth it more later with the Edge Touchup tool if needed, as described below. Click the Preview button to make the background disappear.

In the Preview section at the bottom of the dialog box, you can change the Display setting to a color that contrasts with the original background of the photo. This will give you the best indication of how good your extraction is. If you don't find a workable color in the Display menu, choose Other and pick a color; we picked a red to contrast with the original green **3b.** By switching back and forth between Show Extracted and Show Original in the Preview section, you can compare the extracted edge with the original **3c.**

To make repairs, in the Extracted view use the Cleanup tool ("C" is the keyboard shortcut) on the edge to erase excess material **3d.** What's really exciting is that *you can also use the Cleanup tool with the Alt/Option key held down, to bring back material that was lost in the extraction.* Besides using the bracket tools to change brush size, you can change the pressure (or opacity) of the tool as you work by pressing the number keys ("1"through "9" for 10% to 90%, and "0" for 100%). Use a low opacity setting for a softened edge. In general, using a fairly low opacity and "scrubbing" with the tool gives good results. The Edge Touchup tool can be used to smooth the edge. It automatically removes or consolidates edge pixel debris.

As you touch up the edge and get ready to leave the Extract dialog box, keep in mind that it's better to have too much image material than not enough, because you can further trim the edge after extraction (as described in step 4), but it can be a lot harder to add back. When

Bringing in the new background image

The transparency mask loaded as a selection

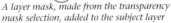
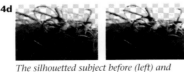

A layer mask, made from the transparency mask selection, added to the subject layer

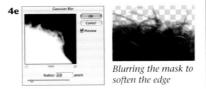

The silhouetted subject before (left) and after adding the layer mask

Blurring the mask to soften the edge

you've examined and fine-tuned the entire edge as well as you can, click OK to finalize the extraction and close the Extract dialog box **3e.**

4 Combining the subject with the new background. Use the Move tool to click in the new background image; then drag and drop it into the portrait file. In the Layers palette drag the imported layer's name to a position under the extracted layer **4a.** Use the Move tool to reposition the image if you like. Or scale it by pressing Ctrl/⌘-T (for Edit, Free Transform) and dragging a corner handle. You can also blur the image (Filter, Blur, Gaussian Blur) to soften the focus if needed, as we did here.

Now that the new background is in place, you may want to further refine the edge of your extracted subject. A flexible, nondestructive way to do that is to make a layer mask that exactly fits the subject and then modify the edge of the mask. First make a selection by loading the transparency mask that's inherent in the subject layer (Ctrl/⌘-click on the layer's thumbnail in the Layers palette) **4b.** Then add the layer mask (click the Add A Mask button at the bottom of the palette) **4c.** Because of the semi-transparency at the edge of the transparency mask, the layer mask that you've made from it will automatically be a bit smaller than the transparency mask, so the layer mask will trim the edge slightly. This change by itself may smooth the edge or get rid of unwanted background color **4d.**

If you need to refine the edge further, you can now paint black on the layer mask to hide more of the extracted image (try the Airbrush with a low Pressure setting). Or use the Blur tool on areas of the edge that you want to soften; we did this for the sweater on the shoulders. Or use Filter, Blur, Gaussian Blur to soften the entire edge **4e,** or just a selected part of it. If you don't like what your painting or blurring did, paint on the mask with white to restore parts of the original extraction edge.

5 Adjusting the ambient lighting. Now you can make changes to the color and intensity of the lighting to make the subject look more at home in the background. To add the warm sunset glow to the ambient lighting of the portrait, we created an Adjustment layer that we could use like a photographic gel. Because we knew what blend mode and Opacity we wanted to try, we held down the Alt/Option key as we dragged on the Create New Fill/Adjustment Layer button (the black-and-white circle) at the bottom of the Layers palette and chose Hue/Saturation from the pop-up menu. (Using the Alt/Option key brings up the New Layer dialog box.) We chose Soft Light for the mode (so we could add a tint without overwhelming the existing color) and set the Opacity at 75% as a first try. We also clicked the Group With Previous Layer box to form a clipping group so the color adjustment would affect only the subject, not the background image **5a** ("Clipping Groups" on page 156 tells more about grouping layers.) Clicking OK opened the Hue/Saturation dialog box, where we clicked the Colorize check box (so the Adjustment layer would act like a sheet of clear, colored plastic over the image) and

5a

Adding a Hue/Saturation Adjustment layer

5b

Coloring and darkening the ambient light

5c

Double-clicking on the name — *not the thumbnail — of an Adjustment layer brings up the Layer Style dialog box. In the Advanced Blending section you can control what part of the image's tonal range is affected by the Adjustment layer. By moving the white-point slider for "This Layer," we limited the adjustment to the shadow tones; we split the slider (by holding down the Alt/Option key and dragging) to make a smooth transition (this technique is described on pages 156 and 157).*

5d

Before *After*

Ambient lighting adjustment made with a Hue/Saturation layer

made sure Preview was selected (so we could see the change in the image as we experimented with the sliders). We changed the Hue to warm up the ambient light. We also reduced the Lightness since the strong backlighting would naturally put the subject more in shadow **5b.** Although in reality the entire face would be shaded, for our ad we limited the adjustment to the shadow tones, leaving the mid-tones and highlights bright enough to print well **5c, 5d.** This was accomplished by using the Advanced Blending option in the Layer Style dialog box ("Blending Options" on page 156 tells more about using the powerful Advanced Blending options).

6 Modifying the directional light. Next we used another Adjustment layer, with a mask, to expand, soften, and color the highlight areas, so warm yellow light would spill over the edges of the face and shoulders. First we made a soft selection of the high-lighted edges, as follows: We again loaded the subject layer's trans-parency mask as a selection (by Ctrl/⌘-clicking its thumbnail in the Layers palette). We shrank this selection inward (Select, Modify, Con-tract), using a setting of 10 for our 1000-pixel-wide image. We soft-ened the selection (Select, Feather, using the same 10-pixel setting as we had used for the Contract command), and then inverted it (Select, Inverse, or Ctrl/⌘-Shift-I), to select just the outer edge of the subject **6a.** We again Alt/Option-clicked the Create New Fill/ Adjustment Layer button and made another Hue/Saturation layer, again choosing Group With Previous Layer to add to the clipping group. We reduced the Opacity, but this time we used Overlay mode to intensify the colors; we clicked OK. In the Hue/Saturation dialog box we turned on the Colorize option, adjusted the Hue to a setting of 40, and boosted the Saturation to 100. Our selection automatically became a mask for the new Adjustment layer **6b,** which changed the color only at the edge of the face and shoulders, where the soft edge of the white part of the mask allowed the adjustment to affect the subject (see the final image on page 162). 🖋

6a

The mask for targeting the second Hue/ Saturation adjustment was made by loading the subject's transparency mask (top) and then contracting, softening, and inverting the selection (bottom).

6b

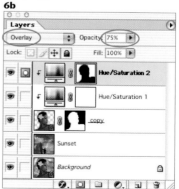

A second Hue/Saturation Adjustment layer was added to color and exaggerate the directional lighting at the edge of the face.

Blending Images & Type

Overview Use Advanced Blending and layer masks to merge images; match shadows, highlights, and film grain to support the composite; add type and rotate it; use a clipping group to mask an image inside the type.

"Cloud-Hand" "before" and "after" files

The original images

Layers

Normal   Opacity: 100%
Lock: Fill: 100%

Phone Hand

Background

Scaling the silhouetted hand image to fit the layout for the composite

JHD / CLOUDS PHOTO © CORBIS IMAGES ROYALTY FREE, DESTINATION TROPICS

THERE ARE MANY WAYS TO BLEND IMAGES in Photoshop. Clipping groups can use the image and masks from one layer to control what parts of other layers are hidden or revealed. In fact, a **clipping group** is Photoshop 7's most flexible and effective way to mask an image inside live type. In the image above, a scaled, clipped copy of the background photo is clipped inside the "AIR TIME" type.

A **layer mask** provides another powerful approach to hiding and revealing. Here the boundaries of a second copy of the clouds image are determined by a screen-shaped layer mask created with the Paste Into command. And a hand-painted layer mask controls how much of the hand is hidden so the clouds from the background can appear to be in front of it.

Instead of masking by *shape* as layer masks and clipping groups do, the **"Blend If"** section of Photoshop's Blending Options (in the Layer Style dialog box) lets you hide or reveal certain parts of the active layer based on the *colors and tones* in the active layer and the image below it. Here "Blend If" was used to help "hide" the hand behind the clouds, but keep it in front of the sky.

1 Preparing the images. Open the image files for the subject and background you want to composite **1**. If necessary, silhouette the subject, removing its background. You may find the following examples of silhouetting, found elsewhere in the book, to be helpful:

2b

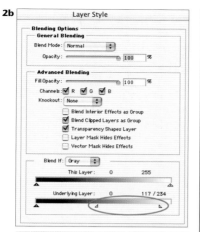

A smooth-edged subject on a contrasting background (the hand used here) in the "Silhouetting with the Magnetic Lasso or Magnetic Pen" tip on page 173

A smooth-edged subject on a busy background (a bike-riding couple in a street scene) in "Silhouetting Images and Type" in Chapter 7

A "difficult-edged" subject (a portrait in which the hair must be selected) in "Extracting an Image" on page 162

2 Merging the two photos.
With both images open on-screen, click in the window of the subject image (here the hand). We selected the hand by opening the Channels palette and Ctrl/⌘-clicking the alpha channel's name to load it as a selection for silhouetting (we had made the alpha channel for this purpose). With the subject selected, use the Move tool to drag it into the background image and release the mouse button to drop it. Use the Edit, Free Transform command (Ctrl/⌘-T), Shift-dragging a corner handle to scale the subject or background proportionally and dragging inside the Transform box until the two layers are arranged the way you want them **2a.** Press the Enter key or double-click inside the Transform box to complete the transformation.

<aside>
AVOIDING SURPRISES

To see the relative size of the images you want to include in a composite, open all the component photos on-screen at the same magnification — for instance, 50% or 100%. If it's necessary to significantly enlarge any of the images to make them work in the composite, you might want to rescan the image at a higher resolution, look for a larger photo, or experiment with a different composition, rather than compromise image quality by scaling up.
</aside>

Using the "Blend If" function reveals the light portions of the clouds where the hand overlaps them. "Masking" done by "Blend If" doesn't show up in the Layers palette.

2c

An airbrushed mask makes sure most of the detail and color in the wrist is hidden.

The next step is to make a layer mask to blend the silhouetted subject with the background. We wanted the hand to be reaching up through the clouds, so we needed to hide the hard bottom edge of the arm and somehow surround the hand with clouds. We decided to try the "Blend If" function of Advanced Blending, which allows you to hide parts of the top layer based on the colors and tones in both layers. We double-clicked the name of the hand layer to open the Layer Style dialog box to the Blending Options section, and then went to work with the "Blend If" sliders. We used the Underlying Layer slider to reveal the lighter colors in the clouds layer so they seemed to be in front of the hand, as follows: We moved the white point triangle slider for the Underlying Layer a little to the left until we could see some of the white from the clouds. Then we *held down the Alt/Option key* so we could split the slider, and we dragged the left half of the triangle farther to the left. This allowed some of the light gray tones from the clouds to show through partially, which softened the transition between the two images and made it look as if some of the clouds were in front of the hand. We fine-tuned the slider positions to get the best result we could **2b.**

3a

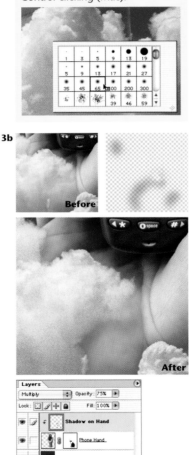

A new layer for painting shadows was added and grouped with the hand layer.

3b

Before

After

Shadows were airbrushed onto the new transparent layer. Since the layer was "clipped" to the hand, the shadows were partly hidden by the "Blend If" settings for the hand layer.

(For more about how the "Blend If" functions work, see "Blending Options" on page 156.)

To hide the cropped bottom edge of the hand photo, we added a layer mask by clicking the Add A Mask button at the bottom of the Layers palette. With this new mask active, we chose the Airbrush. In the Options bar we chose Normal mode, and so that we could build our mask gradually, we set a low Pressure and picked out a soft brush from the Brushes palette. We airbrushed the mask with black to further hide the hand, thereby giving priority to the clouds in the layer below **2c**.

3 Adding details to blend the subject and background. To cast shadows from the cloud onto the hand so hand and clouds would look like they were really (or surreally) in the same space, we added a transparent layer that was grouped with the hand layer below it. Having a separate layer would let us paint the shadows without permanently changing the hand layer. And making this new layer part of a clipping group controlled by the hand would mean that the "Blend If" settings for the hand layer would also apply to the shadows, so the clouds would appear to be in front of the shadows. Also, the only pixels on the shadow layer that would show would be clipped inside the hand, so we wouldn't have to worry about "coloring outside the lines" as we painted the shadows. To add a new layer for the shadows, we Alt/Option-clicked the Create A New Layer button at the bottom of the Layers palette. In the New Layer dialog box, we clicked the check box for Group With Previous Layer and chose Multiply for the Mode **3a.**

Now we could use the Airbrush again. To make sure the shadow would match the larger image, we sampled color from a shadow area in the hand image. We painted a shadow along the edges of the clouds, knowing that the silhouette, layer mask, and "Blend If" settings for the hand layer would hide any stray pixels. We used a low Pressure setting for the Airbrush and gradually built up the shadows until they were a little darker than we would need, knowing that we could adjust the Opacity of the layer to make them more subtle **3b.**

Next we put the cloud image into the phone's screen. We activated the clouds layer by clicking on its name in the Layers palette; we selected part of it with the Rectangular Marquee and copied (Ctrl/⌘-C). Then we used the Polygonal Lasso to make a selection the shape of the screen. With this selection active we could now use the Paste Into command to make a new layer from the clouds image; the new layer would automatically include a layer mask that would reveal the clouds only in the screen area: We made sure the shadow layer was active so our new layer would come in just above it. Then we pasted the image from the clipboard into the selected screen area of a new layer by choosing Edit, Paste Into (Ctrl/⌘-Shift-V). Because Paste Into creates a

3c

Part of the clouds image was "pasted into" the screen selection to make a new layer, and the clouds image was scaled to fit.

3d

In the new layer we linked the image and mask and added an Inner Shadow. The screen image layer was also added to the clipping group.

4a

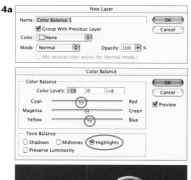

A Color Balance Adjustment layer was added to "cool" the highlights in the hand group.

layer mask that is *not* linked to the image, we could use Free Transform to reduce the image to fit the screen, without shrinking the mask along with it **3c**. To preserve the original highlights on the screen, we put the pasted clouds layer in Overlay mode and reduced its Opacity, settling on 75%. We also added an Inner Shadow effect to the screen to reinforce the strong lighting from the left in the composite, as follows: First we clicked between the image thumbnail and the mask thumbnail in the Layers palette to link the image and mask, so the layer mask's edges (rather than the pasted image's edges) would be used to create the Inner Shadow effect. Next we clicked the "*f*" button at the bottom of the palette, choosing Inner Shadow from the list in the Layer Style dialog box. We clicked the color swatch in the Inner Shadow section of the dialog box and then clicked a dark area of the image to sample a color for the shadow, then clicked OK to close the Color Picker. We dragged in the image to get the offset we wanted for the shadow, and adjusted the Size (to 9 pixels). We made this layer part of the hand-based clipping group (by pressing Ctrl/⌘-G) so it would also be affected by the film grain added in the next step **3d**.

4 Unifying the composite. Next we made adjustments to match the lighting and film grain in the hand image to the background. We wanted to make the highlights in the hand image slightly "cooler," to match the highlights in the sky. We also wanted to add grain to the hand to match the much grainier clouds photo. Since the clouds image in the screen had been scaled down, its grain was no longer apparent and it too would need the grain treatment.

To "cool" the highlights in the hand without affecting the background sky image, we added a Color Balance Adjustment layer to the clipping group, as follows: Hold down the Alt/Option key as you drag on the Create New Fill/Adjustment Layer button at the bottom of the Layers palette, and choose Color Balance. In the New Layer dialog box we chose Group With Previous Layer and clicked OK. In the Color Balance dialog, we clicked the Highlights button and moved the sliders to increase the Blue and Cyan **4a**.

To match the studio shot of the hand (taken with a digital camera) and the photo of the sky (shot with a fast ISO film), we added a Pattern Fill layer, as follows: Hold down Alt/Option and drag on the Create New Fill/Adjustment Layer button and choose Pattern from the pop-out menu. In the New Layer dialog box we chose the grouping option and chose Overlay for the Mode. That way, the gray pattern fill would contribute only its texture, which was created by the tones lighter or darker than the 50% gray that's neutral for Overlay mode. We clicked OK, and in the Pattern Fill dialog box we clicked the little triangle to the right of the Pattern swatch and then chose the Wow 7-Noise Patterns set from the pop-out list (accessible by clicking the arrow icon in the upper right corner of the Pattern Picker). Next we experimented by choosing different

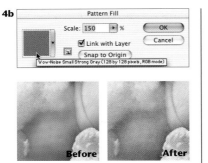

4b

Pattern Fill

Scale: 150 %

☑ Link with Layer

☐ Snap to Origin

Wow-Noise Small Strong Gray (128 by 128 pixels, RGB mode)

OK

Cancel

Before **After**

A "noise" pattern (Wow-Noise Small Strong Gray) in Overlay mode was added to the hand group to simulate film grain.

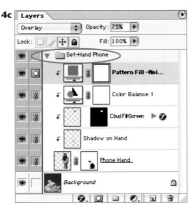

4c

Layers

Overlay   Opacity: 75%

Lock: ☐ ✎ ✛ 🔒   Fill: 100%

Set-Hand Phone

Pattern Fill –Noi...

Color Balance 1

Cloud Fill-Screen

Shadow on Hand

Phone Hand

Background

All the layers related to the hand were linked, and then the linked layers were collected in a set.

5

Type was set in Helvetica Inserat Roman, rotated and assigned a Drop Shadow.

Wow-Noise patterns from the pop-out palette. We settled on Wow-Noise Small Strong Gray (scaled up to 150%) as the best match for the film grain in the cloud image **4b.** For instructions on loading the Wow presets from the CD-ROM that accompanies this book, see page 9.

With our image-matching adjustments complete, we created a layer set so we could collect all the layers related to the hand and tuck them out of the way: First we linked the layers by clicking on the Pattern Fill layer and then dragging downward in the column next to the Eye, from the Color Balance layer down to the hand layer. Then we chose New Set From Linked from the Layers palette's pop-out menu, and chose Orange for the Color, leaving the Mode at the default Pass Through so the blend modes for the individual layers in the set would remain in effect **4c.**

5 Adding type on a vertical baseline. Our next step was to add type and rotate it, then mask a copy of the background image inside it. To set type, choose the Type tool, make sure the Create A Text Layer option is chosen at the left end of the Options bar, and choose a font for the type (we used 120-point Helvetica Inserat Roman). We clicked the color swatch in the Options bar and chose white for visualizing purposes, although the color would be totally hidden when we added the image. Set the type, but don't bother to fine-tune the size or spacing yet — you can do that after you rotate it into place. Now you'll need to get out of type-editing mode by clicking the ✓ at the right end of the Options bar so you can choose Edit, Free Transform (Ctrl/⌘-T). Hold down the Shift key as you drag around outside a corner handle of the Transform box to rotate the type into a vertical position. Then grab a corner handle of the Transform box and Shift-drag up to scale the type for the layout. To complete the Transform, double-click inside the Transform box or press the Enter key. Next drag-select the type (the cursor will turn into the I-beam of the Type tool again when you move it close to the type) and fine-tune the size and spacing **5.** (You'll find pointers for adjusting size and spacing in "Typography, Groups & Layer Styles" in Chapter 7.)

We wanted the type to be readable after the image was masked inside it, so we set the type off from the image beneath with a drop shadow. To add a drop shadow to a type layer, click the "*f*" button at the bottom of the Layers palette. In the Drop Shadow section of the Layer Style dialog, click the color swatch, sample a dark color to be used for the shadow, and click OK to close the Color Picker. Drag in the image to get the offset you want for the shadow, and adjust the Size and Spread if you like.

6 Masking the background image inside the type. To select part of the background image to go inside the type, activate the background layer and select the area you want; we used the Rectan-

6a

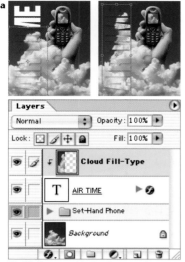

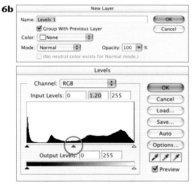

To fill the type with clouds, a new layer made from a selection of the clouds layer was grouped with the type and scaled up.

6b

New Layer	
Name: Levels 1	OK
☑ Group With Previous Layer	Cancel
Color: ☐ None	
Mode: Normal ⬍ Opacity: 100 ▸ %	
☐ (No neutral color exists for Normal mode.)	

Levels	
Channel: RGB ⬍	OK
Input Levels: 0 1.20 255	Cancel
	Load...
	Save...
	Auto
	Options...
Output Levels: 0 255	🖋 🖋 🖋
	☑ Preview

A Levels Adjustment layer was used to lighten the image inside the type.

6c

New Set From Linked	
Name: Set-Type Cloud	OK
Color: ☐ Green ⬍	Cancel
Mode: Pass Through ⬍ Opacity: 100 ▸ %	

Layers
Pass Through ⬍ Opacity: 100 ▸
Lock: ☐ 🖌 ✛ 🔒 Fill: 100% ▸
▸ 📁 Set-Type Cloud
▸ 📁 Set-Hand Phone
Background 🔒

A new layer set was made for the type, and both sets were closed to tidy up the Layers palette.

gular Marquee to select a cloud-filled area behind the type, knowing that we could stretch it so the clouds would fill the letters. Copy the selection (Ctrl/⌘-C), turn the copy into a new layer (Ctrl/⌘-J), and drag the new layer upward in the Layers palette until it's above the type. "Clip" the pasted image inside the type by Alt/Option-clicking the border between the two layers in the Layers palette (or press Ctrl/⌘-G). To stretch the image to fill all the letters, we pressed Ctrl/⌘-T (for Free Transform) and dragged upward on the top handle of the Transform box **6a.**

To help the type stand out from the background, we added a Levels Adjustment layer to the "AIR TIME" clipping group and dragged the midtone (gamma, gray) Input Levels slider to the left to lighten the clipped image **6b.** (At the point when your image-filled type is finalized, you may want to turn the type into a Shape layer by choosing Layer, Type, Convert To Shape so you don't have to supply the font for output.)

As a final bit of housekeeping, we linked all the layers of the type clipping group and created a new layer set from the linked layers, assigning it a different color than the hand set **6c.** *Wow!*

SILHOUETTING WITH THE MAGNETIC LASSO OR MAGNETIC PEN

The Magnetic Lasso and Magnetic Pen are designed to let you select semi-automatically by taking advantage of color contrast anywhere it exists. But you can also substitute manual selection in areas where the contrast breaks down. To use either tool, you click the center of the cursor once on the edge of the element you want to select and "float" the cursor along, moving the mouse or stylus without pressure and without worrying about the precision that would be required to manually drag along the edge you want to select. The tool will automatically track the "edge" created by color contrast. When you use the Magnetic tools, the less well-defined the edge, the smaller the Width setting (the brush size) should be in the Options bar:

- If you're tracing a **well-defined edge**, you can use a large Width and move the tool quickly.

- To avoid confusing the tool, **if there are other edges** or distinct objects near the edge you want to trace, use a small Width and keep the cursor centered on the edge you want to trace.

- For a **soft edge** with little contrast, use a smaller Width and trace carefully. Click to add points when there's *no* contrast.

- You can **change the Width** "on the fly" by typing a number into the Options bar or **use your free hand to operate the "[" and "]" keys** while drawing.

The Magnetic Lasso was used to select the hand (top). The selection was saved as an alpha channel and cleaned up with a hard-edged round Paintbrush (bottom).

If the selection goes off in the wrong direction, press the Delete key and it will "back up" so you can manually set points along the problematic edge. Once you've made the selection, you can save it as an alpha channel for safekeeping (Select, Save Selection) and clean it up as needed.

Assembling a Still Life

Overview *Choose and silhouette the component photos; assemble them in one file and match color and tone; create a background; add matching shadows; distort and mask the shadows to simulate real lighting; adjust the color overall; make final adjustments to unify the scene.*

IMAGE

"Assembly" "before" and "after" files

JHD / ORIGINAL PHOTOS: © CORBIS IMAGES ROYALTY FREE, IN THE OFFICE

1

The original photos

2

Before we used the Background Eraser to silhouette the typewriter, we turned on Protect Foreground Color in the Options bar. We then sampled color from the platen tension lever shown here because it was close to the background color we wanted to erase, but we wanted to protect the lever. The sampled color became the Foreground color and was therefore protected from being erased.

IF YOU'RE ASSEMBLING OBJECTS IN A STILL-LIFE MONTAGE, your first task is to decide whether you want a stylized illustration — strictly to communicate a concept — or whether you also want to fool the viewer's eye into accepting the illusion that all the components are assembled together in a single real (or surreal) space.

1 Choosing your objects. If you're aiming to produce a stylized assemblage, you have a lot of freedom in choosing the elements. However, if something more realistic is what you're after, you'll need to look for elements with matching camera angle, lighting, focus, film grain, and shadow color, as well as similar amounts of detail and appropriate perspective. Some of these matching criteria can be adjusted in Photoshop ("Choosing and Preparing Components on page 152 and "Combining with Light" in Chapter 5 provide pointers). But all of these adjustments take time, so the closer you can come in your choice of photos, the easier the assembly will be.

Often the background image is established before the components are chosen. In that case its lighting will determine the lighting required for the objects. However, for this *Global Economy* still

The five objects assembled over a gradient background

The passport was foreshortened and rotated with one application of the Free Transform command. Then Perspective was applied, along with final scaling, in another transformation.

life we chose to assemble the objects and then add a background ramp later. We chose five photos **1:** The newspaper-and-eyeglasses photo was important in our choice of other items, since it established the camera angle and included a shadow for the eyeglasses that showed that the lighting was coming from above, forward, and from the left. The lighting for the typewriter, globe, and adding machine matched closely enough. The typewriter and adding machine were both angled in a three-quarter view that we could work with, and they were photographed from above. The globe's round surface made the camera angle of this straight-on shot unimportant once we had removed its stand, and its above-front-left lighting matched that of the typewriter and adding machine. The lighting and perspective on the passport didn't match the other photos, but since this was a flat element, it would be possible to change these parameters by rotating the passport and putting it into perspective.

2 Isolating the objects from their backgrounds. The images that we chose from the Corbis Images Royalty Free volume called *In the Office* came with alpha channels and clipping paths already prepared for silhouetting the objects. If the image files you want to use are objects on relatively plain backgrounds but aren't equipped with paths or alpha channels, Photoshop's **Background Eraser** tool can be very helpful. For instance, to isolate the typewriter (for the purpose of demonstration) we chose the Background Eraser in the toolbox. In the Options bar we chose **Contiguous** for the Limits setting so that only pixels whose color continued uninterrupted from the pixel under the eraser's hot spot would be erased. That way if we kept the hot spot slightly outside the edge of the typewriter, the contrasting edge of the typewriter would stop the erasure. With the **Once** setting for Sampling, we could click-drag to sample one of the grays in the background and erase as long as that color continued to do the job, then click-drag again to sample and erase a new shade. We used a low **Tolerance** setting (10%) to restrict the erasure to the grays in the background, so we wouldn't be erasing similar colors in the typewriter. We also clicked the check box to turn on **Protect Foreground Color** so that when we held down the Alt/Option key, the Background Eraser would toggle to an eyedropper that could be clicked in the image to select a new Foreground color. This color would then be protected from erasure, even if it fell within the scope of the Background Eraser's Tolerance and Contiguous settings. For instance, we used this technique to protect the platen tension lever from being erased **2.**

3 Uniting the elements. When all the elements have been silhouetted, drag-and-drop them into one file. This is the time to scale the elements to approximately their final sizes and to do any major color or tone adjustments so that all the elements generally match in appearance. (The matching will be fine-tuned at the end of the assembly process, at step 9.)

5

Drop Shadow
Structure
Blend Mode: Multiply
Opacity: 75 %
Angle: -175 ° □ Use Global Light
Distance: 15 px
Spread: 0 %
Size: 15 px

Adding a drop shadow to the passport to match the existing shadow of the eyeglasses, keeping in mind color, distance, size and angle

6a

Pasting the drop shadow to all the linked layers at once

Layer Properties...
Blending Options...

Duplicate Layer...
Delete Layer

Enable Layer Mask

Rasterize Layer

Copy Layer Style
Paste Layer Style
Paste Layer Style to Linked
Clear Layer Style

At this time we also added a background for our elements to sit on: We clicked the Create A New Layer button at the bottom of the Layers palette and then dragged the new layer's name down to the bottom of the stack. We dragged from corner to corner with the Gradient tool to fill the layer with a light-to-dark-gray Linear gradient **3**.

4 Adjusting position and perspective. Once all the elements are colored, toned, and scaled to feel at home with each other, you can make any necessary changes in position or perspective. The one item that was still out-of-scale and not in perspective with the rest of the elements in our assemblage was the passport. Also, we needed to rotate it so that the highlight along the left edge was angled to match the lighting of the rest of the objects. Although it would have been nice to accomplish the changes with a single application of the Free Transform command, a two-step transformation is required to get the appropriate foreshortened perspective of a rotated object.

First we scaled and rotated the passport (press Ctrl/⌘-T for Free Transform and Shift-drag a corner handle to scale; drag outside the corner handles to rotate). Because of the rotation, the Transform box was now in the wrong orientation to accomplish the final Perspective and Scale operations, so we pressed Enter to accept the changes and then pressed Ctrl/⌘-T again to get a new "straight-up" Transform box. We then used the Perspective command (right-click [Windows] or Control-click [Mac] inside the Transform box to open the context-sensitive menu so we could choose Perspective, dragging on a corner handle to move both that corner and its opposite in or out). Then we opened the context-sensitive menu again and chose Free Transform so we could grab the top center handle and drag downward to foreshorten the passport to its final shape **4**.

Both transformations — Scale-and-Rotate and Perspective-and-Scale — involved resampling, which can make an image look fuzzy. So at this point we compared the passport image to the others and decided to sharpen it slightly (Filter, Sharpen, Unsharp Mask).

5 Starting with a drop shadow. The next step is to create the shadows that will help all the elements appear to be in the same space. Since the newspaper element had a shadow of the eyeglasses within it, we would use the color of that shadow as we manufactured the others. First we would create a shadow for the passport, as described next, and then copy and paste that shadow to the larger elements as a starting point for the cast shadows.

With the passport layer active, we clicked on the Add A Layer Style button (the "*f*") at the bottom of the Layers palette; from the pop-up menu we chose Drop Shadow. We clicked the color square in the Drop Shadow section of the Layer Style dialog box and then sampled the shadow of the eyeglasses by clicking on it in the working window. After clicking OK to close the Color Picker, we again reached outside the Layer Style dialog and dragged the passport's shadow to match the offset of the eyeglasses' shadow. This

6b

Drop shadows pasted into all object layers

TARGETING & LINKING LAYERS

With the Move tool selected and **Auto Select Layer** turned on in the Options bar:

- **Clicking** in the image window will automatically **target the topmost layer that has pixels under the cursor**. (For the layer to be targeted, the pixels have to be at least 50% opaque.)

- If you want **to target the layer of an element lower in the stack**, position the cursor over the element and **right-click (Windows) or Control-click (Mac)** to bring up a list of all layers with pixels under the cursor, so you can choose the one you want to target.

- **To link or unlink the layers for several elements**, hold down the **Shift** key as you click or right/Control-click to choose the layers as described above.

automatically changed the Distance and Angle settings inside the dialog box. Then we experimented with the Size setting until the softness of the shadows also matched **5**.

6 Copying and pasting the drop shadow. To make the shadows cast by the typewriter, globe, and adding machine, we started by copying and pasting the passport's shadow to automatically give us the right color, angle, and softness. To copy the shadow to all the other objects at once, with the passport layer active we clicked in the Layers palette's links column (between the Eye and the image thumbnail) for each of the other layers except the background. With all these layers linked, we could duplicate the shadow to all of them at once, using the following method: Right-click (Windows) or Control-click (Mac) on the "*f*" icon for the layer with the Drop Shadow (in this case the passport layer) to open the context-sensitive menu and choose Copy Layer Style. Then right/Control-click the name of one of the linked layers, and choose Paste Layer Style To Linked **6a**. All linked layers will now have the shadow **6b**.

7 Skewing the shadows. To be able to turn the *drop shadows* into *cast shadows* by skewing them, you'll need to separate the shadows into layers of their own. Since our passport and newspaper were flat items, the Drop Shadow worked fine as it was; we would not need to separate and skew it. But for each of the other elements, we opened the context-sensitive menu for the layer's "*f*" icon and chose Create Layer.

Next, you'll also need to unlink all the object and shadow layers so you can manipulate them individually **7a;** you can do this by clicking all the link icons in the Layers palette, or use the method described in the "Targeting & Linking Layers" tip at the left.

After separating and unlinking, we started with the typewriter's shadow. Pressing Ctrl/⌘-T and opening the context-sensitive menu allowed us to choose Skew. We dragged the top center point of the Transformation box to the right until the shadow was at an angle that looked right for our upper-left-front light source **7b**. (If the light source for an image you're assembling from your own elements is located somewhere other than above-left-front, you'll obviously need to skew the shadows differently.) We noted the "H:" component of the skew angle in the Options bar (–17°) so we could use it later as a starting point for skewing our other shadows. Next

DRAG-AND-DROP STYLES

To copy a Style from one layer to another you can drag the first layer's **Effects** entry in the Layers palette to the second layer's name and drop it. Drag-and-drop also works for a single effect. For instance, dragging and dropping the Drop Shadow entry from one layer to another adds or replaces only the Drop Shadow. **Caution: Transparency settings and blend mode are not included** when a Style is dragged-and-dropped. To preserve these you must copy and paste or use a Style preset. See the "Blend Modes Don't Drag-and-Drop!" tip on page 225.

7a Shadows separated and layers unlinked for the typewriter, adding machine, and globe

7b Skewing the typewriter's shadow

8a Adding machine shadow and globe shadow cast on the background, with both skewed to match the typewriter's shadow, and with the globe shadow foreshortened

8b Masking the typewriter's shadow to keep it from overlapping the globe's shadow

we moved the shadow by dragging inside the Transform box. We used the Distort command from the context-sensitive menu to fine-tune the alignment of the front corners of the shadow with the base of the typewriter; pressing the Enter key closed the Transform box.

Next we targeted the adding machine's Drop Shadow layer and pressed Ctrl/⌘-T for Free Transform. Again we skewed the shadow to match our light source, using the "H:" value we had noted as a starting point. We dragged the shadow and used Distort to align it by eye to the front edge of the machine, and pressed Enter.

8 Visualizing the shadow-and-object interactions. At this point we had to go a step further in visualizing how our elements would actually interact with the light. The globe's shadow would fall on items at three different distances from the globe — the background surface (the farthest away), the adding machine (the middle distance), and the top of the typewriter (right underneath the globe) — and this meant that we needed three copies of the shadow at three different angles.

To make the part of the globe's shadow that fell on the background surface, we dragged the globe's drop shadow layer to the Create A New Layer button at the bottom of the Layers palette to duplicate it and then dragged the copy down in the palette to a position just above the background. We skewed the shadow as we had done for the typewriter and adding machine shadows in step 7. Since the globe is higher above the surface than the typewriter and adding machine are, the angle of the light would be steeper in casting its shadow, and the globe's shadow on the background surface would be shorter. We chose the Move tool and dragged the globe's shadow downward a bit, to create a sense of depth **8a.**

When soft shadows in Multiply mode overlap in Photoshop, the shadow in the overlap gets darker than either contributing shadow. But this isn't usually the way things work in the real world. So some masking is needed to eliminate the overlap. To remove the portion of the typewriter's shadow that overlapped with the globe's shadow on the background surface, we used a layer mask. We knew we wanted to keep the shadow where it fell on the adding machine and the newspaper. So we loaded the transparency masks for these two layers as selections by Ctrl/⌘-clicking on the adding machine in the Layers palette and then Shift-Ctrl/⌘-clicking on the newspaper to add it to the selection. Then we activated the typewriter's shadow layer and clicked the Add A Mask icon on the left at the bottom of the Layers palette **8b.**

To make the globe's shadow that falls on the adding machine, we duplicated the globe's background surface shadow layer that we had just made and dragged the copy above the adding machine's layer in the Layers palette. Then we used the Move tool to drag the shadow up and to the left until it seemed to be in the right position on the adding machine. To eliminate this shadow everywhere but on the

9a

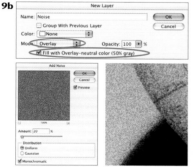

Adding a Hue/Saturation Adjustment layer to adjust color overall

9b

Creating a Noise layer in Overlay mode

9c

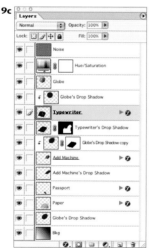

Here is the final Layers palette for the illustration at the top of page 174. "Dark halos" have been added to the typewriter and adding machine, softening their edges and blending them into the atmosphere of the composite image.

surface of the adding machine, we made a clipping group of the adding machine and this new globe shadow by Alt/Option-clicking the border between these two layers in the Layers palette, thus using the edge of the machine to mask the shadow.

We wanted to eliminate the darkening where the globe shadow and the typewriter shadow overlapped on the surface of the adding machine. We added a layer mask on the new globe shadow's layer as follows: With the new globe shadow layer active, we Ctrl/⌘-clicked on the typewriter shadow layer's thumbnail to load its transparency mask as a selection. Then we Alt/Option-clicked the Add A Mask button to make a "negative" layer mask that blocked the globe shadow where it overlapped the typewriter shadow. To get the edges of the two shadows to interact realistically, we had to load the typewriter's shadow as a selection again; with the new layer mask active, we darkened the mask by filling with black.

For the shadow that fell on the typewriter, we could use the original separated globe drop shadow layer as it was, simply clipping it inside the typewriter's shape by Alt/Option-clicking on the border between the two layers in the Layers palette.

9 Finishing touches. To enhance the antique "atmosphere" shared by the assembled objects, we toned down the color and added noise to soften the image overall: First we targeted the top layer, then added an Adjustment layer by Alt/Option-dragging the Create New Fill/Adjustment Layer button, choosing Hue/Saturation from the pop-out list. In the New Layer dialog box we chose Color for the Mode before clicking OK, so that when we reduced the Saturation in the Hue/Saturation dialog box, the contrast wouldn't be affected **9a.**

Above the Adjustment layer we added a new layer by Alt/Option-clicking the Create A New Layer button; this opened the New Layer dialog box so we could choose the Overlay blend mode and also fill the layer with Overlay-neutral 50% gray in the same step. We chose Filter, Noise, Add Noise; we turned on the Monochromatic option and experimented with the Amount and Distribution settings until we had the result we wanted **9b.**

Our last overall addition was a "dark halo" around the three large objects that would help blend them into the atmosphere created by the noise. We copied the Drop Shadow effect from the passport. We pasted it into the globe, typewriter, and adding machine layers and then adjusted the Drop Shadow's Size and offset for each layer.

Now we could fine-tune the separated shadows, blurring the parts that were farthest from the light source **9c**— for instance, at the far edge of the globe's shadow on the background; we used the Blur tool (the water drop) set to 100% Pressure with a soft brush tip, "scrubbing" the shadow more the farther away it extended from the object casting it.

Blending a Panorama

***Overview** Assemble the component photos in one file; straighten and align the component images; create gradient-based layer masks to blend the components; adjust the tonality and color of individual elements and of the panorama overall.*

"**Panorama**" "before" and "after" files

The three component photos, taken with a point-and-shoot camera

Using a horizontal guide and the Free Transform command to straighten the horizon

In order to align details where the "photo 3" layer overlaps the "photo 2" image, the Opacity of "photo 3" was temporarily reduced so "photo 2" could also be seen.

AUTOMATED CAMERAS CHANGE THEIR EXPOSURE settings as the light changes. Ordinarily, this is what the photographer wants. But if you're shooting a panoramic series, the different exposures that happen as you point the camera more directly into the light can cause differences in the overlapping images of the series. This can be the main problem you need to address when you piece the panorama together.

1 Assembling and straightening the images. Open your component images and drag-and-drop them into a single Photoshop file; we assembled three images for our sunset panorama **1a.** You can use the Crop tool to add canvas area so you'll have room to spread the images out to make the panorama: Choose the Crop tool and drag it across the entire image. Then either drag the lower right corner of the window outward or press Ctrl/⌘-Shift-minus (hyphen) to shrink the image without shrinking the window, so that you can see the gray "apron" beyond the edges of the image. Now you can drag the corner handles of the crop box outward into the apron to add as much canvas as you'll need for the panorama.

With the rulers showing (Ctrl/⌘-R is the show/hide toggle), drag a guide down from the top ruler to a position near the horizon in the currently active layer. Use Free Transform (Ctrl/⌘-T) to rotate the image by dragging outside a corner handle until its horizon parallels the guide **1b,** then double-click inside the Transform frame to accept the rotation. Using the same guide, repeat the straightening process for the other layers.

2b

All images rotated and roughly aligned with the guide

2c

Using the Clone Stamp to fill in the empty corner of the "photo 1" layer

3a

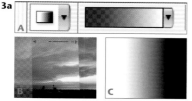

A black-to-white Linear gradient was chosen **A**. The Opacity of the top layer was reduced so the image underneath could be seen in the area of overlap, and with the layer mask active, the Gradient tool was dragged inside the overlap **B** to fill a layer mask **C**.

3b

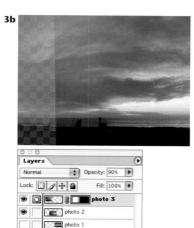

The result of blending the two images with the gradient mask

2 Aligning the images and filling gaps. For all but the bottom image layer, temporarily reduce the layer Opacity so you can see the overlap as you use the Move tool to align the layers so they match up **2a**. When this initial alignment is complete, return to 100% Opacity **2b** and use the Clone Stamp to repair any gaps that must be filled in order to get the final crop you want; we had to fill in the bottom of our right-hand image **2c**. (Alt/Option-click with the Clone Stamp to sample the image you want to use to fill the gap, then release the Alt/Option key and paint.)

3 Blending with layer masks.
Now you'll create a layer mask to control how each layer's image blends with the one below it in the area where they overlap. A black-to-white gradient will form the basis of each layer mask, with details hand-painted as necessary.

Starting with the top layer in your stack, change the Opacity setting to 90% so your image is more solid than at 50% but you can still see the overlap. Click the Add A Mask button at the bottom of the Layers palette. Choose the Gradient tool and, in the Options bar, click the Linear icon and then click the little triangle to the right of the Options bar's Gradient swatch. This opens the Gradient Options palette with the default selection of Foreground to Background. If the gradient is anything other than black-to-white, press "D" for "Default" to reset the Foreground and Background colors.

Drag the Gradient tool's cursor across the overlap to make a black-to-white gradient in the layer mask, starting just inside where you want this layer's image to disappear completely and ending just inside where you want this layer's image to completely hide the underlying layer's image **3a, 3b**. Restore the layer's Opacity to 100% to check the blend. If the first try hasn't produced a smooth transition in the lighting and color of the two layers, you can reduce the layer's Opacity to 90% again and make another try at drawing the gradient. When the general blend is right, you can tackle the details, as described next.

If the blending has caused "ghosting" of details that don't overlap perfectly from one image to the next, you can hand-paint the gradient mask to give priority to one layer over the other. For instance, where we could see a ghost of the people walking on the beach, we used the Airbrush tool at 100% Opacity with white paint

CAN'T ALIGN?

If moving one of two overlapping layers of a panorama series doesn't fix the alignment of details (such as a building in the distance), it may be because the two shots have different perspective. This can happen if the camera was tilted either up or down instead of being held parallel to the ground. (This is where a leveled tripod is invaluable.) To align the two overlapping versions of the element, you may need to select the element on one of the two layers and use the Free Transform command (Ctrl/⌘-T); holding down the Ctrl/⌘ key allows you to drag any of the corner control points to *distort* the element to bring the two images of the element into alignment.

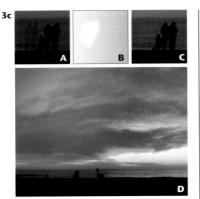

3c

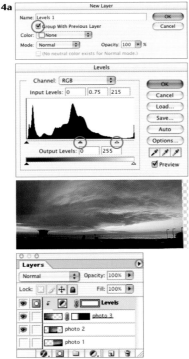

Where the layer mask for the "photo 3" layer was gray, some unaligned details showed through from the "photo 2" layer **A.** *A white "hole" was painted in the layer mask* **B** *to allow the "photo 3" layer to hide the unwanted detail* **C.** *The Opacity of the top layer was then returned to 100%* **D.**

A Levels Adjustment layer was grouped with the top image layer to begin the process of correcting its contrast, exposure, and color.

to lighten that area of the gradient to let the top layer show at 100% opacity, hiding the layer underneath in that spot **3c.**

At this point you can repeat the masking operation for all the other layers except the bottom one; then make color adjustments (as in step 4). Or do as we did: Assess the color and tone of the components, make the necessary corrections, and then finish the masking.

4 Fixing tonality and color. Look at your blended image and decide which of the component photos needs the most fixing, in terms of color, tone, and focus (sharpness or depth of field). We decided that the middle image was the one that looked most like what we were aiming for. The image on the right matched it quite well, but the one on the left (our top image) needed adjustment. If we could adjust the top image to match the middle, the entire panorama should match pretty well.

To adjust contrast and exposure, we added a Levels Adjustment layer **4a.** So that we could keep it from affecting the other layers, we held down the Alt/Option key as we dragged on the Create New Fill/Adjustment Layer button at the bottom of the Layers palette and chose Levels. Using Alt/Option caused the New Layer dialog box to open and we could choose Group With Previous Layer. When we clicked OK, the Levels box opened. We dragged the Input Levels gray slider to the right to darken the midtones and then moved the white slider to the left to bring back the highlights. Because we had grouped the Levels Adjustment layer with the top layer, the adjustments we made affected only that layer.

We used Alt/Option again to add a Hue/Saturation layer to the group **4b** and shifted the oranges toward red as follows: Since "Oranges" isn't offered as a choice in the Edit list at the top of the dialog box, we chose "Reds" (it was the best fit for the oranges we wanted to affect, since they were closer to red than to yellow); then we used the dialog box's "plus" Eyedropper to drag over the orange areas of the sky to define the

4b

Two color adjustments were made with a single grouped Hue/Saturation Adjustment layer: With the Reds range chosen, the Hue slider was moved to push the oranges toward red (top). Then with the Cyans range chosen, the blue-greens were also made more blue.

4c

A Color Balance Adjustment layer was used to "tweak" the color of highlights (shown in this dialog box), midtones, and shadow tones to get the result shown here.

range of colors we wanted to change; finally we moved the Hue slider to the left to accomplish the red shift. Before closing the dialog box, we chose Cyans and used a similar sampling-and-adjusting procedure to shift them toward blue by dragging the Hue slider slightly to the right.

Finally we added a Color Balance Adjustment layer **4c** and made individual adjustments to the Highlights (adding Magenta, Yellow, and Red), the Midtones (adding Magenta and Yellow), and Shadows (adding Red).

5 Adjusting overall color and tone. When you've masked and adjusted each of the separate components — we added a gradient mask to our middle photo but it needed no color adjustments — you can make other adjustments to the entire panorama that will help unify or improve the image. For instance, you can add noise as in step 9b of "Assembling a Still Life" on page 179 or step 6 of "Blurring the Background, but Keeping the Grain" on page 140. Or use a Saturation adjustment as in step 9a of "Assembling a Still Life," or adjust overall color or contrast.

In this panorama the clouds were the "star of the show." To make them look more like the scene we remembered, we wanted to emphasize the bottoms of the clouds where light from the sun at the horizon was reflecting off them. We also wanted to darken their tops, and to keep and even intensify the hot pink highlight on the cloud at the upper left. These kinds of changes seemed to call for dodging and burning different areas of the image. We decided not to use the Dodge and Burn tools — which work on highlights, shadows, and midtones separately, and only on the actual pixels of a single layer at a time. Instead we simplified the operation by creating a "dodge-and-burn layer," as follows: We Alt/Option-clicked the Create A New Layer button at the bottom of the Layers palette; in the New Layer dialog we named the layer "Dodge & Burn," chose Overlay for the Mode, and turned on the Fill With Overlay-Neutral Color option. Clicking OK closed the dialog box and filled the new layer with 50% gray **5a;** because of the Overlay blend mode, the gray appeared completely transparent, or "neutral." By lightening or darkening this neutral 50% gray, we could

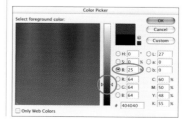

5a

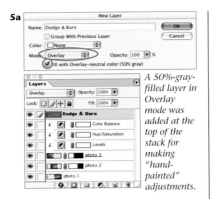

A 50%-gray-filled layer in Overlay mode was added at the top of the stack for making "hand-painted" adjustments.

5b

The "Dodge & Burn" layer (top) lightened the undersides of some of the clouds and darkened their tops.

5c

A final Hue/Saturation layer boosted the saturation of the colors overall and "warmed" the colors slightly.

brighten or darken the image underneath. We used the Paintbrush, stroking and restroking with lighter and darker grays since pure white or black in Overlay mode can oversaturate the colors in the layers below; we set a very low Opacity for the Paintbrush (about 5%) so we would have good control as we slowly built up the effect. If we overdid it with light or dark gray, we could fix the mistake by applying 50% gray **5b.**

Finally, we added another Hue/Saturation layer **5c,** this time for the entire image, by clicking the Create New Fill/Adjustment Layer button *without* using Alt/Option, since we didn't want to group the adjustment with any particular layer. To get the colors as close as we could to the real colors of the sunset without going outside the printable gamut, we increased the Saturation and shifted the Hue a little to the right to warm up the colors. We used the Gamut Warning (as described in the "Unprintable Colors" tip at the right) to let us know when our colors were getting too saturated. When that happened, we could choose the problem color range from the Hue/Saturation box's Edit list and reduce Saturation until the colors came back into gamut. Or, since we've had good luck reproducing color that is technically out of gamut according to Photoshop's Gamut Warning, we could allow some areas to stay "hot."

UNPRINTABLE COLORS

If you plan to increase color saturation, either with the Hue/Saturation dialog box or with the Sponge tool in Saturate mode, it's a good idea to turn on the **Gamut Warning** so you can see where you may have intensified the color beyond what it's possible to print with the current Color Settings.

To toggle the Gamut Warning on or off, choose View, Gamut Warning (or press Ctrl/⌘-Shift-Y). "Unprintable" colors are displayed as 50% gray patches by default, though you can change the color by choosing Edit, Preferences, Transparency & Gamut.

Both the View menu selection and the keyboard shortcut will work, even if a dialog box is already open, so if you forget to set up the Gamut Warning before you open the Hue/Saturation dialog, you can still get to it.

Note: The Gamut Warning tends to be conservative, telling you that some colors are outside the printable gamut when in fact they may print quite nicely.

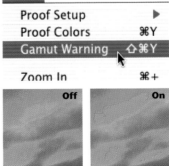

When you turn on the Gamut Warning, the solid gray areas show where there are colors that may be outside the printable range.

Collaging with Masks & Groups

Overview *Create a layout with the type and placeholder shapes; add Layer Styles to the elements; paste and group images with their respective placeholders; adjust color and tonality and sharpen the images as needed; organize with layer sets.*

"**Collage Layout**" "before" and "after" files

1a

▣ Rectangle Tool	U
▣ Rounded Rectangle Tool	U
⬯ Ellipse Tool	U
⬠ Polygon Tool	U
＼ Line Tool	U
⬚ Custom Shape Tool	U

Choosing the Ellipse from the pop-out Shape tools palette

1b

P22 Escher

Setting up the Options bar to create a type layer

1c

Type was set in two layers, one above and one below the circle.

WITH ITS INHERITED TYPOGRAPHIC PROWESS from InDesign and its new spell checker, Photoshop 7 is a now a practical layout tool. For a project such as a website splash screen or a brochure cover, you can design your layout — including placeholders for the images, masking effects, and added Styles — and also set your display type. Then just add your photos and group them with your placeholder layers.

1 Creating the main placeholder shape and type. You can start your layout by opening a new file with a white *Background* and then creating a placeholder for the main image element in your page design. In this case the main element was the central circle — it would frame the largest cat photo, and the display type would curve around it. We chose a medium gray as the Foreground color to create this main element. The gray would be entirely covered by a tiger image later, but in the meantime it would let us design the layout and see the Layer Style as we roughed out different effects. We dragged with the Ellipse (one of the Shape tools) with the Shift key held down to create the circle **1a**.

We wanted the type to accentuate the curves of the central circle, but we didn't need it to fit the circle exactly. The type would have to be in two layers, for two different reasons: first, so that part of the type could be in front of the central circle and part behind it; and second, so that a positive curve could be applied to part of the type (the part above the shape) and a negative bend could be applied to the other part (the type below the shape). To set our top line of type, we chose the Type tool **1b**, and clicked the Palettes button at

4d

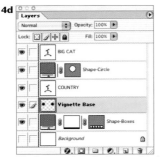

The Layers palette for the completed basic layout

in Multiply mode for a "dark halo" to help the type stand out. You can check these settings also in the **Collage Layout-After.psd** file.

We copied the Layer Style from the top type layer to the other type layer, as follows: In the Layers palette, right-click (Windows) or Control-click (Mac) on the "*f*" icon for the layer with the Style and choose Copy Layer Style from the pop-out menu. Then right/Control-click the name of the layer where you want to copy the Style and choose Paste Layer Style.

We used another Layer Style to color and texturize the background of our layout. First we had to convert the *Background* to a layer that could accept a Style, so we double-clicked its name in the Layers palette, renamed it "Background Texture," and clicked OK. Then we added a Layer Style with Color Overlay and Pattern

A MULTIPLE-STROKE TREATMENT FOR TYPE

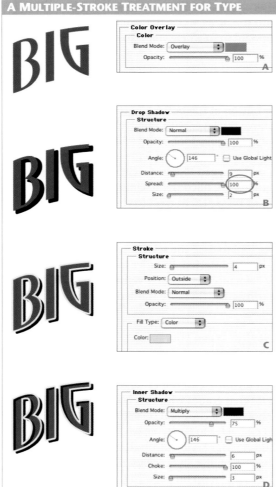

When a non-zero Distance setting is used for Drop Shadow and Inner Shadow, the type looks dimensional.

A **Layer Style** is a great way to add color and character to type or graphics. With the "multiple-stroke" approach described here, you can either create an old-fashioned dimensional look (as shown in the series at the left) or a flat "inline/outline" treatment (shown finished below).

Start with a **Color Overlay:** Activate the layer with the type, click the "*f*" button at the bottom of the Layers palette, and choose Color Overlay from the list of layer effects. In the Color Overlay section of the Layer Style dialog box, click the swatch and choose a color for the body of the type **A.**

Choose **Drop Shadow** from the list at the left side of the Layer Style dialog box. In the Structure section of the Drop Shadow settings, **set the Spread at 100% to ensure a hard-edged "shadow,"** and adjust the Angle, the Distance (which is the offset), and the Size (use a setting that will allow the shadow to extend beyond the width of the Stroke you will add next) **B.** Make sure the Use Global Light box is checked.

Choose **Stroke** from the list at the left side. In the Structure section of the Stroke settings, choose Outside for the Position and use the Size slider to arrive at the stroke width you want **C.**

Choose **Inner Shadow** from the list at the left side. In the Structure section of the Inner Shadow settings, **set the Choke at 100% to ensure a hard-edged "shadow,"** as you did for the Drop Shadow's Spread setting. Make sure the Use Global Light box is checked so the offset will be in the same direction as for the Drop Shadow. Now you can adjust the Distance (offset) and Size as you like **D.**

A Distance (offset) of 0 for the Drop Shadow (Size, 6) and the Inner Shadow (Size, 2) produces an "inline/outline" result.

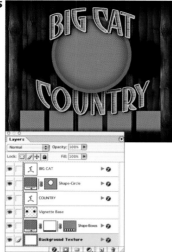

Layer Styles were added to the elements of the basic layout.

Overlay effects **5**. You can check the settings for these effects in the **Collage Layout-After.psd** file.

6 Putting images into the layout. With the layout complete and the type styled, you can bring in your images to be "cropped" by the shapes of the placeholder graphics, such as our central circle, side vignettes, and faded squares. For each photo, the strategy is to select and copy it from its own file, then activate its placeholder layer by clicking its name in the Layers palette of the layout file, and paste in the copied image. The pasted image will come into the file as a layer above the placeholder layer **6a**. To "crop" the photo within the shape of the placeholder, you simply group the two layers (press Ctrl/⌘-G) **6b**. Since the placeholder is the bottom layer of the clipping group, its Style also affects the photo. Repositioning and scaling the pasted photo completes the process of inserting the image — press Ctrl/⌘-T for Free Transform; drag inside the Transform box to move the image, or Shift-drag a corner handle to scale; double-click in the box or press the Enter key to finalize the transformation **6c**. We pasted and transformed the central tiger, the two side cats and the five cats for the bottom squares, each on its own layer **6d, 6e**.

7 Making adjustments. With all the elements in place, you can now look at the layout overall and see where you want to adjust the size, color, or tonality of individual elements or Layer Styles. For instance, you can fine-tune the size of the display type element: Link the two type layers by clicking the name of one of them in the Layers palette and clicking in the column next to the Eye for the

6a

An image pasted into the layout file

6b

The pasted image grouped with its placeholder Shape

6c

The pasted and grouped tiger image was scaled and repositioned.

6d

The pasted images shown ungrouped (top) and grouped with their respective placeholders

6e

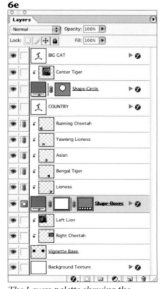

The Layers palette showing the file after all photos had been pasted and grouped

7

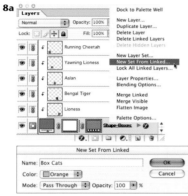

Unsharp Mask was used on each of the images that had been scaled.

8a

Forming a layer set from linked layers

8b

The layer set for the cats in the square boxes

8c

Layer sets were also made for the central tiger and the vignettes.

other one; press Ctrl/⌘-T (for Free Transform) and scale the two type layers slightly by dragging the handles of the Transform box.

You can also balance color and contrast for each image. Or another option is to unify the layout with a not-quite-monochromatic color scheme, as described in the tip at the right.

To sharpen images that may have been softened by the scaling, use the Unsharp Mask filter as needed (Filter, Sharpen, Unsharp Mask) **7**; each image may need a different amount of sharpening. Also, you can adjust the colors, opacity and blend modes of the individual effects in the Layer Styles to work best with the individual images.

8 Organizing the layers. To organize the Layers palette into a more concise form, you can gather related layers into sets, which can be "collapsed" to take up less space in the palette. A quick way to do this is to click on the name of one of the layers you want to assemble into a set, and then click or drag in the Links column (next to the Eye column) to link the other associated layers. Then open the Layers palette's pop-out menu (from the triangle in the upper right corner of the palette) and choose New Set From Linked. In the New Set From Linked dialog box, name the set, choose a color, and leave the Mode setting at Pass Through, to keep the individual blend modes in effect for the layers **8a**. Then click OK **8b**. Repeat the process for any other sets you want to make. We made three sets — for the central cat, for the cats in the side vignettes, and for the cats in the boxes at the bottom of the layout **8c**.

UNIFYING ASSEMBLED ELEMENTS

When you craft a layout from photos or full-color illustrations, sometimes the biggest design challenge is turning a diverse collection of images into a unified set. One approach is to tint the entire assemblage with a single color by adding a Hue/Saturation Adjustment layer at the top of the layer stack, with the Colorize option chosen in the Hue/Saturation dialog box. Also, you can often get the same kind of unifying monochromatic effect while still preserving some of the original color by reducing the Opacity of the Hue/Saturation Adjustment layer.

Clicking the top layer of this layout file in the Layers palette and then clicking the Create New Fill/Adjustment Layer button and choosing Hue/Saturation added an Adjustment layer. With the Colorize option turned on, the Hue was set and the Saturation was reduced. To restore some of the original color, the Opacity of the Hue/Saturation layer was reduced to 75%.

Integrating Type or Graphics

Overview *Add type or graphic to a photo; create a sharp-edged mask to make this element appear to surround the subject of the photo; add shadows to support the illusion; add more type and a "clear" logo element.*

"**Logo Composite**" "before" and "after" files

The original image

Setting the type specs in the Character palette

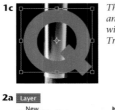

The type was scaled and repositioned with Free Transform.

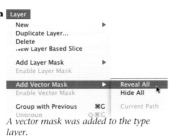

A vector mask was added to the type layer.

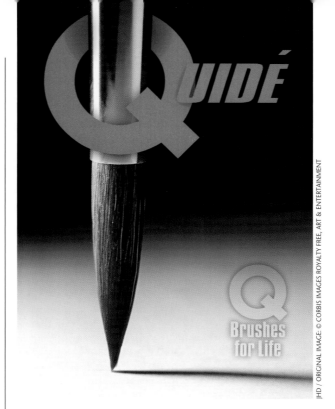

PHOTOSHOP'S LAYER MASKS AND VECTOR MASKS make it possible to integrate type or graphics with a photo. With masks you can put type or graphics *behind* the subject of a photo but *in front of* the background, keeping the type or vector-based shape live and editable. Or, as in the image above, you can even "interweave" the type or graphic and the photo. To achieve an effective composite, you need to tailor a mask to fit perfectly, so it masks the part of the graphic that's "hidden" by the photo, with no telltale edges. And you need to get the shadows right. In the montage above, the masking needed to match the smooth lines of the brush to make it look like the top of the "Q" was behind the brush; we could achieve this by using a vector mask. The rest of the solution consisted of casting the shadow of the "Q" onto the brush and the shadow of the brush onto the "Q."

1 Scaling and aligning. Open the photo **1a** and set your type, or create or import a vector-based graphic. We chose the Type tool and clicked the Palettes button on the Options bar to open the Character palette, where we could choose a typeface (Quicksans Accurate) and a color (red) and specify a size (we guessed at 500 px). We clicked in the image and typed a "Q" **1b.** The letter turned out to be too small, but in order to use Free Transform to scale it up, we first had to "commit" the type (to commit, press the Enter key on the keypad, or click the ✓ at the right end of the Options bar). Pressing Ctrl/⌘-T brought up the Transform box; we Shift-

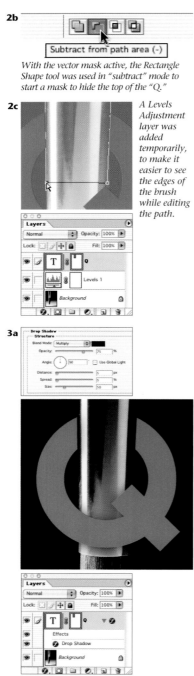

2b

Subtract from path area (-)

With the vector mask active, the Rectangle Shape tool was used in "subtract" mode to start a mask to hide the top of the "Q."

2c

A Levels Adjustment layer was added temporarily, to make it easier to see the edges of the brush while editing the path.

3a

When the vector mask was complete, the Levels Adjustment layer was deleted. A Drop Shadow was added to the type layer.

dragged outward on a corner handle to proportionally scale the "Q," and then dragged inside the box to move it into position **1c.** Finally we double-clicked inside the box to commit the transformation.

2 Adding a vector mask. One way to build the required mask is to add a vector mask that doesn't hide anything and then draw a shape that will conceal the part you want to hide. A vector mask can be added by choosing Layer, Add Vector Mask, Reveal All **2a;** or you can do it by Ctrl/⌘-clicking the Add A Mask button at the bottom of the Layers palette.

The shape that would mask out the part of the shaft where the "Q" overlapped it was almost a rectangle, so we decided to start with the Rectangle (one of the Shape tools) located below the Type tool in the toolbox. We chose the Rectangle and clicked the Subtract From Path Area button in the Options bar **2b.** This would "subtract" the rectangle we were about to draw from the "reveal all" mask. We dragged the tool to make a rectangle that fit the brush as closely as possible; we would adjust the exact shape in just a minute. To make it easier to see the edges of the brush as we edited the edges of the mask, we worked at 100% magnification and added a Levels Adjustment layer just above the photo to boost the contrast and thereby exaggerate the edges **2c.** To do this, click the photo layer's name in the Layers palette to activate it, then click the Create New Fill/Adjustment layer button at the bottom of the palette and choose Levels from the pop-out menu. Move the gamma (gray, middle) slider for Input Levels until the edges are distinct. Activate the type layer again by clicking its name in the Layers palette, then click the mask thumbnail so you can see the path in the working window. Choose the Direct Selection tool and use it to click on and drag the individual control points to reshape the mask. When the mask is complete, delete the Adjustment layer by dragging its thumbnail to the Trash icon at the bottom of the palette.

3 Adding the shadows. To cast a shadow from your type or graphic onto the photo, add a Drop Shadow as follows: With the type layer still active, click the *"f"* button at the bottom of the palette and choose Drop Shadow from the pop-out menu. We used low Distance and Spread settings and a large Size setting to make the shadow soft and diffuse. Because the background around the brush was very dark, the diffuse shadow didn't show up there **3a.** (If the background of your image is a lighter color and shows the shadow, you can use the method described in the next paragraph to paint a shadow for the graphic, restricting the shadow to only those elements of the background image that should actually "catch" a shadow.)

To make the shadow cast by the shaft onto the "Q" where it "went behind" the brush, we activated the "Q" layer and clicked the Create A New Layer button at the bottom of the Layers palette. Then we used the Airbrush with a big, soft brush tip at a low Pressure setting to

3b

A separate transparent layer was added and grouped with the type layer, so the type's mask also hid part of the shadow that was painted onto the new layer. Inset: Shadow and masked type layers viewed without the Background and without grouping.

4

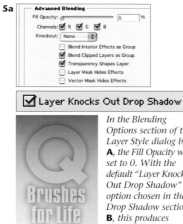

Another type layer was added. The Style from the "Q" layer was copied and pasted to the new type layer.

5a

☑ Layer Knocks Out Drop Shadow

*In the Blending Options section of the Layer Style dialog box **A**, the Fill Opacity was set to 0. With the default "Layer Knocks Out Drop Shadow" option chosen in the Drop Shadow section **B**, this produces "clear" shadowed type.*

paint a shadow onto the top of the "Q." To mask the shadow so it affected only the "Q" and not the brush, we grouped the shadow layer with the type layer (to group adjacent layers, Alt/Option-click on the border between them in the Layers palette) **3b.**

4 Completing the logo. We used the Type tool to add another layer above the shadow layer, and typed "UIDÉ" in the Commador WideHeavy font to finish the logo. We copied the drop shadow from the "Q" and pasted it to this type layer **4,** as follows: right-click (or Control-click on a Mac with a one-button mouse) on the *name, not the thumbnail,* of the layer you want to copy from, and choose Copy Layer Style from the context-sensitive menu that pops up. Then right/Control-click on the name of the layer you want to paste to, and choose Paste Layer Style from the pop-up menu.

5 Adding a "ghosted" logo. We wanted to add a "clear" version of a second logo, with a drop shadow but no fill so the underlying image would show through. This logo existed as an Adobe Illustrator graphic, so we copied it to the clipboard in Illustrator and then pasted it into our Photoshop file as a shape layer (Edit, Paste, Paste As: Shape Layer). We scaled and positioned the logo. Then we double-clicked the new Shape layer's name in the Layers palette to open the Layer Style dialog box to the Blending Options section; there we reduced the Fill Opacity (the *fill* slider just below the *opacity* slider in the Layers palette) to 0; this made the logo disappear. Then we clicked the Drop Shadow entry in the list on the left side of the dialog box to add a shadow **5a**. For the Drop Shadow we used the default "Layer Knocks Out Drop Shadow" and set the Distance to 0 so the dark shadow would spread out evenly around the transparent logo **5b.**

5b

The Layers palette for the finished layout shown at the top of page 191

UNLINKING THE MASK

If you mask a layer that has a Style applied to it, by default the mask is linked to the layer. Any edges created by the mask are treated with any edge effects you've applied as part of the Style. For instance, if the Style includes a Bevel And Emboss effect, the edges created by the mask will also be beveled. One way to avoid this is to unlink the mask from the layer by clicking to turn off the link icon between their thumbnails in the Layers palette.

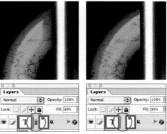

With the mask linked to the layer (left), the masked edges are beveled, which interferes with the illusion of the brush passing through the "Q." With the mask unlinked (right), the illusion is preserved.

 **Q Advanced** files

Wrapping a "Decal"

Overview *Apply an image on one layer (the "decal") to another layer (the "surface"), using the luminance of the surface layer to bend the decal so it conforms to the surface; adjust blend mode and opacity to combine the two layers; use a layer mask to protect part of the surface image from the decal.*

IMAGE

"**Flag Decal**" "before" and "after" files

Original image and flag graphic

The flag was pasted as a new layer above the climbing image; its blend mode was set to Overlay and its Opacity to 50%.

3a

Displace	
Horizontal Scale 10 %	OK
Vertical Scale -10 %	Cancel
Displacement Map:	Undefined Areas:
● Stretch To Fit	○ Wrap Around
○ Tile	● Repeat Edge Pixels

Setting the displacement scales after choosing Filter, Distort, Displace

BENDING, WARPING, AND DISTORTING an image or graphic so it appears to be applied to the textured surface of another image creates a unified visual illusion that can be very powerful in presenting a concept. In Photoshop, the fastest, most flexible, and most convincing way we've found to do this kind of "decal application" is by using the Displace filter with a displacement map that's made from the surface image itself. The Liquify command is of limited use in distorting one image based upon another. For instance, in the case of the image developed here, it can't begin to do the precise, practical work that's required to distort the flag — the amount of hand work required would be enormous, even with Photoshop 7's ability to see what's beneath the layer being liquified.

1 Preparing the images. Choose the image or graphic you want to apply (the "decal" — in this case the flag, which started as an EPS clip art file) and the surface you want to apply it to (here, the same rock surface used in "Carving a Textured Surface" on page 382) **1**.

2 Combining the images. Add the decal to the surface image file as a new layer: We chose File, Place and dragged the placed graphic to scale it, then double-clicked inside its bounding box to accept the scaling. (If your "decal" is a Photoshop file, use the Move tool to drag it from its working window into the working window of the surface image, where it will become a new layer.)

In the pop-out menu at the top left of the Layers palette, choose

3b

After using the Displace filter

4

Masking the graphic layer to protect the climber from the decal

5a

Changing the blend mode to Soft Light (top) lightened and faded the flag. Using Multiply mode (bottom) darkened and faded it.

Overlay for the blend mode. At the top right of the Layers palette, reduce the Opacity for the decal layer until you get the result you want **2. Note**: If your new decal layer is larger than your original photo (as ours was after we had scaled the flag), you'll need to trim away the excess in order for the displacement to work right in the next step. To do this, select all (Ctrl/⌘-A) and then choose Image, Crop.

3 Making and using the displacement map. Prepare a grayscale displacement map from the surface layer as described in step 5 of "Carving a Textured Surface" (we used the same displacement map that we made in that step) and apply it to the decal layer, using Filter, Distort, Displace **3a, 3b** as described in step 6 of that same section.

4 Masking the decal. To remove the decal from a subject in the surface image, so that the subject appears to be in front of the "painted" surface, you can use a layer mask to hide a portion of the decal layer. (In "Carving a Textured Surface" we copied the climber to a separate top layer rather than using a layer mask on the graphic layer, since the edge of the mask would have produced an unwanted bevel around the climber when the Style was applied to the layer. Here, since there's no bevel involved, we can use a layer mask.) To make the mask, first select the subject (see the "Easier Selecting" tip in Chapter 1 for pointers). Then, with the decal layer active, Alt/Option-click the mask icon at the bottom of the Layers palette. Using the Alt/Option key *hides* the selected area of the layer **4,** rather than keeping it visible and hiding the unselected area. This is equivalent to choosing Layer, Add Layer Mask, Hide Selection from Photoshop's main menu.

5 Experimenting with Blending Options. You may also want to experiment with other blend modes, such as Multiply, Soft Light, Hard Light, or Color for slightly different visual effects **5a.** Or choose Blending Options from the Layers palette's pop-out menu and experiment with the "Blend If" section to "wear away" the decal **5b.**

5b

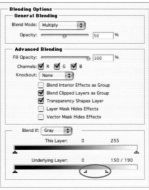

We moved the white point slider inward for the Underlying Layer so the lightest areas of the rock showed through the flag, producing a worn look. Holding down Alt/Option allowed us to split the white point slider to make a smooth transition from flag to rock in these light areas.

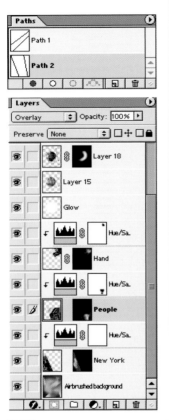

To begin his *CMU* montage, **Henk Dawson** modeled and rendered the globe and metal gridwork in the Electric Image 3D program. Then Dawson started a low-res Photoshop file and dragged in a rendering of the globe and grid. Using the imported rendering as a reference, he clicked from point to point with Photoshop's Pen tool, following the lines of the gridwork to create paths he could use to divide up the background space diagonally. He saved each path and Ctrl/⌘-clicked on its name in the Paths palette to load it as a selection that would limit his airbrushing as he created an intersecting mesh of blue and gold for the background. The small file size of the low-res image eliminated lag time as he used the Airbrush tool, so he could maintain spontaneity in the painting process. And because the airbrushed color transitions he created were amorphous and soft, the quality of this background wouldn't be

degraded when he increased the resolution of the file after he finished airbrushing.

After increasing the resolution (using the Image, Image Size command, with Resample Image selected and Bicubic chosen), Dawson deleted the globe-and-grid layer and replaced it with high-res renderings that he imported and aligned. To get the lighting he wanted for the globe, he layered two different rendered versions, one that was a little too light and one that was dark overall, and contrasty. "Some artists make several renderings of a 3D model," says Dawson, "with a different light used for each rendering." It can be difficult to get the final lighting the way you want it in a 3D program — experimenting with several lights, rendering, experimenting some more, rendering, and so on. It's often much easier to resolve it by making several single-light 3D renderings and combining them in Photoshop as

separate layers using Screen, Multiply, and Overlay modes, and using layer masks to control the composition.

Dawson airbrushed a white glow on a layer below the globe layers. That way he could control its shape and density more directly than with a layer effect or a blurred, white-filled copy of the globe.

The color photos (from Rubber Ball Productions) that surround the globe are on separate layers in Overlay mode; a Hue/Saturation Adjustment layer clipped to each eliminates most of the color by reducing the Saturation. In addition, a layer mask for each photo creates a soft-edged silhouette. In some cases the stored paths that had been used for the blue-and-gold background were also loaded as selections to use in making the masks. Because Photoshop's paths are vector-based, their diagonal edges did not lose any sharpness when Dawson increased the resolution of the file.

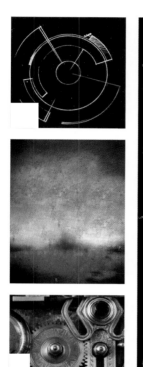

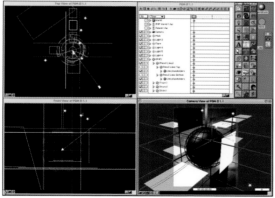

Henk Dawson usually does the final assembly for his three-dimensional compositions in Photoshop, where he can work more spontaneously and adjust lighting and color more easily than in a 3D program. However, for *Connections*, an illustration for a feature article in *Macworld* magazine, he used Photoshop to create textural elements but did the final assembly in Electric Image. To get the depth and perspective he wanted for a unified scene, he needed the light sources and camera angles of the 3D program.

The globe, metal gridwork, and 3D type were created in Electric Image. The Photoshop elements that were imported and used as texture maps included a circular pencil drawing that was scanned, converted to negative, duplicated and positioned both above and below the globe; a background painted with acrylics on canvas, scanned and modified; graphs and charts, scanned and in some cases inverted; a photo of a string; and a stock photo of gears (PhotoDisc). Dawson used alpha channel masking in Electric Image to create partial transparency of some of the imported elements.

Alicia Buelow created *Convert* as an illustration for an article in *Internet* magazine about converting traditional published media into electronic media for the Web. By working with many layers, blend modes, and layer masks, she created a multilevel illustration with a great deal of depth.

To create a textured background, Buelow started with a photo she had taken of a painted wall and combined it with overlying layers containing stock photos of a rust texture and peeling paint. Some areas of the peeling paint image were masked out with a layer mask, and the layer was blended in Overlay mode.

To illustrate turning pages, Buelow took three pieces of paper, curled the edges, and laid them on her flatbed scanner. The resulting scan was blended into the background using a layer mask and Hard Light mode, with Opacity reduced to 93%. Likewise, the open book image was created by scanning a book laid open on the scanner and was blended using Luminosity mode.

The jumbled words and letters in the lower left were cut out of a magazine, pasted onto a piece of paper, then scanned and blended into the background using Color Burn mode. Buelow's use of blend modes had the

effect of pulling all the overlaid elements toward the warm palette of the background. Though she had a sense of the effect that would be produced by each mode, many of her choices resulted from trial-and-error experimentation, influenced by how the color palette of each layered image blended with that of the others.

The web page images were "ghosted" with layer masks. Using painted masks for these and other layers made it easy to bring back parts of the images after checking how they looked in the overall composition.

The background for **Katrin Eismann's** *Fleeting* image was a photo of bamboo taken with a medium-format camera, scanned in Kodak PhotoCD format, and opened in Photoshop. The artist photographed her own sunlight-projected shadow silhouette with a Leica S1 Pro scanning camera, opened it in Photoshop, and dragged it into the background file with the Move tool; Multiply was chosen for the blend mode. Eismann wanted to add a layer mask that would hide parts of the shadow and also make the bamboo-and-shadow interaction look more realistic. To start the layer mask, she loaded the luminosity of her composite bamboo-and-shadow image as a selection. ▶ *You can make a selection based on the composite of all visible layers by pressing Ctrl-Alt-~ (Windows) or ⌘-Option-~ (Mac), or by Ctrl/⌘-clicking the RGB Channel in the Channels palette.*

With the shadow layer active, Eismann added a mask based on the *inverse* of this selection. ▶ *To turn an active selection into a layer mask, click the Create New Layer button at the bottom of the Layers palette; to make the inverse mask (with the selected area dark and the unselected areas light), simply Alt/Option-click the button.*

Eismann's layer mask lightened the silhouette shadow where it fell over highlighted portions of the bamboo. She also painted parts of the layer mask with the Paintbrush tool to hide artifacts at the edges of the shadow. At 100% Opacity the shadow layer didn't produce a dark enough effect, so she duplicated the layer and moved the Opacity slider to the left, stopping at 10% when she saw the result she wanted.

The medical illustration of the hand was a stock image from Visual Language. Eismann selected and rotated the thumb to open the hand a little, then used the digital camera again to photograph her own hand in a similar position. She layered the two left hands together in a file of their own, flipping them to produce a right hand instead, then made a merged copy (by choosing Image, Duplicate, Merged Layers Only) and dragged this into her main image file. She added layer effects — an Outer Glow and Pillow-style embossing — to give the hand dimension and separate it more distinctly from the background.

A

B

C

D

E

To make the *Waikiki Kids* composite image, **Jack Davis** started with two different shots taken on the same morning, in the same basic location. (We all know it's physically impossible to have two children on two moving objects, smiling, facing the same direction, at the same time!)

Davis decided the main shot would be the one with the mandatory Diamond Head in the background **A.** The chore was to add the image of the boy (Ryan) **B** to the photo of the girl (Rachel). To simplify this

process and to allow a degree of flexibility (if the images were to be moved or changed later), the masking of Ryan was done in two stages.

First, a selection of Ryan and the air mattress was made (not worrying about the foreground because that would be hidden in the next step), and then the Add A Mask icon was clicked to isolate him from his background **C.**

Second, the right edge and area above Rachel was selected where Ryan was going to be limited to. But rather than

adding this selection to the existing mask for Ryan (which would mean his position would be "locked" into that location), a Layer Set folder was created (click on the Folder icon on the bottom of the Layers palette.) The Ryan layer was then dragged into this folder, and with the folder Layer active, the Create Layer Mask icon was clicked again **D.** This allowed for the two separate masks to be used on the same image and allowed Ryan's position and scale to be manipulated without affecting the edge that was hiding the overlap with Rachel **E.**

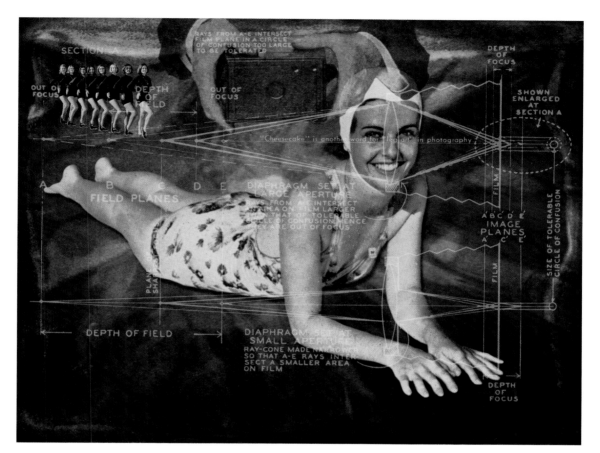

Darryl Baird's *Aqueous Humor #14*, part of a series of
humorous commentary on American culture, is composed
of five black-and-white elements: Baird used three
silhouetted vintage 1940's photos, a diagram, and reverse
typography — each in a separate layer — over an abstract
background that was painted in watercolor and scanned.

To mimic the hand-tinting done in the era when the photos were
taken, Baird added a color-filled layer above each separate black-
and-white element, and then made a clipping group of each
color-and-element pair by Alt/Option-clicking on the border
between the two layers in the Layers palette. As a result the
bottom layer of each pair (containing the grayscale information)
acts as a mask for the solid color layer above it. So each color layer
could tint its element layer below without covering up the image
detail, Baird set three of the color layers to Soft Light mode (those
for the swimmer, reverse type, and chorus line) and two to
Multiply mode. In addition, the tonality of the layer containing the
black-and-white diagram was reversed (Image, Adjust, Invert) and
the layer was set to Screen mode at 60% Opacity, which allowed
the white type and lines to become part of the image but made
the dark background of the layer almost invisible.

USING FILTERS

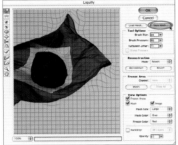

The Liquify command (now residing in the Filters menu) opens a dialog box that lets you move pixels around interactively. The function and setup of this dialog box are like some of Photoshop's more complex filters, such as Lighting Effects, 3D Transform, and Extract. One of the welcomed new features in Photoshop 7's Liquify filter is its ability to perform distortions on a low-resolution file. Save the manipulated "mesh" (see highlighted area above), then load that same mesh back into a high resolution version of the same image (or even a different image), thus allowing you to work much more quickly on initial experimentations.

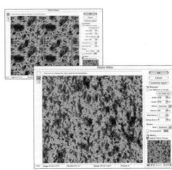

New to Photoshop 7 is the Pattern Maker filter, useful for extending selected textures to fill larger areas or, depending on the source, it may be useful for creating seamless tile patterns to be used in web applications.

GROUPED IN PHOTOSHOP'S FILTER MENU are many small "subprograms" that can be run on an entire image layer or a selected part of one. Some can also be run on individual color channels and on layer masks, a Quick Mask, Adjustment layers, and alpha channels. Filters modify the color or position of pixels in the image, with sometimes practical and sometimes astounding results:

- A few "workhorse" filters — Unsharp Mask, Gaussian Blur, and the Noise filters — can do a lot to improve the quality of scanned photographs, and even illustrations. You'll find these productivity-enhancers used in techniques throughout the book. Their workings are described in detail in the next few pages, in the "Sharpen," "Blur," and "Noise" sections, named for the Filter submenus where they can be found. Also covered here are the less productivity-oriented members of their families, which have specialized uses.

- Many of Photoshop's other filters are designed to add special effects, dimensional treatments, or the look of artists' materials. For a brief visual "catalog" of what these filters can do, see "Filter Demos" starting on page 232. You'll also find examples of their use in tips and techniques elsewhere throughout the book.

- Lighting Effects and other filters of the Render submenu have great potential for synthesizing environments and creating very convincing dimensional effects.

continued on page 204

FILTER SHORTCUTS

Three keyboard shortcuts can save time once you've applied a filter:

- **Ctrl/⌘-F applies the last filter you used**, with the same settings.

- **Ctrl-Alt-F** (Windows) or **⌘-Option-F** (Mac) **opens the dialog box for the last filter you applied**, so you can change the settings and run it again.

  Both of the above commands remain available until you run another filter. *(But neither of them work with the Extract, Liquify, or Pattern Maker "filters.")*

- **Ctrl/⌘-Shift-F** (the shortcut for Edit, Fade) brings up the Fade dialog box so you can adjust the blending mode and Opacity of the filtered image as if it were on a layer above the original unfiltered one. The Fade command is available only immediately after the filter is applied. As soon as you do anything else to the file, Fade is unavailable.

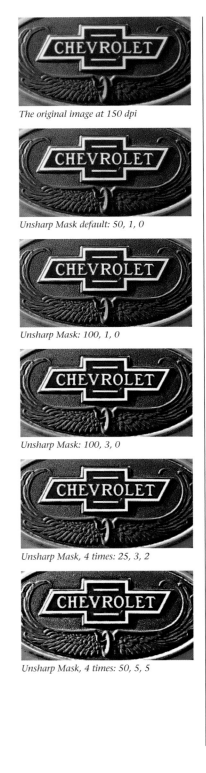

The original image at 150 dpi

Unsharp Mask default: 50, 1, 0

Unsharp Mask: 100, 1, 0

Unsharp Mask: 100, 3, 0

Unsharp Mask, 4 times: 25, 3, 2

Unsharp Mask, 4 times: 50, 5, 5

- Now in Photoshop 7, in the Filter menu, the filter-like Liquify command (described on page 213 and in "Liquifying a Shadow" on page 226) also provides its own "mini-studio" where you can prod, smear, and swirl your images.

SHARPEN

Photoshop provides four sharpening filters — Sharpen, Sharpen More, Sharpen Edges, and Unsharp Mask — but for sharpening an image to improve its quality, **Unsharp Mask is the one to use.**

Unsharp Mask

Unlike Sharpen and Sharpen More, which can accentuate blemishes, film grain, and image-editing artifacts, Unsharp Mask accentuates the differences primarily at "edges," exactly where you want the differences to be distinct. And unlike Sharpen Edges, it gives you precise control. To use Unsharp Mask, choose Filter, Sharpen, Unsharp Mask. This opens the Unsharp Mask dialog box, where you can set:

- The **Amount** (how much the difference at an edge is enhanced by the filter).
- The **Radius** (how many pixels in from the color edge will have their contrast increased). Increase the Radius with increasing resolution, because at higher resolutions the individual pixels are smaller relative to the components of the picture.
- The **Threshold** (how different the colors on the two sides of an edge have to be before the filter will recognize it as an edge and sharpen it). Use higher settings for images that are "grainy" or have subtle color shifts, such as skin tones, so the filter won't sharpen the "noise."

The use of Unsharp Mask comes up again and again throughout the book, but here's a quick list of sharpening tips:

Use Unsharp Mask on scanned images. As a rule, run the Unsharp Mask filter to see if it improves a scanned photo by getting rid of blurriness from a poor original or from the scanning process.

Use Unsharp Mask on resized or transformed images. Use Unsharp Mask whenever you use Image, Image Size with Resample Image turned on, or when you use Scale, Rotate, Skew, Distort,

SHARPENING LUMINOSITY

Sharpening can cause changes in color as the contrast is increased, especially at edges. The more intense the sharpening, the greater the changes. To minimize color changes, apply the Unsharp Mask filter. Then go to Edit, Fade, and change the blending mode of that applied filter to Luminosity.

Photo at 100 dpi, before sharpening

100 dpi photo with Unsharp Mask applied: 200, 1, 0

Resolution increased to 200 dpi without sharpening

Resolution increased to 200 dpi; then Unsharp Mask applied: 200, 1, 0

Perspective, or Numeric functions from Edit, Transform or Edit, Free Transform. Any such change involves *resampling* — that is, creating or recoloring pixels based on calculations — and this is bound to "soften" the image.

Use Unsharp Mask more than once. Running Unsharp Mask more than once at a lower Amount can sharpen more smoothly than if you run it once at a setting twice as high. (Note that Sharpen More and Sharpen shouldn't be run twice, since they worsen the artifacts they create if you apply them more than once. It's best to stay away from them altogether.)

Use Unsharp Mask last. Because it can generate artifacts that can be magnified by other image-editing operations, Unsharp Mask should generally be applied after you've finished editing the image.

Use a "repairs" layer for pinpoint precision. You can get handheld control of the Unsharp Mask filter for touch-ups to an image (an example is shown in the "Adding Depth" tip on page 206). First duplicate the image to another layer and sharpen this new "repairs" layer with the Unsharp Mask filter. Then add a black-filled layer mask by Alt/Option-clicking the mask button at the bottom of the Layers palette, and apply the sharpening where you want it by painting with white. (If you don't use the Alt/Option key, you get a white-filled mask that lets the entire sharpened image show. A black-filled mask, on the other hand, hides the contents of the layer so you see the original image underneath, until you paint on the mask with white to reveal parts of the sharpened image. The process of using a "repairs" layer is described step-by-step on page 134.)
If your computer's memory is limited, **an alternative is to**

EVALUATING SHARPENING

Too much sharpening can give a photo an artificial look, so you don't want to overdo it. But if you're preparing an image for the printed page, keep in mind that sharpening tends to look much "stronger" on-screen or on a laser print than it will when the image is finally printed at much higher resolution on a press.

FILTERING 16-BIT IMAGES

For critical color in Photoshop 7, you can work with images with more color depth than the standard 8 bits per channel (which is called *24-bit color* or *millions of colors* for an RGB file). Not only do many of the Image, Adjust commands used for color correction work on 16-bit images, but now most of the "workhorse" filters — Unsharp Mask, Gaussian Blur, Add Noise, Median, and Dust & Scratches — can also be applied. That means you can use these filters to treat the 16-bit images produced by some scanners and digital cameras (this option is usually referred to in the scanner interface as *billions of colors,* or in the camera as *raw*). The two drawbacks to working with 16-bit images are (1) your file size will increase dramatically, and (2) Photoshop doesn't allow layers in 16-bit files. So you'll typically convert to the 8-bit RGB standard after taking advantage of the 16-bit file for color adjustment and some filtering.

With the Unsharp Mask filter, you can use a masked duplicate of the image to paint the sharpening exactly where you want it. You can control the amount of sharpening you want overall by varying the Opacity of the layer. And you can get less sharpening in some areas by painting the mask with shades of gray instead of white.

PHOTO: © CORBIS IMAGES ROYALTY FREE, BUILDINGS & STRUCTURES

The original image (top) was oversharpened for a special effect (bottom; Unsharp Mask: 500, 50, 50)

PHOTO: © CORBIS IMAGES ROYALTY FREE, BUILDINGS & STRUCTURES

The original image (left) was converted to Lab Color mode and then oversharpened for a special effect (right; Unsharp Mask: 500, 20, 0)

use the History Brush for pinpoint control of sharpening, rather than adding an entire duplicate layer and mask. This technique is presented step-by-step in "Retouching with History" on page 122. It's also useful for image files with more color depth than 8 bits per channel, since these files can have only one layer.

Using the masked repairs layer or the History Brush gives you several advantages over using the Sharpen tool, which shares a spot in the toolbox with the Blur (water drop) and Smudge (finger) tools. When you "paint" the Sharpen tool back and forth over the area you want to sharpen, you can't tell that you've reached the optimal sharpening until you see that you've gone too far; then you have to undo the repair and start over, or step backwards through the states in the History palette. With the Unsharp Mask/repairs method, you can preview the sharpening in the filter's dialog box, so you can see the maximum result in advance, and you can paint, erase, and repaint the mask with white and black until you get the effect you want, without doing any permanent damage to the image.

Use Unsharp Mask at very high settings for special effects. Oversharpening can produce artistic effects like those shown at the left.

BLUR

Photoshop's blurring filters can be used to soften all or part of an image. Blur and Blur More (which is three or four times as strong) smooth an image by reducing the contrast between adjacent pixels. With the **Gaussian Blur** filter, the transition between the contrasting colors occurs at a particular mathematical rate, so that most of the pixels in a black-to-white blur, for example, are in the middle gray range, with fairly few pixels in the very dark or light shades.

Gaussian Blur

With Gaussian Blur, unlike Blur or Blur More, you can control the amount of blurring: Raise or lower the **Radius** value to increase or decrease blurring. Here are some practical applications for Gaussian Blur:

Use Gaussian Blur to make the background recede. A common error in Photoshop montage is combining a sharply focused

Sharpening or blurring can help add depth and form. Sharpen the areas of the image that extend toward the viewer and leave unsharpened (or even blur) the areas that are farther away.

After Francois Guérin painted a still life of fruit in Painter (left), he sharpened the parts of the pear nearest the viewer (right).

Blur the background (right) to reduce the apparent depth of field and to focus attention on the foreground.

A

B

C

D

The Gaussian Blur filter is extremely effective for evening out the color noise irregularities in a digital photograph, especially those that have been "overworked" by dramatic adjustments A. Simply duplicate the original photograph layer (⌘/Ctrl-J) and run the Gaussian Blur filter just enough to get rid of the "clumps" of colored noise B. Then set the Blending mode of this layer to Color C. Your "after" image will be cleaner, more balanced, and have less noticeable noise D.

subject with an equally sharply focused image used as the background. You can make the composite look more like a single photo by blurring the background slightly to simulate the depth of field a real camera lens might capture, as in "Extracting an Image" on page 162. You can also apply this background-blurring technique to a single photo to reduce the perceived depth of field and focus attention on the foreground subject, as described in "Blurring the Background, but Keeping the Grain" on page 140.

Use Gaussian Blur to smooth out flaws in a photo. You may be able to do some photo repair work (such as eliminating water spotting) by using Gaussian Blur on one or all of the color channels.

Use a "repairs" layer with a layer mask for precision. For pinpoint control of blurring, you can use the "repairs" layer approach described for Unsharp Mask on page 205. Or use the History brush and a Snapshot from the History palette as described in "Retouching with History" on page 122.

Use Gaussian Blur to control edge characteristics in masks. The Gaussian Blur filter can be run to soften or smooth out the transition between black and white in a layer mask or an alpha channel — for instance, to smooth a black/white edge that's sharp and pixelated. The filter creates "gray matter" in between the black and the white. Then the Image, Adjust, Levels function can be run to fatten or shrink the mask or to harden the edge as shown in the two figures at the left. Or a filter can be run on the blurred mask to create an artistic edge treatment, as described in "Filtered Frames" on page 218 and also "Framing with Masks" on page 128.

Smart Blur

The **Smart Blur** filter, used at high settings, will leave edges sharp while it blurs the other parts of an image. The result can be a kind of posterization of the non-edge areas — the number of colors is reduced, detail is lost, and the image is presented as blobs of flat colors. Here's how the settings in this filter work:

- The higher the **Threshold** setting for Smart Blur, the less "smart" the filter is about recognizing edges — that is, the more different the color and tone of adjacent areas have to be in order for the difference to be recognized as an edge. And since the filter blurs everything that isn't an edge, the higher the Threshold setting, the more blurring occurs.

- At a given Threshold setting, the higher the **Radius,** the farther away from the edge the original color is preserved. A low setting preserves very little, resulting in a lot of blurring. (The exception to this is at the very bottom of the Radius scale, below 0.5 pixels, where the filter seems to be inactive.) A higher Radius setting

The Smart Blur filter can be used to give an image (left) a "cartoonlike" look (right).

To turn an image into a drawing, Smart Blur was used in Edge Only mode (left). Then the tonality of the image was inverted and the file was converted to grayscale.

ORIGINAL PHOTO © PHOTODISC, SPORTS & RECREATION

To emphasize the energy in this Karate match, a copy of the original high-speed photo was treated with the Motion Blur filter and dragged beneath the sharp original; a black-filled layer mask was added to the sharp original layer and was painted with white to sharpen parts of the athlete on the left.

preserves more of the edges, maintaining more of the image detail. (But once all possible edges are preserved for a given Threshold setting, increasing the Radius more has no effect.)

- For a particular combination of Radius and Threshold, changing the **Quality** changes the degree of posterization, with Low producing the most colors and High producing the fewest.
- The Edge Only and Overlay Edge **Mode** settings were designed mainly for use in the preview window of the dialog box, to help you see where the filter is identifying edges with your current Radius and Threshold settings.

Here are some applications for Smart Blur — for touching up images and for creating artistic effects:

Use Smart Blur at "mild" settings for "cosmetic" purposes — to subdue wrinkles in a portrait, for instance, or hide the freckling of a ripe banana.

Use Smart Blur as an interactive "posterization" tool; it reduces the number of colors by removing detail, but it creates smooth transitions between the remaining colors, rather than the sharp breaks you get with Image, Adjust, Posterize. Experiment with the Threshold and Radius sliders and the Quality setting to get the degree of "posterizing" you want.

Use Smart Blur, then Gaussian Blur and a Levels adjustment to produce a drawing from an image as shown at the left: Run the Smart Blur filter in Edge Only mode to generate a white-on-black line drawing. Invert to black-on-white (Ctrl/⌘-I). Then smooth the jagged lines by running the Gaussian Blur filter at a low Radius setting and using the Input Levels black and white sliders in the Levels dialog box (Ctrl/⌘-L).

The Other Blur Filters

The other three Blur filters fall into the special-effects category:

- **Motion Blur** lets you set a direction and an amount for the blur. It produces an effect like taking a picture of a moving object, as shown in the photo of the Karate match. Motion Blur can also be a good source of streaks in creating textures, as described in "Textures and Backgrounds" in Chapter 8 and in the "Creating Textures" tip on page 238.
- **Radial Blur** provides two options: With **Spin** you can simulate the effect of photographing an object spinning around a center that you specify in a Blur Center box, as shown in the photo of the tire swing on page 209; **Zoom** simulates the effect of zooming the camera toward or away from the center you define, as shown in the photo of the runner on page 209.

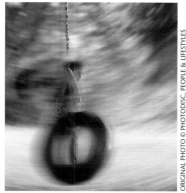

A Radial Blur with a Spin setting enhances the motion of the swing. Extra height was added with the Image, Canvas Size command so the blur center could be defined above the image, where the chain is fastened.

This photo was created using a blurred background and a sharp subject, like the martial artists on the facing page. But this time a Radial Blur in Zoom mode was used, with the blur center near the lower right corner of the photo, to bring the runner forward.

NOISE

Under Noise in the Filter menu, **Add Noise** creates random speckling, while **Despeckle**, **Median,** and **Dust & Scratches** detect edges and then leave these alone while smoothing out less abrupt changes in color. In other words, Add Noise does just that — *adds* noise — and the other three *reduce* noise and can eliminate small blemishes.

Add Noise

The **Add Noise** filter produces several different kinds of speckling effects, depending on the settings you use in the Add Noise dialog box:

- The higher the **Amount** setting, the more obvious the noise becomes — that is, the more contrasty the noise becomes and the more it predominates over the colors or tones that existed before you applied the filter.

- If you check the **Monochromatic** box, instead of drawing from the whole spectrum to change pixel colors, which can lead to an "electronic rainbow confetti" look, the noise that's introduced is a range of grays, with more black and white added as you increase the Amount setting.

- If you choose **Uniform** in the Distribution section of the dialog box, the noise is more obvious in the midtones than in the highlights or shadows.

- Choosing **Gaussian** makes the noise more obvious in the high-lights and shadows, and produces a more clumped noise pattern.

Two of the most common uses for the Add Noise filter are for creating textures and synthesizing film grain.

Adding Noise as the basis for generating a texture. When Add Noise is used with other filters such as Gaussian Blur, Differ-ence Clouds, and Lighting Effects, it can generate some interesting textures. Examples appear in "Textures and Backgrounds" in Chap-ter 8, and in the "Creating Textures" tip on page 238 and the "Mak-ing Marble & Stucco" tip on page 241.

Adding Noise to restore film grain. If film grain is eliminated when part of an image is blurred for repair or for a special effect, you can restore the grain by adding noise in a separate layer or as a Layer Style, and then scaling up the layer or the Style until the noise matches the size of the film grain in the photo, as described in "Blurring the Background" on page 140.

The Other Noise Filters

The three "de-noising" filters give you a range of choices in cleanup operations:

   Median averages the brightness of pixels within an image or selection; you determine the Radius that will be used to select

An example of a film grain pattern made with the Add Noise filter and applied with a Layer Style is shown in "Blurring the Background" on page 140.

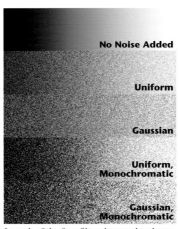

No Noise Added

Uniform

Gaussian

Uniform, Monochromatic

Gaussian, Monochromatic

In each of the four filtered examples shown here, the Add Noise filter was run on the same black-to-white gradient at 200 dpi, with an Amount setting of 40%.

the pixels to be averaged. High Radius settings produce a posterized effect.

Despeckle is like a quick, mild application of Median, without the ability to control the Radius. It can be useful in synthesizing a grainy look, as described in the "Quick 'Clumping'" tip on page 139.

The **Dust & Scratches** filter looks for "defects" (small areas that are markedly different from their surroundings), and it blurs the surrounding pixels into these defects to fix them, without blurring the rest of the image.

- The **Threshold** setting determines how different from the surrounding pixels something has to be in order to be detected as a defect. By setting the Threshold high enough, you can maintain the inherent film grain or "noise" of the original scan while you eliminate the higher-contrast defects.
- The **Radius** setting determines how far from the edge of the defect the filter goes in its search to get the pixels that will be used in the blur.

For images that have more than one or two blemishes, Dust & Scratches works especially well if you use the "repairs" layer approach (as described for Unsharp Mask on page 205 and in step 2 of "Fixing a Problem Photo" on page 134), or if you use the History palette, as described in "Retouching with History" on page 122.

LIGHTING EFFECTS AND OTHER RENDER FILTERS

The filters of Photoshop's Render menu — especially the Lighting Effects filter — are some of the most powerful in the program.

Lighting Effects

The **Lighting Effects** filter offers a dialog box where you can set up both ambient lighting and individual light sources. **Ambient light** is diffuse, nondirectional light that's uniform throughout the image, like daylight on an overcast day. And it may have an inherent color, like daylight underwater. The ambient light will affect the density and color of "shadow" areas that are unlit by any individual light sources that you set up.

- **To set the strength of ambient light,** use the Ambience slider in the Properties section of the Lighting Effects dialog box. The more positive the setting, the stronger the ambient light will be relative to the individual light sources you add in the Light Type section, and so the less pronounced will be the shadows produced by these lights.
- **To color the ambient light,** click on the color box in the Properties section of the dialog box to open the Color Picker.
- **Other settings in the Properties section** — Gloss, Material, and Exposure — also affect the overall environment.

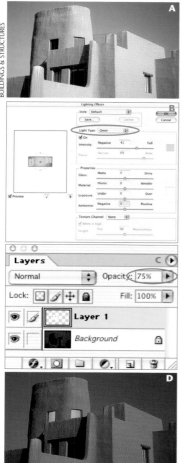

Starting with the original photo **A**, two windows were selected with the polygon lasso, and copied to a new layer (Ctrl/⌘-J). In the Background layer, negative ambient light was set up in the Properties section of the Lighting Effects dialog box. The windows layer (Layer 1) was filled with white with Preserve Transparency turned on, and an orange Omni light was applied to this layer **B**. Finally, Opacity was adjusted **C** to produce the result shown here in **D**.

Lighting Effects spotlights help unify this composite of photos on three layers — top to bottom, a picture frame, a landscape, and a brick wall. A Layer Style with Drop Shadow effect was added to the frame layer.

There are three varieties of **individual light sources** available from the Light Type pop-out list in the Lighting Effects box:

- **Omni**directional lights send a glow in all directions, like a light bulb in a table lamp.

- **Spotlights** are directional and focused. A Spotlight makes a pool of light like its counterpart in the real world.

- **Directional** light sources have a definite direction but are too far away to be focused, like bright sunlight or moonlight on the earth. Directional lights, used in combination with Lighting Effects' Texture Channel option, are ideal for creating textured surfaces and embossed effects.

You can operate the Lighting Effects dialog box like a miniature lighting studio, working on an entire layer or a part you've selected.

- **To add an individual light source,** drag the light bulb icon at the bottom of the palette into the Preview area.

- **To select one of several light sources** so that you can adjust its settings, click on the little circle that represents it in the Preview area.

- **To color a light source**, in the Preview area select the light source and then click the color box under Light Type and choose a color.

- **To move a light source,** drag its central anchor point.

- **To control the direction, size, and shape of a Spotlight,** drag the handles on the ellipse. **To control the angle** without changing the shape, Ctrl/⌘-drag a handle. **To change the shape** without affecting the angle, Shift-drag a handle.

- **To duplicate an existing light source,** Alt/Option-drag it.

- **To turn off a light source temporarily,** so you can see the effect of removing it without actually disrupting its position, click to deselect the On box in the Light Type area of the dialog box.

- **To turn off a light source permanently** (that is, to remove it), drag its center from the Preview area to the trash can icon.

- **To save a lighting scheme** so you can apply it to other layers or files later, click the Save button and name the style. Your new style will be saved with the Lighting Effects Styles supplied with Photoshop, and will be added to the dialog box's pop-out Style menu.

The Lighting Effects filter works well to cast light onto an image as if it were mounted on a wall, as shown at the left. But here are some other ways you can use it to trick the eye:

- To **unify** several fairly different images in a printed or online publication, apply the same lighting scheme to all of them. You can do this by naming and saving the lighting style and then loading it to apply to another layer or file.

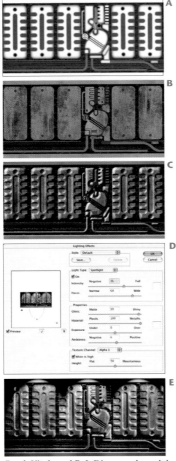

Frank Vitale and E. J. Dixon used an alpha channel **A** as the Texture Channel when they ran the Lighting Effects filter with a Directional light from the upper left on a painted RGB image **B**. The result was a dimensional rendering **C**. Replacing the Directional light with three Spotlights and a subtle blue Directional light from below **D** created more dramatic lighting **E**.

In addition to reorienting pictures of three-dimensional objects, the 3D Transform filter can be useful for applying "labels" to such objects.

- To make light appear to come from **inside** something (such as a bulb in a lamp), position an Omni light at the source, as shown in the lit windows in the illustration on page 211.

- To create a **shadowy area** in an image, use a Spotlight set at a negative Intensity with Ambience set to a positive value.

- To add a **texture** or **embossing** to the surface of an image, set up a light source and choose a Texture Channel to use as a *bump map*. A bump map interacts with the light sources for an image or layer, tricking the eye into perceiving dimension or texture, as shown at the left. The Texture Channel list at the bottom of the Lighting Effects dialog box includes all of the color channels (including any Spot colors) and alpha channels (if any) in the file, as well as the transparency mask and layer mask (if any) of the layer you're working on.

Other Render Filters

In addition to Lighting Effects, there are five other filters in the Render submenu:

- The **3D Transform** filter lets you identify a part of an image — such as a picture of a bottle, a globe or a box — to be treated as a three-dimensional object that you can move and rotate in perspective as if it were solid. Examples of using 3D Transform can be found in "Applying a Logo with 3D Transform" on page 215, and in the "Applying Labels to Glass" tip on page 217.

- The **Clouds** filter creates a cloudlike pattern using the Background and Foreground colors. If you use sky-blue and white, the effect tends to look like high, diffuse clouds. To make clouds with more contrast, hold down the Alt/Option key when you select the filter (an example is shown in the "Rendering a Storm" tip on page 241).

- The **Difference Clouds** filter works the same way as Clouds, except that the cloud effect interacts with the image as if the clouds were being applied in Difference mode. In Difference mode black is the neutral color — that is, black pixels don't cause any change in the target image — and white has the strongest effect, so you can use Difference Clouds with the Foreground and Background colors set to black and white to apply a cloudlike pattern of color inversion. If you apply Difference Clouds over and over, starting with a white-filled layer, you can generate a veined effect like marble, as shown in "Making

FIXING OVERBLOWN LIGHTING

If you've set up several light sources in Lighting Effects and your image is now too bright overall, try reducing the global Ambience or Exposure in the Properties section of the box. Or go ahead and run the Lighting Effects filter and then use Filter, Fade after the fact. Either method is easier than adjusting each light source individually.

The Preview in the Lens Flare filter's dialog box lets you watch what happens as you choose the type of lens and experiment with the Brightness setting.

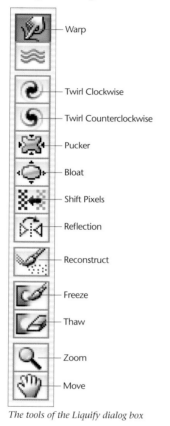

- Warp
- Twirl Clockwise
- Twirl Counterclockwise
- Pucker
- Bloat
- Shift Pixels
- Reflection
- Reconstruct
- Freeze
- Thaw
- Zoom
- Move

The tools of the Liquify dialog box

THE ONLY WAY TO ZOOM

Besides being able to view a *back-drop* to the current layer being liquified in Photoshop 7, you can also scale images with the long-awaited Zoom and Move tools and percentage slider.

200%

Marble & Stucco" on page 241 and in example 2 of "Textures and Backgrounds" in Chapter 8.

- The **Lens Flare** filter simulates the photographic effect you get when a bright light shines into the lens of a camera.

- The **Texture Fill** filter gives you a quick way to import grayscale files to use with the Lighting Effects filter. The process is described in "Using Texture Fills with Lighting Effects" on page 242.

LIQUIFY

The **Image, Liquify** command — like many of the filters — acts to move pixels on either an entire layer, a selected part of a layer, a mask (such as a layer mask, an Adjustment layer, or an alpha channel), or a color channel (including Spot color). The Liquify dialog is very complex, with its own set of tools that operate at the pixel level, with tool options to control how they operate. Liquify allows you to perform a series of distortion operations, all the while previewing the effects, before you click OK to apply the result to your file. Here are some pointers on how the dialog box operates:

- The **Warp tool** operates like Photoshop's Smudge tool but a lot more smoothly and with much better control. In the Tool Options section of the Liquify dialog, the **Brush Size** setting determines how wide a swath of pixels will be affected as you move the cursor around the image, and the **Brush Pressure** setting affects how far the pixels will move as you drag over them, and thus how "smeared" they become as they move.

- The two **Twirl** tools (**Clockwise** and **Counterclockwise**) act like a combination of Photoshop's Airbrush tool and the Twirl filter. Their effect is a bit like twirling a fork in a plate of spaghetti — the pixels "nearest the center of the fork" make the most rotations. Like the Airbrush, the Twirl tools have an effect even without moving them — with the cursor standing still, the longer you hold down the mouse button, the more the area under the cursor is twirled. (Holding down the **Alt/Option** key reverses the direction of the twirl.) The **Brush Size** determines how big an area is affected, and the **Brush Pressure** affects how fast the twirling happens. For better control of the effect, use a lower pressure.

- The **Pucker** and **Bloat** tools affect the image as if it were on a plastic clay surface like Silly Putty™ and you poked the image inward from the front (Pucker) or pushed it outward from the back (Bloat). (Holding down the **Alt/Option** key as you use either of these tools makes it operate like the other one.)

- The **Shift Pixels** tool moves pixels sideways if you move the cursor vertically, and vertically if you move the cursor sideways, according to this scheme: Cursor left moves pixels down; cursor

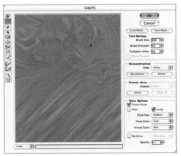

Load Mesh...   Save Mesh...

Tool Options
Brush Size: 64 ▸
Brush Pressure: 50 ▸
Turbulent Jitter: 70 ▸
☐ Stylus Pressure

Reconstruction
Mode: Rigid ▾
Reconstruct   Revert

Freeze Area
Channel: Alpha 1 ▾
Invert   Thaw All

View Options
☑ Frozen Areas
☑ Mesh   ☑ Image
Mesh Size: Medium ▾
Mesh Color: Gray ▾
Freeze Color: Red ▾

☑ Backdrop: All Layers ▾
Opacity: 60 ▸

The Options for the Liquify command are grouped along the right edge of the dialog box. They control how the Liquify tools perform and how the preview looks.

In addition to controlling distortions (bending one layer to follow the contours of another), the Liquify filter is also very useful for adding organic-looking irregularities to fabricated textures, like the bending in the motion-blurred wood grain shown here.

right moves pixels up; cursor up moves pixels left; cursor down moves pixels right. (Holding down **Alt/Option** switches the directions: Cursor left moves pixels up, and so on.)

- When **Revert** is chosen in the Mode menu in the Reconstruction section on the righthand side of the dialog box, the **Reconstruct** tool lets you restore any nonfrozen area of the image to its state before the Liquify dialog box was opened. The Reconstruct tool operates like Photoshop's Airbrush — the reversion continues as you hold the cursor in the same place with the mouse button down, and Brush Pressure determines the rate at which it occurs.

  To restore all nonfrozen areas at once, click the **Revert button** in the Reconstruction section, rather than "painting" the restoration with the Reconstruct tool.

  The choices in the **Mode** menu (other than Revert) control the interaction between adjacent frozen and nonfrozen areas of the image (see the description of the Freeze and Thaw tools below) when the Reconstruct tool or the Revert button is used. (If you're interested in these esoteric interactions, check Photoshop 7's online Help.)

- The **Freeze** tool allows you to paint a mask over part of the image in order to protect it from whatever Liquify changes you apply. You can also paint with the **Thaw** tool in order to erase the protective mask. The area that will be frozen or thawed depends on Brush Size, and the degree of protection depends on Brush Pressure; these tools operate like Photoshop's Airbrush — the effect continues to increase if you leave the cursor in the same place with the mouse button down. The **Freeze Area** section of the Liquify dialog box lets you choose an alpha **Channel,** if the file has any, to define the Freeze area, instead of hand-painting it. The **Invert** button lets you switch the frozen and thawed regions. And **Thaw All** will remove Freeze protection from the entire image.

- The **View Options** section, located in the right bottom corner of the dialog box, gives you options for showing the mask for the frozen areas, showing the image, and showing a mesh — in any one of three sizes — to help you see how the distortions you apply are working. You can also choose from several mask and mesh colors, so you can choose the ones that work best with your image.

Applying a Logo with 3D Transform

Overview *Open a photo of a generally cylindrical object; create or import the logo artwork; apply the art with the 3D Transform filter; fine-tune the placement; set the blend mode and Opacity.*

IMAGE "**3D Transform**" "before" and "after" files

1a **1b**

The original photo   The graphic layer

1c

Once the graphic was positioned and scaled, the graphic layer was duplicated for safekeeping, and the extra graphic layer was hidden by turning off its Eye icon.

2

Making a rectangular selection slightly bigger than the surface where the graphic will be applied

ONE USEFUL APPLICATION for Photoshop's 3D Transform plug-in is to mock up a generally cylindrical object such as a bottle, can, or coffee mug with a label, decal, or other artwork in place (it's not as useful for box-shaped objects). Although 3D Transform can do wonders in bending the artwork around such a cylindrical form, it can be hard to do the final positioning within the filter's interface. So you may want to use Photoshop's Free Transform function for final tweaking.

1 Preparing the graphic. Starting with a photo of a mug or other cylindrical object in an RGB file **1a**, build or import the artwork you want to apply **1b**. Our graphic was a logo designed in Adobe Illustrator, which we placed (File, Place), roughly aligning and scaling it by dragging in the center and on the corner handles of the placement box. Once you have the graphic approximately positioned and sized, duplicate it for safekeeping, in case you decide you need to start over at some point: In the Layers palette drag the graphic layer's thumbnail to the Create A New Layer button at the bottom of the palette. Then turn off the Eye icon for one of the two identical layers and work with the other one **1c**. (The History palette also provides a couple of safekeeping options, but History isn't retained when you close the file, so a duplicate layer is better insurance.)

Dragging the Cylinder tool to make the cylinder outline as wide as the mug and short enough so the bottom center handle stays inside the window

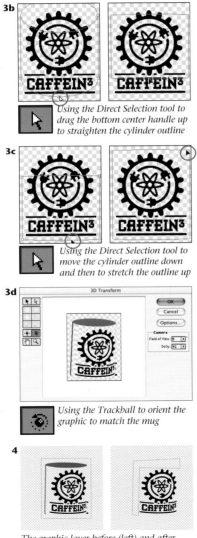

Using the Direct Selection tool to drag the bottom center handle up to straighten the cylinder outline

Using the Direct Selection tool to move the cylinder outline down and then to stretch the outline up

Using the Trackball to orient the graphic to match the mug

The graphic layer before (left) and after cleaning up by selecting with the Polygonal Lasso and pressing the Delete key

2 Selecting the area to transform. The dialog box for the 3D Transform filter only shows the layer you're applying the filter to; it doesn't show you the other layer with the surface you're trying to fit. So before you choose the filter, use the Rectangular Marquee tool to make a selection boundary just slightly larger than the surface where you want to put the graphic; this will give you a frame of reference in the filter's dialog box **2**. (If you experiment with the Camera settings in the dialog box, you can unintentionally scale your image, and without a reference you won't know it.)

3 Molding the graphic. After you've made the rectangular selection, make sure the layer with the graphic is the active layer. Then choose Filter, Render, 3D Transform. In working with the 3D Transform dialog box, the trick is to position the filter's cylinder preview in an upright, centered view *before* you "attach" the graphic to the cylinder for rotation. The steps of this process have to be carried out in a specific order, as follows:

First click on the Cylinder tool and drag from the upper left corner of the preview window, down and over to the lower half of the right edge of the window, making sure to keep the bottom of the cylinder inside the preview window so you can see the bottom center handle **3a**. Rotate the cylindrical shape into a "straight on" view by using the Direct Selection tool (the hollow arrow) to grab the *bottom center handle* and drag it up **3b**. (Using this tool won't rotate the graphic — only the cylinder outline.) Next, drag on the *bottom line* — not the handle — to move the straightened cylinder so the bottom is below the image. Then drag the *upper right corner handle* up to stretch the cylinder up so it encompasses the entire graphic **3c**.

Switch to the Trackball tool. As soon as you choose the Trackball, the cylinder outline will change from neon green to gray. The graphic is now "adhered" to the cylinder geometry, and you can drag to tilt and rotate the cylinder and label to match your object (the mug in this case), visible in the main working window **3d**. (Although we didn't do so, you can also use the Pan Camera tool to move the graphic around; use the Field Of View to switch between wide-angle and telephoto views; or change Dolly settings to get closer or farther away.)

When the graphic fits your object as closely as you can make it (even if it seems like it will need more tweaking), click the Options button and set the Resolution and Anti-Aliasing to High for a smooth result, and click OK. Then click OK to close the main dialog box.

4 Cleaning up the graphic layer. Now remove any excess (gray) material generated by the filter: You can select this material and press Delete, or use the Eraser **4**.

5 Tweaking the fit. If the graphic doesn't align with your object as well as you would like, you can fix that now: With the transformed layer active, choose Edit, Free Transform. We needed to rotate the graphic to match the slant on our slightly askew coffee

5

Adjusting the angle and distortion of the graphic with the Free Transform command

6

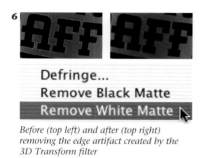

Defringe...
Remove Black Matte
Remove White Matte

Before (top left) and after (top right) removing the edge artifact created by the 3D Transform filter

7

Putting the graphic layer in Overlay mode at 80% Opacity allowed the lighting and surface texture of the mug to show, visually blending the graphic into the ceramic surface.

mug, so we positioned the cursor outside one of the corner handles of the Transform box and dragged **5**. To make final adjustments, you can also hold down the Ctrl/⌘ key and drag a handle for fine-tuned distortions.

6 Checking the details. On close inspection, you may find a visible edge around the graphic, created by the 3D Transform filter. If so, remove it by choosing Layer, Matting and then choosing Remove White Matte if the edge is whitish **6**, Remove Black Matte if the edge is blackish, or Defringe if the edge is another color or if it varies in color.

7 Blending the graphic into the surface. Now you can experiment with the blend mode and Opacity for the graphic layer, to allow the character of the object's surface (noise, grain, texture, or lighting) to show through. This will help the graphic look like it's part of the surface rather than "pasted on." For our black graphic, we used Overlay mode and reduced the Opacity to 80% **7**. For different artwork, you might try Color or other modes. *wow!*

APPLYING LABELS TO GLASS

To mock up a label on a glass jar or bottle, you can add some details that make the transparency of the glass more photorealistic:

- You can make a translucent label with opaque type by constructing the label in two layers, one layer with a solid-filled label shape and another layer above it with the type. Reduce the Opacity of the label shape layer until you get the translucent effect you want, with the photo in the bottom layer showing through. Then, with the type layer active, choose the Move tool and choose Layer, Merge Down (or press Ctrl/⌘-E) to combine the two parts of the label while preserving both the partial transparency of the label shape and the full opacity of the type.

- If there's something inside the jar, you can add a drop shadow on the jar's contents: Click the Add A Layer Style button (the "*f*") at the bottom of the Layers palette and choose Drop Shadow from the pop-out list. In the Drop Shadow section of the Layer Style dialog box, click the color swatch and sample a shadow color from the image. Choose the Angle, Opacity, Spread (density) and Size (softness) to match the light in your photo; choose a Distance appropriate for the physical space between the label and the material it falls on.

The label was made with black type in one layer and a white label shape in a 70%-opaque layer below (top). The two were merged, and a Drop Shadow was added.

IMAGE **"3D Transform Extra"** images

Filtered Frames

Each example shown on these two pages was made by **running a filter on a layer mask** in a 560-pixel-wide image, framed as in the "Framing with Masks" technique on page 128. White and black were used as the Foreground and Background colors. The layer mask was Gaussian Blurred with a Radius of 20 pixels, the black backing layer with a Radius of 2 pixels. Some filters, such as Texture, change even the white areas of the mask, which affects the image as well as the edges.

 "Framing" "before" and "after" files

The four single examples at the top of this page were made with the visibility of the black backing layer turned **off**.

Elsewhere, where there are two examples, visibility of the black layer was **on** for the lower one.

ADDING A LAYER STYLE

If you add a Layer Style to the image-and-mask layer, the effects in the Style will be built using the edge created by the layer mask.

Artistic: Rough Pastels (Stroke Length, 10; Stroke Detail, 10; Texture, Canvas; Scaling, 100%; Relief: 20; Light Dir., Top Left)

Sketch: Graphic Pen (Stroke Length, 15; Light/Dark Balance, 30; Stroke Dir., Right Diagonal)

Distort: Twirl (Angle, 400°)

Distort: Twirl (Angle, 999°)

Pixelate: Color Halftone (Max. Radius, 5; all Screen Angles, 45)

Brush Strokes: Sprayed Strokes (Stroke Length, 12; Spray Radius, 20; Stroke Dir: Right Diagonal)

Distort: Ocean Ripple (Ripple Size, 1; Ripple Magnitude, 12)

Brush Strokes: Spatter (Spray Radius, 15; Smoothness, 5)

Sketch: Halftone Pattern (Pattern Type, Line; Size, 1; Contrast, 25)

Sketch: Water Paper (Fiber Length, 50; Brightness, 50; Contrast, 75)

Texture: Grain (Grain Type, Horizontal; Intensity, 65; Contrast, 75)

Texture: Texturizer (Texture, Canvas; Scaling, 125%; Relief, 10%; Light Dir., Top)

Combining with Light

Overview *Assemble the elements for the collage; create a frame; add type; add depth and unify the lighting with a Layer Style; add drama to the lighting with a masked "spotlight" layer.*

"Combining" "before" and "after" files

The files for the two photo elements (shown above) had built-in paths for selecting them from the background.

The Character palette, opened from the Options bar, was used to fine-tune the type.

3a
- ✓ Extras   ⌘H
- Show   ▶
- Rulers   ⌘R
- Snap   ⇧⌘;
- Snap To   ▶   — Guides
- Lock Guides   ⌥⌘;   — Grid
- Clear Guides   — Slices
- New Guide...   — Document Bounds

Setting up Snap To Grid from the View menu before drawing

JHD / ORIGINAL PHOTOS: © CORBIS IMAGES ROYALTY FREE, MUSICAL INSTRUMENTS

UNIFYING THE LIGHTING for all parts of a montage can be an important part of making it look like all the elements are together in the same space. The Lighting Effects filter is ideal for this purpose. In this assemblage we've also used a Layer Style with Drop Shadow and Bevel And Emboss to contribute to the lighting and to add dimension to the silhouetted photo elements as well as the graphics and type.

1 Preparing the components. Assemble the component photos **1** and make any necessary color or contrast adjustments (for help see "Adjusting Overall Tone and Color" on page 114). Use appropriate selection methods to select each element from its background (for tips on selecting, see Chapter 1).

2 Setting type. With a design in mind for this online album cover, we started a new file (File, New) and then set the type. To set type, choose the Type tool, click where you want the type to start, and

KERNING AND TRACKING

For kerning or tracking you don't have to use the Character palette:

- **To kern, put the Type tool's cursor between** the pair of letters, hold down the **Alt/Option key, and use the right and left arrow keys** to widen or narrow the space. To kern another letter pair, release the Alt/Option key and use the arrow keys alone to reposition the cursor, then kern again.

- **To track, drag the cursor over** the type you want to affect, then hold down **Alt/Option and use the right and left arrows**.

3b

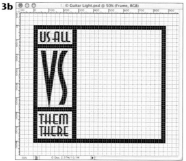

The grid was used to help make a large selection with the Rectangular Marquee tool and then to subtract from the selection by holding down the Alt/Option key as additional rectangular selections were made.

CHANGING THE RULERS

You can adapt the rulers to suit your work as follows:

• **To change the units**, right-click on the ruler (or Control-click on a Mac with a one-button mouse) and choose from the pop-out menu.

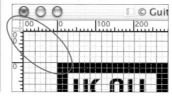

• **To change the 0,0 point** (the origin, from which ruler distances are measured), drag from the upper right corner of the rulers to align the crosshairs inside your work window where you want the new measuring origin.

4

A layer was added above the Background, and each large block of color was made by selecting a rectangular area, choosing a Foreground color, and pressing Alt/Option-Delete to fill.

begin entering the words. You can control some of the type specifications in the Options bar, but for precise control of spacing, open the Character palette **2** by clicking the Palettes button at the right end of the bar. When you've finished setting the type, you can rasterize it (Layer, Rasterize, Type).

3 Making the graphic frame. There are many ways to create a frame. For example, you could use the Line tool with the Weight in the Options bar set to the border width you want. In this instance, however, we used the Rectangular Marquee tool to construct the frame, taking advantage of Photoshop's rulers and grid system to keep the "line width" consistent. To use this method, first set up the "magnetic" grid system by choosing View, Show, Grid and also View, Snap To, Grid **3a**; the grid lines will become visible and will constrain the motion of the selecting, drawing, or painting tools as you use them. Next turn on the rulers (Ctrl/⌘-R), and move the origin (the 0,0 crosshairs) to the point where you want the upper left corner of your frame (see "Changing the Rulers" at the left). Change the ruler units and the grid size to suit your design as in "Changing the Grid" at the right.

Add a layer above the type by clicking the Create A New Layer button at the bottom of the Layers palette. Start the frame by dragging the Rectangular Marquee to outline it. Then, with the Alt/Option key held down, drag to cut out rectangular spaces from this larger rectangle, using the grid to leave borders of equal width all around the spaces. With black as the Foreground color, press Alt/Option-Delete to fill the selection with black; press Ctrl/⌘-D to deselect **3b**.

4 Adding color. Add a new layer below the type and frame by clicking the *Background* label in the Layers palette and then clicking

NAVIGATING TYPE PALETTES

With your type selected, you can use Photoshop's Character and Paragraph palettes to make several changes at once without having to repeatedly move your cursor to the palette:

• Once you click in any field, cycle forward through the fields by pressing Tab, or press Shift-Tab to work backwards.

• When a field is active, press the up arrow key to increase a numeric entry (such as Font Size) or to move up the list (in fields such as Font Family). Press the down arrow key to reduce the number or move backwards through the list.

• Shift-arrow combinations make the changes in a numeric field 10 times as large. In list fields Shift-arrow brings up the last or first item.

CHANGING THE GRID

To change the spacing of Grid lines or change their color, open the General Preferences dialog box by pressing Ctrl/⌘-K or (double-clicking the ruler) and then press Ctrl/⌘-6 to get to Guides & Grid.

5a

The Free Transform command was activated and the guitar was rotated to an upright position. Since it was lit from the right (as shown here), the next step was to flip it so it would fit with the lighting planned for the composite.

5b

The file with all the elements in place

6a

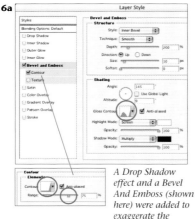

A Drop Shadow effect and a Bevel And Emboss (shown here) were added to exaggerate the directional lighting.

6b

Adding the layer effects used in the Wow-Edge Highlight Style

the Create A New Layer button. Use the Rectangular Marquee and the grid to create areas to fill with color; after selecting each one, click the Foreground color square in the toolbox, choose a color, and press Alt/Option-Delete. We selected and filled four rectangles **4**; the outer edges of the rectangles went all the way to the edges of the frame; the inner edges met underneath the inner "struts" of the frame.

5 Adding the other elements. Drag and drop your other images into the file. Fit the elements to the composition by using Free Transform: Press Ctrl/⌘-T to bring up the Transform box. Shift-drag a corner handle of the Transform box to scale proportionally. Drag around outside one of the corners of the box to rotate. If you need to flip the element to better match the direction of your intended lighting, right-click (or Control-click on a Mac) to bring up the context-sensitive menu where you can choose Flip Vertical or, as in this case, Flip Horizontal. We wanted our lighting from the left, so we needed to flip the larger guitar to get the lighting right **5a, 5b**.

6 Enhancing the lighting with a Layer Style. Now you can use a Layer Style consisting of Drop Shadow and Bevel And Emboss effects to add dimension to both graphic and photo elements. The Style can also exaggerate the directional light source in your composition and thereby enhance the illusion that the elements are together in a single lighted space. We started by clicking on the layer with the larger guitar in the Layers palette and then added a Style. **Note**: You can open the **Combining After.psd** file for reference to the "live" Layer Styles as you follow the step-by-step instructions.

To build a Layer Style like the Wow-Edge Highlight used in this example, click the *"f"* button at the bottom of the Layers palette and choose **Drop Shadow** from the pop-out list of effects. In the Drop Shadow section of the Layer Style dialog box, define the shadow by adjusting the Angle (we used 145°), Distance (20 pixels), Spread (0%), and Size (20 pixels); then adjust Opacity to fine-tune the density of the shadow (we used 50% Opacity).

IS IT STRAIGHT?

If you need to check whether an element is perfectly straight when you're using the Edit, Transform or Edit, Free Transform command, here's a quick way to do it:

Make sure the rulers are visible (Ctrl/⌘-R toggles them on and off). Then drag a Guide from one of the rulers and compare your element to the guide. (The Guide will be visible at least until you release the mouse button. Whether it remains visible after that depends on whether View, Show, Guides is turned on.)

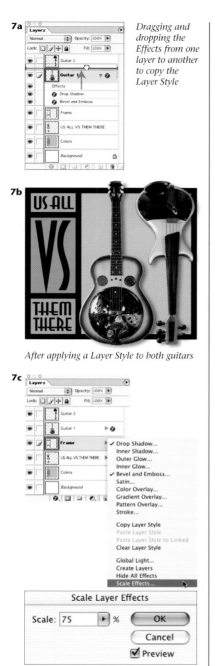

7a

Dragging and dropping the Effects from one layer to another to copy the Layer Style

7b

After applying a Layer Style to both guitars

7c

Scaling the Layer Style to fit the type and the frame

Next open the Bevel And Emboss section by clicking on Bevel And Emboss in the list on the left side of the Layer Style dialog box. The **Bevel And Emboss** effect **6a** has **Structure** settings (at the top of the dialog box) and **Shading** settings (below). In the Structure section, for **Style** we used Inner Bevel, which builds the dimensionality inward from the edge of the element you apply it to. The **Technique** setting determines how sharp the beveled edge will be; we used Smooth for a rounded edge. The **Direction** determines whether the beveling will raise the element above the surface (the default Up setting) or carve it in; we used Up. The **Size** determines how much of the top surface is taken up by the bevel; our setting was 8 pixels. And **Soften** determines how gently or sharply the bevel approaches the top surface; we used 0 pixels for a hard bevel edge.

In the **Shading** section, Angle and Altitude determine the position of the light. If you envision a half-sphere dome over the layer, the Angle determines where around the circumference of the sphere the light will be, and the Altitude determines how far above the surface it will be (between 0° for a light source at the base of the half-sphere and 90° for a light source at the top of the dome). We used 145° for the Angle for lighting from the top left, and we kept the light low with a 0° setting for the Altitude.

The **Gloss Contour** setting helps characterize the material of the element you apply it to. You can choose from the Contours Photoshop offers, or design your own by clicking on the Contour thumbnail and resetting the points on the curve in the Contour Editor dialog box, which operates like the Curves box (see "Correcting Particular Exposure Problems" on page 118 for a description). The higher the peaks in the Curves dialog box, the shinier the highlights; and the lower the valleys, the darker the shadows.

The **Edge Contour,** which is found in its own section when you click the Contour entry in the effects list under Bevel And Emboss, lets you make the edge a little fancier than the Technique setting alone would allow. For this Contour, the curve can be thought of as a cross-section of the "shoulder" of the bevel. The more peaks and valleys in the Curve, the more intricate the "carving" of the edge. Experimenting with the Structure settings and the two Contour settings gives you almost infinite flexibility in designing the edge and lighting characteristics for the Style.

By experimenting with the Contour and Range settings in the Contour Elements section, and the Gloss Contour choice and Altitude in the Shading section, we were able to bring the highlight off the edge of the guitar and onto its top surface and to give the specular highlight the sharp edges characteristic of hard, polished surfaces **6b**.

7 Duplicating the Style to other layers. Once the Style is designed, you can apply it to the other elements in the file by

7d

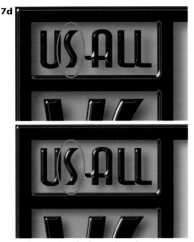

Before (top) and after scaling the Layer Style on the type

7e

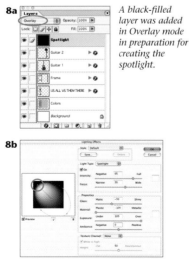

After duplicating and scaling the Layer Style for all layers

8a

A black-filled layer was added in Overlay mode in preparation for creating the spotlight.

8b

Adding a spotlight with the Lighting Effects filter

dragging and dropping: In the Layers palette, look at the entry for the layer that has the Style applied to it. If the little triangle to the left of the *"f"* is pointing to the right, click it to expand the list of layer effects. Then drag the Effects entry to any other layer where you want to apply the Style **7a**. We dragged and dropped to the other guitar layer **7b**, then the frame layer, and finally the type layer. (Not all Layer Styles can be successfully dragged-and-dropped, even between layers in a single file; see the "Blend Modes Don't Drag-and-Drop!" tip on page 225.)

Unless all the elements you apply the Style to are about the same "bulk," you'll need to scale the Style to adjust the bevel details. For instance, the type and frame in this file were thinner than the guitars, so we reduced the Scale value, as follows: Put the cursor on the *"f"* icon for the layer whose Style you want to scale and right-click (or Control-click for a Mac) to open a context-sensitive menu; choose Scale Effects (at the bottom of the menu) and adjust the interactive Scale slider in the Scale Layer Effects dialog box **7c** until you see the bevel you want **7d, 7e**.

8 Reinforcing the lighting with Lighting Effects. For a more dramatic look and to further reinforce the illusion that the elements are in a single space, you can add a spotlight that shines over the entire composition. In order to look right with the lighting already established by the original components and the Layer Style, the spotlight has to come from the same direction. To darken the corners and highlight the central area of our composition, we added a 50%-gray-filled layer in Overlay mode at the top of our file (click the top layer in the Layers palette and then Alt/Option-click the Create A New Layer button;

DUPLICATING ONE EFFECT

You don't have to drag-and-drop an entire Layer Style if all you want is the Drop Shadow (or the Inner Glow or Satin or some other single layer effect). In the Layers palette simply expand the list of Style components by clicking the little triangle to the left of the *"f"* icon of the "donor" layer, and then drag the layer effect you want onto the name of the "recipient" layer.

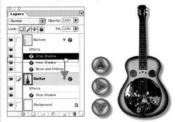

Dragging the Drop Shadow (but not the Inner Shadow or Bevel And Emboss effects from the Buttons layer to the Guitar layer (left) provides the guitar with a matching shadow without rounding its beveled edges.

SCALING LAYER STYLES

Remember that when you scale a Layer Style (Layer, Layer Style, Scale Effects), *all* aspects of the Style are scaled. This may not always be what you want. For instance, you may want to copy a Style from another layer and reduce the size of the bevel but leave the drop shadow, texture, and patterning the same. If that's the case, you can apply the Style and then open the Layer Style dialog (by double-clicking the *"f"* icon for the layer) and change the settings for the specific effect you want to scale.

8c

The composite with the spotlight layer in place and its Opacity reduced to 50%

8d

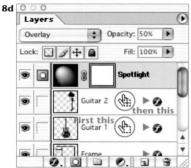

Ctrl/⌘-clicking to load the outline of one guitar as a selection for darkening the mask in the spotlight layer, then Shift-Ctrl/⌘-clicking to add the outline of the second guitar to the selection

8e

Adjusting the Output Levels to darken the selected areas of the layer mask and thus dim the spotlight's effect on the guitars

in the New Layer dialog box choose Overlay for the Mode) and click the check box for "Fill With Overlay-Neutral Color (50% Gray)" **8a**.

Next we chose Filter, Render, Lighting Effects and adjusted the direction of the light to match the light in our composition (by dragging the handle at the intersection of the radius line and circumference in the lighting preview) **8b**. We adjusted the Intensity, Focus, and Properties settings and clicked OK to close the box. After adjusting the Opacity of the spotlight layer to 50%, we were generally happy with the lighting, except that the shadow areas of the guitars were starting to "plug up," or lose detail **8c**.

To partially protect the guitars from the spotlight, we masked the spotlight's effect as follows: To add a layer mask we clicked the Add A Mask button at the bottom of the Layers palette. With the new mask active on the Spotlight layer, we Ctrl/⌘-clicked on the name of the first guitar layer to load its outline as a selection and Shift-Ctrl/⌘-clicked on the name of the other guitar layer to add its outline to the selection **8d**. We chose Image, Adjust, Levels and experimented by moving the white Output Levels slider inward to darken the selected areas of the mask, turning them gray **8e**; this darkening of the mask stopped some of the shadows created by the spotlight from penetrating to the guitars. When the lighting looked right, we clicked OK to close the Levels dialog box. 🖱

Warping with Liquify

Overview *Choose images to merge; combine layers using Opacity, Blend Modes, and Layer Masks; warp one "over" the other using Liquify; unify the two using Soft light effects and Channel Mixing.*

IMAGE

"Warping with Liquify" "before " and "after" files

JHD / MODEL: JENNIFER LUTTRELL / AGENCY: ANDERSON PHOTOGRAPHICS.COM

1a

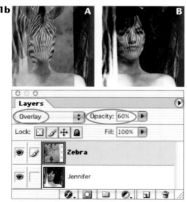

© JHDAVIS DESIGN
© JULIEANNE KOST

The two original photographs we chose to blend together

1b

After transforming the Zebra layer (and reducing its opacity) **A** *to more closely fit our model, we experimented with different Blend Modes to better integrate the two* **B.**

THE APPARENT MERGING OF ELEMENTS can be accomplished by using a variety of functions in Photoshop: Opacity, Blend Modes, Layer Masks, etc. But often it's the subtle adjustments that make the most convincing impression, like bending one image around another using the Liquify filter. With the addition of the View, Backdrop feature in Photoshop 7.0, Liquify has become the most powerful and practical tool for projects like the "Wild" image we've created here (and of course, it works equally as well for "wrapping" elements such as tree bark or corporate logos around other objects).

1 Select and align the images. First choose the photos that you want to merge; make it a point to find images which share consistent lighting, perspective, sharpness, etc. For our two photos **1a,** the view angle in both was almost straight on (by flipping the zebra shot taken by Julieanne Kost, we could get even a little better match), and the lighting for our zebra was flat enough that it could work effectively with almost any photo.

Next we dragged and dropped our zebra photo onto the shot of our jungle-inhabiting model. Then we flipped the Zebra layer (Edit, Transform, Flip Horizontal) and reduced its opacity to 60% so that we could line it up with the Jennifer photo layer below. To move, scale and rotate a layer all at the same time, type Ctrl/⌘-T, for Free Transform. When the control handles appear on the corners and sides of the image, click and drag them (hold down the Shift key to

2a Using Color Range to select the skintones of the model to limit the area where the zebra stripes would appear

2b

Creating a Layer Mask from the resulting Color Range selection

2c

Fine-tuning the Layer Mask with the Paint Brush

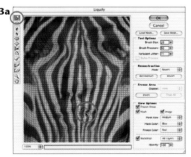

3a

For detailed work such as contouring the stripes around the lips, we used the Warp Tool with a small Brush Size within the Liquify dialog.

3b

We adjusted the View Options in the Liquify dialog to make the Image, Mesh, and Backdrop layers visible, and used the Bloat Tool with a large brush to exaggerate the warping around the tip of the model's nose.

constrain proportions while scaling) until you have the best alignment possible (to rotate a layer with Free Transform, move your arrowhead cursor out of the frame surrounding the image and it will turn into a double-headed bent arrow cursor, showing you that you're now able to click and drag to rotate the element).

Next, experiment with changing the Blend Mode of the layer above. Powerful modes to try when combining images include Overlay, Soft Light, Hard Light, Vivid Light, Linear Light, and Pin Light — all of which use the light and dark areas of the layer above (but not its middle-tone grays) to affect the layers below. We chose the Overlay Blend Mode to achieve our desired striped tattooing effect **1b.**

2 Selecting and Masking. Our next task was to limit the application of the zebra stripes to just the facial skintones of the model in the layer below. To isolate these tones, we chose Select, Color Range. Once the dialog box was open, we chose Sampled Colors from the Select menu, then clicked and dragged with the Plus Eye Dropper over the colors we wanted to select. We set the Fuzziness fairly high (50) to keep a smooth transition between what was being included in the selection and what was being omitted **2a.**

After clicking OK we had the "marching ants" in place for the skintones, and with the Zebra layer active, we clicked the Add Layer Mask icon at the bottom of the Layers palette. This created a Layer Mask identical to the Preview we saw in Color Range — with the white parts of the mask allowing the zebra stripes to show through, and the black portions hiding the rest of the zebra photo. To finetune this mask, we chose a soft-edged paint brush, with black as the Foreground color, and painted on the Zebra layer's mask where we wanted to hide more of the animal (for the area around the model's neck for instance), making sure the Mask Icon (not the Brush Icon) was present in the column next to the eye icon on the layer **2b.** You can Alt/Opt-click on the Mask Thumbnail in the Layers palette to toggle on and off the mask's visibility while you work **2c.**

3 Liquifying the details. Now for the fun part! With the Zebra thumbnail clicked, choose Filter, Liquify. Remember to look for the Brush Icon next to the layer's thumbnail to show that the color portion of the layer is active, and not the mask **3a.** We set our View Options so we could see our Image, the distorting Mesh, and the Backdrop (all the layers below the one being liquified) at 100% opacity **3b.** New to Photoshop 7, the Backdrop option lets you see the "target" below while doing your warping in Liquify, which gives you the ability to control the conforming, rather than just randomly distort. We started with the Warp Tool (located in the upper right of the Liquify dialog) with a large Brush Size (100 for our low-resolution teaching file) and Medium Brush Pressure (50), and moved around the zebra stripes in relation to the major contours of the face below.

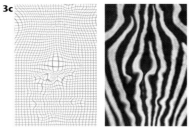

3c

Checking the distortion by toggling on and off visibility for the Backdrop, the Image, and the Mesh

3d

The liquified stripes in position

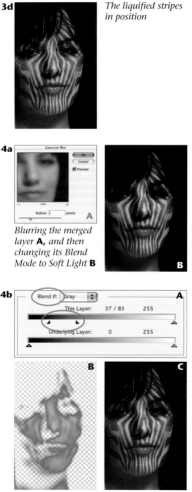

4a

*Blurring the merged layer **A**, and then changing its Blend Mode to Soft Light **B***

4b

*By splitting the sliders in the Blend If portion of the Layer Styles dialog **A**, you can limit the contribution of the dark areas of the Soft Light layer **B** (shown alone) so that your image maintains its shadow detail (shown with all the layers visible) **C**.*

To increase the believability of the warping, we moved the stripes over the eyes inward toward the nose, and the ones over the cheeks slightly outward toward the ears. Then we reduced the brush size down to 25 and adjusted areas of detail around the eyebrows, nostrils and lips **3a**. We finished by changing to the Bloat Tool (6th icon down in the Liquify toolbox) and just clicking on areas like the tip of the nose and chin to make the stripes appear to come forward **3b**. We checked our work by toggling on and off the views for the Backdrop, the Image, and the Mesh **3c** before clicking OK **3d**.

4 Unifying the Parts. With the liquified stripes in place, we could now further enhance the illusion or "unification" of our montage by treating both contributing photos simultaneously. First, we wanted to slightly soften the focus of our montage, while at the same time, enhance its overall density and shading (see "Softening the Focus" on page 130 for more on using this technique).

We started by making a new empty layer at the top of our layer stack (and naming it Soft Light, for the Blend Mode that it would soon be set to) and held down the Alt/Option key while we selected Merge Visible from the pop-out menu in the upper right of the Layers palette. This made a merged copy of what was currently visible onto our new layer while keeping the other layers intact. We applied a Gaussian Blur filter of 5 to this layer, then changed its Blend Mode to Soft Light to allow the layers below to "glow through" **4a**.

The blurred layer gave us the "atmosphere" we wanted, but some of the shadow detail in our image was now getting lost. A quick fix for this problem was to use the Blend If feature within the Layers Styles dialog to limit the "contribution" of the dark areas of this layer to those of the underlying layers. Double-click to the right of the Layer name to bring up the Blend Options portion of the Layers Styles dialog box. Next, drag the black triangle in the "This Layer" section of the Blend If options at the bottom of the dialog. As you move the triangle slider to the right, you will begin to see the dark areas of this blurred Soft Light layer begin to disappear. To soften the transition between what's being hidden and what's continuing to contribute, you can split the sliders by Alt/Opt-clicking and dragging the halves of the triangles apart **4b**. When the shadow detail of the layer below is visible, click OK **4c**.

5 Channel Mixing for Black and White. Finally, we used a Channel Mixer Adjustment layer to reduce the full-color image down to a monochromatic one. To do this, select Channel Mixer from the Create New Adjustment Layer icon at the bottom of the Layers palette and click on the Monochrome button in the dialog's lower-left corner. Now you're able to mix the current colors to achieve the desired tonal balance. One tip (no matter how you balance the colors) is to try to keep the combined percentages total around 100% in order to keep the current luminosity of the image about the same.

4c

The merged, blurred copy in Soft Light Blend Mode

5

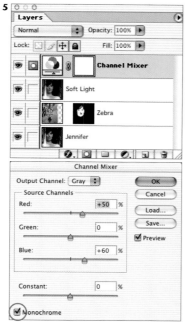

A Channel Mixer Adjustment Layer was added to the image to reduce it from Color to Monochrome. We used these settings shown here for the opening image.

Variation on a Theme. Minor changes can make for major differences in the end product. By simply changing the Blend Mode of our Zebra layer, or varying the settings of our Channel Mixer Adjustment Layer, we arrived with six very different versions of our "wild" montage. The Channel mixer variations are based on the Zebra layer staying in the Overlay Blend Mode, as in our opening image. *Wow!*

Blend Mode Variations

The Zebra layer in Soft Light Blend Mode

The Zebra layer in Hard Light Blend Mode

The Zebra layer in Linear Light Blend Mode

Channel Mixer Variations

Red: +100%; Green: 0; Blue: 0

Red: −30%; Green: +200%; Blue +100%

Red: +150%; Green: −50%; Blue: 0

16-bit Mode Manipulation

Overview *Starting with a high bit-depth Raw digital camera capture or flat bed scan; adjust global tonality and color; use the History Brush and snapshots to selectively Dodge & Burn; as well as to apply the High-Pass filter in Overlay Blend Mode.*

"**16 Bit Maui**" "before " and "after" files

1a

The challenges of working in 16-bits-per-channel mode: no layers, masks, or styles

1b

Auto Color Correction Options
Algorithms
● Enhance Monochromatic Contrast
○ Enhance Per Channel Contrast
○ Find Dark & Light Colors
☐ Snap Neutral Midtones
Target Colors & Clipping
Shadows: Clip: 0.10 %
Midtones:
Highlights: Clip: 0.01 %
☐ Save as defaults

OK Cancel

Within the Levels, Auto Color Correction Options dialog, we selected a new Algorithm and reduced the amount of Shadow and Highlight Clipping

1c

Before and after our Levels and Hue & Saturation global adjustments

ORIGINAL PHOTO: © JHDAVIS DESIGN

IF YOU'VE EVER TRIED TO WORK in the 16-Bits/Channel Mode in Photoshop, then you probably discovered that some of the program's most powerful functions aren't available in that mode. There are no Layers (and the Adjustments, Masks and Styles that go along with them) **1a,** limited filters, and not even Copy and Paste! So just what are "high bit-depth" images and what is it about them (and this mode that lets you use them) that makes them worth all the extra effort? In a word — information.

Specifically, the information contained in a 16-bit-per-channel image has a tonal range for each primary color of a potential 65,000 variations! In comparison, an 8-bit-per-channel image is limited to 256 shades per red, green, and blue channel.

This additional plethora of image information provides many benefits. First, shadow and highlight detail is increased because of the thousands of possible tones per channel (if you have ever tried to coax detail from an underexposed photo in 8-Bits/Channel Mode, you know the challenge). Second, Color Balance is much easier to adjust, while maintaining quality results, when you have billions (16 Bits per channel x 3 channels equals, well . . . a heck of a lot of colors!) of total possible colors at your disposal. Third, when you convert a 16-Bit/Channel color image to monochrome, you can get a higher quality grayscale image than you would with a typical 256 shade grayscale file.

So how *do* you make targeted adjustments to an image without the use of Adjustment Layers or masks, and how do you apply filters and take advantage of Blend Modes? One answer is Photoshop's History Brush and History palette.

1 Global Adjustments. Start by opening the Levels dialog to make sure you have the desired tonal range in your image. A quick way to do this is to use the Auto button, which instantly "maps" the darkest and lightest areas in your image to full black and white. If your image's color and tonality isn't improved with this "insta-fix," click the Options button and adjust the settings for Algorithms and Clip. For our Maui photograph, we clicked the Enhance Monochromatic Contrast button so that Auto would *not* attempt a color adjustment as part of the Auto process, then we reduced the percentages of Shadow and Highlight Clipping to maintain more detail in those areas **1b.**

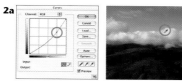

2a

Targeting and adjusting the tones in the Highlights using Curves

2b

*Saving a History Snapshot **A** of the Darkening "Burn" Curves Adjustment and setting it as the source for the History Brush **B**, then undoing the global Curves adjustment **C**, then applying the Snapshot with the History Brush **D**.*

2c

*Taking another Snapshot of a Level's "Dodge" adjustment **A** and using it to lighten the foreground **B***

3a

*Running the High Pass Filter on our photo **A** and taking one final snapshot **B** before undoing the filter*

3b

We applied just the light and dark attributes of the High Pass filter's Snapshot by changing the Blend Mode of the History Brush to Overlay before painting.

After using Levels, we also made a Hue and Saturation adjustment to slightly increase the overall saturation **1c.**

2 Targeted Adjustments. Next we wanted to target specific areas for different types of adjustments. We wanted to darken (or burn) the clouds and sky, and lighten (or dodge) the foreground landscape.

We started by choosing Adjustments, Curves, and when the dialog box opened we Ctrl/⌘-clicked with the cursor on the gray areas of our clouds to automatically set a control point for those specific highlight tones on the Curves diagonal line. Then we tapped on the Down Arrow on our keyboard, thus moving the point downward until we had the desired darkened detail **2a.** We didn't worry that the foreground was also darkening during this procedure because its tonality would be brought back in the next steps.

Next we moved to the History palette and clicked the Make Snapshot camera icon at the bottom of the palette (and gave it a descriptive name when the New Snapshot dialog appeared) **2b** to temporarily save the current state of the Curves' adjusted image for use with the History Brush. Once the new Snapshot appeared in the top portion of the palette, we could now Undo (Ctrl/⌘-Z) the Curves adjustment, knowing that it would still be available via the History Brush. Next we clicked in the column to the left of its thumbnail to set this state of the document as the source for our next step of painting with the History Brush.

Selecting the History Brush in the Tools palette, and a large (300 pixels) Soft Brush from its Options bar, we clicked and dragged across our clouds and sky to apply the Curves Adjustment just where we wanted it.

We used the same 5-step procedure (Adjustment, Snapshot, Undo, Set Source, and History paint) to perform a targeted Levels lightening adjustment to the foreground of our photo as well **2c.**

3 High Pass Filtering. This same History Brush technique can also be used with filters, such as High Pass, found under Filter, Other. At larger settings (here we used 30), this filter can be used for an instant global Dodging & Burning effect, which is what our image needed. We followed the same procedure as outlined in step 2, except instead of adjusting Curves or Levels, we ran the High Pass filter **3a,** took the Snapshot, set it as the source for the History Brush, then typed Ctrl/⌘-Z to Undo. Now the real magic of the High Pass filter comes into play with the addition of Blend Modes, and the fact that certain modes have neutral colors (colors or tones that have no effect on the layers below). Because 50% gray happens to be one of these neutral colors for the Overlay (as well as the Soft Light) Blend Mode, we set the Mode in the Options bar for the History Brush to Overlay **3b,** then applied the instant dark and light edge enhancement effects of the filter without any of its gray components. By choosing a hard-edged brush and setting its size to 1000 and its Opacity to 50%, we could click and drag the brush over the entire image in one pass, which applied the filter everywhere at 50% strength. We then used a smaller, softer brush, with an even greater reduction in opacity to further enhance specific areas.

Filter
Demos

Overview *For any Adobe Photoshop filter you want to use, open an image; select the area you want to filter (make no selection if you want to filter the entire active layer); choose Filter and select a filter from the pop-out submenus.*

This is the original image used for the filter demos, before filters were applied. The image is 408 pixels wide, or 1.8 inches wide at 225 dpi.

MAKING YOUR MARK

Choosing Filter, Digimarc, Embed Watermark opens a dialog box that lets you embed a registered noise pattern, to deter unauthorized publication of your work. But some artists feel that a watermark durable enough to survive changes made to the file by an unauthorized user is also strong enough to interfere with the integrity of the image.

Bert Monroy, whose work appears in the "Gallery" pages of Chapters 6 and 7, uses both a copyright notice and a "type ID" in a different spot in each published copy of an image. If he later sees the image used without permission, he can tell where the file came from.

THE FOLLOWING PAGES PROVIDE A CATALOG of many of the available filters showing the effects of applying them to two kinds of images — a photo and a drawing made from the photo by tracing with one of Adobe Illustrator's dynamic brushes and put on a background made by scanning a marble flooring sample. The unfiltered test image is shown at the left; a filtered version (using Filter, Artistic, Watercolor) is shown above on the left and on page 234.

Where numerical settings are shown in the captions of the catalog images, they are listed in the order they appear in a filter's dialog box, from upper left to lower right. If the default settings were used, no settings are shown.

Where an alpha channel was needed in order to run the filter (as for embossing with the Lighting Effects filter, shown above on the right), or when a selection was required, we used only the drawing and the marble background.

Besides showing you the results of applying the filters themselves, this catalog includes tips for using filters efficiently and creatively. *WOW!*

NOT ALL FILTERS WORK IN ALL COLOR MODES

If you need to produce your Photoshop file in CMYK, Grayscale, or Indexed Color for the output process you'll use to publish it, it's often a good idea to do your creative work in RGB mode and then make the color mode conversion afterwards. One reason for this is that all of Photoshop's filters can be run on images in RGB color mode, but in other color modes the choice narrows, eliminating some of the most powerful.

- Among the first to be eliminated are Lens Flare and Lighting Effects, which work only in RGB Color mode — not even in Grayscale.

- In CMYK Color mode, you lose the entire Artistic, Brush Strokes, Sketch, and Texture menus, as well as Smart Blur, several of the Distort filters, and 3D Transform.

- In Indexed Color, as in Bitmap mode, the entire Filter menu is unavailable.

In CMYK mode many of Photoshop's best filters are "grayed out" in the Filter menu because they're unavailable.

Adobe: *Artistic*

Most of the Artistic filters simulate traditional art media. But the Plastic Wrap filter provides highlights and shadows that can add dimensionality and a slick surface texture.

Artistic: Colored Pencil

Artistic: Cutout

Artistic: Dry Brush

Artistic: Film Grain

Artistic: Fresco

Artistic: Neon Glow

Artistic: Paint Daubs

Artistic: Palette Knife

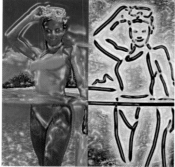
Artistic: Plastic Wrap

Artistic: Poster Edges

Artistic: Rough Pastels

Artistic: Smudge Stick

Artistic: Sponge

Artistic: Underpainting

Artistic: Watercolor

Adobe: *Blur*

TESTING A BLUR

For the Radial Blur filter use a Quality setting of Draft (quick but rough) to experiment with the Amount and the blur center; then use Good (or on a very large image, Best) for the final effect.

Equivalent settings for Smart Blur are Low, Medium, and High.

Blur: Blur

Blur: Blur More

Blur: Gaussian Blur (5)

Blur: Motion Blur (45/30)

Blur: Radial Blur (Spin)

Blur: Radial Blur (Zoom)

Blur: Smart Blur

Blur: Smart Blur (Edges Only)

Adobe:
Brush Strokes

The Brush Strokes filters simulate different ways of applying paint. Like the Sketch filters, some of the Brush Strokes filters produce results that can be effectively composited with the original image (see the "Compositing with Sketch Filters" tip on page 244).

Brush Strokes: Accented Edges

Brush Strokes: Angled Strokes

Brush Strokes: Crosshatch

Brush Strokes: Dark Strokes

Brush Strokes: Ink Outlines

Brush Strokes: Spatter

Brush Strokes: Sprayed Strokes

Brush Strokes: Sumi-e

Adobe: *Distort*

The Distort filters add special effects and textures to an image.

DISPLACEMENT MODES

If you get an uninteresting effect when you use Stretch To Fit mode for the Distort, Displace filter, try applying it in Tile mode. (Many of the displacement maps that Adobe supplies are small, and Stretch To Fit mode badly distorts them.)

Distort: Diffuse Glow

Distort: Displace (Honeycomb 10%)

Distort: Displace (Random strokes 25%)

Distort: Displace (Streaks pattern)

Distort: Glass (Blocks)

Distort: Glass (Custom texture/lightened)

Distort: Ocean Ripple

Distort: Pinch (+100%)

Distort: Pinch (−100%)

Distort: Polar Coordinates (Polar to Rect.)

MORE DISPLACEMENT MAPS

The standard Photoshop 7 installation provides two sets of files to use with Filter, Distort, Displace: one — Displacement Maps — is in Plug-ins; and two — Textures — is in Presets. Additional files can be found in Textures For Lighting Effects on the Adobe Photoshop 7 CD-ROM. You can also create your own displacement maps, as in "Carving a Textured Surface" on page 382.

Distort: Polar Coordinates (Rect. to Polar)

Distort: Ripple

Distort: Shear

Distort: Spherize (+100%)

Distort: Spherize (−100%)

Distort: Twirl

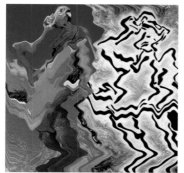

Distort: Wave

Distort: Zigzag (Pond Ripples)

FANCY FRAMING

Some filters can be used to create a custom edge treatment for an image. A few good candidates are Ocean Ripple, Wave, and Twirl from the Distort submenu; and Spatter and Sprayed Strokes from the Brush Strokes submenu; and Underpainting from the Artistic submenu. The process involves making a layer mask for the image, blurring the mask's edges, and applying a filter to distort the blurred part. The technique is described in detail in "Framing with Masks" on page 128, and examples are shown in "Filtered Frames" on page 218.

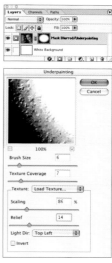

Adobe: *Noise*

One of the Noise filters (Add Noise) can be used to "roughen" an image, and the other three (Despeckle, Dust & Scratches, and Median) are used for smoothing, or eliminating irregularities.

Noise: Add Noise (Gaussian, 50%, Mono)

Noise: Add Noise (Uniform, 50%)

Noise: Despeckle

Noise: Dust & Scratches (4/0)

Noise: Median (5)

REDUCING A FILTER EFFECT

You can reduce a filter's effect if you choose Edit, Fade *immediately* after running the filter. The result is as if you had filtered a duplicate in a layer above the original and were now reducing that layer's Opacity. (Fade also works for the Image, Adjust commands, and for any tool that applies or removes color: Airbrush, Paintbrush or Pencil, Stamps, History or Art History Brush, Erasers, Gradient or Paint Bucket, Blur, Sharpen or Smudge.)

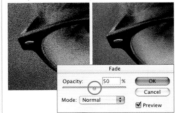

The effect of applying Add Noise (left) was reduced (right) by choosing Edit, Fade. Although we didn't do so here, the Fade dialog also lets you change the blend mode.

CREATING TEXTURES

The Add Noise filter can be useful in creating natural-looking textured surfaces:

For instance, make brushed metal **A** or the start of wood grain by filling a layer with gray (Edit, Fill, 50% Gray) and running Add Noise, then using the Motion Blur filter to create streaks, and finishing with a subtle application of Lighting Effects.

Or make rough paper textures for painting **B** by running the Add Noise filter at a low setting, then Blur or Blur More (used here), and then Emboss (from the Stylize submenu). Or try using Facet (from the Pixelate submenu) between the blurring and embossing steps. Use Image, Adjust, Levels to whiten the paper and reduce contrast.

Find more texture-making tips in "Making Marble & Stucco" on page 241 and "Textures and Backgrounds" and "Seamlessly Tiling Patterns" in Chapter 8.

Adobe: *Other*

The Other submenu houses the eclectic collection of filters shown on this page.

Other: Custom

Other: High Pass (10)

Other: Offset

Other: Maximum (2)

Other: Minimum (2)

MAKING YOUR OWN

It's possible to design your own filters with the Custom interface. When you get an effect you like — by hard work or by chance — save it so you can load it later and use it again.

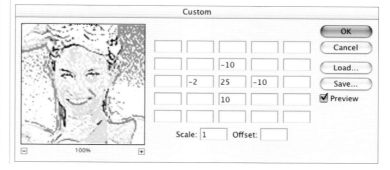

Adobe:
Pixelate

Most of the Pixelate filters turn an image into patterns consisting of spots of flat color. For all but Facet and Fragment, you can control the size of the spots, producing very different effects depending on the size settings.

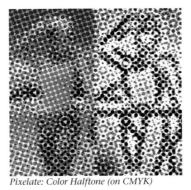

Pixelate: Color Halftone (on CMYK)

Pixelate: Crystallize

Pixelate: Facet

Pixelate: Fragment

Pixelate: Mezzotint (Coarse Dots)

Pixelate: Mezzotint (Fine Dots)

Pixelate: Mezzotint (Short Lines)

Pixelate: Mezzotint (Short Strokes)

Pixelate: Mosaic

Pixelate: Pointillize (white Background color)

Pixelate: Pointillize (black Background color)

Adobe: *Render*

The Render filters create "atmo-sphere" and surface texture. Two of them act independently of the color in the image: Clouds creates a sky, and Texture Fill fills a layer or channel with a pattern. The 3D Transform filter applies an image to a sphere, cube, or cylinder. A step-by-step procedure for such an application is given in "Applying a Logo with 3D Transform" on page 215.

Render: 3D Transform

Render: Clouds (with blue Background color)

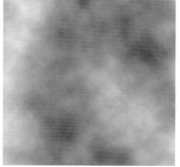

Render: Clouds (with default colors)

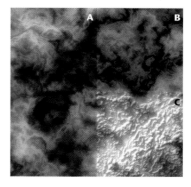

Render: Difference Clouds

RENDERING A STORM

Holding down the Alt/Option key as you choose Filter, Render, Clouds produces a more dramatic cloud pattern with more contrast.

RENDERING OPTIONS

Clicking the Options button in the 3D Transform dialog box before you click OK to render the transfor- mation lets you control the render- ing process — balancing the need for good quality with the desire to shorten the rendering time. Since you can't save your 3D Transform settings between applications of the filter, you may want to set the Reso- lution and Anti-Aliasing higher than the default settings.

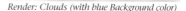

MAKING MARBLE & STUCCO

The Difference Clouds filter can generate a veined, marble look: In the white- filled Background layer of an RGB file, with black and white as the Foreground and Background colors, choose Filter, Render, Difference Clouds. Then press Ctrl/⌘-F repeatedly to build the degree of marbling you want **A**. Colorize the marble by adding an Adjustment layer (click the Create New Fill/Adjustment Layer button at the bottom of the Layers palette). Choose Color Balance from the pop-out list, and adjust the sliders in the Color Balance dialog box **B**. Produce a stucco-like texture **C** by treating the uncolored marble **A** with the Lighting Effects filter as fol- lows: In the Channels palette look at the individual color channels (Red, Green, and Blue) and note which one shows the most contrast. Apply the filter (Filter, Render, Lighting Effects) using Directional as the Light Type and choosing the high-contrast color channel from the Texture Channel menu, with White Is High turned on.

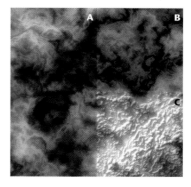

Render: Lens Flare

Render: Lighting Effects (Soft Spotlight)

Render: Lighting Effects (Blue Omni)

Render: Lighting Effects (Directional; Red channel as Texture)

Render: Lighting Effects (Directional; alpha channel as Texture; White Is High on)

Render: Lighting Effects (Directional; alpha channel as Texture; White Is High off)

Render: Lighting Effects (Directional; Blistered Paint as Texture)

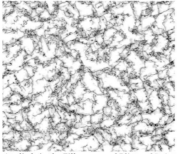

Applied via the Fill command Blistered Paint

USING TEXTURE FILLS WITH LIGHTING EFFECTS

Adobe Photoshop 7 comes with numerous files designed as seamlessly repeating patterns. Here's how to use one of these textures as a "bump map" for creating surface relief for the Lighting Effects filter's light to act on: Open the Channels palette for the image you want to run Lighting Effects on (Window, Show Channels) and click the Create New Channel button at the bottom of the palette to make an alpha channel. With this channel active, choose Edit, Fill. In the Fill dialog, click on the arrow to the right of the Custom Pattern Swatch and select a set of patterns from the menu. We chose the Blistered Paint pattern from the Texture Fill set. Click the OK button to fill the alpha channel with the pattern. Then click the RGB channel's name to make it active, and choose Filter, Render, Lighting Effects, picking your texture-filled alpha channel as the Texture Channel in the Lighting Effects dialog box.

Adobe: Sharpen

Although there are four Sharpen filters, the one you'll use most is Unsharp Mask, because it's the only one that lets you vary the parameters of the effect (see "Sharpen" on page 204 for tips on using Unsharp Mask).

Sharpen: Sharpen

Sharpen: Sharpen Edges

Sharpen: Sharpen More

Sharpen: Unsharp Mask (100/1/0)

NAVIGATING UNSHARP MASK

In the preview window of the Unsharp Mask dialog box (as well as Gaussian Blur and some others), you can use key commands to **zoom in** (**Ctrl/⌘-click** the preview) or **zoom out** (**Alt/Option-click**). Or **move to a particular area of the image by clicking the cursor** there in the working window (the cursor becomes a square when you move it out of the dialog box and into the working window).

Adobe: Sketch

The Sketch filters include a number of artistic effects. Some of them imitate drawing methods, while others simulate different dimensional media. The Sketch effects shown here were produced with black as the Foreground color.

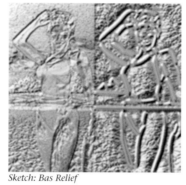

Sketch: Bas Relief

Sketch: Chalk & Charcoal

Sketch: Charcoal

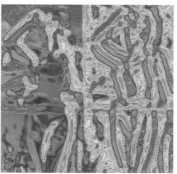

Sketch: Chrome

Sketch: Conté Crayon

Sketch: Graphic Pen

Sketch: Halftone Pattern (Dot)

Sketch: Halftone Pattern (Line)

Sketch: Note Paper

Sketch: Photocopy

Sketch: Plaster

Sketch: Reticulation

Sketch: Stamp

Sketch: Torn Edges

Sketch: Water Paper

COMPOSITING WITH SKETCH FILTERS

Some of the Sketch filters are ideal for making filtered layers that can then be composited with the original image. Here we've layered an image filtered with Reticulation over the original, then reduced its Opacity and used the Color Dodge blend mode to create a glowing effect. The Hue/Saturation Adjustment layer with a mask was added to darken the edges.

Adobe: *Stylize*

The Stylize filters are a diverse collection of edge treatments and other special effects.

NEUTRAL EMBOSSING

To eliminate the color from an image that has been treated with the Emboss filter, keeping only the highlights and shadows, use Image, Adjust, Desaturate.

Stylize: Diffuse

Stylize: Emboss

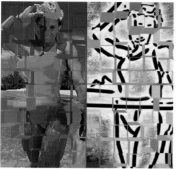

Stylize: Extrude (Blocks)

Stylize: Extrude (Pyramids)

Stylize: Find Edges

Stylize: Glowing Edges

"SOFTENING" A FILTER

If you run a filter and the result seems too strong, you can undo the filter (Ctrl/⌘-Z) and try again. Or you may want to choose Edit, Fade and use the Opacity slider in the Fade dialog box to "soften" the effect. With Fade you can also control the blend mode of the filtered image. But Fade only works if you use it immediately after you apply a filter; the change becomes permanent once you do any other work on the image. For more flexibility later, use a two-layer approach to softening the filter effect, as described in "Compositing with Sketch Filters" on page 244.

*The original photo **A** was filtered with Stylize, Glowing Edges **B**. Then the two images were blended by reducing the Opacity of the filtered image and putting it in Luminosity mode, to produce a subtler effect **C**.*

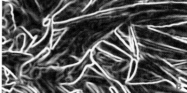

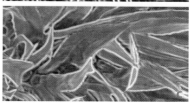

Stylize: Solarize

Stylize: Tiles

Stylize: Trace Contour

To get the look of hand-painted tiles, start by running Filter, Stylize, Tiles on the image. (Or for a mosaic look with each tile a single color, try Filter, Texture, Stained Glass.) Next create an alpha channel (click the Create New Channel button at the bottom of the Channels palette), repeat the filter on this channel (Ctrl/⌘-F), and blur slightly (Filter, Blur, Gaussian Blur). Working in the RGB composite channel again (Ctrl/⌘-~ activates the composite), choose Filter, Render, Lighting Effects; set up a Directional light source and choose the alpha channel as the Texture Channel. If the grout in the alpha channel is white, turn off White Is High.

Filtered and blurred alpha channel　*Tiles and Lighting Effects applied*

Stylize: Wind (Stagger)

Stylize: Wind (Wind)

Adobe:
Texture

Most of the Texture filters create the illusion that the image has been applied to an uneven surface. But Stained Glass remakes the image into polygons, each filled with a single color.

Texture: Craquelure

Texture: Grain

Texture: Grain (Clumped)

Texture: Grain (Enlarged)

Texture: Grain (Speckle)

Texture: Grain (Stippled)

Texture: Grain (Vertical)

Texture: Mosaic Tiles

Texture: Patchwork

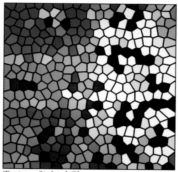

Texture: Stained Glass

Texture: Texturizer (Brick)

Texture: Texturizer (Canvas)

TRYING OUT TEXTURIZER

Choosing Filter, Texture, Texturizer brings up the Texturizer dialog box, which is sort of like a mini version of the Lighting Effects filter. Texturizer doesn't have Lighting Effects' flexibility in setting the type of light source; all its lighting is directional. And it doesn't let you add extra lights or define surface characteristics like shininess. But it's easier to operate, it does let you use images in Photoshop file format as the texture pattern for embossing (through its Load Texture option), and it lets you scale the pattern down to 50% or up to 200% so you can control how many times it repeats. To get a smaller pattern with more repetitions, start with a texture file that's smaller in relation to your background image. To get a rounder edge, apply a slight Gaussian Blur to the texture file before you run the Texturizer filter.

For the image on the left, the Photoshop file used as a texture was scaled to 100%, so it kept its original size relationship to the background image. For the version in the center, it was scaled to 50%. For the image at the right, the texture file was given a slight Gaussian Blur before the filter was applied, which resulted in smoother embossing.

Texture: Texturizer (Sandstone 200/10)

Mark Wainer creates limited-edition prints of his painterly landscapes from his own original photography. His goal is to create images that simulate natural media and do not easily reveal their computer heritage.

Mark begins the process by taking his 35-mm film and scanning it to a 27MB file. (when he uses his digital camera, the files are resampled up to 27 megabytes). After initial color and tonal adjustments are made, the Simplifier filter from BuzzPro 2.0 filter set is applied to a duplicated layer of the adjusted original **A.**

The opacity of the filtered layer is reduced in the layers palette to return the desired amount of the original detail **B.** The image is then resampled up to 81MB in 10% increments using a Photoshop action **C.** Then the image is "sharpened" using the Dry Brush filter, which can be applied more than once if necessary. For some images, sharpening can also be performed by duplicating the flattened image on a new layer and applying the High Pass Filter, then changing the Blend Mode of the layer to Soft Light **D.**

Extensive retouching with the clone tool or healing brush is then applied to achieve the hyper-real, yet stylized and painterly end-result. The images are printed with archival inks on 24- by 30-inch coated watercolor paper.

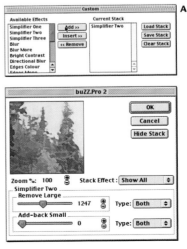

A

Muse No.1 by **Jay Paul Bell** began with a 35mm color photo of a woman wearing a pair of wings from a novelty shop. Bell silhouetted the figure and placed it over a background composed of elements from other original color photographs of pillars, columns, ground surfaces, and landscape textures. To create the impression of an interior space with depth, he used repeating elements that decrease in size and appear to recede into the distance.

To introduce a geometric element, on a separate layer Bell drew lines over the composition, using the Pen tool to create paths. Then, using a brush size and color that worked visually with the composition, he stroked each path with the Airbrush tool. ▶ *You can stroke an active Work Path or named path by Alt/ Option-clicking the Stroke Path button at the bottom of the Paths palette and choosing a tool from the pop-out menu in the Stroke Path dialog box. Or, if a painting, cloning, or toning tool is already chosen, simply clicking the Stroke Path button will stroke the path with the current brush tip for the tool.*

Bell applied the Seamless Welder from the Corel KPT 6 filter set to rectangular, oval, and irregular selections to make some of the line elements repeat. He made a merged copy of the image at this point (add a transparent layer at the top or the stack and choose Layer, Merge Visible

with the Alt/Option key held down) and filtered the copy to produce a neonlike effect on the drawn lines and a solarized and textured effect on the figure and background (Filter, Stylize, Glowing Edges). A copy of the Seamless Welder/Geometric Line layer, with the Mode set to Difference and the Opacity set at 100%, was placed above the new Glowing Edges layer, which produced a blue cast on the figure. To restore some of the original skin tones, Bell duplicated the original figure photo and moved it to the top of the stack in the Layers palette. He deleted all but the head, arm, and torso using the Eraser tool and put this layer in Difference mode also. The hair area had become flat because of the filtering, so Bell repainted it with the Airbrush tool to restore texture.

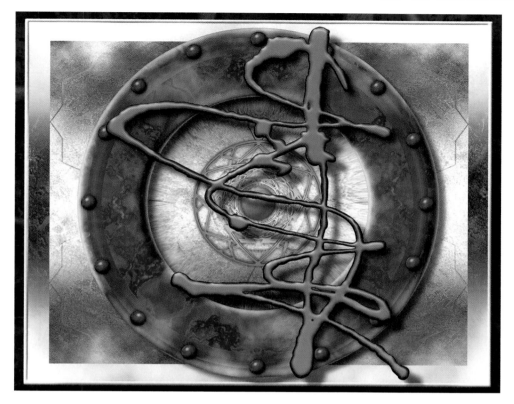

The illustration that **Greg Klamt** used in the cover design for his *Fluxus Quo* CD (Spotted Peccary Music) began with a scan of a drip of black paint from a mixed-media painting **A**. In Photoshop Klamt embossed the scanned shape (an embossing process using the Lighting Effects filter is described in the stucco section of "Making Marble & Stucco" on page 241) and also treated it with the Plastic Wrap filter **B**. Klamt also added a drop shadow and a color gradient to the shape **C**. ▶ *Three Overlay effects in Photoshop (Color, Gradient, and Pattern) allow you to apply color as part of a Layer Style, without permanently changing any pixels in the image, and thus with the flexibility to change your mind. To apply a solid color, a gradient, or a pattern, target the layer by clicking its name in the Layers palette and choose an Overlay effect from the pop-out menu of the "ƒ" button at the bottom of the palette.*

The background for *Fluxus Quo* was created by filling the file's *Background* layer with a multicolor gradient and then running several Corel KPT filters to generate texture. Klamt used Photoshop's Radial Blur filter in Zoom mode on a circular selection in the center of the background. He also added an empty layer and ran the Clouds filter on it (Filter, Render, Clouds), then used the Edit, Fade command to reduce the transparency of the clouds. Finally he erased the middle section of the clouds layer, leaving the clouds only along the top and bottom edges, and experimented with blend modes to get the effect he wanted.

A border area was created by choosing Select, All and then Alt/Option-dragging with the Rectangular Marquee tool to subtract a large rectangular area in the middle. Klamt inverted the color of the selected border area (by choosing Image, Adjust, Invert or pressing Ctrl/⌘-I) and then reducing the intensity of the color (by choosing Image, Adjust, Hue/Saturation and moving the Saturation slider to the left).

The large circle, on a layer of its own, was embossed (like the drip of paint) but was colored by adding a texture-filled layer above it. The texture-filled layer and circle layer were combined in a clipping group so that the color showed only on the ring. Klamt experimented with the blend mode until he had the effect he wanted with the color from the texture layer and the dimensionality from the circle layer. ▶ *To form a clipping group, Alt/Option-click on the border between the two layers in the Layers palette.*

The blue mandala was hand-drawn, scanned, traced in Macromedia FreeHand and imported into Photoshop, where a Radial gradient was applied.

The red sphere in the center was created with the KPT Spheroid Designer. This filter was also used to create one of the small spheres that appear around the edge of the circle. This small sphere was duplicated several times to make the others.
▶ *To duplicate an element, you can select it, switch to the Move tool, hold down the Alt/Option key, and drag.*

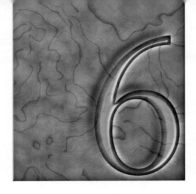

PAINTING

NOW MORE THAN EVER, PHOTOSHOP 7 provides powerful computer artmaking tools for painting from scratch, reproducing parts of an existing image, or drawing with technical precision. To understand better what their strengths are, we can categorize these tools according to how they apply color, transparency, or pattern, or how they reproduce an image. These categories are briefly presented here and are discussed in more detail later in this introduction to the chapter:

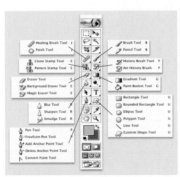

Photoshop's tools for stroking with paint and pattern are the Paintbrush, Pencil, Eraser, Smudge, and Pattern Stamp. The cloning tools, for applying a copy of an image stroke-by-stroke, are the healing Brush (and its sibling, the Patch Tool), Clone Stamp (and its counterpart, the Pattern Stamp Tool), the History Brush, and, in a roundabout way, the Art History Brush. The filling tools — Paint Bucket and Gradient — "pour" color into a layer or a selected area. Unlike all these pixel-based tools, the drawing tools — Shapes and Pens — create vector-based objects whose edges and other attributes don't deteriorate, no matter how many times you resize, rotate, or skew them. These vector-based tools are covered in Chapter 7.

- **Painting tools** are operated freehand, applying or erasing color as you click or drag them, like traditional brushes, airbrushes, pencils, erasers, and so on. Photoshop's painting tools include the **Paintbrush, Pencil, Eraser, Smudge,** and **Pattern Stamp.**

- **Cloning tools** in Photoshop 7 have taken a giant leap forward with the addition of the **Healing Brush** and **Patch Tools.** They are covered extensively in Chapter 3, but basically, cloning tools take a sample from one area of an image and then reproduce the sampled material elsewhere. In addition to the Healing Brush and Patch Tools, Photoshop's cloning tools include the **Clone Stamp, History Brush,** and **Art History Brush.** (The Art History Brush, added in version 5.5, is a specialty tool that samples and uses the color in the image but doesn't actually reproduce the sampled image faithfully; instead it produces automated brush strokes based on the color in the sampled image.) In Photoshop this duplicating can work in both space (from one area of a picture to another) and time (from one version of a file to another). That is, when you clone pixels from one area of an image — either from one layer or from all visible layers — and reproduce them somewhere else, you aren't limited to the current version of the file. By using the History palette and the tools designed to work with it, you can go backwards in time and clone from an earlier stage within the current working session.

- **Filling tools** "pour" color or pattern into a layer or a selected area. Photoshop's filling tools include the **Paint Bucket** and **Gradient**.

- **Vector-based drawing tools** provide a unique opportunity to construct and refine artwork that isn't subject to the "softening" that happens when pixel-based elements are resized or reshaped. Just as important, the artwork produced by these tools is *resolution-*

continued on page 255

The world of **Wow Presets** holds a lot more than just Styles — from painting to retouching to eye-popping special effects, all done with one-click Presets. If you followed the instructions on page 9, you'll find these **Wow 7 Presets** in your Photoshop menus:

• In the pop-out menu of the **Tool Presets** palette are the **Wow 7-Art History Brushes (A)**, **Wow 7-Art Media Brushes (B)**, and **Wow 7-Pattern Stamp Brushes (C)** with more than 60 tools for simulating traditional artists' media — including Pastel, Chalk, Oil, Watercolor, Sponge, Stipple, and Dry Brush. See pages 260-261 for samples of these Presets for the Pattern Stamp and Art History Brush.

• Also available in the **Tool Presets** palette's menu are the **Wow 7-Image Fix Brushes (D)**, Presets for the Brush tool, for correcting color and tone, removing red-eye, whitening eyes and teeth, and neutralizing redness on the skin. See "Using the Wow! Image Fix Brushes" on page 10 for pointers.

• Finally, **Wow 7 Presets** for the Rectangular **Marquee Tool** and **Crop Tool (E)** will help you make selections at many popular sizes and crop images to those dimensions.

• The **Wow 7-Actions** — for production shortcuts; enhancing paintings, photos, and graphics; and fixing images — are covered on page 11.

• There are **Wow 7-Patterns** for printed Fabric, Marble, Media substrates, Miscellaneous Surfaces, Noise (which can be used for artistic treatments or to simulate film grain), and Organic materials such as wood and woven fibers. The **Wow 7-Patterns** will be available from the pop-out menu anywhere the Patterns palette occurs; for instance, in the Fill dialog box, in the Pattern Fill dialog (opened when you click the "Create new fill or adjustment layer" button at the bottom of the Layers palette), in the Options bar for the Pattern Stamp or Paint Bucket tool, or in certain Style components that use Patterns (such as the Pattern Overlay, the Stroke, and the Texture "subeffect" of Bevel And Emboss).

• Using the **Wow 7-Gradients** is described starting on page 265

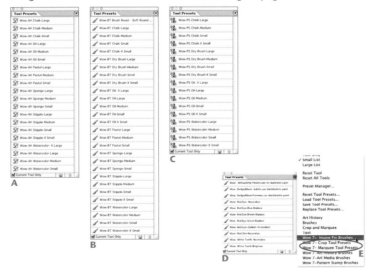

A

B

C

D

E

Turn an existing photo into a painting with the **Wow 7-Pattern Stamp** or **Wow 7- Art History Brushes.** Or paint from scratch on a blank canvas with the **Wow 7-Art Media Brushes** (below). All three brush sets have matching brush tips, so you can seamlessly switch back and forth between the three.

The **Wow-Art Media Brushes Presets** were designed for creating paintings without cloning a photo. (The names of these Presets start with "BT," which stands for "Brush Tool," which is the tool you choose in the Tools palette in order to work with these Presets, chosen from the Tool Presets palette.) Of course, these brushes can also be used for adding the finishing touches to a cloned painting. Strokes made with the **Wow-BT** brushes are shown here:

Wow-BT Chalk

Wow-BT Dry Brush

Wow-BT Oil

Wow-BT Pastel

Wow-BT Sponge

Wow-BT Stipple

Wow-BT Watercolor

Strokes painted with the seven kinds of **Wow-Art Media Brushes**. *In each case the top stroke was produced with the mouse and the bottom one with a Wacom Intuos tablet.*

Continued from page 252

independent, so if it's saved as a Photoshop file, in an EPS (encapsulated PostScript) format, or as a PDF and sent to a PostScript output device, it will be printed or imaged with razor-sharp edges — the best edges the printer or imagesetter is capable of producing.

Because of their vector-based nature, the drawing tools are covered in Chapter 7, "Type, Shapes, Paths & PostScript." Briefly, though, some of Photoshop 7's drawing tools are predefined **Shapes** that essentially draw themselves when you drag the cursor; these are the **Rectangle, Rounded Rectangle, Ellipse, Polygon, Line,** and **Custom Shape.** Other drawing tools are designed to let you create lines and shapes from scratch. These Bézier curve–drawing tools include the **Pen** tool and its "relative," the **Freeform Pen**, which operates freehand like a painting tool. For more about operating the Shape and Pen tools, see Chapter 7.

THE PAINTING TOOLS

Each of the painting tools — the Paintbrush, Pencil, Eraser, Smudge, and Pattern Stamp — behaves in its own unique way. The differences you'll find in the painting tools are summarized below. Many of the controls for the painting tools (Brush Shape, Blend Mode, Opacity, Flow, and the Airbrush toggle), can be found in the Options bar as soon as you choose one of these tools. But for fine-tuning existing brush presets or creating your own elaborate media brushes, you'll need to dive into Photoshop 7's new Expanded View Brush Palette **A.** But for now, here is a list of the tools that take advantage of these new painterly capabilities:

- By default, the **Paintbrush** lays down a smooth-edged (antialiased) stroke of color as you drag. If you click without dragging, it leaves a single footprint of the brush shape. By default, no matter how long you hold the Paintbrush in one place, the color doesn't build up or spread out.

- The **Pencil** operates like the Paintbrush. However, the stroke edges are not soft or even antialiased. Because Photoshop doesn't have to do the calculations required for antialiasing, there's no delay between when you move the cursor and when the stroke appears on the screen, so the Pencil can seem like the most "natural" of all the tools for doing quick sketches. But pixelation can be seen in the "stairstepping" of curved or slanted edges.

- The **Airbrush** is now a Settings option for the paint brush — it's a toggle you turn on and off via an icon in the Brush's Options bar. It works by

With a pressure-sensitive stylus and drawing tablet (such as the Wacom Intuos used for this painting) Photoshop's painting and cloning tools respond more like their traditional counterparts. (See the "Using a Tablet & Stylus" tip on page 258 and "Painting 'Wet on Wet'" on page 272.)

*With the ability to change the Texture **B** (just one of the hundreds of possible variables in Photoshop 7's Expanded View of the new Brush Palette **A,** accessible from the pop-out Options menu in the upper right corner of the palette **C**), there is no medium that can't be imitated with a little finessing. See the projects in this chapter for step-by-step lessons in using these new capabilities.*

MARKER EFFECTS

To get the look of felt-tip markers, use the Paintbrush with Wet Edges chosen in the Options bar. To get the look of a highlighter, as shown here, use the Paintbrush with Wet Edges in Multiply mode. We used the Pastel Light 120 Pixels brush tip.

With Photoshop 7's painting tools you may customize the Fade Control settings throughout the many options available in the Expanded View of the new Brush Palette. For example, by setting the Control settings in Shape Dynamics, Color Dynamics and Other Dynamics to Fade, with different numbers of Steps, you can shrink the brush size **A,** fade to transparency, and change the color (from the Foreground to the Background color) all at different rates with a single brush stroke.

"spraying" color, like its real-world counterpart. The longer you leave the Airbrush in one place, the more the "paint" builds up, till it reaches 100% opacity.

- The **Eraser** removes pixels or changes their color. By default it leaves the Background color (if you're working on a *Background* layer) or transparency (on other layers). It can operate like a Paintbrush, Airbrush, or Pencil, depending on what you choose from the Mode menu in the Options bar. Another Mode choice is Block. This was the only mode the Eraser had in early versions of the program; it's not very useful compared to other modes.

There are also two other versions of the Eraser — the Magic Eraser and the Background Eraser. The **Magic Eraser** "pours" transparency (see "The 'Unfill' Tool," a tip on page 264). The **Background Eraser** can be instructed to erase only a certain range of colors and protect others. It can be very useful in silhouetting a subject from a background, as described in step 2 of "Assembling a Still Life" on page 174.

- The **Smudge** tool smears color as you drag it. If the Finger Painting option is chosen, it starts the smear with the Foreground color. Otherwise, it starts each stroke by sampling the color under the cursor, and it paints with that color. At any Opacity setting other than 100% the process can be very slow; but at 100% it can be very effective for moving around pixels with a "painterly" result,

The **Wow Patterns Presets** *found on the CD-ROM that comes with this book provide patterns that can be used with the Pattern Stamp, the Paint Bucket, the Fill command, or a Pattern Fill layer. They can also be used in a Layer Style, either as a Pattern Overlay or as the Texture in the Bevel And Emboss effect. And perhaps most importantly, they can be loaded in as part of a brush's attributes to significantly enhance the "sensory experience" of imitated natural media.*

If an image has an active selection or if it has more than one layer, Photoshop's painting, cloning, and fill tools will work only *inside the selection* and *on the active pixel-based layer or layer mask.* If a painting tool isn't working:

- It may be because there's an **invisible active selection** — either outside the window, or hidden because you've pressed Ctrl/ ⌘-H to temporarily hide the "marching ants" selection border.

- Or the area you're trying to paint may be protected because the layer's **transparency or pixels are locked** (you can tell by looking at the check boxes for the Lock icons at the top of the Layers palette).

- Or you may be trying to paint on a **Shape** or **type layer**, which doesn't accept pixels.

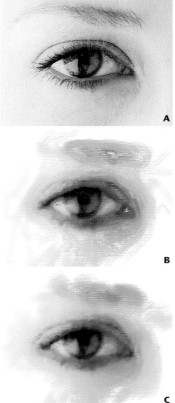

*The settings in the Options bar for Photoshop 7's Art History Brush include the blend Mode, Opacity, painting Style (which sets the length and shape of the strokes **A),** and Area (which specifies how big an area will be filled with strokes when you click the tool once). See "Art History Lessons" on page 276 for examples of how the settings work.*

*Starting with the same source image **A** and the same brush tip, the Art History brush generates different results depending on the settings in the Options bar. By changing the Style setting from Tight Long **B** to Tight Short **C,** the automated brushing process more closely follows the contours of the source image — good for images with a lot of detail that you want to maintain.*

as demonstrated in "Painting 'Wet on Wet'" on page 272.

- The **Pattern Stamp** paints with a pattern rather than with a solid color, using the pattern currently chosen in the Options bar. Besides filling with a preset pattern such as those supplied with Photoshop or on the Wow CD-ROM that comes with this book, you can make your own geometrically repeating pattern, or make a seamless pattern for a texture whose repeat isn't obvious, as described in "Seamlessly Tiling Patterns" in Chapter 8.

THE CLONING TOOLS

Photoshop's cloning tools provide a way of reproducing part of the current image, another image, or a previous stage in the development of the current image. The tools that can clone are the new Healing Brush, Clone Stamp, History Brush, Art History Brush, and Pattern Stamp, as well as the Eraser if the Erase To History option is turned on in the Options bar. Many of the choices in the Options bar are the same as for the painting tools. Other options are specific to the individual tools, as described below.

- As the backward-pointing arrow in its icon suggests, the **History Brush** can use a previous version of the image as a source. Working from a version stored in the History palette, the History Brush applies the former colors and details to the current image stroke-by-stroke. Its operation in relation to the Snapshots and states of History palette is discussed in Chapter 1.

The **Impressionist** option has returned in Photoshop 7 as an option within the Pattern Stamp Tool. It is very useful for converting a reference photo to a "hand-painted" work of art by applying brush-like smears of color based on the colors in the reference. The hidden trick to successfully using this tool is that you must make a "pattern" of your *entire* image first, then use this as a source for your cloned painting. We developed the technique shown on page 281, which turns a photo into a faux painting, by using this capability with hand-held control of each brush stroke.

TWO HISTORY BRUSHES

The **Erase To History** option for the Eraser tool gives you an easy way to keep two different History Brushes ready to paint: You can **choose a different brush tip for each of the two tools** and quickly switch back and forth between the two by using the keyboard shortcuts: "**E**" for the Eraser and "**Y**" for the History Brush. (Both brushes will use the same History state for the source.)

HISTORY "ON-OFF": SWITCH

Holding down the Alt/Option key, while brushing, toggles the Eraser in and out of Erase To History mode.

ORIGINAL PHOTO: © CORBIS IMAGES ROYALTY FREE, BACKGROUNDS FROM NATURE

*Starting with the original photo **A** in the Background layer, the Clone Stamp was used with the Use All Layers option turned on and the Aligned option turned off to cover one of the flowers with greenery **B**. Then two more flowers were added, also with Align turned off **C**.*

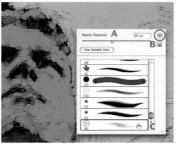

*By right-button clicking (or Ctrl-clicking on a single-button Mac mouse) anywhere within your canvas window, you can automatically call up your Brush Preset Picker **A**. Now select a method to display the brushes by choosing from the Options pop-out menu in the upper right **B** (here we are viewing by "Stroke Thumbnail"), then pick a brush **C** and begin painting.*

- The **Eraser** with the **Erase To History** option turned on paints with the currently chosen Snapshot or state in the History palette.

- The **Art History Brush** is an automated painting tool that can lay down several strokes with a single click. The strokes automatically follow the edges of color or contrast in the Snapshot or state chosen in the History palette. (For information on how this palette works, see Chapter 1.)

Success with the Art History brush depends on controlling the tool's automation. It's helpful to be able to see the original image as you paint, because where you click determines which of the color edges in the source will be given the most weight in determining the shape and color of the strokes that are laid down.

Besides choosing from a limited set of blend Modes and controlling the Opacity, you can set the Stroke Style and Tolerance. The **Style** is the relative length of the strokes and how closely they will follow the color boundaries of the source image. The **Area** is how big an area will be covered by brushstrokes when you click once with the brush. According to Photoshop 7's online Help, the **Tolerance** setting controls how different from the source image the current version has to be in order for the Art History brush to be allowed to paint on it; this can generally be left at the default, 0. "Art History Lessons" starting on page 276 provides step-by-step instructions for taming this tool so the results look "painterly" rather than

simply "filtered." The samples on page 261 show the results of using the Art History Brush with different Wow-AH Tool presets.

- Photoshop's **Clone Stamp** paints with a portion of a sampled image. The source area is sampled by holding down the Alt/Option key and clicking. Samples can be taken from any open image, from all layers as if they were merged (if Use All Layers is turned on), or from the active layer only.

continued on page 262

MAKING AN "OBJECT STAMP"

You can use the Clone Stamp tool as a "brush" to apply multiple copies of an isolated image element, such as the grape shown here.

1 In your image, select the element you want to duplicate and copy it to a transparent layer of its own. Apply a drop shadow if it's appropriate for your image by clicking the Add A Layer Style button (the "*f*") at the bottom of the Layers palette and choosing Drop Shadow from the pop-out list; in the Drop Shadow section of the Layer Style dialog box, click the color swatch and then sample a shadow color by clicking in the image; adjust the other parameters so the direction and intensity of the manufactured shadow also match the image.

2 Use the Rectangular Marquee to make a selection big enough to include the element and its shadow (be careful not to trim the shadow). Then make a merged copy of the selection (Edit, **Copy Merged**, or Ctrl/⌘-Shift-C) and paste it into a file of its own (press Ctrl/⌘-N for File, New; then click OK and press Ctrl/⌘-V to paste). The reason you need to use the Copy Merged command instead of just the Copy command is that Copy won't capture the Layer Style along with the element.

3 Choose the Clone Stamp in the toolbox, and in the Options bar, pop out the Brushes palette (by clicking the little triangle next to the Brush "footprint"), and click the largest brush in the top row of the default set — a round, hard-edged brush. If the cursor doesn't show the shape of the brush when you move it into the working window, go to the Display & Cursors section of the Preferences dialog box (you can do this by pressing Ctrl/⌘-K, then Ctrl/⌘-3); under Painting Cursors choose Brush Size. With the cursor showing the size of the brush, center the cursor over the element and press the right bracket key (**]**) to enlarge the brush until it's big enough to completely include your element. Then Alt/Option-click to define the element as the clone source.

4 Make sure that Aligned is turned off in the Options bar so you can control exactly where the elements are painted. Then just click, click, click with the brush to position the copies.

Object Stamp.psd
layered file

We wanted to add more red grapes to this tray of grapes and cheese.

CORBIS IMAGES ROYALTY FREE, MODERN CUISINE

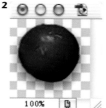

We used the Pen tool to select a single grape, copied it to a layer of its own (Ctrl/⌘-J), added a Drop Shadow, selected the grape and shadow, merge-copied the selection, and pasted it into a new file.

We chose the Clone Stamp tool and enlarged a hard-edged round brush, making it big enough to encompass the grape and shadow. We Alt/Option-clicked to define the clone source, then clicked once to paint each grape.

Using the "loaded" Clone Stamp with our enlarged brush tip, we clicked repeatedly to create new piles of grapes.

On these two pages are paintings made from the photo below **A,** using the **Wow 7-Pattern Stamp Brushes** and **Wow 7-Art History Brushes.** These paintings were produced using a Wacom tablet and using the techniques discussed in the projects starting on pages 276 and 281. The label under each picture tells which Tool Preset and Texture Style (from the **Wow 7-07 Texture Styles B)** were used.

With the **Wow 7-Pattern Stamp (PS) Brushes,** you hand-paint each cloning stroke. The **Wow 7-Art History (AH) Brushes** are set up to apply strokes that automatically follow the contrast and color features of the source image. They clone much faster than the PS tools, but the automation means you have less creative control.

A

ORIGINAL PHOTO: © JHDAVIS DESIGN

Wow-PS Watercolor + Texture 01   **Wow-PS Oil + Texture 03**

Wow-PS Dry Brush + Texture 02   **Wow-PS Chalk + Texture 07**

WATERCOLOR TIPS

Here are some tips for using **Wow-PS Watercolor Presets** described in "Pattern Stamp Watercolors" beginning on page 281:

- To imitate a wash, use one continuous stroke rather than starting and stopping.

- Don't let colors touch or the details will blur.

- To add density to your watercolor, duplicate the painted layer (Ctrl/ ⌘-J) so the partially transparent colors build, and then adjust the Opacity of this top layer to taste.

B

Styles

Wow 7-07 Texture Styles

Wow-Texture 01*
Wow-Texture 02*
Wow-Texture 03*
Wow-Texture 04*
Wow-Texture 05*
Wow-Texture 06*
Wow-Texture 07*
Wow-Texture 08*
Wow-Texture 09*
Wow-Texture 10*

The **Wow 7-07 Texture Styles B** *are a set of Pattern Overlays and Bevel & Emboss Textures that have been built into ten different Layer Styles, useful for adding subtle "dimensional character" to any Photoshop layer (other than the Background). The samples above show the application of some of those styles (which were painted using some of the different Wow Brush Presets included on the CD-ROM that accompanies this book). These texture styles can also be used on photographs or illustrations. See page 12 for more on working with Layer Styles. To the right are the textures that are part of the* **Wow 7-07 Texture Styles,** *numbered 1–10.*

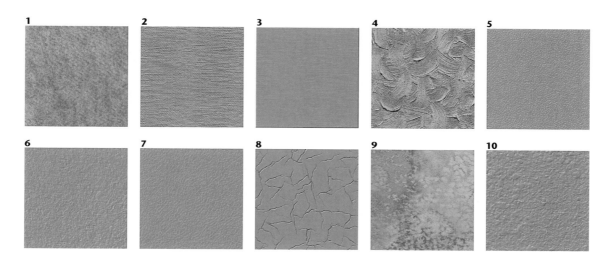

Wow-AH Watercolor + Texture 01

Wow-AH Oil + Texture 02

Wow-AH Pastel + Texture 01

Wow-AH Chalk + Texture 07

Wow-AH Stipple + Texture 10

Wow-AH Sponge + Texture 09

1

2

3

4

5

6

7

8

9

10

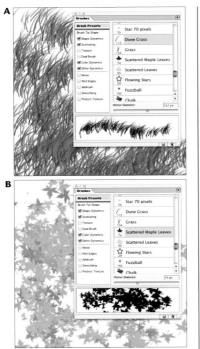

The world-renowned illustrator Bert Monroy has created a number of custom brushes that ship with Photoshop 7. By experimenting with your selection of Foreground and Background colors in your Tool Palette and the Settings in the Color Dynamics portion of the Expanded View Brush Palette, you can achieve amazing instant illustrations. For the Dune Grass preset **A,** we chose 2 versions of green for our Foreground and Background colors, and for the Scattered Maple Leaves preset **B,** we went into the Color Dynamics Settings and set the Foreground/Background Jitter amount to 100% to "give the brush permission" to randomly "jitter" back and forth between our Foreground and Background colors of yellow and orange.

Once the sample has been collected, you click or drag the tool to clone the sampled image. The **Aligned** option works in much the same way as for the Pattern Stamp tool: With the Aligned box checked, the Clone Stamp acts as if it were erasing to reveal the sampled image; with the Aligned box unchecked, each stroke starts a new copy of the source image, beginning at the point where the original sample was taken.

CHOOSING, EDITING, AND CREATING BRUSHES

In Photoshop 7 the brush tips for the painting and cloning tools are all made available through the **Brushes palette** in the Options bar.

- To **choose a brush** from the currently loaded brush presets, click the tiny triangle to the right of the Brush (or Painting Brush) swatch near the left end of the Options bar to open the palette, and then double-click on the brush you want. (Or single-click to select a brush, then click somewhere outside the Brushes palette to close the palette.)

- To **add a custom brush shape,** construct your brush's footprint (see "Brush Tip-Making Tips" on page 263 for ideas) or rasterize a shape made in Adobe Illustrator (File, Place) or choose an area of an existing image. Then surround the new footprint with the Rectangular Marquee and choose **Edit, Define Brush.**

- You can **delete brushes** from the palette one by one by Alt/Option-clicking on the ones you want to remove.

- You can also name and **save** a particular palette of brushes (choose Save Brushes from the Brushes palette's pop-out menu), or **load** a palette you've previously saved instead of the current set of brushes (choose Replace Brushes), or **add** a set of brushes to the current one (choose Load Brushes), or replace the current palette with the **default brushes** (choose Reset Brushes).

CYCLING THROUGH BRUSHES

When you're painting, clicking on the Brushes palette to choose a new brush tip can interrupt your work flow. Instead, you can cycle the Brush swatch by using the **caret keys** as described below.

- Use the > (or period) key alone **to cycle forward** through the palette

- And use the < (or comma) key alone **to cycle backwards** through the palette

Here's a method for making your own brush tips for Photoshop's painting tools:

1 Open a new Photoshop file with the default white *Background*. Choose the Paintbrush tool and one of the soft round brush tips from Photoshop 7's default Brushes palette, opened by clicking the little triangle to the right of the Brush swatch near the left end of the Options bar. Also in the Options bar set the Mode to Dissolve. Click the Foreground color square in the toolbox and choose a dark gray. Then click once with the Paintbrush on the white background. To make more than one brush tip, change brush sizes by choosing other soft round tips in the Brushes palette and click with each one to make a separate footprint.

2 Edit the brush footprints you've painted by using the Eraser with a tiny brush tip to remove some of the "bristles." Or "soften" the brush by selecting a footprint and blurring it (choose Filter, Blur, and choose a type of blur).

3 For each brush you want to make, select one of the brush footprints by surrounding it with the Rectangular Marquee. Choose Define Brush from the Edit menu and give it a name. The new brush will be added to the current Brushes palette.

4 In the Brush Palette Expanded View, choose the new brush tip under the Brush Tip Shape portion of the palette and click on it to make it the current brush. Change any of the available options within the palette (start with the Spacing setting, also in the Brush Tip Shape section of the Brush Palette). Click outside the palette to close the palette, and try the brush to see if it produces smooth, brush-like strokes. If it doesn't seem smooth enough, try a lower Spacing setting. Keep in mind, though, that the lower the setting, the slower the brush will operate. This can cause a delay between when you paint the stroke and when it appears on-screen, which can interfere with the "natural media" feel of the painting. When the brush is behaving as you want it to, choose New Brush from the Options pop-out menu in the upper right of the palette.

Brushes that you define are added to the current Brush Palette, but they will be lost if you ever choose Reset Brushes from the Brush Palette's pop-out menu. To save them permanently as a custom set of Brush presets, choose Edit, Preset Manager, Brushes and Shift-click the brushes you want to save; then click the Save Set button, and when the Save dialog box opens, name and save the set.

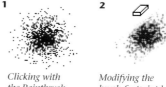

1 Clicking with the Paintbrush in Dissolve mode

2 Modifying the brush footprint by blurring it and then erasing some of the "bristles"

3a

Selecting one of three brush footprints

3b

Defining the brush by choosing from Photoshop 7's Edit menu

4

Giving a name to and saving the new brush footprint

While you paint, you can quickly change the size or hardness of any standard round brush that's currently chosen in the Options bar as follows:

• Use a **bracket key** ([or]) to decrease or increase the **size**.

• Use a **Shift**-**bracket** combination to decrease or increase **hardness**.

5

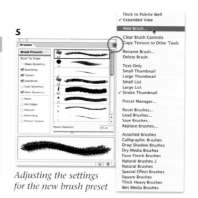

Adjusting the settings for the new brush preset

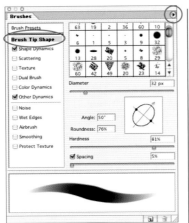

When a round (or "round-based") brush tip is chosen from the Brush Palette's Brush Tip Shape section by clicking on the Brush swatch, it lets you edit the brush itself. You can change its Diameter, Hardness, and Spacing (how often a new "footprint" is laid down). You can also slant and pinch the brush by changing the Angle and Roundness settings or by dragging in the Angle diagram. To save the new brush, make the changes you want and then select New Brush... from the pop-out menu in the top right corner of the palette.

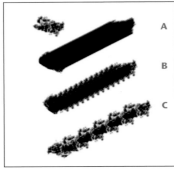

For the Charcoal 58 Pixels brush shown here, the default Spacing (1% of the width of the "footprint") creates a fairly smooth, continuous stroke **A**. At a setting of 25%, the stroke looks rougher **B**. And at a setting of 75%, gaps become apparent **C**. If you turn off Spacing altogether by using the check box, the rate at which footprints are laid down is controlled by how fast you drag the cursor — slower dragging produces more continuous strokes; faster dragging leaves gaps.

- To **save a limited palette of brushes,** choose Edit, Preset Manager, Brushes and Shift-click the brushes you want to save; then click the Save Set button, and when the Save dialog box opens, name and save the set.

THE FILLING TOOLS

Photoshop's filling tools — the Paint Bucket and Gradient — differ not only in *what* they use as a fill, but also in *how* the fill is applied.

The Paint Bucket

The **Paint Bucket** uses a solid color or a pattern. It fills areas that are chosen based on a sampling of color where you Alt/Option-click — either the composite color of all layers (if **All Layers** is turned on in the Options palette) or of the single layer that's active when the tool is used.

With the **Contiguous** check box checked, clicking with the Paint Bucket replaces pixels that are the same color as and continuous with the pixel that the tool's hot spot is clicked on. With Contiguous turned off, all pixels of the clicked-on color throughout the layer or selection will be replaced with the color applied by the Paint Bucket, whether or not the original color is contiguous. The edges of the fill can be **Antialiased** or not. And the fill can be

COLOR-FILLING SHORTCUTS

- To fill with the **Foreground** color, press **Alt/Option-Delete**.
- To fill with the **Background** color, press **Ctrl/⌘-Delete**.
- To open the **Fill dialog box**, where more choices are available, press **Shift-Delete**.
- To fill with the Foreground or Background color as if **Lock Transparent Pixels** were turned on, add the Shift key — that is, press **Alt/Option-Shift-Delete** or **Ctrl/⌘-Shift-Delete**.
- Pressing **Delete** alone fills with **transparency on a transparent layer** or with the **Background color on the Background layer**.

THE "UNFILL" TOOL

The Magic Eraser, which shares a space in the toolbox with the Eraser, is like a Paint Bucket that "pours" clear transparency instead of color. Like the Paint Bucket, it can "fill" Contiguous or noncontiguous color areas and have Anti-Aliased edges or not. It can base its fill region on the composite color if Use All Layers is turned on.

The Magic Eraser can be used to remove color in the same way that the Paint Bucket fills with color.

Although their illustration styles are very different, both Lance Hidy (top) and Steve Conley color their artwork by using the Paint Bucket or Gradient tool or the Edit, Fill command — all with the Anti-aliased option turned off — to fill selections with color. You can see more of Conley's work in the "Gallery" at the end of this chapter.

limited by an active selection, so that whether Contiguous is turned on or off, the filling stops at the selection boundary.

The Gradient Tool

The **Gradient** tool fills an entire layer (or a selected area) with a blend from one color to the next, using two or more colors. The direction of the color change is controlled by the direction in which the Gradient tool is dragged. Choosing Photoshop's

SAMPLING COLOR

For the Paintbrush, Airbrush, Pencil, Paint Bucket, and Gradient, holding down the Alt/Option key toggles to the Eyedropper tool so you can sample color by clicking. The area sampled — Point Sample (a single pixel), 3 By 3 Average, or 5 By 5 Average — is determined by the current Sample Size setting in Options bar for the actual Eyedropper tool.

OTHER WAYS TO FILL

Besides the Gradient and Paint Bucket tools and the Edit, Fill command, there are two other ways to apply fills:

• You can add a **Fill layer** by choosing from the top of the list when you click the Create New Fill/Adjustment Layer button at the bottom of the Layers palette. Depending on which kind of Fill layer you choose, an entire layer is assigned a color, pattern, or gradient. The layer includes a layer mask that you can modify to control where the fill shows up. With a Fill layer you can change the color, pattern, or gradient easily, without worrying about leaving behind remnants of the previous fill.

• Still another way to fill an area is to use a **Color, Pattern,** or **Gradient Overlay** as part of a Layer Style. This makes it easier to control the interaction of the Fill and other effects in the Style, such as glows, drop shadows, and bevels. The Overlay effects are introduced in "Anatomy of a Layer Style" in Chapter 8 and are used in techniques throughout the book, but especially in Chapter 8.

A white-to-gray gradient in a layer mask lets this Pattern Fill layer in Screen Mode fade, from full visibility at the top to almost invisible at the bottom.

The Layer Style applied to this "live" type includes a Pattern Overlay that colors the type.

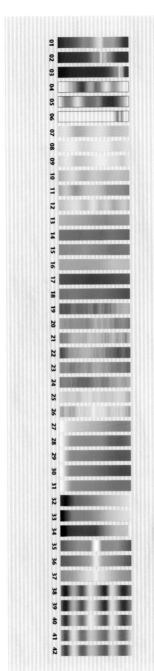

The numbered gradient swatches 01 through 42 are shown in the left column.

Gradient tool brings up Options bar choices that let you further specify what type of Gradient geometry you want — **Linear, Radial, Angle, Reflected,** or **Diamond.** New color gradient effects can now be achieved with a Gradient Fill Layer or with a Layer Style using the Gradient Overlay effect or even the Stroke effect. Gradients can also be used in converting an image to a limited color palette through the new Gradient Map feature, described on page 269.

The Options bar also shows you the currently selected gradient and lets you choose whether to **Reverse** the order of the colors, whether to **Dither** (jumbling the pixels slightly at the color transitions, to prevent the gradient from appearing as distinct bands of color when it's printed), and whether to include any **Transparency** that's built into the gradient or to reproduce it as opaque colors.

You'll find Gradients used in artwork throughout the book. In "Using Gradients" on pages 270–271 there are several examples of applying gradients for special effects.

Using the Gradient Editor

If you click the Gradient swatch in the Options bar, the Gradient Editor dialog box opens. You can use the **Presets section** of the Gradient Editor to:

- **Build a new gradient based on an existing one,** by choosing a gradient from the Presets section and changing any or all of the settings, then adding it to the currently displayed Presets. (The methods for building Photoshop 7's two kinds of gradients are described in **"Building a Solid Gradient"** (below) and **"Building a Noise Gradient"** on page 268.)

- **Rename a gradient** by double-clicking it in the Presets section and entering a new name.

- **Remove a gradient** from the Presets section by Alt/Option-clicking its swatch.

- **Add another set of preset gradients** to the Presets section by choosing from the list at the bottom of the menu that pops out to the right of the Presets section, and then clicking Append in the Caution box. Or click the Load button, and find and load the presets file you want.

- **Replace the current set of gradients** in the Presets section by choosing from the list at the bottom of the menu that pops out to the right of the Presets section and clicking OK in the Caution box. Or choose Replace Gradients from the pop-out menu, and locate and load the presets file you want.

Building a Solid Gradient

To use the Gradient Editor to create your own custom gradient, choose the Gradient tool in the toolbox and then click the gradient swatch itself in the tool Options bar. The Editor will open with the Gradient Type set to either Solid or Noise, depending on which type

With the Linear Gradient (far left) you apply colors by dragging from where you want the gradient to start to where you want it to end. The other four types — Radial, Angle, Reflected, and Diamond — are built by dragging outward from the center.

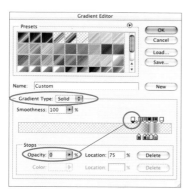

The Gradient Editor set up for making a standard Solid type of gradient with transparency built in. The stops for color are **below** the gradient bar, and the stops that control transparency are **above** the bar (one is circled here).

of gradient was displayed in the swatch when you clicked it. Make sure Gradient Type is set to Solid.

Each of the little house-shaped *stops* below or above the gradient bar represents a color or degree of opacity, respectively. When you click on any of these icons, tiny diamonds appear between the icon you clicked and its nearest neighbors. The diamonds represent the midpoints in the transition between each pair of colors or opacities, the point where the value is halfway between those of the two stops.

- **Change a color** by clicking its stop icon and then choosing the Foreground or Background color from the pop-out next to the Color swatch. Or click the color swatch to open the Color Picker so you can choose a color. Or click in any open file, or in the Color palette (Window, Show Color) or Swatches palette (Window, Show Swatches), or the gradient bar itself to sample a color.

- **Change an opacity value** by clicking its stop icon and then using the interactive slider that pops out next to the Opacity swatch. Or click in any open file, or the gradient bar itself to sample opacity.

- **Reposition a color or opacity stop** by dragging it to a new position along the bar or by typing a percentage of the bar length into the Location field.

- **Add a color (or opacity) stop** by clicking between any two existing stops, just below (or above) the gradient bar.

- **Remove a color or opacity stop** by dragging it downward or upward, away from the bar, or by clicking it and clicking the appropriate Delete button.

- **Change the rate of a color or transparency transition** by dragging the midpoint diamond toward one of its two stops.

- **Reduce the potential for banding** (the appearance of the colors as distinct bands

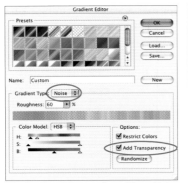

The Gradient Editor set for making a Noise type of gradient with transparency built-in

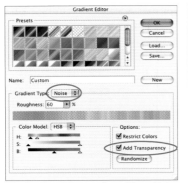

*For a Noise gradient, setting the Roughness higher **A** makes a gradient with more and sharper color bands. At lower Roughness settings there are fewer bands and smoother transitions **B**. With Restrict Colors turned on, the colors in the gradient are limited to those that can be printed with CMYK inks **B**. Moving the sliders on the color bars **C** limits the range of colors in the gradient. Here Hue is restricted to the red-yellow-green range, and Saturation is limited to fairly intense, rather than muted, colors.*

rather than soft transitions) by increasing the Smoothness setting.

When you finish building the gradient, click the New button to add it to the current Presets palette. Use the Save button to save the modified Presets set for future use.

Building a Noise Gradient

To use the Gradient Editor to create your own Noise gradient, choose the Gradient in the toolbox, click the gradient swatch in the Options bar, and make sure the Gradient Type is set to Noise.

- **To set the range of colors that *can* appear in the gradient,** use the color sliders at the bottom of the dialog box. Different sets of sliders appear, depending on the Color Model you choose. The **HSB model** (as shown at the left) provides a fairly intuitive way to limit the range of the three components of color — hue (for instance, to a red-orange range), saturation (to vivid or muted colors), and brightness (to bright or dark shades).

  The range settings you specify by moving the sliders on the Color Model bars will determine the "outside" limits of the colors that *can* appear in the gradient. In fact, your gradient will often include a significantly narrower subset of colors within the range you've set.

- **To limit the colors** to those that can be printed in process **CMYK inks,** turn on Restrict Colors by clicking its check box.

- **To control whether** the color changes in a Noise gradient are **many and abrupt** or **fewer and smooth,** enter a high or low number for Roughness, or use the pop-out slider to experiment.

- **To generate an alternate Noise gradient** within the range of Roughness and colors you've specified, click the Randomize button. You can keep clicking it until you see a particular combination you like.

- **To add transparency to the gradient,** you *can* use the Add Transparency check box in the lower right corner of the dialog box. This introduces random variations in transparency. If you've generated a Noise gradient with colors that you like,

DITHERING

To prevent banding (distinct color steps) in gradients, you can turn on the **Dither** option using the checkbox in the Gradient tool's Options bar. At each color transition, it mixes the colors slightly so that the edge is less distinct and there won't be bands of color when the gradient is printed.

☐ Reverse ☑ Dither ☑ Transparency

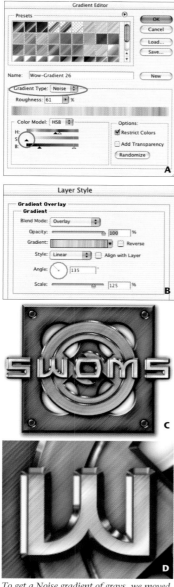

adding random transparency will probably introduce more variability than you want to cope with. If you need to control the transparency of your Noise gradient, it's often more effective to use a layer mask when you apply it than to try to get what you want with the Add Transparency option in the Gradient Editor.

When you finish building the gradient, click the New button to add it to the current set of presets. Use the Save button to save the modified Presets set for future use. *Wow!*

THE GRADIENT MAP

One of the choices in the pop-out list of Adjustment layers and in the Image, Adjust submenu is Gradient Map. The Gradient Map translates the light-and-dark information in an image to the colors of a gradient you choose from the pop-out presets palette in the Gradient Map dialog box. The color at the left end of the gradient swatch replaces the darkest shadow color in your original image; the color at the right end replaces the lightest highlight color; and the intermediate colors of the gradient replace the range of midtones in between.

The Gradient Map provides a way to "translate" a color or grayscale image to a limited color scheme.

To get a Noise gradient of grays, we moved the Saturation slider all the way to the left **A**; we set the Roughness at 50% to get streaks that are distinct but not too sharply defined. We applied the gradient as a Gradient Overlay component of a Layer Style, angled and scaled **B** to create a streaked metal look **C**, **D**. This technique is described step-by-step in "Styled Steel" in Chapter 8.

 "Styled Steel" "before" and "after" files

Using Gradients

Shown on these two pages are a few examples of the ways you can use gradients in Photoshop 7 — either preset gradients or those you design yourself in the Gradient Editor, opened by clicking the gradient swatch. The swatch is found in the Gradient tool's Options bar, the Gradient Fill or Gradient Map dialog box, and several sections of the Layer Style dialog box — the Gradient Overlay, the Inner and Outer Glows, and the Stroke.

MOVING THE GRADIENT

In order to reposition the gradient in a Gradient Fill layer or in the Gradient Overlay component of a Layer Style, you have to open the appropriate dialog box, which can be done in the Layers palette by double-clicking the Gradient Fill layer's thumbnail or double-clicking the entry for the Gradient Overlay in the expanded Effects list for the Style. **Once you open the Gradient Fill dialog box or the Gradient Overlay section of the Layer Style dialog box**, the Options bar tells you that **you can now drag to reposition the gradient**. As you drag, the end color of the gradient fills in behind the trailing edge, so that you never have a blank area.

Click and drag to reposition the gradient.

Gradient Map Layer

Working in RGB, CMYK, or Lab Color mode, you can replace the tonal information in an image with the colors of a gradient: Use the Gradient Map command (from the Image, Adjust submenu) or use a Gradient Map Adjustment layer. To add a Gradient Map Adjustment layer, click the Create New Fill/Adjustment Layer button at the bottom of the Layers palette and choose Gradient Map from the pop-out list. Then choose the gradient you want from the pop-out palette in the Gradient Map dialog box. The colors of the gradient (left to right) replace the colors or tones of your image (darkest to lightest). With an appropriate gradient you can achieve a duotone-like effect, as described on page 87.

 Kids Gradient Map.psd

Gradient Fill Layer

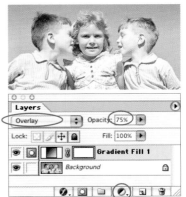

Gradients can be used for extreme or subtle effects. Here we added subtle color by applying the Wow-Gradient 15 in a Gradient Fill layer in Overlay mode at 75% Opacity. (To add a Gradient Fill layer, click the Create New Fill/Adjustment Layer button at the bottom of the Layers palette and choose Gradient from the top section of the pop-out list.) Using a Gradient Fill layer provides flexibility in experimenting with positioning the gradient, as described at the left in the "Moving the Gradient" tip.

Gradient-Filled Mask

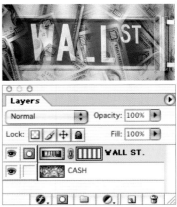

Here two images were combined by using a layer mask filled with the Transparent Stripes gradient that comes with Photoshop. In a mask this gradient becomes black-and-white. After the Gradient tool was used to fill the mask, a Gaussian Blur was applied to soften the edges of the stripes.

Masked Gradient

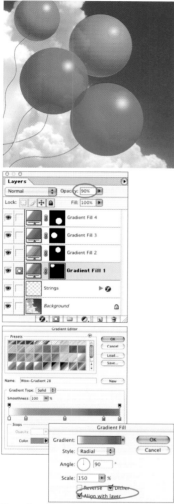

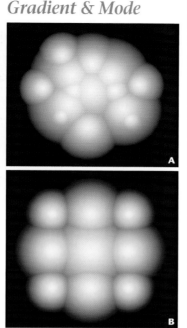

Click and drag to reposition the gradient.

To make each balloon, a Radial gradient was applied in a Gradient Fill layer with an elliptical mask; Opacity was reduced to create a translucent look. The highlight was positioned by dragging as described in "Moving the Gradient" tip on page 270. We experimented with the Scale setting to control the shading on the balloons. The Wow-Gradients 27-31 used in this image are more complex than a simple white-to-color blend. In each gradient the first color transition (from white to a light version of the color) is more abrupt than the other color changes; also a shadow tone is inserted near the right end of the gradient to create the rounding of the balloons.

 Gradient Balloons.psd

Gradient & Mode

You can get a "molecular" look with Radial gradients: First set white and black as the Foreground and Background colors (pressing "D" for "default" and then "X" for "eXchange" is one way to do this). Then apply a Foreground To Background Radial gradient in Normal mode (set in the Options bar) to make a central white molecule and the black background. Next make similar Radial gradients around it but with Lighten mode chosen in the Options bar, which stops the spread of the gradient when its increasingly dark grays can no longer lighten the pixels it encounters **A**. Starting the Radial gradients on Grid points (choose View, Show Grid to make the Grid visible) can create symmetrically packed "atoms" **B**. You can add color to the layer with Image, Adjust, Variations or with a Gradient Map, as described for the photo of the children on page 270.

Gradient & Layer Style

There are many ways that a gradient can be applied as part of a Layer Style — as an Inner Glow (as in "Crafting a Neon Glow" in Chapter 7), as an Outer Glow, as a Gradient Overlay (as shown here), or in a Stroke (see the "Stroke Magic" tip on page 311 or the "Quick Neon" technique in Chapter 8). Here a Linear Gradient was applied as a Gradient Overlay as part of the Layer Style for the front surface of a logo and dragged into position to achieve the lighting we wanted. The same Gradient Overlay, but with the gradient dragged to a different position, was also applied to the black-filled circle that became the recessed areas of the logo.

 Gradient Logo.psd

Painting "Wet on Wet"

***Overview** Add a noise pattern layer in Overlay mode, a "ground" canvas layer, and an empty layer; paint it with the Smudge tool; add an embossed copy of the painting in Overlay mode; add more brush texture with a Pattern Fill layer.*

IMAGE

"Wet on Wet" "before" and "after" files

ALTHOUGH IT STILL CAN'T QUITE MATCH the "natural-media" feel of Procreate Painter, Photoshop 7 offers its devotees at least four great ways to stroke "paint" onto "canvas":

- You can start with a blank canvas and "hand paint" with the Paintbrush.
- You can use the Art History Brush to automate the process of turning a photo or other image into a painting (as described in "Art History Lessons" on page 276).
- With Photoshop 7 the Impressionist option has been resurrected and now resides in the Pattern Stamp tools option bar and is an excellent way to "clone" a photograph into a natural media masterpiece (as described in "Pattern Stamp Watercolors" on page 281).
- Or you can also use an existing image as the basis for hand-painting your own brush strokes by using the Smudge tool as described here.

When painters work wet-on-wet in oils or acrylics, especially in the rapid, outdoor "plein air" style, their brushes pick up color from previous strokes, and the colors mix. Wet-on-wet painting tends to be informal and quick, as artists seek to capture the light in a landscape painted on-site. The paint stays wet during the painting process, and in order to keep the colors pure, it has to be put on thick. Using Photoshop's Smudge tool, your "brush" can be responsive, and the strokes spontaneous, as long as you have a powerful enough computer and you work with the Smudge tool *at 100% Pressure*; lower Pressure settings require the computer to do even more calculation, and the painting will lag behind your brush. A pressure-sensitive tablet and stylus like the Wacom Intuos also makes the process more like traditional painting, giving the strokes more "personality" as the pressure you apply to the stylus scales each stroke on the fly.

1a

The original image and enhanced version

1b

Adding a Pattern Fill layer

1c

Putting the Pattern Fill layer in Overlay mode

1d

The Wow-Reticulation pattern chosen as the Pattern Fill and scaled to 50%

1e

The Pattern Fill layer in place

1f

Before (left) and after adding Wow-Reticulation Patterns as a Pattern Fill layer

2

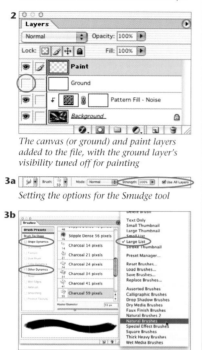

The canvas (or ground) and paint layers added to the file, with the ground layer's visibility tuned off for painting

3a

Setting the options for the Smudge tool

3b

*The Charcoal family of brushes, chosen from the **Natural Media** set for painting*

4a

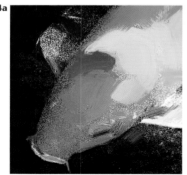

A detail of the "Smudge" painting in progress. With visibility for the ground layer turned off, it's hard to tell where there are gaps in the paint, since the original image shows through from below.

1 Preparing an image for painting. Choose an image and adjust the color (using Hue and Saturation for instance) and crop to taste **1a**. Next, to variegate the "paint" so your "wet-on-wet" brush strokes will show "bristle marks," add a Pattern Fill layer with the Wow-Reticulation Pattern preset as a pattern overlay, as follows: (If you haven't yet loaded the Wow 7 Presets, see page 7 for instructions.) Then choose Layer, New Fill Layer, Pattern **1b**. In the New Layer dialog box choose Overlay for the Mode (you can also turn on the Group With Previous Layer option; with the way this file is structured, grouping won't affect your painting, but it can help to visually organize the Layers palette) **1c**. When you click OK, the Pattern Fill dialog will open. Now load the Wow-Noise set from the pop-out menu that is located on the right of the Pattern swatch. Then choose Wow-Reticulation and set its scale to 50%. This overlaid noise pattern adds subtle irregularities to the original image that will enhance the appearance of individual brush "bristles" when the smearing begins. (If the pattern names aren't listed, open the menu of options from the upper right corner of the palette and choose Small List) **1d, 1e, 1f.**

2 Preparing the canvas and paint layers. Next click the Create A New Layer button at the bottom of the Layers palette and fill this new "ground" layer with the color you want for your canvas. For example, open the Swatches palette (View, Show Swatches), and click white as used here, or black, or a color that contrasts with the colors in your image; then press Alt/Option-Delete to fill the layer.

Again click the Create A New Layer button. Leave this new layer empty. It will hold the brush strokes you paint. Double-click on the name of any of these layers and type in a new name if you like.

Turn off visibility for the Ground layer by clicking its Eye icon at the left edge of the Layers palette **2**. (If you didn't do this, the Smudge tool, which you'll be using to paint, would sample the canvas color instead of the image/Noise composite underneath.)

3 Setting up to paint. Choose the Smudge tool — it's the fingertip icon nested with the Blur (water drop) and Sharpen (pointy triangle) tools in the toolbox. In the Options bar leave Normal as the Mode, set Pressure at 100%, and turn *on* the Use All Layers option, **3a;** this will let you paint on the transparent top layer, but sample color from all the visible layers below. Also make sure that Finger Painting is turned *off*. At the right side of the Options bar, click the brush icon to pop open the Brush Dynamics palette. If you have a pressure-sensitive tablet and stylus, for the Size option choose Stylus, and for Pressure choose Off. If you don't have a tablet, both should be Off. Back on the left side of the bar, click the triangle next to the Brush swatch to pop out the Brushes palette, and locate a set of brushes to use; we chose a set from the **Natural Brushes.abr** library **3b.**

4b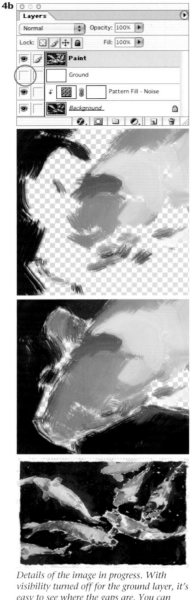

4 Painting. Now choose a fairly large brush and drag with the Smudge tool to paint **4a,** keeping the following tips in mind:

- To make the best use of the color and shapes in the source image, **keep your strokes short** so that you sample color frequently.

- To add detail, switch to **smaller brushes** in the same family you've already chosen.

- **Temporarily turn on the ground layer's visibility** from time to time by clicking in its Eye column. This hides the original image and noise so you can check the progress of your painting **4b.**

- You can intentionally leave **unpainted gaps** between your strokes in order to **add contrasting color** later, as follows: Click the ground layer's name in the Layers palette to target it and turn on its visibility. Click the Foreground color square in the toolbox and choose your first accent color. Looking at both ground and paint layers, you can quickly use the "regular" Paintbrush (not the Smudge tool) on the ground layer to fill the "holes" in your painting **4c.**

5 Adding an "impasto" effect. You can make your paint appear as though it was thickly applied ("Impasto") by making a copy of your finished painting and using it to "emboss" your brush strokes, as follows: With the paint layer active in the Layers palette, create a new empty layer for the embossing by clicking the Create A New Layer button. Then turn this layer into a flat (or merged) copy of your image by pressing Alt-Ctrl-Shift-E (Windows) or Option-⌘-Shift-E (Mac) or by holding down the Alt/Option key as you choose

Details of the image in progress. With visibility turned off for the ground layer, it's easy to see where the gaps are. You can then turn visibility back on for the ground layer and continue painting, or leave visibility off and simply smudge the existing color you have already laid down to fill the gaps. Or leave the gaps and fill them later with accent colors applied to the ground layer (see 4c). Notice the transparency showing through on some edges of the finished Paint Layer (bottom image).

4c

To fill the intentional gaps in the Painting layer, we used the Smudge tool on the Ground layer to quickly "push around" existing color and then the Paintbrush to apply accent colors – without worrying about disturbing the Paint layer above.

The Ground layer alone

The Ground layer showing through the transparent (unpainted) parts of the Paint layer

5a

Using the Alt/Option key and Merge Visible to make a composite copy in the empty layer

5b   Running the Emboss filter

5c

The embossed, desaturated copy of the painting, viewed in Normal mode

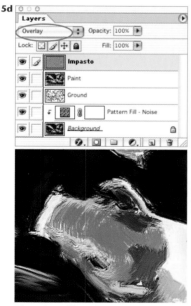
5d

The embossed layer in Overlay mode raises the brush strokes.

Merge Visible from the Layers palette's pop-out menu **5a**. (Without these keyboard gymnastics, Merge Visible would flatten all visible layers into one.) Change this layer's blend mode to Overlay, desaturate the layer (Image, Adjust, Desaturate), and run the Emboss filter (Filter, Stylize, Emboss) **5b, 5c**. In Overlay mode the 50% gray in the layer will become invisible, and the darker and lighter tones of the embossing will "raise" the brush strokes, giving them the "impasto" look **5d**.

6 Enhancing the impasto. To further "fool the eye" you can experiment with adding more textured strokes; they can either seem to be part of the painting or part of the "gessoed" canvas that the paint has been applied to. Create another Fill layer (as in step 1), but this time set the blending mode to Linear Light and the Opacity at just 10% and fill with one of the Wow-Canvas+Brush patterns, which are seamlessly repeating patterns made from scans of real brush strokes on real canvas **6a**. Experiment with the Opacity slider to get the degree of texture you like. If you don't like how some of the strokes in the pattern fall on your image, you can hide them by painting with black on the mask for the new Fill layer **6b**. 🌊

6a
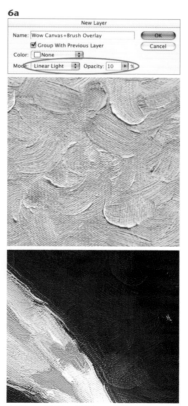

Adding a Pattern Fill layer with scanned, embossed brush strokes

6b
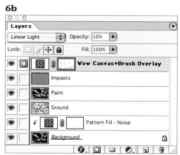

A painted mask on the Wow Impasto Pattern layer removes the brush strokes from areas where they obviously don't match the content of the image.

Art History Lessons

Overview *Enhance the image you want to turn into a painting and take a History Snapshot; add a "Ground" layer to represent the paper and a transparent layer to hold the "paint;" use Wow Art History Brush Presets to paint from the Snapshot, adjusting the settings to control stroke size and shape; add details by hand with the Paintbrush; add a Photocopy Edge effect.*

IMAGE
"**Art History**" "before" and "after" files

JHD, ORIGINAL PHOTOGRAPH © JHDAVIS DESIGN

1a

Original photo, 1000 pixels wide

1b

Power lines removed, saturation boosted and brown "paper" edge added before taking the History Snapshot

PHOTOSHOP'S ART HISTORY BRUSH generates brush or pencil strokes—several with each click of the mouse—that automatically follow the color and contrast contours in an image. At some settings the result can look like a simple filter application, but if you choose your settings carefully and add detailing with other painting tools, you can turn a photo into a very convincing "hand-crafted" painting or drawing.

1 Preparing the photo. Choose a photo **1a** and retouch out any elements you don't like. (We used the Healing Brush to remove the power lines and pole.) Now adjust its color and tonality to the colors you want to see in the final image **1b.** We exaggerated the overall saturation by using Image, Adjust, Hue/Saturation. We used the Marquee tool to select the central 95% of the image, and then chose Select, Inverse to switch the selection to be the outer 5% edge. We filled this outer-edge selection with a foreground color of dark brown (Edit, Fill) using it as our paper color.

2 Setting up the History source. Once you have the image the way you want it, open the History palette (Window, History) and take a Merged Snapshot of the photo: Choose New Snapshot from the palette's pop-out menu in the upper right corner and then select Merged Layers in the New Snapshot dialog box **2**.

3 Setting up the paper. The plan for this painting was to start with a "colored paper" and allow small portions of this background color to show through, for contrast with the colors of the "chalk."

Making a Merged Snapshot to serve as the source for the Art History Brush

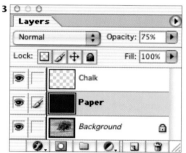

A contrasting "Paper" layer at 75% Opacity allows a view of the image beneath. A separate transparent layer is added for painting or drawing.

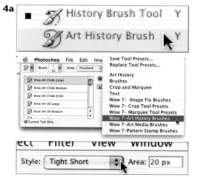

After selecting the Wow 7–Art History Brush Presets from the Presets pop-out menu, choose the specific preset: Wow AH Chalk Large, which uses a tight, short style and an area of 20.

For maximum control and flexibility, set up a separate "Paper" layer filled with the color you want for your final background. Begin by clicking the Create A New Layer button at the bottom of the Layers palette; then we chose the same dark brown color used for filling the outer-edge selection in the beginning, which would show through any gaps in the painting to make the colors of our image jump. Finally, Alt/Option-Delete to fill the new layer with the current Foreground color. Reduce the Opacity of the "Paper" layer somewhat (we used a setting of 75%); this will let you see through to the image below so you can place your strokes intelligently. Finally, add another new layer above the "Paper" for holding the paint, or in this case, chalk **3**.

4 Choosing brushes. Next choose the Art History Brush from the toolbox (Shift-Y toggles between the History Brush and the Art History Brush). Selecting the Wow 7–Art History Brushes from the Presets pop-out menu, choose the specific preset: Wow AH Chalk Large, which uses a tight, short style and an area of 20. Then examine the choices in its Options bar **4a**. We set the options as follows to start the chalk drawing:

- The **Mode** was set to Normal. Later, for detail strokes, it could be changed to Lighten or Darken to add more dramatic contrast in the highlight and shadow areas.

- The **Style** was set to Tight Short. The Style controls the length and shape of the strokes (Long, Short, Medium, Curl, or Dab) and how closely they follow the color contours in the source image (Tight or Loose). Applied overall, styles other than Tight Long, Tight Medium, and Tight Short can produce an effect that looks more like a filter than like hand-painting. If we were imitating a paint technique we would use Tight Long strokes for roughing in color and then switch to Tight Short later to paint details. But for this expressive chalk sketch style, we kept the stroke set to Tight Short.

- **Opacity** was set to 100%. The **Tolerance** was also left at 100%.

- The **Area** was set at 20 pixels for this 1000-pixel-wide image. This meant that with each click of the Art History brush, only a few quick, short strokes would be generated, to cover an area approximately equivalent to a circle with a diameter of 20 pixels, though the "painted" area is not actually circular. We would use this fairly low Area setting for all of the drawing to help the Art History brush "keep up" with our sketching. If your computer isn't lightning-fast, you'll probably want to make the Area setting even smaller so you can get more immediate response as you paint. With a smaller Area to fill, the paint will follow the cursor more closely, so there will be less delay between when you make the stroke and when the paint appears on-screen.

4b

One of the most important options that is integral to the Wow Media Presets (in this case, the AH [Art History] Chalk Presets) is the texture setting where custom Wow patterns have been loaded. All these patterns are taken from fine-tuned scans of real media.

5a

To begin the drawing, we used the Wow–AH Chalk–Large preset, with the Area set to 20 and the paint style set to Tight Short. The first click on the transparent painting layer laid down many "roughing in" strokes. The semi-transparent black "Ground" allowed the image to show through for comparison with the developing painting and to help with placement of the "anchoring" strokes.

- If you use a Wacom tablet for painting (which we highly recommend), you can set the **Stylus** controls in the Brush Dynamics palette so that Size or Opacity will vary with pressure. (The Brush Dynamics palette pops out if you click the little triangle on the painting brush button on the right-hand side of the Options bar. Here "Size" means the size of the *brush tip*, rather than the size of the Area, as defined earlier.)

If you open the Brushes palette by clicking on its icon located on the right side of the Options bar, you will find all the "secrets" to the Wow Chalk Presets, specifically the custom Wow Pattern that has been loaded into its texture option. The coarse texture has been set to Subtract Mode, which gives this technique its characteristic "dry media over rough surface" look.

ART HISTORY WITH A TABLET

To work faster and with more creative control when you use the Art History Brush (or any of Photoshop's brushes) you can use a pressure-sensitive Wacom tablet, thus enabling you to vary the strokes by changing the stylus pressure or angle, without having to make changes in the brush's Options bar or choose different brush tips. In the Brush Dynamics section, which pops out with a click of the Brush palette button at the right end of the Options bar, choose Stylus for the Size setting and Off for Opacity. This gives you dynamic control over the painting process. Start off with heavy pressure for large, long strokes. Then lighten your touch to paint areas of detail with smaller, shorter strokes. For almost photorealistic detail (many small brush strokes that will follow the History Snapshot faithfully) let the stylus tip just "feather touch" — almost float above — the tablet.

With the Style set to Tight Long and the Area set to 50 pixels, a single brush tip (here Charcoal 24 pixels) can be used to make short, thin strokes (with very light pressure) or longer, thicker strokes (with more pressure).

5b

After other large strokes had been laid down, more were added with the same Style and Area settings but with a medium-size brush Wow Preset.

5c

Here Wow–AH Chalk-Large was used to quickly rough in large areas of color.

5d

To bring out more detail, we switched to the Wow–AH Chalk-Small brush tip.

5e

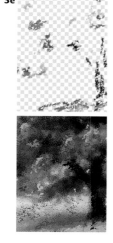

The regular Paintbrush tool was used to hand-paint highlights and detail that couldn't be added with the automated Art History strokes. These "detail" strokes are shown here on a transparent layer (top) so they can be distinguished from earlier strokes.

5 Painting. As you work with the Art History Brush, here are some tips that will help you get good results:

- It's helpful to **"anchor" your strokes** by clicking the brush in an area of color or contrast that has a clear edge, so the strokes will follow the detail that you want to emphasize. This is especially useful when using the Wow presets.

- In general, **paint with Tight Style strokes** set in the Options bar to follow the contours of your image **5a**. If you have a pressure-sensitive tablet, both the size of the brush tip and the length of the stroke can be controlled simultaneously by choosing Stylus for the Size setting in the Brush Dynamics box (see the "Art History with a Tablet" tip on page 278).

- Try a quick **experiment** each time you change the settings — click once with the brush to see if you like the results. If not, undo (Ctrl/⌘-Z), change the settings, and try again.

- Once you have settings you like, you can **click** each time you want to generate a series of strokes. Or **hold down** the mouse button (or stylus) and watch the strokes pile up until you have the result you want. Or **drag** the brush to set down several sets of strokes.

- Don't forget to do some **hand-detailing with the regular Paintbrush,** for fine-tuning that can't be effectively generated automatically with the Art History Brush **5e**. To unify the artwork, use brushtips from the same family of Wow Presets (like Chalk, for instance) for the Paintbrush as you used for the Art History Brush. (With a pressure-sensitive tablet and stylus, you can also get the fine detail by "floating" the stylus tip over the image as described in the "Art History with a Tablet" tip on page 278.)

When you've finished painting, restore the Opacity of the Ground layer to 100% so your original image is hidden by your canvas color.

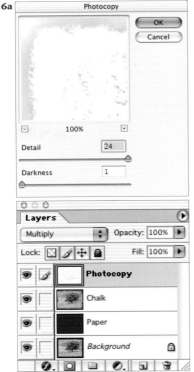

6a

Photocopy

OK

Cancel

100%

Detail   24

Darkness   1

Layers

Multiply ⧫   Opacity: 100% ▶

Lock: ☐ ◢ ✦ 🔒   Fill: 100% ▶

👁 ◢ ▢ **Photocopy**

👁 ☐ Chalk

👁 ☐ Paper

👁 ☐ Background 🔒

The finished chalk layer was duplicated, and the copy was put in Multiply mode and the Photocopy filter was applied to exaggerate edge color and detail.

6b

Result of the Photocopy layer, shown in the detail above and in the final image on page 276

6 Enhancing the drawing. Target the Chalk layer in the Layers palette and duplicate it by typing Ctrl/⌘-J, then (with foreground and background colors set to their defaults of Black and White) filter the new layer using Filter, Sketch, Photocopy, with the Detail setting high and the Darkness setting low **6a**. Then change the Blend Mode of this Photocopy layer to Multiply to combine just the dark portions of this filtered copy with what's below, thus exaggerating the contrast and detail of both the "drawing" and its texture **6b**.

Experimenting. Once you get the feel of creating with the Wow-AH Chalk presets, try the other Wow-AH Presets for additional media effects ranging from Oils and Sponge to Stipple and Watercolors. 🖌

LAYERING THE PAINT

When you're building up strokes in a drawing or painting, it pays to preserve your work in stages so that if you don't like a particular "experiment" you can recover your earlier work. One approach is to paint in layers. When you get to a point where you're happy with the strokes you've laid down so far and now you want to do some experimenting — with a different Area setting or brush tip, for instance — start a new layer by clicking the Create A New Layer button at the bottom of the Layers palette. Now you can add more strokes on this new layer without permanently changing the painting you've done previously. When you're satisfied with the painting on the new layer, you can merge it with the layer below if you need to conserve RAM. Simply choose Merge Down from the Layers palette's pop-out menu (or press Ctrl/⌘-E); then add another new layer and paint some more, merge down, and so on. If you have plenty of RAM, you can maintain the separate layers, without merging, for maximum flexibility.

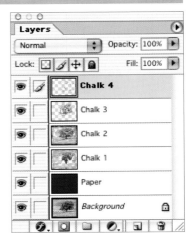

Layers

Normal ⧫   Opacity: 100% ▶

Lock: ☐ ◢ ✦ 🔒   Fill: 100% ▶

👁 ◢ ▢ **Chalk 4**

👁 ☐ Chalk 3

👁 ☐ Chalk 2

👁 ☐ Chalk 1

👁 ☐ Paper

👁 ☐ Background 🔒

A work in progress: The Art History Brush is being used to reproduce the photo in the Background layer as a drawing above a brown background. Brush strokes are built up on several layers — from least detailed on the bottom to finest detail on the top — for maximum flexibility in making corrections.

Pattern Stamp Watercolors

Overview *Prepare a photo for cloning by exaggerating the color; define image as a source pattern for painting with the Pattern Stamp tool. Create a "canvas" surface; use the Wow-PS Watercolor Presets and paint with various sized brushes; enhance painting with filters.*

"**Pattern Stamp Painting**" "before" and "after" files

1a

The original "before" image

1b

The prepared image with exaggerated colors and white border

2a

In the Pattern Name dialog box, type in a name and click "OK."

2b

To set up a new Pattern as the cloning source for the painting, choose the Pattern Stamp from the Tools palette (it shares a space with the Clone Stamp).

IN PHOTOSHOP 7 YOU CAN FINALLY PAINT! With the new capabilities built into Photoshop's Brush engine and the settings you can save as Tool Presets, you're able to get spectacularly realistic simulations of watercolor, oils, pastels, and other media, either by working "from scratch" with the Brush tool or by "cloning" a photo as a painting with the Art History Brush or the Pattern Stamp with the Impressionist option turned on.

Of the two cloning tools, the Pattern Stamp provides more control than the Art History Brush. With the Pattern Stamp you paint stroke-by-stroke, pulling color, but not detail, from the source image. To create a painting like the Yokohama Bay watercolor shown here, start with the source photo from the Wow CD, along with the custom Wow Pattern Stamp Tool Presets and custom Actions and Styles for enhancing the painting. (If you haven't loaded the Wow Presets from this book's companion CD-ROM, see page 9 for instructions.) If turning a favorite photo into a believable painting sounds like fun, you're right!

1 Preparing the Photo. Choose the photo you want to turn into a painting — you can use the **Pattern Stamp Painting-Before.psd** file from the Wow CD or use a photo of your own **1a.**

If you're starting with a photo of your own, here are some changes you might want to make:

- Exaggerate the color and contrast until you have the colors you want. Remember, this is supposed to look like a painting, not a photograph – be expressive!

- If you want your painting to have an "unfinished edges" look, make a selection of the edges and fill it with white **1b.**

2 Loading "paint" into the brush. To make the image the source for painting with the Pattern Stamp tool, define the entire exaggerated image as a Pattern by choosing Edit, Define Pattern. In the Pattern Name dialog box, type in a name and click "OK" **2a.**

Now set up this new Pattern as the cloning source for the painting: Choose the Pattern Stamp from the Tools palette (it shares a

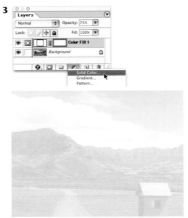

In the Pattern Stamp's Options bar, click the little arrow to the right of the Pattern swatch to open the palette of samples so you can choose the Pattern you just defined.

3

Create a new Fill Layer to act as a canvas, then reduce its opacity to help with tracing the original underneath it.

The painting-in-progress is shown with the Solid Color layer's Opacity set at 75% (top) and at 100% (bottom).

space with the Clone Stamp) **2b.** In the Pattern Stamp's Options bar, click the little arrow to the right of the Pattern swatch to open the palette of samples so you can choose the Pattern you just defined. Make sure the Impressionist option is checked **2c.**

3 Making a "canvas" (or painting surface) layer. This step will add a surface layer above your image to make a foundation for your painting and to serve as a visual barrier between the photo and the painting layer, so you'll be able to see your brush strokes clearly as your painting develops. One way to do this is to click the "Create new fill or adjustment layer" button at the bottom of the Layers palette, then choose Solid Color and click on white in the Color Picker. *(One reason for using a Fill Layer over a regular layer filled with white is that Fill Layers take up no memory in the file or in RAM.)* When the new layer appears in the Layers palette, reduce its Opacity so you can see the photo through it **3.**

4 Preparing a paint layer and painting. Click the "Create a new layer" button at the bottom of the Layers palette to add a transparent layer for painting. Then, with the Pattern Stamp still chosen, in the Tool Presets palette (opened by choosing Window, Tool Presets), choose **Wow 7-Pattern Stamp Brushes** from the menu that pops out at the top right corner of the palette. Then click in the palette to choose the **Wow-PS Watercolor-Medium** tool ("PS" stands for "Pattern Stamp").

Begin painting while keeping these pointers in mind:

- In general, start with a larger brush tip and then use smaller ones as you add finer details (see the tip on page 283, "Varying the Brush Size").

- Don't "scrub" over the image; instead make brush strokes that follow the color and shape contours of the original. Just as in a real watercolor, don't let colors touch, or the "paint" (details) will blur.

- To imitate a single color watercolor wash, use one continuous stroke over an area, rather than starting and stopping.

From time to time, temporarily increase the Opacity of the Solid Color layer back to 100% to hide the original image completely so you can see how the painting is developing **4.**

5 Enhancing the painting. When the painting is complete, you may want to try one of these techniques to further enhance the natural media effect:

- Increase the density of the color by making a copy of the paint layer. Target the paint layer by clicking its name in the Layers palette, and then duplicate it (Ctrl/⌘-J) **5a.** This extra layer will build up any strokes that are partially transparent, to intensify the color, so it's especially effective for watercolor paintings. You

5a

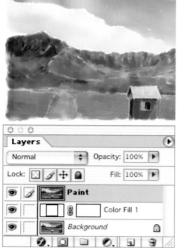

Increase the density of the color by making a copy of the paint layer (target the Paint layer by clicking its name in the Layers palette, and then press Ctrl/⌘-J to duplicate it).

5b

This extra layer will build up any strokes that are partially transparent to intensify the color and density, so it's especially effective for watercolor paintings. You can adjust the Opacity of this top layer to taste, and then merge the two paint layers together (with the top paint layer active, press Ctrl/⌘-E to merge the two paint layers together).

can adjust the Opacity of this top layer to taste **5b,** and then merge the two paint layers together (with the top paint layer active, press Ctrl/⌘-E.)

- Target the paint layer in the Layers palette and open the Actions palette (Window, Actions) **5c.** Then choose **Wow 7-Paint Enhance Actions.atn** from the palette's pop-out list, clicking on the Wow-Paint Edge Enhance Subtle Action, and click the "Play" button at the bottom of the palette. This Action works by making a copy of the paint layer, filtering the new layer using Filter, Sketch, Photocopy, and changing the Blend Mode to Color Burn to combine the filtered copy with the layers below.

- You can make the paper texture that's built into the brush more apparent by applying the Wow-Texture 01 Style to the paint layer **5d.** This Style uses the same tiling watercolor paper pattern that's included in the custom Wow-PS Watercolor-Medium Brush Preset. To apply the Style, target the paint layer in the Layers palette, choose **Wow 7-07 Texture Styles** from the Styles palette's pop-out menu, and click on the Wow-Texture 01* Style in the palette. *Wow*

5c

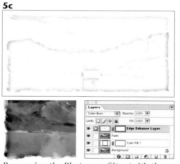

By running the Photocopy filter (with the foreground and background colors set to Black and White) on a duplicate of the Paint layer in Color Burn mode you can get the effect of the watercolor pigments actually pooling along areas of contrast.

5d

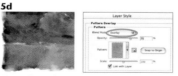

By applying the Wow-Texture 01 style to the Paint layer, the same texture used in the brush is applied as a pattern overlay (in Overlay Blend Mode), therefore exaggerating the impression of pigment on paper.

VARYING THE BRUSH SIZE

For painting in Photoshop 7, using a Wacom pressure-sensitive tablet and stylus definitely gives you a better feel and more options for controlling a brush than using a mouse. But even if you currently have only a mouse, you can vary the size of the brush tip by keeping your fingers on the keyboard's bracket keys and toggling the brush size up and down. Tapping the [key makes a brush tip smaller; tapping] enlarges the brush tip.

A

B

C

D

For *"Moorea Canoe,"* **Jack Davis** started by creating a rough collage from several original photographs: the landscape; the canoe; and the clouds. With his composition set and his "color palette" chosen, he made a Pattern (Edit, Define Pattern) from what was currently visible **A.** This pattern would become the source for the cloned painting by using the Pattern Stamp tool and its Impressionist setting.

Using the techniques described in "Pattern Stamp Watercolors" on page 281, Davis began following the contours of the original collage while painting on an empty layer above **B.**

To further the intended illusion of a watercolor over an ink sketch, Davis used the Style, Find Edges filter and a Threshold adjustment on a copy of the original collage layer **C.** He then blended this duplicated layer with the completed painting layer below by setting its Blend

Mode to Multiply **D.** (For a shortcut to this "sketching" process, use the **Wow-Linework Alone** action in the "Photo Enhance" set of **Wow Actions** on this book's companion CD-ROM.)

Davis then applied a Layer Style with a Pattern Overlay of "Salt Stain" (Wow-Texture 09) to the final Paint layer, along with an edge enhance treatment using the Photocopy filter. See page 281 for more on using this process.

A

B

C

D

Starting with an original photograph of a famous bronze statue in coastal California, *Santa Cruz Portrait* was created using a similar technique to *Moorea Canoe* on page 284 and the Yokohama Bay project on page 281.

For this piece, Davis used his **Wow-PS Dry Brush** Presets and the Pattern Stamp tool, which had two unique settings as part of the Presets. First, he generated a custom canvas *Texture* in order to exaggerate the impression of paint skimming over the surface of coarse cotton canvas. Second, he set the *Angle Control* to *Direction* in the *Shape Dynamics* portion of the Brushes dialog **A,** which allowed the angle of the brush to rotate interactively with the directional motion of the mouse (or in this case, a Wacom Stylus). That way, the "hairs" of the brush also followed the angle of each brush stroke, which nicely complemented the chiseled angles of the statue **B.**

Davis built up the paint strokes on their own transparent layer **C.** When finished he exaggerated the edges and contrast by duplicating the Paint layer, filtering it using Photocopy **D** and setting the resulting layer's Blend Mode to Color Burn. Finally the background "canvas" color was set to black (a technique he often uses with his "analog" paintings) to heighten the intensity of the colors where the black "ground" was intentionally allowed to show through the colored strokes.

For *The Swimmer*, based on a
Michelangelo sculpture, **William
Low** did most of his painting with the
Paintbrush tool with round, hard-edged
brushes in large sizes. But the water highlights were created by starting with a very
soft brush with white at 100 percent
Opacity. Low varied the Opacity setting
for the Paintbrush by clicking in the Opacity box and then using the arrow keys as
he painted. He mixed colors by painting
over one color with another color at low
opacity, the way a traditional painter
builds up a glaze. To use this new color
in other areas, he would sample it with
the Eyedropper and paint at full opacity.
For example, to add a blush to the
swimmer's cheek, Low applied a red with
the Paintbrush in Multiply mode at 5%
Opacity, going over the area until he
liked the result. Then he sampled the
new cheek color, switched the Paintbrush to Normal mode at 100% Opacity,
and painted the nose.

O ne of the techniques that **Sharon Steuer** uses in developing her digital paintings is to layer her changes, so that in repainting some parts of the image, she doesn't destroy what's underneath. This allows maximum flexibility in blending the images as the painting is being developed. Steuer also uses the Save As command (File, Save As, Save As A Copy, with Layers unchecked) to save flattened stages of the painting so she can go back to an earlier version if needed.

Both *Louis Armstrong* (above) and *Mark Twain* (left) were painted in Grayscale mode, using a Wacom Intuos pressure-sensitive tablet and Photoshop's Paintbrush (with and without the Airbrush option), and Eraser tools. Steuer set up the stylus so that pressure controlled only opacity.

Before Steuer flattened it for printing, the final portrait of *Louis Armstrong* was a stack of three layers — one fairly complete painting and two layers of changes.

For *Mark Twain*, Steuer finished painting the portrait on a white canvas and then added a layer above it in Multiply mode, where she painted the background. Where the lighter gray strokes of the top layer overlapped darker areas in the portrait beneath — at the edges of the hair and shoulder on the right side, for instance — the Multiply mode kept the light background from covering the foreground. In contrast, the slight overlap of the dark background strokes on the left side added the appropriate shadows at the edges of the hair and shoulder.

© Bert Monroy 1999

For the highly detailed, photorealistic paintings in his signs series, **Bert Monroy** did his composition in Adobe Illustrator and then used the paths in Photoshop as guides for stroking, filling, and creating friskets for airbrushing. For example, in *The Sidelines*, he used imported paths to make masks, which he stored in alpha channels and then used for painting the neon tubing. (Monroy's method for importing paths from Illustrator is described in the Chapter 7 "Gallery" section. Also described there are some of the processes Monroy uses for creating his photorealistic textures.)

Shown on this page is the development of the first "S" in "Sidelines": First, to define the tube Monroy created a new alpha channel by clicking on the Create New Channel button at the bottom of the Channels palette. He activated his imported path by clicking its name in the Paths palette, then used the Path Component Selection tool (solid arrow) to click the "S" to activate its path.

With the "S" subpath active, he chose the Paintbrush, picked the largest hard-edged round brush tip from the Options bar's pop-out Brushes palette, and modified it.

▶ *Decreasing the Spacing for a large, hard-edged round brush tip can make its stroke smoother when you paint with it.*

Since he was working in an alpha channel, white was the default Foreground color, and clicking the Stroke Path button at the bottom of the Paths palette painted a smooth, white stroke to define the "S"-shaped tube **A**.

Since it was daytime and the neon sign wasn't lit, the slick glass tube would be tinted by reflections of the colors around it, and its roundness would create shadows. To make a mask that would limit the color as he painted reflections and shadows with the Airbrush tool, Monroy first duplicated the alpha channel he had just made (by dragging its name to the Create New Channel button). Then he blurred this new channel (by choosing Filter, Blur, Gaussian Blur) **B**. He used the Move tool with the arrow keys to offset this channel a little down and to the right.

Finally he used the Image, Calculations command to create a third alpha channel (his painting mask) by subtracting the blurred, offset channel from the sharp one **C**.

Monroy created a layer for the "S" (by clicking the Create New Layer button at the

bottom of the Layers palette. He loaded the sharp channel **A** as a selection (by Ctrl/⌘-clicking its name in the Channels palette) and filled it with the light base color of the neon tube. Then he loaded the mask channel **C** as a selection and used the Airbrush to apply yellow paint for the reflections of the yellow wall behind the tube and dark paint for the shadows.

Along with their neon tubes and weathered exteriors, the paintings in **Bert Monroy's** signs series show other fascinating photorealistic details. The "Cinequest" banner in *The Studio Theater* was drawn and typeset in Adobe Illustrator and imported into Photoshop. To ripple the banner, Monroy painted a displacement map file with the Airbrush and black and white paint on a 50% gray background, to use with the Displace filter. He also used this painting as a layer in Overlay mode above the banner layer to add highlights and shadows to match the ripples.

Paths for the neon tubes in *The Alibi* were drawn as Bézier curves in Illustrator, but all the other lettering in this image and in *Hotel Arcata* was typeset in Illustrator, converted to outlines and modified to match the lettering on the actual signs.

In *Hotel Arcata* Monroy created the brick wall to match the extreme perspective in the image. He began by using Illustrator's Blend tool to create intermediate yellow strips between a narrow yellow band at the top and a larger one at the bottom. To make it easy to add the vertical strips of mortar, he split the yellow strips between two layers by Shift-selecting every other strip and moving these to a new layer. When he opened his layered file in Photoshop, he could quickly add the vertical mortar by locking transparency for the first of the two brick layers and painting straight strips of mortar across all the yellow bands. Then he did the same for the other bricks layer, but he offset these painted mortar strips so that the two layers together created a realistic brick-and-mortar pattern.

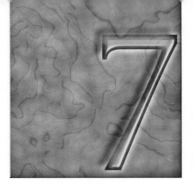

7

TYPE, SHAPES, PATHS & POSTSCRIPT

Photoshop's tools for creating and editing type and vector-based graphics include the Type tool, the Shape tools and Pen tools, and the path-editing

▶ Path Selection Tool	A
▶ Direct Selection Tool	A

▭ Rectangle Tool	U
▭ Rounded Rectangle Tool	U
○ Ellipse Tool	U
○ Polygon Tool	U
＼ Line Tool	U
✿ Custom Shape Tool	U

⌽ Pen Tool	P
⌽ Freeform Pen Tool	P
⌽₊ Add Anchor Point Tool	
⌽₋ Delete Anchor Point Tool	
⌐ Convert Point Tool	

tools, some of which share a toolbox space with the Pens. The Shape tools create vector-based objects whose edges and other attributes don't deteriorate, no matter how many times you resize, rotate, or skew them.

Type   Pixels   Shape

Photoshop's type and vector-based graphics are resolution-independent. On a PostScript output device such as the imagesetter used to make the printing plates for this book, they produce smooth outlines, no matter what the native resolution of the image file. In this demo illustration the resolution was set at 38 pixels per inch to produce exaggerated pixelation in the image. But the outlines of the type and vector-based Shape are smooth. Layer Styles, which provide the coloring and translucency, have smooth edges, but the pixel-based pattern built into the Style is coarse, produced at the file's native 38 pixels per inch.

PHOTOSHOP HAS ALWAYS BEEN ABLE TO EXCHANGE ARTWORK with vector-based PostScript drawing programs such as Adobe Illustrator, and to export artwork for use in PostScript-based page layout programs such as Adobe InDesign, or QuarkXPress. Photoshop 7 has an impressive array of vector-based drawing capabilities and sophisticated typesetting features of its own, that rival some of the best features of these other programs. This means you can use Photoshop to produce:

- **Type** (now including the long-awaited **spell checker)** with **advanced paragraph-formatting controls** that can remain **"live" and resolution-independent** all the way to the output device.

- **Vector-based Shape layers,** a form of artwork that's also resolution-independent and can be scaled without the "softening" and deterioration of edges characteristic of pixel-based artwork. When combined with Layer Styles that apply color, dimensionality, and lighting in procedural rather than pixel-based ways, the vector-based art can remain entirely resolution-independent.

- **Vector masks** (formerly called *layer clipping paths*) for sharp-edged silhouetting of individual layers, which are described in Chapter 4.

- **Vector paths** that can be stored with a file and activated for selecting or silhouetting an entire file.

This chapter tells how to use Photoshop's "vector power." It also points out when it works better to rely on dedicated PostScript-based illustration and page layout programs, and how to move your work smoothly between these programs and Photoshop.

"TWO-PHASE" OPTIONS BARS

One of the key concepts in understanding how the Type tool and the vector-based drawing tools operate in Photoshop 7 is that they have "two-phase" Options bars. Choosing the Type tool, a Shape tool, or one of the Pens brings up the **first (creating) phase**. When you've made choices from the bar and used the tool, the **second (editing) phase** of the Options bar appears. Both phases offer a fairly large number of choices, and it's important to under-

continued on page 292

Photoshop can produce scalable, resolution-independent art using vector-based graphics. Color, lighting, and dimensionality can be applied as Layer Styles. See "Designing for Scalability & Animation" on page 332.

COMMITTING & CANCELING

The keyboard shortcuts for committing or canceling the current typesetting, Shape-making, or path-drawing operation are to press the **Enter key to commit** or the **Escape key to cancel**. For the drawing tools you can use the Enter/Return key on the main keyboard; but, of course this key has a special meaning in typesetting — it starts a new line. To commit type, you'll need to use the other Enter key.

stand them in order to be able to choose and use these tools. So it's worthwhile to be familiar with how the two phases work before getting into the specifics of operating the tools.

While you're in the editing phase, many of Photoshop's other functions — menu choices, tools, and so on — won't work. Basically, you're "trapped" in the editing phase until you **commit** (accept) the typesetting/drawing changes you've made since choosing the tool, or until you **cancel** the operation. Until you get used to this, it can be confusing and annoying, but it actually makes sense in terms of the logical order of operations in Photoshop. Besides starting a new type or Shape layer, another way you might get into editing mode is by activating an existing type layer — by clicking its name in the Layers palette, for instance — and choosing the Type tool. Or you could activate a Shape layer and choose a drawing tool or one of the path-editing tools.

A sure sign that you're in editing mode — and the key to getting out of it — is the presence of the *check* button on the righthand side of the editing phase of the Options bar; often the *check* is accompanied by the *cancel* (circle and line) button. The *check* lets you commit the type or drawing you've been working on, and the *cancel* (circle and line) lets you cancel, as if you'd never done it.

TYPE

Photoshop's typesetting functions are used in techniques presented throughout this book, but they are covered most thoroughly in "Typography, Groups & Layer Styles" on page 308 and "Warped Type" on page 314. In the yellow tip boxes in these two sections, you'll also find many keyboard shortcuts for operating the **sizing** and **spacing** controls. The typesetting controls are spread among the Options bar, the Character and Paragraph palettes, and their pop-out menus. "Typesetting Options" on page 295 shows these controls and tells what they do.

In Photoshop, under most conditions, you can maintain type as "live" (editable) and still be able to control its color, opacity, special effects, and how it blends with other layers in the file:

The "Two-Phase" Option Bar

Polygon Options
Radius:
☐ Smooth Corners
☑ Star
Indent Sides By: 50%
☑ Smooth Indents

*The **"first-phase"** Options bar for the Shape tools lets you choose whether to create a new layer for the Shape you are about to create, or whether to create a Work Path or pixels instead. You can also choose which of the Shape tools you want to use, and you can set parameters for that tool in the pop-out palette (shown here is the Polygon tool and the result of its settings). You can choose a preset Layer Style to be added to the Shape as you draw it, or you can add a Style later via the Layers palette or Styles palette.*

Sides: 30   Style: Color:

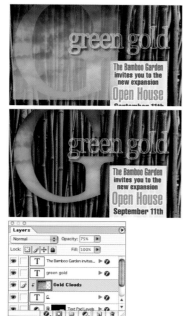

To mask an image inside live type, you can turn the type layer into the base of a clipping group by Alt/Option clicking the border between the image and type layers in the Layers palette or by typing Ctrl/⌘-G.

- **Color** can be added with the color swatch on the Options bar or in the Character palette.
- **Images** can be masked inside of type by using a clipping group with the type as the base layer, as shown at the left.
- **Bevels, patterns, textures, glows, strokes,** and **shadows** can be added with live Layer Styles.

And *all* these changes can be made without having to convert the type to a non-editable form. If you save the file in **Photoshop PDF** format, it's possible to open it with Acrobat Reader with the resolution-independent type outlines intact, even if the fonts you used aren't present on the system where the file is being used. You can also reopen it in Photoshop if you ever need to edit the type further. The **Photoshop EPS** format can retain the vector information but cannot be edited — either outside of Photoshop or inside if the file is reopened (because it will have become a flattened, single-layer file.)

Setting Type

Photoshop 6 brought us the ability to set type right on the canvas instead of in a dialog box. And you can control the color, font, size, and style of each character independently. But there are other important features to be discovered, including automatic wrap to the next line with sophisticated paragraph controls.

To begin setting type, choose the **Type tool**. Before you start typing, though, it's a good idea to check to make sure that the default **Create A Text Layer** option (the farthest left button on the Options bar) is chosen; otherwise, instead of setting type you'll be making a type-shaped selection, an option that was important in previous versions of the program but that has limited usefulness now. Just to the right of the Text Layer/Selection buttons are the **Horizontal** and **Vertical** orientation buttons, which let you set type left-to-right or top-to-bottom. The reason it's important to

Live type can be given a "glowing" stroke by specifying a gradient for the Stroke effect of a Layer Style.

As soon as you start to use the Type tool or one of the drawing tools, the "second-phase" Options bar appears, with editing options. Shown here is the second phase of the Options bar for the Shape tools.

For both **point type** and **paragraph type,** *Photoshop 7 lets you control the specifications — such as color, size, font, spacing, and baseline shift — for each character individually. The Character palette, opened by clicking the Palettes button in the Type tool's Options bar, makes all these character specifications available.*

STARTING A NEW TYPE LAYER

If a type layer is active and you click with the Type tool anywhere near the existing type to start a new, separate type layer, Photoshop may assume that you want to edit the type under the cursor instead. If no type layer is active but the cursor is over any visible type, clicking over the type with the Type tool can auto-select the layer for that type.

To let Photoshop know that you want to start a new type layer rather than edit an existing one, click away from any existing type. If you don't have room to click away from the type, you can either:

• Temporarily turn off visibility for any type layers that are interfering,

• Or create an empty transparent layer by clicking the Create A New Layer button at the bottom of the Layers palette, or press Ctrl-Alt-Shift-N (Windows) or ⌘-Option-Shift-N (Mac). Then type, and the transparent layer will turn into a type layer.

check these settings before you start to type is that as soon as you start typing, Photoshop creates a new type layer and the editing phase of the Options bar comes up. At that point if you find yourself setting selections instead of type, or a vertical stack of characters instead of a line, the only way out is to cancel and start over.

When you have the Options bar set up the way you want it, you can make the next choice: whether to set ***point type*** or ***paragraph*** (box) ***type***. You communicate that choice to Photoshop by **clicking on your canvas for point type** or **dragging to define a text box for paragraph type**. With both point type and paragraph type, you can set more than one line of type; you have complete control of the font, style, color, spacing, size, and other parameters of individual characters; and you can specify how you want the type aligned (left, right, or center). The most obvious difference is that with paragraph type your type is constrained within the box you've drag-defined, though you can always resize the box by dragging one of its handles with the Type tool.

The benefits of using point type are that you can freely manipulate the type — character by character, word by word, or line by line — without having the size and shape of a text box take control of spacing or word wrap. The **benefits of using paragraph** type are:

• Automatic **word wrap** (the text automatically starts a new line when needed to fit within the box)

• The ability to control **justification** (whether one or both sides of the text block are straight with the edges of the box)

• **Hyphenation** (whether and how words can be hyphenated at the end of a line in order to make the text fit within the box)

• **Hanging punctuation** (punctuation marks can extend slightly outside the box for better visual balance and alignment)

• A text box that acts like a transform box, so you can **scale, skew,** or **flip** the block of type with the Type tool

When it comes to hyphenation and justification, Photoshop offers more sophisticated controls than many page layout programs with its **Adobe Composer** options (see the facing page).

Editing Type

To edit type or change its specifications, you activate the type layer and choose the Type tool. **Before you click or drag,** the first phase of the Type tool's Options bar is open and you can **make changes to *all* the type** in the layer at once, without selecting the actual type to highlight it; you can change specifications such as the font, style, size, type of antialiasing, alignment, and color. You can also use the type palettes to make additional overall changes.

When you **click or drag in the type**, the editing phase of the Options bar will appear. You can add or change characters by typ-

continued on page 296

TYPESETTING OPTIONS

Photoshop 7's sophisticated controls for creating and editing text with the Type tool are spread among the Options bar, the Character and Paragraph palettes, and several dialog boxes. For a more detailed description of the settings, choose "Using Type" from Photoshop's online help, and zero in on a topic.

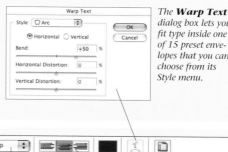

The **Warp Text** dialog box lets you fit type inside one of 15 preset envelopes that you can choose from its Style menu.

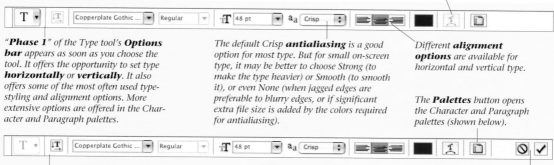

"**Phase 1**" of the Type tool's **Options bar** appears as soon as you choose the tool. It offers the opportunity to set type **horizontally** or **vertically**. It also offers some of the most often used type-styling and alignment options. More extensive options are offered in the Character and Paragraph palettes.

The default Crisp **antialiasing** is a good option for most type. But for small on-screen type, it may be better to choose Strong (to make the type heavier) or Smooth (to smooth it), or even None (when jagged edges are preferable to blurry edges, or if significant extra file size is added by the colors required for antialiasing).

Different **alignment options** are available for horizontal and vertical type.

The **Palettes** button opens the Character and Paragraph palettes (shown below).

The "**phase 2**" Options bar (the **editing** phase) appears as soon as you click or drag with the Type tool. It offers many of the same options as phase 1, but doesn't allow you to start a new block of type.

Clicking the "**check**" **icon commits** the type and returns the Options bar to phase 1. Clicking the "**no**" **icon** "**escapes**" to phase 1 without implementing any typesetting or editing you've done.

The **Character palette** lets you style selected characters. You can select a word or series of words that you don't want to break at the end of a line (**No Break**). And you can turn off **Fractional Widths** to ensure that characters set in small sizes for on-screen display don't run together.

The **Rotate Character** option, available for Vertical type only, lets you set type on a vertical baseline, or make a vertical stack of letters, each of which is in its usual horizontal orientation.

Many of the sophisticated options in the **Paragraph palette** are available only for paragraph (box) type. For instance, the **Justify Last** buttons let you control the alignment of the last line of type independently of the rest of the justified paragraph.

The **Adobe Single-line Composer** option fixes unattractive spacing and hyphenation by choosing the best-looking spacing option for each line separately. It relies on word spacing first, then hyphenation, then letter spacing, with compressed spacing being preferable to expanded spacing.

Roman Hanging Punctuation lets opening or closing punctuation (such as quotation marks, hyphens, and commas) extend outside the margins. Since these marks are small, the type can look odd if they are aligned and justified with the bigger characters.

The **Adobe Every-Line Composer** can change spacing in the entire paragraph, if necessary, to make any adjustments needed to solve a spacing problem in any one line. Even spacing is given the highest priority.

The **Justification** dialog sets acceptable ranges for the spacing in justified text. You can control letter and word spacing, and even the horizontal scaling of the type.

You can specify what multiple of type size to use for **Auto leading**, chosen in the Character dialog box

In the **Hyphenation** dialog you can choose whether to automatically hyphenate standard text or capitalized words. You can specify how many letters of a hyphenated word can be alone on a line, how many lines in sequence can end in hyphens (**Hyphen Limit**), and how far from the right margin a word has to start in order to be eligible to be hyphenated (**Hyphenation Zone**).

Here's a tip from Russell Brown of Adobe Systems: To change the type specifications — font, color, size, or any other characteristic — of several type layers at once, do this:

Activate one of the type layers by clicking its name in the Layers palette. Then click in the column next to the Eye icon of the other type layers to link them all together. Finally, hold down the Shift key, choose the Type tool, *and without clicking on the canvas,* make the changes you want in the Options bar.

With the "Music" layer active and no text selected, holding down the Shift key and choosing a new font changed the font in all the linked type layers.

The Warp Text command can provide a good start (center) for integrating type into an image. See "Warped Type" on page 314.

ing, and you can make changes to the selected characters, through the choices in the Options bar or the palettes.

Warping Type

Both point type and paragraph type can be reshaped using the **Warp Text** function, which bends, stretches, and otherwise distorts type to fit within an "envelope." When a type layer is active, the Warp Text dialog box can be opened by clicking the **Create Warped Text** button in the editing phase of the Type tool's Options bar, or by choosing **Layer, Type, Warp Text,** or by right-clicking the type itself to open a context-sensitive menu (Control-click on a Mac with a one-button mouse). In the Warp Text dialog box you can choose a type of envelope from the Style list, and then set parameters for bending and distorting.

- The **Style** shows you the general shape of the envelope — for instance, an Arc.
- The **Bend** controls the degree to which the type is distorted into that shape — for instance, is it a shallow arc (a low setting) or a more pronounced arc (higher setting)?
- And the **Horizontal** and **Vertical Distortion** settings control where the effect is centered — left or right, up or down.

Warping is applied to the entire type layer; you can't select and warp individual characters. Unfortunately, there's no way to reshape the envelope as a Bézier curve, editing the outline point-by-point. In some simple cases the Arc Style of the Warp Text command can do a pretty good job of imitating type on a curve, a type-setting feature that Photoshop lacks. But for more sophisticated curve-fitting, you'll need to do the shaping in a dedicated drawing program such as Adobe Illustrator, Macromedia FreeHand, or CorelDraw.

When To Convert Type

Keeping Photoshop type "live" and editable as long as possible is a good idea because it provides a great deal of flexibility. And with clipping groups, Layer Styles, and the ability to save in PDF and EPS formats, you rarely have to rasterize the type or even convert it to a Shape layer for output. However, there are some exceptions:

- **To run a filter** on type, you have to rasterize the type layer first (Layer, Rasterize, Type).
- **To edit the shape or tilt** of individual characters in a type block, you have to convert type to a Shape layer. Then you can select and manipulate the individual character outlines, as described in "Silhouetting Images & Type" on page 338.
- If your type has **to exactly match** a Shape version or rasterized version of the same type — for instance, if you're using type to

If you need to tilt or distort individual characters in a text block, the type first has to be converted to a Shape layer.

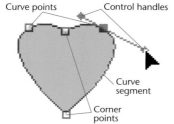

Curve points   Control handles

Curve segment

Corner points

The paths produced by the Shape tools in Photoshop 7 are Bézier curves defined by anchor points and control handles.

Vector mask for the active Shape layer | Stored path | Unsaved *Work Path*

Fill Path

Stroke Path

Load Path as Selection

Make Work Path from Selection

Create New Path

Delete Path

The Paths palette provides everything you need for storing, filling, and stroking paths; converting selections to paths and vice versa; and making clipping paths (via the palette's menu that pops out from the upper right corner) for exporting silhouetted areas.

A subpath is a single component of a path. It can be selected and manipulated independently of other subpaths in its path.

create a knock-out layer for type in a Spot Color channel — it's safer to convert your live type to a Shape layer. That's because Spot Color channels can't include live type, and even slight variations in the name or tracking values of the font on the system where the file is output can cause a mismatch between the live-type knock-out and the pixel-based spot color. You'll find an example in "Spot Color Overlays" on page 100.

- Anytime you want to be sure that your file will open or print as expected, whether or not the font is present on the next system that handles the file, you can convert the type to Shape layers to avoid complications (Layer, Type, Convert To Shape).

THE VECTOR-BASED DRAWING TOOLS

The **Shape** tools and **Pen** tools produce artwork as a series of straight or curving segments that stretch between *anchor points* to make up a *path*. How each segment of the path bends between its two anchor points is determined by *control handles,* located at the anchor points, that put more or less tension on the wirelike segment, making its curve steeper or flatter. (The paths produced with this approach in Photoshop and many other programs are called *Bézier curves.*)

Path Lingo

The term *path* has several overlapping meanings in Photoshop 7. In its general use a ***path*** is any vector-based outline made up of anchor points and curve segments. In that sense, all of the following are paths:

- A ***vector mask*** *(formerly a "layer clipping path" in Photoshop 6)* that defines the shape outline in a Shape layer. It also temporarily appears in the Paths palette whenever that Shape layer is the active layer.

- A ***vector mask*** that is used as a vector-based mask on a transparent layer or a type layer. It also appears in the Paths palette whenever that transparent or type layer is the active layer.

- The current ***Work Path,*** which is independent of any layer and appears in the Paths palette until you start a new *Work Path.*

- A saved ***Path,*** which is named and permanently stored in the Paths palette and, like the *Work Path*, is also independent of any layer. A Path can be made by converting a *Work Path* or duplicating a *vector mask* anytime its name appears in the Paths palette.

A path can include more than one component, or ***subpath***. A subpath is produced when a you draw one Bézier curve and then start drawing another without first creating a new Shape layer or layer clipping path, or a new named Path or a new *Work Path*. A subpath can be selected, so that it can be treated independently of other components of its path. Although there are several ways to select a subpath, the following always works: In the Paths palette, click the

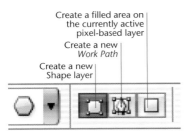

Create a filled area on
the currently active
pixel-based layer

Create a new
Work Path

Create a new
Shape layer

When you choose a Shape tool or a Pen tool, you first choose a mode of operation.

Arrowheads

☑ Start   ☐ End

Width: 500%

Length: 1000%

Concavity: 20%

Custom arrowheads can be automatically applied to lines drawn with the Line tool. Click the little Geometry Options triangle to the right of the Shape tool choices in the Options bar and set the Width and Length (as percentages of the line weight) and the Concavity. A negative Concavity stretches the base of the arrowhead away from the tip, as in the two arrows above on the right. The arrow on the far left was made by clicking with the Line tool to place the starting arrowhead and then dragging toward the tip rather than away from it.

House

Bend O Flex Logo

Hand

Toxic Logo

Photoshop's Custom Shape tool comes with a library of presets, which can be resized without becoming fuzzy and can be printed at the resolution of the output device. You can add your own vector-based graphic elements such as logos, icons, or signatures to the presets.

name of the path. Then use the Direct Selection tool or the Path Component Selection tool to click the subpath in the working window.

SHAPE TOOLS AND SHAPE LAYERS

The **Shape tools — Rectangle, Rounded Rectangle, Ellipse, Polygon, Line,** and **Custom Shape** — are grouped in a single space in the toolbox. Once any Shape tool is chosen, all the others become available in the first phase of the Shape tools' Options bar. The Options bar also gives you a choice of creating a vector-based Shape layer, drawing a vector-based *Work Path*, or creating a pixel-based shape filled with the Foreground color on the active layer. For any of these tools you can create the shape by dragging the tool.

A **Shape layer** specifies a color fill and has a vector mask that defines exactly where this color is revealed and where it's hidden. The Shape tools' Options bar lets you control the Mode and Opacity of the color assigned to the layer, and you can choose a Layer Style to be added to the shape as you draw it. The Style will be applied to everything you draw on that Shape layer.

Of the other two drawing options besides a Shape layer, making a vector-based **Work Path** is more flexible than making a pixel-based filled shape because you can edit the resolution-independent path and convert it to a permanent saved Path (by dragging the *Work Path* name to the Create A New Path button at the bottom of the Paths palette). Then you can use the saved Path to create a filled or stroked area on a pixel-based layer, or to make a selection.

Making a **filled shape** is a *raster* option, and as such it can only be used on a pixel-based layer — that is, a transparent layer or the *Background*. It's a quick and easy way to draw a shape, and because it's pixel-based you can filter or paint on the result immediately. You can set the Mode and Opacity for the fill and choose whether the edges will be Anti-aliased.

Also in the first phase of the Shape tools' Options bar, you can pop-out a palette of specifications for the particular Shape tool you've chosen by clicking the tiny triangle to the right of the tool choices in the Options bar:

• For the **Rectangle, Rounded Rectangle, or Ellipse** you can **Constrain** the shape to a square or circle. You can choose a **Fixed Size** or a **Proportional** relationship between Width and Length, or choose to draw **From the Center** outward rather than diagonally. For the Rounded Rectangle the Options bar also offers a **Radius** setting to determine the roundness of the corners.

• For the **Polygon** tool, the **Radius** (size) is set in the pop-out palette. So instead of controlling the size of the polygon, dragging the tool rotates it, determining its angle. You can also choose whether to have pointed or **Smooth Corners,** whether to **turn the polygon into a star** by choosing to **Indent the Sides By** a percentage of the diameter, and whether to **Smooth the In-**

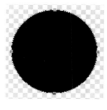

A Shape layer was started by Shift-dragging with the Ellipse tool, chosen from the Shape tools that share the spot next to the Type tool in the toolbox.

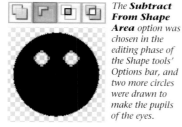

*The **Subtract From Shape Area** option was chosen in the editing phase of the Shape tools' Options bar, and two more circles were drawn to make the pupils of the eyes.*

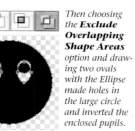

*Then choosing the **Exclude Overlapping Shape Areas** option and drawing two ovals with the Ellipse made holes in the large circle and inverted the enclosed pupils.*

*The Pen tool was chosen and the **Subtract** option was chosen again to draw the mouth.*

SAVING THE WORK PATH

To convert the current **Work Path** to a named, saved Path, double-click its name in the Paths palette.

dents. Both the Polygon and the Line (described next) can be
rotated as you draw them, simply by changing the direction of dragging.

- For the **Line** tool — which produces not actually a line but a long skinny rectangle — the line **Weight** is chosen in the Options bar; in the pop-out palette you can choose to add **Arrowheads**, and you can specify their shape.

- The **Custom Shape** tool lets you use choose from shapes that have been stored as presets. In the pop-out palette you can constrain the Custom Shape to its original Defined Size or Defined Proportions, or specify a Fixed Size. You can choose a different preset shape by clicking the Shape icon or the little triangle next to it to open a palette of shapes. Other preset libraries can be added to the palette via the palette's pop-out menu: **Add to the palette by choosing Load Shapes;** choose **Replace Shapes to substitute.** You can also add any path to the current palette of Custom Shape tools by clicking its name in the Paths palette (where stored paths and any active Shape layer paths are listed) and choosing Edit, Define Custom Shape.

Once you have an active Shape layer, *Work Path,* or saved Path, the Options bar switches to its editing phase and offers you a different set of choices. You now have the option of **adding** the next Shape or path you draw to the current Shape layer, **subtracting** from it, making the **intersection** of the two, or making a combination of the two that **excludes** the intersection. As with the Type tool, clicking the "check" or "no" icons at the right end of the editing phase of the Options bar commits or cancels the changes and releases you from the editing phase.

PEN TOOLS

The Pens and several of the path-editing tools share a spot in the toolbox. With the tools in the Pen family — the **Pen**, **Freeform**

DRAWING HELPERS

To draw a shape outward from its **center** rather than the default edge-to-edge, hold down the **Alt/Option** key as you drag.

To **constrain** the shape to 1:1 height:width proportions (for a square or a circle, for instance), hold down the **Shift** key as you drag.

Use both keys together for both effects at once.

To **move** the Shape while drawing it, hold down the **spacebar**, then release the bar to continue drawing.

CYCLING CUSTOM SHAPES

As they can with so many palettes, the bracket keys can cycle through the Custom Shape tools in the Options bar: Press **]** to cycle to the next Custom Shape after the current one in the palette and **[** to cycle to the one before it in the palette. Adding the Shift key cycles to the end or beginning of the palette.

Here a Shape layer was created by drawing the same figure as on page 299, but with a Layer Style chosen in the Options bar before the drawing began. (You can't add a Style via the Options bar once the drawing has begun, but it's easy to add a Style to the Layer by clicking the Add A Layer Style button — the "f" — at the bottom of the Layers palette.)

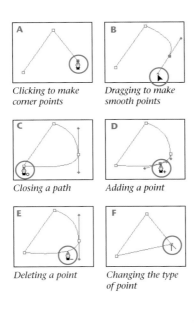

Clicking to make corner points

Dragging to make smooth points

Closing a path

Adding a point

Deleting a point

Changing the type of point

Pen, and **Magnetic Pen** — you can create your own Bézier-curve paths by clicking and dragging. The Pen's first-phase Options bar lets you choose between making a Shape layer and drawing a *Work Path* by pressing one of the buttons at the left end of the bar.

The Pen

With the **Pen** tool, as shown at the left, you can:

A Click to set a corner point.

B Drag to place a smooth (curve) point and to shape the curve.

C Close the path by moving the cursor close to the starting point and clicking when you see a little circle next to the cursor.

You can make path-editing easier by turning on **Auto Add/ Delete** in the Options bar's first phase. With this option turned on:

D The Pen automatically turns into the Add Anchor Point tool whenever you move the cursor over a curve segment.

E The Pen becomes the Delete Anchor Point tool when you move it over an anchor point.

F To change the curve type — from a smooth curve segment coming into a point to a straight segment coming out of it, or vice versa — hold down the Alt/Option key and click the point again; with the Alt/Option key depressed, the Pen toggles to the Convert Point tool, which changes the point. Then release the key and proceed to set the next point.

LOOKING AHEAD

To preview the next segment of the path *before* you click to set the anchor point, turn on the Rubber Band option in the Options bar's first phase.

The Freeform Pen

The **Freeform Pen** lets you drag to create a curve as if you were drawing with a pencil; anchor points are automatically added where they are needed to control the curves. As with the Pen tool, you can choose Auto Add/Delete

CONSTRAINING PATHS

To constrain the click or drag of a Pen tool or a path-editing tool to any 45° or 90° angle, hold down the Shift key and then click or drag with the tool.

in the Options bar. You can also set the **Curve Fit** tolerance — **to determine how closely the path will follow the movement of the cursor;** with lower settings the curve will follow the cursor movements more closely, with more anchor points than at higher settings.

The Magnetic Pen

Magnetic is another choice in the Options bar for the Freeform

If you choose View, Show, Grid and View, Snap To, Grid, you can make the Pen tool follow the grid as you draw a path, snapping points and handles to the Grid points to draw symmetrical shapes. Once the path is drawn, it can be saved as a Custom Shape preset for future use (Edit, Define Custom Shape).

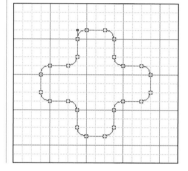

The Magnetic Pen is available as an option in the Options bar of the Freeform Pen tool. Through its pop-out palette, you can customize its edge-tracing settings.

Pen. This choice actually **turns the Freeform Pen into the Magnetic Pen**, which creates a path by automatically following color and contrast differences in an existing image. To operate the Magnetic Pen, click the center of the circular cursor somewhere on the edge you want to trace and then "float" the cursor along, moving the mouse or stylus without pressing its button. The tool will automatically follow the "edge" created by color contrast. The way the tool performs depends on the settings in the palette that opens when you click the Magnetic Pen Options button, which becomes available in the Options bar when you choose the Magnetic option. You can set Width, Contrast, and Frequency and turn Stylus Pressure on or off.

- **Width** is the radius of the area where the tool looks for the edge as you float the cursor along. The smaller the Width, the more discriminating the tool is about finding the edge, but the slower it operates and the more eye-mouse coordination is required.

- **Frequency** specifies how often a fastening point is automatically laid down. Fastening points are not exactly the same as the final anchor points in the path. They simply "tack down" the path and determine how far back the path will be "unraveled" if you press the Delete key.

- **Edge Contrast** specifies how much contrast the tool should look for in finding the edge. The default setting usually works well.

- The Free Form Pen's **Curve Fit** setting (described on page 300) also applies when the tool is operating as the Magnetic Pen.

Here are some tips for setting the Width and operating the Magnetic Pen:

- Use the left and right **bracket keys to change the Width** as you operate the pen, with the] key increasing the Width and the [key decreasing it. **If you're tracing a well-defined edge** with no other edges or distinct objects nearby, use a large Width and move the tool quickly. **If there are other edges or distinct objects** near the edge you want to trace, use a small Width and keep the cursor carefully centered on the edge you want to trace. **For a soft edge** with little contrast use a smaller Width and trace carefully.

- If there is **no contrast** for the pen to follow for Magnetic operation, you can operate the tool as the regular Freeform pen, clicking to set a point or dragging to make a freeform curve.

- Use the Delete key to "undo" misplaced fastening points. To trace a **complex, detailed edge,** set the **Frequency low** to

When you use a Pen tool, you can end a path by clicking the "check" icon in the Options bar. But it's possible to end a subpath so you can start a new one without starting a completely new Shape layer or Working Path:

• The **Freeform Pen** ends a subpath as soon as you release the mouse button.

• With the standard **Pen** tool, you can end a path by closing the path (clicking again on the starting point) or by holding down the Ctrl/⌘ key to turn the Pen into the Direct Selection tool and then clicking somewhere off the path.

• With the **Magnetic Pen,** as with the Magnetic Lasso, end a subpath by pressing the Enter/ Return key.

create more fastening points so you don't have to backtrack too far when you press Delete. To trace a **smooth edge** you can set the **Frequency higher** to use fewer fastening points.

EDITING SHAPES AND PATHS

The Photoshop 7 path-editing tools let you edit the outlines that you've already created with the drawing tools. Some are found with the Pen tools in the toolbox; these are the Add and Delete Anchor Point tools and the Convert Point tool. Two other path-editing tools — the Path Component Selection tool and the Direct Selection tool — share a space above the Pens. Once you've drawn a path, you can edit it as follows:

• **To add another anchor point so you have more control in reshaping a part of a path,** use the Add Anchor Point tool to click on the segment where you want the point.

• **To reduce the complexity of a path** or to smooth it, choose an anchor point you want to eliminate and click with the Delete Anchor Point tool.

• **To turn a corner into a smooth point, or vice versa,** click it with the Convert Point tool (the caret).

• **To reshape a curve,** use the Direct Selection tool to click the anchor point you want to work with. Then to reshape the curve on both sides of the point at once, drag a control handle. To reshape the curve on only one side of the point, hold down the Alt/Option key and drag the appropriate control handle.

• **To move a path,** drag it with the Path Component Selection tool.

• **To invert the nature of a Shape layer** so that the solid area becomes a "hole" and vice versa, activate the vector mask component of the Shape layer (by clicking its thumbnail in the Layers palette once or twice, until the thick border appears around the thumbnail). Then, in the working window, use the Path Component Selection tool to click the particular path(s) you want to invert, and click the Add or Subtract button on the Options bar.

• **To combine closed subpaths into a single subpath or path,** you should

Instead of going to the toolbox to switch between the **Pen** and the path-editing tools, you can do it by holding down a helper key to toggle the tool:

• Hold down **Alt/Option** to switch to the **Convert Point** tool.

• Hold down the **Ctrl/⌘** key to switch to the **Direct Selection** tool.

The easiest way to switch to the **Add Anchor Point** or **Delete Anchor Point** tool is to let Photoshop do it for you automatically, by turning on **Auto Add/Delete** in the Pen tool's Options bar.

A single path can produce a variety of different results, depending on how the Fill Path options are set up. To open the Fill Path dialog box, Alt/Option-click the Fill Path button at the bottom of the Paths palette, where you can choose to fill with solid color or a pattern, choose the Blending Mode, and set the Opacity and Feather Radius.

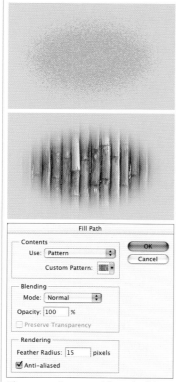

The same path was used for each of these three examples. The path was filled with the Foreground Color in Dissolve mode with a Feather of 15 (top). The other fill was made with a custom pattern used with a soft feather, as shown in the dialog box.

first make sure the positive and negative attributes for all the subpaths are set the way you want them. To reset these attributes, click each subpath with the Path Component Selection tool to select it and then click the appropriate button in the Options bar — Add, Subtract, Intersect, or Exclude. Then Shift-select the ones you want to combine permanently, and click the bar's Combine button.

- **To align subpaths,** Shift-click them and choose Alignment options from the icons in the Options bar.

STROKING AND FILLING PATHS

Photoshop 7 offers a wide range of options for filling and stroking paths. In order for a path **to be filled or stroked with pixels,** a *Work Path* or saved Path has to be selected and a Background layer or a transparent layer or its layer mask has to be active (selected in the Layers palette). These layers are the only ones that will accept a pixel-based fill or stroke. To fill or stroke a path, first select the path in the Paths palette. (If you want to fill or stroke *some* components of a multipart path, but not all, you can select or Shift-select the part(s) with the Path Component Selection tool.) Then:

- **To fill a path,** click the Fill Path button at the bottom of the Paths palette. Or Alt/Option-click the button to open the Fill Path dialog box, where you can specify other fill colors or patterns, as well as the Blending mode and Opacity for the fill and even a Feather setting to soften the edges of the area to be filled.

- **To stroke a path** with the Foreground color, select it in the

Photoshop 7 provides plenty of opportunities for reusing a path to build a single element. You can stroke and restroke a path with different tools, brush sizes, or colors to layer the paint. To choose a tool for stroking a path, Alt/Option-click the Stroke Path button at the bottom of the Paths palette to open the Stroke Path dialog box.

Styled Strokes.psd file

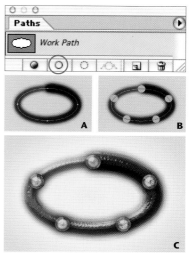

On one transparent layer the oval path was stroked with the Paintbrush using a large Spray brush tip, with Fade set for Opacity and Size in the Brush Dynamics **A**. Then, on another layer, it was stroked again with a 30-pixel hard brush tip with spacing set to 350% to produce the dots **B**. Finally, a Layer Style was applied to each layer **C**.

To some degree, type, Shape layers, the *Work Path*, and saved Paths can be converted into each other. And all four can be rasterized into pixels.

The active **type layer** can easily be converted to a Shape layer (by choosing Layer, Type, Convert To Shape) or to a path (by choosing Layer, Type, Create Work Path. Then it can be named and saved by dragging the *Work Path* name in the Paths palette to the Create New Path button at the bottom of the palette. Or it can be converted directly to pixels (by choosing Layer, Rasterize, Type).

The active **Shape layer** can be duplicated as a saved Path (by dragging its name in the Paths palette to the Create New Path button at the bottom of the palette) or converted to pixels (by choosing Layer, Rasterize, Shape).

A saved **Path** or the **Work Path** can be duplicated as pixels by first making sure that a transparent layer or the *Background* is the active layer, then clicking the path in the Paths palette, and Alt/Option-clicking the Fill or Stroke button at the bottom of the palette.

You can also **duplicate a saved Path or the Work Path as a Shape layer** by clicking its name in the Paths palette and choosing Edit, Define Custom Shape; then choose the Custom Shape tool and choose the new Shape from the pop-out Custom Shape palette in the Shape tools' Options bar, and drag to make the Shape layer. Then if you don't need your new Custom Shape anymore, just Alt/Option-click its symbol in the Custom Shapes palette to remove it.

Paths palette and click the Stroke Path button at the bottom of the palette. Or Alt/Option-click to open the Stroke Path dialog box, where you can choose from a pop-out menu of the tools you can use to make the stroke.

If a path is part of a Shape layer, it can't be filled or stroked with pixels as described on page 303. But it can be assigned a Layer Style, which can include a Color Overlay, Gradient Overlay, or Pattern Overlay for filling the shape, as well as a Stroke for outlining the shape. Fills and strokes assigned as part of a Layer Style can be changed without affecting image quality. And except for the Pattern Overlay and the Texture component of the Bevel And Emboss effect, they are resolution-independent and can be enlarged without deterioration in quality. Layer Styles are addressed in "Typography, Groups, and Layer Styles" on page 308 and are covered extensively in Chapter 8.

USING PHOTOSHOP WITH OTHER POSTSCRIPT PROGRAMS

How do you decide when it makes sense to combine Illustrator (or other PostScript vector-based) artwork with an image created in Photoshop? And when it does, how do you decide whether to import a Photoshop illustration into Illustrator, or an Illustrator drawing into Photoshop, or when to assemble the two in a third program? These pointers can help you make the decision:

- The Pen and Shape tools in Photoshop can draw smooth Bézier curves, and the path-editing tools make it easy to modify the curves it draws. The Grid and Guides allow exact placement and snap-to precision. And the Edit, Transform Path command allows easy scaling, skewing, and rotating. But object-oriented drawing programs such as Illustrator, FreeHand, and CorelDraw still excel at all drawing tasks that require layered constructions, automated spacing or copying, or transformation from one shape to another through several intermediate steps.

- In Photoshop 7 you can keep type live and editable between working sessions, and the type can be scaled, skewed, rotated, and otherwise distorted without degrading the quality of its edges. Still, for really designing with type or fitting type into a particular shape or along a path, PostScript drawing and page layout programs have greater capabilities.

- For a multipage document, or to assemble a number of items with precise alignment, and especially if you need to set large amounts of text and spell-check it, bring both the Photoshop files and the PostScript artwork into a page layout program. A page layout program also provides a way to assemble Photoshop files of different resolutions.

A layered file in Adobe Illustrator **A** can be exported in Photoshop PSD format, with layers preserved, by choosing File, Export, Format, Photoshop PSD (in Illustrator 9 it's Photoshop 5 PSD), and then choosing the desired color model and resolution and enabling the Write Layers option **B**. When the file is opened in Photoshop 7, Layer Styles and other treatments can be applied to the individual layers **C**. (For more about this process, see "Coloring Clip Art" on page 324.)

ILLUSTRATOR TO PHOTOSHOP

Although it's possible to import encapsulated PostScript (EPS) files from other PostScript illustration programs, it's only natural that Adobe Illustrator shows the greatest compatibility with Adobe Photoshop. So the best way to make illustrations available for use in Photoshop may be to save them in (or convert them to) Illustrator EPS format.

- Files from **FreeHand 8** and later versions can be dragged and dropped or copied and pasted directly into Photoshop as pixels or paths. Or they can be exported as Illustrator files or rasterized — converted into pixel-based images — in Photoshop format.

- **CorelDraw** files can be saved in Adobe Illustrator format by using the program's File, Save As, Adobe Illustrator command, or they can be rasterized at the resolution you specify by choosing File, Export, Adobe Photoshop.

  (Translation of a complex file from one PostScript drawing program to another may not be completely accurate. If possible, files translated into Illustrator format should be checked in Illustrator before they are imported into Photoshop. Also, keep in mind that type will not be "live" when an Illustrator file is opened or placed in Photoshop.)

Importing Illustrator Objects as Vector-Based Art

You can **transfer Illustrator paths** into Photoshop, keeping their vector-based nature, in one of these ways:

- **Drag and drop** the artwork as **paths** by holding down the Ctrl/⌘ key as you drag from the open Illustrator file to the open Photoshop file.

- Select the paths you want to transfer, **copy** them to the clipboard, and then **paste** them into Photoshop, choosing **Paste As Shape Layer** or **Paste As Paths** in Photoshop's Paste dialog box. To center, hold down the Shift key as you paste (see tip on page 306 for working with Illustrator 10).

> **LOST IN THE TRANSLATION**
>
> You can transfer objects from Illustrator to Photoshop and retain their vector-based nature. But there are some things that don't transfer successfully. Any strokes or fills assigned to an object are lost when it's copied and pasted or Ctrl/⌘-dragged and dropped. Also, live type can't be imported into Photoshop from Illustrator. It first has to be converted to outlines (in Illustrator: Type, Create Outlines). (See tip on page 306 for more on pasting objects from Illustrator 10.)

Rasterizing Illustrator Artwork into Photoshop

Besides importing Illustrator 9 or 10 art in a vector-based format, you can also *rasterize* it into Photoshop, turning it into pixels:

When you paste an Illustrator object from the clipboard into Photoshop 7, the Paste dialog box lets you choose it as pixels, or bring it in as a path, or import it as a Shape layer. The graphics for this logo were designed in Illustrator, copied to the clipboard, and pasted into Photoshop as a Shape layer. Then the elements were separated onto different layers so that a different Layer Style could be applied to each.

PASTING FROM ILLUSTRATOR 10

In Illustrator 10, the AICB option must be checked in the Files & Clipboard section of the Preferences dialog in order to paste shapes or paths into Photoshop.

- **Export** the file from Illustrator 10 **with layers intact** in Photoshop PSD format (File, Export, Photoshop PSD, Write Layers; in Illustrator 9 this format is called PSD 5). This will produce a Photoshop file with the objects rasterized on layers, according to the original Illustrator layer structure. Then open the file in Photoshop (File, Open).

- **Open** an Illustrator file to rasterize the entire file into Photoshop as a single-layer file at the resolution you choose (File, Open).

- **Place** the file to rasterize all its objects on a single layer of an existing file with the option to align and scale while placing (File, Place).

- **Drag-and-drop** artwork from an open Illustrator file to an open Photoshop file by selecting the Illustrator objects you want to import and dragging from the Illustrator file to the Photoshop file, where they will be rasterized as a new layer. To **center** the imported art in the Photoshop image, hold down the Shift key while dragging.

- Select an object or objects, **copy** them to the clipboard, and then **paste** them into Photoshop, choosing **Paste As Pixels** in Photoshop's Paste dialog box.

Importing Complex Graphics

A fairly common workflow is to construct a complex graphic in Illustrator and then bring it into Photoshop for treatment of its individual components with Layer Styles. The goal is to separate all the individual elements onto their own layers, keeping them in register as in the original graphic. One approach to this process is

DELETING PATHS

If you want to delete all but a few of the subpaths of a path, you can select all of the subpaths, then Shift-click to deselect the subpaths you want to keep, and press Delete to get rid of all the others.

described in "Coloring Clip Art" on page 324 — saving a layered Illustrator file in Photoshop PSD format, with the elements sorted onto layers according to how they will need to be treated in Photoshop. This results in raster artwork on transparent layers.

A second approach is to select all in Illustrator, copy to the clipboard, and paste into a Photoshop file as a single Shape layer; then duplicate this layer as many times as you need layers for separate elements, and delete the unwanted elements from each layer. This method results in vector-based artwork and is described in "Designing for Scalability & Animation" on page 332.

There's also a third possibility. Once you've copied and pasted as a Shape layer, instead of duplicating the Shape layer and then deleting the unwanted parts, you can click the ✓ and start a new Shape layer by choosing any Shape tool and drawing a Shape. Then select and copy the path that you want to put on a layer of its own,

To fit type, the Photoshop file was dragged and dropped into Illustrator, where type was set on a path and converted to outlines. Then the outlines were copied and pasted into the Photoshop file as a Shape layer of its own so a Layer Style could be added later.

The title was designed to fit with the cyclists in a Photoshop file. Then the title and figures were exported as two separate files, each with its own clipping path, so they could be layered and the arrangement fine-tuned in a page layout program.

activate the Shape layer you just added, and paste. The path will appear in exactly the same position where it was when you selected and copied it. Finally, select the temporary Shape you used to create the Shape layer and delete it, leaving only the pasted Shape.

PHOTOSHOP TO ILLUSTRATOR

If you want to import a Photoshop image into Illustrator in order to add type or geometric elements, or to trace parts of it to produce PostScript artwork, there are at least three ways to do it:

- One way is to save the Photoshop file in one of these formats: **TIFF, GIF, JPEG, PICT, PDF, Photoshop** (turn on visibility for all layers you want to include in the imported image), or **EPS** (include a Preview so you can see it on the screen). If you plan to transform the Photoshop art in Illustrator (for example, rotate it), or if you plan to color-separate and print from Illustrator, use EPS, and *link* the imported image rather than embedding it. Then drag it into Illustrator and drop it, or use Illustrator's **Open** or **Place** command to import it onto a printing or nonprinting layer.

- If your objective is **to fit type** to a particular part of your Photoshop image, the simplest way may be to open the file in Illustrator, make a path to fit, set type on it, convert the type to outlines (Type, Create Outlines), and then copy the converted type and paste it back into the Photoshop file as a Shape layer.

  Or use Photoshop's Pen tool to create a path in the shape you want to fit, then export the file (File, Export, Paths To Illustrator), and open it in Illustrator (File, Open). The path will be invisible in Illustrator's Preview mode, being stroked and filled with None, so work in Outline mode. With the imported path selected, choose Object, Compound Path, Release. Then you can use Illustrator's Path Type tool to set the type. Convert the type to outlines (Type, Create Outlines), and then select all, and copy and paste, Place, or drag-and-drop the Illustrator art into the Photoshop file. When the Illustrator type on a path is placed back into the Photoshop image, it comes in exactly in register with the original Photoshop path.

- If you want to use a silhouetted photo and display type together in a page layout, you can set the type in Photoshop, right in the image file with the photo you'll be silhouetting so you can design the elements together. Then export the type and silhouetted photo separately, for maximum flexibility in arranging and layering them in the page layout program. You'll find an example in "Silhouetting Images & Type" on page 338.

Typography, Groups & Layer Styles

Overview *Lighten an area for small display type with a masked Adjustment layer; create two large display type elements; group a photo with one character and add special color effects to the other type element; set several lines of paragraph type in several colors.*

"Text Panel" "before" and "after" files

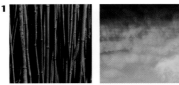

The original photos of bamboo and golden clouds

2a

Setting up a Levels Adjustment layer to lighten an area that was selected for the text pad

2b

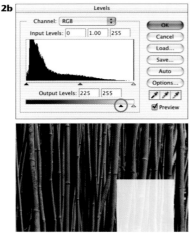

Lightening an area by adjusting Output Levels

WITH IMPRESSIVE TYPE HANDLING, editable Layer Styles, and a new spell checker in Photoshop 7, it's possible to design and produce any simple page layout that consists entirely of images and display type. Here we've put the large type directly over the background image, "clipped" a photo inside the large "G," and also created a lightened panel area that allows the background image to show through but still provides good contrast for the smaller display type.

1 Preparing a background. Choose File, New to open a new Photoshop file the size and resolution you need for your layout. When you set the Width and Height, be sure to include the edge area you need for any bleed (usually 0.125-inch on each side on the final print job).

Now prepare the photo files **1** and drag-and-drop the background photo into your layout. Use Ctrl/⌘-T (for Free Transform) to scale the image up or down, but keep in mind that you shouldn't scale it up more than about 10% and still expect it to look good. When scaling, always use Unsharp Mask afterwards, even if just a little (see "Sharpen" on page 204 for tips on settings).

Be sure the Layers palette is open so you can use it in the steps that follow (choose Window, Show Layers to open it if necessary).

2 Making a pad for type. Drag with an unfeathered Rectangular Marquee to select the area you want to lighten as a pad for the type (you can check the Feather setting in the Options bar; it should be "0 px"). To create an Adjustment layer so you can lighten the text pad area, Alt/Option-click the Create New Adjustment Layer button at the bottom of the Layers palette and choose Levels from the pop-out list. (Using the Alt/Option key opens the New Layer dialog box, where you can name the layer.) Click OK to close the New Layer box **2a,** and when the Levels dialog box opens, move the black point on the Output Levels slider to lighten the selected areas **2b.**

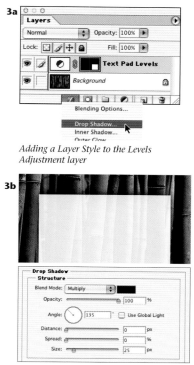

3a

Adding a Layer Style to the Levels Adjustment layer

3b

A Drop Shadow is added to the Adjustment layer and its mask.

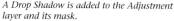

4a

Adding a large "G" with the Type tool

4b

The Type tool automatically creates a separate layer above the currently active layer. The "T" thumbnail indicates that the type is live, or editable.

Image detail will be maintained, but contrast will be reduced so the image won't interfere with the type you'll be putting on the pad.

There are many other ways you can make a lightened pad for type. However, using an Adjustment layer produces a panel that you can easily fine-tune and re-position (by dragging with the Move tool) in case you want to experiment with the layout.

3 Adding a halo. To add a dark halo, click the Add A Layer Style button (the "*f*") at the bottom of the Layers palette and choose Drop Shadow from the pop-out list **3a**.

To make a "dark halo" rather than an offset shadow, we set the Distance to 0, set a large Size (25 pixels), and clicked OK to close the Layer Style dialog box **3b**. Notice that the shadow effect appears only outside the pad. That's because by default the "Layer Knocks Out Drop Shadow" feature is turned on, as described in the tip at the right.

4 Setting the largest type.
Three type elements were used for the postcard: the large "G," the "green gold," and the block of type on the lightened pad. These had to be set separately so they could be individually positioned.

To set a large letter like the "G," choose the Type tool, and in the Options bar make sure the Create A Text Layer option is selected at the left end of the bar. Click the bar's Palettes button to open the Character palette. Choose the font and type-style you want, and enter a value for the font size, then type the letter on the image. If the letter that appears on the image is too small or too big, select it (you can do this by dragging across it) and enter a new size value. Moving the cursor away from the type turns the cursor into the Move tool (or hold down the Ctrl/⌘ key to toggle to the Move tool), and you can drag to move the type into position where you want it.

You can change the color used for the type without changing Photoshop's overall Foreground color — just click the color swatch in the Character palette to open the Color Picker. We chose a pastel orange **4a** that would stand-in for the colors we would add later, so we would be able to develop the Layer Style (in step 6) before we finally clipped the golden clouds photo into the type (in step 9).

5a

As part of the process of fitting the type into the postcard design, a negative tracking value was entered to pull all the letters closer together.

5b

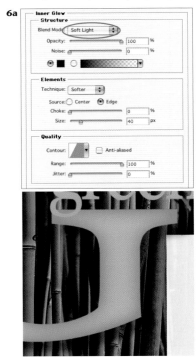

The Free Transform command was used to make final size adjustments for "green gold."

6a

A soft brown Inner Glow in Soft Light mode added subtle surface variations to the "G." A Drop Shadow was added with a 50% Opacity, a Distance offset of 30 pixels at an Angle of 135°, and a 15-pixel Size setting.

When the type is set, sized, colored, and positioned the way you want it, click the ✓ button in the Options bar or press the Enter key **4b**. If you want to change the type later, you'll be able to reselect the type and open the Type tool's Options bar by just double-clicking the "T" symbol for its layer in the Layers palette.

5 Setting type to a specific line length. We wanted the "green gold" type to sit on the platform created by the "G" and to extend as far as the right edge of the text pad. To set type to a specific line length like this, first start another type layer by clicking in the image with the Type tool (see the "Adding Another Type Layer" tip at the right for pointers). Then set the type and adjust its size, position, and color. Work with the type to get as close as you can to the right line length, including any letter-pair kerning and multiple-letter tracking you need **5a**:

- To **kern**, or adjust the space between a **pair** of letters for a more visually consistent result, click the I-beam type cursor between those letters, hold down the Alt/Option key, and use an arrow key (left to tighten the space between letters or right to expand it). Using the arrows overrides the built-in metrics for the font so the space between the two letters can be adjusted. By pressing Ctrl/⌘-+ you can zoom up to see kerning details. Note that kerning is controlled separately for each pair of characters. (Kerning can also be done in the Character palette. Enter a value in the kerning box — a negative number to pull the letters closer together, a positive number to spread them apart.)

ADDING ANOTHER TYPE LAYER

The Options bar for the Type tool allows you to cancel (⊘ icon) or commit (✓ icon) the type you've been setting or editing. **After you've canceled or committed**, if you click again with the Type tool, one of two things will happen, depending on where you click:

- **If you click on or near any of the type** you've already set, you'll be back in editing mode in that type layer, and anything you type will become part of that layer.

- But **if you click away from the existing type**, a new type layer will be started.

The tricky part is that if your existing type happens to fill most of the canvas of your file, there may not be room to click far enough away from it to start a new type layer. In that case you can **temporarily turn off visibility for the existing type by clicking its Eye icon** in the Layers palette. Then use the Type tool to start your new type layer. When you finish typing, click the Eye again to toggle the other type layer's visibility back on.

If your type fills up your canvas, you can temporarily turn off its visibility (as shown here) in order to be able start another type layer, rather than edit the existing one.

6b

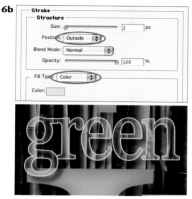

A 2-pixel Color Stroke was added.

STROKE MAGIC

The **Stroke** effect, part of Photoshop 7's Layer Styles, offers some exciting options — especially when you choose **Gradient** for the **Fill Type**. Like the Gradient found elsewhere in the program, this one offers the usual Linear, Radial, Angle, Reflected, and Diamond options. But it also offers **Shape Burst**, which is found nowhere else. The Shape Burst is like a radial gradient that conforms to the shape of the element.

Applying a Shape Burst Gradient Stroke effect with Position set to Outside can produce some interesting inline/outline effects. See also "Quick Neon" in Chapter 8.

• To adjust **tracking**, which means uniformly adjusting spacing between **all** the letters in a selected block of type, select the characters you want to track, and enter a tracking value in the Character palette (negative to tighten the spacing, positive to increase it) or hold down the Alt/Option key and press the left arrow (to tighten) or right arrow (to spread).

When the line length is close to what you want, you can use Free Transform (Ctrl/⌘-T) to finish scaling the type block to exactly the right width **5b.** The type layer remains "live" — an editable, *vector-based* entity — so applying transformations such as scaling, rotation, or skewing won't affect the quality of the edges.

Since we planned to use Overlay mode for the "green gold" layer as explained next in step 6, we chose a lighter-than-medium gray color for the type. The Swatches palette (Window, Show Swatches) provides gray swatches in 5% steps.

6 Applying shadows and color variation to the type.

Drop shadows and glows were applied to the type with Layer Styles. For the "G" layer we applied a Drop Shadow in the same way as we had for the text pad in step 3 but with different settings for Opacity (50%), Distance (30, for the offset) and Size (15, so it wasn't as diffuse). Then we clicked the Inner Glow entry in the list on the left side of the Layer Style dialog box and built the glow, using a soft brown color and Soft Light for the blend mode **6a.** We clicked OK to close the Layer Style box.

Three blend modes for layers — Screen, Overlay, and Hard Light — can be especially useful for allowing glowing color to interact with the image in layers below. For "green gold" we chose Overlay from the blend mode list at the top of the Layers palette. The "green gold" type was lighter than 50% gray, which is the neutral (invisible) color for Overlay mode. So the Overlay setting simply lightened the overall color of the background image under the type. The color and intensity of the effects in the Layer Style, described next, would add impact.

First we added a Drop Shadow, setting the Opacity (75%), Distance (16 pixels), and Size (13 pixels). For the glow inside the edges

AVOIDING TYPE DISTORTION

Resizing won't affect the edge quality of vector-based type. But it *can* affect the type's aesthetics. That's why it's important to get the size and spacing close to what you want using the Type tool, Options bar, and Character palette, rather than depending on the Transform functions. Big changes in type size require adjustment in the spacing relationships between characters in order to look good; proportions that look good small don't necessarily look good big, and vice versa. Also, drastically scaling a block of type horizontally or vertically to make it fit a certain space can differentially distort the thick and thin strokes, ruining the proportions designed into the characters.

6c *The Layers palette after Layer Styles were applied to both type layers*

7 *Setting the invitation type*

8a

Coloring a single line of type

8b

A yellow Outer Glow in Screen mode made the type stand out.

we used an Inner Glow again; we chose a golden color and experimented with the blend mode and Opacity, arriving at Hard Light mode with an Opacity setting of 30% and a smaller Size of 10 pixels. Hard Light interacted well with the Overlay mode for the layer.

Next we added a yellow stroke that would make a bright, sharp outline: We chose Stroke from the bottom of the list at the left side of the Layer Style box. In the Stroke section of the Layer Style dialog box, we chose Outside for the Position of the stroke so it would add to the characters rather than cutting into their shapes. We chose a yellow color and left the blend mode and Fill Type at the default, Normal and Color, to get a solid stroke **6b,** then clicked OK to close the dialog box **6c.**

7 Setting several lines of centered type. To set the type for the invitation, we added another type layer. But we set the color to a dark gray **7,** chose Helvetica UltraCompressed, and clicked the Center Alignment button in the Options bar. We dragged with the Type tool to define a rectangle approximately the width and depth of the area we wanted the type to fall within. We set the type, then adjusted the size and leading to match the line breaks and spacing we wanted.

8 Coloring individual lines in a block of type. To color the type, we started by drag-selecting the "Open House" type and using the color swatch to color it orange (see the "Hiding the Highlight" tip below) **8a.** Then we drag-selected the top line of type and colored it green. We added a Style to the layer, chose Outer Glow from the pop-out list, and built the glow using yellow in Screen mode with a 10-pixel Size **8b.**

9 Clipping a photo inside type. To put the golden clouds photo inside the "G," we first targeted the "G" layer, because we wanted the clouds to become a layer just above the "G." Then we clicked the clouds file's window to make it the active file, and used the Move tool to drag-and-drop the clouds into the postcard. We

---

HIDING THE HIGHLIGHT

To color type, you need to select it, then click the color swatch in the Options bar or Character palette, and choose the color you want. But the selection highlight inverts the color of the selected type and makes it impossible to see its real color. To hide the highlight, press Ctrl/⌘-H. (Notice that this is the same keyboard shortcut that works for hiding the marching ants of a selection boundary or hiding the bounding box made by the Crop tool or the Free Transform command.)

*Selected type **A**; selection highlight hidden **B**; type recolored and still active, with the highlight still hidden **C**.*

9a

9b

Adding the golden clouds image in a layer above the "G"

The finished composite after making the clipping group

reduced the Opacity of this new layer so we could see the "G" underneath. Then we used Free Transform (Ctrl/⌘-T) to scale the pasted image (by dragging or Shift-dragging a corner handle) and reposition it (by dragging inside the Transform box); we double-clicked inside the Transform box to finish the transformation **9a**.

To make it so the clouds image would show only inside the "G," we formed a clipping group (you can do this by pressing Ctrl/⌘-G or by Alt/Option-clicking the border between the image you want to "clip" and the layer directly below, which provides the clipping shape). We experimented with the Opacity but found that we liked the 75% setting **9b**. The final result is shown at the top of page 308.

CONVERTING COLORED TYPE TO SHAPES

If you want to make sure that a type layer will print as expected at the resolution of your PostScript output device, even if the correct fonts aren't available when it's output, you can easily convert it to a Shape layer by choosing Layer, Type, Convert To Shape. However, if your type layer includes more than one color of type, you have a problem to solve: Each type layer is converted into only *one* Shape layer, but each Shape layer can have only *one* color. One way to solve this problem without duplicating different lines of type to different layers is to convert the type layer to a Shape layer and then put the colors in another layer above, grouped with the Shape layer. The vector-based Shape layer will still define the high-resolution edge when the file is output in EPS, DCS, or PDF format, just as the live type did. And the fill colors will be based on the colors in the layer above.

Here's how to do it: First convert the type to a Shape layer (Layer, Type, Convert To Shape). Then add a new empty layer and create a clipping group (you can do this all in one step by Alt/Option-clicking the Create A New Layer button at the bottom of the Layers palette and clicking the "Group With Previous Layer" box in the New Layer dialog box). Working on this new empty layer, select an area just big enough to surround a piece of type you want to color, and fill the selection with the color of your choice. (Pressing Alt/Option-Delete fills an active selection with the Foreground color; click the Foreground color square in the toolbox if you want to choose a new Foreground color.) Repeat the selecting-and-filling process for each piece of type you want to color.

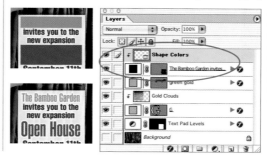

A clipping group was made to color two lines of a block of type that had been converted to a Shape layer. The image is shown here without clipping (top) and with clipping (bottom and Layers palette).

Warped Type

Overview *Set type in an image file; use Warp Text to accomplish the general distortion you want to fit the image; use the Character palette to foreshorten the type and the leading; use Free Transform for final positioning and orientation; mask out areas of the image that should appear in front of the type.*

IMAGE "Warped Type" "before" and "after" files

1a

1b

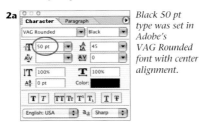

The original photo

2a

Black 50 pt type was set in Adobe's VAG Rounded font with center alignment.

2b

The image with the type layer added

JHD/ORIGINAL IMAGE: © CORBIS IMAGES ROYALTY FREE, TROPICAL ESCAPE

BESIDES BEING A FUN STARTING POINT for Web animations, the type warping function in Photoshop 7 can also help fit type to an image. If you're familiar with the "styles" available for the Warp Text function, the Arc style seems like an obvious approach to fitting type to this fish-eye view of a beach. As the project develops, however, it becomes obvious that there's more to the solution than the Warp Text command.

1 Exploring the Warp Text function. It's worth a little time to experiment with Photoshop's Warp Text, so you'll know what "envelopes" are available and how they can be reshaped to fit type to an image. To experiment, choose the Type tool and make sure the Create A Text Layer and the Horizontally Orient Text buttons are pressed at the left end of the Options bar **1a**. Then click or drag in the working window and type some characters. (**Clicking creates point type,** set line by line; you have to press Return to start each new line. **Dragging defines a bounding box for *paragraph type;*** text wraps automatically to fit within this box. When you've set some type, click the Create Warped Text button (the "T" on the arc) in the Options bar. In the Warp Text dialog box, explore the Style choices, the Horizontal and Vertical options, and the amount of Bend, Horizontal Distortion, and Vertical Distortion. That way, when you come across an image of a flag or a balloon or a curved surface like this beach photo made with a fish-eye lens **1b,** you'll have an idea how the Warp Text function can help you add display type.

A SLIGHTLY DIFFERENT WARP

Point type, which is set by *clicking* and typing with the Type tool, is spaced slightly differently than **paragraph type**, which is set by *dragging* with the Type tool to define the paragraph shape and then typing. Because of the different spacing, the Warp Text function produces slightly different results. To see if point type or paragraph type produces more pleasing results, it may be worth setting and warping type layers in both modes.

3a

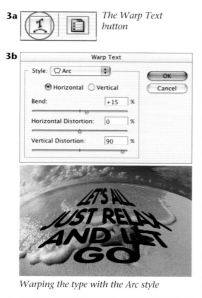

The Warp Text button

3b

Warping the type with the Arc style

4a

Reducing the size of the type line-by-line

CLICKETY-CLICK

Instead of drag-selecting type, you can accomplish many type-selecting tasks simply by clicking the mouse button:

- A **single click positions the cursor**.

- **Double-click selects the word**, defined by a space or punctuation mark or a space/punctuation combination.

- **Triple-click selects the line** of type.

- **Quadruple-click selects the paragraph** (a paragraph is defined when the Return key is pressed to start a new line).

- **Quintuple-click** (that's five!) **selects the entire text block**.

2 Adding the type. To add a type layer, choose the Type tool in the toolbox; make font, style, size, and alignment choices from the Options bar or with keyboard shortcuts, some of which can be found in the yellow tips on the next two pages.

Set up for *point type* as described in step 1. Type the characters you want, pressing the Return key to start each new line and pressing the Enter key when typesetting is complete. Spacing between lines and fine-tuning adjustments such as kerning, tracking, and baseline shift can be accomplished in the Character palette **2a,** opened by clicking the Palettes button on the Options bar. We chose VAG Rounded for the font, pressed the Caps Lock key, and typed. When your type is set, select all of it (Ctrl/⌘-A) and experiment with the size until the block of type is approximately the right size for the image **2b.**

TRYING OUT FONTS

With your Type layer active (you don't have to actually select the characters if you've *committed* the type by pressing Enter or clicking the ✔ at the right end of the Options bar), click to **highlight the font name** in the Options bar and use the **up or down arrow key** to change the font by scrolling backward or forward through the list.

HIDING THE HIGHLIGHT

To get a better look at your type as you modify it, temporarily **hide the highlighting** that shows it's selected: **Ctrl/⌘-H** is a toggle for hiding and showing the highlight.

3 Warping the type. Click the Create Warped Text button in the Options bar **3a** and choose a warping Style; we chose the Arc. Then adjust the sliders to curve the type to match the image **3b;** we used 15% Bend and 90% Vertical Distortion. Notice that the type curves as if it were on a flat horizontal surface. The warping doesn't provide the perspective that's needed in order to make the type look like it's receding. For instance, the letters don't look foreshortened — the ones at the top (in the distance) don't look shorter than the ones in the front.

4 Adjusting perspective. With the technically difficult part of the type-fitting done by the Warp Text command, you can now make a series of changes, in the order described next, to develop more realistic perspective. The values we used were arrived at by experimentation, as we kept in mind that the farther away the line of type, the greater would be the change due to perspective.

- From the next-to-bottom line to the top line, we selected each line of type and made it smaller by changing the **overall size** — 45 pt for "AND LET," 40 pt for "JUST RELAX," and 35 pt for "LET'S ALL" **4a.** (To select a line of type, you can drag the cursor over it, or use the click

CHANGING POINT SIZE

To change the point size of selected characters, use the caret keys: Press **Ctrl/⌘-Shift- >** to **increase** the size or **Ctrl/⌘-Shift- <** to decrease.

To move the cursor around in a block of text, use any of the four directional **arrow keys**.

To select characters starting from the cursor position, hold down the **Shift key with any arrow key**.

4b

Scaling the height of each line

4c

Adjusting the space below each line interactively with the baseline shift control

4d

Enlarging and slightly rotating the type

4e

Adjusting the space below each line interactively with the baseline shift control

system, as described in the "Clickety-Click" tip on page 315 or the "Type Tools Cursor Controls" tip at the left.) As you make changes to the type, you can use Ctrl/⌘-H to hide the selection highlight and get a better view of your changes.

- Next we changed the **vertical scale**, first typing a guess into the vertical scaling box and then fine-tuning with the arrow keys. Leaving the "GO" line at 100%, we changed the other lines in order — 90%, 80%, and 70% **4b**.

- The lines of type were now the right sizes, but the **spacing between lines** (the leading) hadn't changed. Instead of entering leading values in the upper left section of the Character palette, we used the baseline shift control in the lower left corner, lowering the baseline with the down arrow key **4c**. This made the process interactive — we could see the changes immediately instead of the change-and-check, change-and-check approach required for the leading box. As you change the leading, remember that you can use Ctrl/⌘-H to hide the highlight.

LEADING & BASELINE SHIFT

To reduce or increase the leading for a line of type, select one or more characters and press **Ctrl-Alt** (Windows) or **⌘-Option** (Mac) along **with the up or down arrow**.

To shift the baseline of one or more characters, select them and press **Alt/Option-Shift and the up or down arrow**.

- With the overall shape of the type panel and the size and spacing of the characters determined, we pressed the Enter key to accept the changes. For **final sizing and positioning**, we chose Edit, Free Transform. Shift-Alt/Option-dragging a corner handle outward enlarged the type block from the center outward; the W(idth) and H(eight) values in the Options bar showed that the size had increased to 130%. Dragging around outside a corner handle rotated the type 2° counterclockwise **4d**.

- The final tweaks were made by clicking between "AND" and "LET," and increasing the value in the **kerning** box in the Character palette to increase space so that when we masked the starfish (in step 6), the words would still be readable. Drag-selecting individual words, then clicking in the **tracking** box and using the up and down arrow keys completed the fine-tuning **4e**.

KERNING & TRACKING

To kern, put the Type tool cursor between the pair of letters, hold down the Alt/Option key, and use the right and left arrow keys to widen or narrow the space. To kern another letter pair, release the Alt/Option key and use the arrow keys alone to reposition the cursor, then kern again.

To track, drag the Type tool cursor over the type you want to affect, then hold down Alt/Option and use the right and left arrows.

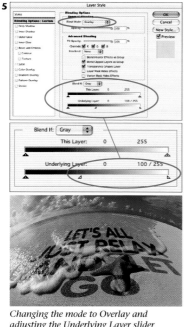

5 Blending the type into the background image. By double-clicking the name of the type layer, you can open the Layer Style dialog box to the Blending Options section. Here you can experiment to choose the blend mode for the layer, and you can also control how the type blends with the background by making changes in the Blend If section. For this image, with black type and a sandy background, we chose Overlay for the mode; it made the type darken and blend with most of the sand but allowed the lightest grains to shine through, contributing to a wet and shiny look. Because the sand is speckled light and dark, moving the Underlying Layer white slider to the left eliminated the type from the lighter specks of sand; holding down the Alt/Option key allowed the slider to split so the transition from "blended" to "non-blended" grains of sand within the letters was smooth and gradual **5.** (Soft Light mode without the Blend If changes also worked fairly well, but we preferred the higher contrast of Overlay.)

Changing the mode to Overlay and adjusting the Underlying Layer slider caused the type to blend into the sand.

6 Masking the type layer. To complete the illusion that the type is printed on the sand, we created a layer mask that fades the type with distance and that makes the starfish and water seem to be in front of the type **6.** First we added a layer mask to the type layer by clicking the Add A Mask button at the bottom of the Layers palette. Then, with black and white as Foreground and Background colors, the Gradient tool (with the Foreground To Background gradient chosen in the Options bar) was dragged from top to bottom of the mask to gradually fade the type. The starfish was outlined with the Pen tool, with the Create New Work Path icon chosen in the Options bar. The path was turned into a selection by clicking the Load Path As Selection button at the bottom of the Paths palette (opened by choosing Window, Show Paths); then the selection was filled with black by pressing Alt/Option-Delete. The water is clear, so the illusion could be completed by hand-painting the mask with the Airbrush to hide the type in areas of nearly opaque white foam.

Adding a layer mask to fade the type and "erase" it from the starfish and foam

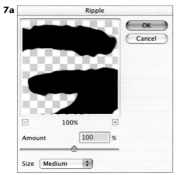

7 Rippling the type. To apply a filter to the finished type so it seemed to ripple with the wet sand, we clicked the type thumbnail in the Layers palette to activate the type itself rather than the mask and chose Filter, Distort, Ripple. A Caution box warned that the type would be rasterized; we clicked OK to proceed **7a, 7b, 7c.** *mau*

Applying the Ripple filter to the rasterized type layer using Medium for the ripple Size

After applying the Ripple filter

The Layers palette for the finished file, showing the rasterized, filtered type layer. The result is shown at the top of page 314.

Organic Graphics

Overview Import and rasterize a PostScript graphic; use the Photocopy filter on a duplicate layer to create shading; starting with another duplicate layer, separate the line work and color into two layers; add an organic background; "texturize" the graphic with a Pattern Fill layer in Overlay mode.

"**Organic Graphics**" "before" and "after" files

The original Adobe Illustrator artwork

© JHDAVIS DESIGN

The Photocopy filter was run on a duplicate of the artwork in another layer.

JHD / © TRAVELWELL MEDICAL SERVICES

THERE ARE TIMES WHEN YOU WANT to take a crisp PostScript graphic out of its slick-lined, flat-colored environment and bring it into a space with a little more texture and personality. Whether you start with clip art or with something you created yourself, once you develop a treatment that you like, you can use it to stylize an entire series of graphics. The step-by-step process presented here allows you to treat line work, color, and background separately. For a quicker, though less sophisticated, approach to customizing clip art see "Fast Filter Embellishing" on page 322.

1 Importing the PostScript artwork. Open or place your PostScript artwork in Photoshop. We opened an Illustrator file, rasterizing it at a little over 1000 pixels wide and high **1.** Our artwork was on a white background, which can be important, since some filters work differently on transparency. An approach for enhancing PostScript art using a layered file with transparency is presented in "Coloring Clip Art" on page 324.

2 Shading the edges. It's a good idea to keep an untouched version

2b

The filtered layer was put in Multiply mode at 75% Opacity.

3a

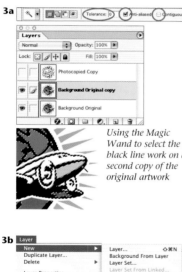

Using the Magic Wand to select the black line work on a second copy of the original artwork

3b

Cutting the selected black line work to a new layer also left the color on a layer of its own.

of the imported artwork available throughout the process of developing the Photoshop file; you can use it as the master graphic for duplicating and manipulating later, and it can also be the quickest way to recover from a mistake. So start by duplicating the artwork (drag its thumbnail to the Create A New Layer button at the bottom of the Layers palette).

Make sure black and white are the default Foreground and Background colors by pressing the "D" key. Then instantly turn this new layer into a shaded black-and-white version of the art by running the Photocopy filter (Filter, Sketch, Photocopy) **2a.** To let the color show through from below, put this filtered layer in Multiply mode. We reduced the Opacity of the layer to 75% to further soften the effect **2b.**

3 Separating the line work from the colors. Next you'll isolate the black lines on one layer and the colors on another so you can easily treat them separately. Duplicate the original artwork layer again. In the new layer, select the black line work with the Magic Wand, using these settings in the Options bar: 0 for the Tolerance, so that only 100% black will be selected when you click on a black pixel; Anti-aliased turned on, for a smooth edge; and Contiguous turned off, so that all black line work will be selected, whether it's connected to the pixel you click or not **3a.** With these settings the Magic Wand selection won't be perfect. It will be slightly smaller than the original line work overall, leaving behind thin dark edges around the color areas. But this won't be a problem because the Photocopy layer above will actually define the edges of the line work. Once the black is selected, separate it onto its own layer by choosing Layer, New, Layer Via Cut (or press Ctrl/⌘-Shift-J) **3b.**

NEW LAYERS FROM SELECTIONS

To make a **new layer by copying** a selected area of an existing one, press **Ctrl/⌘-J**.

To make a **new layer by cutting** a selected area of an existing one, press **Ctrl/⌘-Shift-J**.

3c

Visibility was turned off for the Background Original layer, Opacity was reduced to 50% for the Isolated Black Lines layer, and the Isolated Colors layer was put in Multiply mode.

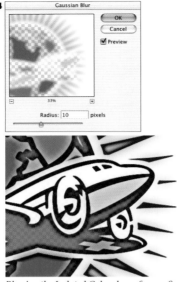

At this point we did some "housekeeping." We renamed all the Layers (to rename a layer, you can Alt/Option-double-click its name in the Layers palette to open the Layer Properties dialog box). Turn off visibility for the Background Original layer, since it won't be part of the developing artwork. Leave the Isolated Black Lines layer in Normal mode, but reduce its Opacity to 50%. In preparation for adding a new background (in step 5), change the blend mode of the Isolated Colors layer to Multiply. This will allow the new background to show through the white areas of the Isolated Colors layer and also to combine with the colors **3c**.

4 "Airbrushing" the artwork. For a soft, subtle airbrushing effect, blur the Isolated Colors layer (Filter, Blur Gaussian Blur); we set the Radius to 10 pixels to get the degree of blurring we wanted **4**.

Blurring the Isolated Colors layer for a soft, "airbrushed" look

5 Adding a new background. To create the new background layer, click on the original artwork layer, then click-drag the Create New Fill/Adjustment Layer button (the black-and-white circle) at the bottom of the Layers palette and choose Pattern. In the Pattern Fill dialog box, click the little black triangle to the right of the pattern swatch to open the palette of available patterns. We chose Wow-Wood 06 from the **Wow 7-Organic Patterns** set **5**. (If you haven't yet loaded the Wow presets from the

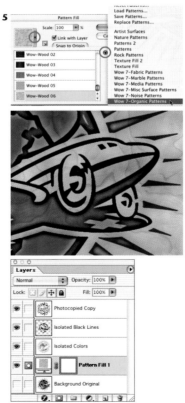

Adding a Pattern Fill layer to create a new background

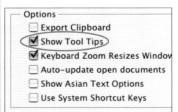

FINDING PATTERNS BY NAME

When you're looking for a particular pattern in the Patterns palette wherever it occurs in Photoshop 7, you can see all the names as well as the swatches by choosing Large List from the palette's pop-out menu. Even without using one of the List modes, if you have Show Tool Tips turned on (Edit, Preferences, General), you can see the name of a particular pattern by pausing your cursor over the swatch.

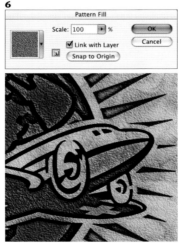

Adding a Pattern Fill layer in Overlay mode to "texturize" the entire graphic

Wow CD-ROM that comes with this book, see page 9 for instructions on how to do this.)

6 Adding texture. To add an overall texture to the graphic, activate the top layer and add a Pattern Fill layer above it. Try the Stucco pattern from the **patterns2.pat** presets file that comes with Photoshop 7, and put this gray-stucco-filled layer in Overlay mode so it contributes only its texture to the composite **6**. The result is shown at the top of page 318.

Experimenting with other textures. With your texture in a Pattern Fill layer in Overlay mode, it's easy to try out other textures — almost like having a "live" filter layer. Double-click the thumbnail for the Pattern Fill layer and choose other patterns from the various Wow Patterns presets. We tried some from the **Wow 7-Noise Patterns** set, as well as from the **Wow 7- Media Patterns** set and the **Wow 7-Organic Patterns** set — the same pattern used for the background — which exaggerated the wood grain and brightened the colors.

*Substituting from the **Wow 7-Noise Patterns** set in the top Pattern Fill layer results in a somewhat subtler texture.*

*Using Wow-Canvas+Brush Overlay-Medium from the **Wow 7-Media Patterns** set in the top Pattern Fill layer adds the look of thick paint or a hand-stuccoed wall.*

*Applying Wow-Wood 06 from the **Wow 7-Organic Patterns** set in the top Pattern Fill layer enhances the wood grain created by the same pattern used as the background.*

Fast Filter Embellishing

Some of Photoshop's filters are especially good for turning flat PostScript line art or rasterized Shape layers into something more organic, textured, or dimensional. Several of these filter treatments are shown on these two pages, along with the settings used to achieve them; in the toolbox the Foreground and Background colors were set to the default black and white. These treatments won't give you the individual "personalities" for line work, color fills, and background that are developed in "Organic Graphics" on page 318. But one of them may offer a quick solution, applied to one graphic or to a series.

IMAGE **Fast Filters.psd** file

© JHDAVIS DESIGN

We started with the Travelwell logo (shown above), which was created in Illustrator and rasterized by using Photoshop's File, Place command as described in "Organic Graphics" on page 318. Then choices were made from the Filter menu.

Artistic: Neon Glow (Glow Size, 5; Glow Brightness, 15; Glow Color, default blue)

Artistic: Rough Pastels (Stroke Length, 6; Stroke Detail, 4; Texture, Canvas; Scaling, 100%; Relief, 20; Light Dir., Top Left)

Brush Strokes: Spatter (Spray Radius, 5; Smoothness, 10)

Distort: Pinch (Amount, 100%)

Artistic: Plastic Wrap (Highlight Strength, 20; Detail, 7; Smoothness, 7)

Artistic: Sponge (Brush Size, 0; Definition, 25; Smoothness, 1)

Distort: Diffuse Glow (Graininess, 10; Glow Amount, 10; Clear Amount, 20)

Distort: Spherize (Amount, 100%; Mode, Normal)

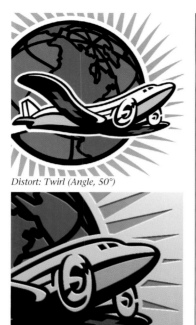

Distort: Twirl (Angle, 50°)

Pixelate: Color Halftone (Default)

Pixelate: Pointillize (Cell Size, 5)

Render: Lighting Effects (Light Type, Spotlight, from upper right; Texture Channel, Green)

Sharpen: Unsharp Mask (Amount, 300%; Radius, 50 pixels; Threshold, 100 levels)

Sketch: Chalk & Charcoal (Charcoal Area, 6; Chalk Area, 6; Stroke Pressure, 1)

Sketch: Conté Crayon (Foreground Level, 11; Background Level, 7; Texture, Canvas; Scaling, 100%; Relief, 4; Light Dir, Top Right)

Sketch: Halftone Pattern (Size, 1; Contrast, 10; Pattern Type, Line)

Sketch: Note Paper Image Balance, 26; Graininess, 15; Relief, 10)

COMBINING FILTER EFFECTS

If you find two filters that you like, but neither is *exactly* right, try layering them, reducing the Opacity of the top layer.

Diffuse Glow at 75% Opacity, layered over Color Halftone

Neon Glow at 75% Opacity, layered over Plastic Wrap

Coloring
Clip Art

Overview *Divide the artwork into the layers you'll need for treating elements with separate Layer Styles; create a white-filled base so you can add color on a separate layer in Multiply mode; apply Layer Styles to add dimension.*

"Color Embossing" "before" and "after" files

IHD

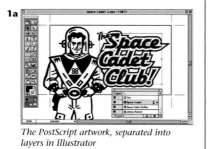

1a

The PostScript artwork, separated into layers in Illustrator

1b

Saving the file in Photoshop PSD format from Illustrator

1c

The layered file opened in Photoshop, with a white-filled background layer added

YOU CAN START WITH YOUR OWN EPS ARTWORK created in a Post-Script drawing program, or take advantage of the zillions of clip art files out there just waiting for the kinds of coloring and special effects that Photoshop can do so well. We started with a clip art space man and a custom-designed logotype, then separated the artwork into the appropriate layers in Adobe Illustrator, and finally moved to Photoshop. The exact step-by-step coloring process will depend on the complexity of your original artwork and how it was created. But two concepts covered here can be useful regardless of the file you start with: (1) isolating shapes that can be filled with color on a separate layer in Multiply mode so there are no gaps between the color and the black "linework" and (2) using Layer Styles to add more color, dimension, and lighting.

1 Preparing the art. The first step is to create and organize the artwork in Illustrator and save it in Photoshop PSD format. We designed a logotype and added it to the Image Club Graphics space man. We used Illustrator's layers to sort the objects that made up the file, using as few layers as we could that would still isolate the areas that would need independent color fills or different Layer Styles. We ended up with four layers, three of which contained various parts of the logotype, and one with the Johnny Rocket artwork **1a.**

Next we exported the file in Photoshop 5 PSD format (we used Illustrator 9, but in Illustrator 10 it's called simply Photoshop PSD), choosing RGB for the Color Mode, setting the Resolution at High, and clicking the check boxes to turn on Anti-alias (for smooth edges) and Write Layers (to translate the Illustrator layers directly into Photoshop layers) **1b.** The resulting Photoshop file kept the same layer names. We added a white-filled layer called Background by Alt/Option-clicking the Create A New Layer button at the bottom of the Layers palette, naming the layer and clicking OK, then press-

2a

Making only the Johnny Rocket artwork layer visible

2b

Ctrl/⌘-clicking on the composite color channel to load the luminosity of the Johnny Rocket layer as a selection

2c

The inverted luminosity selection filled with black on a new transparent layer to make artwork that could be acted on by a Layer Style later

3

The finished white base layer, viewed alone

ing "D" for Default Foreground/ Background colors and pressing Ctrl/⌘-Delete to fill with the Background color. In the Layers palette we dragged the new layer to the bottom of the stack **1c.**

2 Making black-on-transparent artwork. The original Post-Script artwork for the space man had been composed of stacked black-filled and white-filled shapes, a typical way of creating a vector-based drawing and a format that often results when ink drawings are scanned and autotraced in a PostScript drawing or tracing program. There was no easy way to delete the white shapes and still keep the black artwork intact in Illustrator. But in our Photoshop file we needed to have the black artwork on its own transparent layer so we could use its shapes to apply Layer Styles.

To isolate the black "line work," we loaded the luminosity of the Johnny Rocket layer as a selection, as follows: First we clicked to turn off visibility for all layers except Johnny Rocket **2a.** Then in the Channels palette we Ctrl/⌘-clicked on the RGB composite channel's name to load its luminosity as a selection **2b.** That selected all the white areas in the layer and left the black unselected. We inverted the selection (Ctrl/⌘-Shift-I) so that the black was selected. Now we added a new layer above the Johnny Rocket layer by Alt/Option-clicking the Create A New Layer button; we named this layer "Johnny Rocket Lines." In this new layer, with black as our Foreground color in the toolbox, we pressed Alt/ Option-Delete to fill the selection with black **2c.**

3 Making a white base layer for the art. Now we had the black linework isolated on its own new Johnny Rocket Lines layer, and the black-and-white art on the original Johnny Rocket layer below. The process of adding color to the artwork (in step 4) depends on using Multiply mode so that solid color will extend all the way to the black "lines," so there won't be a fringe of antialiasing between the color and the black. But in order for Multiply mode to work, there has to be something opaque underneath for the color to affect. The white-filled Background layer would have worked in this example, except that we wanted to use a color gradient in this layer eventually. What we needed was a white-filled shape that would underlie the space man and logotype but sit above the background.

The original Johnny Rocket black-and-white artwork was still in the layer just above the white-filled background. To turn this layer into a white base for the space man, we activated the layer by clicking its name in the Layers palette. With white as the Background color in the toolbox we pressed Ctrl/⌘-Shift-Delete to fill all the nontransparent areas on this layer with white. (Including the Shift

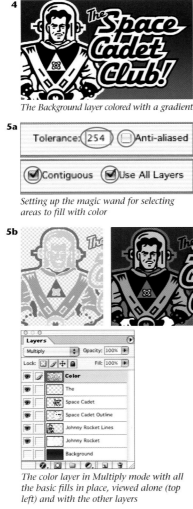

4

The Background layer colored with a gradient

5a

Tolerance: 254   ☐ Anti-aliased

☑ Contiguous   ☑ Use All Layers

Setting up the magic wand for selecting areas to fill with color

5b

The color layer in Multiply mode with all the basic fills in place, viewed alone (top left) and with the other layers

6a

Turning on Preserve Transparency during "fine-tuning," to keep paint from going outside the color-filled shapes

key in the keyboard shortcut temporarily turns on the Lock Transparent Pixels function, so the transparent areas stay transparent.)

With the developing white base layer still active, we next Ctrl/⌘-clicked on the Space Cadet Outline layer, and Shift-Ctrl/⌘-clicked the "The" layer. This loaded these layers' transparency masks as a combined selection, which we could then fill with white in our developing base layer **3**.

4 Coloring the background. With a white base pad in place, you can color the background layer. To make a gradient-filled background, we activated the Background layer, chose Foreground and Background colors, and used the Gradient tool (with Linear and Foreground To Background chosen in the Options bar) to fill the layer with a gradient **4**. (We might have used a Gradient Fill layer here instead, but we needed a pixel-based layer because we planned to add some painted stars later, so we used the Gradient tool on the existing background layer.)

5 Coloring the artwork. Next add a layer for the color. We activated the layer at the top of the Layers palette, added a new layer above it by clicking the Create A New Layer button, and chose Multiply for the new layer's blend mode.

The next step is to select and color each enclosed shape in the artwork. First set up the magic wand, as follows **5a:** Choose the Magic Wand in the toolbox. In the Options bar turn on Contiguous and Use All Layers, turn off Anti-aliased, and set the Tolerance at 254.

• The **Contiguous** setting will limit the selection to the single black-line-enclosed area clicked with the wand.

• The **Use All Layers** setting will let the wand "see" the artwork in all layers below to make the selection.

• **Turning off Anti-aliased** will make a selection that will fill entirely with opaque color, rather than including some partially transparent pixels at the edges. This will prevent the edge from getting messy if you select and reselect, fill and refill a selection as you experiment with color.

• Setting the **Tolerance at 254** means that if you click on a white area, all pixels except solid black ones will be included in the selection — in other words, the selection will encroach into the black linework to include all of its antialiasing pixels, thus making the color-filled area overlap the black "line work" slightly, trapping the color-and-line interface.

Click each black-line-enclosed transparent area with the magic wand, Shift-clicking if you want to add another area to a selection to be filled with a particular color. Then choose a Foreground color and press Alt/Option-Delete to fill the selection **5b.** You can temporarily switch from Multiply to Normal mode and reduce the

6b

Tolerance: 254 ☐ Anti-aliased

☑ Contiguous ☐ Use All Layers

Setting up the magic wand to select filled areas on the color layer only

6c

Filling the area behind the type with a gradient

6d

Range: Midtones ▾ Exposure: 50% ▸

Fine-tuning the color layer, with dodge-and-burn shading (Note also the airbrushed highlight on the helmet.)

6e

The finished, fine-tuned color layer, viewed alone (top) and with the other layers

Opacity of the color layer to see how the edges of the colors overlap the black lines. (The reason to use the Magic Wand and then fill, rather than using the Paint Bucket at the same settings mentioned, is that you can be sure of what areas will be filled *before* you do the fill. This can save some undoing and experimenting.)

6 Refining the color. To fine-tune the color, Lock Transparent Pixels for the color layer (by clicking the leftmost box near the top of the Layers palette) **6a** to prevent "coloring outside the lines." Use the Magic Wand again to select the individual color patches if you need a selection to fill, but this time turn off Use All Layers in the Options bar, so the wand will only "look at" the active layer — the color layer in this case — as it makes selections. Leave Contiguous turned on and leave the Tolerance at 254 so that each click of the wand selects *all* the color that's inside the clicked area and surrounded by the transparent gaps — even if you've filled the area with a gradient, as we planned to **6b.** Select and paint or refill as you like. We started by adding a yellow-to-green Linear gradient to the outline area around the "Space Cadet Club!" type **6c.** We clicked with the Airbrush and white paint to make a highlight on the helmet. And we used the Dodge and Burn tools with a soft brush tip at a low Exposure setting, set to Midtones because of the particular colors we were working on, to lighten and darken various areas to create shading **6d, 6e.**

7 Adding a Layer Style. When you think the coloring is complete — because of the way you've constructed the color layer, you

7a

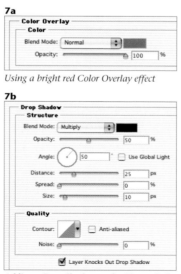

Color Overlay
Color
Blend Mode: Normal ▾
Opacity: ──────── 100 %

Using a bright red Color Overlay effect

7b

Drop Shadow
Structure
Blend Mode: Multiply ▾
Opacity: ──────── 50 %
Angle: ⟲ 50 ° ☐ Use Global Light
Distance: ── 25 px
Spread: ── 0 %
Size: ── 10 px
Quality
Contour: ▾ ☐ Anti-aliased
Noise: ── 0 %
☑ Layer Knocks Out Drop Shadow

Adding a Drop Shadow to the "Space Cadet Club!" logotype to make it seem to stand out from the elements behind it

7c

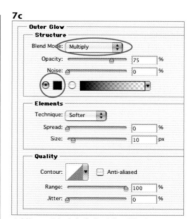

Outer Glow
Structure
Blend Mode: Multiply ▾
Opacity: ──────── 75 %
Noise: ── 0 %
⊙ ■ ○ ▾
Elements
Technique: Softer ▾
Spread: ── 0 %
Size: ── 10 px
Quality
Contour: ▾ ☐ Anti-aliased
Range: ──────── 100 %
Jitter: ── 0 %

Adding a "dark halo" with a black Outer Glow in Multiply mode

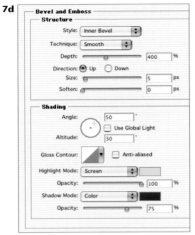

7d

A Smooth Inner Bevel with a yellow Highlight in Screen mode and a Purple shadow in Color mode added dimension and more lighting to the logotype.

8

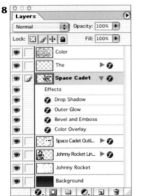

The final Layers palette, with Layer Styles applied to the separate elements of the artwork

9

Close-up of the finished artwork with Color Overlay, Drop Shadow, "dark halo" (provided by an Outer Glow), lighting from above and below (provided by an Inner Bevel), and stars painted onto the gradient-filled background

can always go back and recolor later — you can add dimensionality with Layer Styles. Because we had separated the art and logotype elements into Illustrator layers at the beginning of the project, we could fine-tune the Layer Style for each element separately, adding to the back-to-front layered effect we were creating in the artwork.

You can add a Layer Style by clicking the Add A Layer Style button (the "*f*") at the bottom of the Layers palette and choosing from the pop-out menu of effects. The most pronounced layer effects in our artwork were added to the main "Space Cadet Club!" logotype. We assigned color to the logotype with the Color Overlay effect **7a,** which made it easy to experiment with the main fill color as we adjusted the dimensional effects, all within the Layer Style dialog box.

We chose Drop Shadow from the pop-out menu and dragged in the working window to offset the shadow down and to the left, resulting in a relatively large Distance setting (25 pixels). We reduced the Opacity to 50% to soften the lighting **7b.**

To make a "dark halo" around all sides of the lettering to help add dimension, we clicked on Outer Glow in the list on the left side of the dialog box. In the Outer Glow section of the Layer Style dialog we changed the Blend Mode from the default Screen to Multiply (so the "glow" would darken rather than lighten); we clicked the color swatch and chose black, the same color we had used for the Drop Shadow **7c.**

We used Bevel And Emboss to detail the edge, choosing the Inner Bevel and using yellow for the Highlight and a bright purple for the Shadow color, putting the Shadow in Color mode to override the Color Overlay color on the shadow edge of the bevel, to make it look as if another light source was shining from below **7d.**

8 Adding more Layer Styles. A shadow and slight embossing were applied to the Johnny Rocket line work layer. The Drop Shadow was given a lower Distance setting (5 pixels) than for the logotype; this adds to the illusion that the artwork is closer to the card surface than the logotype is. The Bevel And Emboss Inner Bevel was used with a magenta Highlight in Screen mode and a violet Shadow, also in Screen mode, which again looked like additional light sources. Using a lower Size setting (3 instead of 5) made the bevel look narrower than the bevel on the logotype, so the logotype looks like it stands up farther off the card.

Drop Shadow and Bevel And Emboss effects were also added to the outline behind the logotype and "The" type layers, which also included an outline. The Drop Shadow for each was almost identical to the one for the logotype **8.**

9 Finishing. To finish coloring the artwork, we added stars to the background layer **9.** *Wow!*

Crafting a Neon Glow

Overview *Prepare the type or Shape; add a Layer Style with Inner Glow (to light the neon tubing) and Outer Glow and Drop Shadow (to light the wall); reshape the "tubing" with the Pen tool; add the wall supports.*

"**Neon Glow**" "before" and "after" files

1a

The paths drawn in Illustrator, stroked, and given round end caps and joins

1b

Uniting the paths after outlining the strokes

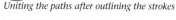

1c

Pasting the copied path as a Shape layer

1d

Scaling the new Shape layer

IN PHOTOSHOP 7 THERE ARE MANY WAYS TO CREATE NEON effects for type or graphics, including the one shown in "Quick Neon" in Chapter 8. But the neon for the sign shown above comes from a Shape layer treated with a Layer Style. The Style consists of an Inner Glow based on a gradient to simulate the neon gas glowing inside glass tubes, as well as a solid Outer Glow and a Drop Shadow in Color Dodge mode to light up a textured surface. The neon is vector- and Style-based so we could easily scale it down and change the Style to create an "off" state and a partly lit state in order to create an animation. ***Note***: You can open the **Neon Glow-After.psd** file for reference to the "live" Layer Styles as you follow the step-by-step instructions.

Here the goal is to communicate the concept of flashing neon, but with additional hand-detailing the neon could be made more photorealistic (Bert Monroy, master of photorealism, adds the "grunge" and other detail needed to make neon tubes look real; you can see some of his neon sign work on pages 288–289.)

1 Preparing the "tubes." Start by importing shapes or creating them in Photoshop, or setting type to serve as the basis for your neon tubing. We drew the custom lettering and symbol in Adobe Illustrator, using a series of stroked,

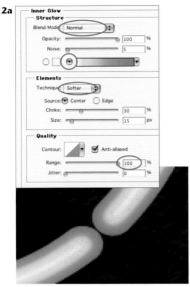

2a

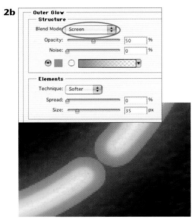

Lighting and rounding the neon tube with an Inner Glow

2b

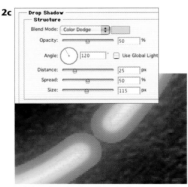

Casting light on the wall with an Outer Glow

2c

Brightening the detail in the background

single paths, with round end caps set in Illustrator's Stroke palette to simulate the tube ends **1a.**

We wanted to import the stroked paths into Photoshop without losing either their strokes or the vector-based characteristics that would make it possible to reshape and resize the neon. However, if you copy stroked paths from Illustrator and paste them into Photoshop as Shape layers, the strokes are lost in the translation. So we prepared the Illustrator artwork by converting the stroked paths into outlined shapes (Object, Path, Outline Stroke).

Next, to make the shapes into a unified graphic without overlapping paths, we selected all the paths (Ctrl/⌘-A) and used the Unite button in the Pathfinder palette **1b.** We copied this graphic (Ctrl/⌘-C), and pasted it into a Photoshop file (in Photoshop choose Edit, Paste, Paste As: Shape Layer) **1c** (See tip on page 306, "Pasting from Illustrator 10"). If you need to scale the Shape layer after pasting, use Free Transform (Ctrl/⌘-T) **1d;** you may need to enlarge the working window beyond your canvas area to see the corners of the Transform box so you can Alt/Option-Shift-drag to shrink the new Shape layer toward the center to fit the canvas. Double-click inside the Transform box or press the Enter key to finish the transformation.

Our background was a scanned texture, with dramatic spotlighting added with the Lighting Effects filter. (For pointers on using this filter, see "Lighting Effects and Other Render Filters" on page 210.)

2 Creating the neon Layer Style. With your graphic in place and its layer active, click the *"f"* button at the bottom of the Layers palette and choose **Inner Glow** from the pop-out list, to open the Layer Style dialog box to the Inner Glow section. In the Structure section of the box, set the Blend Mode to Normal and the Opacity to 100%, so the neon gradient you add will completely override the existing color of your graphic. Click the button to choose the **Gradient** rather than solid color, and choose or create a gradient that goes from white-hot to your darkest color (in our gradient this was red), through one or more intermediate colors (in this case yellow and orange). You can click the tiny triangle to the right of the gradient swatch to open the Gradient palette. If you don't find the gradient you want in the palette, click the circled triangle at the top right, choose Wow 7-Gradients; or you can close the palette and click the active swatch itself to open the Gradient Editor and build your own neon gradient.

In the Elements section of the Inner Glow section, choose **Softer** for the Technique, because this choice will apply the gradient to look less like parallel stroking and more like variable glowing. Choose **Center** for the Source (so the gradient goes from white in the center of the tube to color at the edges); if you've accidentally built your gradient in reverse, you can use Edge instead of Center. In the Quality section, set the **Range** to 100% so the entire gradient will be available for coloring the tube. Then, back in the Elements

3a

Editing the path to create "creases"

3b

The completed neon tubing

4

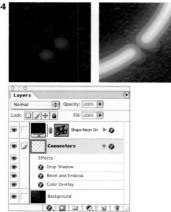

The connectors layer completed the neon image shown at the top of page 329. The "styled" connectors are shown here without (top left) and with the neon layer.

section, set the Choke at 0 temporarily, and adjust the Size until the white-to-color transition at the center of your neon looks right; then adjust the Choke to control how wide the outermost color will be, before the gradient transition begins. You can "jockey" the **Size and Choke** until you get the result you want. We found that for our thin neon tubes and our gradient, using a Choke setting of 30% worked well to "round" the tubes **2a.**

When the Inner Glow is as you like it, choose **Outer Glow** from the list at the left side of the Layer Style dialog box. Set the Blend Mode to Screen so the glow will light up the dark background behind the neon. We used a solid red color, with the **Spread** set to 0 to make the glow as "soft" as possible and minimize any abrupt halo effect. We set the Opacity at 50%, though you can increase this if you're working on a very dark background or if you want a more dramatic glow. We experimented with the Range and settled on the 50% default setting **2b.**

To make the glow outside the tube more realistic, we added a yellow **Drop Shadow**. Since the **Color Dodge** blend mode lightens the color in layers underneath and intensifies contrast, it worked with the yellow to create the effect of the lit neon tubing lighting up the surface, showing off its inherent detail **2c.** For a "straight-on" view, the Distance (the offset) should be set at 0, but since we were trying to create the illusion of looking up at the sign, we set the Angle and Distance to shift this additional glow to the right and down. We set the Size quite large (115) and used a Spread of 50%.

3 Fine-tuning the tubes. With the tubes lit, you can now make adjustments to their shapes to add realism. Activate the Shape layer by clicking its rightmost thumbnail in the Layers palette; the path will also show in the working window. (If you started with live type in Photoshop, you can convert it to a Shape layer in order to alter the characters; choose Layer, Type, Convert To Shape.) Choose the Pen tool; the Options bar will be in Edit mode. Hold down the Ctrl/⌘ key to toggle the Pen to the Direct Selection tool (the hollow arrow) and click on the path to show the control points. To make the Layer Style follow the creases characteristic of bent tubing, we added a point on each side of each point that controlled a sharp inner corner of the cocktail glass. Then by holding down the Ctrl/⌘ key again, we could move these points and the original point to make the crease **3a** and complete the neon tubes **3b.**

4 Connecting the tubing to the wall. To simulate the connections to the wall, you can simply create round dots at the attachment points and add a Layer Style **4.** We made ours by activating the background layer and adding another layer above it by clicking the Create A New Layer button at the bottom of the Layers palette, then painting with the 19-pixel hard round brush and black paint. We added a Style to apply a simple bevel and shadow for dimensionality. *Wow!*

Designing for Scalability & Animation

Overview *Import vector-based artwork and separate it into components; treat each component with a scalable Layer Style; create a layer for each frame of a planned animation; transform the "frame" layers to put the animation into perspective; scale the graphics for multiple uses.*

"Scalable Design" "before" and "after" files

1

The original Adobe Illustrator elements

2a

Paste

Paste As:
- ○ Pixels
- ○ Path
- ● Shape Layer

[OK]
[Cancel]

Pasting the copied graphic into the Photoshop file from Illustrator

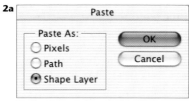

2b

The Shape layer created by pasting the graphic

A TYPICAL LOGO PROJECT MIGHT START OUT as a color graphic designed for a business card and stationery — about an inch to an inch-and-a-half across at 300 dpi. But then you might need a version for a CD-ROM splash screen, which means it can be the same pixel size (about 350 pixels) but at 72 dpi. And now the client wants it animated. You might as well use the animated version on the Web site, too, but it will have to be smaller — say about 100 pixels. Next you'll need a brochure cover, a poster, and — who knows? — maybe a billboard!

Because of the scaling required for the CAFFEIN³ logo's different uses, and because we would need to distort and rotate portions of it for the animation, the smart approach was to create the design using Shape layers and Layer Styles, both of which can be changed repeatedly without the deterioration that's typical when you manipulate pixel-based images.

1 Planning. We wanted to take our flat graphic **1** and turn it into something dimensional and dynamic. Even in its flat state, the gear wheel implied energy and motion. But by combining the central parts of the design into a sphere and tilting the gear forward to rotate around it as shown above, we could give all that energy more purpose and direction. Getting the gear to rotate in perspective takes some advance thinking and planning — you have to create the rotation frames *before* you tilt the gear into position. That's because it's easy to rotate a graphic in the plane of your canvas, but it's pretty much impossible in Photoshop to do the rotation in any plane that extends into and out of the image.

2c

The graphic layer duplicated three times

2d

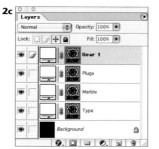

You can delete a graphic element by selecting it with the Direct Selection tool and pressing Delete twice.

2e

Before

After

Removing all the components except the logotype from one of the layers

3a

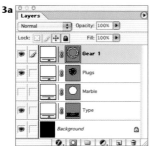

All four component layers after the deletions

2 Deconstructing the graphic into its components. Create or import the graphic you want to "dimensionalize." Working in Adobe Illustrator we designed the logo components, selected all (Ctrl/⌘-A), and copied to the clipboard (Ctrl/⌘-C). (See Illustrator 10 tip on page 306). In Photoshop we set the Foreground color to white. Then we started a new file with a black-filled *Background*. We pasted the copied graphics as a Shape layer (Edit, Paste, Paste As: Shape Layer) **2a;** the Shape layer was white (and therefore so was the graphic), since white was the current Foreground color **2b.**

After the graphic is pasted in, you can scale it if necessary (press Ctrl/⌘-T for Free Transform, Shift-drag a corner handle to scale, and double-click in the Transform box to complete the transformation).

To separate the individual elements of the current single Shape layer into multiple Shape layers, you can first duplicate it to make as many layers as you will have parts, and then delete all the unwanted elements from each layer, leaving behind the appropriate component. For instance, we wanted to be able to handle the gear, the electric plugs, the circle-soon-to-be-sphere, and the type separately, so we needed a total of four Shape layers. You can make the duplicate layers in the Layers palette by simply dragging the Shape layer's *name* or *Fill* thumbnail (*not* the vector path thumbnail) to the Create A New Layer button at the bottom of the palette. If you want to name each layer as you create it, instead of dragging, just right-click (or

To delete elements from a multi-component Shape layer, first make sure the vector mask is active (click its thumbnail in the Layers palette once or twice, until you see a double border around it). Then use the Direct Selection tool to select one or more paths by clicking, Shift-clicking, or drag-surrounding the paths. Finally, press the Delete key twice.

The Direct Selection tool

As you delete parts of a compound path that makes up the vector mask of a Shape layer, Photoshop will automatically invert the positive/negative relationship of the elements. That is, as you eliminate a positive (filled) shape, the negative (transparent) shape inside it becomes positive (filled), the one inside that becomes negative, and so on. A compound path can occur when you paste a complex graphic from the clipboard as a Shape layer (Edit, Paste, As: Shape Layer). Inside Photoshop you create such a path when you make cut-outs in a Shape layer by choosing Exclude Overlapping Shape Areas in the Options bar when you use the Shape or Pen tools to add to the Shape layer. (If instead you create cut-outs with the Subtract From Shape Areas option, this positive/negative relationship doesn't occur.)

The graphic on the left is formed by a white-filled Shape layer over a black background. When the large white circle is deleted, the plugs and the atom rings become white-filled, as shown on the right.

3b

*Layer Styles applied to the graphics layers. (See **Scalable Design-After.psd**.)*

4a

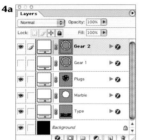

The Gear layer was duplicated to begin the process of creating frames for the animation.

4b

Rotating the Gear 2 layer

Control-click on a Mac with a one-button mouse) on the name of the Shape layer to open the Duplicate Layer dialog box. There you can name the layer according to the part of the graphic it will hold and click OK **2c.**

To delete parts from a layer, click the vector mask thumbnail once or twice — until you see a double border around the thumbnail and you see the path in the working window. Now you can click with the Direct Selection tool (the hollow arrow) **2d** to select a part you want to remove, or drag around more than one part at once; or Shift-click or Shift-drag to add more parts to the selection. Then delete them by pressing the Delete key twice (the first Delete removes the specific segment of the path you clicked on, and the second Delete removes the rest of the selected path **2e).** As we deleted parts, the positive/negative relationship of the parts changed — when we deleted the outer positive (white) gear shape, the interior circle became the positive shape and filled with white, and the elements inside it (atom and plugs) became transparent, allowing the black background to show through (see the "Deleting Compound Paths" tip on page 333).

3 Styling the parts. With the separate graphic layers prepared **3a,** now you can add color, dimension, texture, and lighting by applying a Layer Style to each of your graphics layers. For each layer you can choose a Style from the Wow presets, or design your own custom styles as we did here. ***Note***: For reference to the details of the "live" Layer Styles used in this piece, you can open the **Scalable Design-After.psd** file.

Knowing that we wanted to be able to scale our Styles along with the graphics, we were careful not to use any pixel-based effects in our Layer Styles. The Pattern Overlay and Texture effects include pixel-based patterns and consequently are subject to the same "softening" or deterioration that any pixel-based elements suffer.

For all the styles, the Bevel And Emboss Altitude was set high (70°), to bring the bevel highlights created by the Bevel And Emboss effects on the Marble and Gear layers up off the edges and onto the surface **3b.**

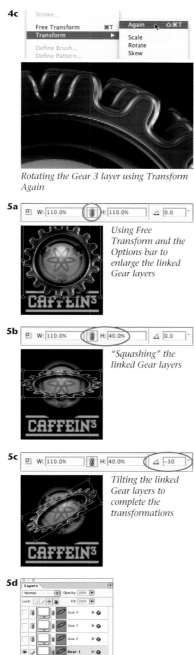

4c

Stroke...

Free Transform   ⌘T   Again   ⇧⌘T
Transform   ▶   Scale
Define Brush...   Rotate
Define Pattern...   Skew

Rotating the Gear 3 layer using Transform Again

5a

W: 110.0%   ⓛ   H: 110.0%   △ 0.0

Using Free Transform and the Options bar to enlarge the linked Gear layers

5b

W: 110.0%   ⓛ   H: 40.0%   △ 0.0

"Squashing" the linked Gear layers

5c

W: 110.0%   ⓛ   H: 40.0%   △ -30

Tilting the linked Gear layers to complete the transformations

5d

The file with all the layers in place after transforming the linked Gear layers

4 Creating the "frames" for the animation. Now the planning that was done in step 1 becomes important. In the CAFFEIN[3] logo the layers required for animating the gear wheel needed to be made at this point while the wheel was still parallel to the plane of the canvas. We needed only enough frames to produce a smooth clockwise rotation of the gear from one position to the next — that is, to rotate the gear until the tooth in the top position had moved to coincide with the next tooth position. When we animated the rotation in ImageReady, we could simply replay these frames continuously for a smooth rotation. We figured that the total angle we needed to rotate was 20° (360° in a circle ÷ 18 teeth = 20° per tooth position). We needed the smallest number of frames that would produce a smooth rotation and that would divide into 20 evenly; we settled on four frames (20° ÷ 4 frames = 5° per frame).

The Gear 1 layer itself would serve as the first frame. To get the second frame, we Alt/Option-dragged the name of the Gear layer to the Create A New Layer button at the bottom of the Layers palette and gave the layer a name ("Gear 2") in the Duplicate Layer dialog box **4a.** To rotate this new layer we used Free Transform, pressing Ctrl/⌘-T and typing "5" for the Set Rotation value in the Options bar **4b.**

We made the third Gear layer by Alt/Option-dragging the second Gear layer's name to the Create A New Layer button. To rotate this new gear layer 5° more, we used Transform Again (you can choose it from the Edit menu, or press Ctrl/⌘-Shift-T) **4c.** We created the fourth Gear layer by duplicating Gear 3 and rotating the copy another 5°.

5 Putting the rotation in perspective. Once all the rotation layers are complete, you can then scale and skew the whole set of rotation elements. First link all the layers in the rotation; we linked our four Gear layers by clicking on the name of one of them to make it the active layer, then clicking in the column to the right of the Eye in each of the three other layers. Then we turned off visibility for three of the Gear layers (by clicking their Eye icons) for a better view of the transformations to come. We transformed the linked Gear layers, first enlarging them to put a little more space between the gear and the sphere, then "squashing" to get the look of a ring-shaped object in perspective, and finally tilting. We did this as follows: Choose Edit, Free Transform or press Ctrl/⌘-T; in the Options bar click the link button between the W(idth) and H(eight) boxes for proportional scaling. Then enter a value for either parameter (we used 110%) **5a.** Next click the button again to *unlink* the two dimensions, and enter a reduced "H" value (we used 40%) **5b.** Finally, enter a Set Rotation angle value (we used –30°) **5c,** and finalize the transformation (you can do this by clicking the ✓ at the right end of the Options bar, or press the Enter key) **5d.**

6 Cleaning up. At this point you may need to rearrange or adapt some of the elements of your design to fit with the new orientation

6

The rearranged and cropped logo

7a

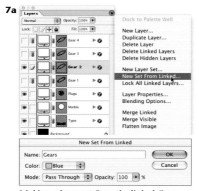

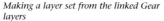

Making a layer set from the linked Gear layers

7b

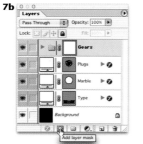

A vector mask was added to the layer set by Ctrl/⌘-clicking.

7c

Selecting the vector mask of the Marble layer, to be copied and pasted as the layer clipping path for the set

7d

The vector mask showed the gear wheel only inside the bounds of the marble.

of the rotating element. For instance, we used the Move tool to drag our type upward, closer to the bottom of the sphere. We also used the Rectangular Marquee to select the logo and just a little space around it, then chose Edit, Crop to get rid of the extra margins **6**.

7 Masking the rotating element. The next challenge was to make the rotating element (our gear wheel) seem to surround the central graphic. To make a single mask that would accomplish this for all four layers that comprised the rotating gear, we would collect the Gear layers in a layer set and then mask the set. With one of the Gear layers active, we chose New Set From Linked in the Layers palette's pop-out menu **7a**. We also color-coded the other elements in the composition by Alt/Option-double-clicking on each layer's name to open the Layer Properties dialog box, where we could choose a color.

Then we used the path from the Marble layer as the basis for creating the mask for the Gears set, as follows: In the Layers palette we first clicked on the folder icon for the layer set and Ctrl/⌘-clicked the Add A Mask button to add an empty vector mask to the folder **7b**. (Without the Ctrl/⌘ key a pixel-based layer mask would have been added instead of a path-based vector mask.) Then we clicked on the vector mask thumbnail for the Marble layer to show its path in the working window; we used the Path Component Selection tool (the solid arrow) to select the path **7c**. Then we copied it (Ctrl/⌘-C), clicked on the thumbnail for the mask for the layer set, and pasted the copied path (Ctrl/⌘-V). At this point the mask "clipped" off the edges of the gear, showing the gear only *inside* the circular outline of the Marble **7d**. To invert the vector mask so that what was currently revealed became hidden and vice versa, we activated the vector nask and clicked the Subtract From Shape Area button in the Path Component Selection tool's Options bar **7e**.

Now we needed to modify the vector mask so that it hid only the part of the gear ring "behind" the marble and revealed the front. We knew we could remove half of the circle from the vector mask by deleting one of the four control points from its path. To remove a "tilted" half **7f**, we first rotated the circular path to the same –30° tilt as the gear (with the vector mask active, press Ctrl/⌘-T and enter –30° for the Set Rotation angle in the Options bar), so the bottom point would be in the right place in relation to the tilt of the gear. Then we used the Direct Selection tool to select this bottom point and pressed Delete **7g**.

8 Resizing the file. To make the 100-pixel-high file we wanted for the Web site, we needed to resize the file without messing up the Layer Styles and having to scale the Style for each layer to get our effects back. Because of a quirk in the way Layer Styles respond to file size changes, we had to do it this way: We first duplicated the layered file (Image, Duplicate) and then chose Image, Image Size. In the Image Size dialog box **8,** we made sure that both Constrain

7e

Inverting the mask made by the vector mask on the layer set

7f

*Rotating the vector mask **A** and removing the "bottom" half of the mask by selecting the bottom control point **B** and deleting it **C** so the rings show in front*

7g

The finished logo

8

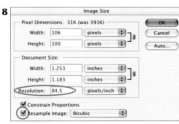

Changing only the Resolution to scale the graphic

Proportions and Resample Image were selected. *We didn't touch the pixel values in the Width or Height boxes at the top of the dialog box.* Instead we experimented by entering lower values for the Resolution until the Height value at the top of the box was 100; then we clicked OK to close the box. We now had our 100-pixel-high file for taking over to ImageReady. We went through a similar process to make the 600-pixel-high file for print, but entered higher Resolution values.

Developing the animation. Animating the two versions (300 and 100 pixels) is described in "Animating with Actions" in Chapter 9.

RESIZING A "STYLED" FILE

Photoshop's Layer Styles have a strange and wonderful relationship with Resolution. If you resize a file that has one or more Layer Styles applied to it, the method you use to resize can make the difference between success and failure. The secret is to **change the Resolution dpi, not the pixel dimensions**. Here's a safe way to proceed:

1 Figure out a target pixel dimension for either Width or Height. For instance, you may need to make the file exactly 100 pixels high for use on a Web page, so a Height value of 100 is your target. Or you may want to print the image 2 inches wide at approximately 300 dpi, so your target for Width is approximately 600 pixels.

2 Once you have your target size, choose Image, Image Size. In the Image Size dialog box, **be sure Resample Image is turned on.**

3 In the Image Size dialog box **Don't touch any of the Height or Width settings!** — not the ones at the top of the dialog box, and not the ones in the middle. **Instead, change the Resolution** until the critical setting (Height or Width) at the top of the box matches the number you figured out in step 1. You can use decimal fractions for the Resolution to arrive at exactly the right Height or Width number.

4 Click OK to complete the resizing and close the dialog box. The image will have been resized, with the Style scaled along with it. Since the Size, Distance, and other settings in the Style have to be in *whole pixels*, there can be some **"rounding error."** For instance, if the Distance setting for a Drop Shadow was 5 pixels for a 400-pixel-high file and you reduce the file to 100 pixels high, the new Distance value would be 1 pixel because it can't be 1.25. So the shadow would look a little less offset than in the original, and you might need to do some fine-tuning to "balance" the settings.

Don't touch — just watch

Don't touch — ignore

Touch — experiment

Silhouetting Images & Type

Overview Make a clipping path for the subject you want to silhouette; save a copy of the file using the clipping path; set or import type and add a Layer Style; add a color-filled layer below the type; convert the type to a Shape layer; make a permanent path from the Shape layer; make the path into a clipping path.

IMAGE

"**Silhouetting**" "before" and "after" files

JHD / ORIGINAL PHOTO © CORBIS IMAGES ROYALTY FREE, EUROPEAN VACATIONS

WITH PHOTOSHOP 7'S TYPE CONTROLS and its special effects that can be applied through Layer Styles, it's easy to create illustrative display type right in Photoshop. You can also export the display type for use in a page layout program, with perfectly smooth, razor-sharp edges based on the vector outlines of the type. Since it's also possible to eliminate the background when exporting images, you can export a "backgroundless" photo *and* type to go with it. That means you can use Photoshop to arrange the basic composition of silhouetted photo and type, and then export the photo and type separately — each with its own clipping path. That way you'll be able to further tweak the composition in your page layout — for instance, putting the type behind the image or in front of it, or arranging both on a custom background. There are a few tricks you can use to customize the display type, including converting the type to a Shape layer and then converting the Shape to a clipping path.

1 Selecting the subject of the photo. Open the photo whose subject you want to silhouette. Since your aim is to create a clipping path, the best way to select the subject may be with the Pen, which draws paths. (The Magnetic Pen can be helpful in automating the selection task; you can choose it by clicking the Freeform Pen tool in the Pen pop-out in the toolbox and then choosing Magnetic in the Options bar.) Though other kinds of selections can be converted to paths, the fit will not be as good as with a path created and fine-tuned with one or more of the Pen tools.

After we made our initial outline with the Pen **1a**, we refined the fit by moving points, curve segments, and direction line handles with the Direct Selection tool (the hollow arrowhead in the toolbox; press Shift-A to reach it) **1b**. We also added more points where we needed them; with Auto Add/Delete turned on in the Options bar, the Pen automatically becomes the Add Anchor Point tool when you move its cursor onto a curve segment, where you can then click to add a point. (For more about the Pen tools, see page 299.)

1a

The original photo with a Work Path drawn to select the subject

1b

Adjusting the path

2a

Save Path
Name: Couple Path   OK   Cancel

Double-clicking the Work Path designation in the Paths palette opens the Save Path dialog box, where you can name the Path to save it.

2b

Using the Paths palette's pop-out menu (top) to make a clipping path for export

2c

On the Mac the outlined Path name in the Paths palette shows that the Path is currently designated as the clipping path for export of the file. (On Windows the name appears bold.)

2d

Saving a copy of the file for exporting the "backgroundless" image

3a

Using the Character palette to adjust the baseline of a letter (selected by dragging with the Type cursor)

2 Making a clipping path for the subject. When you've finished drawing and editing the path, name it and save it: Double-click on the *Work Path* name in the Paths palette to open the Save Path dialog box, type a descriptive name, and click OK **2a.** In the Paths palette, choose Clipping Path from the pop-out menu **2b.** Select your new Path from the Path list. You can leave the Flatness setting blank so that the imagesetter will set it appropriately for the output resolution. When you click OK, the name of this Path will be outlined (Mac) or bold (Windows) in the Paths palette, indicating that it's the clipping path to be used for export **2c.** Finally, choose File, Save As, Save: As A Copy and save the file as a TIFF, a format that's commonly used by page layout programs and that supports a clipping path **2d.** You may want to check with your output service provider to see which format (TIFF or EPS) for clipping path export they prefer.

3 Setting the type. Choose the Type tool and click the Palettes button in the Options bar to open the Character palette. There you can control the color, size, tracking, kerning, leading, stretch, and baseline shift. We typed our title in three lines, using the Return key to start each new line. We condensed the type by setting the character width to 60%. To "bounce" the individual characters, we selected each one and adjusted the baseline shift (the setting in the lower left corner of the Character palette) **3a, 3b.**

IMPORTING TYPE FROM ILLUSTRATOR

You can use Adobe Illustrator's extensive facilities for setting and manipulating type, and then import your type as a Shape layer in Photoshop 7: Set and customize the type in Illustrator, convert it to outlines (Type, Create Outlines), select it, and choose Edit, Copy. Then in Photoshop, choose Edit, Paste, Paste As: Shape Layer. The converted type will retain its vector-based curves as it's imported as a Shape layer. (See tip on page 306 for working with Illustrator 10.)

4 Adding a Layer Style to the type. To add special effects to the type:

- Click the Add A Layer Style button (the *"f"*) at the bottom of the Layers palette and choose an effect from the pop-out menu. Then work within the Layer Style dialog box to customize that effect and set up others as well.

- Or click on one of the thumbnails in the Styles palette to apply a Layer Style (a preset mix of effects).

3b

The finished typesetting, before treatment with a Layer Style

4

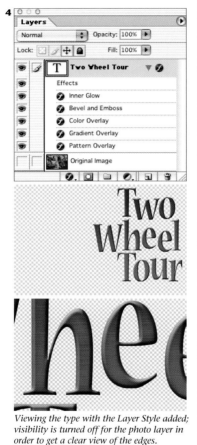

Viewing the type with the Layer Style added; visibility is turned off for the photo layer in order to get a clear view of the edges.

5a

Setting up the Eyedropper to sample color from the type

Whether you build your own Layer Style or use a preset, keep in mind that any effect that extends beyond the actual type edges will be eliminated when you "clip" the type to export it (in step 8). So, for instance, a Drop Shadow, Outer Glow, or Outer Bevel will be removed. Once your Layer Style has been applied, you can turn off visibility for the photo layer (by clicking in the Eye column) to view the type alone **4**.

(We added the Layer Style to the type before converting the type to a Shape layer. But it isn't crucial that you do it in this order. Instead, you can convert the type to a Shape layer first and then add the Layer Style.)

5 Adding a color layer to protect the edges. If you will need to turn your display type into a Path that can be used for export as we did, it's a good idea to create a color-filled layer directly below the display type layer. Filling this layer with the same color as the body of the type will ensure that any semi-transparent pixels at the edges of the letters will pick up a matching color, rather than a potentially contrasting color from the photo. (The same technique will work if you're creating your type without a photo underneath.) To do this, activate the layer that's currently below the type layer by clicking its name in the Layers palette. Then click the Create New Layer button at the bottom of the palette. Choose the Eyedropper tool, and in the Options bar choose "5 by 5 Average" from the pop-out Sample Size menu **5a**; this will "average" any color variations in the area you sample. Then click in the body of the type, and press Alt/Option-Delete to fill the new layer with the chosen color **5b**.

6 Converting the type to a Shape layer. Making a Shape Layer will be necessary if you want to further modify the characters in the display type, making changes that aren't possible with live type (as described next, in step 7). To do this, first convert the type layer to a Shape layer (choose Layer, Type, Convert To Shape) **6a**. Notice that the appearance of the layer's thumbnail changes in the Layers palette. Also, as long as the Shape layer is the active layer, the display type outlines now appear as an entry in the Paths palette, with the name in italics and the term *"vector mask"* as part of the name **6b**.

7 Modifying the shape outlines. Before making a clipping path from the Shape layer, you can use the Path Component Selection tool (the solid arrow in the toolbox), or Direct Selection tool (hollow arrow) to modify the letters. Click on an individual letter to select its outline, and then make changes. For instance, to slightly rotate individual letters such as the first "e" in "Wheel," we clicked on the letter and then chose Edit, Free Transform Path (Ctrl/⌘-T) and dragged outside the upper right corner handle in a counter-clockwise direction **7**. Pressing the Enter key completed the trans-

5b

A color-filled layer was added below the type layer.

6a

Convert live type to a Shape layer by choosing Layer, Type, Convert To Shape

6b

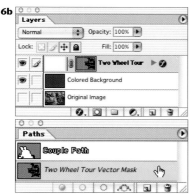

When type is converted to a Shape layer, the layer thumbnail changes in the Layers palette and the name of the Shape layer also appears in the Paths palette with the somewhat confusing designation.

formation. (***Note***: It's important to make any transformations now, *before* the Shape information is turned into a permanent path in step 8. If you try to make the changes to the permanent path instead of to the Shape information, the clipping path that you generate in step 8 won't match the transformed letters.)

8 Making a clipping path for the display type. Once any transformation or reshaping is complete, you'll need to save the Shape information as a permanent path, or you won't be able to use it as a clipping path for export. To turn the Shape information into a permanent path, double-click the italicized path name for your Shape layer in the Paths palette, and use the Save Path dialog box as you did in step 2. We called our new path "Type Path" **8a.**

Next make a clipping path for export by choosing Clipping Path from the Paths palette's pop-out menu **8b.** As in step 2, save the file as a TIFF or EPS, choosing a different name for this new file.

9 Arranging the elements in a page layout. Open your page layout program and import the two copies of the file that you saved in steps 2 and 8. Now you can arrange the two imports to match your Photoshop composition, and then freely experiment with changes to the layout by moving one or both elements or changing their "stacking order" to move one in front of the other **9.**

7

Using the Free Transform command to tilt individual letters

8a

```
Paths
  Couple Path
  Type Path
  Two Wheel Tour Vector Mask
```

A permanent Path was made from the Shape layer.

8b

```
Clipping Path
Path: [Type Path ▼]          [ OK ]
Flatness: [    ] device pixels  [ Cancel ]
```

```
Paths
  Couple Path
  Type Path
  Two Wheel Tour Vector Mask
```

Turning the "Type Path" into the clipping path to be used in saving a second copy of the file

9

Positioning the silhouetted subject and type files in a page layout program

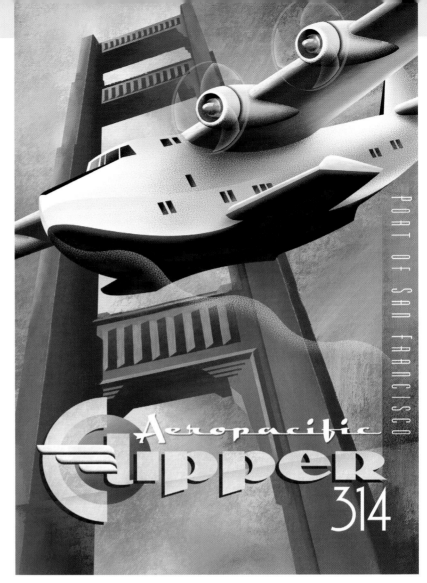

PORT OF SAN FRANCISCO

Aeropacific
Clipper
314

Mike Kungl's art deco posters, such as this *Aeropacific Clipper 314*, are produced with Adobe Illustrator, Photoshop, and procreate Painter. Kungl does his drawing in Illustrator, creating a working layout of shapes filled with flat color. When the Illustrator layout for Clipper was complete, Kungl selected all the elements, copied them to the clipboard, and in Photoshop pasted them as paths into a file created to exactly the same height and width dimensions as the Illustrator file. The paths showed up in Photoshop's Paths palette as a *Work Path*. Kungl selected each outline (in Photoshop 7 this can be done by clicking the appropriate subpath with the Path Component Selection tool) and loaded it as a selection (this can be done by clicking the dotted circle button at the bottom of the Paths palette). He then saved the selection in an alpha channel (by clicking the Save Selection As Channel button at the bottom of the Channels palette). When he had all the shapes saved as alpha channels, he saved the file and opened it in Painter.

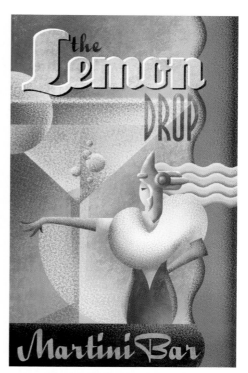

Mike Kungl's posters for the fictitious *Deco Coffee*, *Lemon Drop Martini Bar*, and *Nitro Cafe* were created with the same processes used for *Clipper* (on the facing page). Kungl creates the lettering for his posters in Illustrator, starting with a font from Adobe or another maker, converting the type to paths (the command in Illustrator is Type, Create Outlines), and modifying the individual characters.

▶ *For tips on bringing Illustrator artwork into Photoshop, see "Illustrator to Photoshop" on page 305 and "Coloring Clip Art" on page 324.*

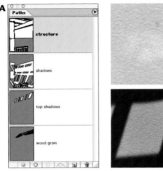

© Bert Monroy 2000

Bert Monroy began *Shadowplay* by composing the image in Adobe Illustrator. For the walls, beams, and railings, he drew a separate shape for every visible surface. He also composed four shadow shapes, one for each of the walls, one for the shadow on the railing, and one for the shadow on the wooden beam. Each shadow was drawn as a crisscross of intersecting shapes that were then combined with the Unite function from Illustrator's Pathfinder palette. Monroy selected all the paths and copied them to the clipboard.

In Photoshop he created an RGB file the same size as the Illustrator file (about 8 x 12 inches) at 300 dpi. Then he pasted the paths into this new file (Edit, Paste, Paste As: Paths), where he would use them to create his "painting." The pasted paths appeared as the temporary *Work Path* in Photoshop's Paths palette. Monroy double-clicked the *Work Path* label to make the pasted paths into a permanent, named Photoshop Path. Then he separated out subpaths that he could use to create the walls, shadows, and wooden elements: First he duplicated the named Path several times (by dragging its name to the Create New Path button at the bottom of the palette); then for each of these copies, he used the Path Component Selection tool and Delete key to remove parts. In this way he made a "structures" Path, two "shadows" Paths, and a "wood grain" Path **A**.

To create the art for each of these elements, Monroy started by making a layer and activating the Structures Path (by clicking its name in the Paths palette). Then he used the Path Component Selection tool to click the particular subpath he

wanted to fill, loaded it as a selection (by clicking the Load Path As Selection button at the bottom of the Paths palette), and filled it with color.

He created the texture for the wall surfaces **B** by adding a small amount of Noise to the color (Filter, Noise, Add Noise), to create just a touch of graininess. He consolidated and increased this texture with the Craquelure filter (Filter, Texture, Craquelure). To create each of the darker or lighter splotches on the wall, he lassoed an area and copied it to a new layer (Layer, New, Layer Via Copy, or Ctrl/⌘-J). Then he lightened or darkened this new splotch layer using Image, Adjust, Levels. Finally he used the Eraser tool in Airbrush mode and with a soft brush tip (chosen from the Options bar's pop-up Brush palette) to shape the splotch and make it blend seamlessly with the wall in the layer below. For other discolorations on the walls, he used the Dodge and Burn tools.

Before applying each of the shadows, Monroy wanted to modify their edges a little. So he used each Shadows Path to load a shadow selection (using the process described earlier for the wall surfaces), then saved the selection in an alpha channel (Select, Save Selection, New Channel). Now he could customize the shadow edges in the alpha channel: To match the photo he was using for reference, Monroy applied Filter, Blur, Motion Blur, setting the Angle in the Motion Blur dialog box parallel to the vertical edges so that it left these edges sharp, but blurred the horizontal ones.

Finally, to make each shadow **C**, Monroy loaded his altered alpha channel as a selection (by Ctrl/⌘-clicking its name in the Channels palette), created a new layer above the appropriate wall or beam layer, and filled the selection with black. He could control the density of each shadow by putting its layer in Multiply mode and setting its Opacity.

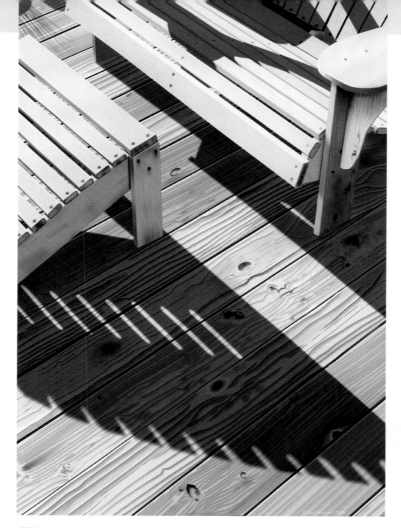

A

B

For *Bodega Shadows* **Bert Monroy** used the same basic construction and shadowing techniques as for *Shadowplay* (opposite), except that he used a dark blue instead of black for the shadows and treated the shadows' edges a bit differently. Instead of using Motion Blur on the alpha channel for the shadows, he selected only the forward edge of the shadow and used Gaussian Blur to soften it **A**, leaving the rest of the shadow sharp **B**.

The rough, weathered wood for the deck in *Bodega Shadows* (and for the wooden beams in *Shadowplay*) began as board shapes filled with gray and treated with the Add Noise filter to create a little texture. The wood grain itself started as a series of paths in Illustrator. After pasting the grain paths into Photoshop, Monroy used them to make three sets of strokes, each set on its own layer. He chose the Airbrush and activated the Grain Path by clicking it in the Paths palette. For each set of strokes he made a new layer by clicking the Create New Layer button at the bottom of the Layers palette; then he chose a brush tip from the Options bar, chose a Foreground color in the toolbox, and clicked the Stroke Path button at the bottom of the Paths palette. On the top layer were thin dark strokes to define the grain, made with a hard-edged brush tip. On a layer below were thicker, softer strokes in white for the highlight, offset a little by dragging the layer slightly toward the light source in the image. Below that was a layer of even thicker and softer black strokes offset in the opposite direction to make the shadows cast by the rough grain of the weathered wood **A, B**.

To complete the wood, Monroy added cracks, knots, and discolorations by painting with the Airbrush tool and using the Smudge tool on some of the grain **A**.

The much smoother grain of the wooden slats of the chair **B** was constructed in a layer above the layer that held the slats. Monroy made the texture by creating color-filled shapes that were longer than the slats beneath them, adding noise (Filter, Noise, Add Noise, Monochromatic), then blurring the noise into streaks (Filter, Blur, Motion Blur); the Angle setting in the Motion Blur dialog box established the direction of the grain along the slats. (He used shapes larger than the slats because the Motion Blur filter's effect fades out at the ends of any area it's applied to.) Monroy clipped this texture inside the slats by Alt/Option-clicking between the texture layer and the slats layer in the Layers palette to make a clipping group. Finally he clicked on the texture layer and merged it with the slats layer (Layer, Merge Down, or Ctrl/⌘-E). To complete the wood textures, he added highlights and shadows with the Dodge and Burn tools.

J **ack Davis** "painted" the logo for the *Danish Chalet Inn* in Adobe Illustrator using a Wacom Intuos tablet and the Paintbrush tool with a stroke but no fill to create a layered file with the type, graphics, and painted elements on separate layers. Then he exported the artwork in Photoshop format (File, Export, Photoshop 5 PSD) so he could open it in Photoshop with the various elements rasterized on their individual layers. With the parts on separate layers he could apply a different Layer Style to add dimension and lighting to the type and to the oval that surrounds the painting. He used soft drop shadows on the type layers (achieved by balancing the Size and Spread in the Drop Shadow section of the Layer Style dialog box) and pillow embossing on the oval (applied by choosing Pillow Emboss for the Style setting in the Bevel And Emboss section of the Layer Style box). He saved the design at high resolution for use on a custom-printed T-shirt, and reduced the size of a copy for use on the Web.

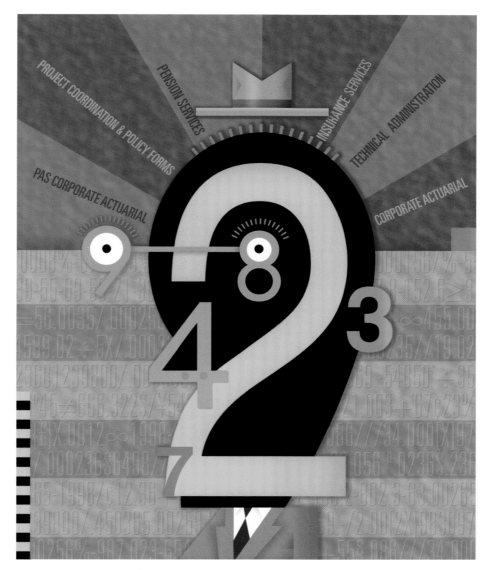

Gordon Studer used a layered file to work out the composition and develop the central figure for *Hire Math: The Actuarial Student Program*, created as cover art for *Topics*, a publication of the pension-planning service TIAA-CREF. The "man" was composed of numbers and other vector-based elements. ▶ *In Photoshop 7 arched elements like the eyebrows can be created by setting a series of "I's" in a sans serif font and then applying a Text Warp using the Arc style, with the degree of arching controlled by the Blend setting in the Warp Text dialog box.*

To help unify (and also soften) the vector elements, Studer scanned a cork texture, then applied Photoshop's Blur and Add Noise filters to create a texture that shows through the geometric stripes and radiating shapes of the background. This mottled texture, as well as a grid of typed numbers and letters in another layer, are used at about 30% Opacity to add surface interest. In addition, a green drop shadow behind the man helps wed this flat element to the textured background.

SPECIAL
EFFECTS
FOR TYPE
& GRAPHICS

MOST OF THE SPECIAL EFFECTS in this chapter are designed to simulate what happens when light and materials interact — from a simple drop shadow to the complex reflections and refraction of chrome, brushed metal, or glass. In Photoshop 7, creating "live" special effects for graphics and type has become almost exclusively the province of Layer Styles, with occasional help from Adjustment layers, masks, and filters. With the continuing evolution of Layer Styles, Photoshop 6 and 7 have made the biggest leaps forward in the way flat graphics can be turned into lighted, solid-looking, even glowing objects since layers were added in Photoshop 3.

The primary change to Layer Styles in Photoshop 7 is that more Blend mode options have been added to the different Layer Style effects; the same options have been added to the Blend modes in the Layers palette. Additionally, the way effects are applied to vector-masked layers has been altered slightly.

With Layer Styles you can create entire dimensional lighting and coloring treatments and apply them wherever you want to. A Style, with all its component effects, can be copied to other layers or other documents — it can even be named and saved as a **preset** for future use. When you apply these portable Styles to other layers, they can be scaled to fit the new elements you apply them to, with a single easy **scaling** operation that adjusts all the component effects at once. In many cases the several Styles applied to the layers of a file can even be **resized automatically along with the file** if you're careful how you go about changing the file size (as described in the "Resizing a 'Styled' File" tip on page 337). This can be a big timesaver for a multilayer, multi-Style file.

WORKING WITH LAYER STYLES

Layer Styles can help you produce artwork that meets all the criteria for Photoshop success: speed in getting the job done, high-quality results, and flexibility to make changes easily or to reapply your creations later. With a Layer Style you can edit and re-edit your special effects without degrading the interior or edge of the element you've "styled." That edge is defined by the **outline of the layer's content** — in other words, the transition between what is transparent and what is opaque on a layer, or the "footprint" of the pixels, type, or Shape on the layer. The outline may also be modified by a

*Most of the **Wow 7-Styles** supplied on the CD-ROM that comes with this book were designed at **225 dpi**, except for the **Wow 7-20 Button Styles** (shown above) that were designed at **72 dpi**. If you want to apply one of these Styles to a file that has a different resolution, prepare your file like this: Choose Image, **Image Size** and make sure the **Resample option is turned off**. Then **change the Resolution** to 225 or 72 dpi to match the Style's "design resolution," and click OK to close the Image Size dialog box. In the Layers palette target the layer you want to "style" and click a thumbnail in the Styles palette to apply a Style. Then you can change the resolution back if you like, again using the Image Size dialog box with the Resample option turned off.*

continued on page 350

Turning a flat graphic or type into a glowing, translucent dimensional object is just one of the things you can accomplish with a Layer Style. The Layer Style used for the type above is described in "Anatomy of a Layer Style" on page 366.

A mask on a layer set can be used to hide part of all the layers in the set. Whether it is linked or not, the mask on the layer set is not affected by the Style on any of the layers in the set. Here the mask hides part of each of the "styled" layers designed to animate the spinning gear, as described on page 336.

layer mask or **vector mask**. As a default, both of these masks become part of the layer content's outline; it is this outline (or transition between what is opaque and what is transparent) that is used to define the edge for the Layer Style.

Photoshop 7 comes with collections of **preset Styles** that can be loaded for use by opening the Styles palette (Window, Show Styles) and choosing from the menu that pops out from the upper right corner of the palette. The bottom part of the menu lists all the preset files in the Styles folder, which is created inside the Presets folder in your Photoshop 7 folder when you install the program.

A preset Style can be applied to any active unlocked layer (except the *Background*) by clicking the Style's thumbnail in the Styles palette. Or you can copy it (by choosing Layer, Layer Style, Copy Layer Style) from a layer where it has already been applied and pasting it to another layer.

You can also develop your own custom Styles. Start by applying an existing Style and editing it in the Layer Style dialog box, or start by activating any layer in the Layers palette, then opening the Layer Style box. The box can be opened by choosing Layer, Layer Style and choosing Blending Options or one of the effects listed below it in the pop-out menu. Or you can simply click the "*f*" button at the bottom of the Layers palette and choose from the pop-out list. Or double-click the layer's name and choose an effect from the list on the left side of the Layer Style dialog box.

UNDERSTANDING STYLES

A Layer Style can consist of as many as 12 different component effects, along with the Blending Options that govern how the effects interact with the content of the layer and how the layer interacts with other layers in the file. Most of the effects (and the Blending Options) have many individual parameters you can change. There are *millions* of possible combinations of settings. You can think of a Layer Style as a cross between a magician's kit and an Erector Set of special-effects components. Once you understand the basics of what's in the Layer Styles kit, you'll be able to think in new and creative ways about building a wide range of dramatic dimensional treatments.

The next few pages present the fundamentals of how the component effects of Photoshop's Layer Styles work. Then "Anatomy of a Layer Style" on pages 366–369 leads you through an examination of the components of a sample Style, showing how the individual effects are set up and how they work together. The step-by-step special-effects techniques that make up the rest of the chapter give you instructions for creating highly tactile dimensional treatments of your own.

Color Overlay

Gradient Overlay (Solid)

Gradient Overlay (Noise)

Pattern Overlay

Drop Shadow

Inner Shadow

Outer Glow

LAYER STYLE OPTIONS

A Layer Style can be made up of any or all of the 12 effects shown here: There are three **Overlays** for coloring the surface, two **Shadows** and two **Glows**, a **Satin** effect, and a **Stroke**. The **Bevel And Emboss** effect has five different categories of bevel structures, as well as a **Contour** to shape the bevel. The structure and lighting in the Bevel And Emboss effect also control the "bump mapping" added by the **Texture** effect.

Inner Glow: Edge

Inner Glow: Center

Satin

Stroke: Color

Stroke: Shape Burst Gradient

Bevel And Emboss: Inner Bevel

Bevel And Emboss: Outer Bevel

Bevel And Emboss: Emboss

Bevel And Emboss: Pillow Emboss

Bevel And Emboss: Stroke

Bevel And Emboss with Contour

Bevel And Emboss with Texture

All the effects that you can incorporate in a Layer Style are listed at the left side of the Layer Style dialog box. Clicking in the check box next to the name of an effect turns visibility on or off for that effect. Clicking on the name of an effect opens the appropriate section of the Layer Style box so that you can edit the settings for that effect.

Styled Circle.psd

An "f" icon next to a layer's name in the Layers palette means that a Layer Style has been applied to the layer. By clicking the little triangle to the left of the "f," you can display the list of effects used in that particular Style. The circular "button" above was developed by adding a Layer Style to a dark-gray-filled circle.

GO AHEAD! EAT YOUR DESSERT FIRST!

For each technique in this chapter, "before" and "after" versions of the artwork are provided on the Wow CD-ROM. As in other chapters, you can use the "before" version as a starting point for following the step-by-step instructions to arrive at the final result, as a "practice run" before applying the technique to your own graphics or type.

However, for the techniques in *this* chapter it's also important to **open the "after" files at the *beginning* of the step-by-step process,** so you can explore them as you construct the Styles. All of the different effects and Blending Options that make up a Layer Style interact with one another, and if you don't get the settings right, the overall Style may turn out differently than you expect. If one or two little settings are left unmodified, or if your Blending Options are set up differently, instead of translucent blue glass, you could end up with black plastic. The layered-and-styled "after" files offer a compact, interactive, and interesting way for you to pick up the details and see how the effects interact.

Also, if your goal is simply to *use* a particular Style rather than learn exactly how it's put together, you can apply the Style by copying and pasting from the "after" file, as described in the "Drag-and-Drop Style Caution" tip below.

LAYER STYLE COMPONENTS

Many of the individual components of a Layer Style are named for the specific effects they were designed to create — Drop Shadow, Inner Shadow, Inner Glow, Outer Glow, and so on. But if you can get beyond the names and understand how each component can interact with the others, you'll greatly expand the creative potential that Layer Styles offer.

Exploring the Layer Style Dialog Box

One way to learn about how the settings in a Shadow or Glow or any other effect work is to make a type or Shape layer, then click

---

DRAG-AND-DROP STYLE CAUTION

Individual effects can be successfully copied to other layers and even other files **by dragging and dropping** their line entries in an expanded Style in the Layers palette.

But to copy an entire Style by dragging and dropping the Effects line entry is risky: The settings in the Blending Options section of the Layer Style dialog box — such as Opacity, Blend Mode, Knockouts, and other blending options — aren't copied when the Effects line is dragged and dropped and aren't removed if you delete the Style. To copy an entire Style including Blending Options, in the Layers palette you can right-click (Windows) or Control-click (Mac) on the "f" icon for the "donor" layer and choose Copy Layer Style from the context-sensitive menu. Then right/Control-click on the "recipient" layer, this time choosing Paste Layer Style. (The "Layer Style Tune-up" tip on page 334 tells what you can do if the Style looks different than you expected.)

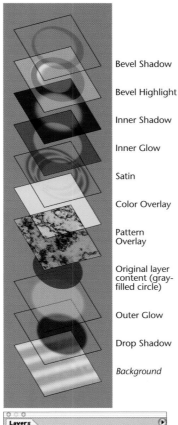

Bevel Shadow

Bevel Highlight

Inner Shadow

Inner Glow

Satin

Color Overlay

Pattern Overlay

Original layer content (gray-filled circle)

Outer Glow

Drop Shadow

Background

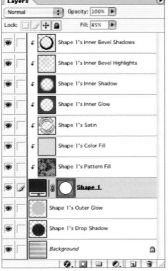

*The Create Layers command renders the effects in a Layer Style as separate layers, as shown here for the **Styled Circle.psd** file shown on the facing page.*

the "*ƒ*" button at the bottom of the Layers palette, and choose an effect from the pop-out list. Once the Layer Style dialog box is open, for each effect that you want to explore, click its name in the list on the left side of the dialog box to open its section of the box. Then try setting Opacity to 100%, setting Blend Mode to Normal, and setting all other parameters to 0. Experiment by slowly increasing the settings one at a time and in combination, seeing what each one does and how it interacts with the others.

Taking a Style Apart

Another experiment that can provide insight is to set up several effects to create a Style and then rasterize the effects (Layer, Layer Style, Create Layers). Each effect will be separated into a layer of its own — some effects will even create two layers. Notice where the new layers fall in the Layers palette — some will be above and some below the layer you applied the Style to. The order of the layers can be enlightening. The "effects" layers that are above the original layer will be included in a clipping group with your original layer serving as the base (as shown in the Layers palette at the left), so the effects show only inside the outline created by the original layer. If you now Alt/Option-click in the Layers palette on the border between the original layer and the one just above it in the Layers palette, the layers will be released from the clipping group, and you'll be able to see what the clipping group was accomplishing. Now experiment by clicking the Eye icons for individual layers.

LOST IN THE TRANSLATION

Not all the combinations of effects that you can create with a Layer Style can be successfully rasterized into separate layers. For that reason, when you choose Layer, Layer Style, Create Layers, a Caution box will warn you that something may be lost in the translation. You'll see the box even for simple effects that will translate perfectly.

GETTING INSIDE THE BOX

You can open the Layer Style dialog box by:

• Choosing Layer, Layer Style and choosing an effect.

• Clicking the Add A Layer Style button at the bottom of the Layers palette and choosing an effect.

• Double-clicking a layer's name in the Layers palette.

• For a layer that already has a Style applied to it, double-clicking the *layer's "ƒ" icon* in the Layers palette.

• In an expanded list of effects for a layer that already has a Style applied to it, double-clicking the Effects line (opens to the last section used), or double-clicking a specific effect line.

Once you're "inside the box," you can move from effect to effect and also set up the Blending Options by choosing from the list on the left side of the box.

By changing the **Color Overlay**, you can adapt a single button Style for different navigation functions. See Chapter 9 for more about Styles for buttons.

 Color Overlay.psd

STYLING IN STAGES

A shadow created with the *Drop Shadow* component of a Layer Style can be separated from its graphic element and rendered as a layer of its own (by choosing Layer, Layer Style, Create Layer). Then it can be distorted with the Free Transform command to produce a cast shadow. Another Layer Style can then be added to the graphic element to create dimensionality and surface characteristics that can remain "live" and editable.

A Layer Style was used to add a Drop Shadow to the Shape layer. Then the Style was separated to create an independent shadow layer that could be manipulated. Then a new Style was added to the Shape layer to build dimensionality, lighting, and surface characteristics.

 Separate Shadow.psd

OVERLAYS

The three Overlay effects provide an easy, very flexible way to apply a solid color, a pattern, or a gradient, with complete freedom to change them at any time, regulating their content, opacity, and blend mode. The Overlays interact as if they were stacked in the same order they occur in the Layer Style dialog's list: Color Overlay (a solid color fill) is on top, then Gradient, then Pattern. Here are a few of the things you can do with **Color Overlay**:

- Darken a recessed element, as if it were in a shadow created by carving it into the surface.

- Create a series of matching buttons or a set of button states (Normal, Over, and Down, for instance) by copying a layer with a button graphic that has been treated with several Layer Effects and changing only the Color Overlay of each one.

- Store color information that you have to apply often — the corporate color for a logo, for instance — so you can apply this Color Overlay wherever you need it.

For the **Gradient Overlay** if the **Align With Layer** box is **checked, the gradient starts at the edge of the layer content.** With the box checked it's as though the entire gradient is "poured into" the outline created by the layer content. With the box **unchecked the gradient will be aligned with the edge of the document.** (The edge of the document may be outside the canvas if any layers are oversized or have been moved partly "offstage.") With the box unchecked it's as though the layer was filled with the gradient and the layer content outline was used as a cookie cutter — only part of the gradient falls within the outline. **Angle** sets the direction of the color changes, and **Style** offers the five gradient types. ("The Gradient Tool," starting on page 265, tells about the gradient types.) The **Scale** slider can be used to compress or expand the gradient, filling the edges with the end colors when the Scale is less than 100%.

For the **Pattern Overlay** if the **Link With Layer** box is **checked,** the pattern starts at the upper left corner of an imaginary bounding box around the **layer content.** With the box **unchecked,** the pattern starts at the upper left corner of the **document** instead. The **Scale** slider lets you shrink or enlarge the pattern independent of the layer content. ***Note:*** Since patterns are pixel-based rather than procedural (instruction-based) like the other effects, a Pattern Overlay can "soften" with scaling. This is also true of the Texture effect, which is pattern-based.

SHADOWS AND GLOWS

Like most of the effects in a Layer Style, both Shadow and Glow effects work by duplicating the outline of a layer's contents — whether pixels, type, Shape, layer mask, layer clipping path, or a

The Global Light setting in the Bevel And Emboss dialog box was designed to make it easy to coordinate lighting angles for all effects in a Layer Style and all Layer Styles in a file, so that the light always seems to be coming from a single direction. However, unless/until Adobe separates Global Angle from Global Altitude, it may be wiser not to use Global Light for any Styles you plan to save as presets that can be loaded into the Styles palette and applied to other files.

The problem is that when a Style with Global Light is applied, it automatically *takes on the Global Light settings that already exist* in the file. If no custom Style has been applied to the file, the intrinsic default Global Light — Angle, 120° and Altitude, 30° — will take over. This may be fine for coordinating the lighting *direction*, but it can ruin the *material characteristics* that can be simulated with the Altitude setting. So a shiny surface that depends on a high Altitude setting can become dull.

To protect your Altitude settings, your best bet is to **leave the Global Light option turned off** for Bevel And Emboss — and for all other effects in the Style as well.

In Photoshop 7 if you design a Layer Style that takes advantage of Global Light, you run the risk that the Global Light native to the file could produce different surface characteristics or inconsistent lighting.

combination. The duplicate is then either filled with color or used as a hole in an overlay that's filled with color, and the result is blurred. Once you visualize the blurred duplicate as the starting point, you can begin to look at the differences between Shadow and Glow effects, and to see what each one does with the blurred result. The two main differences between Shadow effects and Glow effects are:

- A Shadow can be *offset,* but a Glow radiates evenly in all directions.
- A Glow has the option of using a *gradient* or a solid color; a shadow can only use a solid color.

Distance and Angle

The **Distance** setting in a Shadow effect determines how far offset the shadow will be. You can change the Distance setting by using the slider, typing a value into the box, using the up and down arrow keys on the keyboard, or simply dragging in the working window while the dialog box is open.

You can individually set the **Angle** that determines where the light source is located for each Shadow effect and for other effects in your Style, such as Bevel And Emboss. Or you can turn on **Global Light**, which will **apply the same lighting Angle to all of the effects** in your Style. Anytime you change the Angle for one effect, the change will also apply to all the other effects, not only in the one Layer Style you're working on, but *in all Layer Styles in the entire file that are set up to Use Global Light.* The Global Light option makes it easy to ensure that the directional lighting in your image is consistent — you won't accidentally end up with drop shadows going one direction on one layer and another direction on another layer. Using Global Light has potential drawbacks, however, as explained in the "Lighting: Global or Not?" tip at the left.

Glows cannot be offset, and they aren't subject to Global Light. If you choose one of the Glow effects in the list on the left side of the Layer Style dialog box, you'll see that there's no Distance setting and no Angle.

Blend Mode, Color, and Gradient

Though we think of shadows as dark and glows as light, Shadow and Glow effects can both be either dark or light, depending on the color and Blend Mode setting you choose. By default, Shadows are set to dark colors and are in Multiply mode, while Glows are light colors in Screen mode. But you can reverse that if you want to, or use other modes. A light-colored Shadow in Screen mode with a Distance setting of 0 creates a glow. A dark-colored Outer Glow in Multiply mode becomes a centered shadow or "dark halo."

What **Glows** lack in offset ability, they more than make up for in their ability to use gradients. Instead of simply offering a color swatch for you to click to choose a color (as in the Shadow sections),

To color this type, a Pattern Overlay was used to create the fill, and a yellow Stroke was added. To create the hard-edged black shading for this type, the Inner Shadow and Outer Shadow were used with Choke and Spread (respectively) set to 100%. Step-by-step instructions for building the lettering can be found on page 188.

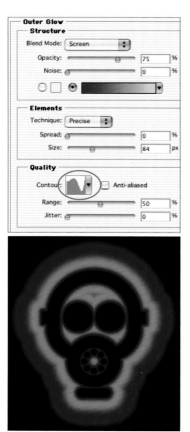

The Contour setting can be used to "remap" the tones in a Shadow or Glow effect.

 Glow Contour.psd

the Glow sections also offer a gradient choice, which, with the right combination of colors and transparency in the gradient, can be used for some fairly complex multicolor radiant effects. There are three additional controls for **Gradient glows. Noise** introduces a random pattern of light-dark variation that can prevent the obvious banding that sometimes happens when gradients are reproduced in print. **Jitter** mixes up pixels of the colors in the gradient so the color transitions are not as well-defined. If you push the Jitter slider all the way to the right, you'll reduce the gradient to a mixture of sprinkles of color. The **Range** setting determines what part of the gradient is used for the Glow.

The Difference Between Inner and Outer

Logically enough, the outer effects (Outer Glow and Drop Shadow) extend outward from the edge of the layer content you apply them to. You can also think of them as filled and blurred duplicates of the outline, placed *behind* the layer — that is, below it in the layer stack.

Inner effects (Inner Shadow and Inner Glow) happen *inside* the edge. The **Inner Shadow** and the **Inner Glow with Edge** as the Source radiate inward from the edge. One way to think of an Edge glow is as an overlay of color with a hole cut in the middle in the shape of the layer's content; the overlay with hole is then blurred, and the result is "clipped" within the layer content's outline. The **Inner Glow with Center** as the Source radiates color from the center outward, getting thinner as it extends toward the edge.

Size, Spread, and Choke

In shadows and glows the **Size** determines the **amount of blur** that's applied to the color-filled copy that makes the shadow or glow. The greater the Size setting, the more the shadow or glow is blurred into the surrounding transparency. This means that at greater Size settings, the shadow or glow is more diffuse — it's thinner and it spreads out farther.

Spread and Choke interact with the Size setting. Increasing the Spread of a Shadow or the Choke of a Glow makes the effect denser, or more concentrated, by controlling where and how abruptly the transition is made from dense to transparent within the range established by the Size.

Contour

A **Contour** setting for a Shadow or Glow is like a Curves setting. It **"remaps" the intermediate tones** or colors that are created by the blur. If the default Linear (45° straight-line) Contour is chosen, the tones or colors stay the same as when they were generated by the blur, proceeding from opaque at the outline to transparent as they extend away from the outline — either inward or outward (except for the Inner Glow with Center as the Source, which is

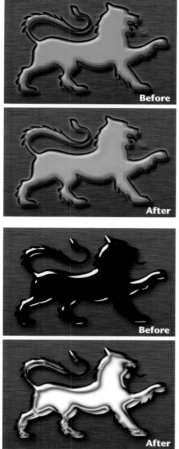

The interior lighting added by the Satin effect can be subtle (top) or dramatic. Shown here are "styled" graphics before and after the Satin effect was added to the Layer Style.

IMAGE Satin.psd

This button was created by reducing the Fill Opacity of the white button graphic shown on the left to 0, and adding a Stroke with a Gradient Fill Type in the Shape Burst style. The difference between the two button states on the right is the color of the gradients and the Inner and Outer Glows. The technique is described in "Quick Neon" on page 381.

IMAGE Neon Stroke.psd

more opaque in the center and gets "thinner" as it goes from the center to the outline).

If you choose a Contour other than the default, the intermediate tones are changed according to the Curve. By applying a Contour with several extreme peaks and valleys, you can get some fairly wild banding in a Glow or Shadow.

SATIN

The **Satin** effect is created by the intersection of two blurred, off-set, reflected copies of the outline of the layer content. It can be useful for simulating **internal reflections** or a **satiny finish**. **Size** controls the amount of blur as in other effects. **Distance** controls how much the two blurred and offset copies overlap, and **Angle** determines the direction of offset. As in other effects, the **Contour** remaps the tones created by the blurring according the Curve you choose.

To get an idea of what's happening when you change the settings for the Satin effect, try this:

1 Use the Ellipse tool (one of the new Shape tools) to create a layer with a filled circle or oval.

2 Double-click the layer's name in the Layers palette to open the Layer Style dialog box to the Blending Options section. In the Advanced Blending area, make sure the Blend Interior Effects As Group box is *not* checked, and set the Fill Opacity to 0. (The filled circle will disappear.)

3 Open the Satin section of the Layer Style dialog box by clicking the Satin entry in the list at the left side of the box. Experiment with the Size (blur), Distance (amount of overlap), and Angle. Pop open the Contour palette by clicking the little triangle to the right of the Contour swatch, and try different Contours. For some fun, watch what happens when you choose a really complex Curve, such as the Ring-Double Contour (one of the presets that comes with Photoshop 7) and vary the Distance.

STROKE

For the **Stroke** effect, the **Size** is the width of the stroke around the outline. The **Position** determines whether the width of the stroke is built from the layer content outward or inward, or is centered, with half the width in each direction. The Stroke's width can be filled with a solid color, a pattern, or a gradient, depending on the **Fill Type** you choose. If you choose the solid color, the pattern, or any of the usual five gradient styles (Linear, Radial, Angle, Reflected, and Diamond), it's as if the Stroke were a slightly larger copy of the layer content, placed behind the layer and filled. But the Stroke's Gradient also offers one additional Style that occurs nowhere else in Photoshop — **with a Shape Burst gradient**

Besides its obvious application for creating bevels, the Bevel And Emboss effect can also be useful for subtle shading and sculpted edges. Dimension was added to the ball by using an Inner Bevel with large Depth, Size, and Soften settings and with Highlights and Shadows in Overlay mode.

To create a solid-looking Outer Bevel that doesn't let the background surface show through, you can use a Stroke, with the Size set exactly the same as the Size for the bevel, as shown in "Styled Steel" on page 405. This technique can be especially helpful for beveling type, since using an inner bevel can reduce the weight of the type too much.

The Emboss style of the Bevel And Emboss effect builds the bevel partly inward and partly outward, letting the color from the layer below show through as well as the color of the current layer. Here the Emboss was applied to the layer with the black graphics, and the beveling also affected the yellow in the layer below.

 Emboss Bevel.psd

the colors follow along the outline, which can create a quick neon effect (see page 381), an inline/outline effect for type (see page 311), or a multicolor glow if the gradient includes transparency at the outer edge. Patterns and gradients can be scaled within the Stroke width. The Stroke can be useful for filling in an Outer Bevel when you don't want the layer below to show through it (see the "Bevels — Inner & Outer" tip on page 408).

BEVEL AND EMBOSS

The Bevel And Emboss dialog box is complex, and takes some getting used to. But if you remember the filled, blurred duplicate idea, it can be easier to grasp how it works. To create the highlight and shadow effects that simulate the bevel shading, blurred dark and light versions are offset and trimmed. The highlights and shadows are partly transparent, even when you set the Opacity at 100%, so they blend with the color underneath. This blend creates the illusion of the bevel.

Like the Shadows and Glows, the Bevel And Emboss effect has tremendous potential beyond what its name implies. When you experiment with Bevel And Emboss, start with the Contour and Texture options in the list on the left side of the dialog box *turned off*. They add complexity, so it's easier to explore them after you understand the basics of the bevel. Explore the Structure panel of the Bevel And Emboss section. Then move on to the Shading section, which controls the lighting.

Structure

Choose the **Direction**: the default **Up** raises the object from the surface; **Down** sinks it into the surface.

Then choose the **Style**: The **Inner Bevel** builds the beveled edge *inward* from the layer content's outline, so the highlight and shadow it generates will blend with the color of the layer content underneath. The **Outer Bevel** builds the beveled edge *outward* from the outline, so the bevel blends with whatever is "behind" the layer, outside the outline of the layer content. The material that's beyond the outline can be the layer below, or it can be a band of color created by the Stroke effect, as shown in the "SW" at the left. In the **Emboss** Style, the bevel "straddles" the outline, building the bevel half outward and half inward to create the kind of bevel seen in license plates and street signs. **Pillow Emboss** is a kind of double bevel, with a bevel extending away from the outline in both directions, like a quilted effect. If you've added a Stroke effect, the **Stroke Emboss** builds the bevel using only the width of the Stroke.

Size, which again is the degree of blurring used to create the effect, determines how far inward or outward the bevel goes — how much of the shape or the background is consumed by the bevel. **Soften** controls what happens to the edge that's away from the

A high Altitude setting (70°, shown at the right) can add thickness to a beveled graphic and can simulate a strong reflection from the surface. The Layer Style for the image at the left uses Photoshop's default Altitude setting, 30°.

 Altitude.psd

outline — whether this edge is sharp and angular or round. A higher Soften value makes it rounder.

Depth determines how steep the sides of the bevel are. A greater Depth setting increases contrast between the tones used for the highlights and shadows and makes the bevel look steeper.

Shading

The **Angle** and **Global Light** settings operate the same way as for the Shadows. The Angle determines the direction of the light and the Use Global Light check box indicates that if you change the lighting here, it will also be changed for all the effects in the file that have the Global Light option turned on.

The **Altitude** setting can also be part of the Global Light. If you envision a circular dome over your layer content, the Angle setting determines where around the circle the light is positioned. The Altitude is how far up the dome the light is hung — from 0° (at "floor"

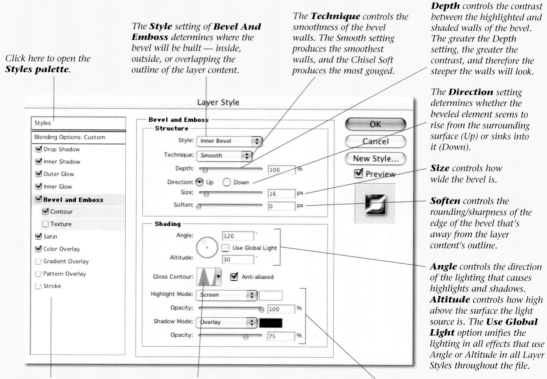

Click here to open the **Styles palette**.

The **Style** setting of **Bevel And Emboss** determines where the bevel will be built — inside, outside, or overlapping the outline of the layer content.

The **Technique** controls the smoothness of the bevel walls. The Smooth setting produces the smoothest walls, and the Chisel Soft produces the most gouged.

Depth controls the contrast between the highlighted and shaded walls of the bevel. The greater the Depth setting, the greater the contrast, and therefore the steeper the walls will look.

The **Direction** setting determines whether the beveled element seems to rise from the surrounding surface (Up) or sinks into it (Down).

Size controls how wide the bevel is.

Soften controls the rounding/sharpness of the edge of the bevel that's away from the layer content's outline.

Angle controls the direction of the lighting that causes highlights and shadows. **Altitude** controls how high above the surface the light source is. The **Use Global Light** option unifies the lighting in all effects that use Angle or Altitude in all Layer Styles throughout the file.

Clicking the **name** of an effect opens its section of the dialog box. Clicking the **check box** toggles the visibility of the effect on or off.

Gloss Contour controls the shininess of the surface, from matte to highly polished, by remapping the tones in the highlights and shadows.

Mode, Color, and **Opacity** settings for the bevel highlights and shadows can be controlled independently.

The Gloss Contour in the Bevel And Emboss section of the Layer Style dialog box was important in creating the dark and light "reflections" that make the surface of the Chrome look shiny and curved. The Gloss Contour was also important in simulating the material placed inside the chrome setting. These effects are described step-by-step in "Custom Chrome" on page 389.

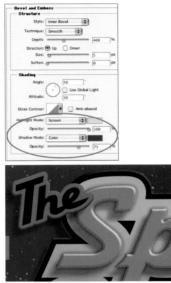

The type was colored with a red Color Overlay and then "lit" with a Bevel And Emboss effect. In the Bevel And Emboss section of the Layer Style dialog box, yellow in Screen mode was used for the bevel highlights and purple in Color Mode for the shadow, to simulate two colored light sources shining on the red type.

SEEING NAMES OF PRESETS

If you turn on Tool Tips (Preferences, General, Show Tool Tips) you can see the name of each Pattern, Contour, Style, or other preset when you pause the cursor over its thumbnail in a palette.

level of the dome) to 90° (at the top of the dome). By increasing the Altitude, you can move the "bevel highlight" farther onto the front surface of the element to which the Style is applied. The result is that surfaces seem more polished with the harder highlights created by higher Altitude settings.

Gloss Contour remaps the tones in the bevel highlight and shadow to make the surfaces seem more or less glossy. The Gloss Contour can be useful for imitating highly polished surfaces with multiple highlights.

The **Color, Mode,** and **Opacity** settings for the Highlight and Shadow let you control the characteristics of highlighted edges and shadowed edges independently. So you can use them to simulate two different-colored light sources if you like, rather than a highlight and a shadow, as shown in the colorful type at the left.

CONTOUR

Just below Bevel And Emboss in the list on the left side of the Layer Style dialog box you'll find **Contour**. This Contour has to do with the Structure of the bevel. It defines the shape of the bevel's "shoulder." To explore its effect, you can start with a gray Shape, add the default Bevel And Emboss, and increase the Size to make the bevel wider. Then click Contour in the list at the left side of the box and make choices from the Contour palette that pops out when you click the little triangle to the right of the Contour swatch. You'll be able to see that the bevel changes as if the Contour swatch were the cross-section of the bevel. Experiment with the Range slider, which controls how much of the bevel is "sculpted" by the Contour — in other words, how much of the bevel is consumed by the "shoulder." Low Range settings make the "shoulder" smaller and move it away from the outline created by the layer content.

TEXTURE

Below Contour in the effects list is **Texture**. The Texture effect embosses the pattern you choose from the Pattern swatch in the Texture section of the Layer Style dialog box. This swatch is like the one in the Pattern Overlay section of the dialog box except that here the patterns appear in grayscale. That's because only the lights and darks of the pattern are used — to simulate bumps and pits in the surface. For an Inner Bevel the embossed pattern goes inside the outline of the layer content. For the Outer Bevel the embossed pattern goes outside, so it appears on whatever is in the layers below the layer with the Style. For Emboss and Pillow Emboss the embossed pattern extends both inside and outside, and for Stroke it appears only within the stroke width. The pattern emboss is affected by the Depth (contrast) and Soften settings for Bevel And Emboss and by all the settings in its Shading section.

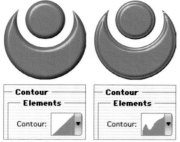

The Contour addition to the Bevel And Emboss can be used to shape the bevel "shoulder." Here the default Linear Contour is shown on the left and a custom Contour on the right.

IMAGE Bevel Contour.psd

BLENDING OPTIONS

The **Blending Options** section of the Layer Style dialog box governs how the layer interacts with other layers. In the **General Blending** section at the top of the dialog box, you can change the Blend Mode and the Opacity. These changes are reflected in the **Blend Mode** and **Opacity** settings that appear at the top of the Layers palette. (Blend mode is discussed in Chapter 2, "Color in Photoshop.")

The settings in the **Advanced Blending** section are a bit more complex. Starting at the bottom of the box, the **"Blend If"** settings allow you to give priority in compositing to certain ranges of tones or colors in the active layer or the image below (see "Blending Options" on page 156).

At the top of the Advanced Blending section is the **Fill Opacity** slider. This control allows you to reduce the Opacity of the layer's "fill" without reducing the opacity of the entire layer. That means, for instance, that you can make the fill partly transparent but leave its shadows or glows at full strength. The two check boxes under the Fill Opacity slider control whether certain inner effects

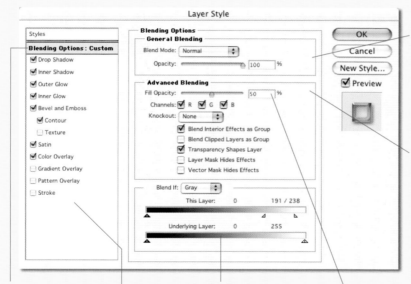

*In the **General Blending** section of Blending Options you'll find **Blend Mode** and **Opacity** settings. These are the same controls that are found at the top of the Layers palette. Changing a setting here also changes it in the Layers palette and vice versa.*

*The Layers palette shows no evidence of the customized settings in the **Advanced Blending** section.*

*The **Shallow** and **Deep Knockout** options can make a "hole" in underlying layers. So if you reduce the Fill Opacity, you'll be able to see through the active layer to what lies below.*

Blending Options are part of the Layer Style, but they don't transfer if a Style is dragged and dropped.

*Applying any of the **effects** in this list causes an "f" icon to appear to the right of the layer's name in the Layers palette.*

*The **Blend If** sliders define the ranges of tone or color where a pixel from the active layer has priority over the pixel from the image underneath, and vice versa. The black and white sliders can be split by holding down the Alt/Option key to make a softer transition so the pixels blend rather than completely replace each other.*

*The tricky thing about **Fill Opacity** is specifying what constitutes the Fill. With both of the "Blend . . . As" options unchecked, the original layer content constitutes the entire fill. With the **Blend Interior Effects As Group** option turned on, any Overlay effects, the Inner Glow, and the Satin effect are considered part of the Fill. With the **Blend Clipped Layers As Group** option turned on, any clipped layers are also treated as part of the Fill.*

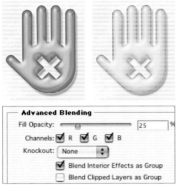

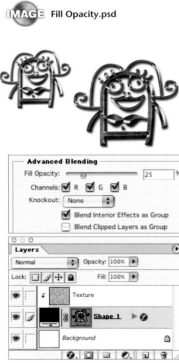

are considered part of the Fill for purposes of adjusting Fill Opacity. With the **Blend Interior Effects As Group** box checked, the Inner Glow, any interior bevel highlights and shadows, the three Overlays, and the Satin effect — all of which are effects that fall within the layer content's outline — are considered part of the fill when the Fill Opacity is reduced. (The Inner Shadow isn't considered an Interior Effect for purposes of blending.)

The **Blend Clipped Layers As Group** checkbox controls whether any layers that are part of a clipping group with the "styled" layer as the base are treated as if they became part of the layer before or after the Layer Style was added. With this option turned on, it's as if the clipped layer becomes part of the fill *before* the Layer Style's effects are applied. So a Color Overlay, Gradient Overlay, or Pattern Overlay will cover or change the clipped image. Blend modes of the various layers also play a role, of course, and it gets complicated quickly.

If you want a layer to cut a hole in the layers below, you can reduce the Fill Opacity and choose the Shallow or Deep option for **Knockout**. If you choose **Deep**, the knockout can go all the way down to (but not through) the *Background,* or to transparency if there is no *Background.* If the **Shallow** option is chosen, the knockout only goes as far as the first logical stopping point — the bottom of the clipping group or the layer set, if either exists. If no stopping point exists, then the knockout goes all the way to the *Background* or transparency. These results are modified by the settings in the two "Blend . . . As" check boxes and by whether the layer set is in Pass Through mode, not to mention the blend modes of the individual layers. Again, it gets complicated quickly.

ENHANCING LAYER STYLES

Once you have a Layer Style in place, it may be easier to make a color or lighting change by adding an Adjustment layer or using Lighting Effects than to "remix" all the effects in the Style. For highly polished surfaces created with Layer Styles you can also add "environmental" reflections by using Distort filters to bend a reflected image to fit the styled element. Filters can also be useful for roughening the edges of a surface to which a texture has been applied, for a more realistic look.

Adjustment Layers

Levels, Curves, Color Balance, and Hue/Saturation can be varied through Adjustment layers to change the color or brightness of a layer to which a Style has been applied, without the need to go back into the Layer Style box and make changes. You can set the Adjustment layer to affect just the interior of the styled element, or the interior and exterior effects, or the interior, exterior, and all visible layers below. Just be sure that the two "Blend . . . As" check boxes in the Advanced Blending section of Blending Options in the

When Blend Interior Effects As Group is turned on, the Color Overlay, Satin, and Inner Glow are treated as if they became part of the surface of the shape before the Fill Opacity was reduced. Since there is no clipping group in this file, the Blend Clipped Layers As Group setting has no effect.

IMAGE   Fill Opacity.psd

Here the marble image is "clipped" by the graphic, Blend Interior Effects As Group is turned on, and Blend Clipped Layers As Group is turned off. It's as if the marble surface goes on top of the Color and Gradient Overlays and other interior effects that create the gray metallic look.

IMAGE   Clipped.psd

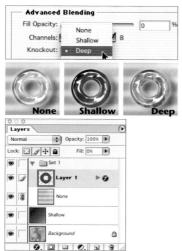

With Knockout set to None, the striped surface shows behind the styled "glass" graphic. With Knockout set to Shallow, the graphic knocks out through the striped surface since it's included in the layer set with the graphic, to show the gradient beneath. With Knockout set to Deep, the graphic knocks out all the way to the Background.

IMAGE Knockout.psd

The middle button shows the original color of all three buttons. To change the color of the left button without changing its Outer Glow or Drop Shadow, a Hue/Saturation Adjustment layer was grouped with the button layer. To change the color of the right button, we used a Hue/Saturation Adjustment layer with the same settings, but it was included in a layer set whose mode was changed from the default Pass Through to Normal.

IMAGE Color Adjustments.psd

Layer Style box are set up so that the Adjustment layer will act on the interior effects and clipped layers if that's what you want.

- If the Adjustment layer is made part of a clipping group with the styled layer serving as its base, the Adjustment Layer will **act only on the interior of the element**. If Blend Interior Effects As Group is turned on, it will affect any Overlay, Inner Glow, or Satin effects along with the original fill.

- If the Adjustment layer is not "clipped," it will affect not only the **interior** of the element but also any **exterior effects**, such as Drop Shadow or Outer Glow, and any **other layers** that are visible below it.

- You can set up your file so the Adjustment layer affects **a number of consecutive layers, even if they are not at the bottom of the layer stack and are not grouped**. To do this, make a layer set, with the Adjustment layer as the top layer in the set and set the blend mode of the layer set to Normal. (A layer set can be made by activating one of the layers and linking all the others you want in the set by clicking in the column next to the Eye in the Layers palette; then choose New Set From Linked from the pop-out menu in the upper right corner of the Layers palette. You can then unlink the layers if you wish.)

Lighting Effects

With the Lighting Effects filter you can create pools of light exactly where you want them by adding Spotlights. A way to apply Lighting Effects with flexibility is to add a 50%-gray-filled layer in Overlay mode and run the filter on that. Because 50% gray is neutral (invisible) in Overlay mode, only the lightened or darkened areas of the layer show up to light the composite. To use Lighting Effects in this way, Alt/Option-click the Create A New Layer button at the bottom of the Layers palette, and in the New Layer dialog box choose Overlay for the mode and click the check box for Fill With Overlay Neutral Color (50% Gray). In the Lighting Effects dialog

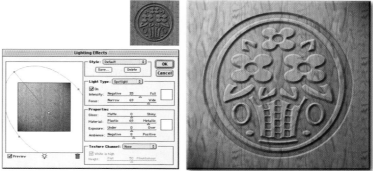

After a Layer Style was used to create a carved effect (top), the Lighting Effects filter was used to add a spotlight to enhance the lighting. (These Style and Lighting Effects techniques are presented step-by-step in "Carving a Smooth, Patterned Surface" on page 387.)

An image of palm trees was treated with the Glass filter and layered above the styled graphic in this chrome treatment. The techniques are described in step 4 of "Custom Chrome" on page 389 and in "Chrome Reflection Variations" on page 394.

The initial "carving" of the rock was done by applying a Layer Style to a black-filled graphic on a transparent layer, using Bevel And Emboss and Shadow effects. The "styled" layer was modified with the Displace filter to make the beveled edge follow the crevices and outcrops of the rock. The technique is described step-by-step in "Carving a Textured Surface" on page 382.

box (Filter, Render, Lighting Effects) you won't be able to see the image — only the gray — as you set up your spotlights. But once you click OK to leave the box, you can add a layer mask or change the Opacity of the layer to fine-tune the lighting. You'll find an example of this use of Lighting Effects in "Combining with Light" on page 220. Lighting Effects can also be very helpful for creating patterns to use as Pattern Overlay or Texture effects (see page 241).

Other Filters

The **Glass** filter (Filter, Distort, Glass) can be extremely useful in distorting environmental images to look like reflections in polished metal or glass surfaces. You can find examples on pages 389–398 in this chapter. The **Displace** filter, also in the Distort "family," can augment carved and chiseled effects by distorting the layer content to make it conform to the textured surface you want to "carve" into, as shown at the left.

Other filters, such as Spatter, can be used to modify the edge of a graphic so its texture matches the roughness introduced by the Texture effect in a Layer Style. An example is shown on page 365. And the Texturizer, Noise, Clouds, Tile Maker, and other filters can be very useful for producing patterns, as shown on pages 378–380.

PHOTOSHOP AND THE THIRD DIMENSION

There are times when you need to go beyond the dimensionality offered by Photoshop's Styles to create an image with a true 3D look. In addition, three of Photoshop's Edit, Transform functions (**Skew, Perspective,** and **Distort**) allow you to select part or all of an image and telescope or "bend" it to exaggerate perspective; the **Spherize** filter can also create depth illusions. And the **3D Transform** filter lets you select an element of your image and treat it as though it was projected onto a 3D object, changing the perspective as you turn it with the filter's trackball tool. (Using the 3D Transform filter is explained step-by-step in "Applying a Logo with 3D Transform" on page 215.)

Stand-alone 3D programs create solid objects by *modelling.* Two of the simplest ways to model are to *extrude* or *revolve* two-dimensional vector-based artwork into a 3D shape. They also allow you to *stage* an entire scene by arranging the models you make, and then quickly change the viewpoint or lighting to produce a new perspective. All 3D programs can also *render,* producing a photo-like view of the scene that assigns surface characteristics to the models and includes the interaction of light and shadows with these textures.

Zaxwerks' 3D Invigorator, a plug-in for Photoshop — provides many of the functions of a stand-alone 3D program. By extruding elements in Photoshop, the Invigorator allows you to create and render elaborately surfaced 3D imagery without ever leaving Photoshop. There are two ways that Photoshop can work with the artwork from 3D programs or plug-in filters. It can serve as

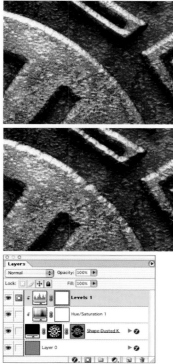

In this corroded metal effect, two Adjustment layers were used to brighten and "neutralize" the color of the graphic to make it stand out from the rusted background (top). Then the Spatter filter was applied to a matching layer mask to "roughen" the edge to match the surface corrosion that had been applied by the Layer Style. The technique is described step-by-step in "Rusted & Pitted" starting on page 399.

Zaxwerks 3D Invigorator is a Photoshop plug-in that provides many of the modelling and rendering functions of stand-alone 3D programs.

the recipient of an object or scene modeled and rendered in three dimensions, so you can then retouch or enhance it. Or it can serve as a generator for images to be used as surface maps to add color, texture, and detail to a model in a stand-alone 3D program.

Photoshop to 3D

All 3D programs accept color files that can be applied to 3D models as flat surface textures (called *texture maps*), for tactile effects (called *bump maps*), or for other "mapping" purposes. Photoshop's Lighting Effects filter can be useful to quickly test out *bump maps* to be used in 3D images. Some programs can also generate 3D models from grayscale images created in Photoshop, translating the shades of gray as different distances above or below a surface, to create mountains, canyons, or other 3D models.

3D to Photoshop

Programs like Adobe Dimensions are designed to make relatively simple 3D models from type or from artwork drawn in PostScript programs such as Adobe Illustrator, Macromedia FreeHand, or CorelDraw. They can extrude or revolve models around the height, width, or depth axes and they can create perspective views, but they can't provide the complex texture, lighting, and shadowing effects of more powerful 3D programs. Effects such as highlights, shadows, and embossed textures can be added by hand to Dimensions artwork with Photoshop's filtering and layering techniques.

Even if you use a more sophisticated 3D program or plug-in with advanced modelling and rendering functions, starting and ending with Photoshop can still save you time. Setting up your models, lighting, and camera angles in a 3D program is time-consuming, and rendering can take a long time. So if you want to change the color or brightness of a 3D image once it's rendered, it may make sense to adjust Color Balance or Hue/Saturation for all or part of the image in Photoshop instead of going back to the 3D program to change the lighting and render the scene again. Also, some kinds of shadows and minute details may look more convincing if applied "by hand" with Photoshop's airbrush or other techniques than by a 3D program's rendering algorithms.

In addition to full-color rendered images, most 3D programs can produce a mask that accompanies the file, appearing as an alpha channel when the file is opened in Photoshop. This channel can then be used in any of the ways Photoshop masks are applied — for instance, to isolate parts of an image so the color can be changed, to apply a blur or another filter selectively, or to silhouette the image for compositing into a new background.

Anatomy of a Layer Style

The Layer Style dialog box offers almost limitless combinations of settings within the 12 layer effects listed at the left side of the box.

These four pages examine the **Wow-Plastic 06** *Layer Style (inspired by Apple Computer's omnipresent aqua interface components and used in "Clear, Colorful Plastic" on page 370). This section explains the fundamentals of how the component effects work. To explore the individual effects, open the* **Plastic P.psd** *file that you'll find on the Wow CD-ROM, then open the Layers palette and double-click the* **"f" symbol to the right of the "P" layer's name** *to open the Layer Style dialog box.* **In the list on the left side of the Layer Style box,** *you can click on the name of each individual effect as you read its description here.*

Plastic P.psd

Layer Content

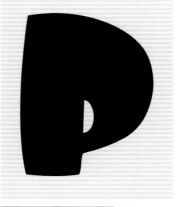

We started by setting type in the BeesWax font above a white Background. The Layer Style could have been applied directly to the live type. But in the **Plastic P.psd** *file the type has been converted to a Shape layer, so you can explore the Layer Style without encountering a Caution box if you don't have the font installed on your system.*

Color & Blending

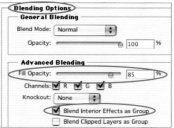

When you put together a Layer Style, it's good to start with the effect that will bring about the biggest change. Then you can watch the Style develop as you add the subtler effects. In this case we started by applying color using the **Color Overlay** *effect; we clicked the color swatch to open the Color Picker and chose a light blue. By applying the effect in Normal mode at 100% Opacity, we could ensure that the Style would always produce the light blue color, completely replacing whatever color had originally been assigned to the type or graphic.*

Since we knew we would be building a Layer Style that included several interior effects — the Color Overlay, Inner Glow, and Satin — we made sure that **Blend Interior Effects As Group** *was turned on in the Blending Options section of the Layer Style box. With this choice, the Blending Options settings would act on the interior of the "P" as a unit, applying to these interior effects combined. For instance, reducing the Fill Opacity to make the "P" more transparent would also make these interior effects more transparent.*

Drop Shadow

With the most significant effect in place, the **Drop Shadow** was a good next step, to begin creating dimensionality. Here the Drop Shadow effect makes a blurred offset copy "behind" the "P." One goal for the Drop Shadow here was to contribute to the illusion of transparency by making it look as if light is passing through the blue type and coloring the shadow. So we clicked the color swatch to open the Color Picker, moved the cursor into the working window to sample the color of the "P," and then chose a darker, less saturated blue. To light the "P" from the top, we set the Drop Shadow's Angle at 90°. It would have been convenient to turn on Use Global Light so that this Angle could automatically carry over to all other effects that use a lighting Angle setting. But using Global Light could have caused problems with maintaining the finished Style's shiny surface quality, if the Style was applied to another file (see the "Lighting: Global or Not?" tip on page 355). We also made sure that the default Layer Knocks Out Drop Shadow was turned on, so the shadow wouldn't show through and darken the "P," which was at 85% Fill Opacity.

Shading the Edge 1

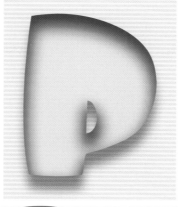

The **Inner Shadow** effect, a blurred offset copy that's created inside the edge, was used here to help round the edges of the "P." We made a soft transition for a gentle rounding (the Size setting controls how soft, or diffuse, a blurred effect will be). So that it would darken the color already established by the Color Overlay, we left the Inner Shadow in its default Multiply mode. We set the Angle at 90°, the same as for the Drop Shadow. (The Inner Shadow is often used for a "cutout" or carved-in, effect. But because a drop shadow was already in place making the "P" look like it was floating above the background, the Inner Shadow didn't create the cutout illusion.) **Note**: Although the Inner Shadow occurs inside the outline of the layer content you apply it to, it isn't blended with other interior effects (Overlays, Inner Glow, and Satin) when you turn on the Blend Interior Effects As Group option.

Shading the Edge 2

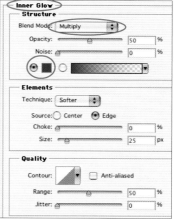

We used the **Inner Glow** to enhance the rounding of the edge that had been started with the Inner Shadow. We changed the Blend Mode from the default Screen to Multiply and used approximately the same blue as for the Inner Shadow. In Multiply mode the dark Inner Glow darkens the shading already established inside the "P" by the Inner Shadow. But unlike the Inner Shadow, the Inner Glow is not an offset effect, so its dark "halo" also darkens the edge areas that were not shaded by the Inner Shadow — for example, the lower edges of the "P."

Adding a Highlight

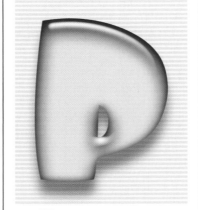

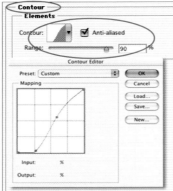

Here we used the **Bevel And Emboss** effect, not so much for bevelling but to add reflective (or specular) highlights on the surface of the "P." Working in the Structure section of the dialog box, we used Inner Bevel for the Style. In the Shading section we used the default white Highlight in Screen mode. But because we had used the Inner Shadow and Inner Glow to control the shading, we could effectively turn off the Shadow by setting its Opacity at 0 (using the bottom slider in the box). Changing the Altitude setting to 65° was very important, because it pulled the highlight off the top edge of the plastic "P" and onto the front surface. Again we set the Angle at 90° to keep the lighting consistent with the Drop Shadow and Inner Shadow.

Refining the Shine

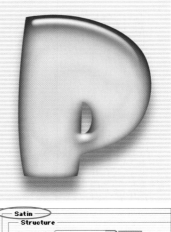

In the list of effects at the left side of the Layer Style dialog box, we clicked on **Contour**. In the Contour section we clicked the Contour thumbnail and customized the curve in the Contour Editor box as shown above. We also changed the Range to 90%. These changes sharpened and narrowed the highlight and pulled it farther up and off the edge of the "P," so it looked even more like a reflection on a hard surface.

Shading Irregularities

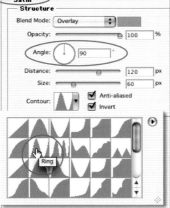

The **Satin** effect was applied in light blue in Overlay mode, creating an offset, manipulated copy of the "P." The Distance setting scaled the copy, reducing it vertically because of the 90° Angle setting. This setting determines the angle of distortion of the Satin duplicate. A 90° setting squashes the duplicate vertically, making it shorter and fatter. As in the other sections of the Layer Style box, the Size setting controls the amount of blur, making the effect subtler by blurring the copy. We clicked the little triangle to the right of the Contour thumbnail and chose a Contour ("Ring" from Adobe's default set) that provides light-dark-light variation in the blurred, squashed duplicate, making it look as if light is bouncing around inside the thick plastic shape.

Refraction Glows

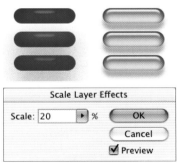

*Finally, the **Outer Glow** effect in light blue was applied in its default Screen mode. We used Softer for the Technique setting for a more diffuse and irregular look than the alternative Precise setting would have produced. Because the glow is in Screen mode, it affects only the parts of the shadow that are darker than itself, and it affects the light background only slightly. As a result, it lightens and colors the Drop Shadow close to the edge of the "P." This makes it look as if light is being focused through the plastic, brightening the shadow beneath. The degree of brightening could be controlled by adjusting the glow's Opacity.*

CONTROLLING TRANSPARENCY

To reduce the opacity of an element without reducing the opacity of exterior effects in the Layer Style, such as a Drop Shadow or Outer Glow, use the Fill Opacity control in the Advanced Blending area of the Layer Style dialog box, rather than the Opacity control in the General Blending Section or in the Layers palette.

SMART SCALING

Whenever you apply a preset Layer Style, be sure that the first thing you do is to scale it to fit. This is necessary because if the Style was designed for a different-DPI file or for a different-size element than the one you're applying it to, it will look entirely different until you resize it.

In Photoshop 7 there's no need to tackle the Herculean task of resizing each individual effect by resetting all its parameters and checking the resulting interactions of all the effects at each step. Instead, simply choose **Layer, Layer Style, Scale Effects**, or right-click the Effects line in the Layers palette to bring up a context-sensitive menu where you can choose Scale Effects (Control-click the Effects line if you're using a Mac without a two-button mouse). Now watch the changes in your image as you adjust the Scale slider — all the effects are scaled at once.

The Scale Effects command doesn't affect the Color Overlay effect (since there's nothing to scale). And remember that a pixel-based Pattern Overlay or Texture effect will look pixelated if you scale it up too much. It can lose detail if it's scaled down very much, especially if the Scale percentage is other than 50% or 25% setting (or some other even reduction).

*The **Wow-Plastic 06** Style looks very different (top left) until it's scaled down to fit the buttons (top right).*

Clear, Colorful Plastic

Overview *In a 225-dpi file, set type; apply the* **Wow-Plastic 06** *Layer Style; add other artwork layers; copy the Style from the Type layer to the artwork layers, and scale the Style appropriately for each layer's artwork; modify the color of some elements with Adjustment layers.*

IMAGE

"Clear Plastic" "before" and "after" files

1

The letter "P" was set in the BeesWax font at about 640 pixels high.

2a

The Wow-Plastic 06 Layer Style (found on the CD-ROM that comes with this book) was applied to the "P" (see "Anatomy of a Layer Style" on page 366 for more about this Style).

2b

Shading	
Angle:	90
	Use Global Light
Altitude:	67

The lighting Angle was set to 90° for every effect that included lighting. The Altitude (found only in the Bevel And Emboss effect) was set to 67°.

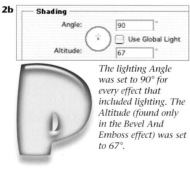

ONE OF THE FEATURES THAT MAKES Photoshop's Layer Styles so useful is that once you've developed a Style you like, it's so easy to apply it to other elements. The ability to scale Styles greatly increases its versatility because it means you don't have to reset individual parameters for all the layer effects. Simply scale the entire Style to fit your new elements (see the "Smart Scaling" tip on page 369 for the how and why of scaling). We manufactured the logo above by developing a Layer Style and then scaling the Style to fit various elements in the logo. We used Adjustment layers as a quick, easy way to change the color and intensity of some of the elements.

1 Setting type. Open a new 225-dpi file with a white *Background*. Choose the Type tool. With the Type tool active, the Options bar lets you choose the font, size, and style you want. We used BeesWax, a shareware TrueType font for Windows by Kevin Woodward, available from **fontfiles.com** and other Web sites; we used the TTFConverter utility (a Web search should turn up sources) to convert it for the Mac. If you don't have BeesWax, you may want to use an ExtraBold or Black typeface such as Helvetica Black. Click with the Type tool in the working window where you want your character to be, and type a letter **1**. If you look at the Layers palette, you'll see that a new type layer (represented by a "T" icon) has been added to your file, and that its name consists of the letter you typed.

If you want to change the specifications for your type, highlight the letter by dragging over it with the Type tool, and then make the changes to the specifications in the Options bar. Or if you'd like even more control over your type, you can click the Palettes button in the Options bar to open the Character palette. (For help with

3

The lower "P" was repositioned with the Move tool and then highlighted with the Type tool and changed to an "E.".

4a

The developing logo after the circle of dots was pasted in

4b

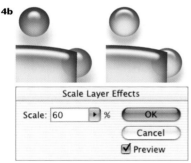

Scaling the copied Layer Style to turn the "marbles" (top left) into flatter "dots" whose dimensional effect matches the type

4c

The logo after scaling the Style on the "dots" layer

operating the Type tool, see "Type," starting on page 292.)

2 Adding a Style. Now you can turn your flat black type into a piece of transparent blue plastic by assigning a preset Style: Open the Styles palette (Window, Show Styles). If you haven't already loaded the **Wow Presets** (found on the Wow! CD-ROM), refer to page 7 for instructions. Once you have loaded the **Wow Presets** and restarted Photoshop, you'll notice that the pop-out menu, accessible from the arrow in the tab of the styles Palette, now has all the available Wow Styles listed at the bottom of the menu. Select the Wow 7-12 Plastic Styles from the menu, then select Wow-Plastic 06 from the newly loaded set **2a, 2b.** Or you can copy the Style from the "P" layer of the **Clear Plastic-After.psd** file as follows: In the Layers palette of the **Clear Plastic-After.psd** file, right-click (Windows) or Control-click (Mac) directly on the "*f*" icon *on the "P" layer* and choose Copy Layer Style from the pop-out menu; then in the Layers palette for the file where you want to add the Style, right/Control-click in about the same place on the entry for the layer you want to "style" and choose Paste Layer Style. **Note:** If the type you've used is very different in size or structure from the BeesWax font we used in our example, you may need to scale the Style, as described in the third paragraph of step 4.

3 Adding a second letter. To add a second letter to the logo, you can copy the first and then edit the copy: We duplicated our type layer by dragging its name in the Layers palette to the Create A New Layer button at the bottom of the palette. Then we targeted the lower of the two identical type layers by clicking on its name. Now we could use the Move tool to drag the lower "P" into position approximately where we wanted our second letter to be (you can toggle from the Type tool to the Move tool temporarily by holding down the Ctrl/⌘ key, or simply by moving the Type tool's cursor far enough away from the type). We used the Type tool to select and edit the type we had moved, changing the character

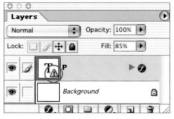

5a

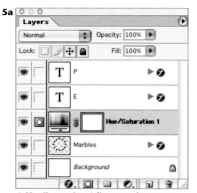

A Hue/Saturation Adjustment layer was added above the dots.

5b

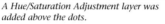

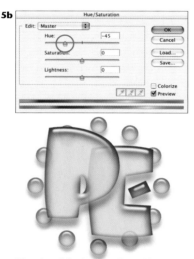

The color of the dots was changed by moving the Hue slider; the Colorize feature offered by the dialog box wasn't needed in this case.

from "P" to "E" **3.** If you need to fine-tune the position of the new letter, activate the Move tool again and press the arrow keys.

Note: One of the features of the Wow-Plastic 06 style is a setting of 85% for Fill Opacity in the Blending Options section of the Layer Style dialog box. With the "Blend Interior Effects As Group" box checked, the reduced Fill Opacity makes the type partially transparent while maintaining the appropriate intensity of the highlights and shadows. In Photoshop 7, the Fill Opacity setting is now located directly within the Layer palette.

4 Adding and styling another component. Now add the next element to your logo. We had produced our ring of dots in Adobe Illustrator, so we copied them there, and then targeted the *Background* of our Photoshop file and pasted (Edit, Paste, Paste As: Pixels) **4a.** This put the dots on a layer above the white *Background* and below the type.

To assign the same "material" and lighting specifications to your new element, copy the same Style used for the letters: Use the method described in step 2 for copying and pasting a Style, with the original "P" layer as the "donor" and the duplicate layer as the "recipient."

Now examine the newly styled artwork to see whether you need to scale the Style. In our case, the dots, which were quite a bit smaller than the letters, looked spherical when the Style was applied, like marbles. To make them look flatter and thus more like the plastic letters, we scaled the Style **4b, 4c:** Right-click on the little "*f*" icon *to the right of the layer's name* (Control-click for a one-

6a

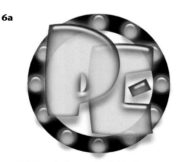

A flat black ring was pasted in from Illustrator.

6b

The Layer Style was copied from one of the type layers to apply it to the ring.

6c

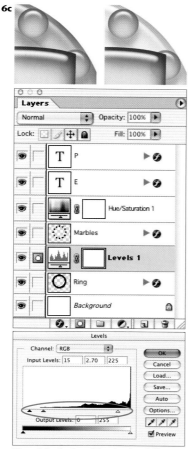

The original color of the ring (top left) was changed (top right) by adding a Levels Adjustment layer and moving the Input Levels sliders to lighten the color overall while maintaining good contrast.

6d

The logo after lightening the ring

button Mac mouse) to bring up the context-sensitive menu where you can choose Scale Effects. Now, with the Preview box checked, you can change the Scale number and watch your image change as you experiment with different percentages (see "Tweaking Numbers" on page 372 for shortcuts).

5 Adjusting color. You can use a Hue/Saturation Adjustment layer to change the color of the elements on the lower layers of your file — without having to recolor each of the effects that make up the Style. To maintain the blue color of the type layers but shift the color of the dots toward green, we added an Adjustment layer immediately above the dots by clicking the Create New Adjustment Layer button (the black/white circle) at the bottom of the Layers palette and clicking Hue/Saturation in the pop-up menu **5a.** We changed the color by moving the Hue slider. This retained the subtle brightness and color differences that we had built into the Style **5b.**

6 Adding and coloring more art. Add any other art needed for your logo, and apply the Style. We again targeted the white *Background* and pasted a ring that we had copied in Illustrator **6a.** We copied and pasted the Style from one of the type layers **6b,** as in step 4. We decided the Style didn't need to be scaled this time, but to lighten the ring, we used a Levels Adjustment layer above the ring but below the dots **6c, 6d.** By using Levels we could lighten the color but retain the highlights and shadows.

Finally we added a new type layer just below the other type layers, where it wouldn't be subject to the Adjustment layers lower in the stack. We clicked the color swatch in the Options bar and chose a blue for the type, then typed "PLASTIC ELASTIC," and reduced the Opacity of this layer to 50%. The reduced Opacity would let the color of the type blend with the highlights and shadows of the dots and ring. This would make it look as if the type was below them.

LIMITING A COLOR CHANGE

You can use an Adjustment layer to change the color in a single layer without affecting *all* the layers below, as shown in this button file. The middle button shows the original color of all three buttons. To change the color of the left button without changing its Outer Glow or Drop Shadow, a Hue/Saturation Adjustment layer was grouped with the button layer. To change the color of the right button, we used a Hue/Saturation Adjustment layer with the same settings, but it was included in a layer set whose mode was changed from the default Pass Through to Normal.

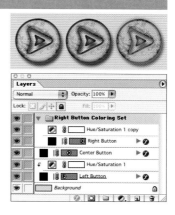

Textures & Backgrounds

***Overview** Create textures for type and graphics and for backgrounds, using patterns, filters, or Layer Styles.*

"1849" "before" and "after" files; **Brick.psd, Stone.psd, Steel.psd,** and **Rust.psd** files

1a
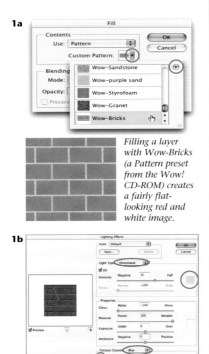

Filling a layer with Wow-Bricks (a Pattern preset from the Wow! CD-ROM) creates a fairly flat-looking red and white image.

1b

Using tinted Directional lighting and the Matte setting for the Gloss property to "emboss" with texture information from the Blue channel

1c
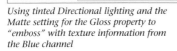

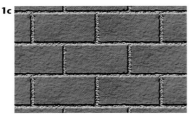

*A close-up of the finished textured **Brick.psd***

PHOTOSHOP 7 GIVES YOU A MAGICIAN'S KIT of filters, patterns, Actions, and Layer Styles that's a great place to start when you're looking for some "raw material" to support a concept or extend an image. With these tools you can invent textures out of thin air, either for making backgrounds or for turning plain, flat type or graphics into believable solid objects.

Before you begin, be sure to load all the Wow! Presets (Patterns, Gradients, Styles, Shapes, and Contours) from the **Wow! Presets** folders on the CD-ROM that comes with this book. This can be done by dragging the folder of Presets from the ***Photoshop 7 Wow! CD*** into the Photoshop 7 Presets folder and restarting Photoshop.

Example 1: Starting with a preset pattern. A Pattern preset can be a great resource for creating a surface texture. You can generate the dimensionality you need by running the Lighting Effects filter using one of the color channels (Red, Green, or Blue) as the Texture Channel. The Lighting Effects filter, especially with a Texture channel, can create dramatic dimensional effects that are hard to achieve any other way, because this filter lets you specify the type and color of one or more lights, as well as material properties of the environment, such as color and gloss.

We made our textured bricks by filling a layer with the Wow-Bricks preset Pattern fill. To do this, target the layer you want to fill and choose Edit, Fill. Then choose Pattern from the Use pop-out menu, and choose **Wow 7-Misc Surface Patterns** from the pop-out arrow in the upper right corner of the Custom Pattern pop-out, then select Wow-Bricks from that set **1a**. Wow-Bricks is a preset Pattern fill that's roughly based on Adobe's Bricks Action, from the **Textures.atn** set that comes with Photoshop 7. This Action uses the Add Noise and Clouds filters to generate a basic brick texture; it roughens the edges between brick and mortar using the Spatter filter, and uses Craquelure for additional texture. We stopped the Action before the Craquelure filter was applied, and used the resulting flat brick image (with some hand retouching, Noise filtering,

2a

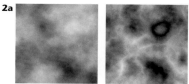

Running the Difference Clouds filter created clouds (left). Running it a second time created dark and light patterning that would work well with the Lighting Effects filter for making a stone texture.

2b

We duplicated the Red channel so we could use it as a Texture Channel for embossing a gray-filled layer.

2c

In the Lighting Effects dialog box we set up a Directional light with a tan color and chose a darker brown for the ambient lighting. The alpha channel made from the Red channel was used as the Texture Channel with White Is High turned on.

2d

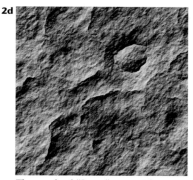

The completed "Stone" texture. The background for the "1849" illustration at the top of page 374 was created using this method.

and color tweaking) to define a seamlessly repeating pattern as described in "Seamlessly Tiling Patterns" on page 378.

Next enhance the surface texture: Choose Filter, Render, Lighting Effects and set the Light Style and Properties parameters **1b**. For the Texture Channel, choose a channel with good texture detail (we used the Blue channel). Make sure that White Is High is set appropriately (we turned it off, since we wanted the light-colored mortar to recede rather than come forward). Click OK **1c**.

Example 2: Creating a texture from scratch. You can

generate a variety of stone surfaces by starting with the Difference Clouds filter and using the result for "embossing" with the Lighting Effects filter. Open a new RGB file (Ctrl/⌘-N), and in the Contents section of the New dialog box, choose White. With black and white chosen as the Foreground and Background colors in the toolbox, choose Filter, Render, Difference Clouds; repeat the filter (Ctrl/⌘-F) as many times as needed to achieve the detail you want for your texture, with a pleasing mix of black elements to make depressions in the rock surface and white elements to create ridges. We applied the filter twice **2a**.

Now use your Difference Clouds image for embossing. You could use the method described in Example 1 to emboss the image itself (some examples of this are shown in the "Creating Textures" tip on page 238 and the "Making Marble & Stucco" tip on page 241). But if you don't want the black, white, and grays of the Difference Clouds image to appear in the final rock image, create a new gray-filled layer as a starting point, as we did here: Click the Create A New Layer button at the bottom of the Layers palette; choose Edit, Fill. In the Blending section of the Fill dialog box, make sure Mode is set to Normal and Opacity to 100%; in the Use section choose 50% Gray; click OK.

If you were to run the Lighting Effects filter on this layer using the Red, Green, or Blue channel as the Texture Channel (as in Example 1), no texture would be created; that's because the color channels are all filled with the flat tones that make 50% Gray. So you need to create a special texture channel: Turn off visibility for the gray-filled layer. Then open the Channels palette, and drag the name of one of the color channels to the Create New Channel button at the bottom of the palette; this will duplicate the color channel as an alpha

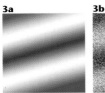

3a

3b

Starting with a Linear version of Adobe's Silver gradient to set the lighting

Adding Noise to create texture

3c

3d

Turning the noise to streaks with the Motion Blur filter

Widening the layer to get rid of the edge artifacts

3e

*The finished "**Steel**" image, colored by several spotlights in the Lighting Effects dialog box (A less dramatically lit steel is shown in the "Creating Textures" tip on page 238.)*

MIXING METALS

For some interesting metallic lustre effects, try running Adobe's Metal gradients on two different layers and at two slightly different angles. In the Layers palette, set the blend mode for the upper layer to Multiply, Screen, Overlay, or Soft Light mode (as shown below) with or without Transparency (Transparency can be set in the Options bar when the Gradient tool is selected).

channel **2b.** Back in the Layers palette, target the gray-filled layer by clicking its name in the Layers palette; choose Filter, Render, Lighting Effects, and choose your new alpha channel as the Texture Channel in the Lighting Effects dialog box **2c.** We used a Directional Light type at Full Intensity, with Matte and Plastic settings in the Properties section of the box to dull the surface. We colored the stone by clicking the color swatches and choosing colors for both the Directional light and the ambient (Properties) lighting **2d.**

Example 3: Using Noise to create a brushed metal texture.

We used Adobe's Silver gradient as the basis of our metallic lustre: Choose the Gradient tool and open the pop-out list of presets by clicking the little triangle to the right of the gradient swatch in the Options bar. Then click the circled triangle in the top right corner of the presets list, choose **Metals.grd** from the list and click Append to add Adobe's metallic gradients to the pop-out list of presets. We chose the Silver preset from the list (if you don't know how to view the names of the presets, see "The Best Presets Displays" tip on page 375); in the Options bar we chose the Linear gradient format and Normal mode, and dragged from a point near the top left corner toward the bottom right to make a kind of "vertical diagonal" gradient **3a.**

With the sheen established, start the texture by choosing Filter, Noise, Add Noise **3b.** We chose Gaussian and Monochromatic in the Add Noise dialog, with Amount set at 50% for our approximately 400-pixel-square file.

To convert the noise to streaks **3c,** choose Filter, Blur, Motion Blur. We used a Distance setting of 50 pixels at an Angle of 0° (for a horizontal blur effect). To get rid of the edge artifacts introduced by the Motion Blur, stretch the layer enough to make the odd edges disappear beyond the boundaries of the image **3d:** We chose Edit, Transform, Scale, and then changed the width (W:) setting in the Options bar to 110%. To complete the transformation operation, double-click in the image or press the Enter key.

Finally, we applied Lighting Effects, using one of the color channels as the Texture Channel (as in Example 1) and adding sheen and color with several colored spotlights. (To add another light, in the Lighting Effects dialog box, drag the little light bulb icon into position, and set the Light Type characteristics, including color) **3e.**

ANOTHER WORKHORSE FILTER

The Texturizer (Filter, Texture, Texturizer) can be used to create surface relief. Although this filter lacks the full "lighting studio" sophistication of the Lighting Effects filter, it has the advantage of being able to load any Photoshop (.psd) file as a repeating embossing texture (see the "Trying Out Texturizer" tip on page 247). Photoshop 7 comes with a Texture fill.pat file (inside the Presets, Patterns folder) containing patterns that can be loaded via this filter's dialog box.

4a

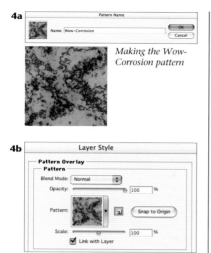

Pattern Name

Name: Wow-Corrosion

OK
Cancel

Making the Wow-Corrosion pattern

4b

Layer Style

Pattern Overlay
Pattern

Blend Mode: Normal

Opacity: ▬▬▬▬ 100 %

Pattern: ▼ ⬚ Snap to Origin

Scale: ▬▬▬▬ 100 %

☑ Link with Layer

Choosing the Wow-Corrosion pattern for the Pattern Overlay component of the Layer Style

4c

Layers

Normal ▾   Opacity: 100% ▶

Lock: ☐ 🖉 ✛ 🔒   Fill: 100% ▶

👁 🖉 ▮ **Layer 0** ▾ 🔵

👁   Effects

👁   🔵 Drop Shadow

👁   🔵 Bevel and Emboss

👁   🔵 Satin

👁   🔵 Pattern Overlay

👁   ▯ *Background* 🔒

🔵 ▾ 🔲 ☐ 🔵 ▾ 🔲 🗑

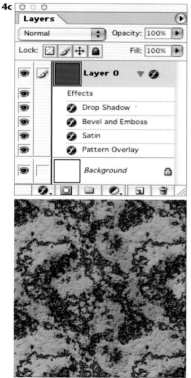

The Wow-Rocks 19 style, with its incorporated Wow-Corrosion pattern, applied to a simple gray-filled layer. The Wow-Corrosion pattern was used as a basis for the Style applied to the "1849" lettering at the top of page 374; see the 1849-After.psd file on the Wow! CD-ROM.

Example 4: Using a pattern in conjunction with a Layer Style. The most powerful tool in Photoshop 7's kit of special effects is the Layer Style. It provides millions of potential combinations for fine-tuning a special-effects treatment. But even more important is the ability to save these creations for repeated use. Styles can be scaled — quickly and easily tailored to fit any file you're working on — so they're extremely practical.

To make the seamlessly repeating custom pattern shown here, we created the basic color and contrast using Corel Texture 6, then opened the file in Photoshop. We made this image into a pattern **4a,** as described in "Seamlessly Tiling Patterns" on page 378. Then we used this pattern to build a Layer Style, as follows:

We filled a layer with a flat medium gray. To begin building the Style, we clicked the Add A Layer Style button (the "*f*") at the bottom of the Layers palette to open the pop-out list of effects, where we chose Pattern Overlay. From the Pattern list (opened by clicking the little triangle next to the Pattern swatch), we chose our newly-saved pattern **4b.** Now we could add other effects to the Layer Style: In the Layer Style dialog box, we chose Bevel And Emboss from the list on the left, clicked the Texture box underneath it, and then chose the same saved pattern we had used for the Pattern Overlay. Here the Pattern showed up as grayscale, since only the luminance is used for a Texture effect.

Then we set up the other components of the Style — Satin, Color Overlay, and Gradient Overlay — and saved the Style by clicking the New Style button and naming the Style **4b.** (To see the settings we used for Bevel And Emboss and other effects in the Rust sample **4c,** double-click the Effects line in the Layers palette of the **Rust.psd** file on the Wow! CD-ROM and explore the Layer Style.) For a step-by-step explanation of how layer effects work, see pages 352–362 and "Anatomy of a Layer Style" on page 366. Here's a brief description of the effects in the Wow-Rocks 19:

- **Pattern Overlay** applies the Wow-Corrosion pattern.

- **Bevel And Emboss,** with **Texture** turned on and Wow-Corrosion used as the Pattern, adds dimension to the texture.

- The **Satin** effect provides tone and color variations throughout the image. It does this by blurring and duplicating the basic shape of whatever the Style is being applied to (in this case a layer filled to the edges of the file). The effect can be subtle or dramatic.

- **Gradient Overlay** adds more overall light-and-dark effects.

- **Color Overlay** adjusts the color.

- The mandatory **Drop Shadow** for occasions when the style may be applied to type or graphics. 🖋

Seamlessly Tiling Patterns

Overview *Use the Offset filter to see the "seam" that your image would create if used as a tile; use one of three methods to hide the seam and make the tile — a tile-making filter, the Clone Stamp, Healing Brush, Patch tool or "hand patching" with selected parts of the texture; define the tile as a pattern.*

IMAGE

Yin Yang.psd file

1

The Offset filter was run with the Wrap Around option to make the "seam" obvious.

2a

Using ImageReady's Tile Maker filter in Blend Edges mode

2b

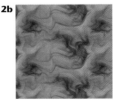

A 500-pixel-wide square filled with the Wow-Tortoise Shell pattern by choosing Edit, Fill, Pattern

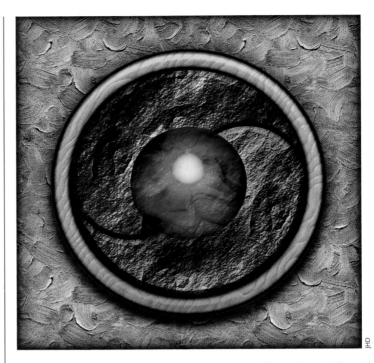

THERE ARE SO MANY WAYS TO USE PATTERNS in Photoshop 7 that it's good to know how to generate your own. If you want to turn an image into a seamlessly tiling texture, you need to first assess the seam that would be generated if you simply defined the entire image as a pattern. Then choose a method for hiding the seam. Once you've used the chosen method, check the result and do further hiding if necessary. And finally, define the altered image as a pattern tile. The assessing and defining steps of the procedure are always the same. But there are at least three good approaches to hiding the seam.

1 Assessing the seam. Open and crop the image you want to make into a seamlessly tiling pattern. You need a single-layer file that includes only the area you want to use for the tile. Use the Offset filter to find out how bad the seam would be if you did nothing to hide it: Choose Filter, Other, Offset and enter pixel dimensions for Horizontal and Vertical that are roughly a third to half the width and height of your file; set the Undefined Areas to Wrap Around and click OK to run the filter. The unmatched "seams" will now be plainly visible near the middle of your image **1.** Next you need to evaluate the patterning and texture of your image and the severity of the seams, and figure out which of the methods (step 2, 3, or 4) you want to use to hide them.

2 Using a tile-making filter. If your image is one that would allow the seams to be successfully hidden by blending, the **Tile**

3a

After running the Offset filter

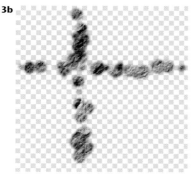

3b

The completed "repairs" layer viewed alone

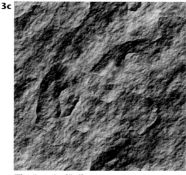

3c

The "repaired" tile

3d

A 500-pixel-wide file filled with the Wow-Rock pattern (Edit, Fill, Pattern)

Maker filter may do the job. You can run the filter in ImageReady or in Photoshop. Start by undoing the test you made with the Offset filter (press Ctrl/⌘-Z or choose File, Revert). To run the filter, choose Filter, Other, Tile Maker (if you don't see Tile Maker at the bottom of Photoshop's Other submenu, see the "Loading Tile Maker" tip at the right).

In the Tile Maker dialog box **2a,** make sure the Blend Edges option is chosen and set the Width percentage, which determines how far into the image the blended edges will overlap. The default 10% often works well. (The "Resize Tile To Fill Image" option can be turned off; this will make a tile that's a little smaller than the selected area because of the overlap where the edges are blended. With it turned on, the image is enlarged slightly to make up for the overlap, but the enlargement may cause overall blurring.) Click OK to complete the filtering.

Eliminate any transparency at the edges by Ctrl/⌘-clicking on the layer's name in the Layers palette to load its transparency mask as a selection. Then choose Edit, Define Pattern, name the pattern, and click OK. The pattern will automatically be added to the presets that appear in Photoshop's Patterns palette **2b.**

3 Using the Clone Stamp, Healing Brush, and Patch tools. If the texture in your image is quite random and "fine-grained," after running the Offset filter at step 1 you can probably hide the seam **3a** by painting cloned material over it as follows: To make it easier to fix any mistakes you might make in the seam-hiding process, add a "repairs" layer by clicking the Create A New Layer button at the bottom of the Layers palette. Choose the Clone Stamp and in the Options bar turn off the Aligned option, turn on Use All Layers, and choose a medium-hard brush from the Brushes palette that pops out when you click the tiny triangle to the right of the Brush swatch. To sample and paint, hold down the Alt/Option key and click on the image to "load" the tool with the "source" image material. Then release the Alt/Option key and click in the seam area to paint over it, trying not to change any of the current edges of the image with your editing. Repeat the sample-and-paint process until the seam is no longer visible **3b.** (If you see a mistake, you can use the Eraser or select the offending dab with the Lasso and delete it from the "repairs" layer.)

To fine-tune the correction with the Healing Brush or Patch tools (which can only work on the layer being fixed) and to make

LOADING TILE MAKER

The Tile Maker filter that comes with ImageReady is designed for making seamlessly tiling patterns for Web backgrounds. But you can also use it in Photoshop. Locate the Tile Maker plug-in (in the Adobe Photoshop 7, Plug-ins, Adobe ImageReady Only, Filters folder) and drag the icon into the Filters folder (Adobe Photoshop 7, Plug-ins, Filters), which holds plug-ins that are shared by Photoshop and Image-Ready; then restart Photoshop. You'll find Tile Maker in the Filter, Other submenu.

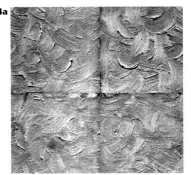

4a

After running the Offset filter

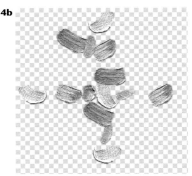

4b

Some of the "patches" viewed alone

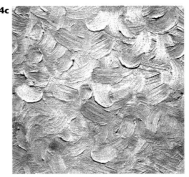

4c

The patched tile

4d

A 500-pixel-square file filled with Impasto Pattern 500 Px (Edit, Fill, Pattern)

sure there are no new seams (there shouldn't be if you were able to stay away from the edges), flatten the file (Layer, Flatten Image), run the Offset filter again with the same settings as in step 1, and again check for seams in the middle. Now make your subtle correction using the Healing Brush or Patch tool (see page 137 for more on retouching with these effective Photoshop 7 additions.) When the image is "seamless," choose Edit, Define Pattern, name the pattern, and click OK **3c, 3d.**

4 Copying bits and pieces. If your image is a photo or scan of a texture that isn't especially fine-grained and doesn't lend itself to blended edges **4a,** the best way to cover the seam may be to copy and overlay selected parts of the image. This method often works well for photos of discrete items, from pebbles to cherries to clouds or brush strokes. Start by selecting a feature; we used the Lasso to select one of the paint dabs in our scan of a hand-painted canvas. Copy the selected element to a new "patch" layer (Ctrl/⌘-J). Use the Free Transform command (Ctrl/⌘-T) to reposition the element over the seam (by dragging) and rotate, scale, or flip it by right-clicking (Control-clicking on the Mac) inside the Transform box and choosing from the menu of transform options, then dragging on a handle, keeping in mind not to change the apparent direction of the light for the copied elements in a way that would "clash" with the lighting in the original image; press Enter to complete the transformation. You can now duplicate this element (Ctrl/⌘-J) and transform the new layer to cover another part of the seam. If you use the same selected element too many times, the repair will be obvious and the element can become blurred from repeated transforming. So instead you can activate the original image layer again by clicking its thumbnail in the Layers palette, then make another selection, copy it to a new layer, and so on. Try to keep your repairs from touching the edges of the file **4b.**

When your seam is hidden **4c,** flatten the file (Layer, Flatten Image) and run the Offset filter again with the same settings as in step 1 to check for new seams. If necessary, create more "patches," then flatten the file again **4d.**

Applying the patterns. To make the illustration at the top of page 378, the patterns developed here were applied to graphics layers as the Pattern Overlay and Bevel And Emboss Texture components of Layer Styles (you can explore the result in the **Yin Yang.psd** file on the Wow! CD-ROM). In addition to the patterns developed in steps 1–4, the Wow-Wood 01 pattern was developed with the Wood filter from Eye Candy 4000 and was used on the ring. *Wow*

Quick Neon

Overview *Set type or create a graphic; add a Layer Style and reduce the Fill Opacity to 0; add a Shape Burst Gradient Stroke and other glows to the Style.*

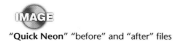

"**Quick Neon**" "before" and "after" files

1

Type set on a transparent layer in the Cheap Motel font

2

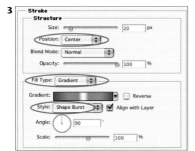

Reducing the Fill Opacity to 0 in the Blending Options section of the Layer Style dialog box, to hide the interior of the type. (The Blend Interior Effects As Group option must be turned off in order for the Inner Glow, added later, to work.)

3

Adding a Stroke effect with a Gradient Fill Type and a Shape Burst Style

IF YOU DON'T HAVE THE PERFECT NEON FONT, such as Eklektic shown on page 329, and you can't take the time to draw the glass tubing by hand as in "Crafting a Neon Glow," also on page 329, you can still communicate the concept of a neon sign by using a Layer Style with a Stroke effect on any font or shape you like.

1 Preparing the type or graphic. In a file with a dark background, set the type or create the graphic that you want to turn to neon **1**; the fill color won't matter, since you'll be eliminating it in the next step. Be sure to leave enough room between the characters or elements of the graphic to allow for the stroking effect.

2 Eliminating the fill. Click the "*f*" button at the bottom of the Layers palette and choose Blending Options at the top of the pop-out list. The Layer Style dialog box will open to the Blending Options. In the Advanced Blending section **2**, set the Fill Opacity to 0 and make sure the Blend Interior Effects As Group option is unchecked. This will make the type or graphic disappear, but its outline will still exist for the Stroke (added next) to act upon.

3 Adding a gradient stroke. From the list at the left side of the Layer Style dialog box, choose Stroke. Choose Center for the Position; choose Gradient for the Fill Type and Shape Burst for the Style **3**. You'll need a "double" gradient that goes from a light color or white in the center to a color at each end. You can pop out the Gradients palette by clicking the little triangle to the right of the gradient swatch; if you don't see the gradient you want in the palette, click the swatch itself to open the Gradient Editor dialog box and create your own gradient, as described in "Building a Solid Gradient" on page 266. You may have to adjust the Color Midpoints of the gradient (in the Gradient Editor) and the Size (in the Stroke section of the Layer Style dialog) to get the rounding you want for the tube.

Completing the lighting. An Inner Glow was added to light the interiors of the letters (see the **Quick Neon-After.psd** file). The same Outer Glow and Drop Shadow effects described in "Crafting a Neon Glow," as well as the dot connectors, were also added.

Carving a Textured Surface

Overview *Add a Layer Style to a graphic to "carve" the graphic into a background image; make a displacement map from the background image to use with the Displace filter to bend the graphic to conform to the background.*

"**Carving**" "before" and "after" files

The original surface image

The climber was selected and copied to a separate layer (Ctrl/⌘-J).

3a

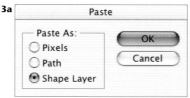

The graphic was copied in Adobe Illustrator and pasted into Photoshop as a Shape.

SOMETIMES ALL YOU NEED TO CREATE THE ILLUSION of the third dimension is an edge, defined by subtle highlights and shadows that can make a shape look carved or cut-out. In Photoshop 7 an excellent way to accomplish this is to use a Layer Style consisting of a Bevel And Emboss effect to create the cut edges, an Inner Shadow to add depth to the carving and match the lighting on the surface image, and a Color Overlay to control the overall shading of the recessed areas. But for a rough surface like the rock face shown above, adding the Displace filter can make the difference between a convincing illusion and a "near miss." Used with a displacement map made from the image itself, the Displace filter can "disrupt" or bend the smooth edges of the carved graphic to conform to the surface texture of its environment.

1 Preparing the surface photo. Open the image of the surface you want to carve into. Many kinds of surface images will work. If you choose a smooth, nonpatterned surface, the carving is simple — you can stop after step 4. If you choose a smooth but patterned surface, you'll work through step 4 and then follow the method in "Carving a Smooth, Patterned Surface" on page 387. If you choose a textured surface, choose an image in which the light and dark features — especially the large features — are created by the high-lighting and shading of raised and sunken areas of the surface rather than by color differences that are independent of the texture. For instance, in the case of the rock wall shown here **1**, the darkest areas are the shadows within the crevices. Although there is

3b

Pasting in the graphic and scaling it to fit the image

a strong *color difference* between the gray and orange areas of the rock, there isn't much *brightness difference* between these two colors, so the color difference won't cause the Displace filter (used in step 6) to create high and low areas. (An example of a surface that wouldn't work well with the Displace filter might be a photo of a zebra. The white and black stripes would create dramatic "peaks and valleys" independent of the texture, shape, or shading of the animal.)

2 Isolating any foreground elements. Since there was a subject in our image (the climber) who would need to be in front of the carving in the rock face, we duplicated her on a separate foreground layer, so we would be able to put the graphic between the subject and the background image (in step 3). Use a selection method appropriate for your image. For this photo we used the Magnetic Lasso as described in "Easier Selecting" tip at the left. The selection doesn't have to be perfect, since the original image will still be underneath and will match up with the selected subject. Once you've made the selection, choose Layer, New, Layer Via Copy (or use the Ctrl/⌘-J shortcut) to copy the selection to a new layer **2**. (***Note***: The "Before" version of the "Carving" file on the CD-ROM includes an alpha channel for selecting the climber; simply Ctrl/⌘-click the channel's thumbnail to load it as a selection.)

3 Adding the graphic to be carved. The other thing you'll need is a shape to use for carving, typically a graphic or typographic element created in Photoshop or imported. We chose an icon from the *Design Elements* CD-ROM from Ultimate Symbol, Inc. Working in Adobe Illustrator 9, we copied this icon (Edit, Copy). Then in Photoshop we targeted our surface image layer (*Background*) and pasted the graphic into the file (Edit, Paste, Paste As Shape Layer) **3a.** We used the Move tool to scale the graphic (by dragging a corner handle of the frame surrounding the graphic) and to position it relative to the climber (by dragging inside the frame) **3b.** *Note:* The Paste As Shape Layer option works differently from Illustrator 10. (See page 306 for tips on pasting from Illustrator 10.)

4 Carving. To carve the graphic, you can construct a Layer Style for its layer, with Bevel And Emboss, Inner Shadow, and Color Overlay effects, as described next. ***Note***: The description that follows results in a Style like the one in the **Carving-After.psd** file. An alternative to constructing the Style yourself is to copy and paste the Style: In the Layers palette of the **Carving-After.psd** file with the Shape 1 layer active, right-click (Windows) or Control-click (Mac) directly on the "*f*" icon for the layer and choose Copy Layer Style. Then in the Layers palette of your "recipient" file, right/Control-click in about the same place for the layer where you want the Style, and choose Paste Layer Style from the context-sensitive menu.

So that you'll be able to see the result of the other effects as you

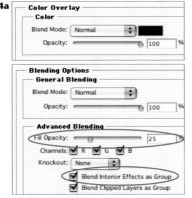

4a

Adding a Color Overlay (top) and setting up Advanced Blending (in the Blending Options section of the Layer Style dialog box) to reduce the Opacity of the graphic so that it just slightly darkens the recessed areas of the "carving"

4b

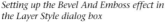

Setting up the Bevel And Emboss effect in the Layer Style dialog box

4c

Adding an Inner Shadow effect. Color is sampled from the image, and the Choke is adjusted to regulate how quickly the shadow transitions from solid to soft.

add them, start with the Color Overlay: Click the "*f*" button at the bottom of the Layers palette and choose Color Overlay from the pop-up menu. The Color Overlay provides a flexible way to darken the recessed areas of the carving. Matching the shadows for the carving to the shadows in the image will make the effect more realistic. So click the color swatch next to the Blend Mode and click in the image to sample color from a shadow area; set the Blend Mode to Normal and the Opacity to 100%. In the Blending Options section of the dialog box (opened by clicking its name at the top of the left-hand list), make sure to turn on Blend Interior Effects As Group. Photoshop will now treat the Color Overlay and the fill on the layer as if they were a single entity, and you can now change the Fill Opacity here; we reduced Fill Opacity to 25% **4a.** (For more about controlling the Opacity of Color, Gradient, and Pattern Overlays, see the "Opacity and Interior Effects" tip on page 385.)

Next click on Bevel And Emboss in the list at the left side of the Layer Style dialog box. Bevel And Emboss will shape the edge, doing most of the "carving" **4b.** Set the Style, Technique, and Size for the Bevel And Emboss; we used Outer Bevel, Chisel Hard, and 9 pixels for a thick, hard edge. Click the color swatch next to the Shadow Mode and click in the image to sample color from a shadow area; when the shadow color is sampled in this way, the Blend Mode can be set to Multiply and the Opacity to 100%. We set the Highlight Mode to Overlay. Unlike the default Screen mode, Overlay preserves the texture details in the highlighted edges of the bevel. Sample the color for the highlight from the image, as you did for the shadow.

Finally, click on Inner Shadow in the list **4c.** The Inner Shadow will add to the depth of the carving and provide a slight undercutting at the bottom edges. Set the Blend Mode to Multiply, sample a color from the image, and adjust the Opacity until you like the degree of shading. Experiment with the Choke to adjust the width of the shadow **4d.**

What you do next depends on the nature of your surface image:

- If the surface is smooth rather than textured and plain-colored rather than patterned, your carving is complete.

- If there's a distinct color pattern in the smooth surface, however, you may want to offset the interior of the carving, creating a "jump" in the pattern, which will add to the illusion that the carved area is recessed. See "Carving a Smooth, Patterned Surface" on page 387 for a method.

- But if your surface photo is highly textured (like the one in this example), you'll want to go on to steps 5, 6, and 7, to conform the edges of the carving to the surface contours.

5 Creating the displacement map. Next you'll make a Grayscale displacement map that you can use in step 6 to distort the graphic so it looks like it's actually affected by the surface topography. A dis-

4d

The layer effects have created the highlights and shadows necessary for the carved graphic, but the carving seems to be independent of the texture on the rock surface.

5a

Ctrl/⌘-clicking the composite (RGB) channel in the Channels palette (left) creates a "luminance" selection that can then be saved as an alpha channel by clicking the Save Selection As Channel button at the bottom of the Channels palette (right).

5b

The alpha channel is blurred (right) to smooth out details in the texture.

placement map works by shifting the pixels of the surface photo in one direction where the displacement map is light, and in the opposite direction where the displacement map is dark. If you create the displacement map from the surface image itself, the map will distort the graphic so the carved surface appears to dip where it goes over dark crevices and rise where it goes over raised, highlighted areas. By making the displacement map Grayscale, you'll be able to see the lights and darks clearly and predict exactly where the dips and rises will be created. (Although the Displace filter can use an RGB file as a displacement map, the effect is harder to predict, since the contrast in the Red channel creates the horizontal displacement and the contrast in the Green channel creates the vertical shift.)

To make a Grayscale displacement map from the surface photo, in the Layers palette, start by clicking the Eye icons next to the names of the graphic layer and the foreground (climber) layer to turn off visibility for these layers, leaving only the original surface photo visible. Then open the Channels palette (Window, Show Channels) and Ctrl/⌘-click the composite (RGB) channel name at the top of the palette **5a.** This will make a selection based on the

---

OPACITY AND INTERIOR EFFECTS

In the Color Overlay section of the Layer Style dialog box, the Opacity setting controls how much the Color Overlay contributes to the final color of pixels on the layer to which the Style is applied. For instance, if you apply a red Color Overlay to a layer with a black graphic and set the Opacity of the Color Overlay to 100%, the result will be a bright red graphic — the red substitutes 100% for the black. But if you set the Opacity of the Color Overlay to 50%, the result will be a dark red, produced by mixing 50% black and 50% red. The Opacity settings in the Gradient Overlay and Pattern Overlay sections of the Layer Style box operate in the same way.

You can further modify the opacity of Color, Gradient, and Pattern Overlays in the **Blending Options** section of the Layer Style box:

If you want to make the overall fill color more transparent and *also reduce the opacity of any other effects applied to the layer,* use the **Opacity** setting (in the General Blending section).

However, in most cases you'll want to use the **Fill Opacity** (in the Advanced Blending section, now located in the Layers palette), because it changes the fill *without reducing the intensity of any other layer effects you may have included in the style,* such as the intensity of highlights and shadows created by Bevel And Emboss or Drop Shadow.

- With the **Blend Interior Effects As Group option turned on,** the Fill Opacity setting makes the element more transparent, without changing its color. So, for instance, in our 50% red example, the dark red graphic stays the same color but becomes partially transparent.

- With the **Blend Interior Effects As Group option turned off,** the Fill Opacity controls only the original color of the pixels, leaving the Color Overlay intact. So in our 50% red example above, only the black component would be reduced by reducing Fill Opacity. At a setting of 0%, the result would be a 50% transparent red graphic, with no black component.

5c

Duplicating the alpha channel to create the displacement map

6a

Choosing Filter, Distort, Displace on a Shape layer brings up a caution box that warns you that the Shape must be turned into pixels before the filter can be run.

6b

A close-up of the carving after running the Displace filter

luminosity (lights and darks) of the visible image. Turn the selection into a grayscale image in an alpha channel by clicking the Save Selection As Channel button at the bottom of the Channels palette. Deselect (Ctrl/⌘-D), and click on the new channel's name to view it.

To make the grayscale image work better as a displacement map, you'll need to get rid of unwanted detail by blurring, and perhaps increase the contrast to exaggerate the light/dark differences. Choose Filter, Blur, Gaussian Blur **5b.** The higher the Radius setting in the Gaussian Blur dialog box, the less sharp and chiseled the edge will look. We used a setting of 2 pixels. If necessary for your image, choose Image, Adjust, Levels and use the Input Levels sliders to darken the shadows (use the left, black-point slider), or lighten the highlights (use the right, white-point slider), or adjust the midtones (use the middle slider). Now make the new Grayscale file: Choose Duplicate Channel from the Channels palette's pop-out menu **5c;** in the Duplicate Channel dialog box, choose *New* for the Destination Document, and click OK. Close the new document, clicking Save in the Caution box that appears, name the file, and save it in Photoshop format.

6 Running the Displace filter. Back in the Layers palette of the main image file, turn on visibility (Eye icons) for all layers again. With the graphic layer targeted, choose Filter, Distort, Displace. If you've used a Shape layer for your graphic, a Caution box will warn you about rasterizing it **6a;** click OK to proceed. In the Displace dialog box, set the Horizontal and Vertical Scale; we used 10 and –10 respectively. The settings in the Displacement Map section of the box are irrelevant, since the displacement map is exactly the same size as the image and so there will be no need for tiling or stretching. Click OK, then locate and select the displacement map you made in step 5, and click the Open button **6b.**

7 Finishing touches. If you want to further exaggerate displacement of some elements of the carving, try the Liquify command: First, make a flattened copy of the file (Image, Duplicate, Duplicate Merged Layers Only). Then choose Filter, Liquify **7.** ("Liquify" on page 213 tells how to work the Liquify dialog box.) Finally, you may want to further unify the carved-in graphic and the surface by sharpening the flattened image slightly (Filter, Sharpen, Unsharp Mask).

7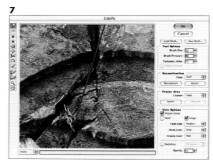

Using the Liquify command to exaggerate the displacement of certain features in a flattened version of the finished image

Carving a Smooth, Patterned Surface

Overview *Apply a Layer Style to a graphic to "carve" it into a smooth, patterned surface image; offset a copy of the surface image, masked with the graphic, to add to the illusion of depth; use the Lighting Effects filter to further exaggerate the dimensionality of the carving.*

"**Wood Carve**" "before" and "after" files

The graphic and wood image, assembled into a two-layer file

A Layer Style was added, with Inner Shadow, Bevel And Emboss, and Color Overlay effects.

The Highlight Mode for Bevel And Emboss (shown here), as well as the Color Overlay, Advanced Blending Options, and Inner Shadow of the Wow-Halo 09 Style are set up very much like those shown in step 4 of "Carving a Textured Surface" on page 382.

"CARVING" A GRAPHIC INTO A SMOOTH SURFACE that has distinct color markings such as wood grain or marble can be enhanced by offsetting the interior of the carving. This creates an obvious "jump" in the markings that adds to the illusion that the carved area is recessed.

1 Preparing the images. Choose the surface image you want to carve into and the graphic to use as the carving and layer them in a single Photoshop file **1.** We opened a clip art graphic in Adobe Illustrator, copied it to the clipboard, and pasted it into a scan of a piece of wood (Edit, Paste, Paste As Pixels).

2 Adding a Layer Style. To carve the graphic into the wood, we began by applying the Wow-Halo 09 Style from the **Wow 7-18 Halo Styles** set that comes with this book (it's very similar to the style created in step 4 of "Carving a Textured Surface" on page 382). To apply the Style, make sure the graphic layer of your carving file is active, and click the Wow-Halo 09 icon in the Styles palette. Then scale the Style to produce the effect you want (Layer, Layer Style, Scale Effects) **2a.** If you're using an image other than the Wood Carve file supplied on the CD-ROM, you can customize the settings for your particular image by opening the Layer Style dialog box (double-click the "*f*" icon for your graphic layer in the Layers palette) and make the following changes: One by one open each of the three effects used in the Style — the check-marked Inner Shadow, Bevel And Emboss, and Color Overlay sections of the dialog box — by clicking their

3a

Cut	⌘X
Copy	⌘C
Copy Merged	⇧⌘C
Paste	⌘V
Paste Into	⇧⌘V
Clear	

The Paste Into command was used to create a masked copy of the wood layer, with the mask unlinked and the image active.

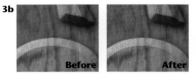

3b

Before   After

Shifting the new layer to the right creates a break in the wood grain, which contributes to the illusion that the carved area is recessed from the surface of the wooden plaque.

3c

The file after carving the surface and offsetting the recessed area

4

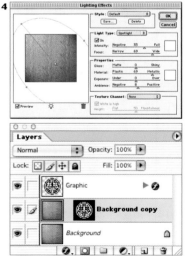

A Spotlight, without the use of a Texture Channel, was applied to both wood layers.

Using a different image for the recessed areas

names in the list at the left of the box. In each case click the color swatch for the shadow color and sample a shadow color from your surface image, and, if you like, adjust the settings that control the extent and darkness of each of the shadow types **2b**.

3 Offsetting the recessed area. To shift the recessed area to enhance the illusion of depth, create a masked duplicate of the surface image: Target the surface image layer (here the *Background*) in the Layers palette; select all (Ctrl/⌘-A) and copy (Ctrl/⌘-C). Then load the graphic as a selection by Ctrl/⌘-clicking on its thumbnail in the palette. Finally, choose Edit, Paste Into (or press Ctrl/⌘-Shift-V). The result will be a duplicate surface image layer with a graphic-shaped mask, which you can leave "as is" or "roughen" as in step 3 on page 401.

By default, when you use Paste Into, the image is active and the mask is *not* linked to it **3a**, so you can offset the image while the mask stays in place. Choose the Move tool and drag in the working window until the image is shifted as much as you like **3b, 3c**.

4 Enhancing the lighting. To liven up the carved image, we applied a Spotlight with the Lighting Effects filter to the masked layer (Filter, Render, Lighting Effects), then activated the original wood layer and applied the filter again with the same settings (Filter, Last Filter, or Ctrl/⌘-F) **4**.

Finishing the carved plaque. To produce the image at the top of page 387, we added a beveled edge and drop shadow to the entire carved piece of wood. First we made a flattened copy of the file (Image, Duplicate, Duplicate Merged Layers Only), saving the layered original in case we wanted to make changes later. In this new file we double-clicked the *Background* label in the Layers palette and clicked OK in the New Layer dialog box; this converted the *Background* to a layer with the capacity for transparency so we could add a Layer Style. Double-clicking the thumbnail in the Layers palette opened the Layer Style dialog box so we could open the Drop Shadow and Bevel And Emboss sections to add the edge treatments.

Layering two materials. To add a second surface material to the carving as shown at the left, replace the surface image that you masked in step 3 as follows: Target the layer you masked in step 3 by clicking its thumbnail in the Layers palette. Open the image file you want to use for the second surface, and drag and drop the image into the carving file. It will appear as a layer above the masked layer. Press Ctrl/⌘-E (or choose Merge Down from the Layers palette's pop-out menu); in the Caution box that appears, click the Preserve button.

Custom Chrome

Overview *Using a graphic (or type) on a transparent layer, build a Layer Style to create a chrome effect; make a displacement map from the graphic, and add an "environment" image to be reflected in the surface of the chrome, using the displacement map to "warp" the image inside the graphic; add a polished "gemstone" surface within the graphic.*

IMAGE

"Chrome" "before" and "after" files

1

The graphic was pasted into the image file as a transparent layer.

2a

A black Color Overlay was added. It didn't change the look of the file, but it would contribute to the "portability" of the Layer Style.

THE TRICK TO IMITATING THE UNIQUELY SHINY SURFACES of chrome is in getting the reflections right. The challenge is to re-create the complexity and distortion of the environment that's mirrored in the rounded, curving surfaces of the polished object. One way to create convincing chrome in Photoshop 7 is with a Layer Style that turns a flat graphic or type into a highly reflective, dimensional object. This transformation is the subject of step 2 below. You can take the chrome simulation even further by using the starting graphic to distort an image of the outer world that's reflected in the shiny surface. In Photoshop you can do this by using the Glass filter with a displacement map file created from your graphic. This method of warping a reflected image on the surface of the chrome object is described in steps 3 through 5.

Besides the subtle highlights and shadows it uses to simulate the reflections and refractions of glass, Photoshop's Glass filter works like its cousin the Displace filter, used in "Carving a Textured Surface" on page 382. The Glass filter moves the pixels of the layer it's applied to, with the distance depending on the luminance (or brightness) of the corresponding pixel in the displacement map. Any image in Photoshop format except a bitmap can serve as a displacement map. When you use a grayscale file, white pixels move their corresponding pixels in the filtered image the maximum distance in one direction, black pixels produce the maximum displacement in the opposite direction, and 50% brightness produces no displacement at all.

1 Preparing the file. Open the file you want to use for the background behind your chrome object. Import the graphics or type that you want to turn to chrome, or create them in Photoshop on a transparent layer. We started with a 1000-pixel-wide wood image and added the "Quest" logo, which had been created in Adobe

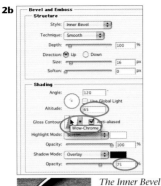

2b

The Inner Bevel included a high Altitude setting to reposition the highlight, a custom Gloss Contour, and reduced Opacity.

2c

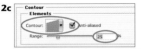

Changing the Contour and Range settings for the bevel brought the highlight farther onto the top surface of the logo and added "underside" highlights.

2d

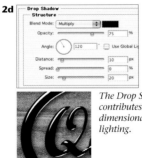

The Drop Shadow contributes to the dimensionality and lighting.

2e

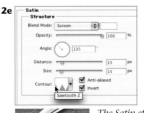

The Satin effect, with the Sawtooth 2 light/ dark Contour setting and relatively small Size and Distance, adds the chrome surface highlights.

Illustrator, copied to the clipboard, and pasted it into the Photoshop file (Edit, Paste, Paste As: Pixels) **1**.

2 Styling the chrome. To create the dimensionality and shininess of the chrome, we built a Layer Style for the graphic, as described next. ***Note:*** You can open the **Chrome-After.psd** file for reference to the "live" Layer Styles as you follow the step-by-step instructions.

With the graphic layer active, we clicked the *"f"* button at the bottom of the Layers palette and chose **Color Overlay** from the pop-out list. This opened the Color Overlay section of the Layer Style dialog box, where we accepted the default settings of Normal for Blend Mode, 100% for Opacity, and black for the color, since our chrome Style depends on starting with black **2a**. Although our graphic was already black, setting the color with Color Overlay would ensure that the Style could be reused on type or graphics of any color, without unpleasant surprises.

Next we started building the dimensionality by choosing **Bevel And Emboss** from the list of effects at the left side of the Layer Style dialog box. In the Structure section we used Smooth for the Technique, to create a rounded edge. We chose Inner Bevel for the Style so the bevel would be built inward from the edge of the graphic, rather than being built from the edge of the graphic outward to the background. (Important differences between Inner and Outer bevel styles are explained in the "Bevel Differences — Inner & Outer" tip on page 408.)

In the Shading section of Bevel And Emboss we tried different Altitude settings and Gloss Contours to create a bright, sharp highlight, settling on 65° for the Altitude and on a custom Gloss Contour.

We also set the Shadow Mode to Overlay. This made no difference now, but it would become important when we added the Satin effect, since Overlay mode increases the contrast of the light/ dark banding that Satin creates **2b**.

We clicked on the **Contour** option (from the list at the left side of the dialog box), which controls the shape of the edge created by the Bevel And Emboss. In this case we customized the contour by clicking on the icon to change the angle to one with a more subtle slope, and reduced the Range percentage in order to increase the complexity of the highlight and let some highlights "pop up" on the shaded side of the object **2c**.

We chose **Drop Shadow** from the list at the left and adjusted the Distance (the offset, 10 pixels) and Size (the extent, 20 pixels), leaving the Spread at 0 for a soft, diffuse shadow **2d**.

Next the **Satin** effect was used to "color" the chrome. We chose white for the color and Screen for the Blend Mode, for an overall lightening effect. For the Contour we chose Sawtooth 2, to get the light/dark striping that's characteristic of multiple light sources reflected in a polished curved surface. We wanted to use Satin's full

2f

The interplay of Inner Shadow and Inner Glow, both black and in Multiply mode, added complexity to the developing chrome.

2g

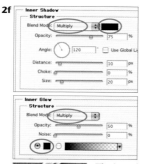

A gray Outer Glow in Multiply mode added a "dark halo" to help set the graphic off from the background.

2h

The "quick and dirty" chrome is completely determined by the Layer Style on the graphic layer.

potential for interacting with the shape of the element it's applied to, so we experimented with Distance, keeping the setting low enough (15 pixels) to get well defined repeats of the graphic's shapes inside the letters and the oval ring. We increased the Size enough to nicely blur the repeats (also 15 pixels), without blowing them out entirely **2e.**

We experimented with the **Inner Shadow** and **Inner Glow** to increase the complexity of the highlights and shadows in the chrome and to enhance the edge definition of the graphic. We used black in Multiply mode for both, adjusting the Distance and Size settings until the interaction of these two shadows with the Satin created the effect we wanted **2f.**

To further "pop" the graphic off the background, we used the **Outer Glow** in Multiply mode to add a "dark halo" **2g.** At this point, the "quick and dirty" version of the chrome was complete **2h.** (You'll find other "quick and dirty" Style-based chrome treatments in "Chrome Style Variations" on page 394.)

3 Building a displacement map. The strategy in reflecting an "environment" in the chrome is to "warp" a "glass-ified" version of the environment photo onto the surface of the chrome object. The first step is to make a displacement map from the graphic, to be used in the distortion. To begin that process, load the outline of the original graphic as a selection by Ctrl/⌘-clicking its thumbnail in the Layers palette. Open the Channels palette (Window, Show Channels) and save the selection as an alpha channel by clicking the Save Selection As Channel button at the bottom of the palette. This channel will serve as safe storage for the white-on-black graphic. Make a copy of the channel for development of the displacement map by dragging the new channel's thumbnail to the Create New

3a

Blurring a copy of the alpha channel

3b

Duplicating the blurred alpha channel as a separate file for the displacement map

4a

Positioning and scaling the clouds image

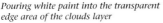

4b

Pouring white paint into the transparent edge area of the clouds layer

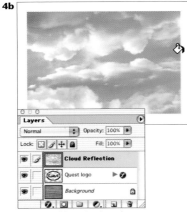

4c

Running the Glass filter with the displacement map made from the graphic "embosses" the graphic on the clouds layer.

Channel button at the bottom of the palette.

Now blur the duplicate channel (Filter, Blur, Gaussian Blur), using a Radius that's half the Size setting for the Inner Bevel created at step 2; since our Size setting was 16, we used an 8-pixel Radius **3a.** The "gray matter" created by the blur will produce a smooth, rounded result when the displacement map is applied.

Since a displacement map has to be a separate file, make a file from the blurred channel by right-clicking (Windows) or Control-clicking (Mac) on the name of the blurred channel in the Channels palette, and choosing Duplicate Channel from the pop-out menu. In the Duplicate Channel dialog box, choose New for the Document and name the new file; then click OK. Now save the displacement map file, since it can't be used with the Glass filter until it's saved (File, Save As) **3b.**

4 Adding the reflection. In this next step, when you add the image you want to use as the reflected environment, it's important that it be exactly the same pixel size as the canvas of the developing chrome file, in order for the Glass filter to work correctly. So select and copy the part of the image you want to use, activate the graphic layer by clicking on its name in the chrome file, and paste (Ctrl/⌘-V). With the Opacity of the new layer reduced so you can see the "styled" graphic below, use Free Transform (Ctrl/⌘-T) to scale the image **4a,** and double-click inside the Transform box to complete the transformation. If your scaling results in the image bleeding off the canvas, select all (Ctrl/⌘-A) and choose Image, Crop to trim off the extra. On the other hand, if the image is too small, use the Paint Bucket to pour white paint around the edges to fill the layer to the edges of the canvas **4b.** The white that you add will contribute a strong white highlight to the "glass-ification" that's coming next. If you find that the white highlight effect is too strong, you can undo the filter effect by pressing Ctrl/⌘-Z and enlarge the reflection layer with Free Transform until it fills the canvas. Don't worry about distorting the image, since distortion is part of the glassifying effect.

When the image is in place, sized, and with white around the

ALIGNMENT IS IMPORTANT

When you apply a filter that uses a displacement map, such as Displace or Glass, Photoshop aligns the displacement map with **the upper-left corner of the layer**. That means that if your layer extends above or to the left of the canvas, or if its upper-left corner doesn't extend all the way to the corner of the canvas, the displacement map will line up differently than you expect when you run the filter. For instance, if you've made the displacement map from a graphic in the file and you run it on a layer that's too big or too small, the distortion won't align with your graphic. To trim away excess on a layer before running the filter, select all (Ctrl/⌘-A) and choose Image, Crop. For a layer whose pixels don't reach the edge, you'll need to fill in the empty space with pixels or select all (Ctrl/⌘-A) before running the filter.

4d

A close-up of the "glassified" clouds layer

4e

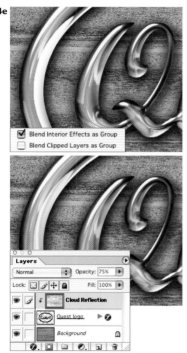

The "glassified" clouds layer was grouped with the graphic layer (top), and its Opacity was reduced to 75%.

5a

The Wow-Gems 04 Style was applied to a black-filled ellipse in the layer below the graphic.

edges if needed, blur it if you like (Filter, Blur, Gaussian Blur), to reduce any detail that can distract from the shape of the graphic. For the soft image of clouds that we used, very little blurring was needed.

Now run the Glass filter (Filter, Distort, Glass). We used the maximum setting (20) for Distortion and 5 for Smoothness (lower Smoothness settings produce sharper edges, but may also produce pixelated breaks in the image; higher settings make smoother distortions, but the edges are softer). For the Texture, choose Load Texture from the pop-out menu, locate the displacement map you made at step 3, and click Open; click OK to apply the filter **4c, 4d.**

To limit the distorted environment image to the graphic itself, make a clipping group: Alt/Option-click on the border between the image layer and the graphic layer, or press Ctrl/⌘-G (for Layer, Group With Previous). Double-click the graphic layer's name in the Layers palette to open the Blending Options section of the Layer Style dialog box. Turn on Blend Interior Effects as Group and turn *off* Blend Clipped Layers as Group. The clipped image will now interact with the edge effects applied by the Style of the graphic layer below **4e.** Experiment with reducing the Opacity of the image layer to arrive at the right blend of the image and the light/dark "striping" created by the Satin effect; we settled on 75% Opacity.

5 Adding an internal surface. At this point we added a "gemstone" surface inside the chrome oval and behind the "Quest" lettering, as follows: We created a new layer just below the graphic layer, used the Elliptical Marquee to make a selection the size of the interior of the logo, and filled the selection with black (Edit, Fill, Use: Black). We added a Layer Style to create a colorful, polished surface; you can examine the Style in the **Chrome-After.psd** file. The Style includes a Drop Shadow with Distance, Size, and Spread settings large enough so the shadow shows around the edges of the graphic in the layer above **5a, 5b.**

5b

The Layers palette for the finished chrome and gemstone treatment, shown at the top of page 389

Variations. The environment image you choose can make a big difference in the way your chrome looks. "Chrome Reflection Variations" on page 396 shows some examples.

Chrome Style
Variations

All the polished metal treatments on these two pages were developed by making changes to the Wow-Chrome 1 Layer Style, developed through step 2 in "Custom Chrome" on page 389, without the use of an "environment" photo. You can explore all these Styles in the **Chrome Style Variations.psd** *file. Each layer is named according to the Style applied to it.*

Chrome Style Variations.psd file

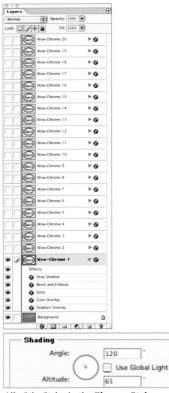

All of the Styles in the **Chrome Style Variations.psd** *file use an Angle of 120° and an Altitude of 65°.*

Wow-Chrome 1

Wow-Chrome 2

Wow-Chrome 3

Wow-Chrome 4

Wow-Chrome 5

Wow-Chrome 6

Wow-Chrome 7

Wow-Chrome 8

Wow-Chrome 9

Wow-Chrome 10

Wow-Chrome 11

Wow-Chrome 12

Wow-Chrome 13

Wow-Chrome 14

Wow-Chrome 15

Wow-Chrome 16

Wow-Chrome 17

Wow-Chrome 18

Wow-Chrome 19

Wow-Chrome 20

Chrome Reflection Variations

The chrome examples on this page were made from the graphic shown below. The only difference from one example to another is that a different "environment" image was used. The Layer Style was set up exactly as described in "Custom Chrome" on page 389, and a displacement map made from the graphic below was used to apply the Glass filter. In each case the Glass filter was run on a layer with white fill around the edges of the image, which in some cases added extra highlights on the left side and top of the "Q" and the right side of the "t."

Chrome Reflection Variatns.psd file

The original graphic

The displacement map

The "environment" image is the same one used in the "Custom Chrome" technique that starts on page 389.

Here a cloud photo with more contrast was used.

A photo of palm trees adds detail and color.

A backlit photo of palm trees includes shape detail and water reflections, but with reduced color.

A low-contrast colorized clouds photo produces limited highlights.

A multistep Linear gradient at 75% suggests an environment, even though no photo is used.

Custom Glass

Overview *Create the chrome effect as described step-by-step in "Custom Chrome" on page 389, adding a "glassified" copy of the background, clipped by the logo; make changes to the Style to brighten the overall effect; reduce the opacity of the reflected image.*

IMAGE

"**Glass**" "before" and "after" files

1a

The graphic and background layers

1b

1c

The displacement map   *The "glassified" background copy*

1c

A Layer Style (Wow-Chrome 03) was applied to the graphic. The filtered background copy was grouped with the graphic layer.

THE GLASS PLAQUE SHOWN HERE is produced using a variation of the "Custom Chrome" technique on page 389, run on a bolder "negative" version of the same graphic. The glass illusion is created by the combination of the background showing through the clear medium and the environment being *reflected* and *refracted* by the surface. The main difference in construction between chrome and this glass is the addition of a distorted copy of the background wood image, clipped by the logo, which makes it seem as if the background can be seen through the transparent shape. Also, the Opacity of the "environment" photo reflected in the surface is reduced, since glass is not as reflective as chrome. A few strategic changes to the Layer Style complete the reflective and refractive character of the glass.

1 Setting up the file. Open the file you want to use for the background behind your glass object. On a transparent layer in this file, create or import the graphics or type that you want to turn to glass. We started with a 1000-pixel-wide wood image and added a logo that had been created in Adobe Illustrator, copied to the clipboard, and pasted into the Photoshop file (Edit, Paste, Paste As: Pixels) **1a.**

To build your new glass style, you can start by applying (or re-creating) the Wow-Chrome 03 Style on your graphic layer as described in step 2 of "Custom Chrome" on page 390. Or copy and paste the Style from the **Chrome-After.psd** file, as follows: Right-click (Windows) or Control-click (Mac) on the "*f*" icon for the chrome graphic layer in the Layers palette and choose Copy Layer Style from the context-sensitive menu. Right/Control-click at the right end of the Layers palette entry for the "recipient" layer and choose Paste Layer Style. Then make the changes described next in step 2 to fine-tune the style.

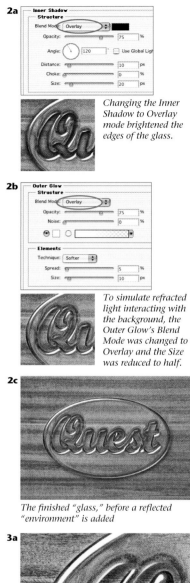

2a

Changing the Inner Shadow to Overlay mode brightened the edges of the glass.

2b

To simulate refracted light interacting with the background, the Outer Glow's Blend Mode was changed to Overlay and the Size was reduced to half.

2c

The finished "glass," before a reflected "environment" is added

3a

To create reflections, an environment image, distorted with the Glass filter, was added to the clipping group and the layer's Opacity was reduced.

Whichever method you use to apply the Style, you may need to scale it once it's applied, to make it fit your graphic. Do that by right/Control-clicking on the "*f*" icon for the layer and choosing Scale Effects from the pop-out list. Adjust the Scale slider until the result looks right.

In the Layers palette, duplicate the background image by dragging its name to the Create A New Layer button at the bottom of the palette. Drag the new layer's thumbnail up in the palette so that it's above the graphic, and make a clipping group of this layer and the graphic by choosing Layer, Group With Previous.

Make a displacement map from the graphic, as described in step 3 of "Custom Chrome" **1b,** and use it with the Glass filter (Filter, Distort, Glass) to "glassify" the duplicate background layer as in step 4 of that section. You can "reflect" light from the surface of the glass logo by lowering the Opacity setting for the "glassified" layer; we settled on a setting of 75% Opacity **1c.**

2 Adjusting the Style. If you've started by re-creating the Style described in step 2 of "Custom Chrome," try these changes to make the logo more glasslike.

- For the **Inner Shadow,** change the Blend Mode to Overlay. This will brighten the edges of the glass graphic **2a.**

- To change the **Outer Glow** from a "dark halo" to a glow that simulates light being refracted through the glass and actually lighting up the wood and shadow beneath, change the color to white and the Blend Mode to Overlay, and experiment with reducing the Size setting **2b.** The glass logo will still cast a slight shadow — thanks to the Drop Shadow effect — which helps with the illusion of the solid, clear material **2c.**

3 Reflecting the environment. To make "environmental" reflections on the surface of the glass, add a "glassified" image layer above the glassified background copy, as described in step 4 of "Custom Chrome." Then, because glass is less shiny than chrome, reduce the Opacity of this layer; we settled on 25% Opacity **3a, 3b.**

3b

The Layers palette for the completed glass file. The finished logo is shown at the top of page 397.

GROUPING

To form a clipping group from the active layer and the layer below, or to add the active layer to an existing clipping group below, press **Ctrl/⌘-G.**

Rusted & Pitted

Overview *Create or import a graphic or type; build a Layer Style to add dimension, texture, and lighting; roughen the edge with a filtered layer mask; copy and paste the Style to the background; use Adjustment layers in a clipping group to change the color and texture of the "styled" element.*

"**Rusted**" "before" and "after" files

1

Pasting paths from Adobe Illustrator into Photoshop 7 created a Shape layer, shown here viewed alone.

2a

Blend Clipped Layers As Group is turned off in the Advanced Blending section.

USING LAYER MASKS AND VECTOR MASKS, along with the Pattern and Texture options of Layer Styles, allows for a tremendous amount of flexibility in creating organic-looking surface and edge effects such as this "weathered" metal logo. You can use this technique with graphics or with live type (although you might want to read the "Advantages of Converting Type to Shapes" tip on page 101).

1 Setting up the file. Start an RGB Photoshop file with a nontransparent *Background* (File, New). We filled our Background with gray (Edit, Fill, 50% Gray) so we could see the effects we would add with a Layer Style in step 2. Some of the effects would be in blend modes other than Normal, and to see them accurately we would need a background underneath. Set type, or create artwork with a Shape tool, or import a design element. Our artwork was created in Adobe Illustrator; the type was converted to paths that were then selected, copied to the clipboard, and pasted into the Photoshop file as a Shape layer (Edit, Paste, Paste As Shape Layer) **1.** (See page 306 for tips on pasting from Illustrator 10.)

2 Creating a Layer Style. Now you can set up the Layer Style that creates the rust. ***Note***: The description that follows results in the Wow-Metals 07 style, which is part of the **Wow 7-Metal Styles** set that can be found in the **Rusted-After.psd** file. Both are on the CD-ROM that comes with this book. As you build the Style "from

2b

Loading the **Wow 7-Misc Surface Patterns**, then choosing the Wow-Rust pattern as a Pattern Overlay

2c

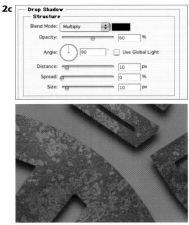

Adding a Drop Shadow

2d

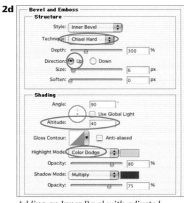

Adding an Inner Bevel with adjusted lighting

scratch," you may want to compare your settings to **Rusted-After.psd**.

To begin to build the Style, click the Add A Layer Style button (the "*f*") at the bottom of the Layers palette. When the Layer Style dialog box opens, find the **Blend Clipped Layers As Group** option in the Advanced Blending section and click the check box to turn it **off 2a**. Turning off this option means that the Adjustment layer that will be added at step 5 will affect the "styled" graphic below, including the features added by the Layer Style. Next use the list on the left side of the Layer Style dialog box to choose each of the effects listed below, and use the settings shown on this page and the next to create the effect.

Here's a general summary that describes what each effect does and how the important settings work. Use these descriptions, the illustrations that go with them, and refer to the **Rusted-After.psd** file to re-create the Style or customize one of your own.

- **Pattern Overlay** is applied first, using the Wow-Rust pattern (part of the **Wow 7-Misc Surface Patterns** set, which can be loaded via the pattern palette that pops out when you click the little triangle to the right of the Pattern swatch) **2b.** To see the names of all the patterns in the palette, choose Small List from the pop-out menu, opened by clicking the triangle in the upper right corner of the palette. If you don't see Wow-Rust in the palette, you can load the **Wow-7 Misc Surface Patterns** set by clicking on the arrow in the upper right corner of the Pattern Picker and selecting that set from the menu. You can resize the pattern with the Scale slider under the swatch, if necessary, to make it look right with your artwork. With the Pattern Overlay in place, it will be easier to see how the other effects are developing.

- The **Drop Shadow** was moved by dragging it in the working window, resulting in a 90° Angle setting that made it look as if the element was lit from the top **2c.** The Size setting was used to dissipate (or soften) the shadow a little. The combination of Size and Distance (which had been established by the dragging) helped characterize the ambient light and set the distance of the element above the surface represented by the *Background.*

- In the **Bevel And Emboss** section an **Inner Bevel** in the Up direction starts the bevel at the edge of the graphic and raises it inward from there. The Chisel Hard choice for Technique creates subtle chisel marks in the edge **2d, 2e.** (The Smooth Technique doesn't produce chisel marks, and Chisel Soft makes the marks very pronounced, as if the edge was being chiseled in relatively soft material.) In the Shading section of the dialog box, using yellow for the Highlight color in Color Dodge mode created warm lighting, and increasing the Altitude moved the light farther up onto the surface of the graphic; a dark brown was

2e

The graphic after the bevel is added

2f

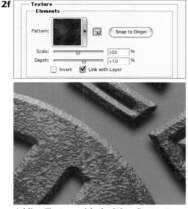

Adding Texture with the Wow-Rust pattern, which appears gray in the Texture section of the Layer Style dialog because only the luminance is used in producing the texture

2g

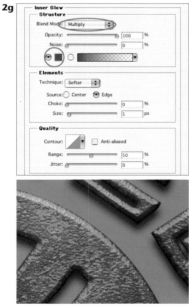

Using a dark Inner Glow in Multiply mode to increase edge definition

sampled from the image for the shadowed edges of the bevel.

- Besides the edge, the **Bevel And Emboss** effect controls the embossing of the **Texture**. We used the Wow-Rust pattern from the pattern palette in the Texture section **2f**. In the Texture swatch, patterns show up in grayscale; this is because only the brightness (or luminance) information — not the color — is used to create the texture.

- An **Inner Glow** of a sampled gray color in Multiply mode was used to add shading inside the edge on the top surface to increase contrast and make edge definition more pronounced **2g**.

- The **Satin** effect, using a sampled dark color and Overlay mode, creates tonal variation that's based on the outline of the element and the Contour (which is like a Curves setting that "remaps" the tonal information according to the particular Contour that's chosen from the palette). Satin can be very useful, as it is here, for changing the surface lighting in an irregular way that distracts the eye from seeing any tiling that might otherwise be apparent in the Pattern Overlay or Texture **2h**.

3 Eroding the edge. The next step is to roughen the edges of the logo without actually doing any damage to the artwork, in case we want to make changes later. An effective way to do that is to add a pixel-based layer mask to the Shape layer and erode the edge of this mask. The Layer Style that we added at step 2 will then use a combination of the layer mask and the vector mask (which was created when we pasted the Illustrator artwork as a Shape) to define the beveled edge, drop shadow, surface shading, and so on.

To add a layer mask, make sure the artwork layer is targeted (click its name in the palette); then load the outline of the artwork as a selection by Ctrl/⌘-clicking its thumbnail in the Layers palette, and click the Add A Mask button at the bottom of the Layers palette **3a**.

To roughen up the edges of the layer mask, apply the Spatter

TWO KINDS OF "MASKS"

There are two kinds of "masks" that can limit how much of a layer's contents will be visible. A layer can have either or both:

A *layer mask* is **pixel-based.** It can include the gray tones that produce soft edges and partial transparency of the layer. And it can be modified by hand-painting, filtering, and other pixel-based processes.

A *vector mask* is **path-based.** It can only be hard-edged and it can't be painted or filtered. However, unlike a layer mask, it can be resized or otherwise transformed again and again without degrading. Outputting from Photoshop, it creates the smoothest, sharpest outline a postscript output device can produce.

To add a layer mask, click the Add A Mask button at the bottom of the Layers palette.

To add a vector mask, Ctrl/⌘-click the Add A Mask button.

2h

The Satin effect completed the Layer Style with tonal variations that hide the pattern tiling.

3a

First this

Then this

To make this

Ctrl/⌘-clicking the vector mask for the Shape layer (top) and then clicking the Add A Mask button created a matching layer mask.

3b

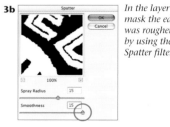

In the layer mask the edge was roughened by using the Spatter filter.

filter (Filter, Brush Strokes, Spatter). In the Spatter dialog box, set the Smoothness at the maximum (15) so you can get a rough but not crumbly edge, and then adjust the Spray Radius until you get the edge effect you want (we used 15). As you look at the preview in the Spatter dialog box **3b,** you won't be seeing exactly what will happen to the edge outline of your graphic or type. That's because *two* masking elements have a role in defining the edge — the roughened pixel-based, filtered layer mask and the hard-edged vector mask that was formed when the artwork was first created or pasted in. Where the filter "eats *into*" the edge of the layer mask, its effects will show in the final artwork. But anywhere that the filter spreads the edge of the mask *outward*, the mask edge *won't* have an effect, because the hard edge of the layer clipping path will mask out these protrusions **3c.** This is a good thing for our degrading effect, because when a metal edge erodes, it is in fact eaten away, not splattered outward.

4 Texturing the background. To turn the *Background* into a plaque made of the same material as the logo, first turn it into a layer that can have transparency and therefore have a Style applied (double-click the *Background* name in the Layers palette and click OK in the New Layer dialog box). Then copy the Layer Style by targeting the artwork layer and right-clicking or Control-clicking (on a Mac with a one-button mouse) on the "*f*" icon for the layer and choosing Copy Layer Style from the pop-out menu **4a.** Apply the

3c

The roughened edge of the layer mask was "clipped" by the vector mask (top). This "ate away" at the edge of the "styled" graphic.

4a

Copying the Layer Style from the graphics layer

4b

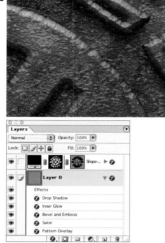

The copied Style was pasted onto the background layer to add texture.

5a

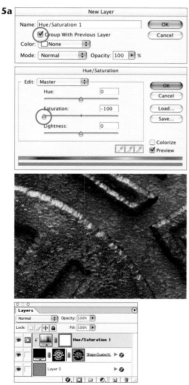

Grouping a Hue/Saturation Adjustment layer with the graphic layer to "decolor" the graphic

Style by targeting the background (now Layer 0), right/Control-clicking its name, and choosing Paste Layer Style **4b.** (Instead of copying and pasting, you can drag-and-drop the Style; step 7 and related tips in "Combining With Light" on pages 224–225 present the pros and cons of drag-and-drop.)

5 Changing the surface characteristics. With the artwork element and the background "styled," it's easy to experiment with the texture and color of either layer. To turn our rusted logo into pitted (but not rusted) iron, we got rid of the color in the logo layer and increased the contrast to emphasize the texture, as follows:

To remove the color we targeted the artwork layer and created a Hue/Saturation Adjustment layer by Alt/Option-clicking the Create New Adjustment layer button at the bottom of the Layers palette and choosing Hue/Saturation from the pop-out list. Using the Alt/Option key had opened the New Layer dialog box, where we could choose Group With Previous Layer **5a** so the Hue/Saturation adjustment would affect only the artwork layer, not the background. We clicked OK to close the New Layer box; when the Hue/Saturation dialog opened, we reduced the Saturation to –100 (the minimum setting) and clicked OK.

5b

Adding a Levels Adjustment layer to the clipping group to brighten the metal completed the artwork at the top of page 399

To increase the contrast we added another Adjustment layer, Alt/Option-clicking the button, choosing Levels, and again grouping. In the Levels dialog box, we moved the Input Levels white slider to the left to increase the contrast until we had some true white highlights **5b** The result is shown at the top of page 399.

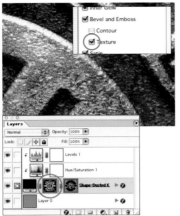

Layer mask turned off to smooth the edge

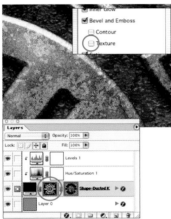

Layer mask and Texture effect turned off to smooth both the edge and the top surface

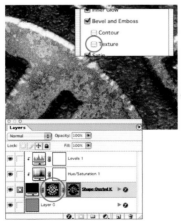

Layer mask turned on but Texture turned off for a rough edge and smooth top surface

Experimenting. We could now experiment with various components of our degraded edge and pitted surface. You can follow along with your file, or open **Rusted-After.psd** from the CD-ROM:

- To smooth the edge, Shift-click the layer mask's thumbnail in the Layers palette to turn off the mask. (This is a toggle — Shift-clicking the red "X" on the layer mask thumbnail will turn it back on.)

- To smooth both the edge and the surface of the metal logo, turn off the layer mask (as just described) and then turn off the Texture effect also (by double-clicking the Bevel And Emboss styles entry in the Layers palette and clicking the Texture checkbox to remove the check mark). This leaves the surface of the logo stained but not pitted.

- To keep the edge roughness but eliminate the surface texture, turn the layer mask on but leave the Texture off.

- To take away the rust color, try removing one or both Adjustment layers from the artwork layer's clipping group so that both the graphic and the background undergo the same color and contrast adjustments.

Another variation. For hot, glowing metal straight from the furnace, take a look at the **Rusted-Hot.psd** file on the Wow! CD-ROM.

"Unclipping" the Adjustment layers removed the rust color from the background as well as the graphic.

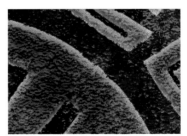

*In the **Rusted-Hot.psd** file, a different Layer Style heats up the metal.*

Rusted-Hot.psd

CLIPPING & UNCLIPPING

You can add a layer to a clipping group directly below it in the Layers palette by targeting the layer you want to add and pressing **Ctrl/⌘-G**.

To remove a layer from the clipping group, along with any grouped layers above it, target it and press **Ctrl/⌘-Shift-G**.

Styled Steel

Overview *Set up Rulers, Guides, and Grid; draw geometric elements with the Shape tools; add a placed graphic; set logo type; add dimension and develop material and lighting characteristics for one element with a Layer Style; copy and modify the Layer Style for other elements; save a flattened copy and sharpen.*

"**Brushed Steel**" "before" and "after" files

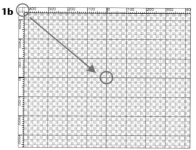

1a

Setting up the color and spacing for Guides and Grid lines

1b

The ruler origin was dragged to the middle of the canvas and Guides were set to cross there.

1c

Snap To Guides and Snap To Grid were both turned on.

2a

The Rectangle tool's Options bar, set up to create a new Shape layer

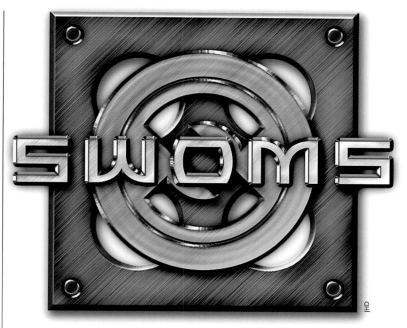

PHOTOSHOP 7'S LAYER STYLE DIALOG BOX provides a kit for turning flat graphics and type — either imported or created within Photoshop — into dimensional elements with color, surface details, and even the highlights and shadows of reflected light. The logo shown here was created with Photoshop's Shape and Type tools, along with a graphic drawn in Adobe Illustrator and pasted into the Photoshop file as a Shape layer. Then virtually the entire Layer Style kit was used, with all ten major effects in play somewhere in the logo:

- The illusion of thickness comes from **Structure** settings in the **Bevel And Emboss** effect.
- Position in three-dimensional space is suggested by a dark **Outer Glow** and enhanced by the **Drop Shadow** effect.
- The reflections were created with the **Gloss Contour** setting of the **Bevel And Emboss** effect and with the **Satin** effect.
- Overlay effects (**Color, Gradient,** and **Pattern**) as well as the **Inner Shadow** are responsible for the "brushed-steel" surface details and shading.
- The **Stroke** effect makes the beveled edges solid and shiny.

Note: You can open the **Brushed Steel-After.psd** file for reference to the "live" Layer Styles as you follow the step-by-step instructions.

1 Setting up to draw with precision. Set up a file with a white *Background* (File, New). We set up our file to be approximately 850 pixels wide by 700 high, a convenient working size for our main application, a printed brochure. Because we would create the entire logo from resolution-independent type, Shapes, and Layer Styles,

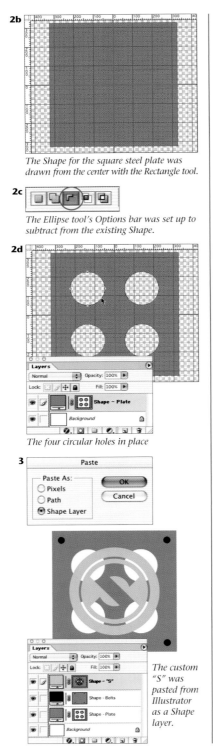

2b

The Shape for the square steel plate was drawn from the center with the Rectangle tool.

2c

The Ellipse tool's Options bar was set up to subtract from the existing Shape.

2d

The four circular holes in place

3

The custom "S" was pasted from Illustrator as a Shape layer.

we could scale it later, as long as we didn't overdo it — the patterns are pixel-based, and could deteriorate if scaled up too much. Since our logo was quite geometric, we started by setting up the Guides, Grid, and Rulers as described next so we could draw with precision.

To make a background for the stylized "S" that we would import from Illustrator, we wanted to draw a square steel plate with four round holes. To be able to work with precision, make the Guides and Grid visible (View, Show Extras) and then set up colors and intervals by choosing Edit, Preferences, Guides & Grid (or press Ctrl/⌘-K to open the Preferences box and then Ctrl/⌘-6 to get to Guides & Grid) **1a**. For the Guides — the lines that would divide the canvas into quadrants — we chose Light Blue from the Color list. For the Grid lines we chose Custom and picked a red from the Color Picker. We set "Gridline Every" at 100 pixels and the "Subdivisions" at 4; this would give us a minor grid line every 25 pixels. Click OK to close the Preferences box.

In the main working window make the Rulers visible (Ctrl/⌘-R) and drag the origin (0,0 point) from the upper left corner where the rulers meet to the approximate center of the canvas. This point can serve as the center of the geometric logo. Set up one horizontal Guide by dragging down from the top ruler into the canvas, until the Guide passes through the 0,0 point. Then drag a vertical guide from the left ruler through the same 0,0 point. The intersection (the center from which graphics will be drawn) is now visible **1b** and can be made "magnetic" by choosing View, Snap To, Guides so that a check mark appears next to the "Guides" listing; make the Grid magnetic in the same way (View, Snap To, Grid) **1c**.

2 Drawing. For almost all of the elements in this logo, the final color would be provided entirely by the Overlays and other effects in the Layer Style, so the initial colors assigned to the graphics weren't very important. But using various shades of gray would keep the colors within the "steel" family; this would be useful for visualizing the design and would also be appropriate if we decided to reduce the opacity of some of the effects and let the original color show through to some degree.

With a color chosen, select the Rectangle tool from the nest of Shape tools in the toolbox. In the Options bar, make sure the Create New Shape Layer option is chosen **2a.** It will be easier to create the rest of the geometric logo if you make the square's outline fall on major grid divisions. Hold down the Shift key and start to drag outward from the 0,0 point; as you drag, hold down the Alt/Option key also. The Shift key constrains the Shape to a square (actually, you may not need this help with the Grid active), and Alt/Option makes the starting point act as the center of the square **2b.**

Now use the Ellipse tool (you can choose it in the Options bar or press Shift-U until it's chosen) to make one of the holes: In the Options bar make sure the Subtract From Shape Area button is

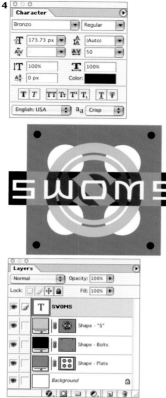

4

A Type layer was added, with tracking expanded to allow for bevels.

5a

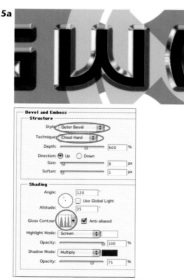

Creating an Outer beveled edge for the type

chosen **2c** (if this option doesn't appear in the Options bar, click the thumbnail for the vector mask of the Shape layer in the Layers palette). Hold down Shift and Alt/Option and drag outward from a grid point in one quadrant of the square. When you have a circle of the size you want, you can choose the Path Component Selection tool and drag the circle into place where you want it, aligning its control points with grid lines. With the circle still selected, you can make each of the other three circles by holding down the Alt/Option key and dragging to make a duplicate, then dragging this copy into place **2d.**

We wanted to be able to apply different Layer Styles to the square plate than to the bolts in the corners. So at this point we started a new Shape layer for the bolts: To get out of editing mode for the current Shape layer, click the ✓ at the right end of the Options bar, or press the Return/Enter key; you'll see that the layer clipping path thumbnail for the Shape layer no longer has a border around it, indicating that it isn't active. Now when you draw a small circle with the Ellipse tool to make the first bolt, a new Shape layer will be started. Make and position three more copies of the circle. To make the bolts a different color from the plate, in the Layers palette you can double-click the thumbnail for the bolts layer and choose from the Color Picker; we chose black.

3 Importing Illustrator artwork. The next step was to import the custom monogram "S." With the "S" file open in Illustrator, we selected the object and copied it to the clipboard (Ctrl/⌘-C). In the Photoshop file we pasted it (Ctrl/⌘-V), choosing the Shape Layer option in the Paste dialog box. We used the Guides and Grid to center the custom shape at the 0,0 point **3.** (See page 306 for tips on pasting from Illustrator 10.)

4 Setting type. We chose the Type tool and set the type for the logo, using the Bronzo font **4.** You can find step-by-step instructions for setting, spacing, and scaling type in step 5 of "Typography, Groups & Layer Styles" on page 308. Be sure to leave enough space between letters to allow for the width that will be added by the bevels.

5 Building the bevel. With the type layer active, we clicked the "*f*" button at the bottom of the Layers palette and chose **Bevel And Emboss** to open the Layer Style dialog box and begin building our "brushed steel" Style. To create the Style, choose Outer Bevel from the Structure section's Style list and Chisel Hard for the Technique. Using an **Outer Bevel** "adds" the beveled edge outside the existing type (in contrast, Inner Bevel cuts into the type to get the material for the edge, which changes the shape of the characters). Using **Chisel Hard** makes a sharp, fairly smooth bevel. The Size setting determines the width of the bevel (we used 8 pixels to get the edge we wanted for the size of the type), and the Depth determines the bevel's "steepness," with higher settings simulating

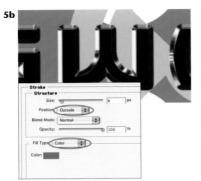

5b

Adding a Stroke to make the bevel opaque

6a

Applying the Wow-Brushed Metal pattern as a Pattern Overlay effect

6b

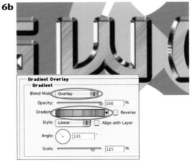

Adding a Noise gradient as a Gradient Overlay

6c

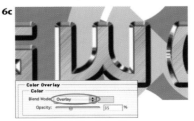

Adding a light blue tint with a Color Overlay

steeper sides by increasing the contrast between highlights and shadows. The lighting is set up in the Shading section, with the **Gloss Contour** and the blend modes and opacities of the highlights and shadows. To produce a highly reflective surface with alternating high-contrast lights and darks, choose a complex Gloss Contour, with multiple ridges such as Ring-Triple **5a**. With Highlight and Shadow Modes set to their default Screen and Multiply modes, you can increase the contrast between highlight and shadow tones by increasing the Opacity settings, as we did for the highlights.

Because the Outer Bevel effect always produces a semi-transparent bevel, as described in the "Bevels — Inner & Outer" tip below, the **Stroke** effect is used to finish the bevel. We clicked the Stroke listing at the left side of the Layer Style dialog box and set up an **Outside** stroke the same Size as we had used for the bevel (8 pixels). We assigned the stroke a "steel blue" color, which showed through the highlights and shadows created by the bevel's Gloss Contour **5b**.

BEVELS — INNER & OUTER

Photoshop's Inner and Outer Bevel effects offer different options for how the beveled edge relates to the shape it's applied to and also how it relates to the background:

The **Outer Bevel** extends outward from the edge of the element it's applied to. And it's always semitransparent, so that whatever is beneath can show through the bevel. This is ideal for **"license plate embossing,"** where the bevel rises from the background and the contrasting color for the type is applied only to the flat top surface **A**.

The Outer Bevel alone lets part of the background show through.

In contrast, the beveled edge of an **Inner Bevel** is built inward from the edge of the element it's applied to, and it takes its characteristics (such as color or pattern) from the element itself — the background doesn't show through (unless the opacity of the element itself is reduced). If you want a solid bevel — for cast metal, for instance — you might be tempted to use an Inner Bevel. However, the Inner Bevel **encroaches on the shape** of the element; this can be a real problem if the element is a delicate shape or if it's type **B**.

The Inner Bevel creates a solid edge but cuts into the shape it's applied to.

To get a **solid outer bevel** (not semi-transparent), you can use the **Outer Bevel with a Stroke** effect added, *whose Size is exactly the same* as the Size for the Outer Bevel, and whose Position is set to Outside. Like the bevel, the stroke will extend outward from the edge of the element. So it will fill in behind the semitransparent bevel, lending its Color, Gradient, or Pattern fill to the edge **C**.

To make a solid bevel without changing the weight of the type, use a Stroke in addition to the Outer Bevel.

6d

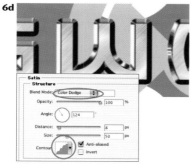

Using the Satin effect to add light/dark variation that reacts to the shapes of the letters

7a

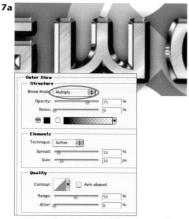

Adding a "dark halo" with the Outer Glow

7b

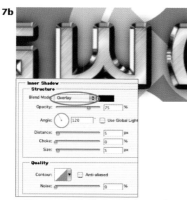

Adding more light/dark variation on the surface with the Inner Shadow effect

6 Coloring the surface of the type. To create the look of brushed steel, we clicked the **Pattern Overlay** listing at the left side of the Layer Style dialog box, then clicked the little triangle to the right of the pattern swatch to open the Patterns palette, and chose the Wow 7-Misc Surface Patterns from the Patterns options menu in the upper right corner of the menu. Then we selected the Wow-Brushed Metal pattern **6a.** (If you haven't yet loaded the **Wow Presets** from the CD-ROM that comes with this book, see page 7 for instructions on how to load these.) This pattern was made by applying noise to a gray-filled layer (Filter, Noise, Add Noise, Mono-chromatic), then applying a motion blur (Filter, Blur, Motion Blur), and finally turning the result into a seamless pattern, as described in "Seamlessly Tiling Patterns" on page 378.

The motion-blurred pattern had produced the short, irregular strokes we wanted. To add more light/dark variation, we next added a **Gradient Overlay** effect in Overlay mode **6b,** using Wow 7-Gradient 26 from the **Wow 7-Gradients** set. (See page 268 for more on Noise Gradients.)

Next we added a **Color Overlay** effect, choosing a light blue in Overlay mode and reducing the Opacity to get the tint we wanted for the surface **6c.**

Finally, we used the **Satin** effect to create some shading that reacts with the contours of the type characters themselves. We chose Color Dodge for the blend mode, which exaggerated the highlighting on the surface. We experimented with the Contour choices that control the light/dark variation of the surface lighting and finally chose Rounded Steps, one of the default presets **6d.**

7 Emphasizing the edges. We used an Outer Glow, Inner Shadow, and Drop Shadow to emphasize the shapes of the charac-ters and pop the type out from the elements behind it. The **Outer Glow** in Multiply mode provided the main "dark halo" shadow effect **7a.** The **Inner Shadow** effect was applied in Overlay mode so that it would interact with the Pattern and Gradient Overlay effects to produce irregular edge shading **7b.** And the **Drop Shadow** was added in Color Burn mode **7c.** Color Burn darkens elements below it in the Layers stack, reacting more strongly with already dark colors than with light ones. So the effect here would be to produce slightly different shadow effects on the light gray custom logo, the darker square plate, and the white background **7d.**

8 Applying Layer Styles to the other layers. Once the treat-ment of the type was complete, we applied the same Style to the custom logo layer. **To copy a Style** from one layer to another, in the Layers palette right-click or Control-click (for a Mac with a one-button mouse) on the *"f"* icon for the layer with the Style and choose Copy Layer Style from the pop-out menu **8a.** Then right-

7c

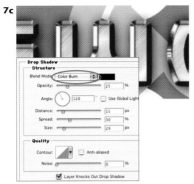

Reinforcing the depth with a Drop Shadow in Color Burn mode

7d

The type layer with its complete Layer Style in place

8a

Copying the Style from the type layer

8b

Pasting the copied Style to the custom "S" layer

click/Control-click the name of the layer where you want to apply the Style and choose Paste Layer Style **8b.**

After applying the Style you can modify it. For the custom logo layer we tweaked the Style by adding an **Inner Glow** in black in Multiply mode to make the shape a little darker than the type **8c.**

Different Layer Styles were applied to the square plate and bolts layers. You can examine the **Brushed Steel-After.psd** file to see the details of the Layer Styles for these layers. The Pattern Overlay effect was not used for the bolts, because we wanted them to be smooth and shiny. A **Texture** was added to the Bevel And Emboss effect, using the Wow-Brushed Metal pattern (the same one used in the Pattern Overlay) to enhance the surface texture **8d.**

Sharpening up the edges. When all the Layer Styles are in place on all the layers, you can save a flattened copy of the file for output purposes by choosing Image, Duplicate and checking the Duplicate Merged Layers Only box. To increase the contrast of the hard metal edges, sharpen the image (Filter, Sharpen, Unsharp Mask). The result is shown at the top of page 405.

8c

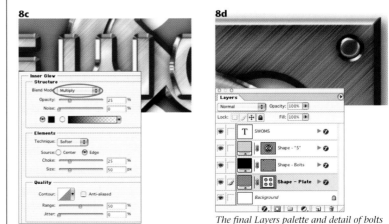

Adding a dark Inner Glow

8d

The final Layers palette and detail of bolts and plate

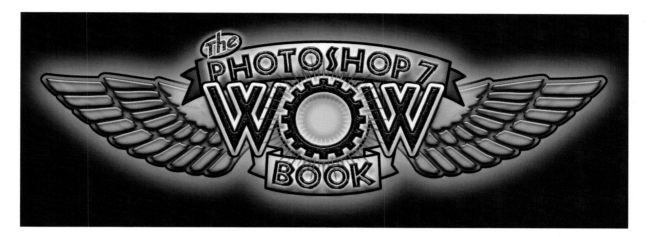

Jack Davis** began his design for the *Photoshop 7 Wow! Book Tattoo*, in Adobe Illustrator, with wings to represent speed and creativity, a cog wheel for "industrial strength," and glows for divine inspiration. He separated the black-filled design elements onto individual layers and then exported the file as a layered Photoshop PSD document. This allowed tremendous freedom when he opened it in Photoshop 7, because he could add color, dimension, and "atmosphere" by applying a custom Layer Style to each element separately, on its own transparent layer.

Having the elements on separate layers also helped when the file was reduced and animated for a Web banner. Each element's Style could be adjusted individually if necessary to fine-tune shadows, glows, and bevels in the reduced artwork, as described in the "Adjusting the Style" tip on page 445. The separate cog wheel layer could also be duplicated and rotated to make additional layers (using the method presented in "Designing for Scalability & Animation" on page 332), which could then be used in ImageReady to produce animation frames to turn the wheel (using the method presented in step 2 of "Animating with Actions" on page 440).

THE WEB & MOTION GRAPHICS

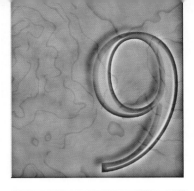

Photoshop 7's toolbox includes Slice and Slice Select tools.

Slice — Slice Select

Image Map tools

Circle — Select

Rectangle — Polygon

Image Map View

Slice View

Preview In Default Browser

Rollover Preview

Unique to ImageReady 7's Tool palette are the Image Map tools and the Preview buttons for viewing slices, viewing image map "hot spots," previewing rollovers, and previewing files in a browser. ImageReady's movable "tearoff" tool palettes allow you to see all the tools that share a spot in the toolbox.

THE COMBINATION OF PHOTOSHOP 7 AND IMAGEREADY can take a Web project all the way from creating the art through automatically writing the HTML and JavaScript for many Web page assembly and linking functions. Though both of these programs share a lot in common and are symbiotic in many ways, they are still very distinct in focus and workflow. Here's a brief summary of the similarities and differences — you'll find more about what these functions mean and how they work in the next 13 pages and especially in the techniques presented in this chapter:

- Both Photoshop and ImageReady have **vector-based Shape-drawing tools** that are so handy for creating button shapes, and that ImageReady has had since version 5.5. The use of the Shape tools is covered in "Shape Tools and Shape Layers," starting on page 298, and elsewhere in Chapter 7.

- Photoshop also has the same **Slice** and **Slice Selection tools** as in ImageReady, and slices can be saved and output directly from Photoshop. Like ImageReady, Photoshop can also create slices automatically from layers, as described in "Creating Button Rollover Styles" on page 449. In ImageReady you can select, name, and save **sets of slices** that you can then quickly load for reselection.

- Both programs make it easy for you to **preview** your Web creations **in a browser.** In ImageReady the Browser Preview button is built into the toolbox (as shown at the left), but in Photoshop the button is inside the Save For Web dialog box (as shown on page 420).

- ImageReady is the only program that allows you to create **instant rollover effects** and the ability to preview this interactivity.

- Both programs have **weighted optimization** based on alpha channels, and now **text and shape layers** as well. You can specify one or all three to control which parts of a file are considered most important in creating a color palette, and which parts of an image are protected from JPEG compression or Lossy GIF compression. This feature helps to minimize unwanted artifacts in areas where they would be most obvious or jarring. "Animating with Masks" on page 443 demonstrates the use of an alpha channel for weighted optimization using Lossy GIF compression.

continued on page 414

The Rollovers palette in ImageReady has been completely redesigned to show all of a file's slices, rollovers, image maps and animations in one organized location.

As in Photoshop 7, preset Layer Styles can be applied to the graphics on a transparent layer in ImageReady 7 by choosing from the Styles palette. A black upper left corner on a thumbnail in ImageReady's palette indicates a combined Rollover Style, with the interactivity and slicing built-in.

- ImageReady has **three Image Map tools** — Rectangle, Circle, and Polygonal — for specifying "hot spots" (links) in a file; it also has an **Image Map Select tool** for moving hot spots and editing their shapes. The Rectangle and Circle Image Map tools are operated like Photoshop's Marquee or Shape tools, and the Polygonal Image Map tool works basically like the Polygonal Lasso. You can also generate **layer-based image map "hot spots."** And you can **assign rollovers to hot spots**.

- In ImageReady 7 you can create and save **combined Rollover Styles** with multiple states built in, so you can apply them to other files by means of ImageReady's Styles palette. "Creating Button Rollover Styles" on page 449 tells how to design, save, and apply combined Rollover Styles. Also, a new **Selected State** has been added, which assists in the creation of navigation bars with simultaneous rollover effects.

- Photoshop (**.psd**) files can be dragged and dropped into **Adobe GoLive** Web pages without going through the Save For Web dialog box. And you can choose to include GoLive-readable code when you save optimized files in either program.

- Both programs have added **dithered transparency options** to simulate transparency or soft edges in GIF files, as well as the ability to **remap** one or more colors to **transparency.**

- Photoshop 7's **Web Photo Gallery** function now comes with even more templates that can be used "as is" or customized to create your own "portfolio" Web site. "Making a Web Photo Gallery" on page 423 includes some suggestions for modifying the frame-based and table-based galleries produced with Web Photo Gallery.

- Perhaps the most notable interface improvement in ImageReady 7 is the **extension of the Rollover palette,** which now gives you the ability to see all of a file's slices, rollovers, image maps, and animations in one place.

ESTABLISHING AN EFFICIENT WEB WORKFLOW

There's a great deal of overlap between the Web-related features in Photoshop 7 and ImageReady 7. Many of the functions you find in the Photoshop Save For Web interface are also found in Image-Ready's palettes. This means that there are many ways to proceed, moving between programs as you develop Web graphics. In general, though, it's often more efficient to **create the artwork in Photoshop,** and then **move to ImageReady if you need image maps, animation, or button rollovers.** Here are some workflow suggestions:

- Photoshop is better equipped for creating and editing images than ImageReady is. (The ImageReady toolbox is missing the **Magnetic Lasso, Background Eraser, History Brush, and Pen tools, and the painting tools are limited compared**

In ImageReady, slices can be constructed from guides pulled in from the rulers as shown here, or from an active selection.

SLICE/SELECT

In both ImageReady and Photoshop the Ctrl/⌘ key toggles between the Slice and Slice Select tool.

A WEB-DESIGN RESOURCE

The Photoshop 7 Wow! Book tells how to put Photoshop and Image-Ready to work in the construction of Web graphics, pages, or sites. A companion book that emphasizes the communication concepts and design principles that underlie effective Web development is *The Web Design Wow! Book* (Davis and Merritt, Peachpit Press), winner of the Computer Press Association Award.

to those of Photoshop. Its selecting and image-editing commands are also limited.) So if you're developing simple **static images** to be posted on the Web, it makes sense to originate them in Photoshop and then use its **Save For Web** command (or ImageReady's Optimize palette) to *optimize* them, which means to balance image quality with file size, for good-looking images and fast downloads. To do this, choose the file format, the type of adaptive palette and number of colors, and the options you want for transparency and for weighting the optimization. (The process of choosing is described in "Optimizing Web Art" on page 419.) You can use the button at the bottom of the Save For Web interface (or in Image-Ready's toolbox) to preview how the file will look when viewed within a Web browser. Finally, save the optimized artwork and the HTML code (if desired) in the **Save Optimized As** dialog box (see "Optimizing Tools" on page 420).

- Since several small image files download faster than a single large image, one way to reduce download time is to *slice* the image file, dividing it into separate files that will be reassembled seamlessly when downloaded. Another advantage of slicing is that you can optimize each slice separately, so you can maximize image quality by using different file formats or color palettes for the various slices.

You can prepare and slice the image file in Photoshop or ImageReady, defining the areas for the separate files using the **Slice** and **Select Slice** tools, or by using **guides** or **selections.** Another way to produce slices is to put the elements you want in your slices on separate layers in your Photoshop file.

Then define layer-based slices in Photoshop or

SLICE LINGO

There are three types of slices you can make in ImageReady; two of these — user slices and auto slices — can also be made in Photoshop:

- **User slices** are the ones that you (the user) draw with the Slice tool or define with guides or selections.

- **Layer-based slices** are made automatically when you choose Layer, New Layer Based Slice. The slice is shrunk to the smallest possible bounding box that includes all the nontransparent pixels in the layer.

- **Auto slices** are the ones that Photoshop or ImageReady make to fill in the rest of the canvas around the user slices and layer-based slices you've made.

It makes sense that user slices are the only ones you can reshape by dragging on a slice handle with the Slice Select tool. Auto slices are reshaped any time you change a user slice or a layer-based slice, to refill the empty area. And layer-based slices are reshaped if you change the layer content.

If you want to edit an auto slice or layer-based slice by hand, you can **promote** it to a user slice. In Photoshop simply click the auto slice or layer-based slice with the Slice Select tool and click the Promote To User Slice button in the Options bar. In ImageReady, click the slice with the Slice Select tool and choose Slices, Promote To User-Slice.

Geno Andrews used a process similar to "Animating by Transforming" on page 434 to create spinning type. First, in Photoshop, he set the type. Then he copied the type layer and rotated the copy, all in one operation (Ctrl-Alt-T in Windows; ⌘-Option-T on the Mac), entering an angle value of 45° in the Options bar and pressing Enter to accept the rotation. He blurred the rotated copy, rasterizing it in the process, by choosing Filter, Blur, Radial Blur, using the Spin method and Amount set to 15. Then he used the copy-and-transform-again keyboard shortcut (Ctrl-Shift-Alt-T for Windows; ⌘-Shift-Option-T for Mac) to make six more copies of the blurred word to complete the 360° rotation. He linked the layers and distorted them (Edit, Transform, Perspective). Then he jumped to ImageReady to make the frames of an animation by using the Animation palette and choosing Make Frames From Layers from the Animation palette's pop-out menu. Finally he turned on the visibility for his bottom most Checkerboard & Face layer and clicked the Unify Layer Visibility icon (the Eye & Lock icon towards the top of the Layers Palette) to automatically add it to each frame. He then deleted the extra first frame that was created with the Make Frames From Layers command and set the timing of the frames as desired.

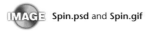
Spin.psd and Spin.gif

ImageReady by activating each layer in turn and choosing Layer, **New Layer Based Slice.** For each layer Photoshop or ImageReady will make a slice that's a "snapshot" of everything that's within the slice, from all currently visible layers, but trimming it as closely as possible based on the content of the active layer.

• To make an ***image map,*** which is a single image that contains multiple "hot spots" (areas that link to other locations), you can prepare the image file in Photoshop, but you have to actually turn it into an image map in **ImageReady**. You can put the artwork for each hot spot on a separate layer either in Photoshop or in ImageReady, and then in ImageReady choose Layer, **New Layer Based Image Map Area**. Or you can delineate the hot spots using ImageReady's **Image Map tools**. Then assign each hot spot a URL link using ImageReady's **Image Map palette.**

• If you're developing an **animation,** you can create the art for the individual frames in Photoshop or ImageReady, but you'll need to use ImageReady's **Animation palette** to assemble and pace the animation, and to save it as an animated GIF file.

For **cel animation,** in which you create separate art for each frame, it makes sense to create all the graphics as individual layers in Photoshop, and then move the file to ImageReady for completion. This workflow is used for "Cel Animation" (page 429), "Animating by Transforming" (page 434), "Animating with Actions" (page 440), and "Animating with Masks" (page 443). When you build an animation using this workflow, you can preview it at every stage of development — in Photoshop by scrolling the Layers palette (as described in the "Photoshop Animation Preview Trick" on page 431), in ImageReady's Animation palette by clicking the Play button, and by previewing in one or more Web browsers, using the Preview In Default Browser button at the bottom of ImageReady's toolbox.

Still another way to animate is to use ***tweening***: You define the starting and ending frames of an animation frame sequence, and ImageReady produces as many intermediate stages as you

It's easy to use Photoshop's Transform command to rotate a circle. But to rotate points around the edge of an oval like the one above, or to rotate an element in perspective such as the "Spin" type on the left, is tricky. To make the points of this burst "travel" around the edge, we first made and rotated several copies of a spiky circle, then linked and "squashed" all the circles into ovals by scaling them vertically. This process is described in "Designing for Scalability & Animation" on page 332.

Oval Anim.psd and .gif

ImageReady's Tween function can tween position, Style, and Opacity, but it can't tween from one shape to another. To "morph" the word "Act" to the word "Now," Geno Andrews set the two pieces of type in Adobe Illustrator, converted them to outlines, then selected the two words and blended them in four steps. He chose Object, Expand to separate the blend elements. Then he put the six stages — two originals and four blended — onto separate layers. He exported the file as a layered PSD document and opened it in Photoshop, where he added a Style to each layer. Then he jumped to ImageReady and produced the animation using the Make Frames From Layers command, as in "Cel Animation" on page 429.

 IMAGE Act-Now.psd and .gif

specify, changing the position, opacity, Layer Style, or text warp. Once the tweening is done, you can add more tweened frames or individual frames to the animation, or edit the frames or the timing. "Tweening & Tweaking," which starts on page 425, shows several approaches to animating in this way.

- If you're developing button graphics that include alternate versions for animated **rollovers** to show the buttons in Normal (rest), Over (when the cursor passes over), Down (pressed), and the new Selected (stays "lit") states, you can develop all the graphics you need in Photoshop. Then assign the rest, rollover, and mouse-down states in ImageReady's **Rollover palette.** Preview the rollover states in your browser and save the automatically generated JavaScript, HTML, and button graphics with the **File, Save Optimized As** command.

  If you produce your button states by making changes to the appearance of a Layer Style only (adding a glow, for instance), ImageReady can even generate a **combined Rollover Style** that you can then save as a Style preset and apply to other buttons simply by clicking in ImageReady's Styles palette. "Creating Button Rollover Styles" on page 449 takes you through the process of developing such a preset, and "Wow Button Samplers" on page 455 explains how to use the 150 Normal-Over-Down Styles and the 50 combined Rollover Styles (a total of 200 different button presets) that are provided on the Wow CD-ROM for instant application to your own buttons.

PLANNING ART FOR THE WEB

No matter what Photoshop/ImageReady workflow you use, planning is essential for designing Web graphics. Almost any effect you can create in Photoshop can be adapted for use on Web sites. Special-effects treatments for text and graphics like those in Chapter 8 make excellent styling for the buttons that activate Web links. Photo treatments and montages like those in Chapters 3 and 4, adapted to meet the special challenges of downloading from the Web, can be ideal for background illustrations or for image maps.

Although many of the same basic rules of design and composition apply whether you're designing for the screen or for print, in some ways designing and creating artwork for the Web or for multimedia is fundamentally different from creating images for the printed page:

- For most people, getting around on a Web site or in a multimedia presentation is still a less familiar and less intuitive process than reading a book or magazine. As a result, one of the goals of most on-screen presentations is to make it clear how a user can get to the information stored at the site or on the disc. Easy-to-interpret **buttons and other navigational "controls"** become essential. (See "Creating Button Rollover Styles" on page

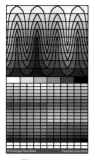

*The **Web Wow Color Pal.gif** file on the Wow CD-ROM provides two "spectrum" layouts of Web-safe colors. It also isolates the four pure grays that exist in the Web-safe palette and provides extra "wells" where you can put colors that are important for a particular job.*

IMAGE Web Wow Color Pal.gif

RUN-LENGTH ENCODING

In run-length encoding, which is similar to the type of compression scheme used in the GIF file format, color data is compressed by reading across the image, one row of pixels at a time, and storing information about color *changes* rather than storing the color of each individual pixel. The fewer color changes there are in each row of pixels — or the more *horizontal color redundancy* there is— the more the file can be compressed. So, for example, a vertical color gradient — one that changes color from top to bottom — contains only one color per row and can be compressed quite small. But a horizontal or diagonal gradient — changing color from side to side or corner to corner — involves many color changes per row and therefore can't be compressed as much. Dithered colors also compress less well than solid colors, since a color change has to be recorded with each color change in the "dotted" mix.

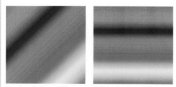

Both of these files are 256 pixels wide, with 256 colors and dither. The diagonal gradient on the left compresses to 20K, while the horizontal gradient compresses to 10K.

449 for button manufacture. Also see the "Wow Button Samplers" on page 455 and the associated layered Photoshop file on the CD-ROM for inspiration and for practical Layer Styles for creating buttons.)

- The **resolution** of on-screen images is a lot lower than that used for print — 1 pixel in the file for 1 pixel on-screen, rather than 3 or 4 pixels in the file for 1 halftone dot on the page. That means you need to take special precautions to ensure smooth edges on type and graphics. When creating low-resolution display type and graphics, you can often get more flexibility in the design process and therefore better-looking results if you **design at twice or four times the size you need** and then scale them down with Image, Image Size.

- **Reduce the dimensions** of each image as small as you can and still achieve the impression you want.

- Restricting colors to the 216-color Web-safe palette isn't as important as it used to be in designing for the Web, because most computers sold in the last few years have at least 16-bit color (thousands of colors). If you need to work with a *Web-safe palette* (for wireless computing applications, for instance), you can choose from a browser-safe Swatches palette such as the **Web Hues.aco** or **Web Spectrum.aco** provided on the Adobe Photoshop 7 application CD-ROM. Or open the **Web Wow Color Pal.gif** file provided on the CD-ROM that comes with this book and use it to sample colors; this file presents the Web colors in an easy-to-use arrangement, as shown at the upper left of this page.

- **Avoid horizontal or diagonal gradients** if you'll be saving files in the GIF format (described on page 419). Because of *run-length encoding-like* methods used to compress images in the GIF format, vertical gradients compress smaller than horizontal or diagonal ones. (The "Run-Length Encoding" tip at the left provides a simplified explanation of how this works.)

ON-SCREEN TYPE TIPS

The Type tool Options bar and Character palette in Photoshop 7 and ImageReady 7 offer several options that will help you produce good-looking, readable type on-screen, especially at small sizes:

- The **Sharp** and **Strong** antialiasing options in the Options bar can make type look sharper or heavier, respectively. For smaller point sizes, **Crisp** gives the type a lighter appearance, and **Smooth** can make small type look blurred or badly spaced.)

- Using The **Underline** option (available from the Character palette's pop-out menu) and turning off antialiasing can make type that's really a graphic or a hot spot in an image map look "live" and interactive.

- Turning off the **Fractional Widths** option (in the Character palette's pop-out menu) can prevent small type from running together on-screen.

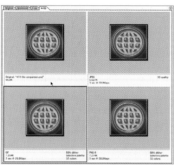

Comparing different file formats and compression options in the 4-Up view

The Optimize To File Size dialog box opens from the pop-out Optimize section of Photoshop 7's Save For Web interface and Image-Ready 7's Optimize palette. Here you can enter a file size as a target. If you choose the Current Settings option, Photoshop will use the file format, type of palette, and Dither currently in the Settings section of the Save For Web interface as a starting point for reducing the file size to hit the target. On the other hand, if you choose the Auto Select option, Photoshop will analyze the colors in the image and choose a GIF or JPEG profile based on the analysis.

- **Use tiled backgrounds.** For an individual Web-page (or frame) background, instead of making a textured or patterned background image file the size of the page, make a small repeating *tile* of the texture or pattern. A Web browser can use this tile to fill the background (see the "Tiling Backgrounds" tip on page 421).

- ImageReady's tweening animation function can tween position, opacity, and effects (including Layer Styles and Warp Text), but it can't "morph" from one shape to another. So you'll want to **plan artwork to take advantage of what can be tweened** (as in the "Tweening & Tweaking" examples starting on page 425), and "work around" what can't be tweened, as shown in the "shape morphing" example on page 417.

- Since ImageReady's **combined button Rollover Style** presets can incorporate only changes made entirely with Layer Styles, it pays to design your rollover states with all Color, Pattern, and Gradient fills applied with Overlay effects, and with dimensioning, glows, and shadows also built with **Layer Style** components.

OPTIMIZING WEB ART

Preparing artwork to be included in Web pages is a balancing act — you're aiming for good image quality and color reproduction but also small file size for fast downloading. Unfortunately, image quality and speed tend to work against each other. The more detail and color subtlety you want to preserve in an image, the bigger the compressed file tends to be, and thus the slower to download. Color reduction (for GIF) and image compression (for JPEG) become all-important.

Choosing a Format

Photoshop's Save For Web dialog box and ImageReady's Optimize palette are designed to help you choose the best file format for good image quality and small size. The most often-used file formats are these three:

- **JPEG** excels at compressing **photographs**. It allows "full" 24-bit color (millions of colors), so people whose computer systems can display 24-bit color (or 16-bit) will see the image at its best (or close to it). (Those with 8-bit systems will see a dithered version.) But JPEG doesn't allow you to make part of the image transparent to let the background of the Web page show through. Also, if applied with too high a degree of compression, JPEG can cause serious image degradation, especially at the boundaries between contrasting colors.

- **GIF** is great for **flat-color artwork** and small elements, but poor for large photos because it supports only 8-bit color at most

continued on page 421

OPTIMIZING TOOLS

Photoshop 7's Save For Web interface (shown at the right) and ImageReady 7 with its working window, Optimize palette and Color Table (shown below), provide the same options, designed to help you balance image quality and file size.

In 4-Up mode (shown here) you see your original image, the format and compression you're currently considering, and two other compression options. The display for each preview includes a listing of file sizes and typical download times. The tools in the Save For Web toolbox — for moving or magnifying the view and sampling color — are found in ImageReady's standard toolbox.

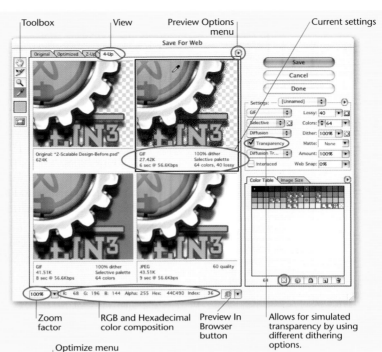

Toolbox | View | Preview Options menu | Current settings

Zoom factor

RGB and Hexadecimal color composition

Preview In Browser button

Allows for simulated transparency by using different dithering options.

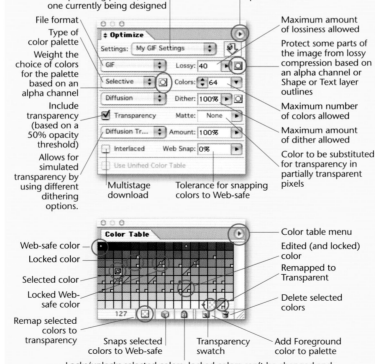

Optimizing presets, or the one currently being designed

Optimize menu

File format

Type of color palette

Weight the choice of colors for the palette based on an alpha channel

Include transparency (based on a 50% opacity threshold)

Allows for simulated transparency by using different dithering options.

Multistage download

Tolerance for snapping colors to Web-safe

Maximum amount of lossiness allowed

Protect some parts of the image from lossy compression based on an alpha channel or Shape or Text layer outlines

Maximum number of colors allowed

Maximum amount of dither allowed

Color to be substituted for transparency in partially transparent pixels

*In the **Optimize** palette you can choose a preset compression scheme or design your own, including the file format, the type of color palette and number of colors to be used, the kind and extent of dithering that will be produced (see the "Run-Length Encoding" tip on page 418). The Web Snap setting determines how close the original color has to be to a Web-safe color before it will automatically snap to the Web-safe palette. With the Transparency box checked, fully transparent pixels remain transparent; otherwise the Matte color is substituted.*

Web-safe color

Locked color

Selected color

Locked Web-safe color

Remap selected colors to transparency

Snaps selected colors to Web-safe

Transparency swatch

Add Foreground color to palette

Color table menu

Edited (and locked) color

Remapped to Transparent

Delete selected colors

Locks/unlocks selected colors; locked colors can't be changed and can't be dropped until all unlocked colors have been eliminated.

*The **Color Table** lets you select and sort colors and lock them so they are the last to be eliminated in the process of reducing colors to decrease file size. Small white diamonds indicate Web-safe colors; a small square in the lower right corner shows that a color is locked; a thick outline means that a color is currently selected. A black dot in the center indicates that the color has been edited by hand and is not Web-safe; edited colors are automatically locked. If the Transparency box is checked in the Optimize palette, the transparency swatch appears as the last "color" in the Color Table.*

If you choose Edit, Preferences, Optimization in ImageReady, you can choose to have the program automatically make its best compromise between file size and image quality, including whether to use GIF or JPEG. You can override the automatic choice at any time by making entries in the Optimize palette.

PROGRESSIVE DISPLAY

For very large JPEG images, you can avoid subjecting the viewer to a long wait before anything happens on-screen by choosing the Progressive option in the Optimize palette. The image will appear quickly (though pixelated) and then build sharp detail.

TILING BACKGROUNDS

To get a textured background for a Web page and still reduce the time needed for downloading, you can use a background tile — a small, repeating element for filling an individual Web page (or frame), starting at the top left corner and proceeding across and down. The smaller the tile, the less time it will take to download. If you make Web background tiles in Photoshop, be sure to try them out with the common browsers at typical download speeds.

The same randomized pattern that was used to make the seamlessly tiled Web-page background was incorporated into each of the graphics on this Web page. The graphics were saved as JPEG files with the same compression settings used for the background tile.

(256 colors), and its compression method is optimized for areas of flat color. It does allow limited **transparency** (including the new **transparency dither** options), however. So you can have graphics that are silhouetted against the Web page background. And it supports **animation**.

- **PNG** (pronounced "ping") allows either 8-bit or full 24-bit color and precise control of transparency (through the use of alpha channels, which can be full 8-bit grayscale masks). It compresses well and also takes into consideration the different gamma characteristics (brightness) of the monitors used on Mac, Windows, and Unix platforms, so that images created on one system are less likely to look too light or too dark when viewed on another platform.

Currently, some of the older browsers don't support all of the options of PNG. So for general distribution, Photoshop's GIF and JPEG formats are still the best bets. However, for incorporating raster-based art into the vector-based Macromedia Flash format, PNG may be a great choice, because the Flash plug-ins for browsers can handle this high-quality, transparency-capable format.

Photographs and Continuous-Tone Images

If you're starting with a photograph or other continuous-tone image, you're likely to get better results with the following format choices:

- **If your image is rectangular and it doesn't have any areas that need to be transparent,** use **JPEG**. Try several Quality settings (or let Photoshop choose them for you automatically), comparing the resulting files for image quality and loading time. Often Low quality works for photos, while Medium may be needed for color gradients. You can use an alpha channel mask to target compression to certain areas of an image.

- **If your image has a shape other than rectangular, especially if it has a soft, feathered edge, JPEG** is still an option if your Web-page background consists of a seamless, randomized texture that doesn't require precise alignment. In that case, transparency can be faked by incorporating the background tile pattern into the image. (See the "Tiling Backgrounds" tip at the left for an example.) Be sure to use the same compression settings for both the tile and the image so the two backgrounds will continue to match.

- **If your image is small and silhouetted,** you'll probably want to use the **GIF format,** realizing that you'll have to compromise color depth in order to get transparency. You can use the GIF conversion process described in "Animating by Transforming" on page 434.

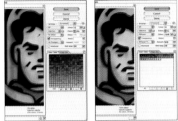

Starting with 256 colors and selecting and locking the important colors (left), then deleting unlocked colors to reduce the palette (right)

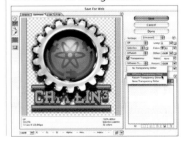
Flat-Color Artwork

For flat-color artwork, **GIF** is the better format. You can reduce the number of colors — and thus the size of the file — as described in "Reducing Color in GIFs," below. If you need **transparency** so the background of the Web page can show through your artwork, or if you want animation, use GIF.

Reducing Color in GIFs

To reduce the number of colors in a GIF file and still keep the image or graphic looking good, start with 256 (the maximum number) as the setting for Colors in the Optimize palette. Then:

1 Choose one of the adaptive palettes (Adaptive, Perceptual, or Selective), based on the nature of the art. An **Adaptive** palette is optimized to reproduce the colors that occur most often in the image. A **Perceptual** palette is like an Adaptive palette, but it also takes into consideration the parts of the spectrum where the human eye is most sensitive. A **Selective** palette — often a good choice — is like the Perceptual but also favors Web colors and colors that occur in large areas of flat color.

2 Select the colors that are important to preserve, by Shift-clicking or Shift-dragging in the image with the Eyedropper tool. In the Color Table the swatches of the colors you chose will be outlined.

3 Click the Lock button at the bottom of the Optimize palette, so that the colors you selected won't be deleted from the palette as you reduce the number of colors.

4 If your file includes transparency and you want to preserve it, turn on the **Transparency** option in the Optimize palette. This option uses the transparency information in the currently visible layers of the image file to create a mask that makes each pixel either fully transparent or fully opaque (called a *1-bit mask*). The **Matte** color determines what color will be used to replace the transparency in the partially transparent pixels at the edges of your element. By choosing the background color of the Web page as the Matte color, you can make the hard edges of a graphic look much smoother (antialiased) and make soft edges blend into the background.

5 Reduce the Colors number as you watch the changes in the Optimized view until the image quality is reduced beyond what you want it to be, and then increase the number of colors until it looks good again. You can use the pop-out Colors menu to reduce the number of colors in large steps — 16 colors at a time, or one row of the Color Table at its narrowest dimensions. Use the tiny up and down Colors buttons to increase or decrease one color at a time.

6 To reduce the file size further you can experiment with **Dither** and **Lossy** compression in the Optimize palette. *Dither* is the

When you're optimizing a GIF file with transparency and with the Transparency option turned on in the Optimize palette, the transparency swatch in the Color Table has a status that's in between locked and unlocked. Although you can lock other colors in the Color Table so they will have priority as you lower the number of colors in the palette, it isn't possible to lock the transparency swatch. But the swatch has a higher priority than unlocked colors. As you reduce the number of colors, transparency will be retained (as the last swatch in the Color Table) until all unlocked colors have been eliminated. So if you reduce colors and find that all the remaining colors are locked but the transparency swatch is still there, you know that you haven't lost any locked colors. If the transparency swatch is gone, use the Colors "up" button to restore colors one by one until transparency comes back, indicating that all locked colors are now present.

ImageReady 7 comes with a number of Actions for creating spinning and zooming animations. Though many of them are not self-explanatory, they're all fast and fun, so give them a try – just be sure to experiment with them on a *copy* of your file!

Actions	
✓	▶ 2-State Button
✓	▶ Constrain to 200x200 pixels
✓	▶ Flaming Text
✓	▶ Frozen Text
✓	▶ Multi-Size & Save
✓	▶ Spinning Zoom In
✓	▶ Spin
✓	▶ Web Page Template
✓	▶ Zoom In
✓	▶ Zoom Out

interspersing of dots of two different colors to create the illusion of a third color. It reduces the number of colors needed in the palette, but because it can interfere with compression, it can sometimes *increase* the size of a compressed file instead of decreasing it. *Lossy* compression allows some image deterioration as file size is reduced, but a setting between 10% and 40% often doesn't degrade the image too much.

USING IMAGEREADY FOR ANIMATION AND ROLLOVERS

Where ImageReady really shines is in generating the JavaScript for rollover states in the Rollover palette and in turning layered files into animations with the Animation palette. The **Animation palette** and the **Rollover palette** share a common way of working. Once you get the hang of it, developing animations and rollover states from imported layered Photoshop files is easy. Briefly, the routine is "**click the page icon and change**, click the page icon and change," and so on.

In the Animation and Rollover palettes, the next graphic (the next frame in an animation or the next state for a button) is created by duplicating the palette's current frame or state and then changing the image file to the way you want it to look for the new frame or state. For instance, if you've created a layered Photoshop file with all the elements you need for your animation or button states, you can duplicate the current frame or state by clicking on the little page icon at the bottom of the palette and then make changes in ImageReady's Layers palette by turning on or off the visibility or changing the settings for layers, masks, Styles, or text warp.

MAKING A WEB PHOTO GALLERY

Photoshop's Web Photo Gallery command automatically makes a "portfolio" Web site from all the image files in a folder, with a banner and interactive "thumbnail" buttons, each of which brings up a larger, potentially captioned version of its image when clicked. The Web Photo Gallery templates provide all the resizing, compression, linking, and HTML coding for the placement and interactivity

For a working demonstration of some of the animated GIFs created with the techniques in this chapter, find Open_in_browser.html file inside the Wow GIF Sampler folder on the Wow CD-ROM and open the file in your Web browser to see all the animations at once.

IMAGE **Open_in_browser.html** and associated files in the **Wow GIF Sampler** folder

PhotoWebber 2 by MediaLab is an amazing stand-alone application that allows you to generate an entire Web page from a layered Photoshop file automatically. Once you design the page as a layered Photoshop file, you can open it in PhotoWebber for automatic slicing, optimizing, creating JavaScript for rollovers, and HTML coding for either a style sheet layout or a table. All you have to do is create the Photoshop file with each separate element on its own layer and add a suffix to the layer name: "_R" for rollover, "_P" for remote pop-up, "_C" for click down, "_M" for the base shape of a menu made from items in layers stacked above it, or no suffix for a static graphic. Then you can choose various options in the Properties dialog box. When you're happy with the layout, you can choose Build to create the entire page automatically.

Go to Medialab.com to find out more about this valuable third-party companion software to Photoshop and ImageReady.

IMAGE

PhotoWebber Sample folder

needed for the site. Eleven templates come with Photoshop 7: Some samples are shown below.

If you're comfortable working with an HTML editor, you can customize a copy of any of the Web Photo Gallery templates to make your own template. But you may also do some customization *without* coding. For instance, for each artwork file, you can use the Caption portion of the File Info dialog box (File, File Info) to create the caption you want for the thumbnail. Also, once you've used any of the templates provided with Photoshop 7, you can customize the results "after the fact" by copying and pasting new images into the thumbnail, background, or navigational arrow files that Web Photo Gallery has stored in the Images and Thumbnails folders it has made. 🎨

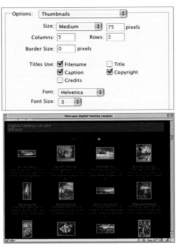

You can caption the thumbnails in a Web Photo Gallery by entering text in the Captions section of the File Info dialog box for the artwork image files before you run the Automate, Web Photo Gallery command. Shown here is a gallery made from the **Simple** *template.*

The new Security feature in Web Photo Gallery allow you to label or watermark (by reducing the opacity of your text) all of the images in your site, depending on your settings.

The thumbnails produced by the Web Photo Gallery are miniature versions of the artwork files themselves. But you can customize them by opening the files in the Thumbnails folder generated by the Web Photo Gallery command, changing their canvas size, and pasting in new images. Here the **Horizontal Frame** *template was used (top). The original thumbnails varied in proportions but all had either a height or a width of 75 pixels. To make square thumbnails, we changed the canvas size of each thumbnail file to 75 x 75 pixels. Then we made new close-up square images of that size by selecting from the original (large) images and copying. Finally we pasted the copied squares into the thumbnail files. On the Wow CD-ROM that comes with this book, you'll find a folder with the resulting gallery, shown above.*

Tweening & Tweaking

Tweening is the process of creating the intermediate frames between the starting and ending frames of an animation sequence. For many GIF animations you can save a great deal of time by letting ImageReady do the tweening automatically. Then, to fine-tune the animation, you may want to go back and make changes to individual frames.

The automated tweening process goes like this: In the Animation palette first select the frame that you want for the beginning or end of your tweened sequence. Then click the Tween button at the bottom of the palette and choose whether to tween this frame with the Previous Frame, the Next Frame, or back to the First Frame. Click OK to create the tweened sequence.

SOME CHANGES WILL "RIPPLE"

If you select a single frame of an animation and change the color, shape, or size of an element (any of the characteristics that can't be tweened) the change will ripple through all the frames. But if you select a single frame and change position, opacity, Layer Style, or Text Warp, or the visibility of a layer or mask (the characteristics that *can* be tweened), only that single frame will change. To change a tweenable characteristic over the entire animation, select all frames first and then make the change.

Tweening Position

We started with a file with a background filled with solid color. The silhouetted tugging hands were dragged-and-dropped from a larger file; when centered they extended beyond the left and right edges of the canvas.

Tug-O-War Banner
.psd and .gif

*In the Animation palette the first frame **A** was duplicated to make the second. Then the hands layer was shifted 4 pixels to the right **B** by choosing the Move tool and tapping the right arrow key.*

A Position Tween of just two steps was carried out by selecting the second frame and choosing to tween with Previous Frame. This made a total of four frames.

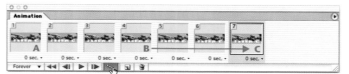

*To set up the tug back to the left, the fourth frame was duplicated to make the fifth, and the Move tool and arrow keys were used to shift the hands layer 8 pixels to the left **C**, to a position 4 pixels to the left of its original starting point.*

Another tween with Previous Frame using Position created two in-between frames for the quick tug to the left.

To complete the basic animation, a two-frame tween with the First Frame was created to bring the hands back to their starting position, and the animation was set to loop Forever. Clicking on individual frames and using the Move tool and arrow keys to nudge each frame up or down added to the struggle in the tug of war.

Tweening a Style

The goal for this animation was to move the position of an apparent light source. We did it by changing just one attribute — the Global Light Angle — of a Layer Style that consisted of a Drop Shadow and a Bevel And Emboss. We turned on Use Global Light for both the Drop Shadow and Bevel And Emboss, and set the Angle at 90° to start, so the light appeared to be positioned at 12 o'clock **A**.

IMAGE Bolt Bulb anim.psd
and .gif files

In the Animation palette, we duplicated the first frame to make frame 2. Next we double-clicked on the Drop Shadow's label in the Layers palette to open the Drop Shadow section of the Layer Style dialog box. Then all we had to do to move our "light source" to a position exactly opposite was to change the Angle setting to –90° (6 o'clock). Since we had turned on Use Global Light, changing the Angle for the Drop Shadow also changed it for the Bevel And Emboss. The shadow and the edge highlights and shading all moved together in response to the change in Angle **B**.

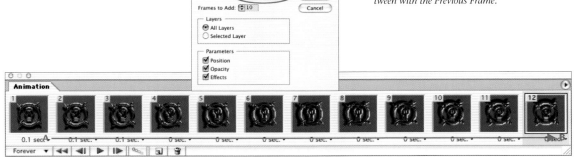

With the second frame selected, we clicked the Tween button and created a 10-frame tween with the Previous Frame.

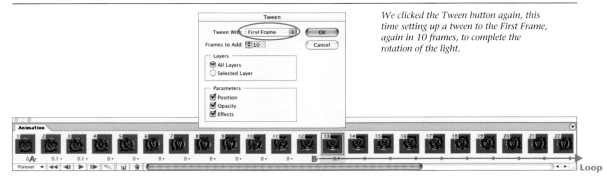

We clicked the Tween button again, this time setting up a tween to the First Frame, again in 10 frames, to complete the rotation of the light.

Tweening Position & Style

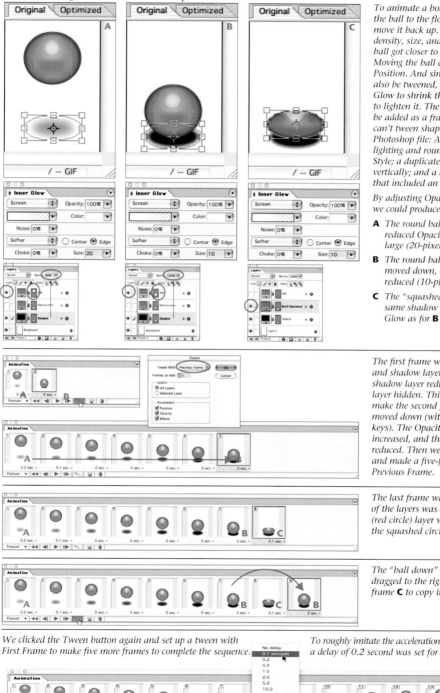

To animate a bouncing ball, we wanted to drop the ball to the floor, distort it on impact, and move it back up. We also wanted to change the density, size, and position of the shadow as the ball got closer to and farther away from the floor. Moving the ball could be done easily by tweening Position. And since Layer Style and Opacity can also be tweened, we would use a tweened Inner Glow to shrink the shadow and tweened Opacity to lighten it. The "squashed" ball would have to be added as a frame of its own, since ImageReady can't tween shapes. We assembled a layered Photoshop file: A red circle Shape layer with lighting and rounding created entirely by a Layer Style; a duplicate layer but with the ball scaled vertically; and a black Shape layer with a Style that included an Inner Glow from the Edge.

By adjusting Opacity, Style, and layer visibility, we could produce these three frames:

A The round ball high in the frame with a reduced Opacity for the shadow layer and a large (20-pixel) Size for the Inner Glow effect

B The round ball on the floor with the shadow moved down, Opacity increased, and a reduced (10-pixel) Size for the Glow

C The "squashed" ball on the floor with the same shadow position, Opacity, and Inner Glow as for **B**

IMAGE Tween Style Ball.psd and .gif files

The first frame was set up with the red circle and shadow layers visible, the Opacity of the shadow layer reduced, and the squashed circle layer hidden. This frame was duplicated to make the second frame, and the ball was moved down (with the Move tool and arrow keys). The Opacity of the shadow layer was increased, and the Size of the Inner Glow was reduced. Then we clicked the Tween button and made a five-frame tween with the Previous Frame.

The last frame was duplicated, and the visibility of the layers was adjusted: Visibility for the top (red circle) layer was turned off and visibility for the squashed circle layer was turned on.

The "ball down" frame **B** was then Alt/Option-dragged to the right of the "squashed ball" frame **C** to copy it to the next frame.

We clicked the Tween button again and set up a tween with First Frame to make five more frames to complete the sequence.

To roughly imitate the acceleration and deceleration of a real bounce, a delay of 0.2 second was set for the first frame. For the second, the last, and the "squash" frame we used 0.1-second.

Tweening a Type Warp

Text Warp is among the effects that can be tweened in ImageReady's Animation palette. Starting with a gradient-filled Background, we created a type layer and set the word "HULA." We added dimension and lighting with a Layer Style. Then we duplicated the layer and flipped the copy, all in one operation, by using the keyboard shortcut for duplicate-and-transform (Ctrl-Alt-T in Windows or ⌘-Option-T on the Mac) and then dragging the top center handle of the Transform frame down to the bottom of the canvas. We added a gradient-filled mask to the duplicate layer to fade the "reflection" **A**.

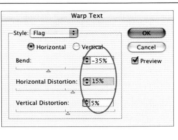

In the Animation palette, frame 1 was duplicated to start frame 2. Then the original type layer was distorted by clicking the Warp Text button in the Type tool's options bar, choosing the Flag Style and setting the Bend and Vertical and Horizontal Distortion parameters, and clicking OK to apply the warp to make the "H down" position. The same Flag Style warp was applied to the duplicate layer, but with opposite Bend settings — negative values were substituted for positive and vice versa **B**.

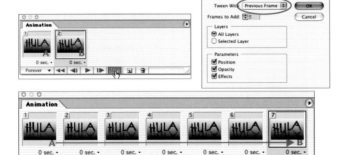

With the second frame selected and both type layers visible, we clicked the Tween button and set up a five-Frame tween with the Previous Frame (the straight type) to tween the position of the letters in both type layers.

The last frame was duplicated to make another. The text warp was changed again to set up the "H up" position **C**. Again the warp for the reflection layer was set with opposite numbers. Then this frame was tweened with the Previous Frame to add 11 frames, and then with the First Frame to add five more frames to complete the animation sequence. The complete, looping animation consisted of 24 frames.

Cel Animation

Overview *Prepare artwork as a series of sequential layers in a Photoshop file; make changes to the artwork to create individual animation frames, temporarily reducing Opacity settings to see several layers at once; create the animation in ImageReady.*

Space Pup.psd "before" and "after" files and **Space Pup.gif** animation

THERE ARE CERTAINLY MORE SOPHISTICATED WAYS of doing animation for the Web (vector-based Flash animation, for example). But creating frames in layers using the Photoshop equivalent of the old animator's onion-skinning process and then turning the layers into an animated GIF in ImageReady can produce a simple "hand-crafted" animation that can be viewed by any browser that supports graphics. Once the frames are painted in Photoshop, the production process is fairly automatic. Here we started with clip art and produced a five-frame "cartoon" of a space pup counting rockets.

1a

The original EPS clip art

1b

Heads cropped and resized

2

Line work thickened and Web color applied

3a

Aligning the second head. A 50% Opacity setting reveals the layer below (left). Restoring Opacity to 100% shows the finished artwork.

1 Preparing the graphics.

You'll build each frame of your animation in a Photoshop layer. We started with a series of clip art images **1a**, opening each of the dogs as an RGB file in Photoshop, then cropping and scaling it **1b**. In order to have some flexibility in the final size of our animation, we started working at approximately 200% of what we thought would be our final pixel dimensions.

2 Coloring the artwork. So

that all the line work from the different source files would match, some of the black-and-white heads were slightly blurred and then treated with Image, Adjust, Brightness/Contrast, using the method described in "Cleaning Up Masks" in Chapter 1. Color was added to the artwork with the Paintbrush with hard-edged brush

2X OR 4X

When you're designing for on-screen display, it's usually a good idea to start out with artwork that's two or four times the pixel dimensions you think you want for the final image. This gives you several advantages: You can see more detail, so it's easier to make selections and fine adjustments; you can make a 1-pixel stroke and it will look like a smooth hairline when you reduce it; you have enough pixels so you can make the on-screen display bigger than you originally planned if you change your mind.

3b

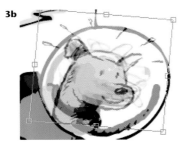

Aligning the last of the heads, with all but the bottom layer at 50% Opacity

3c

Heads aligned and masked

3d

Body composited with all layers

4a **4b**

Using a path to define the arc for the rocket

Stroking the path automatically

4c

Rocket clip art with Web colors added

tips (from the top row of the default Brushes palette), and with Multiply mode chosen in the Options bar so that painting onto the black lines wouldn't change their color **2**. About a dozen Web-safe colors were used (see "Getting Colors Organized" at the right).

3 Using the "onion-skinning" process. Our aim was to animate a sequence of the space pup watching rockets fly over, so we first had to get all the parts into one file at roughly the right size. We selected and dragged-and-dropped each head into the main space pup background file to become a layer of its own, arranging the layers in the appropriate order for the animation.

Visibility was turned off (by clicking the Eye icons in the Layers palette) for all but the bottom layer and the next layer up. The second layer's Opacity setting was reduced to 50% so we could see through to the full dog underneath. The head on the second layer was selected and moved by pressing Ctrl/⌘-T for Free Transform and dragging inside the Transform box; it was scaled by dragging the handles inward or outward, and rotated by dragging around the outside of the box, until it aligned with the dog on the bottom layer. Being able to see through the layer was essential in aligning the frames **3a.**

We made a layer mask by clicking the Add A Mask button at the bottom of the Layers palette and painted the mask with the Paintbrush and black paint to make a smooth transition from the new head to the dog body. Then we turned on visibility for the next layer up, reduced its Opacity to 50%, aligned its head with the body on the bottom layer, and added another layer mask. This process was repeated for the other two heads **3b,** and a copy of the tail was also positioned on each layer by pasting and merging down (Ctrl/⌘-E) **3c.**

Once all the heads and tails had been moved into position, we added a body to the head and tail on the second layer by selecting the body on the bottom layer and duplicating it to a new layer (Ctrl/⌘-J), which appeared in the Layers palette between the bottom layer and the Head 2 layer. This new layer was duplicated (by dragging its thumbnail to the Create A New Layer button at the bottom of the palette), and the copy was dragged between Head 2 and Head 3 in the palette. The duplication and moving process was

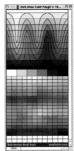

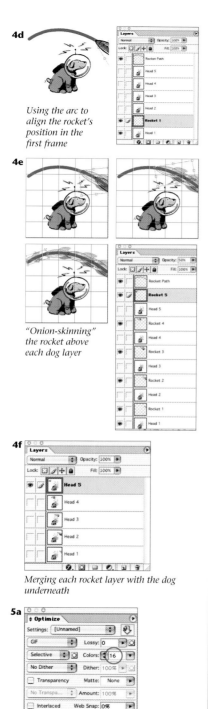

4d

Using the arc to align the rocket's position in the first frame

4e

"Onion-skinning" the rocket above each dog layer

4f

Merging each rocket layer with the dog underneath

5a

We tried reducing the number of Colors to 16, but this resulted in the loss of some colors that were important to the image.

repeated until each Head layer had a body layer underneath it.

We clicked the Head 2 layer to activate it, and then pressed Ctrl/⌘-E (for Layer, Merge Down) to merge Head 2 with the body copy right below it. The merging process was repeated for each of the other Head layers, until all heads had bodies **3d**.

4 Using a guide for motion. If your animation involves an object moving through the frame, sometimes it's helpful to have a guide — an arc for a bouncing ball or for a rocket flying overhead, for instance. To make such a guide for our rocket, we activated the top layer of our file, clicked the Create A New Layer button to add a layer on top of that, and used the Pen tool to form an arc **4a**. To make the arc easier to see, you can stroke the path with paint as we did by choosing a color from the Swatches palette, clicking the path name in the Paths palette to activate it, choosing the Paint-brush tool, and clicking the Stroke Path button at the bottom of the palette **4b**. (The paint stroke layer won't be part of the final ani-mation — it's just a temporary guide.)

We opened a clip art file of a rocket and colored it as we had the dogs **4c**. Then we clicked on the name of the bottom layer of the dog file in the Layers palette to activate it, and dragged the rocket into the file. We used Free Transform (Ctrl/⌘-T), dragging around the outside of the box to rotate the rocket so its nose lined up with the green arc; then we pressed the Enter key **4d**.

To help gauge the horizontal distance to move the rocket in each frame, we turned on the Grid (View, Show, Grid). We dupli-cated the rocket layer, moved the copy up the Layers stack above the next dog, changed its Opacity to 50% so we could see through it to the rocket below, and used Free Transform to move it, rotate it, and scale it **4e**. We continued making copies of the rocket, moving up the stack of layers to the top.

PHOTOSHOP ANIMATION PREVIEW TRICK

Artist Michael Gilmore showed us this trick for using Photoshop's Layers palette to preview an animation whose cels have been created as a stack of Photoshop layers. Before taking the file into ImageReady or another animation program for final preparation, set the Layers palette's thumbnails to the largest size (choose Palette Options from the palette's pop-out menu). Shorten the palette until only one layer's thumbnail shows, and move the scroll box up or down the scroll bar, or press and hold the palette's up or down scrolling arrow, to run the movie as a kind of digital flipbook. If your first frame is in the bottom layer of your file and your last frame is in the top layer, scrolling with the up arrow will run the animation forward; using the bottom arrow will run it backwards.

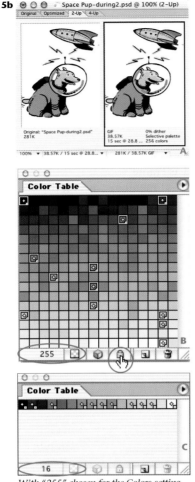

5b

Original: "Space Pup-during2.psd"
281K

GIF
38.57K   0% dither
15 sec @ 28.8 ...   Selective palette
                256 colors

100% ▼ 38.57K / 15 sec @ 28.8... ▼   281K / 38.57K GIF   ▼   A

Color Table

255   B

Color Table

16   C

With "255" chosen for the Colors setting
in the Color Table palette, we used the
Eyedropper tool to click the red of the rocket
fin **A**, then clicked the Lock button **B** so
this color would be preserved when we
reduced the number of colors to 16 **C**.

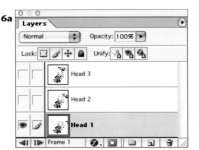

6a

Layers

Normal   Opacity: 100%

Lock: ☐ ✎ ✛ 🔒   Unify:

Head 3

Head 2

Head 1

◀ ▶   Frame 1

In the ImageReady Layers palette, the
image that was to become Frame 1 of the
animation was activated and made visible.

Next we merged each rocket layer with the dog layer below it,
using the same process as in step 3 (Ctrl/⌘-E) **4f.** Finally, we deleted
the layer with the green arc by dragging its thumbnail to the
palette's trash can button. We turned off the Grid (View, Show,
Grid) and saved the file in Photoshop format (File, Save As).

5 Optimizing in ImageReady. Open your layered file in Image-
Ready by clicking the Jump To button at the bottom of Photoshop
7's toolbox or by choosing File, Open in ImageReady. It's a good
idea to choose the type of optimization and compression of your
file before you assemble the animation. That way, as you preview
the animation you can see if problems arise in specific frames.

Start by picking the layer that has the most color complexity —
the most colors and the most broken-up distribution of color
patches. That way you'll know that the compression choices you
make for this image will also work for all the other layers. In the
Layers palette, Alt/Option-click in the Eye column for this layer to
turn on its visibility and turn off visibility for the other layers; also
click its name to make it the active layer.

In the working window, click the 2-Up or 4-Up tab so you'll be
able to see your original and also the current optimized version as
you change the color and compression parameters. Then open the
Optimize palette (Window, Show Optimize) **5a,** choose **GIF** (the
only format that supports ImageReady animation), and set the
Matte color if necessary. There was no **Transparency** in the
space pup file, so the Matte color was irrelevant. (If you don't see a
Matte setting, you can make it visible by choosing Show Options
from the palette's pop-out menu.) **Interlaced** was turned off, since
it's inappropriate for animation.

Then adjust the other parameters to reduce the number of colors
and increase the GIF compression. As you tweak the settings, check
the readouts for file size (K) and download time in the GIF side of
the 2-Up working window.

For the **palette,** we chose Selective, one of the adaptive palettes.
The trick was to find out how few colors we could use and still
maintain the quality we wanted. We had used only a dozen basic
colors for the original illustration, so we "guesstimated" that a **Colors** setting of 16 would provide enough for both the original colors
and some of the antialiasing. But it turned out that at 16 colors we
were losing more of our original color detail than we wanted to, so
we switched back to the full setting of 255 colors temporarily. Then
we locked important colors by choosing the Eyedropper tool and
Shift-clicking the colors in the image that we wanted to preserve,
and then clicking the Lock button at the bottom of the Color Table
palette. Finally we changed the setting in the Optimize palette back
to 16 colors **5b.** With the essential colors locked, the important
color detail was preserved.

6b

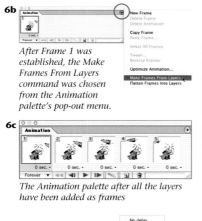

After Frame 1 was established, the Make Frames From Layers command was chosen from the Animation palette's pop-out menu.

6c

The Animation palette after all the layers have been added as frames

7

Using the pop-out menu to set the delay time, and setting the animation for continuous looping

8

Clicking the Play button runs the animation at full size in the working window.

9

Choosing ImageReady's Images Only format to save all the frames as a single GIF file

---

We left the **Lossy** setting at 0 since it provides little benefit with flat colors. (With an image with textures, however, it can help to use a Lossy setting somewhere between 10% and 40%. Sometimes the savings in file size is considerable, and sometimes negligible, depending on the complexity of the image.)

6 Assembling the animation. In the Layers palette turn on visibility for the layer you want to use for the first frame of your animation and turn off visibility for all other layers **6a.** (You can turn visibility on or off by clicking in the Eye column.) Open the Animation palette (Window, Show Animation). You'll find your currently active layer automatically designated as Frame 1.

Open the Animation palette's pop-out menu by clicking the triangle in the circle at the upper right corner of the palette, and choose Make Frames From Layers **6b.** This puts the layers into individual frames in the same order as they appear in the Layers palette **6c.**

7 Adjusting the timing and looping. By putting the cursor over the time delay number at the bottom of any individual frame and dragging upward, you can choose a frame delay time for that frame — the amount of time that frame will be shown before the next one is displayed **7.** Or select all the frames by Shift-clicking the final frame in the Animation palette, or by choosing Select All Frames from the palette's pop-out menu, and then choose a time delay. By choosing the shortest delay (0.1 second) you can ensure that your animation won't flash by too fast on speedier systems. The 0.2-second setting (5 frames per second) is the slowest rate that still produces fairly smooth animation. Use the pop-out list in the bottom left corner of the Animation palette to set the number of times the animation will play — Forever, Once, or a custom Other setting.

8 Previewing the animation. To see the animation running, click on the Optimized tab in the main working window and click the Play button (the triangle immediately to the right of the square Stop button) at the bottom of the Animation palette **8.** If you see something that needs changing, go back to the appropriate palette or window and make the necessary change. The animation will be updated to reflect the change.

9 Saving the file. When the animation is complete, choose File, Save Optimized As. In the Save Optimized As dialog box, choose Images Only as the Format **9.** This will save all the images of the animation as a single GIF file. *wow!*

Animating by Transforming

Overview In Photoshop, isolate the part of the image that you want to put in motion; cut it to a separate layer; duplicate the new layer and use the Free Transform command to change it; continue to duplicate and transform until you have a layer for each frame of the animation you want to create; in ImageReady reduce the number of colors; set visibility of the layers to make each frame; adjust timing; preview in browsers; save the optimized animation.

"Hula Doll" "before" and "after" files

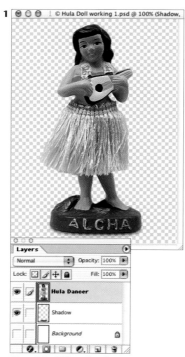

1

The original Photoshop image was silhouetted, and a shadow was created by filling a feathered selection on a layer below it.

PHOTOSHOP'S TRANSFORM COMMANDS can be very useful in creating eye-catching GIF animations. Here we used mainly the Rotate command, taking advantage of the ability to relocate the center of rotation, and to automatically duplicate a layer while transforming again. If the object you're animating is a vector-based graphic, you can transform it repeatedly without noticeable deterioration. With a pixel-based image, you can carry out the transformations in a way that minimizes "softening." Or if the subject calls for it, take advantage of the blurring as part of the animation, as we did here.

1 Preparing the image. Prepare the image that contains the element you want to animate, starting with a file whose pixel dimensions are two to four times what you want the final size of your animated file to be. Creating the animation frames at a larger size and then scaling down can produce a better-quality image than if you start at actual size, and the extra resolution will also give you more options later.

With the goal of animating the skirt to swish from side to side, we started with a silhouetted photo of a hula doll. We created a shadow on a separate layer below the dancer **1** so we would be able to change its opacity and blend mode independently, to make it fit into whatever background it would eventually go on.

2 Isolating the moving object. Select the part that you want to put in motion. We used the Lasso to isolate the skirt **2a**. Because of the transparent background, most of our selecting could be loose — the selection boundary would shrink to fit the pixels. The only places where the selection had to be precise were at the top of the skirt and where the skirt met the legs. Cut the selection to make a new layer (Layer, New, Layer Via Cut, or Ctrl/⌘-Shift-J) **2b.**

If necessary, "repair" the original layer to fill in any gaps that may be created when you put your object in motion. (If you don't get this exactly right at this point, you can make further repairs later.) We used the Smudge tool on the Dancer layer to extend the skin tones so there wouldn't be gaps when the skirt tilted **2c.**

3 Putting the object in motion. Now you can create the frames of the animation by duplicating the layer with your isolated object, then transforming the copy, making another duplicate,

2a

Selecting the skirt

2b

Cutting the skirt to a separate layer

2c

Smudging skin tones down from the waist and up from the legs so there would be no gaps when the skirt moved

transforming it more, and so on. To start the process, duplicate the layer by holding down the Alt/Option key as you drag the layer's name to the Create A New Layer button at the bottom of the Layers palette. Using Alt/Option opens the Duplicate Layer dialog box, where you can name the new layer. As you create each new layer, it's a good idea to name it in some way that describes the animation. Even for a simple animation it's important to keep the file organized and the layers clearly named. For instance, we named our original layer "Skirt-0," our first copy "Skirt-R1" (for the first movement to the right). When we made our second copy (see below), it would be "Skirt-R2" and so on; then we would use "Skirt-L1," "Skirt-L2," and so on for the layers in which the skirt moved left.

With the first duplicate made, transform it to create the change for the first frame of your animation. Choose Edit, Free Transform (or press Ctrl/⌘-T) to bring up the Transform frame, and make the change you want. We wanted to rotate the skirt to the right, but we wanted to center the rotation on the hip, so we dragged the center point of the Transform box to a new position **3a.** We then dragged around outside a corner of the Transform box to rotate the skirt slightly, noting the angle (–5°) in the Options bar **3b.** Double-click inside the box (or press Enter) to complete the transformation.

Continue to duplicate and transform to make additional frames. The best method to use will depend on whether the softening that results from repeated transformation of an image is a benefit to your animation or not. For our animation, the softening could serve as part of a "motion blur," so we used this method: To make

3a

Moving the center of rotation for the Transform box on the duplicated Skirt layer

3b

Rotating the duplicate layer

3c

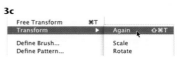

Edit, Transform, Again was chosen with the Alt/Option key held down to duplicate the layer and rotate the duplicate farther. (The keyboard shortcut is Ctrl-Alt-Shift-T on Windows or ⌘-Option-Shift-T on the Mac.)

To repeat the transformation you just made, you can press Ctrl/⌘-Shift-T. To make a duplicate of the element you just transformed and transform the copy again, all in one step, press Ctrl-Alt-Shift-T (Windows) or ⌘-Option-Shift-T (Mac).

3d

Checking the extremes of the animation by viewing the layers for both extremes and reducing the Opacity of one of them

4

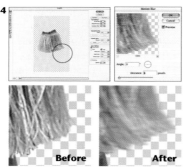

Before **After**

R3 and L3 layers were treated with Liquify's Warp tool with Brush Size at 150 and Brush Pressure at 50 (to add a swish) and the Motion Blur filter to exaggerate the movement.

our next layer, we simply duplicated the duplicate layer and rotated the new copy another 5° by holding down the Alt/Option key and choosing Edit, Transform, Again **3c**.

If we hadn't wanted the softening that comes from repeated rotation, we would have made each duplicate layer from the untransformed original and rotated it "manually" by using a multiple of our original –5°.

For our animation, two duplicates were enough for the motion in each direction, so after creating R1 and R2, we started the motion to the left: We made another duplicate from the original and pressed Ctrl/⌘-T, this time moving the center of rotation to the other hip to create the Skirt-L1 and Skirt-L2 layers **3d**.

To check the extremes of your motion, turn off visibility for all the object layers except the two extremes, and reduce the opacity of the higher layer so you can see both at once.

4 Fine-tuning the motion. You may want to enhance the effect at the extremes of your transformation. For instance, this is the point in a bouncing ball animation where you might squash the ball vertically as it hits the ground. If you want to add enhancements, duplicate and manipulate each of the layers that shows the extreme. We duplicated the R2 and L2 layers, naming the copies R3 and L3. Then we used the Liquify command (Image, Liquify) to pull the bottom corner of the skirt a little farther to the right in R3 and to the left in L3. We also used Motion Blur (Filter, Blur, Motion Blur) on the entire layer, adjusting the Angle so the blur was in the sideways direction of the skirt's motion **4**.

5

The layers were color-coded (for left, right, and center). In preparation for moving the file to ImageReady, visibility was turned on for only those layers needed for the first frame.

5 Preparing the file for ImageReady. Before moving over to ImageReady for animation, you need to make a smaller copy of the file and organize it a bit: Save the file and then duplicate it (Image, Duplicate) and reduce the size of the duplicate. Choose Image, Image Size, and make sure Constrain Proportions and Resample Image are turned on. What you do next will depend on whether you've used Layer Styles in your file. If so, change the Resolution until the critical pixel dimension (Width or Height) at the top of the dialog box reaches the value you want (for more about this method, see the "Resizing a 'Styled' File" tip on page 337). If you haven't used any Styles, you can use a more direct approach: Either change the critical pixel

6a

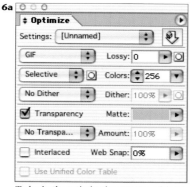

To begin the optimization process, a Matte color was chosen to match the "purple sand" background that would be used on the Web page. Then the Selective palette option was chosen, with 256 colors.

6b

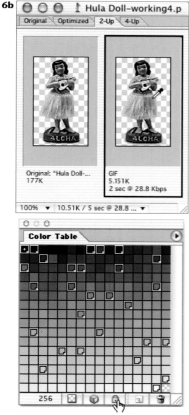

The "important" colors were Shift-clicked in the image to select them in the Color Table. Then all these colors were locked by clicking the Lock Selected Colors button.

dimension at the top of the box, or change the Width or Height in the Document Size section. We changed the Width units to "percent" and entered 25. To reduce softening produced by the resizing, you can choose Filter, Sharpen, Unsharp Mask. We used this filter with an Amount setting of 200% on the Dancer layer, but we left the Skirt and shadow layers soft.

Before jumping to ImageReady, you can color-code the related layers in the file for quicker identification (in the Layers palette Option-double-click the name — not the thumbnail — of the layer to open the Layer Properties dialog box, and choose a color) **5.** Then set up the file to show what you want to see in the first frame. (An exception to setting up the first frame would be if one of your other frame layers includes more colors; in that case you'll want to optimize based on this frame in ImageReady, so you should set up visibility for this frame instead.) For our hula doll we set up the first frame by turning off visibility for all the motion frame layers we had created by clicking in each layer's Eye column. We left visible the Skirt-0, Hula Dancer, and Shadow layers, making sure visibility was turned off for the *Background* also, to retain the transparency around the dancer.

6 Optimizing in ImageReady. When your reduced file is ready, click the Jump To button at the bottom of Photoshop's toolbox to move to ImageReady. Work in the 2-Up view and with the Optimize palette set up for GIF (the only format that can be animated in ImageReady), for a Selective palette, and for 256 Colors. Turn off Interlaced (which doesn't apply to animations) and choose a Matte color (see "Specifying a Matte Color" at right). Turn Transparency on; the Matte color will be used to fill the partially transparent pixels created by antialiasing at the edges **6a.**

Now identify the important colors that you want to preserve in your image by using the Eyedropper tool to Shift-click or Shift-drag in the working window, choosing enough colors to maintain the important color detail. Don't choose more than you think you need, since more colors will mean a bigger file. The colors you clicked will be selected in the Color Table palette, and you can lock all of them at once by clicking the Lock Selected Colors button at the bottom of the palette **6b.**

6c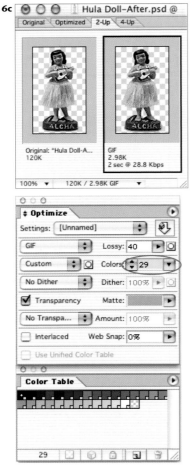

The number of colors was reduced to 29, which was the number of important (locked) colors.

Next see how far you can reduce the number of colors by choosing from the pop-out Colors list **6c**. If your first choice results in a Color Table that includes only locked colors, choose the next higher number from the list. When you get to the point where the Color Table includes some unlocked colors, use the tiny triangles to the left of the list to lower the number until only locked colors (and transparency if Transparency is turned on) show in the Color Table; at this point the Table will include all the colors you locked but no more. We found that 32 colors gave us a few extra, so we lowered this number, settling on 29 colors. We also set the Lossy value at 40%, at the high end of Adobe's 10–40% recommendation.

7 Animating. In the Animation palette make sure that your image looks exactly as you want to see it in the first frame of your animation; if necessary, click in the Eye column of the Layers palette to change what's visible. Then, to start the second frame, click the Duplicate Current Frame button at the bottom of the palette **7a**. In the Layers palette change the visibility of the layers so you see everything you want in this second frame. We turned off visibility for the Skirt-0 layer and turned on visibility for the Skirt-R1 layer **7b.** Continue making frames by duplicating the current frame to start the next one, changing the visibility, and so on. For our animation, after duplicating frame 2 to start frame 3, we turned off visibility for the R1 layer and turned on R2 **7c**. For frame 4 we turned off R2 and turned on R3. To start the swing back to the center, in the fifth frame we turned off visibility for frame R3 and turned on R2 again. Next we made frames for the left swing. We created 12 frames in all **7d,** with the following Skirt layer visibility: 0, R1, R2, R3, R2, R1, 0, L1, L2, L3, L2, L1. We didn't need to go back to frame 0 at the end of the animation because we planned to set it to loop continuously.

Note that when frames are repeated — for instance, when R2, R1, L2, and L1 were used the second time — instead of resetting visibility

7a

Visibility of the layers was set for the first frame, and the first frame was duplicated to start the second frame.

7b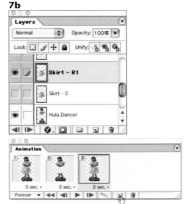

Visibility of the layers was set to show the R1 skirt in the second frame, and the frame was duplicated to start the third frame.

7c

Visibility of the layers was set to show the R2 skirt in the third frame, and the frame was duplicated to make the fourth frame.

7d

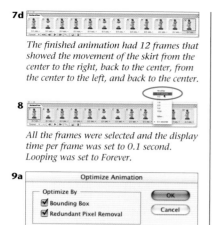

The finished animation had 12 frames that showed the movement of the skirt from the center to the right, back to the center, from the center to the left, and back to the center.

8

All the frames were selected and the display time per frame was set to 0.1 second. Looping was set to Forever.

9a

Setting up to optimize each frame using the smallest dimensions that will hold all the pixels, and eliminating from each frame's optimization the pixels that haven't changed from the previous frame

9b

Setting the background to see how the animation will look against the Web page

9c

Testing the animation in a browser

9d

Saving the animated GIF, with Images Only chosen as the Format

---

in the Layers palette, it's possible to make a new frame based on a previous one. In our example, after making the fourth frame (R3), we could have Alt/Option-dragged the third frame to the right end of the Animation palette to add a fifth frame that was the same as the third. The problem with this approach is that the thumbnails in the Animation palette are small, and it can be very hard to see exactly which frame you want to copy. But if you have to make multiple changes to the Layers palette to set up each frame of your animation, it may be much more convenient to repeat existing frames.

8 Setting the timing. To set the timing initially, choose Select All Frames from the menu that pops out when you click the circled triangle in the upper right corner of the Animation palette (or click on one of your end frames to select it, then Shift-click the other end frame). Then click on the time under one of the frames and change it to set the timing for all the frames. We chose 0.1 seconds **8.** Also set the Looping option in the lower left corner of the Animation box; we chose Forever. Then click the Play button at the bottom of the Animation palette to check the timing. If necessary, click on a particular frame and make a different choice from the pop-out time list. Then recheck the timing.

9 Optimizing, testing, and saving the animation. When you've set the timing for the animation, choose Optimize Animation from the Animation palette's pop-out menu and leave both boxes checked in the Optimize Animation dialog box **9a.** Now you can test your animation over the background it will appear on to make sure that your Matte choice works and that you don't see a color mismatch or an unwanted halo around your animated object: Choose File, Output Settings, Background and click the Choose button to find your background file **9b.** Then choose File, Preview In, or click the Preview In Default Browser button near the bottom of the toolbox (hold the button down to choose a different browser) **9c.** Make any changes necessary based on the preview, check again, and then save the file (File, Save Optimized). In the Save Optimized As dialog box, make sure Format is set to Images Only (since you're saving a file with no links) **9d,** and click the Save button. *Wow!*

TRANSPARENCY & ANIMATION

Using transparency in a GIF that isn't animated makes the file slightly bigger because of the built-in mask that defines the transparency. However, when you animate a GIF that includes transparency, each frame carries a mask, so the additional file size can mount up. If you don't really need transparency in your animation, leave that box unchecked in the Optimize palette.

Using Transparency makes the file size for this animation almost 24K; without Transparency, it's about 9.4K.

Animating with Actions

Overview *Optimize the first version of a file that has been duplicated and scaled to two or more sizes; save the optimization settings; record an Action as you apply the optimization and set up the frames, timing, and looping for the animation; export the file; open the second file; run the Action, and export the file.*

Scalable Design-After.psd, Caf3-350.gif and Caf3-100.gif files

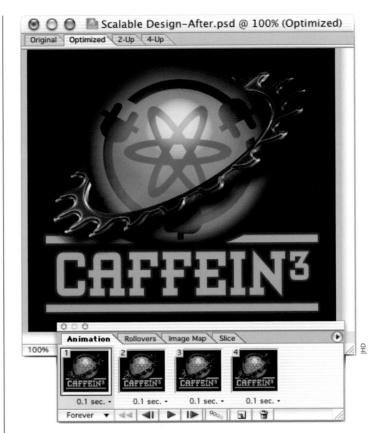

*The larger **Scalable Design.psd** file, opened in Image-Ready and set up with the Gear 1 layer visible and all other Gear layers hidden*

IF YOU NEED TO PRODUCE THE SAME ANIMATION in more than one size, you can save some time — while maintaining high quality — if you produce the different-size files first, then record an Action as you make the frames to animate one of the files. Then you can open another version of the file and play the Action back to animate it. Here we've animated two sizes of the **Scalable Design.psd** file produced in "Designing for Scalability & Animation" on page 332.

1 Optimizing the larger file. When you've finished building your layered file in Photoshop and have saved it in the two or more sizes you want to animate, open the largest version in ImageReady. We had approximately 350-pixel-high and 100-pixel-high versions of the **Scalable Design.psd** file, so we opened the larger file **1a.**

In the Optimize palette, choose GIF for the file format and choose one of the adaptive 256-color palettes: Selective, Adaptive, or Perceptual. We started with Selective because it gives priority to the colors the human eye is most sensitive to *and* to any colors that occur in large areas of flat color, such as the orange logotype in our file. We used Diffusion Dither at 100% (to cut down on the number of colors we would need, since dithering could make some colors

1b

| 32 | | | | | |

Shifts/Unshifts selected colors to Web palette

Snapping the orange color used for the logotype to a Web-safe color

1c

Save Color Table

Save As: Caf3 table.act

Where: Optimized Colors

Cancel   Save

Saving the Color Table

1d

Optimize

Settings: Caf3 GIF Settings

GIF   Lossy: 0

Caf3 table   Colors: Auto

Diffusion   Dither: 100%

Transparency   Matte:

No Transpa...   Amount: 100%

Interlaced   Web Snap: 0%

Use Unified Color Table

Setting up the optimization specifications, with a Selective palette of 32 colors, 100% Diffusion Dither, and no Lossy compression

2a

New Action

Name: Wow-Caf3 Animation   Record

Set: Default Actions.atn   Cancel

Function Key: None Shift Command

Color: None

Creating a new Action in preparation for recording the process of animating the Caffein³ file

2b

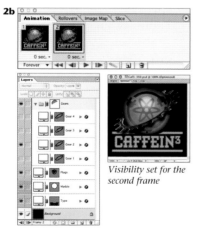

Visibility set for the second frame

by visually mixing others). We set Lossy to 0, effectively turning off this option. Lossy compression generates "noise" in the process of compressing the image. This is not necessarily a problem in the parts of the animation that are moving anyway and therefore changing. But the noise can also cause subtle variation in the static portions of the image, which can be distracting.

We looked at the Optimized view (click the Optimized tab in the working window to show this view) as we reduced the number of Colors in the Optimize palette. In the Color Table palette we clicked on the swatch for the orange of the type and then clicked the Snap Selected Colors To Web button at the bottom of the palette **1b.** This would ensure that this color would not dither regardless of whether the end user's system was capable of displaying thousands or millions of colors or was limited to 256. Then we saved the Color Table by choosing Save Color Table from the palette's pop-out menu **1c.** So that we could apply the same optimization settings to the smaller file later, including our customized Color Table, we saved the settings by choosing Save Settings from the Optimize palette's pop-out menu **1d.**

2 Animating the file and recording the Action. In the Layers palette, set up the visibility in your layered file to show the image you want to use for the first frame of your animation by clicking the Eye column for each layer to turn its visibility on or off. We had made all the component elements of the logo visible, including the folder at the top that included the layer mask, but only one of the Gear layers. We made the *Background,* which would appear in all frames, the active layer by clicking its name in the palette (refer to **1a**). Turning on and off different Gear layers for the different frames of the animation would achieve the rotation we had planned, as described on page 332. Making the *Background* the active layer would prevent the situation in which the active layer was invisible, which can cause problems in recording an Action.

When the file is set up for the first frame, open the Actions palette (Window, Show Actions), and click the Create New Action button at the bottom of the palette. In the Action Options dialog box, name the Action and assign it an F-key shortcut if you like **2a,** and click OK.

As ImageReady automatically records what you do, choose your saved optimization preset (made in step 1) from the pop-out list of Settings at the top of the Optimize palette — even though it's already chosen. Applying it while the Action is being recorded will ensure that its name and all its settings, including the saved custom

REFRESHING THE COLOR TABLE

To update the Color Table each time you change the number of colors in ImageReady's Optimize palette, make sure the Auto Regenerate option is turned on by choosing it from the menu that pops out from the upper right corner of the Optimize palette.

2c

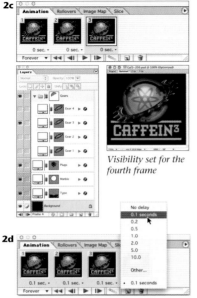

Visibility set for the fourth frame

2d

All four frames were Shift-selected and a delay of 0.1 second was assigned.

2e

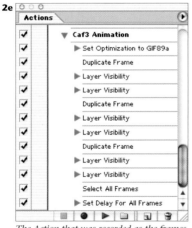

The Action that was recorded as the frames were made and the timing was set

3

Exporting the second animated GIF

Color Table, will become part of the Action. Then duplicate the first frame in the Animation palette to start the second frame by clicking the Duplicate Current Frame button at the bottom of the Animation palette. Adjust the visibility of your layers to show the image you want for the second frame of the animation **2b.** We turned off visibility for the Gear 1 layer and turned on visibility for Gear 2. **Caution**: As you record the Action, wait for the screen to be refreshed to show changes in visibility before clicking on the page icon to make a new frame. This can take some time on a slower computer. Continue to add new frames by duplicating and changing visibility until you have all the frames you need. We made a frame with the Gear 3 layer visible **2c** and another with Gear 4. This completed the frames we would need, since we had designed the graphics with the idea that the animation would loop to continue the rotation of the gear.

With the Action still being recorded, set the timing for the animation: Select all the frames of the animation by choosing Select All Frames from the Animation palette's pop-out menu, and change the timing for one of them by clicking the time value at the bottom of the frame and choosing from the pop-out list **2d.** We chose 0.1 second — the shortest interval available — to prevent the animation from playing back at the fastest speed any particular computer system can achieve at the time the animation was played. Set the looping option (in the lower left corner of the Animation palette). Since we wanted the animation to loop continuously, we left the setting at the default, Forever.

When you've completed the animation, stop the recording of the Action by clicking the square button at the bottom of the Actions palette **2e.** You can check the animation by clicking the Play button at the bottom of the Animation palette.

Preview the animation in a browser by clicking the Preview In Default Browser button near the bottom of the toolbox. Export the animation file by choosing File, Save Optimized As, with Images Only chosen for the Format.

3 Optimizing and animating a smaller version. Open the second version of the file, set the visibility for the first frame, and activate a layer that will appear in all frames (such as the *Background* in our file). Choose the Action you recorded: Click the name of your Action in the Actions palette, and click the Play button. ImageReady will load the optimization settings, create the frames for the smaller animation, and set their timing. Adjust the settings if necessary to get the optimization result you want for this smaller file. If the larger file you animated was much bigger than the second, smaller version, you may be able to economize on your file size by using fewer Colors in the Optimize palette. After adjusting, preview in a browser and export **3.**

Animating with Masks

Overview *In Photoshop create all the layers and Styles necessary for the "on" and "off" states of the neon; create an alpha channel to use later for weighted optimization; scale the file down; adjust the scale of individual Styles if needed; create layer masks; optimize the file by sampling and locking important colors and weighting the Lossy compression with the alpha channel; create the frames needed for the animation; set display times and looping; preview in browsers against the Web page background color; export the animation.*

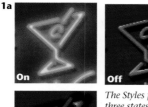

"Mask Animation" "before" and "after" files

The Styles for the three states of the sign — "on," "off," and "sidelit"

JHD

For the "On" state shown in figure 1a, both the "turned off" (base) layer and the "turned on" layer are visible.

TURNING ON AND OFF MASKS is a great way to combine parts of different layers of a Photoshop file to create the frames for a Web animation. For this neon sign, with a cocktail glass that can flash independently of the rest of the sign, we started with the neon sign created in "Crafting a Neon Glow" on page 329. Working in Photoshop, we duplicated the layer with the neon tubes to make two more identical layers, then applied different Layer Styles to them — one for the "off" state of the sign and one for the state of the cocktail glass when the glass flashed off but the rest of the sign was on. In this state the neon tubes of the glass would reflect the light produced by the rest of the sign. ***Note:*** It will be easier to understand the goal of this technique if you play the animated GIF before you begin. The file (supplied on the Wow CD-ROM that comes with this book) is called **Mask Animation-After.gif.** Double-clicking its icon will launch ImageReady (if it isn't already open); click the Play button in ImageReady's Animation palette to put the neon into action.

Reducing the file size for the Web started in Photoshop with cutting the pixel dimensions to a quarter of the original numbers used for the print version. Then in ImageReady we reduced the number of colors used in the file. A weighted optimization was also carried out in ImageReady to give priority to keeping the background color solid when Lossy compression was applied to the graphics and glow to reduce the file size even more.

1 Creating the "on" and "off" states. To create **Mask Animation-Before.psd**, we modified **Neon Glow-After.psd** from "Crafting a Neon Glow" on page 329, as described next. (***Note:*** If you like, you can open **Mask Animation-Before.psd** and skip step 1.) In Photoshop, we first replaced the texture in the *Background* layer with the flat color used for the background of our Web page. To do this you can click the Foreground square in the toolbox and

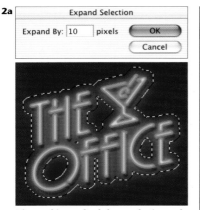

Expand Selection

Expand By: 10 pixels OK

Cancel

The graphic was loaded as a selection and the selection was expanded by 10 pixels.

2b

The expanded selection was feathered 10 pixels and saved as an alpha channel to be used later for weighted optimization.

3

Image Size

Pixel Dimensions: 175K (was 2.74M) OK

Width: 261 pixels Cancel

Height: 229 pixels Auto...

Don't touch

Document Size:

Width: 4.64 inches

Height: 4.071 inches

Resolution: 56.25 pixels/inch

☑ Constrain Proportions

☑ Resample Image: Bicubic

The Resolution was reduced from 225 to 56.25 to scale the file to 25%.

4a

*Adding a layer mask to the "turned off" layer: Selecting the area to mask **A**, and after creating the mask **B**, **C***

enter the appropriate hexadecimal number in the lower right corner of the Color Picker and click OK; then select all by (Ctrl/⌘-A) and fill with this color (Edit, Fill, Foreground Color).

For the flashing neon sign, the frames of our animation would start with the entire sign off, then the entire sign would light up, then the lettering alone would be lit, while the cocktail glass would blink on and off; then the animation would loop, turning the entire sign off as the animation cycle started again. To accomplish this animation, we would create two duplicates of our original graphics layer and apply Styles and layer masks to control the lighting for the sign. Each duplicate was created by dragging the thumbnail for the existing graphics layer to the Create A New Layer button at the bottom of the Layers palette. **Note**: You can open the **Mask Animation-Before.psd** file and double-click the *"f"* icons for the three layers to see the settings for the Styles used to accomplish the different lighting states as you read the description that follows.

For the layer that would show the entire sign turned off, we used a Style without a glow but with the tubes reflecting a little light from above left (this is the Wow-Mask Neon OFF Style) **1a.** A Bevel And Emboss effect created the highlights on the upper left edges, with the Altitude set at 80° to pull the highlight off the edges and around to the front of the tubing. A fairly narrow and faint (50% Opacity) Drop Shadow was used. A combination of Inner Shadow, Inner Glow, Satin, and Color Overlay colored the interior of the tubes. Visibility for this layer would be turned on for all frames of the animation so its shadow could help with the dimensionality of the graphic, with the Styles from each of the other layers adding to it when their visibility was turned on **1b.**

For the layer that would be used when the cocktail glass was lit by the neon glow from the lettering, we used a Style with a denser Drop Shadow that was also more offset to the upper right as if it were cast by the lighted lettering (the Opacity, Size, and Distance settings for the Drop Shadow were all increased). The Angle and Altitude for the Bevel And Emboss were changed to brighten the highlight on the tubes and change the angle of the lighting. In our animation the cocktail glass was the only part of the sign that would ever show this state.

2 Making an alpha channel for the weighted optimization. In the "on" state, the neon sign lights up the background for quite a distance from the tubing itself. In our image this results in many different shades and tones of red, yellow, orange, and brown. The Lossy compression process in ImageReady reduces the number of color changes in neighboring pixels in order to reduce file size, but at higher settings, it also introduces "streaking" that can be very noticeable, especially in areas of flat color. To preserve the solid color of the background so it would seamlessly match our Web page, we would make an alpha channel to use as a mask that

When a Layer Style is scaled — for example, when an entire file is resized — the settings for all the effects are rounded to the nearest whole number. For instance, if you reduce a file to a quarter of its original dimensions, any settings whose value was 5 can't have a value of 1.25 (the value you get by dividing 5 by 4), so they have to be rounded to 1. This kind of rounding can make the Style look different on the smaller file than it did on the original larger one. So it may be necessary to fine-tune the Style for fine lines, type, and other small features. To do this, you can use the Scale Effects command, either by choosing it from the main menu (Layer, Layer Style, Scale Effects) or in the Layers palette by right-clicking (or Control-clicking on a Mac with a one-button mouse) directly on the *"f" icon for the layer* and choosing from the pop-out menu. If your Style depends on a gradient, you may even want to edit the color transitions in the Gradient Editor, opened by clicking on the gradient swatch wherever you find it — for instance, in the Gradient Overlay or Inner Glow section of the Layer Style dialog box.

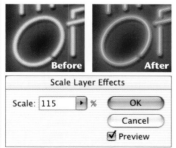

After a file is resized, the Style for each layer may need to be scaled to compensate for rounding errors created by the resizing.

would tell ImageReady to apply its lossy compression algorithm only in the area where there was a lot of color variability already (like the glowing areas), and not in the flat background.

To start the alpha channel mask, load the graphic as a selection. We did this by Ctrl/⌘-clicking on the layer clipping path for one of the graphic layers to load its outline as a selection. To make some space around the graphic itself (for the glow), expand the selection (Select, Modify, Expand). We expanded our selection 10 pixels **2a.** To soften the transition between the areas that would and wouldn't be within the mask for weighted optimization, we feathered the expanded selection (Select, Feather), using a Feather Radius of 10 pixels. Finally, we inverted the selection (Ctrl/⌘-Shift-I) and turned the selection into a black-on-white alpha channel (Select, Save Selection) **2b.**

3 Reducing the size of the graphic. Next we scaled the file down to 25% of its original size, which had to be done in a very specific way in order to scale the Layer Styles along with the graphics: We chose Image, Image Size and made sure that Constrain Proportions and Resample Image were turned on. Since we had produced our original file four times as large as we would need for the Web, our goal was to reduce the pixel dimensions (Width and Height) shown at the top of the Image Size dialog box to 25% of their original values. But because of a somewhat quirky relationship between Layer Styles and resolution, we accomplished this size reduction *not* by changing Width or Height directly, but by calculating that we needed to reduce the Resolution to 56.25, which is 25% of the original 225 dpi of the file, and thus reducing Width and Height indirectly **3;** then we clicked OK to close the dialog box. (A more extensive explanation of scaling Styled files is presented in the "Resizing a 'Styled' File" tip on page 337.) The Resolution (dpi) setting is not relevant for Web graphics — the file will display at 100% of its one-to-one pixel dimensions no matter what its dpi. So we didn't worry about the odd Resolution setting.

Although the Layer Style is scaled along with the file, you may need to fine-tune it at this point, as described in the "Adjusting the Scale" tip at left.

4 Making layer masks. Now make the layer masks that will allow you to turn parts of the neon graphic on and off. We started with the "turned off" layer. We used the Polygonal Lasso to select an area that included the cocktail glass and turned it into a 'hiding' layer mask by Alt/Option-clicking the Add A Mask button at the bottom of the Layers palette **4a.** (Without the Alt/Option key the Add A Mask button makes a layer mask that hides everything *outside* the selection, rather than hiding what's *inside.*)

To make the masks for the other two layers, we Ctrl/-⌘-clicked on the existing layer mask to load it as a selection, then activated

4b

The completed layer masks

4c

Each layer shown with its layer mask turned off (left) and turned on (right)

the layer where we wanted to add the layer mask and either clicked the Add A Mask button (to exactly duplicate the mask on the active layer) or Alt/Option-clicked it (to make the inverse mask) **4b, 4c**. Now we had all the different states for the type and graphics and by turning on and off the visibility and masks for those layers we could control all the possible combinations for the neon sign.

5 Optimizing in ImageReady. Transfer the file to ImageReady by clicking the Jump To button at the bottom of Photoshop's tool-box. Now you can prepare to choose and lock the important colors for each "state" in your animation. Turn on/off visibility of layers and layer masks to create one of the states of the file that you will use in creating your animation frames. We started with only our "turned off" layer visible, by clicking the Eye icons for the other layers to make these layers invisible. Working in the Optimized view, in the Optimize palette we set the number of Colors at 256 so we would have the maximum number of colors to choose from. We chose Adaptive for the palette because it's the one of the three adaptive palettes — Selective, Perceptual, and Adaptive — that chooses its colors giving weight to the part of the spectrum that's most common in the image, which was appropriate for this artwork with its limited number of hues but its many shades and tones of those hues. We also chose 100% Diffusion Dither to help break up the banding in the glows that would otherwise occur when we drastically reduced the number of colors **5a**.

Select the colors that you need to keep: Shift-drag through the important colors in the image, or Shift-click to be more focused and to limit your choice to just those colors needed **5b**. Be sure to include the background color. Then click the Lock Selected Colors button at the bottom of the Color Table palette **5c**.

For each of the other states that will appear in your animation, repeat the process of setting up visibility for the layers and turning

5a

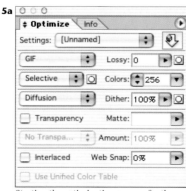

Starting the optimization process for the GIF in ImageReady, with an Adaptive palette, 256 colors, and 100% Diffusion Dither

5b

Shift-clicking with ImageReady's Eyedropper tool to select the most important colors in the "off" state

5c

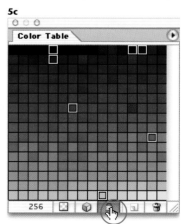

Locking the colors sampled from the "off" state

5d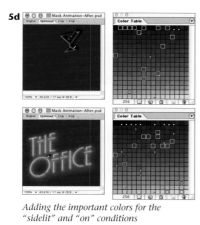

Adding the important colors for the "sidelit" and "on" conditions

5e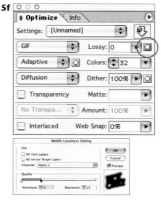

The number of colors was reduced to 32.

5f

Clicking the Use A Channel button opened the Modify Lossiness Setting dialog box, where we could choose the alpha channel and adjust the Maximum Allowable Compression.

6a

Visibility of the layers and masks was set for the first frame to show the "off" state, and this frame was duplicated to start frame 2.

layer masks on and off, then Shift-selecting and locking colors, so all the most important colors for the entire animation are locked **5d.**

Next, working in the Optimized view (chosen by clicking the tab at the top of the working window), reduce the number of colors as much as possible, maintaining color quality: Test different settings from the pop-out Colors list. We reduced the number to 32 colors **5e.**

Now you can check to see if the Lossy setting can help reduce the file size even more. Click on the Use A Channel button to the right of the Lossy setting and in the Modify Lossiness Setting dialog box choose the alpha channel you made in Photoshop **5f.** Experiment with the settings, leaving the left slider at 0 and moving the right slider to the left to choose a setting low enough to keep any "noise" out of the solid-color background. Our alpha channel concentrated the Lossy compression in the areas around the neon tubes (the black areas of the alpha channel) and protected the background areas (the white part of the mask) from the "streaky" artifacts of compression; we clicked OK to close the dialog box. With the important neon and background colors locked and the Lossy compression restricted to the areas that already included quite a bit of color variability, the optimization was complete.

6 Creating the animation frames. Now work in the Layers palette to turn on and off both the visibility for the layers and effectiveness of the layer masks to create the state you want to see in the first frame of the animation **6a.** We wanted to start with the neon entirely turned off, so we turned off visibility for the lit and sidelit layers and also Shift-clicked the layer mask for the "turned off" layer; with the mask "off" (a red X shows that the mask isn't functioning) the entire layer was showing, and the whole sign appeared in its "turned off" condition.

Create the additional frames you need: For each different frame you require, click the Duplicate Current Frame button at the bottom of the Animation palette to start a new frame based on the current one. Then make adjustments in the Layers palette to change the content of this new frame. For our second frame, we turned on

6b

Visibility of layers and masks was set for the second frame to show the "on" state for the lettering.

6c

Frame 2 was duplicated to make frame 3, and the visibility of layers and masks was set to show the entire sign "on."

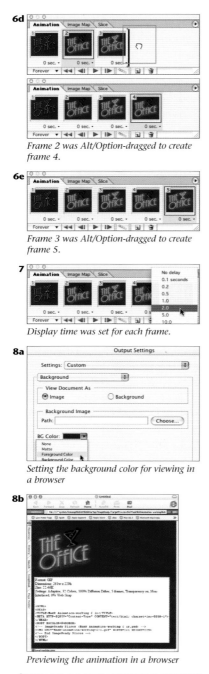

6d

Frame 2 was Alt/Option-dragged to create frame 4.

6e

Frame 3 was Alt/Option-dragged to create frame 5.

7

Display time was set for each frame.

8a

Setting the background color for viewing in a browser

8b

Previewing the animation in a browser

9

Exporting the animated GIF including all images

all three layers, with all the layer masks turned on, to create the condition in which the lettering was fully lit and the cocktail glass was sidelit **6b.** For the third frame, we Shift-clicked the layer mask thumbnail for the "on" layer so the cocktail glass was no longer masked out — the entire sign was turned on **6c.**

After making these three frames, we had all the elements we needed. We duplicated frame 2 to become frame 4 by Alt/Option-dragging frame 2 beyond the last frame on the right **6d.** We used the same process to duplicate frame 3 as the fifth frame **6e.**

7 Setting the timing. Next set the timing for your animation by clicking on the time setting beneath each of the frames in the Animation palette to open the pop-up menu, where you can choose a display time for that frame **7.** We wanted to set our timing so the neon cocktail glass flickered on and off but so the pauses for the flashing of the entire sign were long enough to make the animation interesting rather than annoying. We set the first ("off") frame for 3 seconds, then turned the lettering on by setting the second frame for 3 seconds. We set frame 3 for 1 second (to turn on the glass) and frame 4 for No Delay (so the glass would flicker off for the briefest interval possible), and set frame 5 for 2 seconds. Choose a looping option for the animation, from the lower left corner of the Animation palette. You can preview the animation by clicking the Play button at the bottom of the palette. Make any adjustments you need by resetting the times for individual frames, and Play to test again.

8 Previewing in a browser. When you have the timing adjusted, preview the animation in your browser against the background of your Web page. If your Foreground color has changed since you set it in step 1, reset it. Choose File, Output Settings, Background, and choose Foreground Color from the Color menu, popped out from the small triangle to the right of the Color swatch in the Output Settings dialog box **8a.** Click OK to close the box.

With the Web page background color set, choose File, Preview In and choose a browser, or click the Preview In Default Browser button near the bottom of ImageReady's toolbox (hold the button down if you want to choose a different browser) **8b.**

9 Exporting the animation. If the browser test looks good, you're ready to save the file. Choose File, Save Optimized As, enter a Name, and choose Images Only for the Format. If you plan to use Adobe GoLive for developing the page, be sure the Include GoLive Code box is checked. Then click the Save button **9.**

Creating Button Rollover Styles

Overview *Design a button graphic on a layer in Photoshop; duplicate the button layer enough times so that you have a layer for each rollover state you will need; create a Layer Style for the color, dimensionality, and lighting for each of the rollover states; in ImageReady save the Styles; develop one "master" button layer and use the Rollover palette to apply one of the saved Styles for each of the rollover states; save the combined Rollover Style and apply it to a set of buttons; optimize and save the buttons.*

IMAGE

"**Button Rollovers**" "before" and "after" files

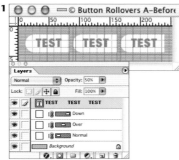

A test button was designed and duplicated twice, creating a separate layer for developing each of the Layer Styles we wanted for our rollover states. Placeholder text was added to help us visualize the real buttons.

The basic color of these buttons would be controlled by the Color Overlay component of each Layer Style.

WITH PHOTOSHOP 7 AND IMAGEREADY 7 you can design and apply a combined Rollover Style preset that can be stored and applied to other buttons with just one click in ImageReady's Styles palette. This Rollover Style not only provides color and dimension for your buttons, but also automatically slices the button file to its smallest possible dimensions *and* writes the JavaScript that adds the interactivity for the rollover states (even ImageReady's new Selected state) you want to include. A Rollover Style preset *can't* include changes in the button's size, shape, or position, but it *can* include changes that result from modifying the Layer Style, and this gives you tremendous creative potential for developing personalities for your navigational elements. Layer-based slices make it easy to work with buttons of any size and shape. And ImageReady's Rollover palette can automatically generate the JavaScript-based interactivity. You can save the entire Style-and-rollover apparatus as a preset Rollover Style that you can then apply to other buttons. The Rollover Style applies the interactive states to the new button. The Style also automatically creates the layer-based button slice to fit the new button's size and shape, and adds the JavaScript that makes the button respond by changing states.

The Photoshop part of the rollover-making process involves designing the button graphics (the button shape and any surface graphics or type) and developing the Layer Styles that give your buttons their personality. You could do the designing in ImageReady, but since Photoshop has more and better creative tools, it's good to start there.

The "styled" file is then taken into ImageReady and the Styles are saved into the Styles palette — you'll need to have the Styles

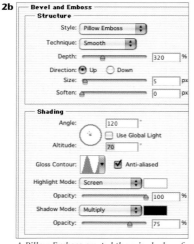

2b

A Pillow Emboss created the raised edge of the button.

2c

The Satin effect created a surface sheen.

2d

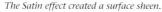

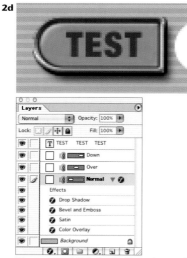

The completed Style for the Normal state of the button

available to create the rollover, which can only be done in Image-Ready, and Photoshop and ImageReady don't automatically share the same Styles palette. The rollover is created and saved as a combined Rollover Style preset. Then you can apply this new preset Style to as many buttons as you like.

1 Setting up the button shapes. In Photoshop design the button shape you want to use for creating your Rollover Style preset. You can use the same graphic that you actually plan to use for a button, or make a test button as we did here. For designing our Styles, we chose View, Snap To, Grid and used the Pen tool (with the Shape Layers option chosen in the Options bar) to make a button shape with one round end and one straight end. This shape would allow us to see what our Normal, Over, and Down Styles would look like on both round and straight-edged buttons.

We duplicated our button layer twice (by dragging its name to the Create A New Layer button at the bottom of the Layers palette), and used the Move tool with the Shift key held down to drag each of the duplicates to the right. Spreading the buttons out in this way would make it easy to see the Styles as we developed them. To further organize the button development, name each layer by double-clicking on its name in the Layers palette and typing a new name. You can name the layers for the rollover states you'll be developing; we named ours "Normal" (the "at rest" state of the button), "Over" (the state when the cursor floats over the button) and "Down" (the "mouse-down" state). We chose not to include a selected state as these buttons weren't going to be used for menus. (The Selected State allows the buttons to remain "lit" until another Selected State button is clicked, which enables it to serve as a label for a section of a website). So that we could see how the button would look with type on it, we also set placeholder type in a layer above the buttons. We reduced the Opacity of this layer to 50% so the type would look more like it was actually part of the button **1.**

2 Designing the "Normal" Style. Starting with the Normal button layer, click the Add A Layer Style button (the *"ƒ"* at the bottom of the Layers palette) and add effects as follows: Click in the list at the left side of the Layer Style dialog box to choose each effect and then set parameters for that effect. We added a Color Overlay for the main color of the button **2a.** We also added a fairly standard Drop Shadow, using the default Angle of 120° for lighting from the upper left. To create the edge of the button, we used the Pillow Emboss Style of Bevel And Emboss with an elevated Altitude of 70° and one of the default Gloss Contour curves (Ring) **2b.** For more shine we added a Satin effect **2c, 2d.** *Note:* To see the Style applied to the Normal layer — as well as the other Styles developed here — you can open the **Button Rollovers-A-After.psd** file from the Wow CD-ROM.

3a

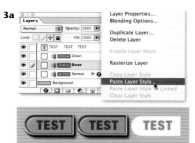

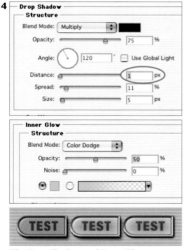

Starting the Style for the Over layer by copying and pasting the Normal Style

3b

The Inner Glow was changed to make the Layer Style for the Over layer.

4

The Drop Shadow and Inner Glow were changed to develop the Style for the Down layer.

5

An Outer Glow was added to the type layer.

3 Developing the "Over" Style. Now you can use the Normal Style you just made as the basis for developing the Over Style. First copy the Style from the Normal layer to the Over layer, as follows: In the Layers palette right-click (Windows) or Control-click (Mac) directly on the *"f"* icon on the Normal layer and choose Copy Layer Style from the pop-out menu. Then right/Control-click in about the same place on the entry for the Over layer and choose Paste Layer Style **3a.** Change the Style to make the button on this layer look like you want your buttons to look when the cursor moves over them. We added a light green Inner Glow with Edge as the Source. We put the glow in Color Dodge mode and reduced the Opacity until we saw the effect we wanted **3b.**

4 Developing the "Down" state. Now start the Down Style by applying the Style from the Over layer, using the copy-and-paste process described in step 3. By typing into the Distance box, we reduced the effect for the Drop Shadow from 5 pixels to 1 pixel to move the shadow closer under the button. We increased the Spread from 0 to 11 to make the shadow more dense, as if the button had been pressed. We also changed the color of the Inner Glow to yellow **4.**

5 Making the type stand out. Though not part of the actual Layer Style for the button, we added an Outer Glow with the default settings to the type layer to increase the contrast and make the letters more distinct. This would help with legibility at the small size used for the buttons **5.**

6 Saving the Styles in ImageReady. To turn the Styles into a preset Rollover Style, you have to first bring the buttons file into ImageReady (click the Jump To button at the bottom of the Layers palette) **6a.** Save each of the Styles as a regular Layer Style preset in ImageReady's Styles palette as follows: Activate the Normal layer by clicking its name in ImageReady's Layers palette. Then open the Styles palette (Window, Show Styles) and click the Create A New Style button at the bottom of the palette. In the Style Options dialog box, name the Style, including its state (Normal) in the name **6b.** Repeat the layer-activating and Style-saving process to make the "Over" and "Down" Styles.

7 Creating the "master" Rollover button. Once all the Styles have been saved, you can turn one of your buttons into the

DO YOU REALLY NEED "DOWN"?

To reduce the file size of your rollover buttons, consider using just two states — Normal and Over. The difference between these two states lets the user know what parts of the interface are interactive. The Down state is just eye candy, unless the response time is so slow that a user might think nothing has happened in response to pressing the mouse button.

6a

Photoshop's Jump To button transfers the file to ImageReady.

6b

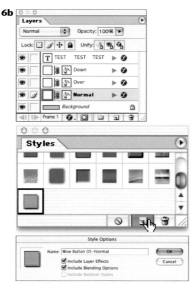

Saving the Normal Style in ImageReady's Styles palette

7a

Removing a Layer Style by choosing from the context-sensitive menu

7b

Styles were removed from the Over and Down layers.

master button that will temporarily store all the Rollover preset information. Start by removing the Styles from the Over and Down layers: Choose Layer, Layer Style, Clear Layer Style **7a.** (It isn't absolutely necessary to remove the Styles, but it will be easier to keep track of what you're doing if you clear the Styles from these layers.) We left the type layer with its glow style alone because it would help us visualize our finished buttons. We also kept the Style on the Normal layer, where it would be used to create the first rollover state **7b.**

Now make a layer-based slice for the Normal layer: Click the layer's name in the Layers palette to activate it, and choose Layer, New Layer Based Slice **7c.** To reduce overlap and minimize file size, ImageReady will automatically make the smallest slice possible based on the layer's content. The layer-based slice command will become part of the Rollover preset, so that when the preset is applied to a new button layer, the slice will be remade automatically, based on that new layer's content.

In the Rollover palette (Window, Rollovers) the button will appear as the Normal state **7d.** Duplicate the Normal state to start the Over state, by clicking the Create New Rollover State button at the bottom of the palette. Then in the Styles palette, click the Over Style you saved to change the button's appearance **7e.**

7c

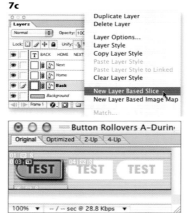

Making a layer-based slice for the "master" button. The slice is just large enough to include the button and the shadow.

7d

The Rollover palette shows the slice, with all visible layers and Styles in place.

7e

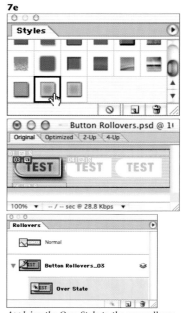

Applying the Over Style to the new rollover state to change the appearance.

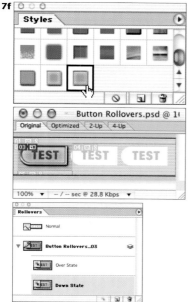

7f

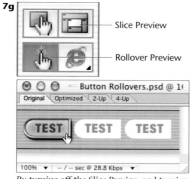

Applying the Down Style to another new state to make the Down version of the button

7g

By turning off the Slice Preview and turning on the Rollover Preview, you can test the interactivity of the button.

8

The new combined Rollover Style was added to ImageReady's Styles presets palette.

Finally, duplicate this state to make the Down state and apply the Down Style to change the button again **7f.**

At this point the master rollover button is complete. Now you can test its operation: Near the bottom of ImageReady's toolbox, turn off the Slice Preview and turn on the Rollover Preview so that when you move the cursor over your master button you can see the Over state **7g;** click to see the Down state.

8 Saving the Rollover style. To name and save the Rollover Style, including its slicing and animation features, with the master button layer active, click the Create A New Style button at the bottom of the Styles palette. Make sure all three boxes are checked in the Style Options dialog box, and give your combined Rollover Style a name; we differentiated our combined Rollover Styles from the regular Styles for our Normal, Over, and Down states by adding the suffix "-All Three." Your Rollover Style will be added to the Styles palette, with a black notch in the upper left corner of its thumbnail to indicate that it's a Rollover **8.** For safekeeping, preserve all your Styles, including the Rollover, by choosing Save Styles from the Styles palette's pop-out menu.

9 Assigning the Rollover Style to another file. At this point we switched from our developmental "test" file to a three-button set of real buttons. Be sure your button file is set up with each button on its own layer so that the Rollover Style with its layer-based slicing can be applied to each button separately and they can operate independently.

For each button, activate its layer by clicking on its name in the Layers palette **9a,** then click on the thumbnail for your Rollover Style in the Styles palette **9b.** This will automatically make a slice for the button and add the Styles and JavaScript that will make it interactive. With the Rollover Preview toggled on, you can check the operation of the buttons.

10 Optimizing the buttons. To make the file sizes for the buttons as small as possible, you can now optimize one of your buttons, then save the Optimize palette settings and apply them to the other buttons. Activate the slice for one of the buttons by using the Slice Select tool to click it in the working window. In the Optimize palette, experiment with optimization settings to get the smallest file size that still looks good for this button. We chose GIF for the file format and our favorite palette, Selective, which gives priority to the colors that the human eye is most sensitive to *as well as* areas of flat color and Web colors. We chose Diffusion Dither at 100% to reduce banding without having to add more colors **10.** Click the Optimized, 2-Up, or 4-Up tab in the working window so you can watch as you reduce the number of Colors as low as possible. Make sure the Rollover Preview is turned on in the toolbox so

9a

In a new file of button graphics, the Back button layer was targeted.

9b
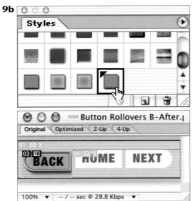
Applying the Rollover Style to the Back button layer applied all three rollover states from the preset and created a layer-based slice.

10
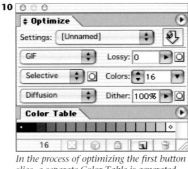
In the process of optimizing the first button slice, a separate Color Table is generated for each of the states in the Rollover Style.

you can operate the button to see how each state looks with the Optimize settings you've chosen. When you've arrived at the best settings, choose Save Settings from the menu that pops out from the upper right corner of the Optimize palette, give the settings a name in the Save Optimization Settings dialog box, and click the Save button. Then apply these optimization settings to each of the other button slices by clicking the button with the Slice Select tool and then loading the saved settings by choosing from the Settings menu at the top of the Optimize palette.

11 Previewing and saving the buttons. Now you can preview your buttons in a browser by clicking the Preview In Default Browser button at the bottom of the toolbox. (You can change to another browser by choosing from the button's pop-out menu.)

Finally, save the buttons, along with the HTML code that provides the interactivity and slice information, as follows: Choose File, Save Optimized As. In the Save Optimized As dialog box, choose HTML And Images for the format.

The Wow Button and Rollover Styles. The Normal, Over, and Down Styles and the combined Rollover Style developed here are included as one of the 50 button design sets in the **Wow 7-20 Button Styles** file on the CD-ROM that comes with this book. The facing page shows the 150 different regular Styles and the 50 combined Rollover Styles with interactivity built-in, and describes the Wow-Button files and how to use them. 🌀

MAKING SELECTED STATES

It's easy to add a Selected State to the interactivity of your button rollovers — for example, when creating navigation bars where a button stays "lit" to act as a label for the current section of a website. In the Rollovers Palette, with the Down State of the current button active, click on the Create Rollover State icon at the bottom of the palette. This will duplicate the "lit" Down State which becomes the new Selected State **A.** Do this for all your navigation bar buttons. Now when you preview the interactivity of your buttons you'll find that the Over States for the buttons work as before, but when you actually click down on a button, it will stay "lit" even while the Over States continue to work on the others **B,** until you click down on another button that has a Selected State and then *it* will become the "lit" button.

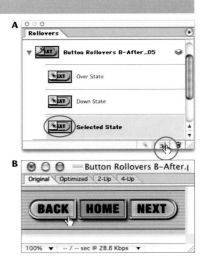

Wow Button Samplers

Shown on this page are 200 Wow Button Styles, designed to work with 72-dpi files, especially for use in turning graphics into on-screen buttons. The **Wow-Button Styles.psd** file (shown at the right) includes 150 individual button layers with Layer Styles — 50 sets with three Styles in each set. The top three rows of each column are different color variations of five Styles.

In the **Wow-Button Rollovers.psd** file (shown below right) there are 50 layers, each with a combined Rollover Style made from three related button Styles, one for each of the Normal, Over, and Down states of the button.

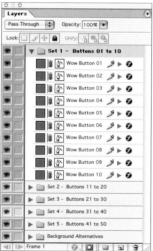

This is the Layers palette for the **Wow Button Rollovers.psd** file shown at the right. You can view the buttons against a light, medium, or dark background by opening the Background Alternatives layer set and turning on visibility for the background you want. The same options are available in the **Wow Button Styles.psd** file shown at the top of the page.

Wow Button Styles

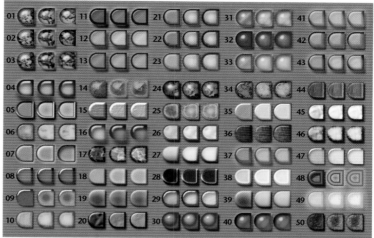

The 150 Wow Button Styles shown above can be loaded into the Styles palette of Photoshop by choosing from the Styles palette's pop-out menu and selecting the **Wow 7-20 Button Styles**. Then the Styles can be applied to a 72-dpi file by targeting a layer and clicking the Style's thumbnail in the Styles palette. Or you can copy and paste the individual styles from the **Wow Button Styles.psd** file, shown above.

Wow Button Rollover Styles

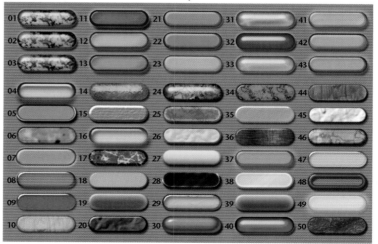

Each of the Wow Rollover Styles shown above includes the JavaScript for Normal, Over, and Down interactivity. You can add the 50 combined Wow Rollover Styles and also the 150 single-state Styles at the top of the page (a total of 200 Styles) to your current ImageReady Styles palette by going to the pop-out menu of Styles palette and selecting the **Wow 7-20 Button Styles**. Then the Styles can be applied to a 72-dpi file by targeting a layer and clicking the Style's thumbnail in the Styles palette. To see all the rollovers in operation in a single array like that shown above, you can open the **Wow-Button-Rollovers.html** file (from the Wow Button Sampler HTML page folder) in a Web browser and operate the buttons by moving the cursor over them and clicking.

After drawing and coloring his online comic strip *Astounding Space Thrills*, www.astoundingspacethrills.com, **Steve Conley** reduces its size for display on the Web, scaling the artwork using the Image, Image Size command. With both Constrain Proportions and Resample Image (Bicubic) checked, the Pixel Dimensions section of Photoshop's Image Size dialog box becomes accessible and Conley types in the Width he wants. He uses 468 pixels because that's the width of a standard banner ad on the Web, and therefore many Web sites are designed to accommodate artwork of that size. Reducing the Width to 468 pixels also automatically scales the Height of the artwork to 190 pixels. He has designed the strip to be 250 pixels tall, including the title and ad above the artwork and the buttons below, because at this size it can be seen without scrolling, even on small screens.

For each strip, Conley starts with a Macromedia FreeHand template file with all the layers needed for the titles, buttons, and artwork. He opens the file in Photoshop, then drags-and-drops his scaled-down artwork into the file.

Speech balloons are then added. ▶ *In Photoshop 7 you can save frequently used shapes as Custom Shape presets, which can then be applied with the Custom Shape tool.* The balloon layer's Opacity is reduced to 80% to allow the artwork to show through. Conley then adds the lettering, using a separate layer for the type in each balloon. He uses fonts of his own design as well as others designed especially for comics. ▶ *A good source for professionally designed comic book fonts is www.comicbookfonts.com.*

Conley does his lettering after the artwork has been resized to its final dimensions because he finds that the type doesn't

reduce well if he adds it beforehand. This means lettering twice, once for the Web and once for print, but the increase in quality makes the extra effort worthwhile.

The buttons at the bottom of the comic strip are mapped to URLs using Image-Ready's image map function.

Before posting his comic strip on the Web, Conley reduces each strip to 45K or less for quick downloading. To do this he uses the 4-Up view in ImageReady's working window. He starts by reducing the number in the Colors pop-out menu of ImageReady's Optimize palette until he gets the file size well under 45K. Then, using another of the four views in the Optimize window, he chooses Diffusion dither and experiments with the Dither slider to see if he can improve the color without making the file bigger than 45K.

Wayne **Rankin** found Photoshop's layers and masks especially helpful in creating an *interactive CD-ROM for Melbourne University Private.* He could assemble the image material in separate layers and then use masks to control how much of each element showed in the final composition of each screen.

To unify the project, Rankin repeated a number of symbols and other graphic elements from screen to screen. For example, a faint grid of receding white circles appears on most screens to create a feeling of depth. The circles were drawn in Illustrator, copied, and pasted as pixels to make a new layer in Photoshop. The concept of "vision" and a focus on innovation, with the client taking a position as "The University for the New Millennium," gave rise to a photo of two eyes in the upper left corner of most screens, with one eye that remains constant, while the other changes through the application of color overlays. ▶ *In Photoshop 7 or ImageReady 7 a Color Overlay can be applied as one of the effects in a Layer Style. In Photoshop another option is to apply it as a Solid Color Fill layer grouped with the layer it colors. In either case it's easy to change the color of the layer without causing any deterioration in the image: For the Fill layer, double-click on its thumbnail in the Layers palette to open the Color Picker and choose a new color. For the Layer Style, double-click the Color Overlay entry in the Layers palette and click the color swatch when the Color Overlay section opens.*

In a rectangular area in the lower left corner of most screens Rankin used luminous color with radiating streaks to convey a sense of innovation. This graphic was created using painting and blurring techniques in Photoshop.

Rankin chose solid black as the screen background because it makes the colors project, looks good on larger monitors, and helps to de-emphasize the rectangular look of the screens, as the combinations of bright graphics define their own overall shapes and patterns.

He developed other graphic devices to communicate the strengths of the University. For example, to convey the idea of a modern institution that retains the underlying strength of experience, he combined old and new images, such as recent photography and scans of old etchings. His use of circles and squares as geometric elements for containing and setting off images and areas of type adds a rhythm and cohesiveness to the composition of each screen and also works to convey a sense of the University's careful planning and systems.

Appendix: Artists & Photographers

Anderson Photo-Graphics
Richard Anderson 147, 226
(Models, Jennifer Luttrell
and Latisha Tolbert)
4793 N.E. 11th Avenue
Fort Lauderdale, FL 33334
954-772-4210
www.andersonphotographics.com
andersonphotographic@mac.com

Geno Andrews 416, 417
www.genoandrews.com

Darryl Baird 201
dbaird@umflint.edu
http://spruce.flint.umich.edu/~dbaird/

Ken Bartle 269
ken@aspennudes.com
www.aspennudes.com

Jay Paul Bell 250
107 Mattek Avenue
DeKalb, IL 60115
www.jaypaulbell.com

Alicia Buelow 198
150A Mississippi Street
San Francisco, CA 94107
415-522-5902
abuelow@sirius.com

Steve Conley 265, 456
steve@steveconley.com
www.astoundingspacethrills.com

Henk Dawson 196, 197
3519 170th Place
Bellevue, WA 98008
425-882-3303
www.d3d.com

Paul K. Dayton, Jr. 118

E. J. Dixon 212

Katrin Eismann 199
Katrin@photoshopdiva.com
www.photoshopdiva.com

Lance Hidy 265
2 Summer Street
Merrimack, MA 01860
lance@lancehidy.com

Greg Klamt 251
greg@gregklamt.com
www.gregklamt.com

Julieanne Kost 226
www.adobeevangelists.com/evangelists

Mike Kungl 60, 342, 343
1656 Orange Avenue, Unit 3
Costa Mesa, CA 92627
949-631-2800
mike@mkungl.com
www.mkungl.com

William Low 61, 286
william@williamlow.com
www.williamlow.com

Jennifer Luttrell 226
(See Anderson Photo-Graphics)

Bert Monroy 232, 262, 288, 289,
344, 345
11 Latham Lane
Berkeley, CA 94708
510-524-9412
bert@bertmonroy.com

Wayne Rankin 58, 59, 457
The Swish Group, Ltd.
251–257 Collins Street
Melbourne, Victoria 3000
Australia
613-9211-5400
wayne.rankin@swish.com.au
www.swish.com.au

Sharon Steuer 287
205 Valley Road
Bethany, CT 06524
203-393-3981
studio@ssteuer.com

Gordon Studer 347
1552 62nd Street
Emeryville, CA 94608
510-655-4256
gstuder@dnai.com
www.gordonstuder.com

Surfnart.com 161
Sterling King
www.surfnart.com

Susan Thompson 148, 149
160 North Elmwood Avenue
Lindsay, CA 93247
559-562-5155
susan@sx70.com
www.sx70.com

Cher Threinen-Pendarvis 54
cher@pendarvis-studios.com
www.pendarvis-studios.com

Latisha Tolbert 147
(See Anderson Photo-Graphics)

Frank Vitale 212
11205 North 26th Way
Phoenix, AZ 85028
602-750-7407
vitalef@home.com
www.vitalef.com

Mark Wainer 248, 249
wainer40@pacbell.net

Tommy Yune 21
Ursus Studios
P.O. Box 4858
Cerritos, CA 90703-4858
tommyyune@aol.com
www.tommyyune.com
www.busterbear.com

Christine Zalewski 108, 109
941-927-7840
www.zalewskiphotography.com

Index

Drop Shadow effect, 102, 147, 176–177, 188, 222, 351, 354–357, 367, 400
in animations, 426
knockouts from, 309
with layer masks, 147
for type, 172, 192–193, 309, 311
See also Inner Shadow
Duotone mode, 66, 68–69, 87–88
duplicate and transform, 26
duplicating a file, 29
dust and scratches, removing, 119–121, 122
Dust & Scratches filter, 120, 122, 134, 135, 139, 210, 238

E

Edge Contour, 223
Edge Highlighter tool, 162, 163, 164, 165
Edge Touchup tool, 162
edges
accidentally cropping, 112
custom, 237
making more distinct, 383
options for, 402
sharpening, 410
using Smart Highlighting for, 162–165
tracing, 301
editing mode, for type and drawing tools, 292, 294, 297
8 Bits/channel, 69
Electric Image 3D program, 196, 197
Ellipse tool, 185, 298, 406–407
Elliptical Marquee, 101
Eismann, Katrin, 199
Embed Color Profile, 80
Emboss effects, 358
See also Bevel and Emboss effects
Emboss filter, 245, 275, 280
embossing, 212, 251
encoding, run-length, 418

Enhance Monochromatic Contrast button, 116, 230
environment, color, 80–81
EPS files, importing to Photoshop, 304–305
EPS format, 255, 293, 307
Equalize command, 76
Erase to History, 257, 258
Eraser tool, 250, 252, 256, 257, 258
even spacing, 25
Exclusion mode, 79
Extract command, 150, 162–164
Extrude filter, 245
EXIF (Exchangeable Image File), 1, 2
Eyedropper tool, 70, 265
EZColor, 83

F

Fade command, 28, 79, 251
with filters, 28, 238, 245
fade settings, for brushes, 256
feathering, 135, 150, 445
felt-tip marker effect, 255
File Browser, 1–2
file formats, 55
for PostScript programs, 304
for Web, 419
file size indicator, 22
files, opening several at once, 21
Fill command, 264–265
Fill dialog box, 264
Fill layer, 153, 171, 320, 321
gradient, 265, 266, 270, 271
solid color, 71, 90–92, 457
Fill Opacity slider, 361, 362, 369, 385
Fill Path dialog box, 303
filling tools, 252, 264–269
fills
for paths, 303
for strokes, 357–358
solid color, 282, 285, 457

film grain
adding, 140–143, 154
reducing, 99
restoring, 209
simulating, 154
filters, 202–251
blurring, 206–208
color mode and, 66
custom, 239
dialogs for, 234
keyboard shortcuts for, 202
noise, 209–210, 238
for PostScript line art, 322–323
reducing, 238, 245
running on layer masks, 218–219
sharpening, 204–206
Find Edges filter, 245
Flash plug-ins, 421
flat-color art, for Web, 419, 421–422
flattening, 159
flipping, of elements, 226
folders, for layers, 157–159
fonts, 315
missing, 371
foreground, blurring, 140, 142
Foreground color, 70, 71
filling with, 264
protecting, 175
four-color process. *See* CMYK
Fractional Widths, 295, 418
frames
creating, 221
fancy, 237
filtered, 218–219
framing with layer masks, 109, 128–129
Free Transform command, 158, 222, 226–227, 435
for fixing perspective, 113
Freeform Pen tool, 255, 299, 300, 302
FreeHand, importing files from, 305
Freeze tool, 214
function keys, 18

Undo, 28
unifying effect, 190, 211, 220–225
Unsharp Mask, 121, 190, 204–206, 243, 323
  following scaling, 308
  using in Lab mode, 204
  using last, 205
  using multiple times, 205
  repairs layer for, 205, 206
  settings for, 204
  for special effects, 206
user interface, 3, 19, 20
user slices, 415

V

Variations command, 76
vector-based drawing tools, 252, 255, 297–299
vector-based layers and paths, 290, 292–304
vector masks, 152–156, 333, 334, 336, 401, 402, 403
views, on-screen, 23
vignetting, 128, 161
visibility, in Layers palette, 153
Vitale, Frank, 212

W

Wacom Intuos Tablet, 255, 258, 260, 278, 287, 346
Wainer, Mark, 248, 249
Warp Text function, 2, 295, 296, 314–317, 428
Warp tool, 213, 227–228
warping, 186, 295, 296, 314–317, 347, 428
watermarks, 5, 232
WBMP format, 5
Web
  cel animation for, 429–433
  comic strip for, 456
  creating motion graphics for, 412–435
Web Design Wow! Book (Davis & Merritt), 415
Web graphics
  buttons for, 449–455
  optimizing, 414–415, 419–422
  planning, 58, 417–419
  sizing, 336–337
  workflow for, 414–417
Web Photo Gallery, 5, 414, 423–424
Web-safe palette, 72, 418, 420, 430
Wet Edges, 255
White Clip, 116
Wind filter, 246
window, enlarging, 112
wood grain effect, 238

Work Path, 297, 298, 338
  converting to pixels, 304
  converting to Shape layer, 304
  saving, 299
working window, 19
Workspace presets, 4
World Wide Web. *See* Web
Wow Actions, 11
Wow Button Styles, 455
Wow Custom Chrome, 394–395
Wow GIF sampler, 423
Wow Gradients presets, 266
Wow Patterns presets, 171–172, 254, 256, 320–321, 374, 409
Wow Extra Styles presets, 460–461
Wow Project Styles Presets, 458–459
Wow Rollover Button Styles, 455
Wow Tool Presets, 10

Y

Yune, Tommy, 21

Z

Zalewski, Christine, 108, 109
Zaxwerks' 3D Invigorator, 364, 365